DATE DUE

MR 15 '96	MY 27 '99		
FE 11 '98	AP 7 03		
MY 26 '98	JY 21 04		
NV 4 '99			
MY 28 '03			
JE 11 03			
DE 15 04			

DEMCO 38-296

Guerrillas and Revolution in Latin America

Guerrillas and Revolution in Latin America

A COMPARATIVE STUDY OF INSURGENTS AND REGIMES SINCE 1956

Timothy P. Wickham-Crowley

PRINCETON UNIVERSITY PRESS

PRINCETON, NEW JERSEY

Library of Congress Cataloging-in-Publication Data

Wickham-Crowley, Timothy P. 1951–
Guerrillas and revolution in Latin America : a comparative study
of insurgents and regimes since 1956 / Timothy P. Wickham-Crowley.
p.   cm.
Includes bibliographical references and index.
ISBN 0-691-07885-8 — ISBN 0-691-02336-0 (pbk.)
1. Revolutions—Latin America.   2. Guerrillas—Latin America.
3. Insurgency—Latin America.   4. Latin America—Politics and
government—1948–   I. Title.
JC491.W53   1991   321.09′4′098—dc20   91-15141

This book has been composed in Linotron Times Roman

Printed in the United States of America
First Princeton Paperback printing, 1993

10 9 8 7 6 5 4 3 2

IN MEMORY OF MY FATHER

whose eyes would never see this filial dedication

Contents

Figures and Tables

Preface

THE WORK that follows is a systematic attempt to blend together an empirically driven study of Latin American revolutionary failures and successes with the social-scientific theoretical treatment of revolutions. Latin America has usually remained the "forgotten region" when general theories of revolution are put forth—Eric Wolf's *Peasant Wars of the Twentieth Century* is the major exception—and I wish to address that lacuna. In blending together revolutionary theory and revolutionary accounts, I found that each body of information inevitably affected the way the other body of information was perceived. As Robert Merton so nicely put it forty-odd years ago, empirical research had a bearing on social theory, yet theory also had its own bearing on empirical research. Without that theoretical literature I would have foundered in a sea of information whose "noise" content always threatened to mask the "signals" within. Without paying attention to the empirics of the Latin American revolutionary process, however, I could not have achieved my recasting of certain crucial concepts. To wit, I could not have amended Jeffery Paige's formal theory of revolutionary movements, James Scott's writings on the moral economy, and Theda Skocpol's comparative study of great revolutions in order to produce concepts more appropriate to Latin American realities.

The sheer number of cases has forced me to divide this book into earlier and later periods, here called "waves." This decision not only protects the reader from mentally juggling a dozen cases within each chapter, it also permits a test of the theory I elaborate. The only method of inquiry appropriate to the problem was the comparative method; the only usable sources of information, for the most part, were nonsusceptible to elegant statistical analyses. While qualitative researchers will only sigh in relief and argue that this feature is all to the good, there is a cost: the comparative study of ten to twelve different cases, which are analyzed structurally and historically rather than simply coded statistically, naturally leads to a discursive expansion of the text, rather than to statistical condensation that then produces correlation coefficients, p-values, and other mathematical shorthands. Whereas Jeffery Paige's theory of rural, third-world social movements can be effectively condensed into one table and one correlation matrix, this work lacks such simplifying devices. Throughout the work, therefore, I try to summarize and resummarize so that the reader will not lose the train of thought, whose length may well prove daunting for those waiting patiently to cross the tracks and move on to some other reading.

I have tried to compensate for such lengthiness throughout by making the text lucid and accessible to those who are not social scientists, but rather Latin Americanists or simply interested literary passersby. For my decision to use simple language I make no apologies; social scientists have done enough damage to the mother tongue without my adding to the carnage. In the end, I hope my fellow social scientists will join me in revealing the best-kept secret of our fields: While the obscure and verbose ministers of fat language often get published in fat books and weighty journals, sociologists, like other mortals, really much prefer to read straightforward prose. Where my prose falls apart in this work, I have no one to blame but myself, for not learning the canons of clear sociological discourse from a master thereof: my former teacher and dissertation advisor, Joseph A. Kahl.

Washington, D.C.
February 1991

Acknowledgments

FOR BETTER OR WORSE, the work that follows is the work of an individual rather than a committee, an offering of what Fernand Braudel might have called *sociologie artisanal*, not *sociologie coopérative*. Yet still I have incurred many debts that are probably uncollectable. First thanks go to my thesis committee members at Cornell University, chaired by Joseph A. Kahl and joined by Thomas H. Holloway and Tom E. Davis; also to Professor Raymond Murphy of the University of Rochester for special kindnesses during this project. For conference criticism of these and related materials, I thank John Womack, Jr., Charles Tilly, León Zamosc, and Manuel Antonio Garretón. For reading and commenting on selected chapters, I thank Jeffery Paige, Theda Skocpol, and Charles Ragin, and several anonymous reviewers who read the entire manuscript and made many useful suggestions to improve the finished product. That product, however, has been most improved by the kind words and constructive criticism I have received from Susan Eckstein since 1984. She is the epitome of what we are called to be: cooperative workers in a community of scholars. The conceptual and empirical comparisons comprising this book would have been far less systematic had she not pressed me to clarify my argument throughout, and to dispense with the introduction of ad hoc and gratuitous "variables" that only muddied the theoretical waters. Thanks to Susan, a scholars' scholar.

For assistance in typing the manuscript at various stages, I would like to thank Laurie Moses of Hamilton College, Janet Smith and Cheryl Williams of the University of Rochester, and various undergraduate assistants to the sociology department at Georgetown, who added bits and pieces. Most particularly I would like to thank Janet Redley, for her able work as my one-term research assistant, in transferring most of the tables and bibliography to computer format; and also Deborah Pokorney, for help in re-preparing work lost on an errant computer disk.

All translations from Spanish, French, German, and Italian are my own; resulting infelicities in style are preferable, I hope, to sending nonpolyglots among the readers scurrying to bilingual dictionaries, which surely would have happened had I left the quotations in their original tongues.

Research support for this book was in part provided by a Summer Research Grant from Cornell University that allowed me to spend a summer doing research at the Library of Congress; it was further assisted by a part-time Postdoctoral Fellowship awarded me by the University of Rochester. To both institutions I give my thanks for the precious spare time those grants gave me, which much improved the final product.

I would like to thank E. J. Brill for permission to use materials that appear here as the latter part of chapter 12; also Butterworth Publishers for permission to reprint some passages on El Salvador that now appear as part of chapter 11; and the University of California Press, for permission to reprint some materials that appeared earlier in a summary article on guerrillas, which here are sprinkled throughout text and tabular material; finally, M. E. Sharpe, Inc., for permission to reprint some passages and tabular data that appear in my book of essays, *Exploring Revolution*.

The human suffering I have encountered in researching this work almost led me at times to that hardening of the heart against which the Psalmist warns us. Yet I have not forgotten those losses. I write this work while recalling and honoring those who died fighting in humane causes, and those still living who grieve for and remember them.

Abbreviations

	Country	Spanish/English/Description
AD	Venezuela	Acción Democrática/Democratic Action/party
ANAPO	Colombia	Alianza Nacional Popular/Popular National Alliance/party created by former dictator Rojas
ANR	Cuba	Acción Nacional Revolucionaria/National Revolutionary Action/Anti-Batista group
AP	Peru	Acción Popular/Popular Action/party
APRA	Peru	Alianza Popular Revolucionaria Americana/American Popular Revolutionary Alliance/party
CAEM	Peru	Centro de Altos Estudios Militares/Center for Higher Military Studies/Army war college
CEBs	Latin America, elsewhere	Comunidades Eclesiales de Base/Ecclesiastical Base Communities/Laypeople's religious organizations, often oriented toward liberation theology
COPEI	Venezuela	Comité de Organización Política Electoral Independiente/Committee for Independent Electoral Organization/Christian Democratic party
CUC	Guatemala	Comité de Unidad Campesina/Committee for Peasant Unity/Peasants'union, 1970s–
DR	Cuba	Directorio Revolucionario/Revolutionary Directorate/Anti-Batista Havana underground, guerrilla group
EGP	Guatemala	Ejército Guerrillero de los Pobres/Guerrilla Army of the Poor/Guerrillas, 1970s–
ELN	Peru, Colombia, Bolivia	Ejército de Liberación Nacional/Army of National Liberation/Unrelated guerrilla groups in each country, including Guevara's Bolivian group
EPL	Colombia	Ejército Popular de Liberación/Popular Liberation Army/Guerrillas
ERP	El Salvador	Ejército Revolucionario del Pueblo/People's Revolutionary Army/Guerrillas

FALN	Venezuela	Fuerzas Armadas de Liberación Nacional/Armed Forces of National Liberation/Guerrillas
FAO	Nicaragua	Frente Amplio Opositor/Broad Opposition Front/Anti-Somoza civic opposition group
FAR	Guatemala	Fuerzas Armadas Rebeldes/Rebel Armed Forces/Guerrillas, 1960s; revival, 1970s–
FAR	Guatemala	Fuerzas Armadas Revolucionarias/Revolutionary Armed Forces/Guerrillas formed by PGT in 1968 after split with original FAR
FARC	Colombia	Fuerzas Armadas Revolucionarias Colombianas/Colombian Revolutionary Armed Forces/Guerrillas
FARN	El Salvador	Fuerzas Armadas de Resistencia Nacional/Armed Forces of National Resistance/Guerrillas
FDR	El Salvador	Frente Democrático Revolucionario/Revolutionary Democratic Front/Civic, mass revolutionary group of early 1980s, allied with FMLN guerrilas
FECCAS	El Salvador	Federacion Cristiana de Campesinos Salvadoreños/Christian Federation of Salvadoran Peasants/Peasants'union
FER	Nicaragua	Federación Estudiantil Revolucionaria/Revolutionary Student Federation/University group linked to FSLN
FIR	Peru	Frente de la Izquierda Revolucionaria/Revolutionary Left Front/Trotskyist front group
FLN	Venezuela	Frente de Liberación Nacional/National Liberation Front/Guerrilla front group
FMLN	El Salvador	Frente Farabundo Martí de Liberación Nacional/Farabundo Martí Front for National Liberation/Umbrella-unity organization for guerrilla groups
FPL	El Salvador	Fuerzas Populares de Liberación—Farabundo Martí/Farabundo Martí Popular Liberation Forces/Guerrillas formed in split from Communist party
FSLN	Nicaragua	Frente Sandinista de Liberación Nacional/Sandinista National Liberation Front/Guerrillas, 1960–1979; governing party, 1979–1990

FUR	Guatemala	Frente Unido de Resistencia/United Resistence Front/PGT front group for original 1960s FAR guerrillas
INCORA	Colombia	Instituto Colombiano de Reforma Agraria/ Colombian Agrarian Reform Institute/Land reform agency
JPN	Nicaragua	Juventud Patriótica Nicaragüense/Nicaraguan Patriotic Youth/Left-wing student group tied to FSLN
JPT	Guatemala	Juventud Patriótica del Trabajo/Patriotic Youth of Labor/Communist youth group
JRN	Nicaragua	Juventud Revolucionaria Nicaragüense/Nicaraguan Revolutionary Youth/Communist (PSN) youth group from which FSLN's founders emerged
M-19	Colombia	Movimiento 19 de Abril/April 19th Movement/Guerrilla group, 1970s–1990
M-26 or M-26-7	Cuba	Movimiento 26 de Julio/26th of July Movement/Castro's revolutionary organization, including guerrillas
MIR	Venezuela, Peru	Movimiento de la Izquierda Revolucionaria/Movement of the Revolutionary Left/Unrelated guerrilla groups; formerly left-wing political splinter groups
MNR	Bolivia	Movimiento Nacionalista Revolucionario/ Nationalist Revolutionary Movement/Party that led and seized power in 1952 revolution and governed until 1964
MNR	Cuba	Movimiento Nacional Revolucionario/National Revolutionary Movement/Anti-Batista group
MOEC	Colombia	Movimiento Obrero-Estudiantil-Campesino/ Worker-Student-Peasant Movement/ Castroist movement that later created ELN guerrillas
MPU	Nicaragua	Movimiento Popular Unido/United Popular Movement/Mass opposition movement linked to FSLN, 1978–1979
MR-13	Guatemala	Movimiento Revolucionario 13 de Noviembre/13th of November Revolutionary Movement/Guerrillas

MRL	Colombia	Movimiento Revolucionario Liberal/Liberal Revolutionary Movement/Liberal Party faction
OLAS	Cuba, etc.	Organización Latinoamericana de Solidaridad/Organization for Latin American Solidarity/Cuba-based group for the Latin American revolutionary left
ORPA	Guatemala	Organización del Pueblo en Armas/Organization of the People in Arms/Guerrillas, 1970s–
PCB	Bolivia	Partido Comunista Boliviano/Bolivian Communist party
PCC	Colombia	Partido Comunista Colombiano/Colombian Communist party (Soviet line)
PCC-M-L	Colombia	Partido Comunista Colombiano Marxista-Leninista/Marxist-Leninist Colombian Communist party (Chinese line)
PCP	Peru	Partido Comunista Peruano/Peruvian Communist party
PCV	Venezuela	Partido Comunista Venezolano/Venezuelan Communist party
PGT	Guatemala	Partido Guatemalteco del Trabajo/Guatemalan Labor party/Communist party
POR	Peru	Partido Obrero Revolucionario/Revolutionary Workers' party/Trotskyist party
PSN	Nicaragua	Partido Socialista Nicaragüense/Nicaraguan Socialist party/Communist party
PSP	Cuba	Partido Socialista Popular/Popular Socialist party/Communist party
UDEL	Nicaragua	Unión Democrática de Liberación/Democratic Liberation Union/Business-backed anti-Somoza group, 1974–1979
UFCO	Guatemala etc.	United Fruit Company
UP	Colombia	Unidad Patriótica/Patriotic Union/Political party formed by (former) FARC guerrillas in 1980s
URD	Venezuela	Unión Repúblicana Democrática/Democratic Republican Union/party
UTC	Venezuela	Unidades Tácticas de Combate/Tactical Combat Units/FALN's "urban guerrilla" wing

PART I

Origins

> Let the sociologists make their detailed studies and exhaustive
> analyses of the causes of the new violence. Confound them, with
> their interesting theories!
>> —Evelio Buitrago Salazar, *Zarpazo the Bandit*

CHAPTER 1

Introduction

> The men of action and conviction have failed enough of late to
> warrant reversing a famous apothegm of Marx: philosophers have
> tried to change the world; now it is time to try to understand it.
> —Barrington Moore, Jr.,
> *Reflections on the Causes of Human Misery*

THINKING ABOUT GUERRILLA WARFARE

Guerrilla warfare is nothing new, and most certainly not a twentieth-century invention found first in the writings of Vladimir Lenin, Mao Zedong, or Ché Guevara. "Barbarian" leaders of many different peoples, including Tacfarinas of the Numidians, Vercingetorix of the Gauls, and Viriathus of the Iberian peninsula all employed guerrilla warfare against the Roman imperial forces in ancient Europe. Francis Marion ("The Swamp Fox") waged guerrilla-style warfare against the British army in the British-American colonies, as did other American armed forces; later the United States' armed forces would suffer similar tactics in their attempts to conquer the various American Indian peoples in the following century. The occupying forces of Napoleon's army in early nineteenth-century Spain would also find themselves harassed by guerrilla forces.[1]

Guerrilla warfare, in fact, is almost surely the most ancient form of warfare, and is best defined in strictly military terms, not in social or political terms. It usually appears when a nation or people is attacked by forces with superior numbers and/or technology. The almost natural military response is to (re-)invent guerrilla warfare: to avoid direct, massed engagements with the enemy and instead to concentrate on slowly sapping the enemy's strength and morale through ambushes, minor skirmishes, lightning raids and withdrawals, cutting of communications and supply lines, and similar techniques. (Precisely because so-called urban guerrillas almost never directly engage the armed forces and often use indiscriminate forms of assault that harm or kill ordinary citizens, the term is a misleading misnomer; we should reserve it for forces that do confront the military. Northern Ireland could well be an exception here.) The central negative feature of traditional guerrilla warfare is thus the avoidance of decisive pitched battles, which they must surely lose; the key positive feature is a heavy reliance on "local knowledge" and local support to compensate for inferior numbers and weaponry.

The true innovations of twentieth-century guerrilla warfare are the transfer of this tactic to internal wars, rather than in external wars against foreign occupiers or colonial powers; the latter form has overwhelmingly dominated the past exemplars of the technique. In most cases of modern guerrilla warfare, including all those discussed in this work, the insurgency is, or intends to become, a civil war in which the populace will eventually (be forced to?) side either with the guerrilla forces or with the government in power. Because of this peculiar feature of many twentieth-century guerrilla wars, for the first time in history the support of the populace for the insurgency—a term I shall use interchangeably with guerrilla war—has become problematic. Since the political enemy is no longer a foreign devil, but armed forces composed of one's own countrymen, guerrillas cannot rely on tribalism or nationalism to provide them with guaranteed allies. Therefore a large part of this work will be devoted to uncovering the social conditions under which such support *is* forthcoming, and those in which it is denied.

In the decade of the 1960s popular fascination with modern guerrilla warfare, guerrilla movements, and the guerrillas themselves reached a level perhaps unprecedented in human history. This period produced a large journalistic and military literature on the theory and practice of guerrilla war—so large, indeed, that it would be merely tedious to list the major works here.[2] This period, however, did not produce a social-scientific literature to match. Only in Vietnam was revolutionary guerrilla warfare the subject of intensive social-scientific study, where a number of scholars examined social conditions, especially but not only in the Mekong Delta, which favored the growth of an insurgent movement.[3] Such detailed analysis had rarely been applied to Latin American guerrilla movements—not even in Cuba—until finally a semblance of such a literature began to appear in the last decade; nonetheless, the corpus of such writings remains insignificant compared to the excellent, indepth literature on Vietnam.

Interest in guerrillas had grown apace with the successes of Fidel Castro in late-1950s Cuba; it later ebbed with the death of Ché Guevara in the Bolivian jungle in 1967, and then waned further still with the fall of Saigon in 1975. The 1979 overthrow of the Somoza government in Nicaragua and the recent revolutionary upsurge in Central America have served to revivify such interests, but certainly not to the levels of the 1960s. The reader may have forgotten the number of posters adorning university walls throughout the world, graced with the quasi-beatific, black-bereted visage of Guevara. "Romantic" interest in Latin American guerrillas was such that Woody Allen saw fit to lampoon them in his own version of a guerrilla diary and in his film *Bananas*, while in *Weekend* Jean-Luc Godard also parodied guerrillas, presenting them as the cannibalistic members of the "Seine and Oise Liberation Front," who first kidnapped bourgeois picnickers, and then ate them.

The romantic, journalistic, and military treatments of guerrillas do not constitute sociological analyses, and we still lack a strong comparative body of social-scientific literature on Latin American guerrilla movements and revolutions.[4] The present study is an attempt to redress that imbalance, by presenting a comparative analysis of guerrilla movements and revolution in Latin America since 1956. The sequence is a simple, if demanding, one. I shall devote parts 1 and 2 to a systematic comparison of the origins and final fortunes of six national guerrilla movements up to the year 1970, in Cuba, Venezuela, Guatemala, Colombia, Peru, and finally Bolivia. In part 3 of this work I shall apply similar logics and analyses to the major guerrilla movements of a later period, in Nicaragua, El Salvador, Guatemala, Peru, and (in part) Colombia. My strategy throughout will *not* be simply to collect a series of case studies, for we already have fine examples of that literary genre;[5] instead, the focus of every case discussion in the book will be its bearing upon theoretical issues in the study of revolution.

Since this book is already overlong, I must leave for others the extremely interesting analytical issue of comparing the *outcomes* of successful revolutions, either with other revolutionary successes, or with similar nations that did not experience revolutions. Fortunately, we are not lacking in such studies, including a variegated but excellent trio of essays by Seymour Martin Lipset (on the United States and Canada), Susan Eckstein (on Latin America), and Theda Skocpol (on the Russian and Chinese revolutions).[6]

Do Strong Movements or Weak Regimes Cause Revolutions?

I do not enter the study of revolutions in a theoretical vacuum, but rather in the midst of an intense theoretical debate over the causes of revolutions. Until quite recently, most observers and scholars would have agreed that revolutionary organizations are indeed the "makers" of revolutions, insofar as their movement-led activities—including urban uprisings, general strikes, peasant insurrections, and guerrilla warfare—have been crucial in producing that rapid social and political transition that we call a social revolution. Such a perspective pervades the *Communist Manifesto*, with its prophecy of massive proletarian uprisings under late capitalism. Yet it also underlies the stance of latter-day, orthodox Marxists who seek to overthrow contemporary incumbent regimes through popular mobilization. Among preeminent social scientists, Eric Wolf has put a substantial stress on "peasant wars" in producing social revolutions in Mexico, Russia, China, Vietnam, Algeria, and Cuba; Jeffery Paige has combined careful statistical analysis with several case studies to demonstrate that certain types of peasantries are likely to participate in revolutionary collective action; and historian-sociologist Charles Tilly in *From Mobilization to Revolution* has constructed an analytical model showing how social unrest in the lower classes can develop.[7]

Such happy agreement that "movements make revolutions" received a jolt with the publication of Theda Skocpol's *States and Social Revolutions*.[8] Her comparative study challenged this perspective in two fundamental ways. First, she rejected the widespread belief that the actions of *revolutionary groups* brought down the old regimes of France (1789), Russia (February 1917), and China (1910–1912); instead she argued that internal structural weaknesses of these regimes plus international pressures led to their collapse. Second, through a series of contrasting case studies of Japan and Prussia, as well as a final contrast with modern, industrial-bureaucratic societies, she was able to argue that *certain types of state or regime are structurally more vulnerable to revolution* than others. In both respects, then, her argument undermined revolutionaries' ambitious claims that they alone were the makers of revolution, and she redirected our analytical noses away from such actions, and toward the social and political *structures* that produce peasant insurrections and weak states.

Despite Skocpol's left-wing credentials and socialist leanings—she acknowledges them in her book—her conclusions have infuriated Marxists, who are probably outraged at the implications of her argument: that revolutionary opposition to certain types of regime is destined to fail. (She further argues that a revolution in a modern industrial society would probably be profoundly different from earlier exemplars and would lack the decisive and dramatic "events" that so enrapture revolutionaries.)[9] Her stance has also been rejected by many students of revolutions who continue to focus on the characteristics of opposition movements, rather than on the characteristics of the states and regimes that those movements confront.

This either/or theoretical debate has been most unfortunate, for Skocpol has directed us to regime characteristics that *must* be faced squarely if we are to understand why some revolutionary movements come to power while others do not. One earlier theoretician neatly transcended this movement versus regime debate, also known as the society-centered versus state-centered debate, even before that debate got started. Walter Goldfrank, in his various writings on the Mexican revolution, has consistently and sociologically analyzed both the characteristics of the rural opposition movements and those of the regime itself.[10] Moreover, Skocpol herself later conceded that revolutionaries' conscious mobilization of a mass opposition—that is, society-centered events—can be added to autonomous insurrection as an alternative path to mass uprisings.[11]

The theoretical deficiencies that arise if we focus only on the strengths of revolutionary movements become immediately apparent when we begin to study revolutions comparatively, especially in Latin America. As we shall see, there is no good evidence that the Cuban revolutionaries of the 1950s had greater military strength or rural support than their 1960s counterparts in Colombia, Guatemala, or Venezuela. That relation holds a fortiori for the 1970s and beyond: the Sandinistas in Nicaragua never fielded an army that matched the size of the ten to twelve thousand Salvadoran guerrilla fighters, the seven thousand or more Colombian insurgents, or even the five thousand soldiers of Peru's Sendero Luminoso. Yet the Cuban and Nicaraguan insurgents achieved their revolutionary ends, while the other insurgents did not. There can be little doubt, therefore, that the Cuban and Nicaraguan revolutions were *not* made by the greater military strength or rural support of the insurgencies.

The Cuban and Nicaraguan regimes were different, and those differences weakened them in the face of revolution. But those differences did not simply exist and operate apart from the insurgencies themselves; here I agree with Robert Dix that such differences served to strengthen the opposition.[12] First, the distinctive traits of the Batista and the Somoza regimes were such as to engender a *cross-class*, *national* opposition to those regimes, throwing radical revolutionaries into an alliance of convenience with more moderate opponents of the regime. We will not see this pattern in *any* other case analyzed here. Second, those same regime characteristics meant that the ruler and the military were increasingly decoupled from civil society itself, and therefore had no taproots of support among any social classes or social institutions; hence, when confronted with a growing revolutionary movement, these regimes *could not mobilize social support* (even international support) for their own continuity. As we shall see, this sharply contrasts with the experience of other nations that did not fall to revolution. Finally, such regimes are virtually defined by their combination of personal rule and a correspondingly personalized military. Yet such military forces become, ipso facto, virtually incapable of drawing on nationalistic and patriotic imagery to maintain the solidarity and fighting morale of the soldiery; hence there is an inbuilt tendency for such military forces to decay in the face of substantial nationalist challenges. Yet in other nations—both in Latin America and worldwide—the military has been the foremost repository of precisely those national sentiments, which serve to steel it for combat and against internal decay.

While all these issues and propositions await their detailed treatment in the chapters to follow, we can now return to our question: Did revolutionary movements or weak regimes lead to social revolutions in Latin America? The answer will soon be clear. Powerful revolutionary movements did indeed "make" revolutions in Cuba and Nicaragua, but only because they faced regimes that exhibited structural weaknesses in the face of an increasingly national opposition. Indeed, it was the nature of the regimes themselves that increased the likelihood that the opposition would unite across classes and despite ideological differences; hence the regime itself served to strengthen the opposition, despite the bloodiness of government repression (especially in Nicaragua).

THE SHAPE OF ARGUMENTS TO COME

Why do these guerrilla movements require comparative sociological analyses, rather than simply a sequence of case studies? While I will give my detailed justifications below, we can observe simply that guerrillas arise in particular countries, appear at particular points in time, and are drawn disproportionately from particular social groups. Thus, in their origins, guerrilla movements demand a comparative sociological treatment to understand such variations, and I provide such analyses in chapters 2 and 3 (for cases up to 1970), and in chapter 9 (for cases after 1970). We can apply similar questions to the later histories of the various insurgencies: Why do some guerrilla movements gain extensive support from regional peasantries, while other guerrilla movements get no such support, and other peasantries are less willing to embrace revolution? How important is the military strength of the insurgency to its success, and how are its chances for success affected by external military aid—to itself or to its governmental adversaries? Finally, the central question of this work concerns the social revolutionary outcome itself. Since both deep peasant support and substantial military strength are found widely among Latin American guerrilla movements, what *other* features can account for the fact that guerrilla-led revolutionaries have seized power only in Cuba and Nicaragua, while failing to do so in Guatemala and Colombia (at least twice in each case), Venezuela, Peru and, most notably, El Salvador?

By far the most interesting issue to most readers, as well as to myself, is precisely that accurate retrodiction of revolution itself. What sociopolitical features of Cuban and Nicaraguan societies led to revolution there, but have stifled such successes in other nations? Three central causes lie behind revolutions in Latin America, which I will simply pose as hypotheses in this introduction:

1. Peasant support is a crucial contributor to revolution, and no revolutionary guerrilla movement—in the Latin American context—is likely to seize power without such support.
2. Guerrilla movements must have enough military power to endure and outlast military repression, and finally to confront the military, or they will be militarily unable to achieve the revolutionary transfer of power. (Such military power is clearly in part dependent upon peasant support.)
3. A militarily strong and peasant-supported guerrilla movement is not thereby guaranteed victory; in this minimal sense, then, "popular support" is not enough to effect a revolution. It is not just (peasant) hearts and minds accompanied by

guns and bullets. Only under specific sociopolitical conditions will such a revolution ensue: when a certain weak type of political regime, confronted with a guerrilla challenge, engenders in the society a cross-class opposition, leading to the appearance of dual power in the political order, and finally a revolutionary overthrow of the old regime. The crucial theoretical linkage here is between a peculiarly weak "old regime" and its tendency to press the elements of the opposition toward an alliance, rather than to aggravate their internal divisions and conflicts.

When those three features converge in a society, the likely outcome is social revolution. Absent any one of those features, revolution will not be the likely outcome. (For example, I disagree with Robert Dix's contention that the peculiar traits of the Cuban and Nicaraguan regimes were sufficient to generate the "negative revolutionary coalitions" that [I agree] caused their downfalls;[13] similar regimes under Duvalier in Haiti, Trujillo in the Dominican Republic, and Stroessner in Paraguay did not lead to revolution.) I will systematically support that pair of contentions in the final chapter of this work. In between, however, we must first address more preliminary issues, the causes of the causes, as it were.

1. What are the social conditions underlying peasant support for revolutionaries in the countryside? Under what social conditions do peasants *not* provide such social support? I address those issues systematically in chapters 6 and 7 for the first wave of revolutions up to 1970, and in chapter 10 for the second wave of revolutions since 1970. For both periods I uncover four different, recurring correlates of peasant support for insurgency.

2. What elements contribute to militarily strong guerrilla movements *or* government armed forces? I will address the issues of internal resources, internal solidarity, and external resources for the first wave in chapter 5. I will not repeat such an analysis for the second wave of guerrilla movements, since each of them clearly fielded strong military challenges to the governments of their respective nations. However, I will consider in chapters 11 and 12 high or low levels of U.S. military assistance to governments, and its relevance to the outcome of insurgencies in Central America since 1970.

3. We must also inquire into the historical origins of those weak political regimes in Cuba and Nicaragua, and further discuss why those regimes were likely to elicit a cross-class opposition from civil society, leading eventually to the creation of dual power and an incipient counter-state (in the guerrilla organizations themselves). The regimes that fell to revolutionaries in Cuba and then Nicaragua were of a peculiar type, which Alain Rouquié has termed the *patrimonial praetorian regime*, which I have termed *mafiacracy*, and which is further clearly suggested by Loveman and Davies's discussions of *Caribbean-style dictatorships*.[14] In chapters 8 and 11 of this work I look into the origins of such regimes in Cuba and Nicaragua, and systematically compare them to contrasting regimes in nonrevolutionary nations of the region. Having traced the origins of those

regimes, I delve into the formation of cross-class oppositions against Batista and Somoza, and finally to the creation of dual power. In contrast, the other, non-revolutionary nations typically leaned toward two other types of polity: mass-based electoral democracy, or collective military rule with the support of the upper class. (Since these concepts are "ideal types," not concrete social realities, actual political regimes only more or less closely approximate each of three types; they do not replicate them.) In those societies, a cross-class opposition to the regime generally failed even to appear, and the creation of bastions of "dual power" was limited, at best, to certain oases of armed rebellion in the countryside.

The analysis that follows will therefore locate the proximate causes of revolution (the first three items listed above), but those causes themselves cannot be simply assumed. The bulk of the work thus consists of an inquiry into the sources of peasant support, guerrilla military strength, and weak incumbent political regimes.

METHODS

Multiple Levels of Analysis

Revolutions happen to entire nations. That commonplace is a domain assumption in virtually every study of revolution ever written. Because analysts inevitably make that domain assumption, their ensuing analyses are deeply colored thereby. When they begin to analyze the events of revolutions, the analytical tools are often pitched at the level of the nation as well. Thus "classes" act or are acted upon in revolutionary moments, whether we speak of a national aristocracy, bourgeoisie, proletariat, or peasantry. Nationwide political institutions—the state and government—are assumed to be the primary foci of revolutionary activity. National social institutions are thought to be weakened, and institutions by definition pervade the entire territory of a given nation.

It is hardly my intent to refute that assumption here; rather I wish to expand it. That revolutions ultimately happen to entire nations is hardly questionable; that revolutions take place ultimately only because of events at the national level is questionable. There are two ways in which we may expand our levels of analysis to deal with that second, dubious assumption. First, we may expand our analysis *beyond* the boundaries of the nation-state and examine how a nation-state's participation in a world system of nation-states might affect the likelihood of revolution within that society. This is the tack that Skocpol chose to take in *States and Social Revolutions*, where she locates the joint causes of revolution in the *international* system of competing nation-states and in the *national* political system where landed upper classes confronted state ministers and bureaucrats over fiscal reforms.[15] The great strength of this approach was to escape the narrow confines of national analysis in a truly innovative way, by introducing the international context of states competing both politically and economically during the worldwide spread of capitalism. Skocpol's work remains weaker, although not fatally flawed, in its lack of attentiveness to *regional variations* in the peasant insurrections so central to her theory.[16] Such regional variations are the second way out of the "national" constriction: one can instead move *within* the nation-state, and begin to pay attention to the different ways in which regionally situated actors or events affect the chances that a social revolution will occur.

Jeffery Paige's theoretical approach in *Agrarian Revolution* manages to address both of these lacunae simultaneously, but only at a price. He places his export crop areas firmly in the context of a worldwide system of market capitalism, in which dependent cultivators produce for foreign markets crops ranging from rice to tea to sugar to rubber. Hence the international market system is firmly implanted in this theory, in his domain assumption that he is only discussing "export agriculture" in the Third World, not agriculture in general. Further, Paige's work clearly compensates for a weakness in Skocpol's book, for his units of analysis throughout the book are *not* nations but agricultural regions, which are coded for the type of crops they export, the types of rural class structures that prevail therein, and the types of lower-class collective action that appeared there. However, while clearly and persuasively addressing the *international* and *regional* aspects of revolution, Paige pays a price: the loss of the national context for "revolution" throughout his book. That context only appears in the case studies of Angola and Vietnam. The result is a work—still the best ever written on revolutionary movements and rural class structures—which is a theory of revolutionary movements, not a theory of revolution. Paige's work therefore is an excellent guide to predicting where socialist and nationalist revolutionary movements will occur; yet since such movements proliferate in the Third World, while social revolution itself does not, his book ultimately does not resolve the *national* question: Which nations will experience social revolutions, and which will not?

The three variables I outlined briefly above seem to span and address those issues well (as do Goldfrank's earlier writings on Mexico).[17] Peasant support for guerrilla warfare, as we shall see, depends fundamentally on the *regional* social contexts that peasants inhabit, moreso than on national or international forces. Yet, as we shall see, one of the sources of the disruption of the peasants' moral economy in the countryside has been the spread of export agriculture there (echoes of Paige), which certainly gives it an international dimension as well. In addition, one source of peasant support discussed in chapters 7 and 10 is not really a regional characteristic, but instead a characteristic of peasant *communities*: the presence or absence in those communities of preexisting organizational bonds linking them to the guerrilla movement prior to the initiation of hostilities. The military power of the government armed forces seems to depend simultaneously on strictly *national* phenomena, such as the state's ability to finance military expansion; on international military aid; and on the military's ability to maintain its solidarity as an organization, perhaps as a "community" of soldiers. There is no reason why we could not apply an analogous line of reasoning to the guerrilla forces as well.

Finally, my focus on regime weaknesses clearly speaks directly to the *national* level of analysis, in inquiring into the structural characteristics that lead to a weakening of the state and incumbent governments. However, one final contributor to the fall of the Batista and Somoza regimes was the withdrawal of *international* support by the United States, even if those withdrawals heavily depended on the peculiar regimes they were, and on the respectable and constitutional oppositions that opposed them.

If I am correct in arguing that those three conditions, when combined, are likely to produce a social revolution, then I have implicitly addressed the analytical issue of levels, which is bypassed by certain earlier treatments. In addressing myself to those three influences upon revolutionary outcomes I have, perhaps only serendipitously, also looked into the international, national, regional, and community influences upon social revolution. If revolutions are indeed things that happen to entire societies, then perhaps it is time we started paying attention to entire societies in our analyses of revolutions, and not just to phenomena that only address the national level of analysis.

What Do We Mean by Comparative Analysis?

Many undergraduate students come eventually to joke about, and a few to dread, those exam essay questions that instruct them to compare different societies with respect to some characteristic, or all. A few thoughtfully inquire into the rationale for such intellectual exercises: What is the purpose? It is not at all clear to me that the professors themselves know the point of such comparison. The object of this work is not simply to compare for the sake of comparison itself, that is, simply to describe the similarities and differences among various societies (cases). Our comparisons instead should have some analytical "bite" to them, to instruct us theoretically concerning the varying outcomes that intrigue us.

Fortunately we now have a clear and insightful guide to the different ways in which social scientists go about doing historical comparisons in "macrosocial inquiry." Theda Skocpol and Margaret Somers have isolated for us three main ways of going about comparative inquiry into historical materials, which they found in the work of macrohistorical sociologists (and other social scientists, too).[18] Although the authors, I think, favor the third such mode, they clearly and with great insight discuss the strengths and weaknesses of each type of comparative analysis.[19] Happily, I can also wed my treatment of this methodological issue to a brief review of the comparative literature on guerrillas in Latin America.

First, comparative history may be approached using the technique of *parallel demonstration of theory*. In this form, a succession of cases is discussed, all of which are intended to provide support for a theoretical position advanced by the researcher. The sheer number of such cases is eventually thought to tell in its favor. To add my own coda to their observations, this particular approach seems to be the one that a sociologist interested in testing a theory would bring to historical subject matters. One can find this approach in S.N. Eisenstadt's *The Political Systems of Empires*,[20] and in a similar form in Karl Wittfogel's *Oriental Despotism*.[21] A different variant is encountered in Paige's *Agrarian Revolution*. We can also encounter a variant of this in studies of Latin American revolutions, particularly treatments of Central America since 1970. The clearest case is Robert G. Williams's *Export Agriculture and the Crisis in Central America*, where he tries to demonstrate, for all five Central American nations, that growing world markets for export crops have increased the physical and economic dislocation of the peasantry; this in turn has resulted in sharpened peasant discontent which, in the most extreme cases, has funneled itself through mass revolutionary movements in Nicaragua, Guatemala, and El Salvador (the last only briefly treated).[22]

A second, and very different, approach is that of comparative history written as a *contrast of contexts*. Here the emphasis is not on the similarities of the cases, but rather on their differences; moreover, such theoretical approaches typically pull back from making causal assertions about the impact of conceptually isolated and hypothetically important "variables" on specifically defined outcomes. Once again I would add my own coda to the Skocpol-Somers discussion: In such work, it is not at all clear just what such works are trying to *explain*, or which analytically separate aspects of history could account for the modern "outcome." This issue clearly arises in two excellent works, Clifford Geertz's *Islam Observed* and James Lang's *Conquest and Commerce: Spain and England in the Americas*, where each examines a pair of contrasting cases. In each study, the author comes close to arguing that the totality of what these societies historically were accounts for the totality of what they later became.

This particular form of argument comes very close to narrative history, rather than sociology. Indeed, I would argue that, if the practitioners of "parallel demonstration of theory" are likely to commit the "sociologists' fallacy"—by trying to force all cases into a single model—the practitioners of "contrast of contexts" are instead likely to commit the "historians' fallacy," by stressing the utter uniqueness of each historical case.[23]

The case-study approach used to analyze virtually all Latin American guerrilla movements can be used with a stress on either of these approaches: to stress the specifics of each case (contrast of contexts), or to demonstrate how they share a strong similarity in their structures and outcomes (parallel demonstration of theory). James Dunkerley, in *Power in the Isthmus*, is one of the more gifted scholars to have written about Central American politics and revolutionary movements to date, and his in-depth research into the twentieth-century history of all five nations has well equipped him to draw theoretical conclusions about the causes of (non-)revolution. Ultimately, though, he chooses to draw back from making firm theoretical statements about precisely that central issue and focuses instead on the "totality" and uniqueness of each individual case. For example, he writes, "[t]he course of events in El Salvador cannot properly be explained through comparison with Nicaragua since it corresponds above all else to a national history with its own logic and only limited relevance to any successful 'model' established by the FSLN [Sandinistas]."[24] No advocate of contrast-oriented analysis could have said it more clearly. Make no mistake about it: throughout his work Dunkerley makes countless sharp and insightful comparative comments about the various national cases; it is perhaps the best work on Central American revolutionary processes, despite the absence of "revolution" from the title. Yet he ultimately shies away from developing a truly comparative and clearly stated *theory* of revolution.

The bulk of the other comparative case studies that appeared since the Cuban revolution have implicitly, more than explicitly, attempted something resembling a parallel demonstration of theory. The focus has almost inevitably been on the failures of the post-1960 revolutionary movements, which are usually explained by the left (and sometimes the right) as due to the U.S. advocacy and support of counterinsurgency in the region after 1960. This focus is implicit in the amount of narrative space devoted to the U.S. role during the period of insurgency.[25] Those works that lie more to the right or the center of the political spectrum are likely to have a longer implicit list of the causes of failure, among which are the ideological extremism, hopeless dilettantism, elitist intellectualism, and/or internecine political divisions of the left.[26] Some critical works are more attentive to the peculiarities of the regimes that the guerrillas faced in the 1960s.[27] Almost all these works, regardless of their political leanings, share the fatal flaw that each one's theory of revolution—if any is to be found—is hopelessly embedded in the narrative, and not to be extracted without the use of deconstructionist theoretical dynamite.

Skocpol and Somers term the third and final "ideal type" of comparison *macro-causal analysis*. Despite her modesty about her contribution,[28] Skocpol's *States and Social Revolutions* is one of the best such analyses ever attempted, and I would group with it Robert Brenner's "Agrarian Class Structure and Economic Development in Pre-industrial Europe."[29] In macro-causal analysis, theorists clearly have an outcome that they wish to account for in a causal fashion (unlike contrast of contexts). Moreover, they systematically attempt to address *both* cases with *and* those without the outcome in question, so as to isolate the "true" causes of the outcome. In doing so, they implicitly tend to resort both to the "method of agreement"—similar outcomes probably have a similar cause—and to the "method of difference"—dissimilar outcomes must have at least one dissimilar condition to account for that difference.[30] That is, macro-causal analyses also systematically address cases that do *not* have the outcome (unlike the parallel demonstration of theory).[31]

I would plant the main lines of my argument firmly in the last school of thought: it is intended as an "exercise" in the macro-causal analysis of revolutionary outcomes in Latin America. Moreover, when I analyze the sources of peasant support for guerrillas in chapters 6, 7, and 10, I always compare regions with high levels of such support to other areas of no support, weak support, or simply no guerrillas; therefore that analysis also stands firmly in the realm of macro-causal analysis.

Nonetheless, Skocpol and Somers also alert us to works of comparative sociology that mix these three different methods of comparative research, and this work is no exception. For example, my detailed and repetitive treatments of the sources of peasant support later in this work only lead to a strong sense that a parallel demonstration of theory is being attempted. Moreover, in the opening section of chapter 11, the case of Nicaragua is recounted, but only along with systematically repeated parallels drawn to the Cuban revolution, which are finally summarized in table 11–1. Those elements of this book therefore pull it out of the realm of pure macrocausal analysis in the direction of "parallel demonstration of theory."

Yet the contrast of contexts is not ignored either. While I do not resort simply to asserting the uniqueness of the Cuban and Nicaraguan cases—and thus opt out of theory building altogether—I do provide detailed discussions of six cases in chapter 8 (Cuba versus the 1960s guerrillas) and five cases in chapter 11 (Nicaragua versus failed revolutionaries in four other nations). Anyone reading those chapters will note the dense discursive quality therein and the strong tendency to emphasize the contrasts between Cuban and Nicaraguan societies, on the one hand, and their failed contemporaries, on the other. Those joint characteristics, careful description of case studies wedded to an analysis that emphasizes contrasts instead of parallels, are precisely those of the "contrast of contexts."

In the end, then, this work does not remain a pure example of macro-causal analysis, although that was my initial intent. Skocpol and Somers metaphorically place the three comparative methods on the three corners of a "Triangle of Comparative History." Works that blend *two* such methods, therefore, we may place on one of the sides of said triangle.[32] By mixing *three* such methods, as this work clearly does, we can only say that it has been pulled into the center of their "Triangle of Comparative History." Let us hope that in the application of those three different methods in this work I shall partake more of their strengths than of the weaknesses of each.

A Brief Historical Overview of the First Wave

Before I begin the analyses that constitute the theory building of this work, I must first render a situation-setting service to those who know naught of or remember only vaguely the political events leading up to guerrilla warfare in the first wave of insurgency (to 1970). Further, I briefly describe the political situation those insurgents confronted, as well as the final (?) disposition of such attempts to effect social revolution in Latin America.

Following the success and socialist transformation of the Cuban revolution, guerrilla movements appeared throughout Latin America in the 1960s, but most died an early death. A few nations have seen a strong resurgence of such activity since roughly 1975: Nicaragua, Guatemala, Colombia, El Salvador, and Peru; the first three cases are linked to and revivals of earlier movements. Although virtually every nation in the region experienced a 1960s movement, the existing literature threw light on few of them, with Venezuela, Colombia, Guatemala, Peru, and Bolivia the most closely scrutinized. Bolivia is the prototype for guerrilla failure, yet we know much about it largely because of Ché Guevara and his famous diary. Other failures left but traces on the written record, too few for the close analysis required here. Since the losers are underrepresented here, my sample is nonrandom, yet the comparative nature of my argument can still contribute to our understanding of the variety of outcomes of such revolutionary action.

In Cuba, Fulgencio Batista seized power in a gradual shadow coup in the years 1933–1934 and dominated Cuban politics off and on for the next twenty-five years. In 1952 he seized power in a coup to stave off probable electoral defeat. In response, one of the disappointed candidates, Fidel Castro, who had stood for a congressional seat, organized a 1953 attack on the Moncada military barracks. Imprisoned but later pardoned, Castro went into exile in Mexico, where he organized an invasion of Cuba. Routed in his December 1956 landing, Castro withdrew into the hills of eastern Cuba, where he built a guerrilla movement. The 26th of July Movement (M-26), as it was known, spread and grew to several hundred rural fighters plus other urban supporters by early 1958, as Batista's troops proved ineffectual in counterinsurgency. Following a failed army campaign, Castro's guerrillas began a summer offensive in 1958, eventually forcing the dictator to flee the country at year's end. Castro assumed and consolidated power, instituted reforms, and declared Cuba socialist in 1961 following a confrontation with the United States over the nationalization of sugar lands.

Venezuela's first experiment with direct electoral democracy began in 1945, following a civil-military coup, but ended in 1948, the victim of another coup. The later military government of Marcos Pérez Jiménez ruled in an increasingly bloody fashion toward the end of the 1950s but, after a period of widespread social unrest and opposition, especially by Communists and left-wing youth, a civilian-military coup ousted the dictator in 1958. Caracas remained in revolutionary euphoria, while the interim government sought to mitigate economic problems with massive welfare spending and subsidies. Returning from exile, Rómulo Betancourt won the presidency in late 1958, brought to power on the strength of his Acción Democrática's ties to the peasant voters, which went back to the 1930s. Over the next three to four years, opposition by students and Caracas residents grew in the face of Betancourt's austerity program, and a dialectic of government and opposition violence ensued. Guerrilla bands appeared in 1962, followed a year later by more systematic guerrilla organization with party backing: the Armed Forces of National Liberation (FALN), sponsored by the Communists, and the Movement of the Revolutionary Left (MIR), organized by a splinter group from the president's own party. From 1963 on, the guerrillas' fortunes declined as agrarian reforms, competitive elections, public distaste, efficient repression, an improving economy, and amnesties gradually took the wind from their sails. Internal splits hastened the decline. By the late 1960s, the guerrillas had all but petered out of existence.

In Guatemala, a decade of reformist government ended with the 1954 CIA-orchestrated overthrow of Jacobo Arbenz, who had carried out a major land reform. A series of dictators followed, generally coming to power under greatly restricted electoral façades. A left-leaning military revolt on 13 November 1960 was suppressed, but two young officers escaped capture, later forming the MR-13 guerrilla movement (Movimiento Revolucionario 13 de Noviembre), and later still the Rebel Armed Forces (FAR). The guerrillas, despite periodic fission and refusion, gained substantial ground in northeastern Guatemala by 1965 but succumbed to an intense U.S.-backed counterinsurgency campaign in 1966–1967. The movement then lapsed into a period of dormancy and urban terrorism, before its revival in the mid-1970s.

In Colombia, a particularly intense period of interparty political violence accelerated with the 1948 assassination of populist Liberal Jorge Eliécer Gaitán. *La Violencia* claimed over 200,000 lives in the next fifteen to twenty years, mostly in rural areas. In response to the violence and to the ensuing dictatorship of Gustavo Rojas Pinilla (1953–1957), Liberals and Conservatives agreed to forego their internecine rivalry and to form a pact, known as the National Front, in which they alternated in the presidency and shared ministries from 1958 to 1974. Government and military soon took notice of the "peasant republics" that had formed during *La Violencia* as quasi-independent zones for self-defense and self-administration in agrarian matters. A military campaign retook those areas in 1964 and 1965. The Colombian Revolutionary Armed Forces (FARC), allied to the Colombian Communists (PCC), rose out of the ashes of those "republics." In 1965, proto-guerrillas returning from a trip to Cuba formed the Fidelista Army of National Liberation (ELN) in Santander, while a few years later Chinese-line Communists formed *their* own guerrilla group, the Popular Army of Liberation (EPL), based in Córdoba and Antioquia. The fortunes and the activities of the various groups waned toward 1970, but would later wax anew in the 1970s.

In Peru, two groups formed parallel Andean *focos* in 1965 and both failed to get off the ground. Héctor Béjar led the Army of National Liberation (ELN), which split from the Communists, and Luis de la Puente led the Movement of the Revolutionary Left (MIR), which left the APRA party (American Popular Revolutionary Alliance). Both unleashed guerrilla movements in the Sierra in mid-year: the ELN in La Mar Province, Ayacucho; the MIR in three sites in Cuzco, Junín, and Piura Departments. Within six months all four had been shattered, although the fronts in Ayacucho and Junín had enjoyed limited success in obtaining peasant support.

Working in the wake of Bolivia's 1952 worker- and peasant-backed revolution and subsequent land reforms, Ernesto "Ché" Guevara organized a Cuban-led *foco* in late 1966 in eastern Bolivia, superseding the objections of the Bolivian Communists. Forced into premature activity and completely lacking peasant support, Guevara's guerrillas split into two groups and never reunited. The army harried each band, and peasants informed on them; they were ultimately destroyed by October 1967, and Guevara himself was killed following his capture. In addition, an even more minor, student-dominated *foco* effort at Teoponte a few years later was rapidly destroyed, and many of the participants died of hunger and exposure.

CHAPTER 2

Who Are the Guerrillas?

> The mandarin character of revolutionaries began with Marx and
> Engels themselves. . . . Who could have been more bourgeois
> than Marx . . . and who more mandarin. . .?
>
> —Alvin Gouldner,
> *The Future of Intellectuals and the Rise of the New Class*

> The intellectuals as such can do little politically unless they attach
> themselves to a massive form of discontent. . . . It is a particularly
> misleading trick to deny that a revolution stems from peasant
> grievances because its leaders happen to be professional men or
> intellectuals.
>
> —Barrington Moore, Jr.,
> *Social Origins of Dictatorship and Democracy*

A SOUND methodological guideline, often ignored by those given to intemperate theorizing, is that facts should be firmly established before attempts are made to theorize about the facts. The necessary process of answering the question posed by this chapter may prove trivial to persons familiar with the study of revolutionaries, yet in this case accurate description must precede explanation, lest we find ourselves engaged in explaining pseudo-facts, a practice against which Robert Merton has cautioned us.[1]

My task here is the relatively straightforward one of establishing the types of persons who became involved in guerrilla movements and demonstrating that they were not randomly drawn from all sectors of the populace. In relatively brief compass I will consider the age and sex distribution of the guerrillas; the class origins and class locations of the guerrilla leadership, and then of the rank and file; and the fragmentary data on race and ethnic distribution.

Appendix A displays data on the sex (inferred from names), age, and class backgrounds of the guerrilla leadership that I have gathered from a wide range of sources. Also included are data on the educational attainment of the principals and their occupations, as well as their political party affiliations. Lacunae as well as data fill the table, yet it is adequate for these modest purposes.

AGE

War has ever been the office of relatively young men (and occasionally young women), and this is true of contemporary guerrilla warfare as well. I have

TABLE 2-1
Average Age of Guerrilla Leadership at the
Peak of the Struggle

Country	Year	Average Age	Number of cases
Cuba	1958	28	7
Venezuela	1963	30	15
Guatemala	1966	25–26	4
Colombia	1965	40	6
Peru	1965	32	9
Bolivia	1967	34	8

Source: Appendix A. Frank País's age for the
Cuban data is 23, due to his death in 1957. Peruvian
data exclude Hugo Blanco and Javier Héraud.

gathered the tabular information on date of birth in order to calculate the average age of the guerrilla leadership during the struggle, shown in table 2-1.

Guerrilla leaders tended to be young men—far younger than national political leaders usually were, as we can see from table 2-1. The Colombian and Bolivian guerrilla leaderships are older than average because each group contained many "war veterans"—the Colombians from *La Violencia*, the Bolivian *foco* those Cubans who were veterans of the Sierra Maestra. In Guatemala, the youthfulness stems from the movement's origin in a revolution of junior officers in 1960. In each case the age is taken at the peak of the guerrilla struggle rather than at time of entry, thereby, if anything, biasing the age distribution upward. In addition, the leadership is almost certainly older than the rank and file—given the age stratification virtually universal to human society—which again biases upward an age estimate for the guerrillas as a whole.

Further evidence of this last point abounds. At a trial of Venezuelan guerrillas in 1962, the "vast majority" were aged eighteen to twenty-eight. Likewise in 1964, a *guerrillera* there noted that the oldest member of her squad was but twenty-five. In Guatemala, the average age was twenty to twenty-two, and the oldest fighter was forty or forty-seven. Bolivia's youngest, by contrast, was twenty-two years of age. Extreme youth is also encountered at times, with documented Peruvian recruitment of young teenagers, and suggestions of similar events elsewhere. One not-too-reliable writer has also described ten Colombian EPL squads composed solely of boys eleven to fifteen years of age.[2]

The high prevalence of youth was not restricted to the urban and highly educated. Four Peruvian peasants tried for MIR guerrilla activity were aged twenty-three, twenty-five, twenty-five, and thirty years. Those Guatemalan guerrillas of average age twenty to twenty-two were composed largely of peasants. In Cuba, Ché Guevara noted the youth and strength of the Sierra Maestra peasant recruits, a situation apparently repeated in Venezuela as well.[3] None of this should surprise, for youth have also predominated elsewhere as well: in the Chinese and Vietnamese revolutions; among rural bandit groups; and among urban terrorists.[4]

GENDER

War since time immemorial has been primarily a male endeavor, and again the guerrilla evidence for the 1960s bears out our expectations. (In the 1970s and 1980s, however, women came to compose one-fourth to one-third of the Nicaraguan and Salvadoran guerrilla combatants, according to some reports.)[5] For the 1960s there was considerable scope in female participation, ranging from zero to 20 percent of the guerrilla leaders. In no case was there female predominance in either numbers or power within a movement, nor did I encounter a single case of a female peasant joining as an arms-bearing guerrilla regular.

Within the Cuban revolution, a special women's battalion was formed in the summer of 1958, whose total casualties were one wounded. Perhaps one in twenty Cuban guerrillas was female at that time. For Venezuela, the 148 guerrilla biographies compiled by Valsalice included but 10 women. Two isolated actions involved three women (of twenty participants) and five (of twenty-five). Reporters visiting the Guatemalan Sierra de la Minas encountered three women in one guerrilla squad, while in another one of twelve was female. If bias exists in these reports, it is likely to be toward overestimation of women's combat participation, since their high newsworthiness increases the likelihood of their gender being noted.[6]

Perhaps more typical of women's participation in the 1960s movements are quite different cases. Of 116 Venezuelans on 1962 trial for guerrilla activity, only 1 was female. A Mexican reporter visiting the Colombian ELN's base camp noted nary a woman among the 60 or so guerrillas present. Only 1 woman—the famous/infamous "Tania," or Tamara Bunke-Bider—took part in the Bolivian *foco*, and I have encountered no evidence of female participation in the 1965 Peruvian guerrillas, despite a substantial series of accounts. The Colombian FARC also lacks evidence of 1960s female participation (there is some later), but there the historiography is much weaker. The Colombian ELN, in contrast, gained a reputation for "feminism" when a woman named "Mariela" took part in the Simacota raid of 7 January 1965. In fact, she is the only *guerrillera* mentioned in ELN narratives until 1974, and she was "seduced and abandoned" by ELN leader Fabio Vásquez, who later forced her expulsion from the group after a period of public humiliation.[7]

Women in guerrilla movements apparently were relegated to typical "support" roles rather than active combat, whether by personal preference or imposition. In this respect their roles resemble those of women in other radical movements of the period, in which men often left them the job of "making the coffee."[8] Among the most famous female revolutionaries were the Cubans Vilma Espín, Celia Sánchez, and Haydée Santamaría. Espín worked as a contact to Frank País's urban support group, while Sánchez worked at Castro's command headquarters in the Sierra Maestra. Santamaría may have worked in both areas. No wonder that women were not more active in combat, when a Marxist female writer on the Cuban revolution wrote only of women who "distributed literature, nursed the wounded, helped fugitives reach embassy asylum, and smuggled arms." Although she adds that women were tortured and killed for such activity, the idea of a more expanded role for women did not seem to be culturally "available" at that time, even for Marxists.[9]

Since, as Weber noted, war conditions tend to impose a "military communism" upon the combatants, and since Marxism often entails radical egalitarianism as well, we might well expect to find outcroppings of feminism within guerrilla movements, in protest against the "coffee-maker" role. And so we do. In Venezuela, Juanita Villavicencio (pseudonym?) commanded a guerrilla unit in Falcón, as did Angela Zago in a hamlet in Lara, while Maria Rangel ("Petra María") may have led the attack on Villanueva, Lara, in December 1964. In Guatemala, "Rose Marie" (Rosa María?) demonstrated that women could even assume the casual attitude toward killing often displayed in war, as the *guerrillera* informed a visiting reporter that she had already executed three villagers suspected of aiding the government.

Fragmentary evidence suggests that women had to fight to maintain equal footing with men in guerrilla movements. Jacinta, a Venezuelan *guerrillera* visiting Zago's Lara camp in 1964, said to her *compañera* that "Women have a very important role in the revolutionary process . . . [and that] in I-don't-know-which front they wish to lower all the women [and that] we should show them what we can do." Zago, for her part, resisted the attempts of male guerrillas to impose standard military drills and discipline within the guerrilla band, insisting in her memoirs that carrying out the revolution and playing soldier were quite distinct activities. The aforementioned Rose Marie gave a talk as well to Guatemalan peasants in 1966, arguing that women could carry guns in the struggle as she did, or learn to be nurses to help the revolution. To learn about one woman's perspective on guerrilla life, one should above all read the memoirs of that thoughtful *guerrillera*, Angela Zago.[10]

I have not intended to imply that repression within the left is the direct cause of lesser female participation therein. To commit oneself to a guerrilla struggle with gun in hand is to adopt an extremely aggressive stance vis-à-vis the "system." Such a stance is too radically aggressive for the vast majority of males or females. Yet men, on the average, are more aggressive than women in human societies.[11] So universal is this phenomenon that scholars suspect, and some research suggests, a biological basis. Given the statistical differences between men and women in aggression, one would expect greater male participation in guerrilla movements on those grounds alone. The Latin American cultural context—less gender egalitarian than northwest European cultures—might be expected to accentuate these differences. Finally, given that guerrillas are heavily recruited from the urban intelligentsia, and given women's underrepresentation in higher education during this period, again we would expect less female participation. Still, heavy female participation in the extreme-left Baader-Meinhof group in Germany (the Red Army Faction) suggests such differences can be transcended.

SOCIAL CLASS

Leadership

While the casual onlooker observing massive (generally rural) revolutionary movements in places as diverse as Russia, China, Cambodia, Vietnam, and Latin America might be prompted to think immediately in terms of peasant revolts, especially originating among the most impoverished and downtrodden peasantry, such portraits of revolutionary movements are now known to be half-truths at best. Alvin Gouldner accumulated in brief compass much of the information concerning the revolutionary leadership in many worldwide revolutions, and he consistently turned up highly educated intellectuals at the center of such organizations and movements.[12]

A mythical interpretation of the rise, in particular, of modern rural guerrilla movements is that they "spring up"—perhaps in some social analogue of spontaneous generation—from the exploitative conditions of rural life in Latin America, as peasants awake to organize and shake off their centuries-old chains and go into battle against their oppressors.[13] In truth, autonomous peasant insurrections can and do occur, but such was not the case in our six nations here.[14] That aforementioned scenario of peasant awakening has more to do with revolutionary poetry than with the realities of the first stage of contemporary Latin American guerrilla movements, which takes place typically in urban areas in the milieus of universities and party politics. Instead, such a portrait only resembles guerrilla movements in their second stage, when urban-educated organizers "go to the countryside."

If we once again examine Appendix A, we can clearly see that the leadership of guerrilla movements was, with few exceptions, drawn from the urban middle and upper classes and from rural elites. In all these groups the university-educated predominated. Of particular interest are the sons and relatives of *hacendados* and plantation owners among the proponents of agrarian revolution, among them Fidel and Raúl Castro of Cuba; Douglas Bravo, Hipólito Acosta, Domingo Urbina, and Argimiro Gabaldón of Venezuela; and Luis de la Puente Uceda of Peru.

The free professions—doctors, lawyers, architects, and engineers—were also overrepresented in the guerrilla leadership, as were students, teachers, and university professors. Given the class selectivity of Latin American universities, it is fairly safe to assume that student status was usually indicative of middle- to upper-class background, even when data on parental class are absent.[15] Students have been a gold mine of cadres for guerrilla movements throughout Latin America, and nowhere more so than in Venezuela where, in the first few months of guerrilla activity, four of every five guerrillas the army captured were students.[16]

Young military officers also played an important role in the guerrilla struggle in Guatemala and Venezuela, because in each country left-wing barracks revolts against the government failed, and the escaped rebels went on to form or join guerrilla movements. Most commonly we find lieutenants or captains in these insurrectionary roles, but at least two lieutenant colonels participated in the Guatemalan *focos* as well. In a unique case, all the Cuban participants in the Bolivian *foco* held officer rank in the Cuban army.

Using the biographical data in Appendix A, we may construct a table indicating the distribution of the guerrilla leaders by socioeconomic status (SES). Where information allows, I place them according to their own education or occupation; where such information is absent, the father's status dictates the placement. I have eliminated Bolivia since all nineteen of the Cuban participants were Cuban army officers. Four of the five for whom we know more were doctors, and the fifth was of peasant stock. Of the thirty-six Bolivian participants, we have SES data on eleven more, distributed as follows: three miners, two doctors, four students, one engineer, and one mining union leader. The two Peruvian participants were a law student and a radio operator.[17] The data in table 2-2 statistically support the claim that guerrilla leaders in Latin America issued from relatively privileged social groups.

Despite the objective evidence of social and economic privilege, some guerrilla leaders tried—in what can only be described an act of reverse snobbery—to identify themselves with the lower classes through an act of sheer will.[18] Most common in this regard was the self-identification of the guerrillas as "popular movements," "forces of the people," and the like, a penchant shared by the movements' uncritical chroniclers. While a self-portrait as a "popular movement" is certainly accurate for the broad-based Cuban opposition to Batista, elsewhere that picture is far more suspect.

Thus Douglas Bravo could refer to his declining FALN guerrillas in 1964 as the "forces of the people," despite a shattering defeat for the FALN at the polls in the December 1963 elections. At that time, the "forces of the people" threatened to shoot anyone who went to the polls—and 90 percent of the

TABLE 2-2
Socioeconomic Status of Guerrilla Leaders, by Country

| Country | Cuba | Venezuela | Guatemala | Colombia | Peru |
Total Identified	29	43	9	19	11
Rural elite	—	4	—	—	—
Urban elite	—	1	—	—	—
Professions	14	10	2	5	5
Doctors	3	2	—	1	—
Lawyers	4	2	—	—	2
Teachers	2	1[a]	—	—	—
Others	5	5	2	4	3
Students	7	14	2	6	5
University	7	12	1	6	4
High School	—	2	1[a]	—	1
Military officers	—	11	5	2	—
Subtotal (%)	*21 (72)*	*40 (93)*	*9 (100)*	*13 (68)*	*10 (89)*
Peasant	2.5[b]	—	—	5	1[c]
Small Businessman	2.5[b]	1	—	—	—
Worker	3	1	—	1	—
Other	2	1	—	—	—
Subtotal (%)	*8 (28)*	*3 (7)*	*0 (0)*	*6 (32)*	*1 (11)*

Source: Appendix A.
[a] Peasant family background.
[b] See Universo Sánchez, Appendix A.
[c] Hugo Blanco.

people turned out to vote.[19] In analogous fashion, Héctor Béjar described the Peruvian ELN as coming from "impoverished and powerless sectors." In a MIR flier directed at soldiers and police engaged in counterinsurgency, Luis de la Puente Uceda, the elite-born leader of the MIR, addressed himself to the police thusly: "Or is it perhaps that you're the son of some *latifundista*, of some banker, or some great industrialist? No. You are poor like us, you are exploited like us. Out of necessity you are wearing a police uniform. . . . We are simple people and we defend simple people, we are poor and we defend the poor."[20]

In a similar fashion, the routine claims that guerrilla movements united within their ranks workers, peasants, students, and the progressive sectors of the bourgeoisie were especially weak on the first group so embraced. Only Castro's Moncada attack of 26 July 1953 included a high proportion of fighters drawn from the working class, and his nascent guerrilla movement in the Sierra Maestra in 1956–1957 was far more middle class in background, a feature accentuated by fifty-eight new recruits sent to him in April 1957 by his support group in Santiago.[21]

Rank and File

Yet my emphasis on the privileged origins of guerrillas only encompasses the first, urban stage of guerrilla movements, which in reality have a bifurcated, two-stage recruitment pattern. In that second stage, the newly formed guerrilla nucleus goes to the countryside and seeks to gain recruits and support from the rural populace. In every case examined here—save the Colombian FARC—planning took place outside the rural *foco* area before the founders tried to forge that revolutionary alliance. (In the case of the Colombian FARC, the guerrillas rose phoenixlike out of the ashes of the peasant republics of south-central Colombia in 1964–1965, following the elimination of their autonomy by a government military campaign.)

This typical two-stage recruitment campaign should not be considered trivial. Writers often identify guerrilla movements as rural explosions comparable to land invasions or peasant revolts, when they are usually rather more complex.[22] They are in fact attempts by revolutionary intellectuals to form class alliances with peasants against those whom one or both parties define as enemies. A more appropriate analogue to such movements is that of the *narodniki*, nineteenth-century Russian intellectuals who went to the countryside both to adopt the peasants' way of life and to fan the fires of revolt.[23] Hugo Blanco attempted to create in Peru a movement much like that which Alexander Herzen had envisaged in Russia a century before.

How successful were the guerrillas in recruiting peasants to their cause?[24] Even allowing for some serious disagreement on the Cuban and Guatemalan data, peasants soon composed a high percentage of the combatants in all cases reviewed here save Bolivia and Peru, where the *focos* endured but half a year.

For Cuba, estimates of peasant participation range from 10 to 75 percent, the last being Castro's own assessment. They may vary because they are taken at different inflection points in the M-26's history. The summer of 1958 is the best point at which to make an estimate, after Castro had recruited for a year and a half, but before his movement benefited from bandwagon enrollments. At that time Castro had about three hundred in the Sierra Maestra, with another three hundred in the other two fronts combined. Over a year before that time, in April 1957, we know that the guerrillas numbered some seventy persons, the bulk of whom were of middle-class backgrounds. We also know that they suffered few casualties in their military history. If none but peasants joined from mid-1957 to mid-1958, the peasant share might have totalled 90 percent. That is an unlikely scenario, and an estimate of 50 to 75 percent seems reasonable for mid-1958, although it is admittedly guesswork.[25]

In Venezuela, the 1962 wave of guerrilla mini-*focos* included mainly students. By early 1963, however, reports already noted a band with a core of 10 criminals and students accompanied by 100 peasants (the latter forced to join, according to the government). By 1964, peasant membership in the "Frente Páez" totaled perhaps 44 percent, and in 1965–1967 various estimates for overall peasant participation in the movement ranged from 70 to 90 percent. Therefore 75 percent seems a reasonable peak estimate of peasant guerrillas for Venezuela. We should note, however, that the peasant share increased from 1964 to 1967 as the absolute number of guerrillas fell from 1,000 to 2,000 to fewer than 300.[26] Their increased proportion may simply indicate a greater commitment to the armed struggle.

Several comparative chroniclers cite Guatemala as the most peasant-oriented guerrilla movement in the region, with perhaps 90 percent peasants, a claim made for the MR-13 in 1965. At that time its counterpart, the FAR, was still allegedly student dominated. Yet in 1966 leader César Montes claimed a peasant majority within the FAR's ranks, even though a 1967 FAR deserter would tally the group's membership at 300 students plus 100 peasants. Still, the deserter conceded, some of those students were only "weekend guerrillas."[27]

Colombia was graced with three separate guerrilla groups, and each shows a distinct pattern. The FARC was composed overwhelmingly of peasants—many with bandit pasts—at its founding in 1965, and it also contained some urban cadres of the Soviet-line Communists (PCC). FARC strength rose to 600 men in the field in the mid-1960s, later losing ground, but then showing even stronger growth in the 1970s and early 1980s.[28]

Its chroniclers usually describe the Colombian ELN as a predominantly student and middle-class movement. Yet I compiled a list of members in the field identified by a visiting Mexican reporter and by a former ELN member (all identified by name so as to avoid redundancy). Of the twenty-four, fourteen were peasants, two were doctors, one a missionary, and seven students—a distribution suggesting that the middle-class dominance may not have extended to the rank and file of the ELN. Whatever its class composition, there is no disagreement on one fact: The ELN generally maintained strong peasant support. A similar picture probably applies to the Maoist EPL guerrillas as well.[29]

In Peru few peasants joined the guerrillas, while in Bolivia none swelled the revolutionaries' ranks. The Peruvian guerrillas did, however, obtain some peasant support briefly in some areas. The sole case of documented support in Peru was that of the Campa Indians for the MIR *foco* in Junín, which even the army conceded (there is less good, yet still persuasive evidence from Béjar's ELN *foco* in Ayacucho). However, the Campas later collaborated with the government in the capture of the guerrillas. Thus peasant participation in the four *focos* was uncommon, and the Peruvian prime minister's estimate that 80 percent of the guerrillas were from universities does not seem absurdly high.[30]

Did peasants ever assume positions among the topmost leadership of these movements? In Cuba, the most notable case was Guillermo García, who reached the highest rank in the Cuban revolutionary army. However, as Theodore Draper showed, those who controlled Cuban politics after the revolution were virtually all university-educated professionals, with nary a peasant or worker among them. In the Colombian FARC we do encounter a case in which peasants probably held a majority of the leadership positions—due surely to the FARC's birth from the peasant republics. Peasant Fabio Vásquez led the Colombian ELN, but his ideological and personal disputes with the urban intellectuals who composed most of the remaining leadership led to virtual warfare within the group, splitting it asunder. Peasant Camilo Sánchez became second in command of the Guatemalan FAR, but he had at least a high-school and perhaps a university education, making him an extraordinary peasant given Guatemalan educational conditions.[31]

Other Latin American guerrilla leaders—predecessors, contemporaries, and successors of those examined here—have also emerged from relatively privileged backgrounds. At least since Toussaint L'Ouverture led Haitians in rebellion against the French shortly after the French Revolution, Latin America's revolutionary leaders have consistently been much more educated than the rank and file, and generally from privileged class origins. Despite his own work in a variety of humble occupations, Augusto Sandino was born the (illegitimate but recognized) son of a rich landowner before later becoming the hero of the resistance to the U.S. occupation of Nicaragua. Of more recent vintage, an Argentine *foco* in Salta in 1963 consisted mainly of students and white-collar workers, an Ecuadoran adventure in 1962 consisted of forty students, and intellectuals and former political guerrillas made up the Colombian MOEC guerrillas at Vichada at the same time. A second Bolivian *foco* attempt at Teoponte in 1970 was again composed mainly of students, many of whom died of hunger and disease. Finally, a survey of guerrilla attempts in Mexico also concluded that almost all the participants were students and that none were peasants.[32]

RACE AND ETHNICITY

The evidence on selective participation by race and ethnic group is extremely fragmentary, but certain parts of it are suggestive. Afro-Cubans did not appear to have exceptionally high or low rates of participation in the Cuban insurgency, given their concentration in Oriente Province, home of Castro's guerrillas forces. One suggestive piece of evidence is the racial composition of the Cuban officers in the Bolivian *foco* of 1967. Of fifteen men described, three are identified as "Negro," somewhat lower than their proportion of all Cubans. Photographs of Peruvian and Venezuelan guerrillas appear to indicate some underrepresentation of, respectively, Amerinds and blacks in the two movements. We do know, however, that the Campa tribe gave support to the Peruvian guerrillas of Junín for a time. In Venezuela, one "Negro Antonio" led a guerrilla squad for a time.[33] In the Bolivian *foco*, not only were the Cuban-led guerrillas ethnically distinct from the Indian and *mestizo* (mixed race) Bolivians, but they even spent time teaching themselves Quechua, the language of many highland Bolivians, rather than Guaraní, the lingua franca of many southeastern Bolivians. Colombia, for its part, is a thoroughly mestizo nation, with some African concentration on the coasts, but the evidence there is scanty on this topic.

Guatemala provides in many ways the most interesting illustration of ethnic barriers. More than 50 percent of all Guatemalans were Indians in the 1960s. In that country, *Ladino* indicates any person who has adopted Hispanic culture, most importantly the Spanish language. Yet virtually all the Guatemalan guerrillas were *Ladinos* and not Indians; the *focos* settled most firmly in the *Ladino* areas of the east; and they failed in attempting to set up a base in heavily Indian Huehuetenango in 1962. Instead, the guerrillas awoke to find themselves surrounded by machete-wielding Indians, who promptly turned them over to the authorities.[34]

Yet in Guatemala, as well as in Peru, we shall see that the barriers to recruitment of Indian guerrillas were breached by the guerrillas of the second wave (See chapter 9). Therefore it will become apparent that guerrillas *can* recruit from indigenous peoples with sufficient effort, command of the language, and favorable structural conditions. Yet that process may be a slow and painstaking one relative to work with other social groups.

SUMMARY

I can now summarize the results of the investigation to this point. First, the guerrillas were young, usually in their twenties, with a slightly older leadership, and their ages showed little variation. Second, the guerrillas of the 1960s were overwhelmingly male, with female participation usually only in supporting roles. Still, evidence from the 1970s suggests much higher rates of female combat participation. Third, in their initial stage, guerrilla movements begin among the highly educated offspring of rural elites and the urban middle and upper classes. In the two cases where there were left-wing military revolts, junior officers from the armed forces were important as well, in Venezuela and Guatemala. Fourth, in the subsequent stage of the movement, peasants come to predominate in numbers, while power remains in the hands of those with higher status and education. Fifth, the Colombian FARC is a major exception to the third and fourth points just noted. Sixth, while evidence is fragmentary, guerrillas don't seem to recruit especially well among ethnic minorities, although the experience of the 1970s in Guatemala and Peru suggests that movements can be built almost totally upon an indigenous rank and file.

CHAPTER 3

The Social and Political Origins
of the Guerrilla Movements

> [T]he first Declaration of Havana . . . was intended to be the spark that would start the fire of South American revolutions.
>
> —Boris Goldenberg

> [E]xternal causes become operative through internal causes. In a suitable temperature an egg changes into a chicken, but no temperature can change a stone into a chicken. . . .
>
> —Mao Zedong

IN THIS chapter we will try to arrive at an understanding of the origins of the guerrilla movements. As we saw in the previous chapter, any attempt to understand them simply as social explosions in the countryside is doomed to failure from the start.[1] Guerrilla movements do not begin among peasants in the countryside but among urban-based intellectuals, especially in the twin milieus of universities and left-wing political parties. Therefore we must focus our attentions in those areas for understanding. The crucial issue of peasant support for insurgency, however, merits detailed treatment, which it will receive in chapters 6 and 7. We wish answers to the following queries:

1. Why did all the important rural guerrilla movements of the postwar period appear only from about 1962 on, with the exception of the Cuban insurgency?
2. Why were guerrilla movements much stronger in some countries than in others?
3. Why did such movements first and most strongly take hold among youth and in universities and political parties?[2]

TIMING

Guerrilla movements appeared in Latin America after 1961 because of the impact of the Cuban revolution upon intellectuals and parties of the political left and center in the region. We need not impute this influence to the principals involved, for both their attitudes and their behavior provide ample confirmation of that thesis. With regard to attitudes, Debray sums up neatly the overall effect of the Cuban revolution on the Latin American Left: "Cuba descended like a clap of thunder on scepticism and legalism." Héctor Béjar of the Peruvian ELN noted that one of the major reasons for his group's formation was unity of admiration for the Cuban revolution, and Douglas Bravo of the Venezuelan FALN evinced similar views. A letter seized from the guerrillas by the Venezuelan authorities reads in part that "the glorious Cuban revolution is the concrete example for our struggle." In Guatemala, a revolutionary wrote in a similar vein, saying that "Developments in our country are greatly influenced by the Cuban Revolution . . . the example of Cuba is directly influencing the revolutionary people in their choice of the *means* of the struggle against the reactionary regime." Finally, a former colleague of Luis de la Puente Uceda, founder of the Peruvian MIR, described him as a "fanatical admirer" of Fidel Castro.[3]

Direct behavioral measures also suggest the impact of the Cuban revolution, the most important of which, of course, is the timing of the latter movements themselves. Too, an enormous number of Latin Americans made the trip to Cuba, which quickly came to resemble a revolutionary Mecca where potential guerrillas would be spiritually prepared—and often militarily trained—for revolutionary struggle. The impact of such trips was especially strong when a cohort of people visited or trained together in Cuba and then returned as a group to follow "The Cuban Road"—precisely the history of the Colombian ELN and of Javier Héraud's ill-fated Peruvian venture at Puerto Maldonado in 1963.[4]

We also encounter more indirect behavioral indices of the Cuban impact. Ideas are generally conveyed in books, and copies of Ché Guevara's writings on guerrilla warfare regularly turned up when government troops overran guerrilla camps. The Venezuelan FALN's kidnapping (for publicity) of a world-famous soccer player in 1963 bears a striking resemblance to Castro's kidnapping of race-car driver Juan Manuel Fangio a half decade before.

All major guerrilla movements in the region appeared, first, after Cuba's confrontation with the United States in mid-1960 and, second, after President Osvaldo Dorticós proclaimed Cuba socialist in April 1961. All guerrilla movements after this phase were dominated internally by Marxist ideologies, though their public proclamations often espoused broader, populist messages.[5] In responding to the radicalization of the *1960s* "Cuban revolution," however, regional revolutionaries moved ever further from the ideology and experience of the *1956–1958* "Cuban revolution." The earlier ideology was, as we shall see later, fundamentally political and classless in content, quite unlike the guerrilla Marxism of the 1960s and beyond. In aiming at the "Cuban Road," guerrillas of the 1960s forgot that the Cuban revolutionaries succeeded in the political climate of the 1950s. The later guerrillas typically lost contact with the moderate left—a situation that Castro never allowed. In addition, changing conditions in Cuba itself may have dismayed the moderate left in the region, as Cuba drew ever closer to the Soviet Union.[6]

How did the Cuban experience implant itself so strongly in the minds of Castro's later imitators? Following Charles Tilly, I would suggest that there was a fundamental shift in the *cultural repertoires* of revolutionary collective action in Latin America following the Cuban revolution.[7] Within any social group certain responses to collective strain are in their current "stock" of available responses, while other responses are not. For example, in Great Britain and Ireland of 1765 the petition march was part of the cultural repertoire, but the sit-in was not. Repertoires can also vary in their flexibility, with additions and subtractions being made to the stock. Some additions can expand the repertoire; alternatively, additions may so dominate the *conscience collective* as to squeeze out of consideration all competing responses.

Quite apart from such cultural repertoires, new events may shape people's perceptions of the possible, whether accurately or not. Peasant land invasions—as in Bolivia in 1952, Venezuela in 1958–1961, and the Peruvian Sierra in 1962–1963—were apparently rational peasant responses to the accurate perception that the balance of repressive forces that had held them in check for so long had fundamentally changed in each nation, when agrarian-reform parties ascended to power. Our perceptions of the possible may change, not only due to new conditions, but also due to new information that leads us to redefine the inevitability of present circumstances,[8] or to recalculate the costs and benefits of possible courses of action.

We may best understand the impact of the Cuban revolution on Latin American intellectuals in precisely these terms. Castro's successes redefined revolutionary possibilities in Latin America. The thought processes of future guerrillas were probably remarkably neat: if Cuba can carry out a socialist revolution under the very nose, and against the resistance, of *yanqui* imperialism, then why not here as well, where the U.S. presence is so much less pervasive? Ché Guevara's second thesis on guerrilla war exemplifies the military corollary of this argument: A guerrilla army can militarily defeat a conventional army.[9]

With regard to cultural repertoires, those of Communist party members by mid-century amounted to little more than patient preparation, sometimes electoral in nature, for the mass uprisings and general strikes in urban areas that could be nurtured under the proper "objective conditions." Indeed, Fidel Castro himself thought that the general strike—and not the guerrilla *foco*— would be the cause of Batista's downfall. But Castro's call for an April 1958 general strike failed, and he and his comrades rethought their strategy. Speeches and writings by Castro, Guevara (and later Debray) from January 1959 onward—culminating in Ché's treatise on guerrilla warfare—were all steps in codifying and simplifying the Cuban experience, and in making it generalizable to the rest of Latin America and beyond. Extreme forms of this new position—glorifying the role of rural guerrilla warfare—were adopted in 1967 at the OLAS (Organization for Latin American Solidarity) conference in Cuba. OLAS was largely preaching to the converted, however, for among

Latin American intellectuals these ideas had already found very fertile ground.[10]

No matter the sociological label we pin on the sudden spread of a new idea—"symbolization," "the development of a shared image of the object," the short-circuiting of thought to create a "generalized belief," or the process by which the "imagination becomes monopolized"[11]—the process is the same: conversion from one way of looking at the world to a radically different one, the adoption of a different frame of reference.[12] In adding guerrilla warfare to its cultural repertoire, the Latin American left did not expand its previous repertoire so much as it narrowed it down, leading to the splitting off of a new left wing of the left, with a repertoire of but two elements: rural guerrilla warfare and urban terrorism.

In retrospect, some of the guerrillas candidly recognized the degree to which they had been seized by an idea. Venezuela's guerrillas had a higher survival rate than others, and the comments of some of the principals were noteworthy. Communist party leader Guillermo García Ponce noted that "The victory of the Cuban revolution spread the illusion of a rapid and heroic triumph, leading to mechanical transplants." Former Communist and guerrilla Teodoro Petkoff spoke ruefully of "absurd deformities in our actions [which] awakened hatred in the population toward us," adding that the guerrillas "intoxicated" themselves with the literature about Mao and Vietnam. Américo Martín, MIR leader, voiced similar views in repudiating his past "errors." In addition, the very act of participating in a rural guerrilla *foco* tended to radicalize the participants more than their urban peers.[13]

In his revolutionaries' *vade mecum, Revolution in the Revolution?*, Régis Debray sought "To Free the Present from the Past." From what we have seen above, it appears as though slavish obedience to old doctrine was replaced by equally inflexible awe for a new one, whose superiority lay more perhaps in its psychological immediacy and temporal proximity than in its political efficacy. As ex-guerrilla Américo Martín put it, "More than an error, it was a tragic mistake into which all fell. From the ideological point of view, the *foquista* concept led to a new orthodoxy, and from the political point of view to a frightening lack of flexibility."[14]

UNIVERSITIES AND GUERRILLA MOVEMENTS

Why did the example of the Cuban revolution have its greatest impact on intellectuals, in both universities and in left-wing political parties? I will consider the university first, and my guiding concern is why people in such a social location are more likely to adopt revolutionary theories and behaviors than people in other social situations. I do not wish to argue that all students were "revolutionary," only that universities tended to produce revolutionaries in greater proportion than other social organizations, classes, and institutions. (Indeed, many students were and are conservative.)

What is the social nature of the university? According to Karl Mannheim, (university) intellectuals have the best chance of providing a "total" view of the social world because they are drawn from a variety of social groups, each with its own relatively restricted cognitive "map" of the world. From this variety of viewpoints—brought together in the context of the university—the intellectual community should then be able to construct a more accurate map of that social world.[15] Yet one suspects that the zestful adoption of guerrilla warfare by so many students has little to do with a better grasp of the nature of society.[16] Indeed, such an inference confuses the act of cognition with moral judgments.

Moreover, Mannheim's view suffers from a fundamental flaw: Intellectuals by and large do *not* come from many and varied social backgrounds. As late as the 1960s, university students in Latin America—and in much of Mediterranean Europe as well—were drawn overwhelmingly from the middle and upper classes of society. In the 1960s Latin American universities obtained very few of their students from the working class and the peasantry. The working-class share of regional university enrollments during this period probably did not exceed 10 percent. As Carlos Rangel has wryly noted, "The proletarian masses whose name is so often invoked in defense of the university do not in fact send their children there, except as cafeteria workers or cleaning women."[17]

Most Latin American universities of the 1960s and 1970s—there are well-known exceptions like Huamanga in Peru and several others in Colombia—thus served more to maintain class purity than to increase class mixture. Yet university students did not behave like the middle and upper classes from which they emerged, tending often to be "revolutionary intellectuals" instead. As Mannheim understood, to try to understand intellectuals' behavior by their class backgrounds is a hopeless task. Rather, he argued, we must recognize that they lie between classes but are not a middle class. In Gramsci's words, they are a derivative social group.[18]

Gláucio Soares and Loreto Hoecker have suggested a structural explanation for student behavior. When social class has minimal behavioral effects, they suggest we seek a social milieu that limits or screens out class influences. Drawing on Goffman's concept of total institutions, they argue that the university resembles one of those organizations in certain ways, especially in its functional autonomy from the larger society, and in the amount of "psychic energy" invested in it by its members—like other total institutions such as military camps, monasteries, asylums, and the like. (There is a key difference: Few students reside on campus, unlike members of those other institutional forms.) Soares and Hoecker further suggest that class analysis is also less justified due to the narrow class-variation within the typical Latin American university.[19]

Barrington Moore has suggested that a key prerequisite for social transformation is social and cultural space within the prevailing order, "protected enclaves within which dissatisfied or oppressed groups have some room to develop distinctive social arrangements, cultural traditions, and explanations of the world around them."[20] The autonomous university in Latin America provides just this type of political enclave.

University autonomy in Latin America has especially flowered since the 1918 reform movement at the University of Córdoba in Argentina. Yet there were elements of institutional independence in the Latin American university long before Córdoba. Spanish and later Spanish-American universities were modeled after those of medieval Bologna, Italy. In that model, the university is structured as a corporate community, composed most particularly of students. The Bolognese model contrasted markedly with the Parisian model, in which the university was controlled by the masters, with the students clearly treated as political and academic subordinates. Several centuries before Córdoba, Spanish students were already electing the rectors of their universities.[21]

The Córdoba movement spread throughout Latin America after 1918. University autonomy guaranteed not only free thought and discussion, which are familiar to students in Anglo-America, but also student election of university administrators, thereby giving them substantial influence on the faculty. Perhaps most important, autonomy protected the university grounds from entry by police without search warrants, even if in direct pursuit of criminals. Such autonomy created a "veritable discontinuity between the University and society." During the guerrilla years, especially in Cuba and Venezuela, demonstrating and rioting students commonly took refuge from the authorities on university grounds. A Peruvian minister and Venezuelan President Raúl Leoni independently characterized the university as a "state within a state." When the latter sent army troops in to occupy the Central University in Caracas in December 1966, he noted that the university grounds would no longer enjoy "extraterritoriality," and immediately proposed legislation limiting those particular areas of university autonomy.[22]

Autonomy gives an impetus to the development of student power, since it facilitates the formation of opposition political organizations during dictatorial or repressive periods. Student power is especially important where vacuums of power appear at the national level for short periods of time, during which student power grows relative to that of other social groups.[23] Significantly, European students by the 1960s sought the university powers that Latin American students had already enjoyed for decades, and Fidel Castro ended university autonomy shortly after coming to power in Cuba—the very autonomy that had been crucial to the Havana resistance to Batista.[24] There would obviously be no such enclave of resistance under his regime.

Autonomy does indeed provide that "space within the prevailing order" of which Moore wrote, and which throughout most of Latin America has produced a distinct political subculture. Comparisons of national and student elections—for student elections run along national party lines—show that students (at least those who vote) are far to the left of the national populace on political issues. In Venezuela, combinations of the Communists (PCV) and the Fidelista MIR consistently garnered 50 to 60 percent of the Central University student vote in the 1960s, while the Venezuelan electorate, if anything, moved to the right of its 1958 vote, in which it gave the PCV less than 10 percent nationwide. Maoist students in Peru won the July 1965 elections at the University of San Marcos, when Marxist parties at best could win a few percentage points in national elections.[25]

Furthermore, some evidence suggests that student radicalism increases the longer the student stays at the university. If one were a proponent of class analysis, one would rather predict that, as entry into the class structure approaches, anticipatory socialization for one's future, privileged position should proceed, evidenced by lesser, not greater radicalism. The evidence of increasing radicalism is more consistent with the "total institution" perspective I have adopted here.[26]

The university affects student attitudes through a straightforward process of political socialization. Aldo Solari writes that "The student movement occupies itself with transmitting to the student the image of a political role and making this part of the socialization of school members." Historically, university students in Latin America have had a self-image as the future saviors of society, an image nurtured by their presence in the vanguard of anti-dictatorial struggles in this century. A "rational man" model of behavior will not carry us far in understanding such a culture, for that ideology's fundamental source is a moral vision of the world, one certainly not reducible to the simple pursuit of self-interest. This is all quite consistent with Mannheim's observation that intellectuals define their positions *against* prevailing social currents, a fact driven home in telling fashion by the 1989 anticommunist "revolutions" in Eastern Europe, in which intellectuals and university students played such central roles.[27]

Intellectuals live in a world of ideas, their battles are generally fought out in that same world, and the ammunition in those battles consists of theories of the world. Just such a theory was provided by the events and ensuing literature of the Cuban revolution. Allemann argues that intellectuals tend to lean toward "voluntarist extremism" because only exceptionally do they have a "practical grasp of the thought patterns [*Denkweise*] of the 'underprivileged' or even personal contact with the mass of the people." In Herbert Blumer's terms, they have "romantic morale" rather than "practical morale."[28]

The isolation of university students from the broader society is thus a door that swings both ways. Students do enjoy a privileged sanctuary in which to rethink the world, yet for their ideas to take effect they must be propagated beyond their original confines. Such propagation requires adjustment of the original ideas to a new audience, one with which the middle- and upper-class students are often acquainted only in the most nominal sense. Their isolation from workers and peasants constitutes, then, a kind of phenomenological barrier between social worlds. Such isolation also encourages a false extrapolation, so that left-wing political influence in the universities is incorrectly generalized to the broader society. As one Venezuelan MIR member noted ruefully, their complete domination of the *liceos* (secondary schools) and universities led them to believe that they had a mass basis for revolution, but "there was absolutely no mass solidarity with the idea of insurrection." Domingo Alberto Rangel, the premier theoretician and cofounder of the MIR, finally noted after withdrawing support for the guerrilla struggle that it was self-deluding to believe that the MIR had influence among youth: "The Left enjoys prestige among students, but is unknown among working-class youth, or the youth of the barrios ."[29]

The evidence that specific university campuses were closely associated with particular guerrillas is impressive. The Cuban Directorio Revolucionario (DR)—the urban resistance to Batista whose members suffered far more casualties than Castro's guerrillas—was centered in the University of Havana, from which its members eventually organized their own guerrilla front in the Sierra Escambray. The Peruvian ELN had ties to the National University of Ayacucho, whose students helped spread agitation throughout La Mar Province in 1965. Various left-wing political parties used the National University in Lima to similar effect on behalf of the MIR in that same year. The Colombian ELN had extraordinary contacts with the Industrial University of Santander in Bucaramanga and were aided in that regard by that studentry's previous radical history.[30]

Despite that impressive list, the closest guerrilla and university links were those between the FALN and MIR guerrillas and the Central University of Caracas, which served as recruitment and financing center, safe area, and ammunition and weapons dump for the operations of the guerrillas' rural and urban wings. So close were the ties that Orlando Albornoz stated flatly that the "Venezuelan guerrilla movement is a university or at least a university-inspired movement."[31]

POLITICAL PARTIES AND THE GUERRILLAS

Yet it is not precisely accurate to say the guerrillas were university based, even in Venezuela, for the movements were consistently spawned by left-wing splinter groups from other political parties and movements. Robert

Lamberg, in particular, has amassed a convincing array of evidence linking guerrilla movements to their political parent organizations.[32]

Fidel Castro's 26th of July Movement (M-26) had several organizational roots, which Castro was able to mold into a single unit in a remarkable display of political dexterity. Eddy Chibás, the charismatic leader of the left wing of the Ortodoxo party, had committed suicide on 5 August 1951 after a fervent moral appeal to the Cuban people by radio. His death was followed by a "galloping disintegration" of Cuban political life, as one writer put it, in the midst of which Batista seized power. Castro was also a member of the Ortodoxo left, from which he drew most of the members for his famous 26 July 1953 attack on the Moncada barracks. Although the attack failed, through it Castro verbally and symbolically assumed the mantle of Chibás, including the leadership of Ortodoxo youth in Oriente, whose support for Castro's M-26 came early on.

A second major source of Castro's guerrillas was the Movimiento Nacional Revolucionario (MNR), an anti-Batista group guided by Professor Rafael García Bárcena. The list of later M-26 members from the MNR is impressive: Frank País, Pepito Tey, Pedro Miret, Faustino Pérez, Enrique Oltuski, Mario Llerena (Castro's PR man and political organizer abroad), and others. After the dissolution of the MNR, País formed a new resistance group, Acción Nacional Revolucionario (ANR). Castro convinced País to place the ANR under the aegis of Castro's M-26 group, and the ANR was probably the source of the first wave of fifty-eight urban recruits sent to the Sierra Maestra during Castro's darkest hours in April 1957.[33]

In Venezuela, the PCV and MIR—the latter an offshoot of the ruling Acción Democrática party—created the Venezuelan guerrilla movements. James Petras in 1968 described the FALN as "independent of and critical of the local Communist Party," apparently in an attempt to portray the FALN as a non-Communist guerrilla group. That description, however, only reflects the *later* split between the FALN guerrillas and the PCV, which did not even begin to show until 1965, when the guerrillas had already passed their zenith. That split culminated in FALN chief Douglas Bravo's loss of his PCV Central Committee seat in summer 1966, and in his eventual expulsion from the party in April 1967. The MIR, for its part, had adopted guerrilla warfare as party strategy in October 1961 with a large majority, although one *mirista* claims it was official only as of January 1964.

In any event, the PCV was the real driving force behind the guerrilla struggle, as numerous memoirs and interviews show. Following the fall of Marcos Pérez Jiménez in 1958, in which Communists played a key role, PCV enrollment swelled from a thousand to over forty thousand members in three years. This influx was heavily weighted toward youth, who then controlled the party until late in the 1960s. The existence of the Fidelista MIR exerted additional pressure on the PCV to move to the left, since the MIR was moving rapidly leftward. Given the pressures of its own youth and of the ideological competition, the PCV was pulled inexorably into organizing guerrilla warfare. Government repression of the left provided an additional push. Gustavo Machado and Jesús Faría, both members of the PCV Central Committee, proudly pointed to Communist participation in "our guerrillas." One other important organizational source of guerrillas was the armed forces, for many officers and soldiers who fled the failed military revolts of mid-1962 joined the guerrillas at the time of the FALN's official formation in February 1963 out of a congeries of guerrilla units.[34]

The initial Guatemalan guerrilla force, the MR-13 (13th of November Revolutionary Movement), was not a creation of the Communists (Partido Guatemalteco del Trabajo, or PGT), but rather of the military men who led the coup attempt of 13 November 1960, directed against U.S. training of Bay of Pigs invaders on Guatemalan soil. Some 120 soldiers had formed the Organization of the Baby Jesus, and this group was at the core of the uprising, according to its leader, Marco Antonio Yon Sosa. The PGT and its youth wing worked along with the MR-13 during the urban unrest of March–April 1962. The PGT joined the guerrilla movement one year later despite internal resistance. The PGT assumed the ideological leadership of the movement and formed a corresponding political arm and front organization called the Frente Unido de Resistencia (FUR—United Resistance Front) in urban areas to correspond to the rural guerrillas, now called the Fuerzas Armadas Rebeldes (FAR—Rebel Armed Forces).

The FUR almost certainly did not control the guerrillas, but it definitely exerted pressure on the FAR, if through no other means than by its role as channel for new guerrilla recruits from the party. However, an October 1964 position paper by Luis Turcios Lima and Luis Trejo Esquivel distanced the FAR from its now-Trotskyist MR-13 offshoot *and* from the orthodox Communists of the PGT. In March 1965, though, PGT pressure led Turcios to read Yon Sosa's now-heretic MR-13 out of "the movement," and the PGT, its youth wing, and the FAR then formed a new central control committee for the revolution. This communist-guerrilla alliance suffered the same fate as its Venezuelan counterpart. The FAR broke with the PGT on 10 January 1968. This split resulted in the FAR's reunification with the MR-13 (now rid of the Trotskyist "disorder"), and also in an internal schism in the PGT, in which it lost half of its upper ranks as well as most of its youth, who supported the guerrilla movement.[35]

Each of the Colombian guerrilla movements had ties to a political party or movement at its inception. The FARC's ties with the Soviet-line Colombian Communists (PCC) derived from the links that the latter had established with the "peasant republics" during their formation in the 1950s. The three organizations were intimately linked together in the 1950s and 1960s. As FARC leader and former Communist Jacobo Arenas would later bluntly recall, "the independent republics were the agrarian and self-defense movements that we [the proto-FARC] directed." Moreover, one guerrilla diarist of the period notes that his FARC guerrillas, in turn, were created "on the orders of the [*por disposición del*] Communist Party of Colombia."[36]

Although many of the FARC peasant leaders held seats on the PCC Central Committee, those seats were apparently ex post facto ways of increasing Communist influence in those regions of the nation prior to 1960. Like their coreligionists, the Guatemalan PGT, the Colombian Communists also apparently jumped aboard an already-moving revolutionary bandwagon, tried to give it organizational shape, and increased their influence through this procedure. (Similar events took place in Cuba in late 1958 as Castro neared power and the Cuban Communists [PSP] finally joined his movement, after years of collaborating with Batista.) Once created, however, the FARC behaved not unlike the sorcerer's apprentice, and over the years sporadically asserted its separateness. PCC influence on the FARC was strong enough, however, to prevent the latter from forming any equal partnerships with the ELN guerrillas, since each group insisted on the subordination of the other.[37]

The Movimiento Obrero-Estudiantil-Campesino (MOEC, or Worker-Student-Peasant Movement) formed shortly after the Cuban revolution and promptly demonstrated its Fidelista leanings by setting up a guerrilla *foco* in Vichada in the early 1960s. MOEC clearly provided the ideological and almost surely the organizational base for the later ELN guerrillas. Robert Lamberg states flatly that MOEC formed the ELN in July 1964. MOEC no longer crops up in chronicles of the period after that time, and it is not unlikely that, reversing the Greek myth of Kronos, the child swallowed up the parent.[38]

The Colombian EPL was simply the armed wing of the Colombian Maoists. This Partido Comunista Colombiano—Marxista-Leninista (PCC-M-L) began as a splinter group from the PCC youth in a year-long process from early 1964 to mid-1965. The EPL guerrillas were formed, mostly of students, on 11 November 1967, and were still in existence in the 1980s, despite some severe early setbacks.[39]

The two Peruvian guerrilla groups, the MIR and the ELN, were both offshoots of existing political parties, and both also began as nonguerrilla organizations. The MIR, like its Venezuelan counterpart, went through a series of steps in its split with its parent reform party. It began as an internal caucus within APRA, calling itself APRA Rebelde; then it moved into open schism, naming itself the MIR; and it finally embraced guerrilla warfare as party policy.[40]

Héctor Béjar's ELN was born in a 1962 break from the PCP (Communists) and was later strengthened by an influx of Trotskyists from Hugo Blanco's former political cover group. Béjar received no help from the Peruvian Communists. In contrast to the Venezuelan Communists, the PCP had been improving its electoral performance at the time of the guerrilla movements, and members wishing to follow the guerrilla path were in an absolute minority in the party from 1961 to 1966.[41]

Planning for the Bolivian *foco* had gone on in Cuba for well over a year with the cooperation of the Bolivian Communists (PCB), but in late December 1966, their chief Mario Monje visited Guevara's camp at Ñancahuazú, apparently demanded but failed to obtain PCB control over the *foco*, and the PCB as a party thereafter did not support the guerrillas. Some writers simply accuse the PCB of betraying the insurgency. Despite the party's policy, the urban contacts of Guevara's ELN were largely composed of PCB militants. In addition, many of the Bolivian guerrillas were recruited from both the pro-Soviet and pro-Chinese wings of the PCB.[42]

If the guerrillas generally formed as a result of political schisms within existing political parties and movements, there were also splits within the guerrilla movements themselves. The following guerrilla movements experienced one or more internal splits in the course of their life cycles: the DR guerrillas in Cuba; both the FALN and MIR in Venezuela; the MR-13 and the FAR in Guatemala; the ELN and later the M-19 in Colombia. At least four guerrilla groups operated in Guatemala by the 1980s, and three were offspring of the original FAR. Guerrilla fission was especially notable in Venezuela, where the internal struggles during their decline belong, as Allemann notes, "less to the history of partisan revolts than to that of the notorious self-flagellation [*Selbstzerfleischung*] of the Latin American revolutionary left."[43]

What is the significance of these deep historical links between political parties and guerrilla movements? Simply this: Guerrilla movements are not best understood as the response of oppressed peoples to government repression, although that was certainly present in several of the cases here. Rather they better fit Theda Skocpol's concept of "marginal political elites," heretofore excluded from full power, who turn to revolutionary organizations. Their revolts are the response of part of the "intrinsic elite" to that exclusion and are an attempt to secure that power through the unorthodox means of a military alliance with the peasantry.[44]

Those who first took up arms against their respective governments—again with the exception of the Colombian FARC—were at or near the upper levels of power, prestige, and material well-being within party or society. The Cuban revolution and certain domestic events raised their expectations tremendously, after which the perceived blockages to power now appeared to be in their own political parties or in the political system itself. This situation in turn led to the splintering of left and center parties into Fidelista and non-Fidelista groups: the cases of the Venezuelan and Peruvian MIR, the Peruvian ELN, Castro's wing of the Ortodoxos, the Guatemalan PGT, and the Bolivian

PCB. Alternatively, such conditions could pull the Communists themselves into active organization or backing of guerrilla movements—as happened in Venezuela, Guatemala, Bolivia, and with both Communist parties in Colombia.

YOUTH

This discussion leads readily into the next topic: the predominance of the young in guerrilla movements. Our full understanding of this fact—especially the case of university students—necessarily involves psychological principles, historical experience, and structural location. Let us deal with each in turn.

According to Piaget, adolescence is a psychologically distinctive stage of the life cycle, during which one constructs plans of world salvation, even interlaced with elements of messianism and megalomania. During this period, the "society that interests him is the society he wants to reform; he has nothing but disdain or disinterest for the real society he condemns." These plans for world salvation are the means by which the adolescent "injects" himself or herself into the adult world. In the course of attempting to put these ideas into practice, a more or less forced reconciliation occurs between social reality and those ideals. Piaget notes that "[e]ffective and enduring work, undertaken in concrete and well-defined situations, cure[s] all dreams."[45] Therefore we would expect that the young would be more vulnerable than the old to the appeal of the guerrillas on psychological grounds alone.[46]

However, generational experience is also an important component of that appeal. For Mannheim, a generation is not simply the fact of birth in a common time period, but the experience of particular historical events at similar points in the life cycle, at similarly impressionable periods of development. This results in a "stratification of experience," such that older and younger generational groups do not experience these events in the same manner. The crucial period for the transmission of received culture is around age seventeen. The critical historical event in question, I would argue, was the Cuban revolution, which decisively changed the political culture of young, politically oriented Latin Americans coming of age from roughly 1958 to 1965.[47]

Combining these two viewpoints, then, we would expect the young to be particularly active participants in guerrilla movements. Yet two problems remain: (1) urban student youth had a far higher rate of participation than peasant youth; and (2) students and young politicians who joined the movements were not solely in their late teens and early twenties, but up to a decade or more older.

The structural location of students in the university accounts for these differences, for the Latin American university experience constitutes, from a Piagetian perspective, an extended period of psychological adolescence. That is, the particular moment at which one "injects" oneself fully into the broader society is delayed for ten or more years. For Piaget, "endless discussion" of one's theories and world views with others is an integral part of the period of adolescent messianic planning, and it would be hard to find a more apt description of university life as well. Such discussions may elicit disagreement among peers on some issues, Piaget adds, but generate absolute consensus on at least one matter: the need for reform.[48] Quite apart from university life per se, the typical stay at a Latin American university was much longer than at its Anglo-Saxon counterpart. Standard program periods of five to eight years were typically stretched 20 to 160 percent, as if the average medical student took twelve to thirteen years rather than seven to eight to complete the degree. With an average length of completion 70 percent above the requirements, one study found the average age of the finishers to be over thirty years, with a range from twenty-six to forty years, depending on the program.[49]

Petras argued that guerrilla leaders tended to be in their early thirties, times of personal and political crisis as they finish their student years and are confronted with hard personal and political choices.[50] Among the political choices made freshly appealing around 1960: the armed struggle. Peasants, by contrast with the studentry, rarely had the luxury of postponing their "injection" into adult society for ten to fifteeen years. Quite the contrary, from childhood on they busily adjust to a life of soil, toil, and poverty, in a gradual transition to adulthood contrasting markedly with the students' sudden expulsion into the "real world." In stark contrast to such a peasant experience, university students live in a world of ideas, that participation may continue literally for decades, and university autonomy plus intense student interaction provide optimal conditions for political mobilization.[51]

RESPONSES TO THE CUBAN EXAMPLE

Rural guerrilla movements appeared in virtually every country of Latin America in the 1960s, clearly in response to Cuba. Yet they took deeper root in some countries than in others. Revolutionaries typically chalked up their failures to "errors" of an ideological or organizational sort. Skeptics may wish rather simply to write off the failures as evidence of radical dilettantism. I wish to suggest instead a sociological explanation for those variations.

The strongest guerrilla movements in the decade following Castro's entry into Havana grew in Guatemala, Colombia, and Venezuela. These countries are randomly distributed on regional measures of development—from very low to rather high—which suggests that a "poverty" explanation of their distinctiveness would not be persuasive. A more fruitful avenue is suggested by the recent political history of each of the three, where we see roughly similar phenomena: the presence of a nationwide revolutionary situation followed by the reimposition of nonrevolutionary if not counterrevolutionary government, in the aftermath of which the guerrilla movements took hold. Indeed, one could make a fair case for the year 1933 in Cuba as the year of the revolutionary situation, frustrated thereafter by Batista and the ineffectual and corrupt presidencies of Ramón Grau San Martín and Carlos Prío Socorrás.[52]

The Venezuelan case is the most interesting. Rómulo Betancourt's government (1959–1964) was Venezuela's most democratic ever, had initiated the most thorough agrarian reform yet seen in nonrevolutionary Latin America, and was achieving advances in literacy and school enrollments similar to those being achieved—with rather more fanfare—in Cuba at the same time.[53] Yet the Betancourt government unleashed the most violent guerrilla reaction of any of the cases under review. Why?

The concept of generations again provides useful clues. Betancourt had earlier led a civilian-military junta (1945–1947) which had instituted the first extensive reforms in Venezuelan history, especially in labor rights, education, and petroleum policy. His Acción Democrática party (AD) consistently polled over 70 percent of the popular vote at that time and, vis-à-vis its political competition, pursued a scornful, anti-accomodationist line, arousing the ire especially of the Christian Democrats of Rafael Caldera's COPEI party. The AD government was overthrown in 1948 in a military coup, from which Marcos Pérez Jiménez rose to power several years later. This experience profoundly affected the "Old Guard" of AD—Betancourt, Raúl Leoni, Gonzalo Barrios, and others—who resolved not to make the same instransigent error again.

However, the youth of AD and other parties forged their political thought in the battle against the increasingly bloody Pérez Jiménez regime. Side by side with the young Communists and other politicized youth, they jointly increased opposition to the dictatorship until the dictator fled the country in January 1958. The country—or at least Caracas—remained in a state of revolutionary euphoria for the next year under the interim government of Wolfgang Larrazábal, who instituted radical welfare spending to soak up unemployment in the capital, in effect beginning a gigantic system of "wage" payments to the jobless under his *Plan de Emergencia* . In the elections held at year's end, Betancourt returned from forced exile and won the presidency with 49 percent of the national vote, but with only 12 percent of the Caracas vote.

The new president assumed power with $1 billion in foreign debts and another $1 billion in frightened capital fleeing the country. Still with memories of the 1948 coup, he pursued a policy of conciliation with other parties—except the Communists (PCV), whom he and the others systematically excluded—and initiated austerity measures, while at the same time shifting government attention more toward the countryside and interior, and somewhat away from the capital. Agriculture was the main beneficiary of the spending shift, but none of these activities endeared him to the Caraqueños, who had already decisively passed their negative judgment on Betancourt at the polls.

The youth of three major parties—AD, the PCV, and Jóvito Villalba's Unión Republicana Democrática (URD)—were at the same time moving to the left. The influence of the Cuban revolution was doubly accentuated because Betancourt and Castro came to power at the same time and the latter visited Venezuela in early 1959. While Cuba moved so confidently leftward toward its self-identification as socialist in 1961, Betancourt merely struggled, trying to stave off military coups from the right and growing unrest on the left, with an economy in a severe recession. The contrasts in results between these two forms of "revolution" seemed obvious to the Fidelistas.

Betancourt's "opening to the right"—for this is how his accommodation with other parties and AD's new "softer" ideology were viewed by some—stemmed from his generation's experience of 1945–1948 and the nation's current economic problems. This "opening" and the government's policy of rewarding its rural supporters (at moderate speed) were in radical conflict with the movement leftward of politicized Venezuelan youth. For them, the key formative experience had been the revolutionary struggle against Pérez Jiménez and the simultaneous impact of the Cuban revolution against *its* dictator, Batista. These opposite political movements would tear the country apart politically over the next decade, and the organizational splits regularly took place along generational lines. AD split three times in the decade after 1958, and each time lost most of its youth. URD also lost a youth wing in a split in the mid-1960s. Even the Communists lost part of their youth in 1967 with the expulsion of guerrilla leader Douglas Bravo and his followers from the party, effectively cutting the PCV's ties to the FALN guerrillas. The PCV lost youth again when ex-guerrilla Teodoro Petkoff left them to form a democratic socialist party in 1970 in the wake of the 1968 Czechoslovakian invasion. It was therefore these circumstances—radical rejection of the regime by party-oriented youth and the citizens of the Caracas barrios—that led to open hostility, demonstrations, repression, bus burnings, riots, and, eventually, urban terrorism and rural guerrilla warfare against the government.[54]

The Colombian revolutionary situation can be summed up in two words: *La Violencia*. This wave of (superficially anomic) violence left the country in a virtual "revolutionary situation" for almost two decades after 1948, the year Jorge Gaitán, charismatic leader of the Liberal party's left wing, was assassinated. Indeed, Marxist historian Eric Hobsbawm described Colombia in just those words, while Major General Gerardo Ayerbe Chaux called conditions "a milieu of insurrection." As we have already seen, the FARC guerrillas rose directly out of the government's attempt to reimpose federal authority over the peasant republics formed in response to *La Violencia*. In the case of the Fidelista ELN, Fabio Vásquez chose as his home ground an area in which left-Liberal guerrillas had operated during *La Violencia*, where he knew he would encounter a favorable social and political milieu for his guerrillas. Further evidence of widespread discontent with traditional Colombian politics came in the mid-1960s, as electoral absenteeism rose anew each time the polls opened, reaching as much as 70 percent of the electorate.[55]

In Guatemala, guerrillas arose in the wake of the overthrow of the quasi-revolutionary government of Jacobo Arbenz. The period through 1954 witnessed the incorporation of massive numbers of heretofore-ignored peasants into the political life of the country, peasants who also benefited from a widespread land reform. This newly politicized peasantry was in places willing to defend the Arbenz government with arms against the 1954 CIA-orchestrated invasion from Honduras, but their weapons never arrived (the armed forces intercepted one shipment from Czechoslovakia at dockside). The post-coup period witnessed a counterrevolution, in particular a near-total reversal of the agrarian reform (see chapter 6 for details on that reversal). The military revolt of 13 November 1960, which gave delayed birth to the guerrilla movement, was directed against the military offspring of that coup and against U.S. training of Bay of Pigs invaders on Guatemalan soil.

In each of our three cases, then, we see the raising and dashing of revolutionary hopes, as radical expectations were dashed on the rocks of routine or counterrevolutionary realities. The contrasts with the political histories of Peru and Bolivia are quite striking. In those two nations, the peasant land invasions associated with their own "revolutionary situations" (Bolivia, 1952 and Sierran Peru, 1962–1964) were at least partially successful in their immediate objectives: getting and holding the land. Hence, at the subsequent period of each country's guerrilla "explosion" in the countryside, many of the rural areas were no longer "ripe" for revolutionary struggles, if they ever had been.

These events in Peru and Bolivia, and the contrasting experiences of Venezuela, Guatemala, and Colombia, both fit into a modified version of the J-curve theory of revolution. In that theory, revolution occurs when a national period of rising expectations and conditions is followed by a sudden reversal of fortunes (the curve forms a partially inverted "J"). This downturn generates a large gap between still-rising social aspirations and newly limited social realities, and a revolutionary situation consequently takes shape. Thus in Davies's theory, *relative* feelings of deprivation (i.e., relative to newly heightened expectations)—rather than absolute deprivation—lead to revolutionary ferment.[56]

Evidence also suggests that not just national politics, but also different national experiences in the university, also distinguish those nations in which there were strong university-guerrilla linkages in the 1960s: Venezuela, Guatemala, Colombia, and Peru. Since students were often the dominant force in these movements, we might well ask whether their lives as students were affected in those four nations in a way distinctive in the region.

TABLE 3-1

Changes in Latin American University Enrollments, 1955–1965
(in rank order by 1955–65 growth rates)

	Enrollments		% Change
Country	1955	1965	1955 to 1965
Venezuela	**7,664**	**43,477**	**467%**
Peru	**16,789**	**64,541**	**284**
Colombia	**13,284**	**44,403**	**234**
Nicaragua	948	3,042	221
Panama	2,389	7,091	197
El Salvador	1,393	3,831	175
Paraguay	2,142	5,833	172
Guatemala	**3,245**	**8,459**	**161**
Chile	18,300[a]	43,608	138
Mexico	56,249	133,374	137
Ecuador	5,845	13,728	135
Costa Rica	2,537	5,824	130
Bolivia	6,280[a]	13,996	123
Brazil	72,652	155,781	114
Dominican Republic	3,161	6,606	109
Honduras	1,107	2,148	94
Haiti	859	1,607	87
Argentina	149,087	222,194	49
Uruguay	14,550	16,975	17
Cuba	24,273	20,573	−15

Sources: United Nations, UNESCO, *United Nations Statistical Year-book* (Paris, France and Gembloux, Belgium: UNESCO), 1966 (pp. 159–61) and 1977 (pp. 336–44).

Boldface indicates strong student-guerrilla linkages in the 1960s.

[a] Interpolated estimates, for Bolivia between 1950 and 1960 data points, for Chile between 1949 and 1957 data.

Let us consider a simple hypothesis: Increasing social density in the university should be associated with generalized student radicalism, one particular form of which might be guerrilla warfare, in extreme cases. Therefore we would expect to find greater radicalism where the relative increases in university enrollments had been the greatest. Furthermore, there is some evidence that enrollments from 1955 to 1965 increased faster than resources spent, indicating a possible further, material source of discontent. Therefore increased student crowding and interaction plus declining "quality" of education might lead to increased student discontent and radicalism.[57]

Table 3-1 presents evidence to support this view. The four nations with the closest and strongest guerrilla-student connections in the 1960s—Venezuela, Guatemala, Colombia, and Peru—are concentrated at the top of Latin America in the relative increase in the size of their university populations. Such a distribution is highly unlikely to occur through chance alone. Hence there was a correlation, even a striking one, between collective student susceptibility to the call of the armed struggle and conditions within the university itself. Especially noteworthy is Venezuela's presence at the head of the list, since the guerrilla-student linkages were closest of all in that nation. I would be remiss if I did not draw readers' attention to Uruguay—home of the Tupamaro urban guerrillas—near the bottom of the list.

Conclusions

I can now recap the preceding arguments. There is little question that the appearance of guerrilla activity in the 1960s is due to the example of the Cuban revolution.[58] Those who lived in the world of ideas—members of political parties and university students—were peculiarly susceptible to the theories and symbols emanating from that Caribbean island. In addition, those persons located psychologically and generationally between childhood and entrance into the routine adult world of everyday work showed a special propensity to go to the countryside. Finally, certain nations showed particularly strong affinities for the Cuban model. Such affinities can be found, first, in the frustration of heightened hopes for domestic revolutionary change, and second, in certain changes in the university itself, as enrollments increased enormously in certain nations in the 1955–1965 decade. The guerrilla movements of the later 1960s showed clear declines in strength, however, which may be directly traceable to the death of Ché Guevara in Bolivia in 1967.

Until now my analysis has focused on the urban origins of the guerrillas. What makes them distinctive, however, is surely the encounter between guerrilla leaders and the peasantry—and the outcomes of those encounters. Therefore I will now shift the focus from the city to the countryside, and from the origins to the outcomes of guerrilla wars.

PART II

Constructing Theory—
The Outcomes of the
First Wave, 1956–1970

As regards this form of fighting, it is unconditionally requisite that history be investigated in order to discover the conditions of environment, the state of economic progress and the political ideas that obtain, the national characteristics, customs, and degree of civilization.
—Vladimir Ilyich Lenin, *Partisan Warfare*

CHAPTER 4

Variables and Models

Hypotheses non fingo. —Isaac Newton

Them that asks no questions isn't told a lie.

—Rudyard Kipling

[O]ne might revise Kipling's statement and assert with equal accuracy and greater relevance that "them that asks no questions isn't told a truth."

—David Hackett Fischer

THE MAJOR working assumption of the remainder of this book is that sociological analysis can help us to understand the outcomes of guerrilla war. We have the gift of knowing who the winners, losers, and the also-rans were. We wish to understand why the Cubans and Nicaraguans won, why several guerrilla movements garnered substantial support yet failed to proceed to victory, and why guerrillas in several instances failed badly to obtain any support whatsoever from the populace, failing militarily as well.

The operating assumptions of the analysis in the following chapters may be summarized as a series of propositions and hypotheses:

1. The degree of peasant support is a crucial determinant of the failure or success of rural guerrilla movements.
2. We can identify areas of greater and lesser peasant support by a variety of indicators, and can make reasonable ordinal and even numerical estimates of such support.
3. Peasant support is not and cannot be—save in overwhelmingly rural societies— the sole determinant of guerrilla success or failure. Other determinants are the military power of the opposition and the relative success that guerrillas or their opponents have in securing the loyalties of the overall populace. This almost inevitably necessitates a far broader political base than the peasantry. Such transfers of popular loyalty, however, appear to depend in good part on the type of regime that the guerrillas confront in each nation.
4. Each of these determinants—peasant support, relative military power, and popular loyalty—is itself an outcome to be sociologically studied, whose analysis will give us, by extension, clues to the outcomes of guerrilla war. Moreover, *their* determinants are also plural rather than singular.

5. The study of guerrilla warfare and revolution entails considering materials from the macro down to the micro level of analysis.

I will consider issues 1 and 2 below under the heading "Measuring Peasant Support." Propositions 3 and 4 will follow under the heading "Multiple Determinants and Functional Substitutes." I have already briefly treated with "Levels of Analysis" in chapter 1 and will return to that subject in the final chapter.

Measuring Peasant Support

Peasant support is a necessary but not sufficient condition for the victory of rural guerrilla movements. While it is fashionable at times in the social sciences to invert, in dramatic style, certain commonly accepted ideas, this is not one of those times. As Eric Wolf and a host of other writers have shown, revolutionary and/or guerrilla movements with peasant support have come to power in this century in Mexico, Russia, Algeria, China, Bolivia, Vietnam, Cuba, Cambodia, and Nicaragua.[1] This is not to deny that peasants themselves often had divided loyalties, or that peasants have often later been the victims of policies made by those very persons whose ascent to the commanding heights was made possible by peasant support.[2] Yet one cannot deny the fundamental truth that a substantial portion of the peasantry backed the insurgents.

Why did it happen so? The answer is simple. How could a rural guerrilla movement possibly survive in a rural area *without* peasant support? Specifically, how could it survive without a peasantry willing to protect guerrillas from army patrols with silence and misdirection; without peasants willing to join the band and give to the group a familiarity with local conditions and persons otherwise impossible to achieve; without peasants willing to provide at least a modicum of food and other resources? If the peasantry turns against the guerrillas, there is no way for them to survive except as bandits. And the latter are usually eliminated by a minor army campaign, then fade off into the limbo of history.

If we can easily agree to the thesis that peasant support is the sine qua non of revolution, the problem of defining peasant support engenders considerably more difficulty. What do we mean by "support?" Following some leads suggested by Tilly in his discussions of loyalty, the measurement of strikes, and collective action in general,[3] I would argue that answers to the following questions will yield, collectively, good measures of degrees of peasant support:

1. How many peasants are willing to commit resources to the guerrillas' cause?
2. What kinds of resources are these persons willing to commit to the guerrillas?
3. Under what range of circumstances will they commit those resources?

The reader will notice that measurements of attitudes are conspicuously absent from these criteria. Analysts as different as Tilly, on the one hand, and Leites and Wolf, on the other, agree that "warm feelings" are of precious little value to a social movement.[4] Peasants, like others, have practical resources to offer to the guerrillas. If peasant sympathy means that a fleeing guerrilla will be offered shelter, or that, even under torture, peasants will not reveal guerrilla locations, then we may consider those actions as indicators of "support," rather than the feelings themselves. Let us discuss each of these measures in turn.

Number of Persons

Guerrilla bands cannot accept all potential recruits, but the number and proportion of peasants acting as combatants is a very strong indicator of guerrilla support in a region. My best estimates of the numbers of peasants who acted as combatants in the guerrilla bands at their peaks appear in table 4-1.[5]

Let us discuss each case briefly. Guevara succeeded in getting no peasant recruits—as his diaries revealed—and thus the Bolivian estimate is certainly our most accurate. For Peru, inside estimates place the total number of guerrillas at about 150. Few in either Cuzco or Ayacucho were peasants, but a substantial number were peasants in Junín. The Peruvian estimate is probably a generous one. Cuban estimates range from 10 to 75 percent peasant composition (see chapter 2 above) for the M-26; my estimate is about 50 to 70 percent. Castro did not need as much peasant support as did other rebel groups because of his recruitment and supply connections with the city of Santiago. The numerical estimate is taken as approximate for June 1958, as Castro's summer offensive began, when he had 300 men, with an additional 300 or so in the other fronts led by his brother, Raúl, and by Ché Guevara. (This count excludes the 2,000 or so "poorly armed irregulars," or *escope-*

TABLE 4-1
Peasant Guerrilla Fighters in Latin America
(Estimates)

Country	Number	Percentage of all Guerrillas
Bolivia	0	0%
Peru	50	20–40
Cuba	300–450	50–70
Guatemala	200	70–80
Venezuela	200–300	20–80
Colombia	500+	60–80

Sources: See text and accompanying notes.

teros, mentioned by Macaulay.)[6] By using the mid-1958 estimate, we avoid counting those who jumped aboard the revolutionary bandwagon in the last few months as Castro's victory appeared imminent.

Guatemalan guerrillas reportedly had the strongest peasant support of all guerrilla movements, but their overall numbers almost surely never exceeded 400 combatants. Some peasants served as occasional militiamen rather than as full-time combatants. The Venezuelan guerrillas may have reached 1,000 or even 2,000 in number in 1962 and 1963, but these numbers may well reflect artificial inflation due to influxes of vacationing and weekend students. In 1962 almost all guerrillas were students. In 1963–1965 in Lara and Falcón, by contrast, as many as 80 percent of all fighters were peasants, according to reliable reports. In other areas proportions were much smaller. This accounts for the variability in the Venezuelan percentage estimates. Finally, for Colombia—by late 1973—there were between 300 and 1,000 guerrillas for all three organizations, and those numbers are almost certainly down from peaks in the 1964–1968 period. (The numbers are once again larger by the early 1980s—in the thousands.) FARC was probably the most heavily peasant-dominated group (as well as numerically the largest), while the ELN had the largest nonpeasant contingent.

What do these numbers mean? They suggest that, by this first measure, Bolivian and Peruvian guerrillas received the lowest degrees of support, followed by the other four countries' insurgents. The degree of peasant recruitment into guerrilla movements in Cuba, Venezuela, Guatemala, and Colombia is uniformly high, and Cuba does *not* stand out as a particularly strong example; such a distinction would probably go to the Colombian movement. It is simplest, and most in keeping with the quality of the data, to designate each of these four nations as having highly successful guerrilla movements in terms of peasant recruitment and support.

Resources Committed

What kinds of resources might peasants commit to the guerrillas? We can posit a simple scale, ranging from active hostility, to positively Swiss neutrality, to all-out support. What actions would constitute lesser and greater degrees of support? I would propose the following sequence of actions, ranging from lowest degree of support to highest:

1. Nonreporting of the guerrillas' presence to the authorities.
2. Offering food and other goods and services to the guerrillas.
3. Offering to serve as guides, lookouts, or errand runners for the guerrillas.
4. Offering shelter to the guerrillas.
5. Offering organizational cooperation with guerrillas at the village level, including making of weaponry, participation in schools and civil defense, etc.

6. Offering occasional armed service to the guerrillas (militia service).
7. Abandoning one's fields and work to become a full-time combatant in the guerrilla unit.

Although most attention in various literatures is given to full-time guerrilla fighters—these are the usual numbers counted when governments or guerrillas claim certain numerical strengths—most supporters of rural guerrilla movements render more modest, if still vitally necessary, services such as levels 1–5 above. For example, one estimate commonly made in counterinsurgency circles is that it takes ten rural supporters to maintain one guerrilla fighter.[7] Therefore, one would err badly in supposing that the number of peasant fighters—a necessarily modest figure given that weapons are ordinarily hard to come by—is the fullest and only measure of the regional peasantry's support for insurgency.

I would argue that these various commitments will distribute themselves on a Guttman Scale: persons showing clear support at any one level will also be highly likely to offer support at lower levels, but not necessarily at higher levels. For example, any person willing to serve occasionally in the "militia" (level 6) would also be willing to supply goods and services of a more modest sort (levels 1 to 5). Persons offering support at level 7—joining as combatants—would almost surely be willing to supply support at levels 1–6 as well.

Let us discuss our six nations, working our way up the scale. In Bolivia, peasants were generally willing not to report the presence of the guerrillas (level 1), but some peasants did not even render this minimal service, instead performing their civic duty by reporting to the authorities the presence of armed foreigners in the region. Other peasants offered goods (level 2) but usually at a substantial price. One peasant who served as a guide (level 3) actually led the guerrillas into an ambush. Ché's *foco* never achieved levels 4 through 7 in Bolivia.[8]

In Peru, the guerrillas fared only slightly better than in Bolivia. In Cuzco, there were a few peasant recruits, but more typically the highest degree of peasant commitment was the transport of goods (level 3) to the guerrillas' Mesa Pelada stronghold—at very good wages. In Ayacucho and Junín, the guerrillas fared considerably better. Béjar's group in Ayacucho gained a few peasant recruits, but the highest degree of support typically received in the locale was the extensive collaboration of the peasantry with the guerrillas' hacienda takeovers (level 5). At least the same degree of support was obtained by the MIR group in Junín, where Lobatón reported in a private message to de la Puente that "the support given by the peasants was unbelievable: supplies, information, new members. The details would fill a book. . . ." Lobatón's group received considerably more new recruits (level 7) than did Béjar's group in Ayacucho and must be considered the most successful of the

Peruvian fronts—although still far inferior to results achieved in our four remaining countries.[9]

In the four other nations, most guerrilla bands received strong influxes of peasant recruits into the movement (level 7), as well as most lesser forms of support (level 6 militias were not universally present). Some particulars are worth noting. In Guatemala, the use of part-time peasant guerrilla combatants (level 6) was apparently commonplace for both the FAR and the MR-13 guerrillas.[10] In Cuba, Castro claimed that he turned away fifty potential recruits for every one that he accepted; however dubious that claim, he did talk entire army units into joining the insurgents.[11] Similar evidence suggests that the Colombian ELN could be selective in its choice of new recruits.[12] In Venezuela, while there is irrefutable evidence of strong peasant support (level 7) for the guerrillas, strong evidence also suggests that the government mobilized other peasants *against* the guerrillas, and even that peasants acted collectively against the guerrillas on their own initiative.[13]

Our measure of the degree of resources committed tends to parallel our measure of the number of supporters: Bolivia and Peru rank low, and the other four countries high, on the greatest degrees of support typically offered by peasants to guerrillas in each country.

Range of Circumstances

It is one thing to offer guerrillas food when they are volunteering to pay several times the going rate for food and supplies—a commonplace in the cases under review. It is quite another to offer to feed them for free, when one remembers that peasants tendering such offers may live on the edge of subsistence. Similarly, it is easy enough *not* to report on guerrillas when they happen to pass through a village; one simply does not bother to hike down to the police post to do so. It is rather more difficult not to talk when confronted by police or soldiers making inquiries, especially when their interrogation is accompanied by bribes or beatings.

Therefore it is most relevant to know how the levels of support given by the peasantry change with circumstances. In Bolivia and in Cuzco, Peru, peasants with no prompting informed on the guerrillas and actively assisted the authorities at times. As we have just seen, there were similar cases in Venezuela where, however, guerrillas also received considerable support from other peasants. In Colombia, the cooperation of the Páez Indians helped the government to subdue the peasant republic of Marquetalia. In Cuba, Colombia, and Guatemala, however, spontaneous peasant collaboration with the authorities was relatively rare (the ability of guerrillas to exact vengeance may be of some importance here).

By offering money, guerrillas in Peru and Bolivia received somewhat more cooperation than they might otherwise have expected. In contrast, monetary offers were relatively restricted in Venezuela, Colombia, and Guatemala. In Cuba, Fidel Castro left a 100-peso note in the hut of at least one peasant who offered him shelter overnight (if word of such a practice spread, he might well have been a very popular boarder). But the Cuban guerrillas did not use "bribery" or "high-price" techniques more generally.[14]

However, governments in Cuba, Guatemala, Venezuela, and Colombia either offered bribes if peasants would inform on guerrillas or bounties for the delivery of certain guerrilla leaders to the authorities. To my knowledge, none of these bounties was ever collected. The Colombian authorities did have some success, however, in obtaining information in exchange for payment.[15] Coercion could also be effective in changing the "natural" degree of peasant support for insurgents. Terror against the peasantry—at times combined with offers of benefits as well—apparently broke the back of peasant support for guerrillas in parts of Peru and Guatemala. However, Cuban, Colombian, and (a more limited case) Venezuelan government terror had the net effect of driving the peasantry deeper into the guerrillas' camp. There was virtually no terror used against the Bolivian peasantry.[16]

Our combined measures of peasant support strongly indicate that the Bolivian guerrillas received the lowest degree of such support, followed by the Peruvian movements. Guerrillas at their peaks in Cuba, Colombia, Guatemala, and Venezuela all received high degrees of support, although there are instances or locations in each of those countries where peasant support was considerably more limited.

MULTIPLE DETERMINANTS AND FUNCTIONAL SUBSTITUTES

Having established the various degrees of peasant support in each nation, we must necessarily lay to rest the illusion that such "popular support" guarantees victory against an opponent. It does not. Experienced revolutionaries certainly do not believe this. Leo Heiman argues this point forcefully, pointing to the failure of the Ukrainian anti-Soviet guerrilla war of 1944–1949, which had the support of at least 60 percent of the rural population.[17]

What, then, are the other determinants of guerrilla success? First of all, military power is of critical import: a shattered guerrilla army can achieve nothing. Charles Tilly, examining the span of modern European history, concludes that "[i]n general, when a European state temporarily trained its full repressive power on its internal enemies . . . the enemies subsided."[18] Yet such full power may *not* be available to the state: as several analysts of revolution have argued, many revolutions have come about because of a weak state or weakly committed colonial power (Mexico, 1910; Algeria) or because wars had greatly weakened the repressive power of the state apparatus (Russia, China, Bolivia, Vietnam, Cambodia).

In Latin America, both states and armed forces have had varying degrees of strength. In both Cuba and Nicaragua, guerrilla forces faced weak, personalistic states with militaries to match. This was not true of the other nations. Let us consider the following thought experiment:[19] What would have been the result had Castro faced, not Batista and his cronyized army, but the Colombian armed forces? Since Castro came within a hair's breadth of destruction on several occasions, saved only by the lack of fighting spirit of Batista's troops, the thought experiment suggests that the Cuban guerrillas would have been destroyed in such an encounter.[20] Varying levels of military strength and of state power can possibly explain why, of four guerrilla movements with high degrees of peasant support, only the Cuban M-26 came to power, while equally supported movements elsewhere failed.

If military power is one element to add to peasant support as a determinant of revolutionary outcomes, a second element to add is mass loyalty. By this we mean, not the loyalty of the peasants of a particular region, but the broader loyalties of the entire populace. Analysts as diverse as Leon Trotsky, George Pettee, and Charles Tilly have all suggested that the shift in popular loyalty from the present government to the revolutionary contenders is the critical element in the decisive revolutionary transfer of power.

If this is so, then we would do well to consider all three of these elements in our analyses of the outcomes of guerrilla war. And so we shall. The role of military power, both internally generated and externally strengthened, is the subject of chapter 5. Shifts in popular loyalty and their effects on (non)revolutionary outcomes are the subject of chapters 8 and 11, and I will analyze four major influences on peasant support in chapters 6, 7, and 10.

Why does the analysis of the causes of peasant support—and, by extension, the outcomes of guerrilla war—require such extensive discussion? While a variety of monisms have been laid to rest in the last century, scholars continue to revivify them, dust them off, and trot them out in new garb. The search for simplicity of understanding via Occam's razor[21] is among the most laudable of goals (certainly preferable, as Peter Berger opined, to Marcuse's shovel), but not at the expense of accuracy. Why should a scholar settle for a simple analysis that accounts for but a third of observed variation, when a more complex analysis can account for half? Current debates on the determinants of peasant radicalism have pitted a series of monisms against one another, among which we can perceive at least four distinct "schools" (cf. chapter 6, below). Rather than embrace one or the other of those "schools" as our alma mater, our goal should be to achieve as full an understanding of the determinants of peasant support as possible. One theory can account for certain patterns of guerrilla history quite well, while not accounting well for other aspects; another theory may show a complementary pattern. Melvin Tumin has suggested that each theory defines certain facets of a phenomenon with a bright light, but only at the cost of casting other facets into the shadows. My use of multiple analyses is an attempt to avoid that particular pitfall through a kind of theoretical triangulation.

Some years ago, Robert Merton requested euthanasia for the idea of "functional indispensability," the notion that a particular social systemic function can be served by one and only one structure. He argued, instead, that our working hypotheses should be based initially on the probable existence of *functional alternatives*, a plurality of structures that can serve similar or identical social needs.[22] My working analysis of the determinants of peasant support has run along analogous lines, but looking at social causes rather than social functions. I consider below the possibilities that peasant support for guerrillas may vary with types of agrarian structure or with changes therein (chapter 6), and thereby consider sequentially the effects of both social structure and social process. Such support may also vary with the strength of social linkages tying peasant to guerrilla, and with regional variations in the historical experience of conflict in rural areas (chapter 7). Were this analysis a multiple regression, the results would be easier to obtain. Since, alas, it is not, I can only trust that the reader will have the patience to work through the implications of each analysis, for I believe that each enriches our understanding of the social roots of differences in peasant support for revolutionary organizations.

CHAPTER 5

The Role of Military Power

> It is the state of the army, of competing armies, not of the working
> class, that has determined the fate of twentieth-century
> revolutions.
>
> —Barrington Moore, Jr.

THE GOVERNING assumption of this chapter is that the success or failure of
guerrilla movements versus government armed forces depends in part on
three variables: the internal "financing" of their respective armed forces; their
internal solidarity as fighting forces supporting or opposing a political system; and the support each army enjoys from actors outside the nation-state.
These three variables, measured for both the government and the opposition
guerrilla forces, will jointly determine the relative military strength of the
guerrillas and their chances of bringing their irregular war to a successful
military conclusion.

We must first confront, though, a curious dichotomy of thought in the
literature on guerrilla warfare. In these writings, the success of guerrilla
movements is often attributed solely to the national animus of "the people,"
while the suppression of such movements is often traced directly to U.S.
imperialism (i.e., military assistance to Latin American governments).[1] Fidel
Castro, in his Second Declaration of Havana, wrote that "Revolutions are not
exported; revolutions are the work of the people." Richard Kiessler retorted
that guerrilla movements cannot act autonomously but are rather subsystems,
with special roles deriving from their location in "global systems of the international revolutionary movement."[2] Few debates concerning the import of
U.S. or Cuban "intervention" in Latin America have risen above the level of
polemics, and neither polar solution offered above is satisfactory.

I will rather adopt an agnostic view, one that insists upon evidence for
either position. From such a perspective, the concept of rendering external
"support" for or against guerrilla movements must be better defined than it
has been to date in the literature, where support can mean anything from good
wishes to shipments of tanks, Kalashnikovs, or napalm.

GOVERNMENTS: INTERNAL MILITARY RESOURCES

Whether or not such external aid is decisive in the outcomes of guerrilla struggles is dependent not only on military assistance itself, but also on the respective military capabilities of governments and guerrillas.[3] This observation is

of fundamental importance, for the military capabilities of Latin American armed forces vary enormously. Let us examine such variations more closely.

The simplest way of comparing the military capabilities of the government armed forces is through the study of military budgets, and the work of Joseph Loftus on defense expenditures is particularly helpful here.[4] Elsewhere I have converted the budgets for our six countries into 1960 U.S. dollars in order to make revealing comparisons about the resources governments were able to commit to counterinsurgency.[5] Venezuela devoted far greater annual resources ($150–250 million) to the military in its guerrilla period than did any of the other five nations. Guatemala ($10–30 million) and Bolivia ($5–12 million) spent far less than the remaining three countries (ca. $50–110 million). Such variation remains even if we compare data for the peak years of guerrilla activity in each country. Each government was typically faced by a group of a few hundred guerrillas, yet their capacities to confront such a challenge—at least as measured by military budgets—exhibited qualitative differences, a point driven home by the data in table 5-1. The ratio of the highest to lowest figures in table 5-1 is more than 25 to 1; even the ratio of the highest to the mean is more than 2.5 to 1.

If one looks closely at Loftus's or my own data, they show that there is no *systematic* tendency for military budgets to increase as guerrilla activity appears or increases. Guatemala, from 1962 to 1966, shows the most pronounced increase in spending, followed by Venezuela (1962–1966), and Cuba (1956–1958). Colombia (1964–1967) exhibits a mixed pattern, and Peru (1965) and Bolivia (1967) show decreases from the previous year. Perhaps more importantly, neither do military shares of government spending show systematic increases in this period. To summarize: "repressive capacity" in our six nations varies greatly, and there is no systematic pattern of increases in military spending—whether in real dollars or in budget shares—in response to guerrilla threats.[6]

TABLE 5-1
Military Expenditures in Years of Peak Guerrilla Activity
(Millions of 1960 U.S. $)

Country/Year	Military Spending	% of Government Spending
Cuba, 1958	$58–64 mil.	13%
Venezuela, 1964	190.2	10
Guatemala, 1966	14.4	11
Colombia, 1965	94.0	26
Peru, 1965	71.0	17
Bolivia, 1967	7.9	16

Sources: Loftus, *Defense Expenditures*, tables 1 and 5; Wickham-Crowley, "A Sociological Analysis of Latin American Guerrilla Movements," chap. 5; see note 4.

If we move instead to *relative* measures of military strength—relative to population, expenditure per soldier, and the like—we still arrive at broadly similar conclusions. If we look at military expenditures per inhabitant, Venezuela again leads the way, followed by Peru, Cuba, and Colombia, with Guatemala and Bolivia again at the bottom, with but a small fraction of the expenditure per person typical of Venezuela.[7] If we consider military expenditure per member of the armed forces, Venezuela leads with $2,809, again followed by Colombia, Peru, and Cuba, all between $1,300 and $1,600 spent per soldier, with Guatemala ($1,115) and Bolivia ($687) spending substantially less than the leaders.[8]

Finally, if we look at the absolute size of the armed forces, and the number of armed-forces personnel per thousand inhabitants, Venezuela is no longer the leader. At the peak of the guerrilla struggles, the Peruvian armed-forces numbered about 70,000, the Venezuelan, Cuban, and Colombian forces numbered about 40,000, the Guatemalans 15,000, and the Bolivians 8,000. Peru and Cuba had the greatest number of soldiers per inhabitant with about six per thousand, followed by Venezuela and Bolivia (four per thousand), and Guatemala and Colombia (two per thousand).[9]

What patterns, then, have we found overall in our quantitative indicators of military strength? First, Venezuela consistently ranked first in any measure of military expenditure, followed rather consistently by Peru, Cuba, and Colombia, and trailed by Guatemala and then Bolivia. That is, richer countries spent more than poorer ones. Second, if we measure repressive power by the relative size of the armed forces, then Peru and Cuba were the leading nations, and Guatemala and Colombia had the lowest numbers of soldiers relative to population. If we conceptualize guerrilla war as a labor-intensive activity, clearly the Guatemalan and Colombian militaries were least prepared for such a conflict, and the Cubans and Peruvians most ready. If we view the ability to equip and train one's soldiery as decisive, then Venezuelan capabilities were superior to those of Peru, Cuba, and Colombia, which in turn outstripped those of Guatemala and Bolivia. I wish to stress that the ranking of countries on military expenditures parallels their ranking on more conventional measures of economic power, such as GNP per capita—Venezuela leads the group of six, and the poorest countries, Guatemala and Bolivia, trail far behind. Both of these ways of considering military capabilities are illuminating yet incomplete, as we shall see.

Yet *qualitative* aspects of domestic military resources should also be examined. How prepared were Latin American militaries to fight a *guerrilla* war, quite apart from U.S. training programs? The answer is straightforward. Only the Colombian armed forces had any appreciable wartime experience, having fought against *La Violencia* for fifteen years (as well as in the Korean War) and thus possessing exceptional anti-guerrilla experience. In contrast to the Colombians, army and national guard patrols in the five other countries were routinely routed in their early engagements with guerrillas. Latin American soldiers simply were untrained to fight guerrilla wars until the United States began training their officers in counterinsurgency strategy and tactics in Panama and elsewhere.

The theory of anti-guerrilla warfare was also generally underdeveloped in the military journals issued by the various armed forces. Colombia's *Revista de las Fuerzas Armadas* clearly stood out for its high quality in this field, and showed considerable foreign influence in the articles published therein. The theory of guerrilla war was also relatively well developed in the *Revista Militar del Peru* and in journals published by the Peruvian Escuela Superior de Guerra (Army War College) and by the Centro de Instrucción Militar (Military Instruction Center). In one instance, officer-students in 1966 were given as a classroom exercise the suppression of a guerrilla movement, the outlines of which are clearly that of the previous year's guerrilla struggle![10] Venezuela's military journals, in contrast to these two, gave considerably less coverage to the problem of guerrillas, and military-theoretical treatment of guerrilla warfare was simply nonexistent in Guatemala and Bolivia.

What of Cuba, the locale where it all began? While there were thirty-nine articles and editorials from 1953 to 1958 in Cuba's *Boletín del Ejército* (Army Bulletin) on the subjects of guerrilla warfare, irregular war, civil war, subversive war, and terrorism, their theoretical foundations were uniformly weak, especially in contrast to similar articles in Peru and Colombia. Two issues in 1958 featured pictures of men on horseback, of all things (including one on the cover), and an article on guerrillas in the Cuban war for independence defined guerrillas as Spanish troops! The sense of unreality is capped by the fact that the *Boletín del Ejército* never acknowledged that the army was engaged in a guerrilla war. The other armed forces committed many errors, but only the Cuban military went so far as to deny the very existence of its opponent (although it was common practice to label the guerrillas bandits).

GOVERNMENTS: MILITARY SOLIDARITY

The preceding emphasis on the purely quantitative strength of armed forces is somewhat misplaced. War is *not* simply a competition between the size of purses or the number of warm bodies that can be fielded, as the United States government discovered in Indochina. It is also a contest of wills, of commitment to the struggle. The control over the instruments of violence is crucial in war, and such control entails the commitment to the cause by those who wield those instruments. Most importantly, soldiers' commitment to the *patria* or to the military as an institution need not be in the service of causes widely held to be "good" or "noble," for the morale and combative spirit of German troops during World War II were exceptionally high.[11] Morale depends on other things.

Loyalty to the government is the most critical qualitative characteristic of armed forces, for the outcomes of rebellions and revolutionary wars hinge on that loyalty. Sociological analysis, especially in its Marxist variants, tends to deemphasize such military forces in favor of attention to long-term social trends and social causes leading to revolutionary success. Contrariwise, Barrington Moore, a longtime student of revolutions, argues that such an overemphasis is misplaced, and that the importance of control over the means of violence—i.e., the loyalty of the armed forces—is better understood by Marxist revolutionaries than by Marxist historians.[12]

In a rigorous analysis of the correlates of modern revolutions, Diana Russell found that high disloyalty of the armed forces toward incumbent governments was well correlated with rebel success, and strong loyalty with failed revolts.[13] In Latin America, significantly, both successful guerrilla movements to date have occurred in countries where the army was perceived to be, and in fact was, the tool of a personalistic dictator, rather than an arm of the federal bureaucracy, with the president merely as titular and temporary commander-in-chief. In Cuba and Nicaragua in the 1930s, the old armies were effectively destroyed, and the new armed forces—in Nicaragua, the National Guard—were rebuilt virtually as the personal armies of Fulgencio Batista (Cuba) and Anastasio Somoza García (Nicaragua). Promotion in these armies was based on loyalty to the national *caudillo* (personal political leader or warlord), who frowned on any independent shows of skill or initiative.[14] The first Cuban military academy did not appear until the 1940s, and those officers with professional military training in the United States were consistently passed over for promotion in favor of Batista's personal favorites. This led to deep political cleavages in the Cuban officer corps. The military's personal loyalty to the younger Somoza was far stronger in Nicaragua (1977–1979) than it was to Batista in Cuba (1956–1958), yet the distinctiveness of these two military histories is striking. That two armies dissolved under the attack of guerrilla units strongly suggests that personalistic military leadership is not conducive to maintaining commitment to battle and the loyalty of the rank and file.[15]

In contrast to these two cases, in those instances where the military can cultivate among the ranks loyalty to the military as an institution and can successfully identify the military as the representative of nationhood (the *patria*), the loyalty of the troops will be far more steadfast. The military, as a total institution, is more capable of generating institutional commitment than any other political organization, to elicit what one author has nicely termed "independent morale." Attempts to understand military behavior through "class analysis" fail utterly to grasp this peculiar capacity of total institutions to suppress class-based differentials.[16] To put it in axiomatic form: The less permeable an organization is to influences stemming from civil society, the more likely that the behavior of the membership will respond to organization-oriented rather than to class-oriented impulses.

In Peru and Colombia, the development of intra-military solidarity appears to have been strong. The military's self-definition of its goals and its stances on key issues in Peru were elaborated in the Centro de Altos Estudios Militares (CAEM—Center of High Military Studies), the rough equivalent of the U. S. Army War College or the military academies. Allemann terms the Peruvian military one of the most "self-defined" armed forces in the region. In the Colombian case, military solidarity was less predicated upon the common organizational experience of the officer corps than on the common combat experiences of the soldiery in the battle against *La Violencia* in the 1950s and 1960s. This campaign against bandits (real and alleged) resulted in a great deal of experience in guerrilla warfare and enhanced troop morale. Soldiers came to see themselves as the last barrier between civilization and complete barbaric anarchy.[17] As the 1960s progressed, however, the Colombian military increasingly found itself defending, as one analyst noted, not civilization, but a particular social order and a particular minority-backed government, creating chinks in that solid morale. Yet the morale of the special elite troops (similar to the U.S. Green Berets), who carried on the bulk of the anti-guerrilla fighting, remained extremely high, supported by special elite perquisites, higher pay, and better training and equipment.[18] Such elite troops appeared elsewhere in Latin America as well and were generally composed of those who had received U.S.-sponsored anti-guerrilla training in Panama.[19]

We have seen that the Cuban army showed very weak internal solidarity when confronted with the guerrillas, while the Peruvian and Colombian armed forces, in contrast, maintained strong institutional coherence. Our other cases lie in the gray area in between. The Bolivian army was composed in its bulk of peasant conscripts who received no pay, but only room, board, and uniforms.[20] Little information exists on Bolivian military solidarity in 1967, save for a few fragmentary items. First, Bolivians have been an extremely nationalistic people—at least since the 1952 revolution. This has implications for soldiers' behavior in a battle against guerrilla forces led by Cubans. Second, the military high command initially resisted, not welcomed, U.S. aid in the suppression of the guerrilla movement.[21] Third, President René Barrientos was an army officer whose major social support stemmed from the Quechua-speaking Bolivian peasantry, who formed the bulk of the armed forces. Fourth, there is no evidence of officer desertions to the guerrillas despite Guevara's highly charitable treatment of captives. All these facts suggest a moderately high degree of solidarity within the Bolivian armed forces in 1967.[22]

There remain the cases of Venezuela and Guatemala, which are distinctive in that military officers contributed either a substantial number of (Venezuela) or virtually all (Guatemala) the early guerrilla leadership. The desertions of junior officers to join a guerrilla movement provide prima facie evidence that military solidarity was considerably less than airtight in these cases (with desertions common in Cuba as well).

In Venezuela, the armed forces had been discredited by the simultaneously inefficient and repressive performance of military governments from 1948 to 1958, including that of Pérez Jiménez. His 1958 overthrow (with military support) had apparently spread social reformist, if not revolutionary, ideas among the junior officers, who could not be immune to the revolutionary currents then coursing through Venezuelan society.

The first three years of the Betancourt presidency (1959–1964) saw his governing AD party trying to accommodate both leftists and right-wing military *golpistas* (coup-makers), the latter staging several coup attempts in that period. The alliance of left-wing junior officers with parties of the radical left—the Communists (PCV) and the Fidelista MIR—grew stronger as Venezuelan society became more polarized up to 1962. The results in 1962 were two military revolts—with some civilian support—at the port cities of Carupano (May) and Puerto Cabello (June). Both were suppressed by loyalist forces, the latter with very heavy bloodshed. Participating officers who escaped the ensuing cleanup joined the nascent FALN guerrillas in the mountainous areas of the interior (see the number of ex-army officers in the Venezuelan guerrillas in appendix A). The decisive suppression of these revolts apparently broke the back of the radical left within the military, which thereafter showed relatively high degrees of solidarity in its anti-guerrilla campaigns, especially in the years 1964 to 1966.

The internal influence of officers-turned-guerrillas on FALN policy was appreciable. In their early days, the guerrillas tried to avoid at all cost the killing of soldiers, trying to limit their opponents' firefight casualties to policemen and members of DIGEPOL (the national police force). In conjunction with this policy, their pamphlets called upon soldiers to desert or to turn their guns back upon their commanding officers. President Betancourt, although apparently under considerable pressure, did not untie the hands of the army and air force until after the guerrillas killed four members of the national guard in an attack on an excursion train in September, 1963. Massive roundups followed, several radical congressmen lost parliamentary immunity and were put under house arrest, and the armed forces were given a somewhat freer hand to pursue the guerrillas. At the time, a MIR leader charged that in fact a shadow coup had taken place, with the military in real control of the government, a charge that Betancourt vehemently denied. Once the FALN had killed the guardsmen—in what was widely characterized as a cowardly attack—attempts by the FALN to distinguish between police and soldiers could no longer be effective. The *cazadores* (hunters or rangers), the elite trained by the United States at Fort Gulick in Panama, apparently were exceptionally strong in their anti-guerrilla feelings.[23] Various guerrilla memoirs indicate the immunity of this group to the guerrillas' "subversive" appeals during the military campaigns of 1964–1966.

Finally, in Guatemala, the fact that the guerrilla movement began as an abortive military coup had great consequences for the nature of the anti-guerrilla campaigns of the 1962–1965 period. Given that Guatemalan Indian peasant recruits were more or less pressed into service in virtual village roundups,[24] a pattern common in Central America, one would not expect high solidarity with the nationalist and institutional appeals of their *Ladino* officers. When one adds the military revolt of 13 November 1960—in which the latter-day guerrilla chiefs had participated—which was nationalist and anti–United States in its origins, one can see that the guerrillas had strong claims on the very symbols that military organizations try to employ, while the military had few solidary foundations. In addition, guerrilla leaders Turcios Lima and Yon Sosa maintained close contacts with their old junior-officer cohorts, and both are rumored to have appeared at officers' parties in the capital during the insurgent period. As a result of these conditions, the anti-guerrilla campaign (until 1966) has been described as "insouciant," and another observer said that the guerrillas were treated "with great indulgence" until the latter period.[25] Yet another source of cleavage in the Guatemalan armed forces was an internal split between the old-line officers (e.g., Carlos Arana Osorio, who directed the brutal 1966–1967 anti-guerrilla campaign) and the graduates of the Escuela Politécnica, among whose ranks was numbered former president Jacobo Arbenz.[26]

This "indulgent" situation changed drastically in the mid-1960s. The campaign of 1966–1967 was apparently guided by U.S. Green Beret advisors who found in Colonel Arana a man who would take their advice, as one observer put it. Army intelligence was gathered by working over revolutionaries, from guerrilla deserters, and from retired NCOs and former soldiers living in the target villages. Indulgence was replaced by very nearly its opposite, which suggests that guerrilla sympathizers had been purged from the army, or that the command structure of the army was transforming otherwise-reluctant soldiers into effective anti-guerrilla fighters. The army became a profoundly conservative organization, perhaps partly in response to the latest of recent attempts by the revolutionary left to arm the peasantry to create a counterforce to oppose the army. (The previous attempt to do so, in 1954, may well have been the prime reason the military leadership stood aside when the Arbenz government was faced with the U.S.-organized Castillo Armas invasion.)[27]

We may summarize our analysis of military solidarity in table 5-2, where I indicate (roughly) the state and trend of solidarity in the armed forces in each nation. The first measure of solidarity is taken prior to the guerrilla struggle, and the second indicates the direction in which solidarity moved in response to the struggle.

Finally, one should not underestimate the impact of the Cuban revolution itself on "closing the ranks" of the armed forces in the other five nations. No military institution will stand aside and watch the government create an inde-

TABLE 5-2
Trends in Military Solidarity in Response to
Guerrilla Conflicts

Country	Changes in Solidarity
Cuba	Moderately low to low
Venezuela	Moderately low to moderately high
Guatemala	Moderately low to moderately high
Colombia	High to moderate
Peru	High to moderately high
Bolivia	Moderate/High (?) to Moderate

Source: See text.

pendent counterforce, such as Arbenz may have attempted to do in Guatemala in importing arms. The fact that Castro had, upon achieving power, destroyed the old armed forces was imprinted strongly in the minds of the officer corps in Latin America. Especially memorable may have been Castro's killing of 600 senior officers of Batista's army. Hence, senior officers in Latin America routinely stressed that the guerrillas' plans involved "elimination of the Armed Forces . . . as happened in Cuba."[28]

GOVERNMENTS: EXTERNAL U.S. MILITARY ASSISTANCE

The literature abounds with (mostly scattered) references to this or that item of the role of the United States in the anti-guerrilla struggle, whether to a yearly purchase of helicopters, the use of napalm, Panamanian anti-guerrilla training, or government-to-government pressure. Rather than survey this largely impressionistic material, I will systematically analyze four forms in which U.S. military aid may have affected the outcomes of Latin American guerrilla struggles: through grants and sales of goods and services, through military training and intelligence, through informal pressures, and through the commitment of troops.

Money and Weaponry: Grants

The United States has provided military assistance to Latin American and other nations in the form of credits and loans for military purchases, surplus stock grants, and military training. It is necessary to put this assistance to Latin America in comparative perspective, as is rarely done in the literature. From 1950 to 1973, the United States' Military Assistance Program (MAP) totaled some $35.9 billion, of which only $0.8 billion went to Latin America. During this same period, the U.S. government and private companies sold and delivered some $13.4 billion worth of war matériel throughout the world as Foreign Military Sales (FMS), about \$0.5 billion going to Latin America.[29] Latin American nations were thus recipients of about 2 percent of all U.S. military assistance and about 4 percent of all U.S. military sales. The region received a far lower share of military assistance and sales, in fact, than it did of U.S. trade, investment, or economic aid.[30] The widely held notion that Latin America was a *special* focus of United States' quantitative military largesse is mistaken.

These broadly sketched figures do not indicate, however, in what way these relatively modest expenditures affected the repressive power of Latin American armed forces. If the United States were funding half of the military budget of Cuba during a guerrilla war, this would have greater consequences than if it were to fund one-hundredth of the Venezuelan military budget in peacetime. We have evidence that some U.S. MAP aid is factored into the budget-making process of Latin American militaries.[31] How important was such aid in funding military activity in our six select nations?

In table 5-3 I have displayed data on U.S. military assistance to our six countries, as a percentage of each nation's military expenditures. All raw data have been transformed into 1960 U.S. dollars as I did earlier. Only in Bolivia during the 1960s and (with large swings) in Peru throughout the entire two decades, does U.S. military assistance consistently exceed 10 percent of a nation's military budget. The idea that the United States "poured in" aid to support Cuba's Batista is shown to be highly misleading from our comparative perspective. In contrast, that the Guatemalan military received substantial U.S. aid in its anti-guerrilla struggle is borne out by the data, as seen in the jumps in aid in the early 1960s. Looking at the guerrilla years, we see that U.S. aid to Peru (1965) actually dropped 25 percent from the previous year, while that to Bolivia (1967) increased by a similar percentage. Aid to Peru and Colombia was very erratic, while annual aid to Venezuela hovered around 5 to 6 percent in the mid-1960s, dropping to less than 1 percent after the guerrilla struggle begins to decline.

It is difficult to believe that military aid amounting to 5 percent or 10 percent of the budget can substantially increase the fighting ability of the military in these countries. Yet an inside look at the data reveals a more important role for U.S. aid than might be inferred from these figures. Unlike the United States military, which may be seen as a "capital-intensive" industry, the armed forces of Latin America are labor-intensive organizations. That is, relatively few of their expenditures are for arming the rank and file or for equipment in general. Various sources indicate that 70 to 90 percent of military budgets in the region were for personnel costs in the 1960s, even in a relatively well equipped army such as Colombia's.[32] Only about 10 percent of the budgets are for arms costs, according to one estimate. In such a situation, military assistance equaling 10 percent of the overall budget may, in Edwin Lieuwen's estimation, increase the *arms* budget of the military by 50 to 90

TABLE 5-3

U.S. Military Assistance as a Percentage of Latin American Military Expenditures, 1953–1970 (Millions of 1960 U.S. $)

    Column A: U.S. Military Assistance
    Column B: Military Expenditures of Country
    Column C: A as a percentage of B

	Cuba			Venezuela			Guatemala		
	(A)	(B)	(C)	(A)	(B)	(C)	(A)	(B)	(C)
1953	0.5	(50)	1%	—	67.9	0%	—	6.2	0%
1954	1.3	(53)	2	—	65.9	0	—	5.8	0
1955	1.8	(51)	4	—	105.3	0	—	7.2	0
1956	1.9	(53)	5	—	131.6	0	0.4	8.2	4.9
1957	2.1	(56)	4	—	106.7	0	0.3	8.6	3.5
1958	3.1	58–64	5	—	174.2	0	0.1	9.2	1.1
1959	0.4			13.5	191.7	7.0	*	9.6	*
1960	0.2			8.3	174.6	4.8	0.2	9.6	2.1
1961	0.1			9.5	147.6	6.4	0.4	9.3	4.3
1962				10.0	156.5	6.4	1.3	9.0	14.4
1963				7.4	183.0	4.0	2.5	9.3	26.9
1964				9.4	190.2	4.9	1.3	10.9	11.9
1965				6.1	221.5	2.8	1.4	14.1	9.9
1966				10.7	233.4	4.6	1.3	14.4	9.0
1967				0.8	266.9	0.3	1.0	16.0	6.3
1968				0.8	264.2	0.3	0.9	15.1	6.0
1969				0.6	249.3	0.2	1.9	14.7	12.9
1970				0.6	253.7	0.2	1.1	26.3	4.2

percent, the latter in some of the smaller countries. (This figure was challenged by one congressional witness, who put the increases at closer to 10 percent.)[33]

Not all MAP aid is in the form of weapons grants, but we can estimate the impact of U.S. military assistance on equipment from the sources used in the previous table. We will assume (generously) that 15 percent of Latin American military budgets are for arms procurement and compare the resulting dollar values to the weapons portion of U.S. MAP aid (i.e., not aid in the form of training, etc.) for the mid-1960s, and the late 1950s for Cuba.

In table 5-4, MAP weapons data are derived from the same source as for table 5-3. After trying to exclude non-weapons aid in the data, the resulting estimates of weapons aid are surely still generous as estimates of arms shipments, for Edwin Lieuwen's report to Congress shows other grant expenses which are included in MAP, such as conferences, seminars, and civic-action programs.[34]

TABLE 5-3 (*cont.*)

	Colombia			Peru			Bolivia		
	(A)	(B)	(C)	(A)	(B)	(C)	(A)	(B)	(C)
1953	4.0	55.0	7.3%	2.6	36.6	7.1%	—	4.2	0%
1954	2.9	62.7	4.6	4.0	33.7	11.9	—	?	0
1955	4.2	63.8	6.6	4.1	35.9	11.4	—	?	0
1956	2.6	62.8	4.1	9.9	59.1	16.8	—	2.4	0
1957	2.4	53.6	4.5	10.7	53.8	19.9	—	2.5	0
1958	2.7	48.9	5.5	7.7	61.0	12.6	0.1	2.1	4.8
1959	2.5	42.2	5.9	4.2	52.3	8.0	0.3	2.8	10.7
1960	2.7	47.3	5.7	3.5	50.1	7.0	*	4.0	*
1961	16.8	54.6	30.8	22.6	51.9	43.5	0.4	4.6	8.7
1962	5.8	90.7	6.4	14.2	51.9	27.4	2.1	4.7	44.7
1963	8.1	90.3	9.0	7.8	80.7	9.7	2.3	6.0	38.3
1964	6.2	85.7	7.2	9.9	78.7	12.8	3.0	4.9	61.2
1965	5.3	94.0	5.6	7.6	71.0	10.7	1.8	9.0	20.0
1966	12.3	94.6	13.0	9.1	70.7	12.9	2.6	8.4	31.0
1967	8.3	97.2	8.5	4.5	89.7	5.0	3.2	7.9	40.5
1968	4.1	127.7	3.2	1.2	89.8	1.3	2.0	7.5	26.7
1969	3.2	73.8	4.3	0.4	?	?	1.6	7.4	21.6
1970	5.6	90.1	6.2	0.5	?	?	1.1	9.7	11.3

Sources: For Column A—U.S. Agency for International Development (AID), Statistics and Reports Division, *U.S. Foreign Assistance and Assistance from International Organizations, July 1, 1945–June 30, 1962* (Revised), pp. 28–50; and *U.S. Overseas Loans and Grants and Assistance from International Organizations: Obligations and Authorizations, July 1, 1945–June 30, 1966*, pp. 25–52; and (same title), *July 1, 1945–June 30, 1975*, pp. 33–61. Column B—Same as for table 5-1.
( ) denotes estimate.
* less than $50,000.

Keeping in mind that the estimates of arms spending in the military budgets are generous, and that the estimates of weapons aid are high as well, table 5-4 exhibits a sharp contrast with the overall data of table 5-3. All countries save Venezuela apparently received substantial portions of their weaponry through outright grants. Bolivia's procurement grew an estimated 150 percent through U.S. grants, while the estimated Peruvian, Guatemalan, and Colombian weapons budgets grew by half in response to yearly aid. Cuba's arms capabilities were increased by about one-fourth. If these data are even roughly accurate, U.S. military-assistance programs had a substantial effect on the military capabilities of five of these six countries.

Certain data should be highlighted. Batista's Cuba did not receive especially large amounts of weapons aid from the United States. Since weapons aid from the United States was such a small percentage of the Venezuelan budget, no argument tracing the suppression of the guerrillas to U.S. weap-

TABLE 5-4

U.S. Weapons Assistance to Latin America as a Percentage of Estimated Arms Budgets
   Column A: Estimated weapons aid in millions of 1960 $
   Column B: Column A as % of estimated military weapons budget, which is estimated at 15% of
   military spending

	Cuba		Venezuela		Guatemala		Colombia		Peru		Bolivia	
	(A)	(B)	(A)	(B)	(A)	(B)	(A)	(B)	(A)	(B)	(A)	(B)
1956	1.7	21%										
1957	1.8	21										
1958	2.7	28–31										
1959	0.3	?										
. . .												
1962			0.2	4%	1.0	71%	5.2	38%	4.0	52%	1.4	200%
1963			0.3	5	1.9	136	7.4	55	4.4	36	1.6	178
1964			0.3	5	1.0	63	5.4	42	8.3	70	2.0	286
1965			0.3	5	1.1	52	4.9	35	6.7	63	1.2	86
1966			0.04	0	0.8	36	9.6	68	6.8	64	1.6	123
1967			0.04	0	1.4	58	7.3	50	3.6	27	2.0	167
1968			—	0	0.6	26	3.4	18	1.1	8	1.1	100
Totals	6.5	25	1.2	5	7.8	58	43.2	42	34.9	44	10.9	149

Sources: Military spending from table 5-1; weapons share of military spending is estimated at 15% of the total—see text; weapons share of MAP grants: for grants themselves, see US-AID sources for table 5-3; for estimate of weapons share thereof, see text.

ons grants can be sustained. The remaining nations all apparently received substantial boosts in weapons capacity from the grants, even though none of the weaponry sent to Latin America during this period was of the latest design, and much of it came from "excess stocks." Bolivia's army is said to have been virtually rebuilt through United States aid since 1952, and the 1960s budget figures support such a picture. Thus, if we see weaponry in general as crucial to waging counterguerrilla war, then Bolivia was helped the most by such aid, followed by Guatemala, Colombia, and Peru, then by Cuba, and last, receiving little or no weapons grants, Venezuela.

We would expect, since these are the nations that experienced major bouts of guerrilla warfare, that they would stand out as targets of military assistance during their guerrilla struggles. In table 5-5 we can examine this hypothesis by comparing military aid in our six countries to the overall Latin American figures for the period 1953–1970.

Aid to this select group of countries, even when taken over this longer period, was 40 percent higher than in the area overall. The other countries in the region received even less aid than the $5.29-per-capita figure would indicate, since our target countries pull up the average. Are these figures "high" or "low?" That is a difficult matter to assess. To put these numbers in one perspective, for example, Soviet military aid to Cuba from 1960 to 1969 was $1.5 billion, just under $200 per capita, $20 per capita *per annum*. Both

TABLE 5-5

U.S. Military Assistance Per Capita in Latin America, 1953–1970 Totals

Country	Military Assistance (millions 1960 $)	Population, 1960 (thousands)	Aid per Capita (1960 $)
Bolivia	$ 20.5	3,696	$ 5.55
Colombia	99.7	15,468	6.47
Cuba*	11.4	6,153 (1955)	3.70*
Guatemala	14.1	3,765	3.75
Peru	124.5	10,199	12.21
Venezuela	76.7	7,394	10.37
6-Nation Average	346.9	47,319†	7.33
Latin America	1,097.9	207,379	5.29

Sources: Military assistance—as for table 5-3; population—from J. Mayone Stycos and Jorge Arias, Population Dilemma in Latin America (Washington, D.C.: Potomac Books, 1966), p. 2. Cuban population in 1955 is interpolated between the 1950 and 1960 figures. "Latin America" includes the twenty nations listed in table 5-8.

* Since Cuba received aid for only half of this period, the per capita figure is doubled to match the time periods of the other five nations.

† Uses Cuba's 1960 population: 6,797,000.

figures were about forty times the average value of contemporary U.S. aid to the Latin American nations.[35]

We can focus our attention even more closely by measuring aid in *annual* dollars of military assistance per capita for the area and for our six nations for the entire period, as well as focusing on the period of guerrilla activity proper. The results of these calculations appear in table 5-6.

The data in this table seem clearer. Per capita military assistance to the entire region grew only slightly in the sixties—supposedly the decade of the U.S. counterinsurgency push in Latin America—but was appreciably higher than average in four of our six countries during their periods of guerrilla activity. Bolivia and Cuba show the highest increases in per capita aid over the norm, while Peru and Colombia show only slight, region-wide increases (these two countries, despite internal violence in the latter, were politically more stable than the other nations during their guerrilla periods). Guatemala and Venezuela show increases larger than the last two countries but smaller than the first pair.

What may we conclude? Although our analysis of overall military aid and military budgets shows that U.S. military grants have no appreciable influence in maintaining overall regional military strength, closer examination shows that such aid may be decisive in the crucial area of weaponry. Table 5-7 summarizes our findings by ranking nations according to the degree that they were helped by U.S. assistance. Interestingly enough, we find a pattern

TABLE 5-6

Annual U.S. Military Assistance to Latin America
(in 1960 U.S. Dollars per Capita)

	1953–1970	Guerrilla Period
Latin America	$ .30	$ .32
Bolivia	.31	.63
Colombia	.36	.37
Cuba	.21	.38
Guatemala	.21	.30
Peru	.68	.72
Venezuela	.58	.74

Source: Tables 5-4 and 5-5; the 1953–1970 column is the last column of table 5-5 divided by 18, except for the Cuban figure, divided by 9. Guerrilla periods are defined as follows: Latin America 1961–70; Bolivia, 1967–68; Colombia, 1964–70; Cuba, 1956–58; Guatemala, 1962–67; Peru, 1965–66; and Venezuela, 1962–68. Population in 1965 is used to calculate per capita figures for the guerrilla period for all countries save Cuba, for which 1955 figures are used. See table 5-5 sources for population data.

TABLE 5-7

Ranks of Six Nations on the Impact of U.S. Military
Assistance on Anti-Guerrilla Fighting Capacity
    Column A: Overall Levels of Military Aid
    Column B: Impact on Weaponry
    Column C: Degree of Response to Guerrilla Conflict

Country	Rank A	Rank B	Rank C	Final Rank and Average
Bolivia	1	1	1	1
Guatemala	3	2	3	2.7
Peru	2	3.5	5	3.5
Cuba	6	5	2	4.3
Colombia	4	3.5	6	4.5
Venezuela	5	6	4	5

Sources: Column A is from table 5-3; column B is from table 5-4; column C is from table 5-6.

opposite to that of domestic military capabilities. The reader may recall that Venezuela consistently ranked first in financial measures of fighting ability, and Bolivia and Guatemala last. This pattern is reversed for military assistance from the United States. Perhaps unsurprisingly, despite all the care and effort involved in the preceding analyses, U.S. military aid went mostly to those countries least financially able to support their own forces and least to those that could, which is precisely the intent of military aid. Sometimes sociology does confirm the obvious, after all.

Money and Weaponry: Sales

Unlike the case of military grants-in-aid, the sale of military equipment to a Latin American government cannot be considered part and parcel of (so-called?) U.S. hegemony in the region. Rather, U.S. arms sales to Latin America are affected by a series of pressures and counterpressures internal to the United States: attempts to make restrictive policies that seek to limit sales to certain types of governments and to certain types of weapons; counterpressures to continue sales to "friendly nations" regardless of political coloring; and commercial pressures to maintain the U.S. position in the Latin American arms market. Latin American governments themselves also mount pressure, by demanding the latest model weaponry, especially when a political rival has or is obtaining more advanced equipment (e.g., Peru and Chile, Brazil and Argentina, etc.).

The failure of the United States to train counterguerrilla forces might conceivably have had great consequences in Bolivia in 1967. But its refusal to sell weapons to Batista in 1958 had little or no effect: he simply bought them from Britain, France, Italy, and Czechoslovakia(!) instead.[36] The option to *buy* arms from a plurality of vendors is clearly distinguishable from (1) the training of soldiers, (2) the influence of military missions, and (3) the provision of arms grants. In all these, the United States had a real or near-monopoly in Latin America.

We can still briefly examine figures on U.S. arms sales to Latin America. From 1950 to 1963 Latin America bought 6.4 percent of U.S. arms sales to the world; if we look at the longer period 1950 to 1970, that percentage falls to 4.0 percent. In the context of the Vietnam war, Latin America was *not* a major purchaser of arms from the United States, although absolute levels of sales were higher in the 1960s than in the 1950s. As we shall see in table 5-8, there is no relationship between arms sales to these countries and the guerrilla movements of the 1960s.[37]

Our five guerrilla nations (excluding Cuba) combined had per capita arms purchases high above the Latin American norm during these two decades, but that is a statistical fluke produced by the continuation of the historically large arms purchases by Peru and Venezuela, which predated, continued throughout, and postdated their experiences with guerrillas. Despite the size of those two nations' purchases, the United States actually supplied less than half of their weaponry in the 1964–1973 period.[38] As table 5-8 suggests, the United States only dominates the arms markets of the smaller countries, especially in

TABLE 5-8
Latin American Arms Imports, 1964–1973:
Total and from the United States
(1960s guerrilla cases in italics)

Country	Total Arms Imports (million $)	Percentage from United States
Dominican Republic	$ 24	100%
Costa Rica	2	100
Guatemala	*30*	*97*
Paraguay	16	94
Nicaragua	15	93
Bolivia	*31*	*87*
Uruguay	37	73
Mexico	30	70
Panama	13	62
El Salvador	15	60
Honduras	14	57
Chile	157	57
Argentina	312	54
Brazil	448	52
Colombia	*173*	*49*
Ecuador	71	45
Venezuela	*259*	*41*
Peru	*360*	*23*
Cuba	311	—
Haiti	1	—
Latin America	*2,319*	*42*

Source: U.S. Arms Control and Disarmament Agency,
*World Military Expenditures and Arms Transfers 1963–
1973* (Washington, D.C., 1975 [?]), p. 70.

the Caribbean and Central America. (The data in table 5-8 may include grants
as well as sales; the source is not clear on this point.) This is consistent with
the historical divergence between U.S. power in the Caribbean area and its
power in South America: near-hegemony in the former area, but only prepon-
derant influence in the latter. Just as in the case of U.S. military grants, military sales show a pattern in which the greatest resources go to (a) small Latin
American countries which (b) are typically close to the United States.

Given this analysis, it is difficult to justify including arms sales by the
United States in the same theoretical framework as U.S. military aid. The
latter is largely responsive to nonmarket forces: social unrest and international political relations. The sale of weapons to such nations, however, ap-

pears to be largely responsive to market position. A purchasing country will obtain arms from whichever vendor is willing to sell, limited only by the size of the former's wallet. The sale of arms by social-democratic Israel to that world pariah, South Africa, or Batista's purchases from socialist Czechoslovakia are sufficient to demonstrate this point.

Military Training and Intelligence

In the postwar period through 5 September 1973, Michael Klare reports that the U.S. Army had trained 33,147 Latin American soldiers in the Army School of the Americas in the Panama Canal Zone. In another table, however, he reports 28,621 trained in both the United States and in the Canal Zone in the 1950-to-1975 period, with an additional 43,030 trained in "other areas" (presumably right at home).[39]

Why is the training of soldiers so relevant? Primarily because guerrilla war is a labor-intensive form of war, in which only limited kinds of weaponry (e.g., helicopters, patrol boats, small arms) are effective. As one Peruvian colonel aptly noted, "Guerrilla war is the place where machines are least able to supplant man." Robert Lamberg, perhaps the closest student of the Latin American guerrillas, argued that the most important element of U.S. military aid was training, not money—and that, overall, U.S. aid was "relatively restricted" but "highly effective."[40]

U.S. training at Fort Gulick in the Panama Canal Zone was oriented both to civic action and to the purely military aspects of counterinsurgency. In the Internal Security Department officers were trained in guerrilla, counterinsurgency, and intelligence operations, while in the Technical Department the school had (by 1965) graduated 11,000 officers in "various areas of technical and logistical support," including auto repair, general mechanics, construction engineering, radio repair, medical care, and other areas.[41] Exceptional students were sent for further training to Fort Bragg, Georgia. Among the alumni of the two schools were Marco Yon Sosa and Luis Turcios Lima, later to become Guatemalan guerrilla leaders. (Of the former, one U.S. spokesman noted ruefully, "You can bet he won't be getting any more scholarships from us.")

From the qualitative point of view, the efficacy of such counterguerrilla training is certainly subject to dispute. One alumnus-turned-guerrilla was "scornful" of the value of such training, calling it "mechanical" in that it merely tries to separate the "fish" from the "water" in its inversion of Mao's dictum. A critic of U.S. military-aid programs claims that such training only serves to produce strident anticommunism, further politicizing the armed forces rather than making them professional.[42] Despite these criticisms, and given the rather impressive performance of the Guatemalan guerrillas for half a decade, it seems unwise simply to write off U.S. training as worthless, for the military backgrounds of the guerrilla leadership were clearly helpful in increasing the longevity and fighting experience of the Guatemalan insurgents.

Was U.S. training of Latin American officers of great importance throughout the region, or was it only important in certain countries, perhaps those that actually experienced insurgency? I attempted to judge the focus of U.S. training programs by comparing the number of officers trained in Panama and elsewhere with the armed forces manpower in 1965. The reader is reminded that it is far from clear that all the Panama graduates received counterinsurgency combat training, as can be seen by the distribution of courses in the School of the Americas.

The patterns of table 5-9 are clear, and have little or nothing to do with guerrillas or with patterns of social and political unrest: yet again, small countries close to the United States receive a disproportionate share of U.S. military "attention." This finding holds true whether or not there is a great deal of unrest in each particular nation (compare Costa Rica and Guatemala). Areas that experienced large-scale guerrilla warfare do not stand out in this table, nor do those such as Brazil, Panama, Nicaragua, and the Dominican Republic, which experienced other forms of social unrest at various times. Very little aid went to Cuba, reflecting the fact that training for counterinsurgency began in earnest only after the success of the Cuban revolution. The U.S. Army trained more Bolivians (600) in Bolivia in four months than it trained Cubans anywhere in a decade. Overall the pattern is, once again, for small, low-GNP countries to receive relatively large amounts of counterinsurgency training, while larger, high-GNP nations receive relatively little. Countries close to the United States (geographically speaking) are also clustered near the top, with the major exception of Mexico.

However, if we step back from the numbers for a moment, evidence of the importance of U.S. training programs becomes somewhat more persuasive. The clearest case is that of Bolivia, 1967. In that country, a Mobile Training Team headed by Major Ralph "Pappy" Shelton was dispatched in April with some twenty Green Berets to begin a crash anti-guerrilla training course for six hundred Bolivian soldiers.[43] In late August the "graduates" went into the field against Ché's guerrillas, and he noted in his diary the improvement in the fighting quality of the opposition. One month later the *foco* had been shattered. Given the evidence of the internal decay of the guerrillas, it is still not clear, however, that the training course was instrumental in Ché's demise.

A second important qualification of the numbers in table 5-9 is that those officers and soldiers trained in Panama and elsewhere by the United States tended to be in the forefront of the fighting wherever the guerrillas appeared. Therefore, their importance in the fighting part of the guerrilla war far overshadowed their relatively modest numbers in the armed forces overall. Judg-

TABLE 5-9

U.S. Counterinsurgency Training of Latin American Officers Compared to
Armed Forces Manpower (1950–1975)

	A	B	C	D	E
	No. of Officers Trained		Armed Forces		
	U.S./Panama	Total	Manpower, 1965	A/C	B/C
Latin America	28,621	71,651	734,500	.04	.10
Panama	60	4,130	3,500	.02	1.18
Nicaragua	808	4,897	5,000	.16	.98
Honduras	388	2,641	4,000	.10	.66
Costa Rica	33	529	1,200	.03	.44
Guatemala	729	3,030	8,000	.09	.38
Bolivia	502	3,956	15,000	.03	.26
El Salvador	239	1,682	6,600	.04	.25
Ecuador	1,601	4,556	18,000	.09	.25
Dominican Republic	782	3,705	19,300	.04	.19
Uruguay	1,120	2,537	14,000	.08	.18
Colombia	2,527	6,200	40,000	.06	.16
Venezuela	1,675	5,341	35,000	.05	.15
Chile	2,811	6,328	46,000	.06	.14
Paraguay	402	1,435	11,000	.04	.13
Peru	3,385	6,734	70,000	.05	.10
Haiti (to 1963)	475	567	5,900	.08	.10
Brazil	7,544	8,448	200,000	.04	.04
Argentina	2,766	3,676	132,000	.02	.03
Cuba (to 1960)	307	521	40,000 (1958)	.01	.01
Mexico	467	738	60,000	.01	.01

Sources: Columns A and B—Klare and Stein, *Armas y poder*, pp. 159–60; column C—Loftus, *Defense Expenditures*, p. 87. Cuban armed forces data are for 1958, based on estimates in the literature on armed forces at their peak under Batista.

ments of the qualitative impact of such training are quite varied. We have already seen that some alumni of the programs did not think they were worth much. In contrast, two former Panama trainees (one later a guerrilla) allegedly were taught to torture prisoners using a combination of brutal and gentle measures and were even told to do away with prisoners when they could not be taken along.[44] These are serious allegations, indeed, but the evidence for them is somewhat thin—unless we consider similar, validated reports from Indochina, in which case they are more plausible.

Finally, the United States military was an important source of intelligence on guerrilla movements in several countries. U.S. military advisors and CIA agents in Bolivia began examining the guerrilla movement there as early as March 1967, reporting back to Washington on the situation in Santa Cruz.

The Guatemalan armed forces, lacking an intelligence section, are said to have relied completely on U.S. intelligence sources during 1966. One might have suspected that two such poor countries might lean heavily on the United States for such help, since it is a relatively refined area of military expertise. Yet in oil-rich Venezuela as well, the United States reportedly "completely" controlled the military cartography section.[45]

To summarize our discussion of the impact of military training on the outcomes of guerrilla war: The quantitative comparative evidence does not support the idea that U.S. counterinsurgency training was critical in defeating the guerrillas, nor was it focused in areas affected by insurgency. However, the qualitative evidence, although only sketchy, suggests greater importance for the content of training, especially in supplying an elite core of manpower that could be directed into counterinsurgency operations, and also for "rounding out" those areas in which Latin American armed forces had limited capabilities.

Informal Pressures

The United States government may also have influenced the course and outcomes of guerrilla warfare in Latin America through government-to-government pressures. While these may have taken place through diplomatic or informal channels, it is likely that the military mission was also a major source of pressure to "do something" about actual or potential "subversion."

If we examine the military missions to the various nations at the end of 1966, we can compare the size of those missions to the size of the respective armed forces, to see if the United States had committed especially large contingents of officers to certain "hotbeds." Petras, for example, argued that these missions "are responsible for the suppression of popular movements," and asserted—wrongly—that the Venezuelan mission was Latin America's largest, with several hundred persons.[46] I found once again the pattern discovered in our previous comparisons: Small, low-GNP nations have a relatively high ratio of U.S. military-mission personnel to armed-forces size, while larger, higher-GNP locales have lower ratios. The total number of mission personnel as of 31 December 1966 was 737, just below the peak of 800 the following year. Venezuela had only 76 such persons (not "several hundred"), and Brazil headed the list with 119. The United States had no military mission personnel in Mexico, Cuba, or Haiti.[47]

Again, though, the systematic and quantitative evidence does not quite address the question asked: How did U.S. pressures affect counterguerrilla operations? There is serious evidence that U.S. influence was greatest in the Guatemalan case, substantial during the Bolivian and Colombian insurgencies, but relatively unimportant in affecting the guerrilla wars in Cuba, Peru, and Venezuela.

In Cuba, the major documented case of informal U.S. influence was the CIA's late-1958 attempt to secure the release of Colonel Ramón Barquín from a Batista prison and have him take over the government in Castro's stead. By then, however, Barquín was already a member of the M-26 and remained subordinate to Castro in his newfound role as head of Havana's armed forces, which he put at Castro's disposal.[48]

In the case of Venezuela, the virulence of political infighting led to charges bordering on hysteria, as when Communist leader Jesús Faría alleged that the "government and the police receive their orders directly from the American Embassy and the CIA." In a similar vein, Douglas Bravo charged that the United States directed the anti-Betancourt coup of 1948. One charge that gained some credence outside of guerrillaphile circles was that the U.S. military mission organized and even supervised the execution of Operation Torbes, a counterinsurgency campaign of January 1963, which failed in its goal of eliminating the guerrillas in Falcón State. The guerrillas made charges that U.S. aides even flew in some of the reconnaissance planes used in that operation.[49] The U.S. mission's response: Our men haven't flown anything more airworthy than desks. Despite all such allegations, the Venezuelan government never formally asked for U.S. assistance in the counterinsurgency struggle (as governments did in Cuba, Peru, and Bolivia), nor did the United States offer any.[50]

The most serious charge the Peruvian guerrillas made was that the United States military sent anti-guerrilla experts to advise the Peruvian armed forces on the 1965 campaign. In fact, Peruvian-American relations were strained during that year due to disputes over the government's expropriation of the International Petroleum Company. Such action led President Johnson into forced invocation of the Hickenlooper Amendment, which forbade the sale of helicopters, etc., to Peru until late in the year, despite Johnson's willingness to help. By then the guerrillas had been all but destroyed.

In these three cases, while the United States certainly favored the anti-guerrilla campaigns—save perhaps in Cuba—its role in the waging of the war was extremely circumscribed, and pressures to speed up or to adjust military strategy were clearly limited.

Such a portrait contrasts somewhat with U.S.-government activity in both Colombia and Bolivia, were such pressures and effects may well have occurred. In Colombia, allegations spoke of CIA agents and external intervention in "purely internal" affairs, similar to Peruvian charges. The U.S. military and the Peace Corps(!) were also charged with "advising" the Colombian military in its 1964 campaign against the "peasant republics." More importantly, a Colombian colonel reportedly said that Operation Marquetalia—the foremost of those campaigns—was inevitable since it was impossible to resist U.S. military mission pressure on the Colombian authorities in the matter.[51] In Bolivia, as noted earlier, a U.S. special mission literally took over the training of Bolivian troops in early 1967, and it was this same group of trainees who hunted down Ché Guevara in October of that year.[52]

The greatest U.S. pressure was applied to Guatemala. Due to the "old-boy network" linkages between the guerrilla leaders and their former fellow officers, anti-guerrilla operations were relatively muted until 1966. Even at the time of the original revolt of 13 November 1960, U.S. military personnel reportedly "harangued" wavering Guatemalan officers into fighting the rebels, even implying that the U.S. Air Force would do so if they didn't. In 1968, Colonel John Webber said that the (terror-filled) campaign in Izabal of 1966–1967 was his idea and had been implemented at his instigation. Colonel Arana Osorio, the executor of that campaign, has been described as a man who would listen to U.S. military advisors. Unsurprisingly, then, Guatemala was also the locale of probably the greatest intervention of U.S. personnel in counterinsurgency in the region.[53]

Military Personnel/Combat Troops

Colonel George S. Blanchard has listed four graduated steps in levels of military assistance for counterinsurgency. First come Military Assistance Advisory Groups (MAAGs), which were present in forty-five countries in 1964. They operate as "efficiency experts," evaluating a nation's counterguerrilla performance and abilities, making recommendations, perhaps even supervising actions carried out by domestic agencies. Second in line are Special Action Forces, groups combining talents in medicine, civic action, engineering, intelligence, and psychological warfare. These units go where local requirements go beyond already-existing levels of U.S. support. Within these SAFs, the Mobile Training Teams (MTTs)—such as the one sent to Bolivia in 1967—are a common form due to their "unique counterinsurgency capabilities," and may number from one to fifty persons. In 1965 alone, fifty-two such special missions went to Latin America. Blanchard's third line is only fuzzily outlined: "the Army is prepared to dispatch other types of support forces to the area," as in Vietnam in 1964.

The fourth and final line is the dispatch of conventional combat troops to a region.[54] This obviously occurred in Vietnam, but there is a (less well known) good chance that Green Berets fought in Guatemala, as well as (less well founded) charges that they fought against domestic guerrillas elsewhere in the region, perhaps in Venezuela and Bolivia. In Peru and Colombia—with one exception—charges by the insurgents referred only to "assistance" and "direction," and not to actual combat.[55] To my knowledge, not even these more modest charges were tendered during the Cuban guerrilla war.

For Venezuela and Bolivia, the sources alleging U.S. combat troops' participation in counterinsurgency are from unreliable guerrilla sources of information.[56] In the absence of any other confirmatory evidence, these reports should be discounted. In contrast, the variety and number of sources suggesting Green Beret combat roles in Guatemala—in the 1966–1967 campaign—is rather more impressive. They include a Catholic priest, a U.S. reporter, various chroniclers of the guerrilla movement, and, of course, the guerrillas themselves.[57] The number of such combatants, however, probably numbered considerably less than the "thousand(s)" mentioned by the insurgents. If certain reports are accurate, the U.S. advisors exercised virtual control over the *fighting* part of the Guatemalan army—through the cooperation of then-Colonel Arana Osorio—as well as over the intelligence services and the secret police. The guerrillas even believed that there was an unspoken policy of "showing" the Green Berets to peasants and insurgents, to intimidate the guerrillas into believing their cause a lost one.[58]

Summary of United States' Influence

While there is no mathematically simple way of calculating the tipping points beyond which U.S. assistance was decisive in defeating the guerrillas, we can make some rough commonsense distinctions. U.S. military aid *cannot* have been decisive where such aid (1) was a small share of the military budget, especially for weapons; (2) did not result in great advances in counterinsurgency training; (3) was not associated with a great deal of influence or control over the armed forces; or (4) did not appreciably improve domestic military strength or solidarity. In addition, the weaker and the more fragmented were the guerrillas, the less importance we must attach to the U.S. for their defeat.

Judging by these criteria, Guatemala and Venezuela lie at opposite ends of our spectrum of influence. Venezuela had domestic military strength greatly superior to Guatemala's; it had much smaller shares of U.S. military aid in its military budget, virtually no weapons aid, and bought its weaponry from a more diverse group of vendors; retained far more domestic control over its military apparatus; and improved its military solidarity after 1962 quite independently of U.S. assistance. It seems absurd to judge U.S. aid of decisive importance in the defeat of the guerrillas, especially given the fact that the governing AD party clearly had more backing from the nation's peasantry than did the insurgents.

Guatemala provides a striking contrast. The United States held a hegemonic position there in military aid, military sales, aid to the police, and other economic assistance; the U.S. military exercised far more influence through training and clout in the armed forces; U.S. military aid increased noticeably as guerrilla activity grew in the mid-1960s; the performance of the Guatemalan armed forces improved markedly during 1966–1967, the period of perhaps greatest U.S. influence; and U.S. combat troops may well have participated in that campaign. Politically, the governing party had little or no popular backing, the 1966 elections had resulted in virtual usurpation of power by the military, and the guerrillas were among the best-prepared and most popularly supported in the region. Given those features, if U.S. support was decisive anywhere, that place was Guatemala in the 1960s (yet as we shall see in our final chapter, there is cause to doubt even that minimalist conclusion).

A superficially strong argument can be made for a similar role in Bolivia. U.S. influence on the Bolivian military and its reconstruction had been at least as large as in Guatemala, and the Bolivian army was as ill prepared for war as its Guatemalan counterpart. However, in strong contrast to Guatemala was the strong peasant support for President René Barrientos, whatever his electoral bona fides for holding that office. Also in contrast is the tragicomedy of errors that constituted the military history of Ché's *foco*, for the group had no popular support and lost several persons in attrition for reasons unrelated to combat or desertion. Ill fed, ill informed, tired, and sick, there was quite simply no way they could have defeated the Bolivian army, sorry as the latter may have been. The peasantry who informed on them throughout the campaign would eventually have brought them to defeat if the army could not have done so alone.

For the remaining cases, U.S. military support could only have been decisive if we view it as the result of *long-term* military training and aid, and not as short-term responses to domestic upsurges. No significant, short-term aid responses to Peru or Colombia can even be remotely viewed as decisive in the defeat of the insurgents (short-term is what those defeats were in Colombia, however). In both cases, as elsewhere, U.S-trained soldiers were at the forefront of counterinsurgency. Despite this, the guerrillas were too fragmented and disorganized in both countries to mount a serious military or political threat to incumbent governments. In Peru, the guerrillas counted on simultaneous, spontaneous strikes and uprisings nationwide to force the military to disperse its forces. Instead, the military picked off the *foco* sites one by one. The dispatch with which the Peruvian armed forces disposed of the insurgents can only be laid at the doorstep of the United States with arguments strained exceedingly thin.

Colombia's military, in contrast, faced several well-armed, popularly supported, experienced guerrilla groups. Here U.S. assistance might have been critical. Yet it was in Colombia that the key element of such assistance— counterinsurgency training—was least required, for the Colombian armed forces had acquired far more experience in fighting guerrillas, in fifteen years of guerrilla-style civil war, than they could possibly gain in a course in Panama. The United States' military in turn pointed to the Colombians as the exemplary Latin American model for counterinsurgency technique. Colombia's soldiery, or at least the elite troops, were sufficiently well trained to head off any hopes of fragmented guerrillas seizing power in the Cuban style.

TABLE 5-10
Military Conditions Favoring Government (+) or Insurgents (–) in
Outcomes of Guerrilla Warfare

	U.S. Training	U.S. Military Aid	Domestic Military Strength	Guerrilla Vulnerability
Bolivia	+ +	+ +	–	+ +
Colombia	+	+	+ +	–
Cuba	0	+	–	–
Guatemala	+ (+)	+ +	–	– –
Peru	+	+	+	+ (+)
Venezuela	+	0	+ (+)	–

Sources: See text and preceding chapter tables.

Let us summarize our discussion, giving a plus (+) to any conditions that aided the suppression of the insurgents, a minus (–) to those that favored the guerrillas, and a zero (0) for a neutral role. Double signs (+ + , − −) indicate particularly strong conditions. The results appear in table 5-10.

We might say, roughly, that U.S. influence could have been decisive when a strong U.S. presence (pluses in the first two columns) was paired with relatively weak domestic armed forces and a strong guerrilla movement (minuses in the second pair of columns). We can now better understand the distinctiveness of the Guatemalan guerrilla war in its international context: strong U.S. aid and training were paired with a weak domestic military and a strong guerrilla movement. The result may well have been the insurgents' defeat.

GUERRILLAS: FINANCES, SOLIDARITY, AND EXTERNAL AID

There exists no a priori reason not to extend the preceding analysis to the *guerrillas'* armed forces. Both analyses would then partake of similar "hydraulic" models; the investigator makes a reasoned judgment as to how much "pressure" each contender can exert on the other, and finds out how that balance changes when the variable of outside assistance to one or both contenders changes the scenario.[59] We have seen that U.S. assistance appreciably increased the fighting strength of some militaries, and this is true for outside support to guerrilla forces as well—some of them benefited more than did others. Our subsequent analyses, however, must be far more qualitative, given the paucity of systematic information available on "underground" aid to insurgent forces.

Yet there are those who oft'times object: outside assistance can *never* be crucial to the success of insurgent movements, whose success derives solely from the popular support they secure. That is, winning the hearts and minds of the people always yields eventual victory to the insurgents. This objection contains more ideology than analysis, for it is not, in fact, true that guerrillas have been successful irrespective of secure lines of outside support. Leites and Wolf argue that rebellions can never be successfully repressed *unless* external aid is somehow denied the rebels. Walter Laqueur argues a similar case in his world-historical survey of guerrillas, citing specific cases, such as the Greek Communist resistance of post–World War II.[60] Notwithstanding its great importance, popular support is not the be-all and end-all of a guerrilla failure or triumph, and it cannot be the sole focus of our analysis.

When we read of "outside" assistance to guerrillas in Latin America, the writer above all usually intends us to think of Cuban aid. How did such aid—paralleling our previous analysis—improve the training, finances, and armaments of the 1960s guerrilla movements? To answer, here is a summary of our following discussion: Outside assistance to guerrillas seems to have been most effective in training new insurgents, but where money was important the Cuban guerrillas of the 1950s, and *not* their 1960s imitators, benefited most.[61]

How many Latin Americans did the Cubans train? Estimates of such numbers vary widely and sometimes wildly. (Here we must take care not to equate a mere trip to Cuba [e.g., the Venceremos Brigade, etc.] with a visit made to secure training in the strategy and tactics of insurgency.) In early 1963, the CIA estimated before Congress that 1,000 to 1,500 Latin Americans had been so trained up to that time. Two years later, a U.S. Army colonel gave a figure of 1,500 for 1962 alone, but his figures included those receiving "ideological indoctrination" as well. By 1966, Gall estimated 1,200 trainees to date; by 1967, another observer placed the cumulative total at 2,500; and by the late 1970s an estimate for the period to 1967 totalled 3,000.[62]

We suspect that by that latter year the peak period of training guerrillas had passed—although it clearly continued well into the 1970s, if not beyond—and that 2,000 to 3,000 trainees for the entire period does not seem like an overestimate. This might seem to pale beside U.S. efforts in training tens of thousands of soldiers. Yet the generally accepted ratio of conventional soldiers needed to confront guerrillas successfully is 10 soldiers for each guerrilla; therefore, the training efforts of the United States and Cuba in Latin America may not have been all that disproportionate.

Estimates of Cuban efforts in each target nation vary widely as well. Whatever the actual numbers, it does appear that the ratio of overall Cuban trainees to the maximum number of guerrillas at any one time was very high, perhaps surpassing one-half (note that this does not mean that one of every two guerrillas was trained there; there were, after all, deaths, desertions, and turnover as well). One source estimates 300 Venezuelan trainees through 1967, under 200 for Guatemala in the same period, and 2,500 overall in Latin America. A Peruvian military source estimated that 1,200 Peruvians were trained in various communist nations by 1965, far more than the 150 or so who participated in the 1965 *focos*. Peru's Haya de la Torre, by 1965 a staunch anticommunist, even estimated the figure at 1,055 for 1964 alone. These last two estimates almost surely conflate guerrilla trainees with left-wing tourists to communist countries, if we are to give them any credence at all. Discrepant figures exist for Colombia as well, where *Time* counted 700 ongoing Cuban trainees in 1965, while another source more modestly counted 200 overall through 1967. Finally, for Bolivia, the U.S. ambassador in 1967 estimated that 250 to 400 Bolivian nationals trained in Cuba from about 1962 to 1967.[63]

Which countries sent the most pupils to Cuba for military training? Here again our numbers are unreliable, but perhaps very roughly indicative. Writing in 1965, Gall thought that the majority were from Colombia and Venezuela, and he is a most reliable source in guerrilla matters. Lamberg, also a reliable source, thought the list of major contributors was larger: Venezuela, Ecuador, Peru, Bolivia, Argentina, and Central America.[64] Despite the disagreement on Colombia, we do see a rough Cuban pattern that mirrors the efforts of the United States in the region: Cuban "military training," like that of its rival to the north, concentrated in the *Caribbean* region, with relatively little attention to most of South America. That Colombia and Venezuela were its "most-favored" targets seems consistent with references in the literature on those two nations, which indicate the routine nature of the "Cuban training course," as well as other routine contacts.

The Cuban revolution of course provides us with a special case, since no "Cuban model" for insurgent assistance then existed. Nonetheless, our analytical tools can help us here as well. In this case, however, money rather than training was of greatest importance to the guerrillas. Castro was well financed by fund-raising campaigns among Batista exiles and American sympathizers in the United States. Indeed, Barquín suggests that Castro's funding amounted to hundreds of thousands of dollars. A single gift from the interim revolutionary government of Venezuela (in 1958) came to $50,000. Near the end of the guerrilla war, in fact, the M-26 apparently had a steady monthly income in excess of $10,000.[65]

The Cuban guerrillas were also quite well supplied with weaponry in their struggle, better than their 1960s imitators, but not so well equipped as some of the later guerrillas. In guerrilla wars where no secure border provides an easy channel for arms shipments, weapons usually come from dead or captured enemy soldiers. In Cuba, however, extensive gunrunning from the U.S. mainland became a major source of arms for Castro's M-26. In 1957, the U.S. government intercepted some $250,000 worth of such shipments yet estimated that more than that had gotten through. Ex-president Carlos Prío Socorrás was among those charged with felonies in the U.S. for such activity. For example, the weaponry used in the Granma landing, as well as the boat itself, was mostly of American manufacture. Dickey Chapelle estimated that about 15 percent of Castro's weaponry was so obtained.[66] At one point in the war, a Costa Rican plane carrying arms to the rebels employed one of the rough Sierra Maestra landing strips to deliver the hardware. Relative to the 1960s guerrillas, then, the Cubans enjoyed fairly long-term and sustained financial and arms assistance from abroad.

Venezuela was the venue of the most publicized evidence of Cuban support to the 1960s guerrilla movements—apart from Ché's Bolivian *foco*. A U.S. congressional report in 1967 concluded that Venezuela was one of four Latin American nations—along with Guatemala, Puerto Rico, and the Dominican Republic—in which Cubans were supporting guerrillas. From 1964 to 1967 the Cubans, for their part, candidly acknowledged their role in training and otherwise assisting the Venezuelan insurgents. Indeed, training was by all indicators a commonplace there, for an internal PCV memo of 1965 suggested training in Cuba for *all* guerrilla cadres who were not from the state in which their guerrilla *foco* was sited.[67]

It is impossible to estimate precisely how much money the Venezuelan insurgents received from abroad, but fragmentary evidence may suggest the magnitude of the operations. In April 1965, three Italian Communists were arrested and charged with attempting to smuggle in $330,000 to the FALN. In that same year, police estimated that the largest single sum delivered to the guerrillas was $300,000, sent from Peking (Beijing). In the period after 1966, Douglas Bravo's Falcón guerrillas were the main recipients of foreign largesse. While submitting requests to Cuba for money in 1967, Bravo received $50,000 from China, and then complained that Castro was spending his money on automobiles instead of supporting "people in the mountains."[68] After a lengthy period of disengagement from support of Bravo's guerrillas, Cuba in 1970 even ended hortatory revolutionary radio broadcasts aimed at Venezuela. Since Cuba was widely cited as the major supporter of the Venezuelan guerrillas, its aid must have been substantial indeed to surpass the sums from China and Italy suggested here. The guerrillas themselves evidently entertained no illusions that "popular support" alone was sufficient to fuel their movement, since their newspaper *Revolución* described aid from the "world revolutionary camp" as something that was "as indispensable to us as the wind is to the sail."[69]

If Venezuela stood out as a focus of external financial support for insurgency, it also was outlined (briefly) as a focus of weapons aid. In November 1963 a farmer found a three-ton weapons cache buried on a beach on the Paraguaná peninsula in Falcón State. At first, the Venezuelan government believed the 4,230 cubic feet of weapons to have been taken from Venezuelan troops and hidden there for future use. Close examination instead revealed them to be of Belgian origin, coming from a Belgian shipment to Cuba some time before. Despite the notoriety of this particular find, Allemann is probably correct in his evaluation of the Venezuelan guerrillas' armaments supplies: they were vastly inferior in weaponry to their governmental opponents, whose weapons purchases were backed by taxing vast oil revenues. Internal documents of the MIR indicated that neither the internal arms market, nor weapons captured from government troops, nor supplies from friendly lands—individually or collectively—ever adequately supplied the guerrillas with a fighting power capable of confronting their opponents. This contrasts markedly with Fidel Castro's situation in Cuba by 1958.[70]

Venezuela is also, again apart from the obvious case of Bolivia, the one country in the hemisphere for which certain evidence of Cuban combat guerrillas is documented. Some Cubans by birth who fought in the FALN were pre-1958 emigrants to Venezuela. They should not be confused with the Cuban assistance corps that landed on the Venezuelan coast in mid-1966; or with a commando raid in May 1967, in which Venezuelan authorities captured three guerrillas identified as Cuban army officers; or with the Cuban guerrilla volunteer whose diary the Venezuelan authorities seized and later published. (In an earlier period, the Communist PCV had rejected Castro's offer to have Ché Guevara come fight in Venezuela. Times had obviously changed.) Still, as with the case of weapons, there is no evidence of sustained, large-scale reinforcements to the Venezuelan guerrillas.[71] Overall, there is little doubt that Venezuela stands out as a major focus of Cuban training, financial and military supply, and combat troop support in the hemisphere during the 1960s. Perhaps indicative of the closeness of the social ties between guerrillas and their foreign benefactor is the Venezuelan FALN, which was officially represented in Havana, complete with its own office and stationery headed República de Venezuela—Fuerzas Armadas de Liberación.

Three of the four proven Cuban interventions in Latin America took place in Venezuela. The fourth, in Guatemala, occurred in 1966 through a Cuban-based group working out of Mexico.[72] However, there is little evidence of more extensive Cuban aid to Guatemala's insurgents. Guerrilla leaders Luis Turcios Lima and Marco Yon Sosa visited Cuba more than once, and many Guatemalans trained there, but little else. Castro reportedly offered both arms and men to Turcios, who declined the offers. Eighty percent of the rebels' weaponry reportedly was taken from the Guatemalan army, both from defeated soldiers and through outright purchases from army stocks through the guerrillas' old-boy networks in the military.[73] Cuban involvement in Guatemala was substantially less, therefore, than in Venezuela.

In Columbia, Cuban aid had some impact in the early 1960s. The peasant republic of Marquetalia received some initial organizing help from Cuban and Chinese instructors. Later on the ELN, usually described as Fidelista in its politics, began with the training of an entire cohort of its leaders in Cuba before returning to Colombia for its first military activity. The Colombian government claimed only that the ELN guerrillas received Cuban money and advice, not arms or military leadership. ELN leader Fabio Vásquez was never satisfied with the level of Cuban aid—in money or weapons—even though an ex-member reported that Vásquez began to base the ELN's strategy on such external aid in late 1967. This may explain the vehemence of Vásquez's break with Castro in 1970, when he termed the Cuban leader a "traitor to the guerrilla cause," while breaking off financial, military, and ideological relations. The text of a government interrogation of a left-wing Mexican journalist, who had just visited the ELN's camp in 1966, also suggests that the guerrillas largely obtained their weapons from Colombian soldiers, and not from Cuban shipments.[74] The level of Cuban aid in Colombia, then, seems more like the Guatemalan than the Venezuelan example.

The Peruvian case also resembles the preceding two instances, differing mainly in the extreme numbers that the authorities claimed had secured training in Cuba (and elsewhere).[75] Evidence suggests that the Cubans arranged some arms shipments through Bolivia, filtered through Czech agents in La Paz. As in the case of the Colombian ELN, a Peruvian cohort of proto-guerrillas trained in Cuba and then returned to begin the revolution: Javier Héraud's ill-fated group of 1963, who entered southeastern Peru near Puerto Maldonado and were quickly wiped out. The extent of the government's claims, including a list of fourteen Peruvians allegedly trained in China, suggests that the training of Peruvians in various communist countries may indeed have been more extensive than in the cases of Guatemala and Colombia, at least up through 1965.[76]

Bolivia, of course, stands out as the sui generis case of Cuban support for guerrilla movements. The *foco* there was led, financed, and armed in such a manner that the Bolivians' participation was more peripheral then central to the movement—more like liaisons than cadres. Guevara had argued that Bolivia was to be but the first stone to fall in a broader continental revolution—but one star in the revolutionary cosmos—and if necessary was to be sacrificed in order to achieve that larger goal. The Bolivian adventure is less notable for its scope—militarily it was the least impressive of the six cases under review—than for the notoriety engendered by Ché's presence. The foreign sponsorship of the Bolivian *foco* was also accompanied by a series of striking Cuban denials (concerning the Cubans' presence) and absurd counterassertions (concerning the scope of American military involvement).[77]

CONCLUSIONS

Cuban aid to the Latin American guerrilla movements of the 1960s was variable, but generally quite limited, therefore having little effect on the outcomes of the region's guerrilla wars. Putting aside the Bolivian case—a virtual Cuban "export" to that nation—Cuba gave its greatest support to the Venezuelan insurgents. After Venezuela, there is little to differentiate the degree of Cuban aid to Guatemala, Colombia, and Peru. In all four of those cases, Cuban guerrilla training must be adjudged of prime importance, if the life courses of the insurgencies were indeed extended for external reasons. Money and weapons assistance was extremely limited, even to Venezuela. Indeed, despite the enormous brouhaha over *1960s* Cuban aid to revolutionaries in the region, there may be better evidence of large-scale aid to the *later* guerrillas, those of the 1970s and 1980s. Indeed, the scale of many of those later insurgencies was substantially greater: the numbers of insurgents, the numbers of dead, the violence of the confrontation (especially the numbing levels of government terror against the peasantry), and the degree of aid supplied by both the United States and Cuba to some of the principals.

Returning to the earlier period, and most interestingly, there is good reason to believe that the greatest degree of external support to a guerrilla movement went to the Cuban insurgents of 1956–1958. The Cuban guerrillas' supplies of both money and weaponry seem to have been both larger and more secure than those of their 1960s imitators. Surprisingly, then, it was a "pre-Cuba" yet Cuban guerrilla movement that was able to elicit the most extensive external support for its cause, and not those later movements whose leaders had most been led to expect regular and massive aid from the "world revolutionary camp" (i.e., wind for their sails), simply because of their Fidelista bona fides.

Finally, in contrast to Cuban assistance, military aid from the United States may have had a decisive impact on the outcome of one revolutionary movement of the 1960s—the Guatemalan—in the lending of critical assistance to a weak, weak-willed, and weakly supported military establishment. However, it is only for Guatemala that such a scenario is even plausible, for even in Bolivia one cannot make a strong case that, absent such U.S. aid, the guerrillas would have prevailed, or even gotten a longer lease on life. This conclusion applies *a fortiori* to Colombia, Peru, and most especially to Venezuela.

This chapter began with an academic brief in favor of taking quite seriously the sociological study of military matters, which too often are given short shrift in the social sciences. Nonetheless, we do not wish to adopt a strictly military perspective on such affairs—to "go native" in Militaryland, as it were—for the outcomes of guerrilla wars hinge on more than the naked ability to inflict losses upon one's opponents. They depend as well on the ability of guerrillas (or their opponents) to secure the support of regional peasantries and the loyalty of the broader populace. To understand the social origins of such support and loyalty is the aim of the next three chapters.

The Sources of Peasant Support I:
Agrarian Structure and Its Transformations

> It is necessary to suppress poverty and misery, which cause shame
> and provoke revolts.
>
> —Confucius, 484 B.C.

THE STATE OF THE THEORETICAL ART

Until recently, the state of our knowledge about the social bases of rural
collective action, especially peasant revolutionary action, had gone little beyond that suggested by Confucius. In the past decade or two, however, theoretical explanations of peasant-based revolution have come to the forefront of
social science. With that advent has come the normal by-product of theoretical fruition, lively and stimulating debate.

One can discern at least four "schools" of thought on the social sources of
peasant revolution. In Jeffery Paige's view, different agrarian *structures* give
rise to different forms of cultivator collective action, and revolutionary action
is to be found when cultivators derive their income from "wages" (rather than
land), in combination with a landholding class that derives its income from
control of land (rather than capital in the form of processing, warehousing, or
transportation investments). In James C. Scott's view, however, peasant revolutionary sentiment is likely to appear when peasant villages and villagers
experience the impact of capitalist market relations in the countryside, for
those relations tend to break down age-old systems of patron-client (i.e.,
landlord-tenant) systems of reciprocity, which protected peasant cultivators
from market risk. Peasants, where they are able, then respond to such historical *processes* that threaten their "moral economy" by rebelling against their
neo-capitalist landlords and the landlords' governmental allies. Similar views
have been aired by Eric Wolf, Barrington Moore, Jr., and E. J. Hobsbawm.
Samuel Popkin, in contrast to Scott, has argued that peasants don't respond
to a moral economy collectively shared by villagers. They respond rather to
their own rational *self-interests*, in a way perfectly intelligible to the economics of utility-maximization. Finally, Theda Skocpol has suggested, roughly,
a plague on all those theoretical houses (except perhaps Scott's). Peasants are
always discontented, she argues, and theorists should rather pay attention to

macrostructural relationships that structurally permit or press peasants toward rebellion. In particular she proposes attention to those rural social structures in which, first, peasant villages show high degrees of solidarity, and second, in which villages are relatively free from landlord influence and control. There, she argues, one can find a revolutionary peasantry.[1]

Nor has the matter rested there, with theories bypassing one another like ships in the night. Paige's work is built in part around a critique of earlier theories, especially those of Wolf, himself a forerunner of Scott. J. Craig Jenkins has compared the retrodictive powers of Paige and Scott on a particular case, found the former wanting, and the latter a good guide. Contrariwise, Popkin's thesis is presented in part as a thoroughgoing critique of Scott's "moral economy" view, for which he would substitute his "political economy." Skocpol, in turn, doesn't think very highly of Paige's perspective, although her own view is rather more congruent with Scott's. For his part, Paige entered the lists by comparing the predictive power of Scott, Popkin, and himself in the case of the second-generation Guatemalan guerrilla movements and found his rivals theoretically wanting.[2]

Thus we have two, three, many theories of peasant revolution. In this chapter I do not wish to enter a special plea for one or the other of these schools, for school making is one of the less appealing aspects of sociological research. I wish rather to suggest, following Merton's suggestion of a half-century ago, that we entertain the possibility that our multifarious social life harbors functional alternatives—in this case, actually, causal alternatives: various structures, each of which can produce the same social outcome. Therefore we may encounter a plurality of social conditions that can produce revolutionary peasantries, and not a unique one unearthed by Paige, Scott, Popkin, or Skocpol alone.

In this regard, my cause is not unprecedented, for both Paige and Skocpol use functional alternatives in their discussions of revolution and related topics. In his discussion of the conditions for agrarian revolts (not revolutions), Paige argues that the structural condition of "serfdom" is not a sufficient condition for an agrarian revolt, but must be joined to an organizational push from outside the system, which may appear in three different forms (functional alternatives). In Skocpol's *States and Social Revolutions*, revolution occurs when the collapse of the state is paired with peasant insurrection. Yet the state's collapse may occur for one (or both) of two causes (functional alternatives): external military defeat or internal landlord resistance to the reform of an agrarian bureaucracy.[3]

In suggesting that peasant revolution may have multiple roots, therefore, my following arguments are not without distinguished precedents. In the pages to follow I wish to make a case for modified versions of both Paige's and Scott's theses. For the former case, I wish to suggest that agrarian structures are indeed related to the revolutionary proclivities of the peasantry, yet add to Paige's theory the coda that *squatters* (as well as his sharecroppers and migratory estate laborers) are likely to be *foci* of revolution. To Scott's thesis—that the socioeconomic dislocation of peasants through the decay of their old patron-client ties is tied to their rebelliousness—I wish to add that *physical* dislocation from one's lands may also be associated with peasant revolution.

AGRARIAN STRUCTURE: ZERO-SUM CONFLICT AND REVOLUTION

Paige's Theory: Exegesis and Extension

Paige distinguishes four main types of collective action engaged in by cultivators: (1) reform commodity movements, in which cultivators seek to control the vagaries of market prices for their inputs or their crops; (2) labor reform movements, where cultivators act like factory workers, in seeking higher wages and benefits and better working conditions, usually through trade union activity; (3) agrarian revolts, in which peasants seek radical but limited aims in the countryside, by invading lands, by refusing to pay landlords for use of the land, or by refusing to work any longer on the landlords' estates; (4) agrarian revolution, in which such radical peasant actions are combined with demands for unconstitutional political changes or are made in alliance with Marxist or Communist political parties.

Paige then proceeds to correlate his measures of agrarian export structures, from all over the underdeveloped world, with the types of collective action engaged in by cultivators in those regions, as culled from newspaper accounts. He uncovers a series of relationships showing that different types of agrarian structure are in fact statistically associated with different types of cultivator collective action during the years 1948–1970: (1) smallholders (i.e., owner-operators of small farms) with reform commodity movements; (2) laborers on capital-intensive plantations (e.g., sugar) with labor reform movements; (3) "serfs"—usufructuaries whose rights to use a plot of land are contingent on their work on the landlord's estate—with agrarian revolts and, finally and most importantly, (4) sharecroppers and migratory estate laborers, who are paid in wages, both with revolutionary movements, the former with socialist revolution, the latter with nationalist revolution.

Where would squatters fit in a model such as this? Clearly squatters derive their incomes from land, rather than wages. At the same time they are usually engaged in a form of conflict that is classically zero-sum: their efforts to resist eviction from the lands that they work and landlords' efforts to oust them from lands to which landlords have legal title. In these two respects combined they resemble Paige's "serfs." Further, following the logic Paige employs in his analysis of serfs, we would expect squatters especially to engage in radical action when some outside force gives an impetus to their organization efforts, and therefore to their capacity for collective action.[4]

What, therefore, do we expect from our modification of Paige's theory? Revolutionary guerrillas should draw their greatest support from areas in which sharecropping is more prevalent, for sharecroppers lean toward such sociopolitical radicalism. Squatters, whatever their partial structural resemblance to serfs, should obey a somewhat different logic, outlined by Eric Wolf, in that their common locations on agrarian frontiers often give them "tactical mobility" and therefore a freedom to act radically unlike the close social controls usually exerted over serfs.[5] Squatters thus are more likely than serfs to be sources of radical support for revolutionaries, at least insofar as that "radicalism" is keyed to access to land—the focal issue in Paige's "agrarian revolts."[6] "Tenants" are a more general case of which sharecroppers are a special instance, and we might expect them to be sources of radicalism as well, as Jenkins has argued.[7] Such a general category may have to suffice when we lack detailed breakdowns on subtypes of tenants, as in the analyses of Guatemala here and El Salvador in chapter 10.

I will largely apply ecological analysis in the following material, just as Paige did, for we lack individual-level data (such as surveys) that might fill in the gaps. If the guerrillas gain support in an area with a *relatively* high prevalence of sharecroppers, squatters, or perhaps tenants, my working assumption is that there is an "elective affinity" between the two, and that guerrillas would *not* have received such support in more ordinary agricultural regions. Whenever possible, I have tried to strengthen this inference through one of two comparisons: either comparing guerrilla strongholds to nearby areas that were not strongholds, or comparing areas of strong and sustained peasant support with other areas in which guerrillas received lesser support. The first comparison is not unprecedented. In his study of support for Chinese Communist guerrillas, Roy Hofheinz initially found no tenancy-support correlation across China's gigantic provinces. Yet within provinces, by comparing adjacent districts, he in fact found that relatively high tenancy in a district was associated with greater Communist influence there.[8] Since guerrillas do not oblige the sociologist by providing experimental conditions—equal guerrilla presence in every rural area of each country—we must make do with these further assumptions, by comparing peasant support across the political units (departments and states), and within those units, comparing adjacent *municipios* and/or districts.

For the following quantitative comparisons I certainly considered employing tests of statistical significance, but they are inappropriate, insofar as the researcher uses them in order to make careful inferences from a sample to a population: these are *census* data of the entire population. I could certainly have used t-tests and other statistical measures focusing on the differences in percentages (e.g., of squatters) in two regions being compared. Yet the sheer numbers involved routinely would have produced "statistically significant" differences even where the differences were substantively small, and one should never confuse those two types of "significance." In other sections of this work I will not shy from such analyses where the data are good and the procedures appropriate.

Cuba

Our data come from the Cuban agricultural census of 1946. Unlike our other nations, we have reason to believe that we can safely exclude tenants from our list of revolutionary possibles, for by the 1950s most of the sugar tenants (*colonos*) in Cuba were legally secure from eviction, and hence protected from that landed insecurity which is the taproot of peasant radicalism. Non-sugar tenants were somewhat less secure but still protected by law. Squatters, however, were not secure, since by law some rent had to be paid on a non-owned plot to secure oneself from eviction. There was one exception, however: By old Spanish legal tradition, continuous farming of a plot for twenty to thirty years—sources differ on the exact time span—was grounds for the establishment of ownership, rent or no rent. Most squatters, however, were outside the law, without title to the land, paying no rent, and with insufficient time on a plot to establish a legal claim to it.[9]

The mountains of Oriente (Sierra Maestra and Sierra Cristal) and later, in 1958, those of Las Villas (Sierra Escambray) provinces were the main loci of rural guerrilla activity in Cuba.[10] Incidentally, both were also the centers of coffee production on the island. As we can see in table 6-1, Oriente is by far

TABLE 6-1
Distribution of Landholdings in Cuba, 1946, by Type of Tenancy
(percentage of units)

| | *Average Landholding* | *Units Taken in Rent* | | | *Squatter Held* |
		All	*Fixed*	*Share*	
CUBA	*57 hectares*	*54%*	*33%*	*21%*	*9%*
Oriente*	51	33	17	15	22
Las Villas*	51	64	46	18	2
Camagüey	117	37	27	11	5
Havana	46	68	54	14	1
Matanzas	52	68	55	13	1
Pinar del Río	42	81	26	55	2

Source: Cuba, Ministerio de Agricultura, *Memoria del censo agrícola nacional, 1946* (Havana, 1951), table 7, pp. 387–93.
* Province with guerrilla movement.

the major center of squatter activity in Cuba, most of it in the two Sierras, as we shall see. Neither province, though, was a center of sharecropping activity, that honor falling to Pinar del Río, at the other end of Cuba. Las Villas was not a center of either activity. The data suggest, then, a strong relationship between the center of guerrilla activity in the hills of Oriente, and the prevalence there of squatters, twenty percentage points higher than in the rest of Cuba. They suggest, however, no such relation for the secondary and later DR guerrilla zone in Las Villas.

If we now look within provinces (table 6-2), the pattern of results remains. Las Villas remains opaque to this structural analysis, while the results from Oriente, if anything, become more pronounced. While it is difficult to separate guerrilla strongholds from other areas of Oriente, where Castro's M-26 grew and flourished, the existing literature allows a rough approximation. Once again the difference in rates of squatting is sharp: 30 percent of all cultivators were squatters in the guerrilla zones of Oriente, but only 9 percent in the rest of the province. Therefore, the squatter structural thesis is sustained for Cuba by our ecological analysis for the key guerrilla zone of Oriente, although not for the secondary zone of Las Villas.

In this case, we are fortunate to have micro-level qualitative data to support the preceding ecological, quantitative analysis. All we have learned so far is that Castro's guerrilla strongholds were also havens for squatters. In the historiography of the Cuban revolution, however, we find that squatters were indeed the first peasants to join Castro's guerrillas in the Sierra, were its staunchest supporters throughout the struggle, and were promised a land reform by Castro in return for that support, a promise that he fulfilled promptly upon attaining power.

Available evidence also indicates a sharp focus of (zero-sum) conflict between squatters and the landowners of the Sierra, as well as bad relations with merchant middlemen and the local and national constabularies. Many estates were run by foremen—the whitest of Cuban agrarian occupations, even in heavily African Oriente—whose major tasks were the eviction of squatters. Lowry Nelson recounts an eviction case in the late 1940s involving 1,200 squatters in El Cobre *municipio* (in the Sierra Maestra), many of whom had in fact lived on the land for more than thirty years. The typical squatter lived on less than one hectare of land (= 2.44 acres), despite Cuba's ample agricultural endowment. Nationwide, Cuban landowners sharpened the level of eviction conflict from 1940 to 1957. The squatters had responded by forming anti-eviction bands—before Castro arrived—which were led by Crescencio Pérez in the Sierra Maestra, the same squatter leader who formed an alliance with Fidel Castro in 1956.[11]

If qualitative analysis supports the thesis of a guerrilla-squatter alliance, it also lends support to the counter-thesis that Cubans in different rural circumstances did not render strong support to the guerrillas. Ché Guevara and Régis Debray were to develop a thesis contrasting the people of the Sierra with

TABLE 6-2
Cuba: Type of Tenancy by Guerrilla Zones

	Number of Units	Squatters		Sharecroppers	
		Number	%	Number	%
Cuba	159,958	13,718	8.6%	33,064	20.7%
Oriente	51,447	11,447	22.3	7,764	15.1
Guerrilla Zones	33,479	9,872	29.5	4,522	13.5
Sierra Maestra	16,468	5,591	34.0	2,481	15.1
Bayamo	4,146	34		965	
Campechuela	686	387		16	
El Cobre	2,550	702		783	
Jiguaní	3,146	264		647	
Manzanillo	2,885	1,701		61	
Niquero	3,055	2,503		9	
Sierra Cristal, etc.	17,011	4,281	25.2	2,041	12.0
Alto Songo	3,803	383		873	
Baracoa	4,181	953		774	
Guantánamo	2,209	1,200		135	
Mayarí	2,621	591		97	
Sagua de Tánamo	2,093	978		91	
San Luis	1,082	17		24	
Yateras	1,022	159		47	
Other Areas	17,968	1,575	8.8	3,242	18.0
Antilla	485	31		29	
Banes	1,020	14		205	
Caney	1,362	73		355	
Gibara	1,395	39		424	
Holguín	6,450	293		1,409	
Palma Soriano	3,675	792		431	
Puerto Padre	1,125	4		57	
Santiago de Cuba	211	30		1	
Victoria de las Tunas	2,245	299		331	
Las Villas	40,182	636	1.6	7,166	17.8
Guerrilla Zones	15,373	197	1.3	3,171	20.6
Cienfuegos	2,702	44		392	
Rodas	1,434	32		38	
San Fernando	793	6		10	
Sancti Spíritus	4,380	31		979	
Santa Clara	4,363	58		1,374	
Trinidad	1,701	26		378	
Rest of Province	24,809	439	1.8	3,995	16.1

Source: Cuba, *Memoria del censo agrícola, 1946*, pp. 408–19.

those of the *llano*, or plain, based on Guevara's experience during Castro's summer offensive in 1958. While the *llano* often refers to the urban resistance, Guevara also decried the relative lack of support obtained in the rural lowlands, contrasting it with the "unanimous support" of the Sierra. He explained it, like a good Marxist sociologist, by the existential factors of life in the lowlands, which "turned these men into slaves." He decried not only their behavior but their attitudes, noting that the social conscience of the Camagüey peasantry was "minimal" and anticipating "numerous betrayals." Allemann notes that the plains peasantry was "simply indifferent to strangers." In addition, Domínguez noted that anti-Castro guerrillas in 1960 were to lodge themselves in the Sierra Escambray (not a squatter haven), while the counterrevolutionary movement against Castro's government in 1963 was rooted on the plain in Matanzas Province.[12] All in all, this discussion strengthens the purely statistical indicators of a link between squatters and support for revolutionary guerrillas.

Venezuela

Venezuela provides an excellent case for evaluating the structural thesis. Not only do we have a superb case study of the guerrillas in Valsalice's work but strong supporting data as well. In addition, the guerrillas were widely dispersed throughout the nation and received varying degrees of peasant support, both of which help to evaluate the theory. Again, just as in Cuba, coffee is a common denominator of the key centers of guerrilla strength; indeed, the correlation is a striking one, especially in the intra-state guerrilla havens of Falcón and Lara.[13]

Table 6-3 displays the relative prevalence of tenancy, of sharecropping, and of squatting by state in Venezuela. Starred (*) states are those with guerrilla *focos* after 1962, according to Valsalice, and are listed in rough order of the strength of peasant support in those locales.[14] Although Mérida, Zulia, and several other states did have some guerrilla activity at an earlier period, they simply are not areas of major fronts after 1962; therefore they are listed in the residual category. Venezuela, however, does approach an "experimental situation," since guerrillas appeared through most of the countryside in the early 1960s, but only took root in certain selected regions. Data come from the 1961 agricultural census.

We do not anticipate a squatter-guerrilla connection in Venezuela, for in that nation the squatters farmed government-owned land, not private land. Therefore that basic locus of zero-sum conflict with private landlords was absent. However, at first glance, even the sharecropper hypothesis seems to suffer. Lara and Falcón were the chief foci of guerrilla activity, but only Lara had substantial sharecropping, as did other Andean states like Mérida and Táchira. When taken collectively, the starred states in table 6-3 have only 9.0

TABLE 6-3
Venezuela: Percentage of Units Held by Nonproprietors, 1960–1961

	Average Landholding	Percentage of Units Rented			Squatter Held
		All	Fixed	Share	
Venezuela	82 hectares	19%	10%	9%	45%
Lara*	54	23	9	14	27
Falcón*	53	7	2	5	15
Portuguesa*	40	29	20	9	48
Trujillo*	18	40	11	29	10
Miranda*	33	24	19	5	52
Yaracuy*	24	22	16	6	53
Barinas*	160	12	11	1	85
Sucre*	12	12	5	7	60
Apure*	685	11	10	0.2	86
Monagas*	57	8	7	1	82
Guarico*	270	11	7	3	74
Anzoátegui	103	6	4	2	83
Aragua	69	38	34	4	45
Bolívar	341	2	2	—	91
Carabobo	33	25	22	2	47
Cojedes	225	38	24	14	54
Mérida	25	23	3	19	17
Nueva Esparta	10	34	5	29	12
Táchira	30	17	7	10	10
Zulia	125	4	4	0.5	29
Federal District	24	39	29	10	43

Source: Venezuela, Dirección General de Estadística y Censos Nacionales, *III censo agropecuario 1961: Resumen general de la república—Parte A* (Caracas, 1967), table 0.1, pp. 2–9.

* State with guerrilla activity after 1962.

percent sharecroppers, versus 8.3 percent for the remaining states; respective tenancy shares of 10.5 percent and 9.2 percent; and private-land tenancy percentages of 7.4 percent and 7.2 percent. These small differences could hardly sustain the thesis of a connection between sharecroppers and guerrillas.

If, however, we examine the political subunits, or districts, of Venezuela, the scenario changes sharply. We will do this in two fashions, first comparing all guerrilla districts nationwide, divided into high support areas and others, and second, looking within each state, separating relatively high-support zones within each state from areas of no or lesser support.

Table 6-4 shows the results of the first district-level comparison, contrasting the agrarian structures of high-support districts and of lower- or no-

TABLE 6-4

Venezuela: Sharecroppers as a Percentage of All Landholders in High and Low Guerrilla-Support Districts

		Number of Units	Number Sharecropped	%
	Venezuela	315,477	27,552	8.7%
State	Guerrilla districts	65,530	7,364	11.6
	High support districts	28,545	5,629	19.7
Falcón	Bolívar	892	246	27.6
	Federación	2,385	91	3.8
	Petit	1,765	360	20.4
Lara	Jiménez	3,709	690	18.6
	Morán	4,314	1,052	24.4
Miranda	Páez	2,920	298	10.2
Portuguesa	Sucre	4,275	666	15.6
Trujillo	Boconó	8,285	2,226	26.9
	Lower support districts	34,985	1,466	4.2
Barinas	Bolívar	2,181	5	0.2
	Osbispos	2,373	43	1.8
Falcón	Acosta	2,910	12	0.4
	Colina	524	4	0.8
	Miranda	625	12	1.9
	Silva	1,089	8	0.7
Guarico	Monagas	2,825	113	4.0
Lara	Iribarren	2,360	582	24.7
Miranda	Acevedo	3,975	107	2.7
	Brión	1,539	12	0.8
Monagas	Acosta	1,257	39	3.1
	Caripe	2,267	3	0.1
Sucre	Ribero	4,640	63	1.4
Portuguesa	Guanare	3,026	462	15.3
Yaracuy	Bolívar	3,394	1	0.0

Source: Same as for table 6-3.

support districts. Although this is a rigorous test of our theory, the results generally conform to our expectations. Sharecropping is only three percentage points greater in all guerrilla districts than in the nation overall. Yet we encounter a striking differential between the high- and low-support districts nationwide, with the prevalence of sharecropping five times as high in the former areas (20 percent versus 4 percent). In Falcón, sharecroppers made up 14 percent of all cultivators in the high-support zones, but were virtually absent from lower-support districts and from the rest of the state.

TABLE 6-5

Venezuela: Percentage of Units Farmed by Sharecroppers—
Intrastate Variations by Guerrilla Influence

State/District	Number of Units	Number of Sharecroppers	%
Lara	*19,140*	*2,690*	*14.1%*
Guerrilla zones	10,383	2,324	22.4
Iribarren	2,360	582	
Jiménez*	3,709	690	
Morán*	4,314	1,052	
Other areas	8,757	366	4.2
Portuguesa	*16,956*	*1,478*	*8.7%*
Guerrilla zones	7,301	1,128	15.4
Guanare	3,026	462	
Sucre*	4,275	666	
Other areas	9,655	350	3.6
Trujillo	*26,012*	*7,599*	*29.2%*
Guerrilla zone	8,285	2,226	26.9
Boconó*	8,285	2,226	
Other areas	17,727	5,373	30.3
Miranda	*17,970*	*901*	*5.0%*
Guerrilla zones	8,434	417	4.9
Páez*	2,920	298	
Acevedo	3,975	107	
Brión	1,539	12	
Other areas	9,536	484	5.1
Barinas	*12,702*	*132*	*1.0%*
Guerrilla zones	4,554	48	1.1
Bolívar	2,181	5	
Ospispos	2,373	43	
Other areas	8,148	84	1.0

In table 6-5 I have presented the results of the second comparison, examining the same high- versus low-support differential for each state separately. The patterns are surprisingly clear. In those states where the guerrilla movements were the largest and strongest (Falcón, Lara, Portuguesa, and Trujillo), we find absolutely high levels of sharecropping, 15 to 30 percent of all units versus a nationwide average of only 9 percent. Except for Trujillo, we also find the greatest differentials in sharecropping when we compare guerrilla strongholds with other areas (including "weakholds"). Boconó, in Trujillo, does not have relatively high intra-state sharecropping proportions, but it has the highest absolute level of any guerrilla district in the nation. Only one "strong" guerrilla district has been omitted from this analysis: Páez in

TABLE 6-5 (*cont.*)

State/District	Number of Units	Number of Sharecroppers	%
Guarico	*15,292*	*497*	*3.3%*
Guerrilla zone	2,825	113	4.0
Monagas	2,825	113	
Other areas	12,467	384	3.1
Monagas	*14,845*	*75*	*0.5%*
Guerrilla zones	3,524	42	1.2
Acosta	1,257	39	
Caripe	2,267	3	
Other areas	11,321	33	0.3
Sucre	*27,915*	*1,817*	*6.5%*
Guerrilla zone	4,640	63	1.4
Ribero	4,640	63	
Other areas	23,275	1,754	7.5
Yaracuy	*14,919*	*951*	*6.4%*
Guerrilla zone	3,394	1	0.03
Bolívar	3,394	1	
Other areas	11,525	950	8.2

Source: Same as for table 6-3.
* Strong guerrilla area.

Miranda State, where the sharecropping percentage was only five points higher than the rest of the state. In contrast to the differences we found in the "strong" guerrilla states, "weak" states exhibited absolutely low levels of sharecropping (at most 7 percent of all units), and few if any differences between guerrilla zones and other areas. Therefore, our district-level analysis supports the theory of a correlation between agrarian structure and revolutionary support, and in Venezuela 10 percent appears to be the "tipping point": when the proportion of sharecroppers rises above that mark, districts are more likely to be guerrilla havens, and no areas of strong support contain fewer than 10 percent working as sharecroppers.

Guatemala

Guatemalan data come from the 1964 census of agriculture. Unfortunately, that census does not distinguish between sharecropping and other forms of tenancy. In Jenkins's reading of Paige, this should pose no problem, for he argues that this is really what Paige is referring to, rather than the special case of sharecropping.[15] Nonetheless, the pooling of all tenancy categories does make our analysis more problematic for Guatemala. The census data do, however, allow us to separate out a category corresponding to Paige's

TABLE 6-6
Guatemala: Percentage of Farm Units Held by Tenants, 1964

| | | Percentage of Units Taken in Rent | | |
	Average Landholding	All	Fixed/ Share	Labor Service
Guatemala	16 manzanas	23%	11%	12%
Zacapa*	25	26	20	6
Izabal*	25	20	15	5
El Progreso*	15	27	27	0.4
Alta Verapaz*	17	55	4	51
Chiquimula*	8	14	14	0.2
Baja Verapaz	14	28	14	15
Chimaltenango	8	16	10	6
El Petén	9	—	—	—
Escuintla	37	43	25	19
Guatemala	11	33	18	15
Huehuetenango	9	8	5	3
Jalapa	11	25	24.7	0.5
Jutiapa	12	24	22	2
Quezaltenango	7	13	7	6
El Quiché	9	13	3	9
Retalhuleu	19	52	34	18
Sacatepéquez	5	15	8	7
San Marcos	7	12	5	6
Santa Rosa	19	37	19	17
Sololá	3	4	3	2
Suchitepéquez	16	58	27	31
Totonicapán	2	0.2	0.2	0

Source: Guatemala, Dirección General de Estadística, *II censo agropecuario 1964—vol. 1* (Guatemala City, 1968), tables 2-2, 5-2 (pp. 209–17, 269–86).
1 manzana = .7 hectare.
* Guerrilla department.

"serfs," a type termed *colonato* in Guatemala, where peasants work usufruct plots in exchange for labor on the estate owner's lands. Table 6-6 refers to them under "labor service." Again, areas of guerrilla influence are starred and placed at the head of the table, in order of the strength of the local guerrilla movement.

Zacapa and Izabal clearly are the standouts in this regard, although the FAR did establish a presence in some areas of El Progreso, Chiquimula, and Alta Verapaz. Guerrilla claims of significant activity elsewhere in the country are not well established. Looking at table 6-6, we see that guerrilla states are areas of relatively high tenancy (meaning, for Guatemala, fixed-price tenants *and* sharecroppers).

TABLE 6-7
Guatemala: Intradepartmental Variations in Land Tenancy
by Zones of Guerrilla Influence

	Number of Units	Number Rented	% Rented
GUATEMALA	417,344	47,026	11%
Zacapa	7,216	1,432	19.8%
Izabal	7,103	1,093	15.4%
Guerrilla zones	5,608	1,002	17.9
El Estor	631	146	
Los Amates	2,708	523	
Morales	2,269	333	
Other areas	1,495	91	6.1
Alta Verapaz	36,892	1,274	3.5%
Guerrilla zone	2,247	343	15.3
Panzós	2,247	343	
Other areas	34,645	931	2.7
Chiquimula	17,199	2,400	14.0%
Guerrilla zones	4,148	893	21.5
Chiquimula	3,312	579	
San José La Arada	836	314	
Other areas	13,051	1,507	11.5
El Progreso	6,848	1,826	26.7%
Guerrilla zones	1,814	356	19.6
San Agustín A.	1,250	211	
San Cristóbal A.	167	32	
El Jícaro	397	113	
Other areas	5,034	1,470	29.2

Source: Same as for table 6-6.

By superimposing maps of guerrilla activity over political and topographi-
cal maps of Guatemala,[16] we can look within the departments, and there see
even more striking results. I treat Zacapa here as a single unit, for reasons
given below. The results of this second analysis appear in table 6-7.

Again the structural hypothesis gains support. If we look only at guerrilla
zones, we see a tenancy minimum of 15 percent and a maximum of 22 percent, versus the 11-percent national average. In particular, the results for
Izabal, Alta Verapaz, and Chiquimula support the theory of a connection
between tenancy and peasant support for revolutionaries, although it does not
hold true for El Progreso (a less important case).

The department of Zacapa might well be called "Guerrilla Central" for this
period, which creates problems for our intra-departmental analysis. The four

TABLE 6-8
Intradepartmental Tenancy Rates in Zacapa, Guatemala,
by Guerrilla Zones

	Number of Units	Number Rented	%
ZACAPA	7,216	1,432	19.8%
Sierra de las Minas	2,949	640	21.7%
Gualán	2,176	594	
Río Hondo	518	11	
Teculután	97	7	
Usumatlán	158	28	
Other guerrilla zones*	2,772	729	26.3%
Cabañas	563	291	
San Diego	588	204	
Zacapa	1,621	234	
Rest of department	1,495	63	4.2%
Estanzuela	188	6	
La Unión	892	48	
Huité	415	9	

Source: Same as for table 6-6.
* Zacapa plus two municipios bordering on an area of an adjacent state where guerrilla presence was confirmed, other than zones in Sierra de las Minas.

municipios containing the Sierra de las Minas (haven of the FAR) also extend down into the plains, and other areas of claimed guerrilla influence extend down into El Progreso, Jalapa, and Chiquimula. The municipio of Zacapa itself was purportedly also a hotbed. These multiple areas leave very little of the department to serve as a control area for our comparisons, but we can essay a tentative comparison of the different zones, presented in table 6-8.

Even given reasonable restraint in interpreting the results, again the results appear to support the hypothesis. While tenancy is quite common throughout Zacapa, the prevalence is markedly less in those areas that were not guerrilla hotbeds, 15 to 20 percentage points lower than guerrilla zones and departmental averages. Whether Zacapa is viewed as a whole, or dissected into subregions, the findings there support a theory connecting tenancy to rural support for guerrillas. Overall, the Guatemalan results lend weight to the Venezuelan and Cuban findings we have already seen: intrastate variations in land tenure are closely associated with variations in support for guerrilla movements.

Some negative evidence from Guatemala also lends support to the theory. An attempt by the incipient guerrillas to set up a 1962 foco in the west in Huehuetenango failed miserably, as the local residents captured the insurgents and turned them in. In contrast, rebels fleeing the military revolt of 1960 were openly welcomed by the peasants of Zacapa and Izabal. The difference may be due to Indian predominance in the west, which created ethnic and linguistic barriers between guerrilla and peasant, yet it may prove illuminating to look at the problem from the viewpoint of agrarian structure.[17]

"Poverty" demonstrates itself to be unpromising as an explanation for revolution, for Huehuetenango was certainly one of the poorer Guatemalan departments. The prevalence of tenancy (4.6 percent) and "serfdom" (3.0 percent), however, were noticeably lower there than the Guatemalan averages, suggesting reasons why the area may not have been receptive to revolutionaries. The guerrillas made their attempt in San Mateo Ixtatán *municipio*. Proprietorship of land (rather than tenancy, etc.) was even more common there than in the state overall. Certainly this was an unpromising venue for revolution, from our structural perspective. Even the inequality of land distribution was not so skewed as in the rest of Guatemala, and 66 percent of all the land was held in plots of less than 44 hectares in Huehuetenango—features reproduced in microcosm in San Mateo. Therefore, the rejection of the guerrillas by the indigenous people of the area was fully consistent with predictions based on Paige's structural theory.[18]

Colombia

As in the case of Guatemala, the Colombian data again do not conform exactly to our theoretical needs, again illustrating that classical gap between conceptualization and operationalization. While the 1960 agricultural census does provide our basic information for the departmental level, the finely tuned tenancy divisions appropriate to our theory are not available at the municipio level in the national summary volumes.[19] (They would have been available in the various volumes issued on individual departments, but the series was apparently never completed, and only volumes for Caldas and Cundinamarca are available.) Therefore, our *intra*-departmental analysis can only proceed (as we shall see) after making some questionable assumptions.

In table 6-9 I have presented data for Colombia by department and type of tenancy, and here we include both squatting and sharecropping (as well as other tenancy forms) in our analysis. Nationwide, sharecroppers make up just over half of all renters, and no other "pure" renter category comprises more than 15 percent of the renter total.[20] As in our other tables, departments with substantial guerrilla activity appear first in the table, are starred (*), and are listed in approximate order of the movements' strength located therein. These are areas of "Extensive Guerrilla Influence." Departments with lesser guerrilla activity appear with a cross (+), are denoted as areas of "Fragmentary Guerrilla Influence," and are placed in alphabetical order with the remaining Colombian departments.

Table 6-9
Colombia: Percentage of Units Held by Renters and Squatters, 1960

	Average Landholding	Percentage Taken in Rent			% Squatter Held
		All	Fixed	Share	
COLOMBIA	23 hectares	23%	11%	12%	4%
Tolima*	23	31	16	15	1
Huila*	29	20	15	5	1
Santander*	20	29	6	23	4
Caldas*	14	32	6	27	1
Valle*	23	22	10	12	4
Antioquia*	16	28	9	19	2
Córdoba*	34	19	15	4	3
Atlántico	23	36	35	1	16
Bolívar†	29	24	22	2	10
Boyacá	22	17	9	8	4
Cauca†	13	15	13	2	3
Cundinamarca†	11	19	14	6	1
Magdalena	59	23	18	5	12
Meta†	196	28	9	19	18
Nariño	8	15	6	8	4
Norte de Santander	21	39	5	34	3

Source: Colombia, DANE, Directorio nacional de explotaciones agropecuarias (censo agropecuario) 1960: Resumen nacional-Part 2 (Bogotá, 1964), pp. 22–23.
* Department with extensive guerrilla influence.
† Department with only localized, fragmentary guerrilla influence.

The data in table 6-9 suggest a substantial link between the prevalence of sharecropping and guerrilla influence. All areas with double-digit sharecropping percentages except Norte de Santander are areas of guerrilla influence. Reversing the logic, every state with strong guerrilla influence has double-digit sharecropping—except for Huila.

If we pool the Colombian results by degree of guerrilla influence, further support for our hypothesis comes forward. We can see that areas of extensive guerrilla influence have sharecropping proportions double those of the rest of Colombia. Areas of nonextensive (or weaker) guerrilla influence, though, have levels of sharecropping well below the national average.[21]

We can now proceed with the intradepartmental analysis, looking at the guerrilla municipios within guerrilla departments. For the ELN's operations in Santander we have excellent data, a list of guerrilla "events" (village seizures-cum-armed-propaganda, firefights, ambushes, etc.) there supplied by a former member. The location of those events indicates that the maps of guer-

TABLE 6-10
Prevalence of Sharecropping in Colombia, by Zones of
Guerrilla Influence

Area	Number of Units	Sharecropping	
		Number	%
Colombia	1,209,672	145,056	12.0%
Extensive guerrilla influence*	545,727	94,502	17.3
Localized, fragmentary guerrilla influence†	298,418	14,196	4.8
Rest of nation	365,527	36,358	9.9

Source: Same as for table 6-9. See table 6-9 for assignment of particular departments to each category, as indicated by "*" and "†" there.

rilla activity supplied by Lamberg and Allemann—normally reliable chroniclers—are misleading, for they both place the ELN largely in the eastern part of the department, when in fact the ELN's operations overwhelmingly took place in the west: San Vicente (especially), Barrancabermeja, Puerto Wilches, Lebrija, Rionegro, Girón, Simacota, and Cimitarra.[22]

For the FARC, we know roughly that they operated in the areas of the old peasant republics. Gott's map of those areas, in combination with the annual reports on guerrilla activity provided by the minister of defense to congress, enable us to locate the mobile FARC's operations area with some precision. We can then select areas of major FARC influence by superimposing a political-divisions map over that of guerrilla activity. While some municipios had different names or were broken off from others in the period 1960 to 1967, the matches were, in general, easily made. The results appear as table 6-11.[23]

As for the EPL, there is broad agreement that their area of operations was northern Antioquia, southern Córdoba, and parts of Bolívar and perhaps Chocó. While their claimed zone of influence is very wide indeed, we will restrict ourselves to areas of specific operations, plus the contiguous areas that fill out the skeleton of the zone. In Córdoba, the municipios are Ayapel, Montelíbano (especially), Planeta Rica, Tierralta, and Valencia. In Antioquia, the area comprises Turbo, Apartadó, Chigorodó, Mutatá, Ituango, Cáceres, Caucasia, Zaragoza, Segovia, and Remedios.[24]

Unfortunately, the national summary volumes provide us only with the land area farmed by each type of cultivator and not, as is usually the case, with the number of units farmed by each. We can proceed very tentatively, however, to estimate the latter item as follows: multiply the municipio sharecropping area by the ratio of the sharecroppers' percentage of units divided by their percentage of lands, for each department. The result gives us an esti-

TABLE 6-11
Areas of FARC Guerrillas' Influence in Colombia, 1965–1970

Department (Intendancy)	1960 Municipios (1970 Name)
Cauca	Corinto, Inzá, Miranda, Páez (Belalcázar), Toribío
Cundinamarca	Arbeláez, Bogotá D.E. [Usme area], (Cabrera), Gutiérrez, Nilo, Ospina Pérez, Pandi, San Bernardo, Tibacuy
Huila	Algeciras, Baraya, Campoalegre, Colombia, Iquira, (Nataga), Neiva, Rivera, Santa María (part of Palermo in 1960), Tello, Teruel, (Tesalia)
Meta	Granada
Quindío*	Calarcá, (Córdoba), Pijao, Génova
Risaralda*	Pereira, Santa Rosa de Cabal
Tolima	Ataco, Cajamarca, Chaparral, (Cunday), Icononzo, Ortega, (Planadas), Rioblanco, Roncesvalles, San Antonio, Villarrica
Valle del Cauca	Alcalá, Caicedonia, Cartago, La Victoria, Obando, Sevilla, Ulloa, Zarzal
(Caqueta)	Puerto Rico, San Vicente de Caguan

Source: See text and accompanying notes.
* Part of Caldas in 1960.

mate, with an unknown bias,[25] of the number of sharecroppers in each *municipio*, which we can then compare to the total number of cultivators. These intra-departmental estimates appear as the last column of table 6-12.

Results for Caldas, Córdoba, Cundinamarca, Meta, and Valle are in the predicted direction, but are of varying degrees of strength. Cauca and Huila yield neutral results, while the remaining results go counter to the theory, in Antioquia, Santander, and Tolima. Overall, the results are inconsistent with the sharecropping version of our theory. That is, our fairly clear departmental pattern is not reproduced at the *municipio* level.

We can, however, now follow Merton's advice and seek functional alternatives to sharecropping: different structures that might produce similar effects.[26] Based on our previous analysis of Cuba, we can round up the most likely theoretical suspects: squatters. There is, I would add, more than Mertonian reason to guide us here, for squatters in Colombia seem both in number and location rather similar to their Cuban counterparts. In fact, Colombian squatters were likely to be concentrated in areas that later became guerrilla strongholds.

Like their sharecropping peers, Colombian squatters do not display a connection with guerrillas in all cases. However, in the three states that demonstrated a *negative* internal correlation between sharecropping and guerrilla influence (Antioquia, Santander, and Valle), we now find a *positive* correlation between squatting and guerrilla influence. Even in Tolima, although the

TABLE 6-12

Colombia: Percentage of Lands Held by Sharecroppers, Guerrilla Zones versus Other Areas
(hectares in thousands)

	Overall Totals		Sharecropping Totals			
					Number of Units	
	Number of Units	Land (hectares)	Land (hectares)	Area %	Number	% estimated
COLOMBIA	1,209,663	27,371.8	1,104.6	4.1%	145,056	12.0%
Antioquia	169,299	2,759.3	103.9	3.8	32,022	18.9
Guerrilla zones	16,993	861.3	16.5	1.9		9.5
Other areas	152,366	1,898.1	87.4	4.6		22.9
Caldas	80,424	1,094.5	195.6	17.9	21,392	26.6
Guerrilla zones	11,200	185.4	40.9	22.1		32.8
Other areas	69,224	909.1	154.7	17.0		25.3
Cauca	73,752	959.0	10.9	1.1	1,634	2.2
Guerrilla zones	11,468	144.3	1.2	0.8		1.6
Other areas	62,284	814.8	9.7	1.2		2.4
Córdoba	48,395	1,657.9	12.4	0.7	2,138	4.4
Guerrilla zones	13,048	655.8	8.5	1.3		8.2
Other areas	35,347	1,002.1	3.9	0.4		2.5
Cundinamarca	145,003	1,525.1	47.3	3.1	8,410	5.8
Guerrilla zones	7,616	109.0	5.8	5.3		9.9
Other areas	137,387	1,416.1	41.5	2.9		5.4
Huila	34,683	997.7	22.3	2.2	1,653	4.8
Guerrilla zones	10,991	443.5	9.4	2.1		4.6
Other areas	23,692	554.3	12.9	2.3		5.0
Meta	15,835	3,108.1	37.5	1.2	2,987	18.9
Guerrilla zones	2,058	88.1	2.7	3.0		47.3
Other areas	13,777	3,020.0	34.8	1.2		18.9
Santander	89,972	1,830.1	186.0	10.2	20,445	22.7
Guerrilla zones	15,624	696.9	49.7	7.1		15.8
Other areas	74,348	1,133.2	136.3	12.0		26.7
Tolima	72,133	1,634.9	114.8	7.0	10,979	15.2
Guerrilla zones	18,859	565.1	26.6	4.7		10.2
Other areas	53,274	1,069.8	88.2	8.2		17.8
Valle	50,817	1,166.6	106.6	9.1	5,873	11.6
Guerrilla zones	7,955	179.8	33.2	18.4		23.5
Other areas	42,862	986.8	73.4	7.4		9.4
Caquetá	(no data reported)					

Source: Colombia, DANE, Directorio de explotaciones, 1960 Part 1, entire, and Part 2, p. 23 for
number of sharecroppers in each department. Intradepartmental percentages of sharecroppers by guerrilla
zones and other areas are only estimates; see text. The estimates are based on the ratio of percent sharecrop-
pers/percent sharecropped land for each department separately. This ratio is then multiplied by the percentage of land sharecropped—guerrilla zone or other areas—to obtain the estimate of the percentage of all units
held by sharecroppers. Summary data in part 2 of the Directorio differ somewhat from individual department data presented in part 1, due to slightly differing definitions.

TABLE 6-13
Colombia: Percentage of Lands Held by Squatters, Guerrilla
versus Non-Guerrilla Zones
(thousands of hectares)

	Total Area	Squatter Area	%
COLOMBIA	27,371.8	3,755.3	13.7%
Antioquia	2,759.3	210.9	7.6
Guerrilla zones	861.3	148.6	17.3
Other areas	1,898.1	62.3	3.3
Caldas	1,094.5	18.1	1.7
Guerrilla zones	185.4	0.7	0.4
Other areas	909.1	17.4	1.9
Cauca	959.0	77.3	8.1
Guerrilla zones	144.3	8.4	5.8
Other areas	814.8	68.9	8.5
Córdoba	1,657.9	60.8	3.7
Guerrilla zones	655.8	57.3	8.7
Other areas	1,002.1	3.5	0.3
Cundinamarca	1,525.1	81.8	5.4
Guerrilla zones	109.0	0.5	0.5
Other areas	1,416.1	81.3	5.7
Huila	997.7	13.3	1.3
Guerrilla zones	443.5	4.3	1.0
Other areas	554.3	9.1	1.6
Meta	3,108.1	1,328.7	42.7
Guerrilla zones	88.1	43.0	48.8
Other areas	3,020.0	1,285.7	42.6
Santander	1,830.1	327.9	17.9
Guerrilla zones	696.9	172.3	24.7
Other areas	1,133.2	155.7	13.7
Tolima	1,634.9	18.8	1.1
Guerrilla zones	565.1	15.7	2.8
Other areas	1,069.8	3.1	0.3
Valle	1,166.6	37.0	3.2
Guerrilla zones	179.8	0.03	0.02
Other areas	986.8	36.9	3.7

Source: Sames as for table 6-12.

magnitudes are small, the difference is in the predicted direction. In the case of Santander, moreover, the "real" differences are in fact understated in table 6-13 for, due to changes in the administrative divisions therein during the 1960s, we had to eliminate Cimitarra (a guerrilla area) from our censal analysis, since it was part of the *municipio(s)* of Bolívar and/or Vélez at the time of the 1960 census. Those two municipios contain 90 percent of the squatter lands not already included in the "guerrilla zones" of Santander in table 6-13.

TABLE 6-14
Fit of Each Colombian Department to the Sharecropper-Guerrilla
or Squatter-Guerrilla Hypothesis
(within-department analyses only)

Department (Guerrilla Group)	Sharecropper Model	Squatter Model	Either Model
Antioquia (EPL)	–	+	+
Caldas (FARC)	+	o	+
Cauca (FARC)	o	o/–	o
Córdoba (EPL)	+	+	!
Cundinam. (FARC)	+/o	–	o
Huila (FARC)	o	o	o
Meta (FARC)	+	o	+
Santander (ELN)	–	+	+
Tolima (FARC)	–	o	o
Valle (FARC)	+	o	+

Source: Tables 6-8 to 6-13.
+ = fits model
o = no relationship
– = negative fit to model

Thus, virtually all squatter-held lands in Santander were in areas that could reasonably be seen as guerrilla zones, and almost no squatters lived elsewhere in the department. Finally, there are also very clear guerrilla-squatter associations in the departments of Antioquia and Córdoba, the EPL's operations area.

Therefore, if we broaden our original monocausal thesis and argue that either sharecropping or squatting or both (as in Córdoba) may contribute to increasing support for guerrillas, then we obtain the results displayed in table 6-14. The two types of agrarian structure appear to be complementary, for only in Córdoba do we find both types associated with an area of guerrilla influence. This should not surprise us, for we would expect squatters to prevail in frontiers or areas of low economic importance, where land resources are not closely monitored. In contrast, we would expect sharecropping under tighter resource conditions, where landlords can demand, and get, a tenure system that markedly increases peasant-borne risk. In short, sharecropping is more likely in a closed-resource situation and squatting in an open resource situation. Yet in both cases the cultivator is likely to be in conflict with landowners, either over the price for and share of the crop, or over the very possession of land itself. Finally, the assertion that squatting is associated with guerrilla zones is not solely statistical, for other students of La Violencia and subsequent guerrillas have made similar observations.[27]

Tolima and Huila, however, remain recalcitrant cases, refusing to fit well with either model at the *municipio*-level of analysis. For Tolima, it may well be mistaken even to attempt intra-departmental analysis, for the *entire* department has been the single greatest focus of first, *La Violencia*, and later the guerrilla movements.[28] Tolima does conform to the sharecropper model, but only when compared to other departments; internal variations remain unimportant in determining guerrilla influence. The events in Huila, however, remain opaque to this structural analysis, for it has been a center of *La Violencia* and guerrillas, yet displays none of the structural characteristics found in the other areas.

To summarize: The Colombian data fit the original model well when viewed across departments. When viewed within departments, however, guerrilla influence conforms only to a modified model and is associated with either sharecropping or squatting.

Peru

With the case of Peru, we find two problems as yet unencountered in our analysis. Until now, "guerrilla zone" has been roughly synonymous with "zone of support for the guerrillas." In Peru this is no longer true. Ayacucho, home base of the ELN guerrillas led by Héctor Béjar, provided at best moderate peasant support, even by Béjar's own admission in his memoirs. Junín Department harbored the MIR *foco* led by Guillermo Lobatón, which also received moderate assistance from the Campa Indians (for a time) and from other peasants. The MIR's Cuzco *foco* (despite claims by some guerrillas and even by military analysts) did not get as much peasant support as either of the aforementioned cases. The MIR *foco* in Piura remains somewhat of a mystery, for it never went into action, and the members fled across the Ecuadoran border before the army arrived. The degree of peasant support, which should involve some "test of fire" before it is to be considered lip service, was probably low, given that the guerrillas took flight so quickly, but this remains conjecture.

Our second problem is far more intractable. The Peruvian census of 1961 would appear to provide a good contemporary data source for testing our theory, but the Sierran land invasions of 1962–1964 made that census prematurely obsolete. A 1964 survey of Peruvian agriculture unfortunately cannot compensate for the superseded census. I essayed an earlier attempt to employ the census data, adjusted by the 1964 survey data[29] but have since concluded that the assumptions involved are too dubious, the adjustments too extensive, and the original census categories too inappropriate to place any kind of faith in the bastard results, no matter how numerical and systematic their appearance. Therefore we will have to make do with more qualitative and less systematic information, and the results will necessarily be more suspect.

Still, we are fortunate in possessing micro-level historiography, journalism, memoirs, and other information available for all our areas of interest. In

Ayacucho, guerrilla actions took place in the area of the enormous Chapi Hacienda, which existed side by side with Indian communities with whom the owners, the Carrillo brothers, had had violent conflicts for many years, involving theft of Indian goods and animals, rape, and outright murder. After the guerrillas took Chapi and executed the Carrillo brothers, with the consent of the local peasants, locals flocked to support the revolutionaries and promptly occupied the hacienda lands. Prior to that time, peasant *comuneros* had typically worked on the hacienda's coffee lands in exchange for usufruct plots.[30]

In Junín we find roughly similar conditions. The guerrillas got their first recruits after their raid on the Santa Rosa mine to steal dynamite. They followed up with seizures of the haciendas Runatullo and Alegría. The peasants on these estates were also usufructuaries, corresponding to Paige's "serfs." When Runatullo was sacked, the hacienda peasants promptly threatened to seize the estate.

As the guerrillas moved eastward deep into Jauja Province they encountered a different situation. The peasants there were also *colonos* (i.e., usufructuaries), again growing coffee on hacienda lands. Yet the warlike Campa Indians, mostly residing in small forest villages, had long-standing claims to the hacienda lands. This claim would put them in conflict not only with landlords, but also with the *colonos* who worked the estate and who desired more land as well. The guerrillas soon received strong support from the Campas, as they promised to help them regain old tribal land such as the Hacienda Kubantia.[31]

Given this information, our micro-level analysis tends to support Paige's theory, but it is his theory of serf-based agrarian revolt. We find the classic conditions here for such a social movement with, as usual, disproportionate power in the grasp of landlords, and (probably) a structurally divided and weak peasantry. Suddenly the *comuneros* and *colonos* found themselves with armed allies in their continued struggles with landowners, who were promptly dispossessed of their estates. This is precisely the outcome predicted by Paige: Serfs will be unable to act effectively unless (1) their strength increases due to outside assistance, or (2) unless their opponents weaken. What is questionable here is whether the peasants would have continued to support the guerrillas in further, more politicized activity. The ambiguity of Paige's theory regarding leadership ideology versus rank-and-file demands becomes evident here. Clearly the guerrillas wanted agrarian revolution, but no evidence suggests that peasants were at all discontent if they could just hold on to their newfound lands. Béjar himself candidly confessed the difficulty his ELN had in attempting to broaden the rebellious peasants' horizons from local land tenure problems in La Mar to national revolution. Béjar also admitted that the guerrillas overestimated the local peasants' firmness of support. In the case of Lobatón's MIR group, they probably lost the Campas' support in Junín when the two groups jointly occupied one of the haciendas desired by the Campas. Lobatón and the estate owner's wife partied into the night, and by morning Lobatón pronounced the estate's books in proper order and left the hacienda intact. The Campas were quite unhappy with that decision.[32]

In contrast to Junín and Ayacucho, La Convención (in Cuzco) by 1965 was an area of small landholders, following the success of the land invasions there in 1962 and 1963. Despite the fact that the MIR had worked in the area all through 1964 and 1965, attempting to gain influence among the local peasantry, their efforts were less successful than in the two cases just discussed. This held true despite their logical efforts to capitalize on the recent radical history of the local peasant federation under Hugo Blanco's leadership. The guerrillas actually encamped on the nearby, precipitous Mesa Pelada rather than in La Convención, and paid peasants to transport supplies to their aerie, at excellent wages. Béjar notes revealingly that the MIR did not in fact obtain any influence in the local peasant federation and, when the army arrived, "wavering elements" went over to the military. Specifically, local peasant leader Albino Guzmán deserted the *foco*, denounced de la Puente for not caring about peasant interests, and led the army patrols to the Mesa Pelada campsites.[33] If the real test of peasant support is willingness to hide the guerrillas or to fight with them, then the MIR's Cuzco *foco* gained no meaningful peasant support.

Finally, in choosing the fourth site in Piura, the MIR chose an area dominated by peasant smallholders, according to a report by an officer involved in the anti-guerrilla campaign. The apparent absence of local peasant support would be theoretically consistent with such agrarian conditions.[34]

To summarize: Censal analysis of the Peruvian *focos* is ruled out by the post-census land invasions of the early 1960s. However, basing our argument on more *qualitative* evidence at the local level, we see that areas of moderate support for the insurgents were, in fact, areas of "serfdom," land hunger, and hacienda-community conflicts over land. In such areas, the peasants' behavior is consistent with either the agrarian-revolt or agrarian-revolution hypothesis. In contrast, areas of lesser or unknown support were dominated by smallholders. The overall pattern of the Peruvian data supports the theory, but it also highlights some of the theoretical ambiguities in Paige's thesis.

Bolivia

The case of Bolivia need not detain us for long. The guerrillas received no support from the rural populace in their area of operations, located in Santa Cruz Department, south of the city of that name, and roughly parallel to the Chuquisaca border. Given that dismal record of no support, we would expect to find the least radical of all cultivators, the smallholder. That is precisely the case.

Bolivia's last agrarian census prior to 1967 was in 1950 which, even more so than the Peruvian census, is useless for our analysis. The Bolivian revolution of 1952 led to periods of more or less intense land invasions and government land title distributions, which destroyed *latifundismo* throughout most of Bolivia. While some areas were more thoroughly changed than others, there is little doubt of the overall, short-term effect: Almost overnight, rural Bolivia was transformed into a nation of smallholders.

Santa Cruz, however, was distinctive from Bolivia of the *altiplano* or of the Cochabamba Valley. Even prior to the 1952 revolution, Santa Cruz was *not* an area of land hunger, "one of the few places in the world where the work of a farm laborer is much more valuable—within a short time—than a hectare of land." Rental rates for sharecropping clearly told the tale: the tenant kept 90 percent of the harvest, turning over only 10 percent to the landlord. Land in the area was essentially "free," and few persons had legitimate titles to their land.[35]

This situation held *a fortiori* after the 1952 revolution. Santa Cruz remained a distinctive area, set apart from the major centers of Bolivian politics and society. Rural production was generally growing more quickly than elsewhere in the nation, and the nascent oil industry supplied jobs that pumped yet more money into the region. All observers agree that it continued to be an area of abundant land. Mercier sums it up most simply when he writes of the Santa Cruz farmers that "there is no poor peasantry to ally against the central government or landowners. They are just simple farmers, without any great resources, but for whom the question of land is irrelevant." As another critic noted caustically, "What was Ché going to offer these peasants, still more land they could not use?"[36]

Bolivia is thus added to the list of generally supportive cases for a modified form of Paige's agrarian theory of revolution. Whatever the limitations of his theory suggested by Skocpol, Jenkins, and others, little doubt remains that his structural orientation sheds a strong light on Latin American guerrilla activity of the 1950s and 1960s. Yet dissatisfaction remains precisely because Paige's model remains largely a static snapshot, because the vague suspicion persists that cultivators respond not *only* to their structural position in the countryside but also to the enormous—one might even say revolutionary—changes that have taken place therein in this century, especially in regard to land tenure and market systems. It is to those structural transformations that we now turn our analytical sights.

Agrarian Transformations and Their Effects

In his work *The Moral Economy of the Peasant*, James C. Scott argues strongly for a historical view of the origins of peasant radicalism. He argues that peasants caught up in certain world-historical transformations—the rise of capitalism, the supersession of old patron-client ties, and the spread of purely market relationships between landlords and peasants—are likely to view such changes as violations of their "moral economy." We can understand their moral economy as a series of "rules of the game" concerning the reciprocal rights and obligations of landlord-patrons and their peasant-clients. The most important of the obligations imposed on landlords in such systems is that they *not* threaten the peasants' subsistence minimum, even if it means that the landlord's crop share may fall in years of bad harvest. In addition, landlord-patrons have other obligations, including seed and tool provision, "godfathering" clients' children, and the like. Problems arise in such a system with the growing importance of market relationships and their unruly ups and downs.

As landlords push more and more toward a purely contractual relationship with their peasant-clients, the protective elements in the reciprocal moral economy tend to be shunted aside, and peasants bear more and more of the risk of a bad harvest. Peasants imbedded in such historical processes, Scott argues, are likely to view these market-related changes as violations of their moral economy, to feel outraged at their increased exposure to risk, and even, where possible, to rebel against landlords and their government backers who support the naked contractual rules of the market instead of the old, risk-limiting moral economy.[37]

I wish here to extend Scott's logic in a commonsense fashion: peasants respond not only to violations of their moral economy, but also to intrusions on their *physical economy*. That is, we might expect peasants to respond to changes in their relations to the land itself, in particular to their gain or loss of lands due to various social or political measures taken by governments and individuals. Just as in Scott's case, the peasants are always measuring their status at any point in time against some kind of "reference group"[38] or measuring stick, usually their own historically specific experience. Where they feel that their lot is worsening relative to that reference group, we are likely to find radical sentiment, just as Scott found when the peasant moral economy began to decay.

We might, then, expect peasants whose situation is showing current improvement, or which portends such, to be very unlikely candidates to be guerrilla supporters. Peasants whose status is somewhat stable at the moment, in contrast, might be more receptive to the guerrillas' siren song—it might well depend on the *kind* of social structure (à la Paige) in which they are enmeshed. Peasants who have been losing ground—literally—to landlords or the state, whose situations have become more precarious, or whose very existence as tillers of the soil is threatened by opponents, are our most likely candidates for radicalism. Indeed, this last scenario is a close match to the situation in Morelos, Mexico, prior to the outbreak there of the Zapatista revolutionary movement.

Two types of evidence are most relevant to these hypotheses, and I will consider each in turn. First, government efforts at land reform—or the lack thereof—may well have some influence upon peasant radicalism in the directions just predicted. In this sense, land reforms meant to turn impoverished, land-poor peasants into stable, comfortable smallholders should create buffers against revolutionary sentiment—the by-now well-established Marxist fear that a bourgeois land reform will turn otherwise radical peasants into conservative "kulaks." Indeed, Paige's work suggests that peasant smallholders are, in comparative context, the most conservative of cultivators, at least in the content of their collective demands.[39]

If government actions in rural areas can affect the peasant propensity to rebel, so too might less formal actions of private individuals. Successful peasant land invasions, on the one hand, should be followed by the "tranquilizing" of peasant radicalism if this logic is sound; on the other hand, ongoing processes of peasant uprooting—perhaps related to the spread of capitalist farming into the Latin American countryside—might be expected to create hotbeds of peasant discontent, as cultivators fight to retain subsistence plots that at times may be of very old lineage—as among Indian communities in the Andes or Guatemala.

Both the governmental and informal processes of agrarian change appear in the discussion that follows, although the relevant mix varies for each country: ranging from Cuba where no government agrarian reform efforts existed and major peasant eviction processes were under way; to Venezuela where both government reforms and land invasions occurred simultaneously (fueling one another); to Peru's Cuzco and to Bolivia, where major agrarian revolts had brought land into the hands of peasants against landlord resistance. I will discuss each nation's experience in turn, and the bearing thereof on the theses concerning agrarian transformations.

Cuba

In Batista's Cuba, unlike our other five cases, agrarian reform attempts were nonexistent; therefore, it is very unlikely that peasants were benefiting from systematic government reforms in rural areas. One governmental action that had benefited the sugar tenants (or *colonos*), however, was a series of recent laws that had made them virtually invulnerable to eviction.[40]

The squatters of the Sierra Maestra and elsewhere had no such legal protection, as I noted above in my discussion of Paige's theory. Not only were they legally insecure on their plots, they were also increasingly the target of eviction attempts—through private force and public lawsuits—which threatened their very ability to survive as cultivators. From 1940 to 1959, landowners were winning 75 percent of their eviction lawsuits in Cuba. Lowry Nelson reported one such case from 1945, where landlords were trying to evict 1,200 squatters who had been living on three estates in El Cobre (in the Sierra Maestra) for as long as thirty years or more, some of whom actually possessed land titles (he does not report the disposition of the case). Eighty percent of the eviction cases in Cuba were centered in Oriente, and they must have been in the two Sierras there—later guerrilla havens—for that is where the squatters lived. Those *precaristas* were quite poor, especially in view of the abundance of Cuban land, and constituted half of all those *microfundistas* with only tiny sub-hectare plots of land.[41]

In addition to routine insecurity and ongoing eviction struggles, the squatters of the Sierra also suffered as special targets of Batista's "cleanup" campaign there following Castro's December 1956 landing. Local landlords directed army troops toward local squatter leaders, further aggravating long-standing landlord-squatter enmity, a hostility that had previously resulted in the formation by squatters of bands armed to resist eviction attempts.[42]

There is little doubt, then, that the squatters fit our image: A peasantry threatened with the total loss of lands, crops, and sometimes life, allied itself with a revolutionary movement that proposed to overthrow the existing regime and institute a land reform to benefit the *guajiros* of the Sierra.

Venezuela

In Venezuela we encounter two related phenomena: a widespread land reform under the Acción Democrática (AD) governments of Rómulo Betancourt (1959–1964) and Raúl Leoni (1964–1969)—largely elected by their party's rural supporters—and land invasions in the late 1950s and early 1960s in response to the overthrow of the military dictatorship and subsequent "depressurization" of the political arena. The land invasions came about in part because a previous land reform under an earlier AD government (1945–1948) had been largely reversed under the military regimes that followed.

In fact, a dialectic ensued after 1958 between the reformist AD government's attempts to control the process of land reform, on the one hand, and constant peasant pressures for the more rapid distribution of lands. Since the peasant invaders were largely supporters of the new government, "order" in the process of agrarian reform was eventually restored by about 1961. It may have been restored because, as John Duncan Powell showed in a statistical analysis of government "attention" paid to rural areas, the federal government was in fact responsive to peasant demands. Eighty percent of the 265 land invasions reported by the Venezuelan Agrarian Institute took place in the states of Aragua, Carabobo, Yaracuy, Trujillo, and Zulia. All were states with strong peasant unions.[43]

How did these processes relate geographically to the guerrilla movements of the 1960s? The areas of early land reform (1945–1948), reversals of agrarian reform (1948–1958), and subsequent land invasions (1959–1961)—roughly related to one another—were *not* the main areas of guerrilla strength in the 1960s, with the possible exception of parts of Portuguesa and Trujillo, and the definite, though minor, exception of Yaracuy. Notably, Miranda

State was passed over in its land reform petitions in the 1940s, was not an area of land invasions, but did provide some support to the 1960s guerrilla *foco* at El Bachiller.[44]

The Venezuelan government published a great deal of systematic information about its land reform efforts in various regions of the nation. While the accuracy of the data has been questioned in many quarters, the relative size of the effort is not, I think, disputable. It is possible, as I have done elsewhere, to try to "milk" the land reform data to explore the possibility that guerrilla hot spots like Lara and Falcón states were *somewhat* passed over by the government's land reform efforts, experienced "relative deprivation" as a result, and consequently harbored guerrilla movements. One might even hypothesize that such government efforts in those two states would have increased during the guerrilla period, in response to the insurgencies there, in order to quiet the countryside. In summary, the systematic analysis of the land reform data mildly supports the first hypothesis, and does not support the second one. However, the relationships are so substantively thin as to merit little detailed consideration.[45]

Indeed, there is little evidence from Venezuela that would unambiguously support my adaptation of Scott's thesis. If we are to seek the roots of peasant support for Venezuelan guerrillas, we would be well advised to seek among the other "functional alternatives" I explore in this chapter and the next.

Guatemala

In Guatemala we can find the clearest case of an agrarian counterrevolution. Between January 1953 and June 1954 the government of Jacobo Arbenz expropriated over half a million hectares of land from private estates and distributed them to roughly 100,000 peasant families. In 1954, the Castillo Armas invasion (organized by the U.S. government) ousted Arbenz from power, and the agrarian reform was subsequently not just abandoned but reversed. By the end of 1956, only 0.4 percent of the reform's land recipients still retained their lands, according to the CIDA survey of Guatemala. While the Guatemalan government nominally continued distributing plots to peasants in the next decade, the efforts were much smaller, and did not make the peasantry forget the reversal of their earlier gains.[46]

Guatemala was therefore notable in several theoretically relevant respects: it had had no effective, lasting agrarian reform, it had a highly skewed land distribution and, by most reports, exploitative relationships between landlords and peasants. Combined with the land reform's reversal, we would expect most rural areas of such a nation to be receptive to revolutionaries. However, since the agrarian reversal was focused on certain regions of the nation rather than others, we would expect the core areas of that reversal to be special hotbeds of peasant discontent.

We do not, in fact, know how many peasants in each Guatemalan *depar-*

TABLE 6-15

Land Distributed under the Arbenz Government in Guatemala,
1953–1954

(hectares)

	(A) Area Expropriated	(B) Area in Farms 1950 Census	(C) A/B
Guatemala	*603,615*	*3,720,833*	*16.2%*
Guatemala	24,402	176,657	13.8
El Progreso	10,866	87,713	12.4
Sacatepéquez	4,397	35,825	12.3
Chimaltenango	21,270	124,863	17.0
Escuintla	151,707	454,712	33.4
Santa Rosa	27,252	262,664	10.4
Sololá	1,442	39,379	3.7
Quezaltenango	6,561	137,517	4.8
Suchitepéquez	30,706	177,877	17.3
Retalhuleu	14,438	135,078	10.6
San Marcos	9,614	227,368	4.2
Huehuetenango	34,944	240,154	14.6
El Quiché	53,299	202,760	26.3
Baja Verapaz	16,466	155,793	10.6
Alta Verapaz	95,286	494,447	19.3
Izabal*	82,767	204,202	40.5
Zacapa*	1,830	117,164	1.6
Chiquimula	731	88,360	0.8
Jalapa	3,151	116,406	2.7
Jutiapa	12,575	206,929	6.1
Totonicapán	—	19,958	0
El Petén	—	15,007	0

Source: CIDA, *Guatemala*, p. 41; Guatemala, *II censo agropecuario 1964* II, p. 21. Original census data on land area were in manzanas; one manzana = 0.7 hectare.

* Guerrilla strongholds. Weaker guerrilla areas were in parts of Alta Verapaz, Chiquimula, and El Progreso.

tamento received lands under the Arbenz reform, but we do know how much land was distributed in each locale, and may use the latter as a surrogate for the former. Since we also know that 99.6 percent of all recipients later lost their lands, we can safely assume that all "reformed" lands were later reclaimed from the beneficiaries of the reform. If our "radical hotbed" thesis is correct, guerrilla strongholds are likely to be those areas where the highest proportion of departmental lands were distributed and then taken back.

Table 6-15 contains the pertinent figures for each department and for Guatemala: land area distributed in the reform, total land area in farms, and the

first figure as a percentage of the second, the last being our ₁
The single leading department—with 40 percent of its lands o.
peasants and then reclaimed—is Izabal, stronghold of the MR-13
led by Yon Sosa. Indeed, Adolfo Gilly reports a conversation from th₁
foco that gives life to our dry theoretical discussion, for there a peasant-₁
rilla pointed bitterly to the plantation lands that had been given his people a
then taken away, which he was intent upon reclaiming, even at the risk of his
life.[47]

Izabal and Escuintla were the twin leaders in reform targeting because they
were the twin seats of United Fruit plantations—Bananera and Tiquisate, respectively. The high percentages of unused lands, foreign ownership, and the
history of political conflicts with UFCO all made its plantations especially
attractive targets. Still, by no means were all the plantations' lands expropriated: the company was left with more than 100,000 of its original 188,339
hectares.[48]

Zacapa was the other major guerrilla stronghold, but it does not fit our
expectation of being a reform focal point. Indeed, Zacapa is near the very
bottom of the rankings, as only 1.6 percent of its lands were touched by the
agrarian reform. Overall, the Guatemalan results divide neatly: Izabal fits the
predicted pattern, Zacapa does not. This is most interesting for, as we shall
see in the next chapter, Zacapa probably fits our model of historic rebelliousness, while Izabal does not. Again the limits of monocausal explanations are
driven home by the stubborn complexities of the social world.

Colombia

The Colombian experience displays some elements of each of our previous
two cases. INCORA, Colombia's agrarian reform and colonization agency,
published data on the distribution of titles and lands in Colombia from 1962
to 1967. We can replicate our Guatemalan procedure and compare the numbers of plots and area in the reform with the total 1960 figures for each department, thereby yielding estimates of those areas most touched by the reform.

As we can see in table 6-16, few rural Colombians were touched by IN-
CORA's 1960s reform efforts. Even these numbers are overestimates of the
proportion of the rural population served, for they exclude the landless laborers whose plight is rarely captured by agricultural censuses directed at the
effective holders of plots of land. To point up the contrast, Venezuela's reform touched about one-sixth of the rural population by 1968, and Guatemala
a similar figure in less than two years. In Colombia, if we take into account
the landless *jornaleros*, less than one-twentieth of the rural populace had benefited by 1967. Further efforts in the next two years only added another 5,000
land titles. Indeed, Ernest Feder singled out Colombia's efforts as a classic
case of *counter*reform in his critique of the region's agrarian reform efforts in
the 1960s.[49]

.₃LE 6-16

Land Reform in Colombia, by Department, 1962–1967

1960 Department	Farms			Farm Area (1,000 hectares)		
	Units in 1960	Titles Awarded	%	Farmland in 1960	Land Adjudicated	%
Colombia	1,209,663	66,511*	5.5%	27,371.8	2,236.6*	8.2%
Antioquia	169,299	4,410	2.6	2,759.3	282.4	10.2
Atlántico	11,902	348	2.9	276.6	1.9	0.7
Bolívar	63,827	2,046	3.2	1,824.5	113.6	6.2
Boyacá	169,276	4,384	2.6	3,761.5	130.3	3.5
Caldas	80,424	551	0.7	1,094.5	20.2	1.8
Cauca	73,752	2,170	2.9	959.0	39.7	4.1
Córdoba	48,395	2,336	4.8	1,657.9	111.1	6.7
Cundinamarca	145,003	1,959	1.4	1,525.1	56.2	3.7
Huila	34,683	8,491	24.5	997.7	85.5	8.6
Magdalena	54,991	5,377	9.8	3,249.2	354.4	10.9
Meta	15,835	5,882	37.1	3,108.1	209.8	6.8
Nariño	90,285	2,747	3.0	692.7	31.5	4.5
Norte de Santander	39,069	1,457	3.7	833.9	75.7	9.1
Santander	89,972	5,262	5.8	1,830.1	224.9	12.3
Tolima	72,133	3,816	5.3	1,634.9	88.2	5.4
Valle	50,817	1,846	3.6	1,166.6	30.8	2.6

Source: Colombia, DANE, Directorio de explotaciones, Part 1, p. 15, and Colombia, Instituto Colombiano de Reforma Agraria (INCORA), Seis años de reforma social agraria en Colombia, 1962–1967 (Bogotá: INCORA, 1968), p. 18.

* Land reform data include territories not included in 1960 census data.

After 1966, Quindio, Risaralda, and Caldas were created from Caldas of 1960. César and Guajira were split off from Magdalena and Sucre from Bolívar.

Unlike our Venezuelan case, though, we do find that the Colombian government *did* accelerate its reform efforts in certain guerrilla regions in the later 1960s. Huila and Meta are the only departments in which INCORA's reforms affected a high proportion of peasants. The border area between the two states was a FARC stronghold (the former "peasant republics" of Guayabero and El Pato), and INCORA's attention accelerates there in 1966 and 1967, shortly *after* the signing of the FARC's formation document.[50] This suggests statistically what the guerrillas argued verbally in a number of documents and reports: that the government directed its agrarian reform efforts to "hot spots" in attempts to reduce the appeal of violence and rural radicalism. (Military civic action efforts during this period also tended to focus on guerrilla zones.) One can overinterpret here, though, for the magnitude of the Colombian reforms was generally too small to have major structural effects throughout the nation.

TABLE 6-17
Colombian Coffee Production by Department, 1874–1956, Selected Years
(thousands of 60-kg. sacks)

Department	Annual Production			Production Increases	
	1874	1932	1953–1956	1874–1932	1932–1956
Colombia	114.2	3,453	5,944	3,339	2,491
Antioquia	1.2	617	1,003	616	386
Boyacá	0.6	23	36	22	13
Caldas	1.3	1,004	1,922	1,003	918
Cauca	1.1	56	148	55	92
Cundinamarca	8.0	405	554	397	149
Magdalena	0.2	21	80	21	59
Nariño	0.2	18	42	18	24
N. de Santander	90.0	270	169	180	−101
Santander	10.0	150	137	140	−13
Tolima	1.0	448	843	447	395
Huila	—	51	220	51	169
Valle	0.6	354	790	353	436
Other areas	—	36	—	36	−36

Source: William P. McGreevey, "Exportaciones y precios de tabaco y café," in Compendio de estadísticas históricas de Colombia, edited by Miguel Urrutia and Mario Arrubla
(Bogotá: Dirección de Divulgación Cultural, 1970), p. 210.

The Colombian experience provides stronger evidence for the second hypothesis: that peasants who are losing ground to land grabbing or evictions are
likely to be radicals. Pierre Gilhodès has suggested that a correlation exists
between expanding areas of modern capitalist agriculture and areas heavily
affected by La Violencia. By extension—due to the geographical overlap of
La Violencia and the FARC guerrillas—we suspect a connection with guerrillas as well. Gilhodès argues that "(w)ithin this context, La Violencia appears
as a brutal purge of pre-capitalist relations of production. . . ."[51] While
Gilhodès does not consider coffee in his analysis, we will consider its spread
as the critical crop that could affect social conditions throughout the Colombian interior.

William McGreevey has collected data on coffee's "migration" across Colombia from 1874 to 1956. He presents his data in terms of sacks of coffee (60
kg. each) rather than in acres planted, but we will take one as a surrogate of
the other. In table 6-17 I reproduce McGreevey's figures for three points in
time: 1874, 1932, and 1953–1956 (the last a three-year average), and the
increases in the two interim periods.

In 1874 the two Santanders produced about 90 percent of Colombia's coffee; by 1932 their share had fallen to just 30 percent while the combined
shares of Antioquia and Caldas had risen to 35 percent. By the 1950s, the

latter two departments produced half of Colombia's coffee, and the southwest departments of Valle and Tolima were the other major producers. In short, over a period of eighty years coffee continued to expand in its earlier centers, but mainly grew through "migrating" south and west from the Santanders.

Like Gilhodès, and in accord with my working hypothesis, we suspect that this migration was not without incident; indeed, I suggest that the incorporation of new lands to coffee accentuated conflicts with the previous residents of these new coffee zones, and in fact created a structural cause of *La Violencia*. Research by a former University of Michigan graduate student indeed suggests that much of *La Violencia* was associated with attempts to expand coffee production in areas where later violence was so intense.[52]

I tested this hypothesis statistically by correlating the expansion of coffee with the number of violent events during the last stage of *La Violencia* (1958–1963), employing McGreevey's departments as the units of analysis. Tolima led all states with 316 such events, followed by Valle (290), Caldas (225), Santander (73), Antioquia (65), Huila (42), and Cauca (36). The remaining departments each had fewer than 25 events, with only Cundinamarca, Meta, and Boyaca having more than 10. Pearson's r correlating absolute coffee expansion (1932 to 1953–1956) and the number of violent events (1958–1963) was $+.75$ ($p < .01$), a strong correlation despite the modest number of cases.[53]

I also checked for spurious effects in several different ways. If violence was itself a response to other violence, rather than a response to structural changes, then those departments with much violence could really be displaying mostly a contagion effect, inflating the "real" structurally caused violence. If we convert the actual number of events in each department to the natural log of that number, we mathematically remove such possible "contagion" from the data. (Sites with one or zero events were both assigned a zero on this measure.) The correlation remains impressively high, at $+.71$ ($p < .01$). I also ran a multiple regression, employing as the second independent variable the preexisting levels (1932) of coffee in each department, to see if the observed results were possibly due to relatively small expansions of coffee lands in coffee-dominated areas. If this were the case, the regression coefficients (Bs) and their standardized counterparts (*betas*) for the new variable would be statistically significant, and those for the previous variable would not be; alternatively, the new variable might be expected to improve the explained variance. Each of these alternative scenarios can be safely rejected. The regression coefficient for the absolute expansion of coffee is large ($+.28$) in the multiple regression, while that for preexisting levels is near zero ($+.01$). Moreover, the r^2 for the simple regression is .55 (that is, 55 percent of the variation in violent events is accounted for by coffee expansion); but the R^2 for the multiple regression is virtually identical, indicating that preexisting levels of coffee production add nothing to our statistical understanding of violence. It is change rather than structure that produced violence during the latter period of *La Violencia* and, by theoretical and historical extension, contributed to differential regional support for guerrilla movements.

One caveat of note: A close look at the data suggests that coffee's migration "explains" the violence in areas that later became FARC strongholds, but not that in Santander (ELN territory), where coffee production declined in the two decades prior to the events counted. In addition, the EPL strongholds in southern Córdoba were not areas of coffee production, although their regions of influence in northern Antioquia were. As a result, the recent history of coffee's migration across Colombia can help us understand *La Violencia* and the later success in the same areas of the FARC guerrillas, but not the successes of the ELN and EPL. In a sense, this statistical observation meshes with the views of previous chroniclers of *La Violencia*, who argued that Santander's violence had "political" causes, while that in Tolima, Valle, and Caldas (N.B.: FARC regions) had greater economic causes.[54]

Peru

In Peru, two historical "events" are critical for our analysis of the effects of agrarian changes on peasant radicalism. First, the series of over 300 Andean land invasions between 1962 and 1965—beginning in La Convención valley—wrought fundamental changes in many areas. Second, President Belaúnde's agrarian reform law promulgated in 1963 established several Sierran areas as reform zones, subject to survey and possible land redistribution. We would expect either successful invasions or the receipt of plots under an agrarian reform to neutralize or limit such peasant radicalism. Even the local expectation of receipt of lands might quell peasant discontent. Reforms might exacerbate local conflicts in one special case, however: In those places where hacienda peasants *and* nearby (Indian) villages (*Comunidades*) both lay moral or legal claim to estate land, reform might sharpen conflicts between *campesino* and *comunero* over land that both need.

In La Convención, as we have seen, land invasions destroyed the hacienda system there by 1963. Peasants later withdrew from many of the invaded lands when informed that agrarian reform laws would not be applied to invaded estates. Cuzco *was* declared a reform zone, and by 1965 formal distribution of lands was proceeding in La Convención. We would therefore expect little support for the guerrillas there, and that is precisely what we find.[55]

To evaluate the other two major guerrilla regions—Junín and Ayacucho departments—we must first consider the impact of land invasions there.[56] Based on half a dozen sources, we can draw the following tentative conclusions. Junín had a great deal of land invasion activity, and Ayacucho an appreciable if lesser amount. While such invasions shattered the hacienda tradition in at least a few areas of the Sierra, such as the area of Tullis's study in Junín, most of the invasions were rolled back by government repression. Peasants may have been somewhat mollified by the naming of Pasco and Junín as reform zones.[57]

Guerrillas in both Junín and Ayacucho received moderate support from the peasants. For Ayacucho's La Mar Province, Béjar's account provides no grounds for believing that the peasantry there had gained ground.[58] Indeed, his account suggests that the major *hacendados* still exercised economic and political control of the region. Hence moderate support for the guerrillas seems consistent with our theory.

For Junín, our picture is more complex. Huizer suggests that land invaders were suppressed there, and that land distribution began there only *after* it became evident that Guillermo Lobatón's MIR *foco* had considerable influence on the peasantry of Concepción Province. As Lobatón's band moved eastward they gained support from the Campa Indians, who certainly had not regained the tribal lands whose loss they still bitterly resented. Again, this pattern seems theoretically consistent with the moderate support afforded the guerrillas in Junín.

One other historical trend might have affected peasants' revolutionary inclinations in the Sierra: the declining terms of trade with the coastal areas. Tullis and McClintock have separately indicated such a twenty-year pattern in which the price of potatoes fell relative to the costs of agricultural inputs and peasant consumption needs. There was one sharp downward inflection from 1963 to 1965, and the later period of the 1970s saw another, this time sustained, drop in the terms of trade, the latter one associated with a subsistence crisis in the Andes (which is apparently linked to the popularity of *Sendero Luminoso* in the 1980s).[59] It is quite possible that the peasants of the mid-1960s experienced an especially strong economic squeeze above and beyond the traditional one imposed by the agrarian structure of the Sierra, and we would expect such a squeeze to be correlated with a willingness to support insurgency, for it closely resembles a problem in the "moral economy" of the region.

Bolivia

We turn finally to Bolivia. We have already established that Santa Cruz Department was an area of abundant land, with labor the commodity in short supply and peasants largely in possession of their lands. It seems hardly necessary to elaborate on the situation to show that it does not display a promising milieu for a radical peasantry. Although Santa Cruz was an area neither of land hunger nor of peasant agitation prior to the 1952 revolution, it benefited disproportionately from official land reform activity thereafter, especially in the mid-1960s. Up to 1966, 26 percent of the rural families in the department had been served by the land reform, versus 21 percent nation-wide. By then one-fourth of its (1950) farmlands had been distributed, a bit less than nationwide (one-third). By 1969, over half of the department's rural households had received land titles, versus 30 percent nationwide.[60] All in all, the area chosen by Ché Guevara was a poor choice on three counts: little pre-1952 land hunger, attention from land reformers up to 1966, and in-creased attention between 1966 and 1969. Small wonder, then, that he re-ceived such scant support from the area's peasantry.

CONCLUSIONS

We need not pose, then, a false choice between different types of theories predicting revolutionary peasantries. Both variations in agrarian structures and variations in the experience of change in those structures are closely asso-ciated with the radical proclivities of certain regions in each of the six coun-tries under review. Our confidence in these conclusions is strengthened by the systematic comparisons of guerrilla strongholds to other areas wherever pos-sible. Such comparisons have suggested again and again that the pattern of strong peasant support for guerrillas does not occur irrespective of agrarian structures or of the peasants' recent experiences of agrarian change.

This is not to claim perfect predictive powers for either thesis. Such phe-nomena are rare enough in sociology, where excessive claims are commonly made for low correlations and small regression coefficients whose signifi-cance levels are made impressive by enormous sample sizes. Here, as well, there are exceptions to theoretical rules. The Sierra Escambray in Cuba, Huila in Colombia, and other regions provide clear exceptions to the predic-tive power of our agrarian structural theory. Nor do agrarian transformations invariably predict radical peasantries to the exclusion of all competition, for the examples of Falcón and Lara in Venezuela and Zacapa in Guatemala—hotbeds all—provide major counterexamples. Therefore, with any inclina-tions to sociological hubris held firmly in check, we can now proceed to two other conditions that produce "revolutionary" peasantries.

CHAPTER 7

The Sources of Peasant Support II:
Rebellious Cultures and Social Ties

> Men are not machines. . . . They are men—a tautology which is
> sometimes worth remembering.
>
> —Gilbert Ryle

MANY CONTEMPORARY political sociologists, especially those whose work is tinted or more deeply colored with Marx's influence, share an affinity for the analyses of the preceding chapter, which are broadly macrosociological in orientation, and class-analytical in actual procedure. Yet many such scholars—but by no means all—in turn reject complementary forms of analysis that tend to focus on cultural distinctiveness or on patterns of social structure not of a "class" type. Such views, at the extreme, suffer from two reductions. First, social structure is reduced to class structure, and other patterns of social organization may be systematically ignored in the broad brush strokes of "class analysis." Second, cultural patterns, or structures, in turn are reduced to class structure, and/or simply treated as epiphenomenal in nature. Such a view was exemplified by a scholar at a session I once attended who opined that "culture doesn't explain anything."

It is clear from the preceding chapter that I am not hostile to macrosociological analyses focusing on the importance of structured social inequalities in producing change. Unlike those just mentioned, though, I wish to resist any premature closure of scholarly inquiry, and furthermore to insist that cultural structure is *not* reducible to social structure, for there are many historical phenomena that are explicable by patterns of cultural communication or diffusion that are not explicable in terms of social structural variations. Two ready examples: George Homans's historical explanation of the distinctive social institutions of Britain's East Anglia, which came about through Frisian rather than Anglo-Saxon settlement; and van de Walle and Knodel's demonstration that the generalized European fertility decline around the turn of the previous century diffused along lines of culture and language, and cannot be explained as a response to economic development.[1] Walter Wallace has systematized this viewpoint, in establishing a model that grants (hypothetically) equal weight to social structure and cultural structure as possible independent variables in social theory, and Jeffrey Alexander has also entered the lists arguing that we cannot reduce the explanation of social action or social order to mere social structural determination.[2]

Moreover, while "class analysis"—vague though it may be on propositional statements—clearly has a place in many analyses, the categories are often too gross and macro to capture regularities at a micro-level of analysis—that is, patterns of social organization that are not class patterns, but that nonetheless influence the size and shape collective behavior displays when it appears on the historical stage. In a number of books, historian-sociologist Charles Tilly has presented briefs in favor of class analysis (of a special sort) as a good key for unlocking historical patterns of collective conflict, contrasting its utility with "useless Durkheim." Yet Tilly is too good a historian not to detect other social patterns relevant to the understanding of collective conflict, as he noted in his analysis of the counterrevolutionary Vendée in France. "The most microscopic information we have on communal politics in Southern Anjou resists forcing into categories of class and locality alone, and calls for hunches about kinship, family friendships, the residues of old feuds, and the like."[3]

In the discussions that follow, I intend to take both cultural structures and Tilly's "microscopic information" and "hunches" most seriously, for there is strong evidence that both cultural and micro-social variations are associated with variations in peasant support for guerrilla movements.

Regional Legacies: Rebellious Cultures

In July 1953, as Fidel Castro and his surviving followers fled from the disasters attendant upon their attack on the Moncada barracks, the rebels marched toward Gran Piedra. Along the way, they met an old black woman who offered to assist them. In order to justify their trust, the woman showed the insurgents a revolutionary credential, indicating that the bearer was a loyal rebel supporter, signed by none other than the leader of Cuba's nineteenth-century war for independence, Antonio Maceo![4]

Do people carry their rebellious histories with them? If so, are there intra-country variations in such histories? If so, are they related to regional propensities to support contemporary revolutionaries? Evidence from Latin America and elsewhere[5] clearly suggests a positive answer to the second question just posed, just as Castro's chance encounter suggested "yes" to the first. As we shall see, a yes answer is suggested for the third as well. As usual, we will examine each nation's experience sequentially, trying where possible to examine the entire nation, so as not to bias the analysis toward finding what the theory predicts.

The Cuban revolution is the sole successful case in our period until Nicaragua twenty years later. It also gives the clearest impression of a connection between guerrilla insurgency and previous regional events. In the nineteenth century, most slave revolts took place in Oriente Province, notably in 1812, 1827, 1843, and 1879. The Cuban wars for independence (1868–1878, 1895–1898) were also fought mainly in Oriente, just as was Castro's later guerrilla war. Of this there is little doubt. No other region of the country was so overwhelmingly involved in the opposition to Spanish colonial authority as the east. The *maquis* during these periods formed especially in the Sierran regions of the province, in Mayari, Jiguani, Baracoa, Palma Soriano, and other municipios. The initial uprising of 1868 was led by the coffee planters of the region, but there is little question of mass resistance to Spanish authority there. Thomas argues that the first war was more or less a formalization of the banditry already endemic to the region, but that the later war involved virtually the entire populace in open or covert opposition to Spain. The Sierra Maestra was haven for Antonio Maceo's guerrillas during the last, successful insurgent campaign.[6]

Oriente's primacy in insurgency continued right up through the middle of this century. A major uprising of four thousand Afro-Cubans in May 1912 there was suppressed only after the landing of U.S. troops. During the 1933 revolution against Gerardo Machado, communist-inspired peasants rose up near Guantánamo, at Realengo 18. They seized the land and declared independent soviets, but were suppressed within a year or two.[7]

Various event counts also support the special character of the Orientales. Domínguez reports that ten of seventeen major Cuban peasant struggles occurred in Oriente, while a second source he cites counts twenty out of forty-five there, and a recent government map of "peasant struggles and revolutionary movements" puts the proportion at ten out of eighteen. Whatever the count, Oriente is clearly historically distinctive.[8]

In addition to the easily counted indicators of Oriente's insurgent past, we have more qualitative ones. A number of scholars have argued for a distinctive cultural tone to Oriente life. Barquín aptly describes the region as marginal to both law enforcement and material progress, and both marginalities shaped cultural perceptions there. Oriente was the center of a type of lawlessness that in the United States we would call "Wild-West" ("Wild-East" would be more suitable here). It was a center of banditry, a haven for refugees from justice, a center of individual resistance to authority. This sense of alienation from government was sharpened by the province's regional backwardness. Meneses wrote that the Orientales were "obsessed by injustice and neglect" and saw their province as a supplier of raw materials to Havana. These subjective feelings were not without foundation, for Orientales were, on average, the poorest, least educated, and least healthy Cubans. Oriente was also the one region in which serious land-tenure conflicts continued into the 1950s.[9] Little doubt exists, then, that Castro's guerrillas chose prime real estate in which to begin a revolution.

Following such detail, the evidence from other nations must surely pale by comparison, yet guerrillas still generally took root in areas historically the foci of resistance to federal authority.

Venezuela's Falcón State, one of two key guerrilla centers, has been a revolutionary "port of entry" since at least 1807, when Francisco Miranda landed there, and it served similar duty for opponents of Gómez (1908–1935), Pérez Jiménez, and Betancourt in this century. As to the last, a number of guerrilla groups originating in Cuba landed there, including the one that buried an arms cache on the Paraguaná peninsula, found in November 1963. Falcón was once, perhaps, a major economic region of Venezuela as well, but since 1875 had suffered a major decline in importance. During its heyday Falcón birthed much *caudillo* opposition to the federal government. Valsalice describes the state as a center for landlord resistance to any "presumptuous" claims made by federal or state governments to exert their powers there. Perhaps in accord with this tradition, Falcón was the scene of vendettas and feuds involving entire clans (more on this below). All in all, there appear to be certain parallels to "hillbilly" regions of the American south, where "revenooers" are rarely welcome.[10]

The state of Lara, the other primary guerrilla locale, was also one with "an old tradition of guerrilla war, that could make it a secure haven," which contributed to its role as home of the "Frente Simón Bolívar" guerrillas. That tradition was reinforced in 1929 when the father of (later) guerrilla chief Argimiro Gabaldón led a rebellion of thousands of peasants in the mountains against the Gómez dictatorship. Here as well there is little question of the proclivity for revolt.[11]

The guerrillas of the Venezuelan *llanos* (plains) did not survive for long. Lack of adequate support or supplies, or lack of lasting guerrilla organization there, may have hamstrung the movement on the plains of Apure, Barinas, and Portuguesa. Yet the plains were historically a major center for anticolonial, and later antigovernment revolts. Guerrilla and *llanero* Antonio Zamora writes that the *llanero* is "by his own initiative . . . a guerrilla. These people are guerrillas, born guerrillas. . . ." Valsalice ascribes the guerrillas' failure in the *llanos* to simple unwillingness to exploit the "natural resource" of the area's insurgent culture. He argues that, as a result, the guerrilla presence in the *llanos* was always fragmentary, and never developed into a true front.[12]

The Andean state of Táchira also had a strong history of caudillistic takeovers of government, but the guerrillas never attempted to turn it into a stronghold. Despite some nineteenth-century *caudillo* activity in the far east of the country, neither the "Oriente" guerrillas nor the *foco* in Miranda State operated in milieus with long histories of insurrectional activity. We did not expect them therefore to furnish fertile soil for guerrillas, and peasant support in those two locales was substantially inferior to that of Falcón and Lara.[13]

Overall, the evidence in Venezuela suggests a fairly good connection between historically important areas of resistance, and those areas that provided strong support to guerrillas of the 1960s.

In Venezuela, regions of historical opposition to central government are plural and easy to locate; not so for Guatemala. My survey of Guatemalan political histories failed to turn up any significant regions of recurring opposition to government there in the last century. Indeed, in contrast to the stormy history of mass collective conflict in rural areas of Cuba, Colombia, Bolivia, and Peru, the countryside of Guatemala was quiet indeed until mid-twentieth century. For the most part, the mobilization of the Guatemalan peasantry to collective action begins with the Arbenz government of the 1950s.[14]

We have some fragmentary evidence, however, that we may consider. A Guatemalan Marxist, in an unfortunately vague passage, argued that "in the rural districts where people are more active politically and where traditions of revolutionary struggle are strong, the guerrilla movement enjoys the support of the population." He then contrasts this support with the lack thereof in regions without such traits. He does not, however, name the areas, yet we already know that the Sierra de las Minas (Zacapa) and portions of Izabal were the guerrillas' main havens. Reinforcing this view, Allemann states outright that the Sierra de las Minas sheltered a traditionally rebellious peasantry and compared its culture to that of the Cuban Sierra Maestra. The evidence is sketchy, then, but tends to support the thesis.[15]

If it is difficult to locate historical areas of insurrection in Guatemala, it is difficult to avoid them in Colombia. Colombia's history of violence in the last hundred years makes its historical experience sui generis in the Latin American context.[16] Quite literally hundreds of thousands of persons have died in political violence in that troubled nation.

We can, however, make some regional distinctions. First, aside from violence surrounding strikes and labor disputes among banana workers in Magdalena, the vast majority of Colombian violence has taken place in the country's interior, especially in areas touched sooner or later by coffee production. Second, while the urban working class has not been quiescent, the majority of collective violence in Colombia has involved the mobilization of the peasantry rather than urban violence. A guerrilla war at the turn of the century in Colombia took place in the coffee areas of the old departments of Tolima and Cundinamarca, which then encompassed part or all of present-day Huila, Caldas, Quindio, Risaralda, and Meta as well—and all these areas became FARC guerrilla zones in the 1960s. Particular foci of that earlier war were the areas of Sumapaz, Viotá, Tequendama, and La Palma—the first three becoming Communist "peasant republics" decades later during La Violencia. During this period, as well as before, Indian tribes were being pushed out of their lands, despite fierce resistance, especially on or near the borders of present-day Tolima. One of the sites of such activity was Marquetalia, later a peasant republic and a FARC guerrilla stronghold. Finally, during the War of a Thousand Days (ca. 1900), there was an early episode of the bloody peasant-v.-peasant, Liberal-v.-Conservative fighting so common later, taking place in Santander, which in the 1960s harbored the ELN guerrillas.[17]

In the decade of the twenties, much police activity was directed against peasant movements, particularly those in Tolima, Cundinamarca, and Valle departments. These areas, later key zones of FARC guerrilla influence, were also among the most turbulent during the 1946 elections, and further erupted with the 1948 assassination of the leader of the Liberals' left wing, Jorge Eliécer Gaitán.[18]

La Violencia, datable roughly from 1948 to 1963, racked virtually the entire Colombian interior, as can be seen in the maps and discussion by Guzmán and his coauthors.[19] Still, certain states were particularly afflicted with violence. The leading areas of violence (in 1958–1963) as we saw in the last chapter were Tolima, Valle, (old) Caldas, Santander, etc. Tolima was the focal state of FARC activity after 1965, while Santander was the ELN's stronghold. The parts of Valle and Caldas most affected by *La Violencia* in this quinquennium were precisely the areas of FARC influence later.[20]

Richard Maullin tried to estimate more exactly the regional overlap between *La Violencia* and the 1960s guerrilla movements. He estimated that, of the 98 *municipios* that experienced insurgent violence in the 1960s, fully 60 percent had likewise been areas of earlier partisan violence. The one guerrilla area we haven't discussed in terms of a history of violence is the EPL's stronghold in southern Córdoba. There, too, "guerrilla" violence prevailed during *La Violencia*, as did a well-organized peasant movement.[21]

Little doubt remains about the continued historical pattern of violence and even insurrection in certain areas of the Colombian interior. We can, however, add a most curious coda to our analysis, for the land invasions that shook Colombia's countryside in the late 1960s and early 1970s were in general *not* located in the *municipios* that were the centers of guerrilla activity. One chronicler recorded over 350 such invasions. Tolima and Valle—FARC strongholds—shared only 15 such invasions between them, while Santander (ELN territory) had but 4. Huila *was* a center of land invasions (with 41), but these, if anything, were concentrated outside the guerrillas' *municipios*. Similarly, Córdoba housed the single greatest area of invasions, with 70, but they mostly occurred in northern areas of the department, with only 4 occurring in the EPL's southern strongholds of Montelibano and Tierralta. Madgalena and Sucre departments were the other major invasion centers.[22] Either the animus behind the land invasions was very different from support for guerrillas, or the two forms of collective action were somehow complementary yet mutually exclusive responses to peasant grievances in rural areas.

In Peru, we arrive at a situation where we expect some differentiation. In Junín and Ayacucho, where guerrillas obtained moderate support from the peasantry, we would expect some insurgent history; in La Convención, however, we would expect little or no such experience.

A survey of peasant movements in Peru makes it quite clear that virtually the entire Sierra has been the site of scattered or intense peasant resistance and agitation for at least the last century. Peasant movements took place in Cajamarca, Apurímac, Cuzco, Pasco, Junín, Puno, Ayacucho, and elsewhere. Even so, La Mar Province in Ayacucho stands out somewhat in this large group, and it also was the later haven of the ELN guerrillas. Over half a century before, by 1895, La Mar already had behind it considerable history of indigenous revolts against authority, and another Indian uprising occurred that year. La Mar was virtually controlled at the time by a single family, the Añaños, with family members holding both formal authority and informal power in the area. They virtually "converted the province of La Mar into an annex of their haciendas," according to Kapsoli. A violent conflict with local Indians over the usurpation of community lands left some 430 peasants dead there in 1923, and the revolt had millenarian overtones as well. By the early 1960s, much of La Mar Province was controlled by the Carrillo brothers, who were also engaged in continual conflict over land and labor rights with local Indian communities. The brothers were singly or jointly responsible for rape, murder, and various assaults in the area. Given this immediate and more distant background, it should little surprise us that local peasants welcomed the aid of the ELN when the guerrillas offered it to them in the struggle against the Carrillos.[23]

In Junín, I could find no evidence so specific as for Ayacucho. Still, Junín did share the more general Andean history of revolt, as evidenced by its importance in the early 1960s' Sierran land invasions. The Campa Indians—from whom the guerrillas received support for a while—had been in constant conflict with white settlers in this century (perhaps before as well) over the usurpation of their old tribal lands. They had been pushed ever farther into the forests of Jauja Province over the decades before 1965, yet retained their resistant, warlike inclinations. They quickly joined the guerrillas when the MIR *foco* offered them support in their quest to reclaim those lands.[24]

La Convención valley in Cuzco had been settled relatively recently, and was a place with abundant land. It was largely isolated from the rest of Peru, and was not really part of the Andean *Kulturkreis*. Much of the land there was not in the Sierra proper, but rather in upper areas of the Amazon jungle to the east.

La Convención's peasant movement from 1952 to 1963 seems to provide an obvious counterexample to our theory, for despite such a background the guerrillas garnered little support there. It provides just the opposite, though. The raison d'être of most peasant movements is the acquisition and retention of land. Despite the capture of peasant union leader Hugo Blanco there in 1963, and despite the repression visited upon the peasants in the Army's campaign against Blanco, the former "serfs" of the valley had, by 1964, succeeding in their goal of destroying the landed elite and acquiring the land for themselves. Therefore, when the guerrillas arrived shortly thereafter, they found a peasantry for whom the basic structural cause of resistance and insurgency had ceased to exist. It was utterly unsurprising that these former serfs failed to respond to the clarion calls sounded from the nearby Mesa Pelada in 1965. Their revolution had already been won.[25]

In Bolivia, we again expect the center of guerrilla activity, Santa Cruz, to have little history of revolt, for Ché Guevara's guerrillas received so little support there. In Bolivia, generally, we find a peasantry with a past history of rebellion, but one that had largely secured land ownership after the 1952 revolution. Prior to that time, however, Bolivia's peasants had a long and unsuccessful history of revolts against landlords, against the outlawing of traditional Indian land tenure institutions, and against the central government in general. One survey counted no fewer than two thousand rebellions or movements there from 1861 to 1944 alone. Indications are, however, that the vast bulk of these peasant movements took place in the highland department of La Paz and in the Cochabamba Valley. The decade prior to 1952 was especially filled with peasant agitation, and with violence and counterviolence.

In contrast to the massive movements elsewhere, "[a]reas of sparse population, such as La Paz north of Lake Titicaca, Beni, Pando, and Santa Cruz, hardly knew the demand for agrarian reform until it was instilled from above." The department of Chuquisaca bordered Guevara's area of operations, and it too was an area with little history of rebellion, in which mobile slash-and-burn peasants at times even resisted the government's attempts to give them land titles. In this area, too, agrarian reform was often an outside import rather than a response to internal pressures. In Santa Cruz, the only real "insurgent" patterns of this century have been those of secessionist movements, often associated with the right-wing Falangists.[26]

The evidence accumulated here is impressive. In every country we encounter an association between strong guerrilla movements and areas with rebellious histories. The prediction that little or no insurgent history weakens the potential support base, and that a substantial such history strengthens it, is borne out strongly by the evidence from Cuba, Colombia, and Bolivia. The evidence from Venezuela, Guatemala, and Peru is neither so abundant nor the fit so clear, yet it still generally supports the twin hypotheses. Latin American guerrillas benefited from their locations in regions with insurgent histories, and at times even chose their *foco* sites precisely because they knew that those particular regions harbored inhabitants likely to be responsive to the guerrillas' appeals for support.[27]

SOCIAL NETWORKS AND PEASANT COMMUNITY SUPPORT

Why do peasants join and support revolutionary movements seeking to overthrow existing governments? The obvious answer would be as follows: Peasants share in the revolutionary (often Marxist) beliefs of the guerrilla leadership and act in accord with such beliefs by joining the revolutionary resistance. In this case, as in many other examples of commonsense analysis, the obvious answer is wrong. Alternative, less obvious answers have also been offered. For example, peasants have specific local grievances, especially against landlords and tax collectors, and are willing to join any group that will further the redress of such grievances. This view is certainly closer to some "truth" than the first—indeed, it is rather clearly a subtext of the previous chapter—but it, too, is limited in its ability to throw full light on the social mechanisms that bring guerrillas and peasants into close cooperation.

Previous studies of incorporation into religious "cults" provide clues for the analysis to follow. A series of studies by Stark and Lofland, and similar works by others, suggest that religious "conversion" is *not* the key to understanding successful instances of recruitment into religious cults. Instead, in almost every case, people who entered such cults *first* began by forming close social attachments to cult members, whose attempts to recruit strangers were unsuccessful. Only later did the process of conversion begin to appear, *working its course via those friendships* established between cult members and outsiders. These studies are relevant because religious conversion is rather clearly similar to other forms of ideological conversion, and we might expect to encounter the same features in recruitment to political movements. Similarly, recruitment to the Nazi party in Weimar Germany did not appear as a sequence of ideological conversion, then incorporation. For example, readership of Hitler's ideological treatise *Mein Kampf* increased *after* party membership rolls increased, rather than before. It appears that the dense social networks created by the early Nazis were social channels by which potential recruits were brought into contact with committed Nazis, and were the paths to later Nazi party membership. Wilson and Orum have also argued clearly that mobilizing people for collective political action depends upon existing social networks.[28]

In this section, I will argue that a variety of such social-network attachments also served to channel peasants into the guerrilla movements, thus paralleling Tilly's findings about late eighteenth-century France. These channels are *not* reducible to class influences; indeed, some of these recruitment channels in fact function best because they cross class lines (see the discussion of Venezuela below). In suggesting this "model" of peasant recruitment, I'm suggesting that we must take a very hard look at micro-level data from peasant communities wherever we can find it, and see how such evidence bears upon the thesis that local attachments were crucial in engendering peasant support for guerrillas.

In suggesting this thesis, I wish to oppose it to a contrary thesis, propagated by none other than Ché Guevara. Guevara's image is rather one of "slow conversion." In this view, peasants initially distrust the guerrillas, and slowly the authorities' bestial behavior and the guerrillas' ethically proper actions lead to a close guerrilla-peasant alliance.[29] In Sartre's unfortunate words, the peasants only became guerrillas after the guerrillas had first become peasants. Note that even Guevara's thesis does not involve *ideological* conversion beforehand. Guerrillas in the field—such as Guevara in Cuba, Béjar in Peru, the FAR leaders in Guatemala, and the FARC and ELN leaders in Colombia—all recognized that peasants joined the guerrillas for their own reasons, and the urban-educated guerrilla leaders typically set out thereafter "to raise the cultural level" (a painfully recurring phrase in guerrilla discourse) of their new recruits, usually through literacy training and Marxist-Leninist indoctrination.

Therefore, I am not without yet more distinguished precedents in suggesting that ideology does not precede conversion. How, then, might social attachments channel peasants into close ties with guerrilla movements? Let us consider the following pure, or ideal typical taxonomy of subtypes. First of all, peasants and guerrillas might be thrown together through common membership in *formal* organizations, or because of more *informal* social organizational ties. Among the former we might include, primarily, political party membership, adding as well membership in local peasant federations, and possibly attendance at schools or even universities in exceptional cases. On the borderline between the formal and the informal, we might consider such institutions as local churches, the ecclesiastical base communities thrown up under the auspices of liberation theology, and the village "fraternities" or *cofradías* of highland Guatemala. At the informal level, we have simple patterns of village membership, in which people are tied together by language, friendship, ethnicity, and the like.

A second distinction, which cuts across the first set (thus creating a fourfold table of "pure" types), is that between *hierarchical* attachments and *nonhierarchical* or lateral attachments among individuals. In the first case, it is possible that preexisting hierarchical attachments between guerrillas and peasants might give extra force to the guerrillas' attempts to mobilize peasants behind a revolutionary movement. Guerrillas might be superordinate to peasants as landlords or the children of landlords; as officers in political parties in which peasants are rank-and-file members; or as officers in peasant federations or formal peasant movements. Any kind of *patron-client* relation would clearly fall neatly into this category. Again on the borderline between the two types, there might be peasants who wield considerable *influence*, rather than power, in a region, and whose opinions and decisions about supporting guerrillas carry local weight by that very influence. Finally, on the nonhierarchical end of the distinction, we have simple patterns of lateral friendships, day-to-day interaction, and ethno-linguistic ties, without the added element of hierarchical control.

What is the hypothesized relation between these attachments and peasant support? We can argue most simply on the theoretical basis of psychological balance theory, which predicts that unbalanced social (dis-)attachments create cognitive dissonance and psychic discomfort, and that people are therefore pressured toward balance in their social relationships.[30] Given that theory, we would expect that "any friend of yours will be a friend of mine" and that "the enemy of my enemy will be my friend." That is, friendly attachments between proto-guerrillas and peasants will serve to channel them into *joint* opposition to the enemies of the guerrillas: the central government and the military. To the extent that guerrillas are tied to peasants by *any* of these mechanisms *before the guerrilla movement proper is born*, those ties will serve to facilitate the growth of that movement on a peasant support base. A *fortiori*, where those attachments are reinforced by preexisting, proto-guerrilla authority (*not* just power) over the actions of peasants, we would expect to find especially strong channels drawing guerrillas and peasants into unified opposition.

Before we proceed to analyze each nation on a case-by-case basis, I should signal to the reader the obvious: that each of these patterns of social ties might be put at the service of counterrevolutionary ends as well. Those same social ties, if tying peasants into nonrevolutionary organizations, could even channel peasants into decidedly reactionary activity. While the structural pressures I discussed in the preceding chapter suggest that a revolutionary peasantry is more likely than its opposite, we must keep our minds open to the possible rather than just the probable, for we will in fact encounter such opposite cases, especially later in El Salvador.

Cuba: Insurgents and the Squatters' Movement

In Cuba, the guerrillas built up their *foco* initially on the basis of an alliance they struck with an informal peasant leader of the Sierra Maestra, Crescencio Pérez. The reader may remember Guevara's description of the first guerrilla-peasant contacts as being highly tentative and distrustful. That description is inaccurate. At least as early as November 1956, Castro's M-26 (not yet a guerrilla movement) had contacted Pérez. In exchange for the support of Pérez and his followers, Castro promised land titles to Pérez and other Sierran *precaristas* (squatters), agrarian reform, and other social- and political-welfare measures.

In Pérez, the guerrillas had thoughtfully sought out and acquired an invaluable ally. If even part of the chroniclers' descriptions of Pérez is accurate—and some of them are a bit excitable—then he was a remarkable man. They describe him as "married" to three sisters, and as the "lawyer, judge, sheriff, counsellor, and patriarch of 50,000 *guajiros* [Sierran peasants]." Even discounting literary hyperbole, Pérez clearly wielded enormous influence among squatters, and a substantial part of this was through his personal kinship network in the Sierra.

Castro's forces landed at Niquero on 2 December 1956 and were rapidly cut up by waiting Batista soldiers. (Crescencio had been waiting to receive them with 100 men and some trucks on the evening of 30 November on the coast, but Castro's rebels arrived two days late.) About 20 persons fled toward the Sierra. At the very first peasant house that Guevara approached after the flight from Niquero, he was received warmly and festively. The local peasants offered to take him to Crescencio, and further informed him that Castro was alive, for the two had been separated in their flight. On 5 December, Sergio and Ignacio Pérez (Crescencio's sons) began to scour the Sierra to find the rebels and offer them shelter and guidance. By 8 December, Crescencio had mobilized his followers throughout the Sierra. On 9 December, Juan Almeida and Camilo Cienfuegos were found and escorted to safe haven. On 17 December, Castro's followers were finally all reunited with their leader at the home of Mongo Pérez—Crescencio's brother. Two peasant combatants were promptly accepted into the guerrillas' ranks, although eight days later Castro had insufficient weapons to accommodate the 30 men who offered to join on the spot; instead he accepted 15 of them into the M-26 auxiliaries.[31]

Clearly, Guevara's image of the "slow conversion" of the peasantry is wildly inappropriate for Pérez and the squatters he led, although Barquín suggests that nonsquatters may have fit that image. This experience was repeated in somewhat similar form over a year later, when Raúl Castro opened up the second front in the Sierra Cristal. There he promptly received offers of service from several irregular peasant-guerrilla bands already operating in the mountains, who were then incorporated into Raúl's command.[32]

Venezuela: Communists and Caudillos

In Venezuela we encounter the strongest, most systematic evidence that preexisting social attachments empowered the most important guerrilla movements throughout the nation. Indeed, Venezuela exhibits most markedly the two hypothetically most important patterns of attachments: hierarchical attachments through formal organizational membership and hierarchical attachments through less formal patron-client ties. Let us discuss them in turn.

We can easily find several examples outside of Latin America in which Communist parties used their rural influence to change the shape or direction of rural collective action, even if they weren't the driving force behind such movements.[33] In a slightly different form in each case, Communist parties in Venezuela, Colombia, and Guatemala also were a (or the) major impetus behind peasant-guerrilla linkages.

By all odds, though, the Venezuelan case is the most important. As Alexander has shown, the PCV (Communists) had influence in many regions of rural Venezuela, even if they did not match the broad influence held there by the governing AD (which won the 1958 and 1963 elections largely on its rural vote). The Communists had even engaged in "civic action" in some areas to ameliorate the conditions of the peasantry.[34] Their greatest influence, however, was clearly in Morán District in the state of Lara. Two *municipios* of that district—Humocaro Alto and Humocaro Bajo—gave the PCV a clear majority of the vote in the 1958 national elections, when the PCV won less than 10 percent nationwide. Angela Zago provided a humorous illustration of the PCV's influence on the peasants, when she was sent to the area to help set up the guerrilla front there. At one of her first stops an old peasant woman asked her, "Are you a Communist?" Zago answered in the affirmative. The old woman replied, "Good, because if you're not a Communist, you don't come in my house."

That area had the single strongest guerrilla front in all Venezuela, and we must surely relate that fact to the preexisting hegemony of the Communist party there, for they were the engine behind the FALN guerrillas, and they (of course) arranged peasant support networks and linkages for the guerrillas throughout the region. Former Lara guerrilla chief Teodoro Petkoff, in a rare interpretative lapse, oddly attributed the *foco's* success to the guerrillas' organizing efforts there ("political work" is the usual idiom). In view of the preceding evidence, it is far more reasonable to assert that the organization was *already* intact, and that the guerrillas exploited it to the hilt. Further evidence for this interpretation is the fact that the front disintegrated quickly after the death of its key commander and with the withdrawal of the PCV from active guerrilla support beginning in 1965.[35]

The Venezuelan guerrillas also built widely on preexisting patterns of patron-client and family loyalties in generating peasant support for the guerrillas. In Valsalice's summary words, "intimate and affective aspects . . . contribute to a kind of identification with the guerrilla war by vast family conglomerates tied through chains of kinship or friendship. In such a manner, territorial bases which the Venezuelan guerrilla war lacks are obtained in a different fashion, on a terrain of family solidarity."[36]

Gilmore has defined *caudillismo* as "the union of personalism and violence for the conquest of power."[37] Such regional political leaders have arisen throughout Latin American history and are marked by the strongly local and personal nature of their followings. If we follow Turner and Killian's definitions, a *social movement* is a collectivity oriented toward a particular goal, while a *following* is instead oriented toward a particular person.[38] The former is largely ideological, the latter largely personal. Especially in Venezuela—but also strongly in the case of Castro in Cuba, Vásquez and Marulanda in Colombia, Guevara in Bolivia et al.—guerrilla movements were shot through with personal followings and personal attachments to traditional or charismatic leaders. Several groups drew strongly on such affective followings to strengthen the guerrilla movement, and nowhere more so than in Venezuela. Many Venezuelan guerrilla leaders in this respect resemble, more than anything else, *caudillos* twice over, for they combined elements of traditional informal authority over peasants with modern authority as the leaders of guerrilla units.

Venezuela was certainly the haven for such activity. In Falcón, at least four guerrilla leaders—Douglas Bravo, Domingo Urbina, Hipólito Acosta, and Pablo "Chema" Saher—were the sons or close relatives of powerful landowners or politicians. The first three were related to landlords, the last the son of Falcón's governor. Bravo and Urbina definitely used their family and peasant (i.e., patron-client) ties to create firm bases of support in Falcón's guerrilla zone.[39]

There was an additional overlay of political feud in Bravo's fight against the AD governments from 1959 to 1969. Bravo's father, an opposition URD supporter, was killed by a member of the rival Hernández clan (old AD supporters), in the latest episode of an old family vendetta. Instead of exacting immediate vengeance, Bravo went on to Caracas to pursue his legal studies and returned only later—still in local dishonor—to set up the guerrillas' *foco* near his aunt's family estate, Los Evangelios. Much of the subsequent fighting in the region was overlain with what Gall nicely terms this "Hatfield-McCoy" type of feud. Valsalice even suggests that such feuds are endemic to the region. The importance of kinship and personal ties can hardly be overestimated for Bravo's front, for he knew virtually everyone in the region, and hundreds more were his relatives. Even his old comrade-in-arms Teodoro Petkoff, despite his Marxist credentials, describes the Falcón front as having been "established . . . on this kind of family-political relationships."[40]

Similar features imbued the fighting in nearby Lara State. We already know that the Communist party organized and strengthened the guerrilla-peasant contacts in the "Frente Simón Bolívar" there. The leader of the *larense* front was Argimiro Gabaldón, whose father, the hacendado and general José Rafael Galaldón, had led a regional rebellion of thousands of peasants against the Gómez dictatorship in 1929. Argimiro himself developed very strong personal relationships with the peasants on his estate and in surrounding areas, and actually initiated attempts to organize estate workers. As a result, when police and army troops told local peasants that Argimiro was a "bandit," they scoffed at the very thought. In one reported instance, the peasants actually held off with knives a police squad that had learned the location of the wounded guerrilla leader.[41]

A second leader of the Lara guerrillas was also a local, José "El Gavilán" Díaz, who had long been a peasant-organizer there for the AD party, living in the mountains during the Pérez-Jiménez regime, and forging strong personal ties with the peasants there. Díaz joined the MIR when it split from the governing AD, and the MIR later organized their own guerrilla group, cooperating with the PCV insurgents in the area. Gabaldón died in a freak gun-cleaning accident in December 1964, and "El Gavilán" came down from the hills eight months later, indicating that, without Gabaldón's leadership, the *foco* was disintegrating.[42]

Even in the relatively weak guerrilla "front" on the plains, or *llanos*, such ties were put to work. Antonio Zamora's memoirs recount in detail his experiences in giving the front there a significant if short-lived revival. Zamora was born and raised in the area, where his father owned two cattle ranches. Zamora's biographer fails to relate those facts to the following descriptions, but we can:

> Antonio's strength was not so much at the operational level, but rather in the realm of tying the guerrilla band into the social milieu, i.e., the real political plan of the guerrilla movement. It was when we entered into a settlement that "el Camarita" was put to the test of truth. There everyone knew and loved him, and it was he—of all of us—who always merited the greatest shows of affection from those simple country people. . . . In the final accounts it was Antonio and not "the invaders" who at length was really welcome in the kitchen, the ultimate refuge of even the most modest *campesino's* hut.[43]

In those same *llanos*, the guerrillas also tied themselves into the social milieu by superimposing their operations over preexisting cattle-rustling patterns. "Ramoncito," a well-known cowboy in the area, joined the guerrillas and brought with him the respect of local peasants, since he had a history of conflicts with local landlords. The brother of Antonio Zamora also helped out the guerrillas, but strictly as a family matter. Similar examples were repeated in other areas of Venezuela.[44] Finally, when Congressman Fabricio Ojeda took to the hills to join the guerrillas, he joined the "El Charal" Front, which just happened to operate in the area of Ojeda's hometown of Boconó, in Trujillo State.

With such strong channels to the peasantry, why didn't the Venezuelan guerrillas fare better throughout the countryside? First, as this work makes clear, peasant support alone is not enough to win a guerrilla war. Second, the FALN and MIR guerrillas certainly had appreciable channels to the peasantry, but in this regard they were overmatched by the AD governments of Rómulo Betancourt and Raúl Leoni during the period of guerrilla warfare. AD's organizing efforts in rural areas dated back to the 1930s, and peasant support was crucial to AD electoral victories in the 1940s, 1958, and 1963. In *most* of the Venezuelan countryside, then, guerrillas faced occupied ground in their attempts to drum up revolutionary support. In addition, those

AD governments carried out a major land reform there in the 1960s. These, more than any other features, spelled disaster for any hopes of guerrilla victory in 1960s Venezuela.

Colombia: The Special Case—Peasant Leaders and Peasant Led

Colombia always provides a special case in one key regard: For the FARC guerrillas—largest of the three sixties' groups—it is highly misleading to speak of urban, upper-class guerrillas trying to establish rapport with rural, lower-class peasants. This theme recurs throughout this book because I must make very clear that the guerrillas and peasants typically came from profoundly different "social worlds," which made highly problematic the forming of "bridges" between those worlds.[45] In Colombia we encounter a fundamental exception to this generalization. FARC's leadership at this time was drawn largely from peasant leaders thrown up in self-defense areas during the course of *La Violencia*, if not before. The FARC itself was born when the government attempted to retake the areas of the "independent republics," and fleeing peasants joined a congeries of fledgling guerrilla bands which later united as the FARC. Given such a scenario, no bridges needed to be built between the guerrillas and the peasantry. As Arenas argued, there was no need for the guerrillas to go the masses, for they were of the masses.[46]

Even so, some of our models of social attachments are still quite relevant to the Colombian experience. The Colombian Communist party (PCC) had by 1948 established a strong rural influence in Viotá, Sumapaz, and Tequendama, all near the Tolima-Huila-Cundinamarca border area. *La Violencia* took them by surprise. Only after the establishment of a multitude of peasant "guerrilla" bands (of various political loyalties and [anti-] social inclinations) did the PCC begin to establish contacts with them, especially in southwestern Tolima and in southwestern Huila. The PCC arranged for many of these peasant guerrilla leaders to enter the upper echelons of the party. Among those rising rapidly in the ranks were Pedro Antonio Marín, a.k.a Manuel Marulanda Vélez and "Tiro Fijo" (sure shot), and Juan de la Cruz Varela, who later was elected to Congress. Marulanda, Isauro Yosa, and Ciro Trujillo all later rose to membership in the PCC Central Committee. FARC in the mid-1960s was a congeries of guerrilla bands headed by persons like Marulanda and linked together by ties and recruitment networks to the PCC in urban areas. The PCC actually remained legal during this period, operating with two faces. Further evidence of the strong peasant-PCC linkage is the fact that 40 percent of the participants in the 1958 Party Conference were peasants or rural wage workers. As in Venezuela, the Communists began to back away from "the armed struggle" in 1966—perhaps influenced by Soviet-Colombian rapprochement—and FARC activity decreased notably for some time thereafter. By the 1980s, Marulanda denied any FARC-PCC ties.[47]

The PCC's influence in rural areas was, however, quite modest compared to that of the major parties. A number of writers have argued that Liberal and Conservative loyalties at the local level dominated village life and often approached the pathological. In such a situation—even granting considerable decay in those loyalties during and after *La Violencia*—the PCC did not have the kind of political ties to the bulk of the peasantry that the main parties had.[48] For its part, the ELN was born through its ties to MOEC, and the EPL was simply the armed wing of the Chinese-line Communists (PCC-M-L). Of these, the MOEC had some preexisting influence on the peasantry in a few areas in Santander, where the ELN later was to center its operations.[49]

Channels between local peasants and guerrillas were also greased by local universities and their ties to the peasantry through agricultural extension and rural development programs. In Colombia, the Industrial University of Santander in Bucaramanga played such a role, as did San Cristobal in Huamanga, Peru for the Peruvian ELN, and universities in Satipo, Junín, and in Cuzco (for the Peruvian MIR). The most important case, to be discussed later, is that of university ties as the foundation for Peru's later movement, *Sendero Luminoso*.[50]

Despite its ties to the peasants, however, even the FARC ran into problems of peasant reliability at times. In this case local hostilities, rather than attachments, were important (although this case, too, meshes neatly with balance theory's predictions). The army actually recruited informers from FARC regions who had "personal contradictions" with the peasant guerrilla leadership. In an earlier case, the army recruited Páez Indians—who had had conflicts with the "peasant republic's" leaders—to scout and guide for the military in its campaign against Marquetalia. Their role was crucial in the army's taking of the region, and the guerrillas noted ruefully that "[w]ithout the support of the Indians, the army would have received some hard blows from the guerrillas."[51]

The most striking single feature of the Colombian guerrilla experience, especially but not only for the FARC, is how thoroughly the entire guerrilla experience has been rooted in local experiences in the countryside. The whole history of violence in a number of rural areas appears to have made them prime real estate for harboring the guerrilla warfare of the 1960s, without the need to import either organization or ideology from the urban-educated revolutionary intellectuals who so thoroughly dominated revolutionary leadership elsewhere.

Guatemala: Contact Men, Cofradías, and Army Cohorts

There is always a danger in this kind of analysis in finding just what you're looking for, the danger of "lumping" together all congenial facts, and ignoring the uncongenial.[52] Let it be said at the start of this section, then, that the Guatemalan case provides the least micro-level information supporting the importance of preexisting social ties in linking the guerrillas to the social milieu. Nonetheless, the existing evidence is worthy of our review.

The role of the Guatemalan Communists (PGT) in the rural armed struggle resembles somewhat that of their Colombian counterparts, although at a more reduced level. In both cases "the armed struggle" began as a surprise to the party; in both, the Communists hastened to board an already-moving revolutionary movement; and in both cases the party provided urban support networks and recruits to the largely rural guerrilla movement. While the Guatemalan Communists lacked the widespread rural ties of the Colombian PCC, or the deep roots in a single area of the Venezuelan PCV, their rural ties did provide some assistance to the guerrillas. A member of the PGT, Estanislao de León, provided a point of contact between the guerrillas, the PGT, and the rural wage workers of the Izabal banana plantations, because he was a union leader in the area near where Yon Sosa's guerrillas later took root. On this basis, Yon Sosa formed a series of peasant support groups in Morales *municipio* and in the Mico Mountains. León was thus simultaneously peasant, union leader, Communist, and guerrilla—thus providing a "hub" for those many spokes. More generally, we can make a stronger statement, more sharply paralleling the Venezuelan experience in Lara. Pablo Monsanto, a guerrilla leader since the 1960s, has declared in retrospect that the guerrillas in *both* Zacapa *and* Izabal built their movements precisely where their PGT allies had achieved earlier successes in organizing the locals in the banana region. In Monsanto's estimation, "the guerrilla movement [*la guerrilla*] could not have formed that social base of support on its own."[53]

Normally, social ties in guerrilla war serve to strengthen the insurgents' ability to resist the army. In the Guatemalan case, in contrast, there is strong evidence that social ties instead weakened the willingness of the army to wage all-out war against the guerrillas until late 1966. The key guerrilla leaders—Turcios Lima and Yon Sosa—were both former army officers who had led the nationalist revolt of 13 November 1960 (hence the name MR-13) against *Yanqui* use of Guatemalan territory to train Bay of Pigs invaders. After the suppression of that revolt, and the proto-guerrillas' escape, Turcios maintained information sources in the armed forces, and guerrillas at times purchased weapons from soldiers in the regular army. One story had it that Turcios even showed up at party thrown for officers in the capital, and was welcome there! Indeed, there seem to be elements of medieval chivalry in the continued cordiality between foes during this period. A number of writers have attributed the laxity ("insouciant" is one term) of pre-1966 counterinsurgency efforts precisely to Turcios's and Yon's maintenance of old army contacts, which violated every army's basic rule against fraternization with the enemy.[54]

If one peasant could tie the guerrillas partly into the social milieu of Izabal, another helped the FAR guerrillas to forge links with the Kekchí Indians in

Alta Verapaz. A member of that ethnic group, Emilio Roman López (a.k.a. Pascual Ixtapá), had been among the disappointed when Arbenz refused to arm the peasantry against the 1954 invasion, and he sought out Turcios Lima after the failure of 1962 uprisings in the capital. López, who could employ his authority as the *alcalde* (roughly mayor) of the town of Rabinal, was then entrusted with the formation of a completely Indian guerrilla column, which he accomplished. This group was then incorporated into the Edgar Ibarra Front (in Zacapa) in November 1963. López was killed in late 1966 and the group destroyed in Guatemala City in October 1967. Schump even argues that López himself convinced Turcios of the need for a peasant-based revolutionary war, rather than another rebel-officer coup.[55]

The FAR guerrillas also enlisted the otherworldly aid of local evangelical missionaries for their worldly pursuits, in a way presaging the role of Liberation Theology in the 1970s. The evangelists compared the guerrillas' struggles for justice to those of the Biblical Maccabees. As Turcios himself exulted, "Those Maccabees! After all these centuries they've turned out to be magnificent allies for us!" Maryknoll missionaries in Huehuetenango apparently also proselytized on the guerrillas' behalf and may even have planned with the FAR to establish a *foco* there, the reason given for their expulsion from Guatemala in 1968. Perhaps the Maryknollers' or others' work took eventual root, though, for by the 1980s Huehuetenango was a primary stronghold of the new Guerrilla Army of the Poor (EGP).[56]

Finally, the Guatemalan FAR and MR-13 made one quite distinctive use of lateral linkages to peasant villages. While neither group evidenced extensive use of preexisting attachments to the peasantry, the guerrillas did attempt to administer Indian locales through the village *cofradías* (guilds or brotherhoods), rather than destroying the local institutions. According to one observer, the *cofradías* had been "bulwarks of resistance" for centuries against the white conquerors. This maneuver by the insurgents may well have been an excellent strategic move in eliciting local cooperation in some areas. However successful the guerrillas were in those home bases, as soon as the army pushed the FAR out of its strongholds in the 1966–1967 counterinsurgency campaign, the guerrillas found themselves without the old peasant contacts, and without support to boot. After this experience the rural wing of the FAR rapidly disintegrated, with tiny offshoots surviving, eventually reincarnated as the "new" guerrillas of the late 1970s.[57]

Peru: Linkages for and Against

Unlike the previous three cases, the Peruvian guerrillas had no solid political party linkages to the peasants they tried to address. Party politics were late in coming to impoverished rural Peru, but by the 1950s APRA had influence in several northern areas, while the Acción Popular (AP) party led by Fernando

Belaúnde Terry had support in the southern Sierra. Belaúnde had nearly won the presidency in 1956 on the strength of the peasant vote in the central and southern Sierra, and did win it in 1963. In contrast, the MIR (an offshoot of APRA) and ELN (an offshoot of the Communists) guerrillas had little or no such party following among the peasantry. Not unlike their Venezuelan contemporaries, then, the Peruvian guerrillas at times faced previously organized peasants ("occupied ground") in their 1965 attempt at insurrection.

In Peru, though, we do have one clear case in which preexisting authority among peasants was put at the service of revolution, and I find it decidedly noncoincidental that it occurred precisely where the guerrillas received the greatest degree of support from the peasantry, of the four *focos* that year. Máximo Velando Gálvez had worked for several years in Junín Department as a peasant organizer before joining the MIR proto-guerrillas.[58] Indeed, he had risen to a leadership post in the Satipo and Concepción peasant organizations. Velando was even accused of orchestrating the land invasions that swept Junín between 1962 and 1965. When the *focos* came to life in 1965, Velando put his established peasant contacts to excellent use in forming a network of guerrilla supporters, in his new role as second-in-command of the *foco*. Unsurprisingly, then, the Junín *foco* received more peasant support than its MIR counterparts in Piura and Cuzco.[59]

Cuzco provides a most interesting case in which peasant contacts can be shown to vary in their effects. Luis de la Puente's 1965 *foco* in La Convención tied itself into the local context in large part through the cooperation of a local peasant leader, Albino Guzmán, who had risen in the local federation when Hugo Blanco guided it to such militant activity (e.g., the first of the land invasions in the Sierra). (Blanco and de la Puente, however, could come to no agreement a few years earlier, when the latter sought Blanco's help in setting up the *foco*.) De la Puente could not speak Quechua, which was the lingua franca of the area. Guzmán, in contrast, as a former Blanco organizer, and as a local native and Quechua speaker, gave the *miristas* superb ties to the local peasants. Guzmán later withdrew his initial commitment to the MIR. Indeed, he and two other peasant leaders who had served analogous roles surrendered to the authorities in early September 1965. At that time, they said they had been tricked into joining the guerrillas by unkept promises, and that the peasants and workers were only being used in the struggle because their "material existence" made many susceptible to "bribery and promises." Guzmán then led the Peruvian armed forces camp by camp to the MIR strongholds on the nearby Mesa Pelada, hastening the *foco*'s history to an early conclusion.[60]

In Peru the army also made use of Indians (the Campa) in tracking down and killing or capturing the guerrillas of the MIR *foco* in Junín—this despite the fact that the Campas had earlier fought *for* the insurgents. The military's Campa support was apparently obtained through a combination of military terror and "civic action" visited upon the inhabitants of the guerrillas' zone of action, although the guerrillas themselves may have alienated their erstwhile supporters by failing to act promptly to restore age-old tribal lands to the Campas.

Here as elsewhere, the insurgents' problem was the fundamentally different social worlds that the guerrillas and their target audience inhabited. Central here was the socially indicative split between the guerrillas' Spanish and the Quechua spoken throughout most of the Sierra. Only a few guerrillas in each front—indeed, only one in Béjar's Ayacucho front—were able to converse with the local residents in Quechua. This contrasted sharply with the earlier, bilingual organizers of the peasant federation in Cuzco and its counterparts elsewhere. Even the guerrillas' year or two organizing campaign in these regions failed to establish secure guerrilla-peasant ties (their own opinions notwithstanding). Radio Havana directed hortatory broadcasts in Quechua at the Sierran audience, and the army also used Quechua in its counterinsurgency campaign. In all three key *focos*, guerrillas made contact with local peasants or even leaders of local peasant organizations. Yet the support thus obtained, as in the case of Albino Guzmán, was neither firm nor long lasting. Indeed, even Hugo Blanco's followers had turned against him in the end, and he had had a far more secure following in the Andes.[61]

Bolivia: Strangers in Revolutionary Paradise?

Ché's guerrillas in Bolivia, we have seen, were hamstrung in several ways by the conditions indigenous to the eastern region in which they operated. Not least of these was the fact that all members of the *foco* were strangers to the chosen site. Guevara and other Cubans were usually the leaders of the ELN, while the Bolivian members were uniformly from the *altiplano*, and none was from the sparsely populated east. Hence the guerrillas' encounters with the Santa Cruz *campesinos* were all encounters between strangers. To sharpen the distinctiveness of such encounters, we should note that the Cubans were obviously *not* Bolivians (most notably the Afro-Cubans)—thereby sharpening any negative nationalistic responses—and the Cubans wasted valuable time trying to teach themselves Quechua (the language of part of the *altiplano*), when in fact Guaraní was often the lingua franca in parts of the east.

Guevara was quite aware of the negative impact a Cuban-led guerrilla band would have on the nationalist proclivities of many Bolivians. He dealt with this by regularly using Inti Peredo and other Bolivians as intermediaries whenever the guerrillas contacted the locals for dialogue, supplies, or assistance. Guevara even posed once as Peredo's assistant. If Lamberg is correct, even this may have been insufficient, for Bolivians in the southeast even tended to view *altiplano* residents, such as tin miners, almost as foreigners. When U.S. officers trained soldiers in counterinsurgency in 1967, those chosen for the training were drawn from the eastern interior and not from the highlands, so that the soldiers pursuing Guevara would have much in common with local peasants. An army squad captained by a man from the immediate vicinity wiped out Joaquín's band in one of the campaign's few major firefights.[62]

Indeed, if any principal could claim to have special contacts with the peasantry, that was President René Barrientos. Barrientos was not only president and head of the armed forces at this time (the latter more solidly than his successors would be), but he also had a strong personal following among the Quechua-speaking peasantry of the Cochabamba Valley, which even the Cuban press acknowledged afterwards. While the Bolivian *foco* was not located there, any expansion into that area would thus have been most difficult. In any event, even the leader of the peasant union in Guevara's locale was a pro-Barrientos man.[63] As in other aspects of the Bolivian guerrilla campaign, the insurgents ran headfirst into some stark social realities that greatly disfavored the nurturing of rural revolution in their Bolivian backwater.

Summary and Conclusions

Overall, Venezuela exhibits the most impressive network of guerrilla-peasant linkages, followed closely by Cuba, then by Guatemala, then Peru, with Bolivia far behind. Colombia remains a special case, for the spanning of discrete social worlds was not necessary in that country to spawn a powerful guerrilla movement.

Balance theory helps us to understand the difference between a peasantry that is "virgin soil" and one that is "occupied ground." If a political party is delivering on its promises in a region to peasants it has organized, or if hacendado-peasant relations are seen by peasants as reasonably reciprocal and paternal, then we may speak of favorable peasant attitudes toward party or landlord. In such a situation, the intrusion of guerrillas hostile to that party or landlord can only create cognitive dissonance; the guerrillas are therefore likely to be rejected.

If, however, peasants are hostile to government or landlord, conditions are more promising for insurgency. Here the guerrillas enter the scene as "the enemy of my enemy," and are likely to be welcomed. That shared hostility toward a common foe provides the basis for cooperative action. The case is more complex if the two groups are ethnically divided. Indian rejection of white-skinned intruders is a commonplace, based on firm historical experience. In such a meeting of worlds, the role of contact person is especially important (e.g., the cases of Albino Guzmán in Peru and Pascual Ixtapá in Guatemala).

Lacking this, guerrillas could use a phenomenological virtuoso. By this I mean a person who can move easily through many "social worlds," and readily communicate with many different types of people. Clearly the rural born and bred have an edge over their urban counterparts in this regard (e.g., Gabaldón and Zamora in Venezuela). Again and again, guerrillas in Peru, Bolivia, and elsewhere complained of their inability to get through to the peasantry, at times comparing them to stones. The social distance between the world of the urban-bred, college-educated guerrillas and the peasantry was enormous, as guerrillas like Héctor Béjar later realized. It should not surprise us, then, that the most successful guerrilla movements were typically led by men from rural areas, especially in Venezuela, Colombia, and Cuba.

In this respect Fidel Castro, scion of a rural estate owner, stands out as *the* phenomenological virtuoso. Many of his chroniclers, friend and foe alike, have remarked on his ability to move easily through many social worlds, to talk easily with both simple peasants and politicians. Perhaps he was assisted in this respect by the cultural homogeneity of Cuban society, an advantage that his counterparts in Indian areas of Peru, Bolivia, and Guatemala lacked. Even so, his personal gifts—charisma if you will—may well have been crucial to the success of the Cuban revolution.

The correlation between the intensity of preexisting guerrilla-peasant linkages and the strength of support for the guerrillas suggests that these attachments were yet one more basis for the expansion of peasant support. Such links are not forged simply through shared ideology, or even through offers of desired "goods and services," or most certainly through guerrilla terror against the peasantry. I have tried to demonstrate that diffuse personal ties involving legitimate authority (both formal and informal), kinship, friendships, personal influence, and shared ethnicity are basic, not peripheral, to understanding the process by which guerrilla leaders forge alliances with peasant cultivators. Parallel to Tilly's findings about the counterrevolutionary French of southern Anjou some 200 years ago, our best knowledge of the micro-processes involved in securing peasant support—i.e., information gleaned primarily from the memoirs of the guerrillas themselves—supports the thesis that such preexisting social ties are a central source of peasant support for guerrilla movements, by extension giving us clues as to the probable outcomes of guerrilla wars.

Thus, neither class structure alone, nor historical changes therein, exhaust the correlates of peasant support for guerrillas. Variations in regional political cultures, especially their sheer "ornery"-ness in the face of exactions and exertions by central government, are also related to regions' propensity to provide haven and support for the challengers to government, including those of the radical left. All three of those *regional* analyses, however, can ignore the micro-level of *community* studies only at their peril, for it is at the community level that the basic decisions—to support or not to support, to join or to remain apart—are made throughout the history of guerrilla conflicts.

Nonetheless, our analyses are not exhausted here (although the reader may be). Ultimately the outcomes of peasant revolutionary exertions, as Eric Wolf has so clearly argued,[64] hinge on events beyond the scope of local or regional rural society: they depend on events and classes beyond the rural milieu itself. The outcomes of guerrilla war behave in like fashion for, as we shall see in the next chapter, they depend fundamentally on the nonrural allies guerrilla movements obtain or lose through the course of the insurrection.

CHAPTER 8

Regime Weaknesses and the Emergence of Dual Power

> Fidel Castro's success wasn't really a military success. It was in
> the first place a moral victory among the people. . . . Castro didn't
> destroy his opponents. They collapsed like a rotten bone.
> —Claude Julien

UNDERSTANDING THE REVOLUTIONARY SITUATION

We have just surveyed the military strength of, and peasant support rendered
to, a variety of 1960s guerrilla movements. We have encountered wide variation in those elements. Yet are military strength and peasant support enough
to push a guerilla movement through to victory? Evidence suggests a negative
reply for Latin America, at least since World War II. Perhaps in other contexts, as in overwhelmingly agrarian China from 1927 to 1949, one could
make a strong case for the sufficiency of those two elements alone. However,
given Latin America's urban-tilted population distribution, and the relatively
small numbers involved in the insurgent conflicts, we are led to believe that
such a "Chinese solution" to the conflict is not possible: the urban sectors
cannot be ignored in light of the "low intensity" nature of the guerrilla wars.

Evidence from Latin America itself further strengthens such a theoretical
position, for we can in fact find cases in which both peasant support and
military strength were appreciable, but where those have not been enough to
bring rebels to the seat of power. In Colombia since the mid-1970s, the guerrillas' ranks have grown greatly, and numbered several thousand by the early
1980s, with fronts scattered throughout the nation. Yet at no time have the
rebels ever posed a serious threat to the power of incumbent governments or
the state. By the early 1980s, the Guatemalan insurgents also had a great deal
of peasant support and impressively large numbers, yet they too still did not
border on the seizure of power. Even in El Salvador, where several thousand
guerrillas and their political allies (in the *Frente Democrática Revolucionaria*—FDR) have come close to such a tipping point from 1980 to 1989, and
where fat rebel coffers plus deep and widespread peasant support keep the
movements' fires well stoked, by 1990 the guerrillas were not any nearer to
power than in 1981. Indeed, they were less near. In each of these cases, the
guerrillas were strongly rooted in parts of the countryside, but only weakly

planted among the townspeople. Why didn't central governments in *those* nations, like Batista's regime in Cuba, collapse in the face of such massive guerrilla opposition?

The element separating the Cuban revolution from those failures of later years is clearly the emergence of what Trotsky called "dual power," and what Charles Tilly has more systematically analyzed as "multiple sovereignty."[1] The distinctive feature of a revolutionary situation is that the incumbent governors no longer remain secure in their claims to rule. Instead, one or more new contenders emerge to challenge those claims. Multiple sovereignty exists when a substantial part of the subject population comes to regard (one or more of) the new contenders as "authority," and they come to obey the new contender's directives rather than those of the incumbent. Thus, in the Russian Revolution Lenin's Bolsheviks led their struggle with the cry of "All power to the Soviets!" In the French Revolution power was decisively shifted in the year 1789 from the monarchy to the newly formed National Assembly (jerry-built from parts of the Estates General). In the Mexican revolution there were multiple contenders for power, including groups led by Madero, Carranza, Zapata, Villa, and others. And in the Cuban revolution, as we shall see, authority shifted from Batista to Fidel Castro's revolutionary movement.

Following George Pettee, I would agree that "the transfer of consent by the passive members, in an advanced society, is a great act, the fundamental constituent act" of a revolution, and that the revolution properly speaking "begins with a sudden recognition by almost all the passive and active membership that the state no longer exists." Pettee further argues that revolutionary battles typically come "late" in the struggle, in the sense that the state has lost already the loyalty of even passive members of the populace.[2] In both Tilly's and Pettee's work, then, subjective and objective aspects of the transfer of authority become central to their analyses. Indeed, in both cases there exists a near-identity between the transfer of authority and/or loyalty, and that revolutionary "tipping point" at which regimes clearly seem to be crumbling.

In contrast, Theda Skocpol's comparative study of the "great revolutions" foregoes such emphases on authority and loyalty altogether. Instead she opts clearly for a "structural analysis" in which subjective views of "authority" have no place whatsoever. In her view, revolutions came about because the collapse of quasi-bureaucratic states in agrarian societies was paired with widespread peasant insurrections. (By states Skocpol means the formal organizations embodied in the executive, the civil bureaucracy, and the military.) New states were then rebuilt by organized revolutionary forces—the French Jacobins, Russian Bolsheviks, and Chinese Communists—who had little to do with those state collapses in the first place (hence the revolutionaries did not "make" the revolutions). Skocpol's states did not, however, collapse in the face of the "transfer of consent" or due to "the emergence of multiple sovereignty," but because of strong external pressures (especially wars) and because landed elites used footholds in the state apparatus to block necessary tax reforms that could strengthen the state.[3] In other words, pressures from external nation-states or from internal landed elites became unbearable, rather than opposition from the masses. As Skocpol makes abundantly clear, therefore, *regime weaknesses* make revolutions likely to occur.

Can we possibly reconcile these radically different views of revolution: the movement- and society-centered version of Tilly with the regime- or state-centered view of Skocpol? It seems that we can, and Skocpol has indicated one way to unite these two views. As she argues in her later analysis of the Iranian revolution against the shah, structural weaknesses (of another type) there did not alone bring down the state, which did fall to a revolutionary movement organized from below. In Iran, therefore, state weaknesses *plus* a conscious revolutionary movement brought down the state and brought in a revolutionary government. Indeed, one could draw certain rough parallels between the weaknesses of the Iranian and the Cuban political structures, and the importance of mass opposition in each case.[4] Although Skocpol doesn't use the term, her own analysis of the Iranian events strongly suggests the emergence of "dual power" there, centered geographically in the urban bazaars and socially in religious leaders, the mullahs.[5]

To unite Skocpol's and Tilly's analyses, then, we must specify the structural weaknesses of certain types of regimes that make them more (or less) vulnerable to revolution (Skocpol). Furthermore, we must convincingly *show* that multiple sovereignty emerged clearly in Cuba before 1959 and contributed to the revolutionaries' success (Tilly). Finally, we must establish some persuasive links between those two features, showing how those very regime weaknesses made it more likely that a mass resistance would emerge, strengthen itself, and bring about a revolutionary situation.[6] To pursue those aims carefully, the following analyses employ a consistent pattern of comparison and contrast between Cuba and our other five cases, highlighting the causes of the Cuban revolution.

Comparisons between Cuban revolutionary success and the Colombian, Guatemalan, and Salvadoran failures discussed above lead us to suspect strongly that some variable heretofore undealt with contributed to the Cuban revolutionaries' success. How, then, was Cuban society distinctive in a way that contributed to the rebels' victory? Some analysts have immediately seized upon two features of Cuban life that were highly distinctive: the overwhelming importance of sugar in the Cuban economy; and the exaggerated role of the United States in Cuban politics.[7] Yet the sugar workers remained largely outside the struggle until the very end, and the regime's major armed opposition came from the urban underground and from the guerrillas in the eastern hills;[8] it seems that no group was more *outside* the revolution than the sugar sector. Yes, Cuba had (and still has) a "sugar economy," yet we cannot glibly trot out that lonely fact to account for every other distinctive feature of Cuban history and society, no more than "the caste system" can explain every distinctive feature of Indian society.[9] As for the presence of the United States, the "expected" anti-imperialist rhetoric was muted throughout the struggle, and the opposition spilled far more ink and words about the 1940 constitution, free elections, and (most especially) the illegality of Batista's rule than it did on the subject of *Yanqui* imperialism.[10] Castro in early 1958 publicly rejected talk about nationalization of any part of the economy, including those portions under U.S. ownership ("at best, a cumbersome instrument" was his phrase).[11] Therefore, there is no proximate link of either the sugar economy or anti-imperialist sentiment to the Cuban revolution. However, as I shall argue below, one can make a case for a more distant contribution of both sugar and the U.S. presence in weakening the chances that Cuba would develop strong political institutions.

Cuban Exceptionalism: The Polity and Society

To understand why the Cuban revolutionaries (alone until the 1979 Sandinista victory) came to power, we must therefore undertake a less superficial *comparative* political sociology of the various cases, in the hopes of revealing those distinctive features of Cuban politics and society that *did* contribute decisively to rebel success. Indeed, since many nations have witnessed militarily strong guerillas with wide and deep peasant support, and since only the Cuban guerrillas had seized power through 1978, these special Cuban conditions might well be considered the "hinge variable" that decisively sealed the insurgents' victory. Moreover, in a later chapter of this work, I will argue that there are sharply defined structural similarities between Cuba and Nicaragua that contributed in *both* cases to the rebel seizure of power.

What are regimes, and what makes some of them weak? By regime I mean a patterned complex relating the state to civil society. Skocpol's agrarian bureaucratic regimes tie the upper class to the state by office-holding and the peasantry to the state through taxation. In democratic regimes, political parties are brought into government, and hence (presumed) control of the state, through mass popular elections. Military regimes, by contrast, tend to operate usually with (sometimes tacit, sometimes open) upper-class support and maintain their control over the state by coercion. Unusually here, part of the state (the military) has seized control over government, especially the law-generating capacity of legislatures and executives. Weak regimes are likely to be present where one or more of the following conditions prevail: (1) small numbers of persons involved in making political decisions; (2) low levels of solidarity among such decision makers; (3) low levels of stable commitment to that group or organization by other members of civil society or the state. Hence a weak regime will be one evincing splits within the polity itself, or weak commitments to the government by its "supporters" (e.g., parts of the armed forces or members of the upper class).

In contrast to national politics and to guerrilla movements in the rest of

Latin America, including our five contrasting cases, the Cuban regime and opposition displayed a number of distinctive features. For the moment I will simply list them, and then try to give some theoretical shape to the resultant "laundry list":

1. *The Cuban middle and upper classes* were both relatively weak and incohesive, even when compared to other Latin American nations. The landed elite was probably weak because ownership of capital (sugar mills and associated rail lines) was more critical to the sugar economy than was ownership of land. In addition, the upper class was socially divided among Cuban, Spanish immigrant, and United States' property owners. The middle class in Cuba was exceptionally weak and has been described as "parasitic" and "dependent."

2. *Cuban political parties* were very weakly institutionalized and never consolidated themselves on a class, ethnic, or religious social base. They were neither oligarchical nor ideological in nature. "Opportunistic," "corrupt," and "venal" are recurring adjectives used to describe them. This applies to the Liberals and Conservatives who emerged following independence, as well as to later political entrants such as the *Auténticos*.[12]

3. *The Cuban military* was institutionally weak and personally controlled. The armed forces, already burdened by a weak command structure, succumbed in the 1930s to the first *sergeants'* revolt in history. Ex-Sergeant Batista then established his personal, very unprofessional control over the military at that time; it became his personal army, ensuring his control over the polity as well. By the time of Batista's return to power in the 1950s he had lost some of that control, but the military was disintegrating from the top down, with loyalties focused at the level of the camp, not the institution.[13]

4. *A patrimonial praetorian regime* or *mafiacracy*[14] emerged out of these peculiar preconditions when Batista consolidated power following his graduated coup of 1933–1934. Such a regime unites personal rule over the military and hence the state; suppression of political parties and their competition; and individualized patrimonial dispensing of rewards and favors, along with massive corruption.

5. *Moderate messages and mass media*: The "revolutionary" opposition in Cuba strongly emphasized constitutional, democratic, and electoral symbols in its ideological struggle with the Batista regime, and deemphasized radical social and economic changes. Mass-media coverage and access strongly favored the fortunes of the opposition in Cuba. Particularly favorable were treatment by the domestic mass-circulation periodicals and by the foreign press.

6. *The mass revolutionary coalition* that eventually overthrew Batista was not a "class-based" movement but drew most heavily from the peasantry and middle class, and on large portions of the working and upper classes as well. It was revolution of national sentiment far more than it was a class war. At the very end, virtually all Cubans supported the dictator's downfall.

What theoretical coherence can we give to that list of Cuba's sociopolitically distinctive features? I have condensed and summarized the argument embodied in the sections that follow as figure 8–1. In brief: (1) The inter-related weaknesses of Cuban class structure and political institutions paved the way for the seizure and consolidation of power by a personal, military dictator. However, the very personalism and corruption of Batista's rule structurally pressed those excluded from power, including the middle and upper classes, into a cross-class alliance with groups in society who were more typically aggrieved. The cross-class nature of the opposition led to a moderation of its programs and rhetoric, and secured it easy access to "re-spectable" mass media. The "revolutionary situation" and "dual power" that ensued pervaded all classes and institutions in Cuba, resulting in the mass overthrow of a dictator, bereft in the end of any secure class or institutional allies. (2) Absent those striking weaknesses in class structure and/or political institutions, regimes emerged in a variety of other forms, including electoral democracy; traditional upper-class oligarchy; or allied military-cum- upper-class rule. Electoral democracy tended to divide the government's opponents into a clear right and left, thus lending such systems "moderating" legiti-macy. The other two types of regime, without the mass desertion of the upper and middle classes that occurred in Cuba, tended to produce a clearer form of class conflict against the government and its supporters, rather than producing a cross-class opposition. Such conflict polarized the parties involved, leading to a radicalization of the guerrilla-based opposition and its consequent relega-tion to the domestic political extreme left, without moderating allies or voices in the mass media.

I will discuss each feature in turn. While focusing in detail on Cuba, I will analyze the other five cases closely enough to bring into relief their contrasts to the Cuban revolution. We can understand as well the relation between those six features named above and my preceding theoretical discussion of Skocpol and Tilly. The first four items limn the structural weaknesses of the prerevolutionary Cuban political regime (Skocpol), while the last two help us to understand why dual power emerged in Cuba under such circumstances (Tilly).

WEAK MIDDLE AND UPPER CLASSES?

> One has the general feeling that Cuban society has not "set" or "jelled."
>
> —Lowry Nelson (1950)

The Middle Class and Politics

The experience of other Latin American nations suggests middle-class pat-terns that could have emerged in Cuba had conditions there been different. Elsewhere in Latin America the middle class, *qua* class, has tended to relate to national politics in one of two manners.

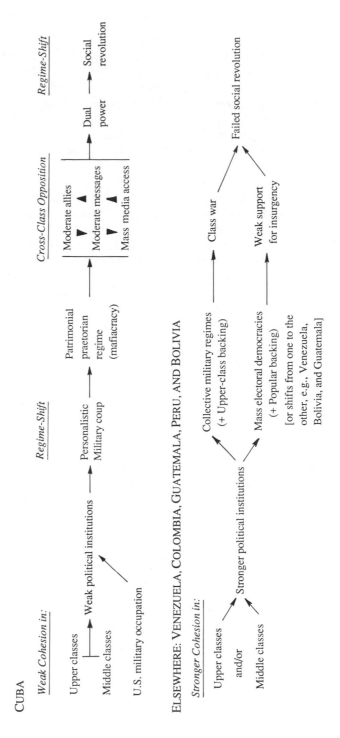

CUBA

Weak Cohesion in:

Upper classes
→ Weak political institutions ——→ Personalistic
Middle classes   Military coup

U.S. military occupation

Regime-Shift

Personalistic
Military coup ——→ Patrimonial
                    praetorian
                    regime
                    (mafiacracy)

Cross-Class Opposition

Moderate allies
Moderate messages
Mass media access ——→ Dual
                        power

Regime-Shift

Dual ——→ Social
power   revolution

ELSEWHERE: VENEZUELA, COLOMBIA, GUATEMALA, PERU, AND BOLIVIA

Stronger Cohesion in:

Upper classes
and/or   → Stronger political institutions
Middle classes

Collective military regimes
(+ Upper-class backing) ——→ Class war

Mass electoral democracies
(+ Popular backing)
[or shifts from one to the
other, e.g., Venezuela,
Bolivia, and Guatemala] ——→ Weak support
                              for insurgency ——→ Failed social revolution

Figure 8-1. Social Origins of Regime Weaknesses in Cuba: A Comparative View

First, they may make their political entrance as the backers of parties pursuing clearly middle-class interests, who campaign against upper-class dictatorial control of the polity, and who often secure working-class electoral allies in their bid to open up the polity to nonelites. As Barrington Moore put it for Europe and the United States: "No bourgeois, no democracy." This pattern seems to fit the nineteenth-century British extension of the suffrage, and also the rise of clearly middle-class parties such as the Radical Civic Union in Argentina, the Radicals in Chile, the Colorados of Uruguay and, in more recent decades, several Christian Democratic parties throughout the region.[15]

A second possible pattern of middle-class entry into the political arena, which seems to have occurred later and in the less developed countries in Latin America, is that of the populist party, led by men of the "rising" middle class, but clearly pursuing more radical programs than our first type, and drawing heavy political strength from the lower classes, including the peasantry at times. Such parties look more like "mass" assaults on "oligarchic" rule than do the middle-class parties and often contain radical or socialistic reform proposals, however watered-down their execution may be once the party comes into power.[16]

This second pattern could take an electoral or a revolutionary form. I will discuss the electoral variant below, yet revolutionary examples are clearly at hand as well, in the cases of both Mexico and Bolivia. In each instance, one could understand the revolution as a populist "explosion" of the masses, with middle-class leadership, against intransigent, upper-class–based, dictatorial regimes in which the middle class had no political leverage.[17]

The Cuban middle class fit neither of these patterns. Neither the middle-class party nor the populist party emerged there. Instead an ex-sergeant exploited the weakness of the middle class as a political actor to gain successive control of the military and the state in the 1930s, thus ending a period of indecisive politics in which no class-based party had firmly ensconced itself in the national political arena.

There is wide agreement among Cubanists that the Cuban middle class did not come to constitute a class for itself, either in the social-psychological sense or in the political sphere.[18] The Cuban middle class was relatively large at 22 percent of the employed population (compare Argentina then at 36 percent and Brazil at 15 percent). However, it was overwhelmingly concentrated in the liberal professions and most especially in the state bureaucracy, the latter often in patronage-plum, make-work, or no-work positions.[19] This bureaucratic-employment pattern was not unusual in Latin America, save perhaps in degree. Cuba's distinctiveness lay in the unprofessionalism and unreliability of such employment, in the face of the massive spoils system that constituted much of government. Domínguez has aptly named it "neopatrimonialism," that is, a modern variant of Weber's ideal-typical political system where government posts and authority are treated as private resources. Political favorites of the regime-of-the-moment prospered from such posts, while the politically outcast might find themselves out of jobs to boot. In Farber's words, the Cuban middle class "sought bureaucratic employment as a way of avoiding poverty" and were "on the whole, dependent and parasitic."[20]

Attempts to consolidate a new, populist, anticorrupt, middle-class party were shattered after the 1951 suicide of Ortodoxo party leader Eddy Chibás, which was followed by a "galloping disintegration" of Cuban political life.[21] Paradoxically, although it was middle class voters who largely brought the winners to victory in national elections, those winners did not represent middle-class interests.[22] Socially and hence politically the middle classes were "fragmented." Once in power, therefore, the governments could safely ignore many middle-class interests with something akin to impunity. One analyst goes so far as to suggest that Cuban governments alternated in pursuing classic conservative policies (such as protection of property and income, we must assume) or in "socializing" policies, such as the protective and regulative legislation under the first Batista government.[23]

In contrast to the Cuban pattern, Colombia's middle class did have a hard entrepreneurial core in Caldas and Antioquia. On the other hand, the bulk of the bureaucratic and professional middle class, Smith argued, was composed of downwardly mobile cadet sons of the Colombian upper class, whose intellectual and political sights were still set firmly on the social world they had lost.[24] Hence their sense of class identity was set firmly by that experience of "sliding." Politically, Colombia's middle class, like all other social classes, had been vertically integrated into one of Colombia's dominant political parties, the Liberals and the Conservatives. These were the most strongly institutionalized parties in all Latin America, dating back at least to 1849 and struggles over the role of the Catholic Church in Colombian society. Each party was headed typically by members of the Colombian upper class but was multi-class in terms of composition and voter support. Middle-class supporters of the victorious party could participate in the patrimonial spoils that each party could distribute upon gaining state power.[25]

In Venezuela, the middle class had entered politics in the second, "populist" manner indicated above, providing the leadership of at least one mass party. The entire Venezuelan "Generation of 28" (drawn largely from middle-class backgrounds) appeared earlier in this century as principled resisters to the historical Venezuelan pattern of regional, *caudillo*, upper-class rule.[26] The most important populist party born during this period was Acción Democrática. AD was a populist party for, despite espousing middle-class interests such as nationalism (in petroleum policy) and expansion of education, it sank deep roots in the organized working class and itself helped organize the peasantry.[27] The results by the early 1960s were as I indicated in chapter 3:

The AD government sustained itself largely through some middle-class (especially professional and intellectual) support, important labor-union backing, and widespread peasant support (the last kept them in power in the 1963 elections).[28]

The Peruvian case also exemplifies the middle-class–led populist party that enters politics espousing a populist program against oligarchic rule. Víctor Raúl Haya de la Torre's APRA party was born in the 1920s and consolidated in the 1930s, stressing its *indigenismo*, anti-Yankeeism, and "mass" opposition to "oligarchic" rule. "APRA first made its appearance as a protest movement, as a campaign to win integration into political life for the new classes which had emerged since 1919 (industrial workers, white-collar workers, students). . . ." The *aprista* leadership of the 1930s was born from newly formed "political clienteles" drawn largely from student and white-collar organizations and from trade unions.[29]

The APRA party *was* the opposition to "oligarchic" rule until the 1950s. While regionally strongest in the north, where it combined blue-collar and white-collar backing, it also had substantial lower–middle-class support in the center and south. Its 1950s policy of *"entente cordiale"* with political actors such as Manuel Prado and General Manuel Odría, however, lost it the support of many students and some middle-class groups, providing political space for other mass parties to compete. APRA's main electoral opponent from 1956 until the 1980s has been Fernando Belaúnde's Acción Popular (AP). If we might say, very roughly, that APRA's white-collar support was from the "old" and the lower middle class, then the AP's leadership came largely from the "new," professional-technocratic middle classes, exemplified by its architect-leader. AP also rapidly became a populist party, however, and in three national elections showed a strong electoral following among the peasantry of the southern Sierra.[30]

In Bolivia we encounter the revolutionary version of populism. The Bolivian revolution of 1952 was led by men of the middle classes and the tin miners, and was consolidated by peasant action in the countryside, as well as by miners' union activism leading to the nationalization of the tin mining industry. All their grievances were focused through the MNR, "a party of intellectuals and young middle-class nationalists, hardened by the struggle into a truly radical force. They carried with them the small urban middle class, and were the *de facto* leaders of the labouring classes . . . they still had very few connections with the peasants."[31] This Movimiento Nacionalista Revolucionario had come into being with the "intention of winning power from the oligarchy," [whom they viewed as] "'the puppet of foreign interests,' for the benefit of a 'national' urban petty bourgeoisie." Through its later agrarian reforms, the MNR developed among the peasantry the strong following that it had lacked in 1952.[32]

Once again, Guatemala remains the odd case out, with a ten-year, truncated experiment in populist rule. Guatemala has never made the decisive breakthrough to middle-class political power. Not that the attempt wasn't made. Prior to 1944, it didn't even take a Marxist to observe in Guatemalan politics that "[g]overnment was manipulated in the interests of the large landowners, the foreign corporations, and the small upper class in Guatemala City."[33] The 1944 ousting of dictator Jorge Ubico, in contrast, was clearly led by the middle class, including students and junior army officers, and it led to a ten-year Guatemalan experiment with middle-class–led populist rule. That honeymoon came to an end with the U.S.-orchestrated invasion of Guatemala in 1954. Ever since 1954, the Guatemalan military, more than *any* social class, has been the "arbiter of Guatemalan politics," as more than one Marxist analyst has been forced to concede.[34] The middle class has thus never established a foothold in the Guatemalan political arena, which is not too surprising given the relatively low level of economic development of highly rural Guatemala. Indeed, that both the Bolivian revolution and the Guatemalan "revolution" [1944–1954] gave way to conservative military coups suggests that their social structures were "too underdeveloped" to sustain such populist regimes.

The Upper Class in Politics

Our comparative treatment of the roles of upper classes in politics requires far less commentary. The traditional stereotype of Latin American societies is one in which the upper class exercises untrammelled hegemony over the masses in national politics, through civilian or military dictatorship, or through its control of dominant "oligarchic" parties.[35] From my preceding comments on the middle class in politics, we can see that such an image is far from accurate for several Latin American societies, yet has still been historically accurate for others at certain times.

The Cuban upper classes never exercised such control over the Cuban polity, and most certainly not in any kind of unified, cohesive manner. They ruled neither before nor during Batista's regimes in any kind of systematic way. A fundamental, tripartite division split that class sharply in a way that strongly impeded unified upper-class action. The three prongs composing that upper class were Cuban entrepreneurs, immigrant Spanish landowners and businessmen, and U.S. businessmen controlling land, capital, and sugar mills.[36] Thus, for the first thirty years of independence, Domínguez could describe a Cuba where the sharp social cleavages between classes had little to do with any political differences.[37] The upper classes slowly yielded whatever collective political clout they had to parties elected largely by middle-class voters, as Raggi observed. Finally, Batista's rule heralded no initiation or return of upper-class rule, for Batista was certainly "not the man of the bourgeoisie."[38]

Virtually all analysts reject the notion that Batista "represented" upper-class rule, and many have documented the turn against Batista within that class, especially beginning around 1956.[39]

If descriptions of upper-class political rule in Latin America often embody more than a bit of caricature, nonetheless there is a large kernel of truth in such descriptions. Not only ideologues, but analysts have written (sometimes to temper such descriptions) of the "Fourteen Families" who ruled El Salvador, the "Twenty-four Families" who governed likewise in Colombia, and of "the oligarchy" who ruled Peru until recent decades. Similar comments have abounded for other nations as well. For our purposes, it is highly indicative that no such commentary appeared about Cuba, for its upper classes had never displayed the kind of unity that could lead even polemicists to such a characterization of the Cuban polity. In contrast, such images at least had the air of plausibility in several of our cases.

Colombia and Peru are both cases in point, although they embody upper-class political cohesion differently. In Colombia, the vertically integrated political parties have always competed for political advantage, but *each* party has been overwhelmingly dominated at the top by men of upper-class background, elected though they might have been by the votes of the middle class, workers, and even peasants.[40] Hence there was a kernel of truth to some Colombians' observations about "Twenty-four Families." In Peru, political domination by "oligarchic" parties or individuals was far less competitive, and the exclusion of meaningful middle-class or populist participation in politics, let alone that of peasants and workers, continued well into this century (the banning of APRA for a quarter century is the most important example). Moreover, Dennis Gilbert has superbly documented kinship, economic, and other social ties among the members of the old Peruvian upper class, putting considerable flesh on the bones of that skeletal concept, "the Peruvian oligarchy."[41] These respective observations, I should add, do not exclude divisions within the Colombian and Peruvian upper classes.[42] In neither of these cases, however, can one detect the absence of upper-class political cohesion that appeared in Cuba.

In Bolivia and Guatemala by the 1940s, one could reasonably describe their political systems as upper-class dominated. The paths those two societies took from that period on have sharply diverged. In Bolivia, upper-class rule was rooted out: with the 1952 revolution; with the nationalization of the tin mines; and with the rural revolution involving land invasions, refusals to pay rents, and continuing agrarian reforms. In Guatemala, however, as I detailed above, a middle-class–led populist assault on upper-class control of the polity began in 1944 and ended in 1954. Since then, the military has been the effective arbiter of Guatemalan politics, described by one group of Marxist analysts as "Garrison Guatemala." Upper-class property owners do retain a great deal of economic power in that nation, however, and a partial merger of that class with the upper ranks of the officer corps since the 1960s has produced a further coincidence of interests in conservative policies.

Finally, Venezuelan politics for much of this century has been dominated by the issue of oil. Since the petroleum was in foreign hands until the 1970s, the ultimate source of national wealth did not create a domestic upper class, but rather a foreign enclave. Petroleum revenues therefore enhanced the power of the state and foreign investors at the expense of the older regional *caudillos*, and the state increased its bargaining power in that "dependent" relationship from the 1940s until the oil was finally nationalized in the 1970s. The long rule of Juan Vicente Gómez (1908–1935) broke the back of regional agrarian *caudillos* in Venezuela, and with increasing federal oil revenues Venezuela came to resemble a "rentier state," with true power residing in the polity rather than in the domestic upper class.[43] It should thus be unsurprising, as I noted above, that no Venezuelan political party identifies itself as conservative (in the classic sense, as in Chile or Colombia), for such conservative parties have been the havens of the traditional upper class in most Latin American societies.

If we look back on these extensive comparative comments, the striking pattern is how politically weak *both* the middle class *and* the upper class were in Cuban society. None of our other five nations displayed such a pattern. More striking still was that Cuba could display such a pattern despite being one of the four or five most developed nations in Latin America, and the most developed tropical nation in the entire world.[44] While Venezuela might have a weak upper class, and while Guatemala was too underdeveloped to have developed a politically strong middle class, only Cuba displayed a striking political weakness in both of those key social classes.

The result of this odd pattern was the opening up of Cuban "political space." In other nations, that ideological and political space was routinely occupied by upper-class parties, upper-class–controlled parties (Colombia), middle-class parties, or populist parties. No such ideological parties emerged in Cuba, and I believe we must trace that failure to the failure of Cuban society to "set or jell," as Lowry Nelson so aptly put it.

Strength and Weakness in Political Institutions

> The failure of parliamentarism in Cuba was a common enough phenomenon. But the complete failure to crystallize durable, substantial political parties was exceptional in Latin America.
>
> —Robin Blackburn

Cuban politics were weakly institutionalized in this century and had weak and incohesive social support bases. By this I mean that each of the political parties lacked a strong history of stable political contention; each lacked a strong ideological basis for its participation in politics; and each lacked a firm, dependable support base in the population, whether based on class, race, or religion.[45] On this matter, Domínguez, Farber, Thomas, and Blackburn are agreed, so it would be foolhardy to disagree with such a strange assortment of analytical bedfellows.[46]

The Cuban state had become a massive, direct provider of individual job opportunities, and since such privileges shifted rapidly with political power-shifts, the bureaucratic middle class could be expected to shift political allegiance readily to whichever party controlled the patronage strings of the moment. This surely in part explains the hemorrhage of post-electoral party switching by just-elected officials that Domínguez has documented for pre-revolutionary Cuba.[47] That is, despite periodic calls for moral and political renewal (voiced by the Auténticos in the thirties and by the Ortodoxos after World War II), a common response of Cuban party members to the electoral (or nonelectoral) success of their opponents was a transfer of party loyalties (generally to the victors), so as to take part in the distribution of state spoils that the government controlled. The strength of this pattern was probably without parallel in Latin America. The Ortodoxos, to whom many Cubans looked in the early 1950s for a moral reforging of Cuban politics, fell apart following the suicide of leader Eduardo Chibás in August 1951, but Fidel Castro tried (with some success) to gather together the remnants of the Chibasist Ortodoxos into his 26th of July movement (M-26).[48]

Why were Cuban politics so weakly institutionalized? Here, if anywhere, sugar and the United States may have played some role. One could argue that the very wealth of the Cuban sugar economy could produce both the incomes and the tax revenues to make Cuba one of the four most prosperous Latin American societies by the 1920s, continuing into the 1950s, despite a slow-growth economy.[49] Some of that prosperity was funneled into government spending in the economy (of which only a fraction went to the military). Much of it supported the massive, patronage-laden, civil-service bureaucracy that dominated Cuban middle-class employment. By the end of 1949 there were 186,450 persons on the active state payroll, plus about 30,000 persons drawing state pensions, all in a society of only six million people. President Ramón Grau San Martín was elected in 1944; by June 1946 there had been 10,000 personnel changes in the Ministry of Education alone, and 4,000 employees therein had no duties whatsoever.[50] There seems to be a link, then, between the taxes generated by King Sugar and the patrimonial bureaucracy so typical of Cuba.

Cuba's late and violent war for independence concluded in 1898, coming at the precise time when United States' power was rapidly growing in the region, a power far greater than the United States had exercised during the earlier wave of Latin American independence struggles (1808–1826). Moreover, Cuba had had strong economic ties to the United States while still a colony.[51] With the United States' intervention in that war, Cuba became a virtual political dependency of the United States from 1898 until at least the 1930s. The Platt Amendment (1901) limited Cuban political sovereignty and gave the United States the right to intervene in Cuban politics under certain circumstances. And intervene it did, regularly, often at the request of Cuban political actors. (Similar patterns of U.S. domination and intervention in Nicaragua, Haiti, and the Dominican Republic in this century also seemed to produce weakened party systems, as well as the eventual rise to power of Batista-like dictators: Somoza, Duvalier, and Trujillo.) Any fundamental attempt to institutionalize political conflict in the form of stable parties with stable support bases could thus be undermined by an external actor who required no such domestic support. Under such conditions—the United States willing to intervene and domestic political losers prepared to invite intervention—political parties could hardly be independent guarantors of politically based rewards to stable constituencies.[52]

The very weakness of such political parties, in Cuba and those other three nations, could make possible a new regime that did not depend on party loyalties. How strikingly weak Batista's political opposition looks up to the mid-1950s, if we compare it to Peronist opposition to Argentine military rule, APRA resistance to Peruvian military rule, or multi-party opposition to military rule in Venezuela during the 1950s. Once dictatorial rule was in place, such institutional weaknesses impeded the formation of any kind of politically powerful, collective opposition. Weak political institutions thus opened the door for a dictator who could close the doors of power behind him after he had entered, yet still continue an individualized patronage system. To ensure control, he could depend heavily on the military, making it by far the strongest, best-organized political actor.[53]

How does this pattern compare to the politics of our other five nations, where the guerrillas did *not* come to power? While the 1960s guerrillas in other countries did face dictators at times, none of the governments they faced were so thoroughly personalistic in both political and military control as was that of Cuba in the 1950s. Presidents Betancourt (1959–1964) and Leoni (1964–1969) of Venezuela and Peru's Belaúnde (1963–1968) were elected in mass popular voting, each with a core of support among the *campesino* population; similar patterns obtained in the more restricted election of Bolivia's Barrientos (1966), in an OAS-overseen vote. The Colombian presidents were all products of the National Front electoral agreement (supported eighteen to one in a national plebiscite in 1957) that parceled out political posts between the Liberals and Conservatives from 1958 to 1974. Guatemala is the exception, since the military or certain factions thereof ruled society through electoral façades from 1954 until 1985; yet even there the one relatively open (1966) presidential election, won by civilian Julio Méndez Montenegro, came at a critical period and politically weakened the insurgents.[54]

Political parties also functioned more effectively in most of the other five nations, to mediate between social groups and the allocation of political power. Colombia had the oldest political loyalties, known there as "hereditary hatreds," to the Conservative and Liberal parties, despite rising abstention rates in the 1960s. In Peru, the diverse interparty competition so visible in the 1980s' national elections took shape in the 1960s, with participation by Communists, military populists (General Manuel Odría's party), erstwhile "revolutionaries" (APRA), and the new techno-populists of Belaúnde's AP. In Venezuela, *Acción Democrática* was born during the depression and grew through mass mobilization in the 1940s and thereafter. Its rival COPEI took shape in the 1940s, broadened its base of support in the 1960s, and captured the presidency in 1968, producing a very strong two-party–dominated system. In Bolivia, mass loyalties to the MNR were born with that party's leadership of the 1952 revolution, and members of that party have been the most prominent ever since (e.g. Victor Paz Estenssoro). In Guatemala, regular elections under military rule highlighted the otherwise obscure divisions within the military, especially between the far-right groups associated with the 1954 invasion and more "moderate" generals.[55]

This comparative overview suggests that only Guatemala had relatively weak political institutions plus weak social support for political actors during the guerrilla period. Given the strength of its guerrilla movement, therefore, we would expect Guatemala, apart from Cuba, to have come closest to a political "tipping point" in the guerrillas' struggle for power. That is precisely what we find. While there was no period in Colombia, Venezuela, Peru, or even Bolivia when the incumbent regime was seriously challenged for power by the revolutionaries, Guatemalan evidence does indeed suggest a strong *political* challenge to the incumbents in 1965–1966, which I will discuss further below. As we know, the guerrillas did not in fact come to power, yet in that year or two the Guatemalan guerrilla movement came closest to mounting a severe challenge to an incumbent government in the entire twenty-year period from Castro to the Sandinistas.

We thus have a continuum: a very strong revolutionary challenge to the state in Cuba, a substantial one in Guatemala, but only weak ones elsewhere. The strength of the revolutionary challenges correlates inversely with the strength of party, military, government, and/or state institutions in those nations. Cuban conditions, combining weak political institutions with a personal rather than collective form of dictatorship, paved the way for the Batista regime to fall to the "revolutionary" opposition. Guatemalan politics combined weak institutions with a more collective form of dictatorship, and that military regime faced a strong revolutionary challenge in the mid-1960s. That challenge, however, weakened in the face of a reform-minded civilian's election to the presidency in 1966 and disintegrated under a concerted military counterinsurgency campaign in 1966–1967. In Colombia, Venezuela, Peru, and Bolivia, however, national (electoral) politics all had strong social bases, and incumbent governments could thus claim to speak for "the people" during their guerrilla struggles. Political rule was collective in most cases, and electoral in all, and hence less vulnerable to political attacks from below. The partial exception, Barrientos in Bolivia, ruled with substantial military collaboration and with strong regional peasant support. Since he had run as the MNR's vice-presidential candidate in the 1964 elections, many peasants identified him as the continuer, guarantor, and even renewer of the MNR's revolutionary rule.[56] He, too, enjoyed at least some of the MNR's revolutionary "halo effect." Even had he lacked such support, moreover, Ché Guevara's guerrillas posed no substantial domestic political challenge.

Although there is more to the political strength of the regimes in our last four cases than elected governments, such elections contributed greatly to the weaknesses of the revolutionary opposition, since the reformist option seemed to provide the opposition with an alternative path (even in Guatemala in 1966). Hence Ché Guevara's early warning, that one should never seek to unseat an elected government through guerrilla warfare, is largely borne out by the evidence. That Ché abandoned this thesis, in order to begin a continental peasant revolution in the jungles of Bolivia against an elected hero of the Bolivian peasantry, only attests to the invulnerability of ideological impulses to accurate social theorizing. The desire for active "praxis" apparently overcame the desire for accurate theory.

THE MILITARY AS A POLITICAL INSTITUTION

> The deterioration of political parties . . . and the relative meaninglessness of suffrage reduced the value of civilian political organizations. The armed forces quickly filled this vacuum. . . .
>
> . . . army leadership was politically and socially afloat, lacking legitimacy in the political, economic, and social sources of power on the island.
>
> —Louis A. Pérez, Jr.,
> *Army Politics in Cuba, 1898–1958*

I wish now to relate the preceding two discussions to the causes, nature, and consequences of military rule in Cuba, in comparative perspective. I wish to argue that Cuba had three distinctive military features that paved the way for the revolutionary successes of the 1950s. First, Cuban military intervention was neither that of upper-class defense nor one in pursuit of middle-class interests, both of which appeared in most Latin American nations in the nineteenth and twentieth centuries, respectively. Second, Cuban military intervention appeared as the occupation of a relative political "vacuum," one in which other collective political actors, especially political parties, were relatively weak. Third, Cuba's military, since its inception, had been constantly politicized by government intervention in institutional matters, and thus had never developed the independent morale and solidarity typical of other Latin armed forces. The second feature "opened the door" for Cuban military intervention, but the first and third features made it highly unlikely that a Cuban military government could defeat a revolutionary opposition.

Above I discussed two paths of the middle class into Latin American politics. However, a third pathway of the middle class into political influence or power is through what José Nun has called the "middle class military coup." Pairing Nun's in-depth treatment of Latin American cases with Samuel Huntington's general theory of political praetorianism, we can argue that, in the later stages of development, middle-class coups that earlier were progressive in bringing the middle sectors into politics, become conservative, or "guardian coups," as they prevent lower-class–based parties from gaining their own power. These theories account well for the highly conservative coups in the relatively developed "Southern Cone" in the 1960s and 1970s.[57] However, despite Cuba's high levels of development, no one has made a persuasive case that the Sergeants' Revolt and subsequent coup in 1933–1934 fit that model, especially given the progressive legislation Batista sponsored in the 1930s and 1940s. The Cuban middle class, as we have seen, was too politically incohesive to generate a compelling clamor for such a *golpe*. Instead, Batista's coup more simply refracted the political weakness of all other collective political actors. If anything, Batista's coup reflects his adroit advocacy of internal "military populism," in setting the enlisted men against the officer corps.[58] Several authors have even noted the revolutionary overtones in lower- and working-class NCOs overthrowing an officer corps whose elite was drawn from the upper class, Batista's military then establishing a political regime pursuing populist programs in the 1930s.[59] Therefore, the military history of twentieth-century Cuba is a *counter*example to the model of the "middle-class coup," distinguishing it sharply from many other Latin American nations, including our five contrasting cases.

With regard to "political vacuums," a number of scholars have suggested that the prominence of the armed forces in politics reflects negative aspects of the social structures of less developed nations. In this view, the absence of any other highly organized social and political actors leaves a political vacuum that the tightly organized and highly disciplined armed forces are tailor-made to fill.[60] In opposition to such a logic, which he terms "the developmentalist model," Nun has argued *against* its uncritical extension to Latin America from its original purpose in interpreting Afro-Asian politics.[61] A century and a half since independence has given to many Latin American countries national political institutions that are often lacking in African nations, in particular. Cuban politics, however, *did* display institutional weaknesses that bore structural similarities to that Afro-Asian model: the Cuban military did indeed occupy a relatively empty "political space."[62] It became strong in politics because other collective political actors were weak. My previous discussion of political parties in our other five cases clearly showed a much higher level of party institutionalization elsewhere. The exception, Guatemala, occurred in a nation where military rule was stabilized by a strong alliance made with that nation's upper class.

There is a last feature of the Cuban military to consider: the weakness of the military as a cohesive, independent institution. This declaration may appear to contradict my previous statement about the Cuban military as a strong political actor in the absence of collectively strong political opponents. Yet each statement is a relative one: compared to Cuban political parties, the Cuban army was a strong political actor; yet compared to the institutional history of other Latin American armed forces, the Cuban army was exceptionally weak.

In Cuba, the military from its birth had been weakened by the attempts of early presidents to politicize and personally control the armed forces.[63] Gerardo Machado (1925–1933) also weakened the army by bypassing the U.S.-trained officer corps through direct, suborning appeals to the sergeants, and one author states simply that the weakening of the army's command structure clearly begins with Machado.[64] Machado continued political turnover of the officer corps as well. Moreover, fully 56 percent of the officer corps had come up through the ranks. This both weakened the authority of the officer corps and led to an unusual reliance upon and strength within the NCO and enlisted ranks.[65]

Following Machado's fall, we must seek the causes for the Sergeants' Revolt of September 1933 in the already weakened officer corps and in the peculiar strength of the army's lower echelons. Both of these patterns seem unique to Cuba within Latin America. In a short period of time the upper levels of the officer corps, drawn largely from the old Cuban upper classes, were effectively dissolved, when they refused to accept an opportunity for reincorporation. A new officer corps was then drawn from the lower and working classes in society.[66]

All observers agree about the aftermath of Batista's seizure of army power: he converted the armed forces into a personal machine for his personal rule.[67] To put it simply, he continued and extended the *machadista* program to its logical conclusion, but with a sergeant rather than a politician in charge. As a direct outgrowth of such control, the army never developed independent institutional morale and solidarity, and could never claim to represent the *patria*, for all Cubans knew otherwise: It was the personal tool of Batista. Batista extended further the privileges and exemptions of the officer corps that Machado had begun, and officers were promoted, demoted, and dismissed on the basis of their personal relationship to Batista, rather than on the basis of military professionalism.[68] Batista did have some problems, however, in bringing the military completely to heel, and especially in his later period of rule (1952–1958) personal factionalism grew while simultaneously demands for professionalization of the armed forces came from the *puros* (purists) in the officer corps.[69] The rebellious bent of the *puros* came to the surface in 1956 with the exposed plot and arrest of Colonel Ramón Barquín López, and in 1957 with the Cienfuegos Naval Revolt.[70]

Nonetheless, the army mostly held together as long as it problems were basically those of controlling civil society. Its unity was based largely on "corruption" and "opportunism," in Farber's estimation. That unity had had little challenge in the early 1950s, for the Auténticos and the Ortodoxos virtually collapsed as organized political opponents after Batista's seizure of power. That fragile military unity, however, could not stand the acid test of the army in the role for which it was, after all, designed. When confronted, not with collecting graft payments or enjoying military privileges and perquisites, but with real combat, the armed forces simply "collapsed" or "just evaporated." Moreover, the army itself began to experience "revulsion" at Batista's terror tactics and suffered a sharp drop in morale when the United States imposed an arms embargo in early 1958.[71]

I will not consider our other five cases in detail but simply sum up Cuba's military uniqueness. In none of our other five countries did the military come so thoroughly to divorce itself from other social groups in civil society as to render it impotent in the face of an armed political challenger. Only in Guatemala did the armed forces have comparable power as a class-independent institution, and there they increasingly worked hand in glove with the upper class from the 1960s onward (joint opposition to the events of 1944–1954 undoubtedly helped to establish and even cement that alliance).

In none of our other nations was a single person's control over the armed forces so thorough and so utterly unprofessional (i.e., based instead on personal loyalty and sycophancy) as in Batista's Cuba, and we must trace this distinctive feature of the Cuban military to the institutional history of the armed forces and to the conditions leading up the Sergeants' Revolt. Elsewhere, the military acted collegially when it seized political power, as in Guatemala, or gave measured collective support to one of its colleagues in power (Barrientos in Bolivia). As a result the Cuban army, whether in political power or not, remained institutionally the weakest army in the six nations under review. While that institutional weakness did not prevent it from ruling a politically disintegrated Cuban society, it critically crippled it in the face of combat against a guerrilla foe. The weakness of the Batista regime then paved the way for the creation of dual power, as the crumbling legitimacy of Batista's rule provided opportunities for the reconstitution of Cuban political life.

Mass Media and Moderate Messages

> I fear the Cologne Gazette more than 10,000 bayonets.
>
> —Napoleon

Napoleon and other warriors such as T.E. Lawrence (of Arabia) understood and stressed the importance of a good press. Modern guerrillas have not ignored it either, for "guerrilla war is also propaganda war, and the guerrilla values a 'good press' no less than arms or supplies."[72] I wish to argue here that the mass media have a strong impact upon the contenders' ability to place their messages before the public. Therefore revolutionary access to the eyes and ears of the populace, as well as the kinds of messages sent through those channels, are important, perhaps central mechanisms in the emergence of multiple sovereignty. Conversely, limited access to the media in combination with less felicitous messages would be expected to limit the appeal of the insurgents and further impede their attempts to bring mass loyalties into the revolutionaries' camp.

If the Cuban revolution stands out from its 1960s counterparts in any manner, that distinctiveness lies in Fidel Castro's access to the media and the messages he conveyed therein. Through his adroit use of the media Castro was able to place himself firmly in the minds of the Cuban people as a romantic, heroic, nationalist, legitimate, and revolutionary alternative to the Batista regime. He was assisted in this pursuit by the high literacy of the Cuban populace and by the wide dispersion of radio listeners and newspaper readers among them. His access to the media was outstanding in contrast to other Latin American guerrilla movements, and that access spread to the United States, where films favorable to the Castro resistance were shown even in junior high schools.[73]

Castro's overwhelming presence in the Cuban and American press, despite Batista's sporadic censorship attempts, can best be described through a brief (and far from complete) "media history" of Castro's guerrilla movement.[74]

1951

5 August: Ortodoxo leader Eddy Chibás commits suicide after an impassioned radio appeal to the Cuban people to reject the old corrupt politics.

16 December: Bohemia political preference poll concerning the upcoming elections, in which Castro is running for Congress and Batista for president, indicates that Batista has the support of only 14.2 percent of all Cubans, but 18.9 percent of the lower classes. His two opponents each have the support of one-third of the Cuban voters.

1952

10 March: Batista seizes power in a military coup prior to the 1952 elections.

1953

26 July: Fidel Castro leads a group of 150 in an attack on the Moncada barracks. He is captured but not killed, as his comrades were. A military tribunal puts him on trial, where he delivers his famous "History Will Absolve Me" defense speech. The text of this speech receives little circulation in Cuba prior to 1959. He is sentenced to fifteen years in prison.

1955

15 May: Castro is released from prison in a Batista general amnesty. The Cuban press flocks around him to interview him, ignoring the other released prisoners. His fame from the Moncada trial is the source of their interest.

29 May: *Bohemia*, *"Mientes, Chaviano!"* ("You Lie, Chaviano!"). In this article, Castro exposes the atrocities committed by Batista's troops in tracking down the Moncada assault team.

Summer: Castro goes into self-imposed Mexican exile. Thereafter, his letters from exile (up to December 1956) impress Cubans with his honesty and lack of desire for personal gain.

25 December: *Bohemia*. Castro proclaims himself free of all sectarian political ties, attacking the old political groups.

1956

19 March: *Bohemia* (?). Castro resigns from the Ortodoxos but argues that "For the Chibásist masses, the 26 July Movement is not distinct from Ortodoxia."

31 August: *Bohemia*. Castro denounces ex-president Prío Socorrás for attempting to form an anti-Batista alliance with Dominican dictator Trujillo.

[M-26 is preparing for its December Granma landing.]

19 November: *Alerta* (Havana daily newspaper, run by a "notorious *batistiano*"). Interview with Castro, who states, "We will be free in 1956 or we will be martyrs," and also that "our men are committed formally to *accepting no* electoral *office*." (emphases in original)

[Granma landing in early December. Invaders are routed or killed. Twenty flee into the hills to regroup. Batista declares all invaders killed.]

December: Castro encounters a peasant who immediately says, "You are Fidel Castro! I saw your photos in the papers." Another old man calls him *"un grande"* ("a great man"), like Antonio Maceo.

21 December: *New York Times* reports that Castro is alive despite government claims.

1957

January: Batista imposes censorship and suspends constitutional guarantees.

8 February: *New York Times*, p. 2. Report on Castro's guerrillas in the Sierra Maestra. The size of the force is inaccurately reported as 500 strong, with reports that 200 soldiers have been killed to date, and that the guerrillas have the backing of peasants and others.

4 March: *New York Times*, p. 75. Herbert Matthews's article on the Cuban guerrillas, with on-the-spot photos and interviews; a result of Castro's invitation. Matthews grossly overestimates actual troop strength, deceived by Fidel's maneuvers to make the band seem larger. The *Times* circulates in Havana, undercutting local censorship, and is believed in preference to the local papers.

13 April–5 May: CBS-TV journalist Robert Taber is in the Sierra Maestra with a camera team, where they film a newsreel, later shown in the States, entitled "The Story of Cuba's Jungle Fighters."

May: *Bohemia* publishes excerpts from Castro's interviews with Taber. Basic political program: "to restore the 1940 Constitution and to hold free elections."

June: *Bohemia* publishes an interview with Matthews, who sees a Batista-Castro impasse.

9 July: *Time* publishes Castro's earlier reform programs, including land-to-the-tiller agrarian reforms and nationalization of public utilities.

28 July: *Bohemia* publishes the "Sierra Maestra Manifesto" which had just been released by the Civic-Revolutionary Front. All talk of expropriation of land or nationalization is strikingly absent. The focus is on political issues. The land reform discussion treats of "establishment of the bases for an agrarian reform" and of the "prior indemnification of any landholders affected."

1 August: Batista imposes tighter press censorship, affecting even *Bohemia's* political coverage. Apparently this is an attempt to cover up U.S. ambassador Smith's negative comments concerning police attacks on female Santiago demonstrators. The pro-Batista press attacks Smith, who is backed by John Foster Dulles, secretary of state.

September: "Radio Libertad," a rebel-created station, gives Batista fifteen days to leave office or be driven out. *October*: "Voice of the Revolution" broadcasts continue calling for Batista's ouster, and the station issues reports on government atrocities.

November: The government seizes two (more) clandestine radio transmitters. *Hispanic American Report* describes M-26 goals as largely political, and notes the disavowal of earlier programs that did not represent Castro's true philosophy. Residents of Havana refer to the movement as "one of the best-dressed revolutions in history."

30 November: Castro authors an article in *The Nation*, "What Cuba's Rebels Want." His program is political, although Castro does discuss the plight of the seasonally employed sugar workers. He calls for adjusting the split in sugar revenues, giving more to the cultivator, less to the mills, and also calls for profit-sharing programs in business firms.

1958

25 January: Batista restores press freedoms, save in Oriente Province.

2 February: *Bohemia*. Castro breaks publicly with the Miami exile group headed by ex-president Prío. The comments between the two are strictly political in nature.

Early (?) 1958. A letter from Raúl Castro to Ché Guevara discussing Marxism falls into the hands of the government, which publishes it as evidence that the guerrillas are Communists. Castro flies into a rage at his colleagues over the incident and instructs them to be far more careful.

February: *Coronet* and *4 February*: *Look*. In articles in two U.S. periodicals, Castro reiterates the moderate reformist goals of his movement, disavowing earlier reports of expropriation of land and nationalization of utilities as central programs. He calls nationalization "at best, cumbersome" and further renounces any political intentions to run for president.

23–24 February. "Radio Rebelde" begins broadcasts, reporting on M-26 programs and government crimes.

March: *Bohemia* publishes an interview with Fidel Castro by Spanish journalist Enrique Meneses, who was in the Sierra Maestra from December until March. The article consists of 30-plus pages of text and photos. A special edition of 500,000 issues is snatched off the stands, at a time when Cuba's population numbers about six million. Batista's immediate tightening of censorship fails to quell the shock wave.

April: The PSP (Communists) offer support to Castro's M-26 rebels. Castro's supporters reject the espousal as unsolicited and unwanted.

[Castro begins his summer offensive.]

June: Raúl Castro kidnaps Americans in retaliation for Batista's use of U.S.-manufactured rockets in air attacks on guerrillas. The U.S. press reaction to the kidnapping is strongly negative.

14 July: *Life*. An on-the-spot report from Raúl's camp. The article and photos emphasize the easygoing, cordial, and even friendly relations between the American captives and the Cuban rebels.

21 July: *Life*. A follow-up story now notes the mutual admiration of captors and captives. A full report on Raúl's front ensues. The reporter notes the presence of some army soldiers lined up waiting to join the rebel forces. Estimate of the rebels' numbers: 3,000 soldiers (a gross exaggeration).

July, August: A series of letters and broadcasts by Castro over Radio Rebelde focuses on government torture and killing. He defends the M-26 ethic of releasing prisoners and contrasts it to Batista's no-prisoners policy.

October: Radio broadcasts by Castro's sympathizers to Cuba from Venezuela are ended by the interim government there, which argues that it must maintain relations with the Batista government.

October: Castro orders a memorial mass said for the late Pope Pius XII.

November: Army reports of hundreds of rebels killed. Castro responds, "The dead who were killed are enjoying good health."

[Batista flees Cuba on New Year's Eve.]

In the wake of this historical record one could hardly argue that Castro did not receive fair reportage in the world's press.[75] The preceding chronicle demonstrates not only that Castro received excellent domestic and foreign press coverage, but also that he retained a great deal of control over the kinds of information filtered to the media. He emphasized official M-26 programs in news and radio broadcasts, issued his own articles published in Cuba and abroad, and secured a series of interviews with the world press that inevitably presented the M-26 guerrillas in a favorable light.

The contrast with the media history of the other guerrilla movements will soon become clear.[76] In detailing the contrasts with the Cuban experience, we should focus on Castro's impressive, sustained access to the mass-circulation Cuban media (*Bohemia*) *in the midst of a revolutionary war*, despite Batista's recurring censorship attempts. Our second focus of comparison should be firmly on the *kinds of messages* that Castro sent. Castro continually resisted and retracted any messages or images that would make the movement seem "too radical" and therefore less appealing to crucial social groups. Overall, Castro's "bourgeois-democratic" ideology and his emphases on political issues—the illegality of the Batista regime and the restoration of the 1940 Constitution—impressed Cuban and non-Cuban alike.[77]

In Venezuela and Guatemala, by contrast, the guerrillas enjoyed brief "windows" of favorable media coverage, but those were never sustained for longer periods. In addition, despite some classless, nationalist imagery in some of their public manifestoes, guerrillas in both countries clearly revealed their Marxist ideology and their (*socialist*) Cuban inspiration, which narrowed their appeal sharply among more moderate (particularly middle-class) groups in the populace.

In Guatemala, we again find a situation most closely approaching that of Cuba; yet again the similarities also fail to persuade us of true analogy. Guatemalan governments from 1954 on were highly repressive and (sometimes pseudo-) dictatorial. In 1966, right-wing terror became established as a weapon to use against the regime's opponents. The guerrillas at the same time, however, were enjoying a relatively good press, which was to a large extent liberal and uncensored through most of the 1960s.[78] A major interview with them appeared in the *Saturday Evening Post*, and usually referred to them as "rebels," rather than as "guerrillas," a term by then loaded with negative connotations in the wake of Cuba and Vietnam. The interview accompanied a CBS-TV special entitled "Undeclared War," aired 15 June 1966 in the United States. Within Guatemala, some newspapers were sympathetic to the FAR, and the foreign press was uncensored. When twenty-eight political prisoners were murdered by the government—it could not account for their whereabouts following their arrest—the Red Cross almost recognized the FAR as a "legitimate force," as did university and professional organizations. Other commentators said that the guerrillas were "rapidly becoming effective government." The press began to publish FAR communiqués—echoes of Cuba—and turned against the incumbent government.[79]

Yet the guerrillas encountered serious media problems. The government elected in 1966 put the local press under censorship, and favorable coverage of the FAR was stifled at a decisive juncture. Moreover, the guerrillas' ideology, although cloaked in nationalist and more moderate language, was correctly identified as Marxist. This was not true at the 1962 birth of the MR-13, but the two main guerrilla leaders, Luis Turcios Lima and Marco Yon Sosa, moved respectively toward Castroist Marxism and Trotskyism, generating a 1965 split that weakened the movement in the very years of its greatest popular support. Therefore the press inevitably labeled the guerrillas correctly as Marxists, and indeed the Guatemalan Communists (PGT) had been intimately tied to the guerrillas since 1962. Articles in the Marxist periodical *Monthly Review* from 1965 to 1967 made this abundantly clear to an American audience. Lest their *fidelista bona fides* be in any doubt, the FAR dispelled them when it was the toast of the Tricontinental Conference in Cuba in 1966.[80]

A final critical blow to guerrilla chances of success was the timing of their challenge to the incumbent regime. Just as the guerrillas were beginning to mount a serious political challenge to the military regime, the "democratic opening" of 1966 occurred, and moderate and liberal candidates contested with conservative military ones for the presidency in the 1966 elections. This election generated an ideological crisis within the revolutionary opposition, as moderate regime opponents went to the polls to vote against the right. The FAR eventually opposed the elections and the liberal candidacy of Julio Méndez Montenegro, and lost some face and support thereby. They succumbed the following year to the military's terror-filled counterinsurgency campaign.[81]

In Venezuela, despite the Betancourt government's (1959–1964) democratic credentials, it maintained a far tighter rein on the Venezuelan press than had Batista in Cuba. Moreover, no periodical nearly so influential as *Bohemia* served the guerrillas' needs for a mass audience. Indeed, the only messages that the FALN could disseminate broadly were its threats to shoot anyone who violated their calls for a general strike and boycott of national elections in late 1963. This is hardly the stuff of positive public relations. Late 1963 is probably the point of inflection beginning the guerrillas' media down-swing, for in September the guerrillas killed four national guardsmen who were riding on an excursion train. The media widely viewed this as a cow-ardly attack, which evoked and was exploited to produce outrage in the gen-eral public: both bloody photos and blaring mastheads pointed to the results of the guerrillas' "revolutionary" actions. In addition, the action led to the first complete entry of the military into the guerrilla war, and to guerrilla declines in subsequent years. Similarly, the urban assassinations of police-men eventually backfired in the FALN's face, and they lost the urban *barrio* support they had formerly enjoyed. By 1964 the newspapers—undoubtedly under government orders—no longer even referred to the FALN by name, but rather to "members of a clandestine organization."[82]

The Betancourt government closed down, or its police raided newspapers several times during the guerrilla era. The victims were a broad assortment, including left-wing, pro-guerrilla papers like *Tribuna Popular*, *Clarín*, *La Hora*, and *La Tarde*, as well as the moderate *El Universal* and a "girlie" magazine, *Venezuela Gráfica*, where "Four Days with the Guerrillas" ap-peared in mid-1964. At still other times it imposed censorship, affecting even ordinary news coverage by papers like *El Nacional*. *The Daily Jour-nal* reported that it was prohibited, under one 1962 decree, from printing news on police or army movements, terrorism, or ongoing investigations. The shutdowns were typically short-lived and temporary but may well have served their purpose of producing the famed "chilling effect" on news reporting.[83]

The guerrillas' ideology superficially presented a moderate approach to politics, but a deeper reading strongly suggests the opposite.[84] From an early stage, most Venezuelans knew that the Venezuelan Communist party was the real driving force behind the armed struggle in general, and behind the FALN in particular. If they didn't already know it, in 1966 PCV leader Jesús Faría trumpeted the overwhelming role of Communists in the struggle.[85] Venezue-lans also knew that the second prime mover of the armed struggle was the AD offshoot, the MIR. While all knew that the PCV was organized *ab initio* around Marxist principles, such was also true of the MIR, whose cofounder and coleader could write in 1963 that "our ideological standpoint, our basic doctrine was Marxism-Leninism," announced at the very time the MIR was founded in 1960. Moreover, he claimed such affiliation in a Communist party organ.[86] Hence, amid the nationalist imagery in the early manifestos and pamphlets of the FLN one can find references to the formation of a "revolutionary, national people's regime" and of the "path to socialism" as "unavoidable." Thus journalist Alfredo Peña could reasonably argue in the 1970s, to ex-guerrilla Américo Martín, that the Venezuelan guerrillas' Marxist-Leninist colors, in contrast to the democratic images used by Fidel Castro, were decisive in their failure to seize power.[87]

Finally, despite their plausible claims that their violence was merely a popular response to violence initiated by the Betancourt government,[88] broader evidence indicates that PCV leader Douglas Bravo was considering guerrilla war as early as 1959, and that other underground groups planned a similar course at least by December 1960.[89] The result was an insurgent left increasingly distant from the moderate views of other Venezuelans, perhaps best summarized by rural guerrilla Angela Zago: "What a strange thing: it had never occurred to me that there are Venezuelans not in this struggle."[90]

Despite national variations, Colombia, Peru, and Bolivia each had a national press best characterized as unremittingly hostile to the guerrilla movements. As such, these cases will require relatively little time and attention here. Moreover, the cases of Peru and Bolivia each displayed highly unpromising rural conditions and peasant support; it is therefore beyond reason to suggest that positive mass media could have compensated for such shortcomings.

Colombia's "great bourgeois press," as it is known to its Marxist critics, reflects the hereditary hatreds of Colombia's reigning parties. Every major newspaper is affiliated with either the Liberal or Conservative party. One does not expect such organs to endorse the policies or promote the ends of guerrilla movements that uniformly treat Liberal-Conservative competition as a form of sham democracy with no ideological content. The Colombian Communists have in the past relied largely on techniques other than newspapers or radio transmission to reach their followers.[91] Even as recently as the early 1980s, the PCC continued to complain of the minimal circulation of its organ *Voz* in competition with 1.5 million daily issues of the "mouthpieces of the bourgeoisie." As for radio broadcasts, by the 1980s the best the PCC could claim was a single weekly forty-five-minute slot prepared by PCC-friendly journalists.[92] *A fortiori*, the guerrillas of the 1960s simply did not expect favorable coverage from the Colombian press, and occasionally remarked on its ideological hostility. We do have one index of press and government hostility: Not apparently until the 1980s would the government permit guerrilla interviews to appear in the national press or books.[93]

Ideologically, the Colombian FARC may have had some moderate tones in its initial document of 1966, but the political filiation of each of the three major guerrilla groups was crystal clear to observers from an early point. The FARC at its inception was allied with the Soviet-line PCC, as much as its leader Manuel Marulanda might wish to deny such ties in later years.[94] The ELN guerrillas followed a revolutionary Cuban line, while the EPL guerrillas were the armed wing of the Chinese-line Colombian Communists. In Colombia, therefore, we encounter the fewest pretenses among the guerrillas to social democratic ideologies and programs, undoubtedly due to the functioning electoral system of Colombia.

In Peru, the major daily newspapers acted, if at all, as gadflies in the government's anti-guerrilla campaign. *La Prensa* continually called, first, for President Belaúnde to *admit* that he had a guerrilla insurgency in the Sierra, and then, second, for him to do more to snuff it out. In a series of articles and editorials throughout 1965, *La Prensa* consistently took a strong, even radically conservative stance on the insurgency, loudly reported guerrilla losses and atrocities (some of them surely false), and continually hammered away at the presumably foreign inspiration, direction, and command of the Peruvian insurgency.[95] One undoubtedly effective ideological tack by *La Prensa* was its contrast between the new agrarian reform law passed by Peruvian legislators, which would eventually give land to peasants, and the putative collectivization of agriculture that would occur should the "red" guerrillas ever come to power: "forced labor for the benefit of a small body of the state . . . a new *gamonalismo*" (which translates roughly as "landlordism").[96]

The guerrillas tried to respond with their own newspaper, *El Guerrillero*, and in pirate radio broadcasts over "Voz Rebelde" (Rebel Voice). Once again we see the Venezuelan pattern, in which claims to represent the national aspirations of all the masses are mixed in with language redolent only of Marxism: the movement is self-described as "anti-feudal" and "anti-imperialist" and proposes to achieve the widely shared aims of democracy and development through a peculiarly Peruvian form of "socialist planning."[97] Moreover, in its July 1965 manifesto from the Sierra, the MIR had publicly rejected the very institutions of representative democracy for which Fidel Castro continually claimed to fight during the Cuban revolution.[98] Clearly times had changed.

Finally, in Bolivia we find the land where newspapers are of slight importance as mass media, due to the nation's high rates of illiteracy, but where radio stations reach a large portion of the populace. Ché's guerrillas, like their Guatemalan counterparts, never really entered into radio-based media competition with the Barrientos government, and hence could not benefit from the technique used with such effect in the Cuban revolution. The single most widely read newspaper in Bolivia was the Catholic paper *Presencia*, which appeared after the Bolivian revolution and preempted some of the market formerly dominated by the papers controlled by the nation's ruling elite.

Throughout the guerrilla struggle, *Presencia* provided surprisingly accurate information about the clandestine guerrillas, and its reports continually prodded the Barrientos government to take further action against Ché's insurgents. Its strongly anti-Communist line tells the tale of its position on the insurgency. Bolivia had also had a strong history of pamphleteering, which had substituted in part for the weakness of the mass media there. Once again, this tool was not usefully employed by the guerrillas, who lacked a printing press or ties to urban support groups. Instead, the Barrientos regime continued the tradition, by dropping a series of propaganda fliers over the guerrillas' area of operations, urging the peasants to defend their lands against those foreign communists who had come to take them away.[99]

To summarize: the more deeply we pursue a comparative analysis of both media access and media messages, the more profoundly does the Cuban experience stand out. Yes, the international climate had also shifted radically with the growth of U.S.-sponsored counterinsurgency programs in the 1960s. Yet that difference should have produced tactical moves by guerrillas to modulate and moderate their revolutionary calls during that decade. Instead, the guerrillas' manifestoes were uniformly *more* radical than the ones Castro had issued from his Sierra Maestra stronghold. Their failure to respond to the changed geopolitics of the hemisphere strongly indicates that guerrilla ideology was less responsive to such rational, game-theoretical maneuvers and more responsive to other forces.

As I argued in chapter 3 above, the clearest force behind that ideological shift leftward was the leftward movement of the Cuban revolution itself from 1958 to 1961 and beyond. As guerrillas identified with Castro the Marxist, they conveniently forgot that the man who defeated Batista was Castro the self-proclaimed restorer of electoral democracy. As the 1960s' guerrillas shifted their ideological stance to conform to Cuban events, they increasingly lost access to the mass media in their own societies, and moderate supporters to boot. A further ideological push leftward came from the political nature of the regimes they faced. Against a traditional rightist dictatorship, Castro's constitutional-electoral-democratic program was a powerful "draw." Against elected governments in Venezuela, Peru, Colombia, and even briefly in Bolivia and Guatemala, such symbols were mostly coopted by the incumbent regimes. Hence the only ideological space in which the leftists could carve out a niche was on the revolutionary wing, declaring themselves against sham reformism, and against "bourgeois" institutions such as elections. With such attacks on bourgeois institutions, we can understand more readily why the "great bourgeois press" was not more willing or more forthcoming with space for the clarion calls of the guerrillas. And with the Cuban case outlined again in high relief, we can now proceed to the question of dual power.

UNDERSTANDING DUAL POWER AND
REVOLUTIONARY SITUATIONS

> The truth is that such a revolution can only be carried out by an
> alliance of several classes under the leadership of mainly one of
> them, and occurs only when almost the entire society has reached
> the point of consent to the destruction of the state.
> —George Pettee (1938)

Before I proceed, I wish to connect the preceding discussions of multiple political weaknesses in the regime and the revolutionaries' use of mass media to the emergence of dual power in Cuba. Regarding in-built structural weaknesses, Batista's patrimonial praetorian regime excluded large portions of a very large middle class and an upper class from effective participation in the Cuban polity. That combination of large numbers and political exclusion was absent in our other five nations: either those groups did participate in electoral politics (Venezuela, Peru, Colombia) or they were small percentages of the populace (Bolivia, Guatemala). Exclusion under Cuban conditions structurally created a *large* reservoir of *moderate* discontent with the Batista regime, which must have been strongly "magnetic" to the far smaller radical opposition. That magnetism worked both ways for, given their own lack of political alternatives, the moderates would find the radicals more attractive. To forge an alliance, all the radicals had to do was downplay their radical goals, emphasize the aims they shared with the moderates—above all, the ouster of the dictator—and begin an oppositional marriage of convenience.

Cuban conditions of personal, exclusionary dictatorship tended to pressure the opposition toward unity, by providing them with a striking symbol to unite them: Fulgencio Batista himself. Once such an alliance was forged, the resulting quantum leap in the opposition's strength, along with furtherance of the prime goal (the dictator's ouster), served to cement the alliance and further pressure the radicals and moderates toward compromise: the alliance *itself* urged the radical "revolutionary" opposition to moderate its ideological appeals. To support this reasoning further, we can also observe that those movements in other nations with the most radical ideological appeals have also been those most separated from working relationships with other groups in society; the epitome is Peru's *Sendero Luminoso*. Extreme radicalism can almost never persist without extreme social isolation to support it.[100]

In Cuba, as a radical-cum-moderate alliance became an increasingly plausible political alternative, the leadership would logically begin to issue more formal and detailed political position papers and put forth its alternatives for the nation's political future. It would, in short, begin to look and act like a political party, as it prepared for its ascent to power, and compete directly with the incumbent regime for the loyalties and obedience of the bulk of the population, seeking a "revolutionary situation" and the destruction of the state via "dual power."

The emergence of mass consent to the destruction of the state can by no means be taken for granted. Sartre referred to such status quos (more properly, *stati quibus*) as the "practico-inert," and critical Marxists, headed by Herbert Marcuse, have increasingly focused on the absence of mass resistance to the modern capitalist order as *the* focal problem for socialist revolutionaries. Charles Tilly has broadened the scope further, for he detects a "deep conservatism" in every polity, and traces it to the fact that the collective action of the masses responds more to (negative) threats against their welfare than to (positive) opportunities for improving that welfare.[101]

The emergence of dual power or multiple sovereignty, therefore, cannot be taken for granted; it requires a deep rather than superficial treatment, documentation rather than assumption. Before we proceed, however, we will allow Tilly to define the issues for us.[102] Multiple sovereignty can emerge only when at least two contenders for central political authority exist, one of them typically the incumbent regime. Such multiple contention does not alone constitute multiple sovereignty, for we must also confirm that "some significant part of the subject population honors the claim" of one or more of the challenging groups, especially through obedience to its directives rather than to those of the incumbent regime. Furthermore, such obedience "must be activated in the face of prohibitions or contrary directives from the government." Tilly's other concept, the revolutionary situation, is closely related to his definition of multiple sovereignty: "A revolutionary situation begins when a government previously under the control of a single, sovereign polity becomes the object of effective, competing, mutually exclusive claims on the part of two or more distinct polities." Both the revolutionary situation and that of multiple sovereignty are ultimately resolved when a single sovereign polity regains control over the political arena. For example, in the Cuban case, the issue of sovereignty was not decided simply by Batista's flight but had to wait until Castro had disarmed or secured the pledges of a variety of groups (some army officers and most of the *Directorio Revolucionario* among them), who had initially resisted Castro's attempt at immediate consolidation of unitary sovereignty over the Cuban polity.[103]

In rendering any account of the emergence of multiple sovereignty in Cuba we must pay attention to that word *multiple*. We seek to document not only Castro's rise but also Batista's decline. We can do so most effectively by analytically "carving up" society in three different manners. First, we can examine the geographical axis of multiple sovereignty, trying to detect urban-rural and regional variations in the emergence of opposition. Second, we can employ an organizational axis for our analysis, identifying the political positions taken by major, formally organized social groups: the U.S. government, the army, political parties, the church or other religious groups, the university, and the labor unions. Finally, we may take the approach favored by Marxist commentators (but employed by almost all analysts of the Cuban revolution) and observe how the question of multiple versus unitary sovereignty was resolved in different social classes. As an added virtue, this approach will also serve us in good stead when we proceed to analyze our other five cases. Along virtually any of these axes, as we shall see, we can discern the emergence of multiple sovereignty and, finally, a revolutionary situation in Cuba; yet we will detect few such processes among "a significant part of the subject population" in any other instance until the Nicaraguan revolution.

The Emergence of Multiple Sovereignty in Cuba

Batista's preemptive coup of March 1952, which derailed scheduled elections, accentuated the "galloping disintegration" of Cuban political life that had begun with the August 1951 suicide of Ortodoxo leader Eddy Chibás. Most commentators are struck by the degree to which Cuban political life simply fell apart, and at the virtual lack of open opposition to Batista's seizure of power.[104] Yet we know that virtually all observers hailed Batista's downfall when it came less than seven years later; that Fidel Castro at that time was supported by the "overwhelming majority of the population"; that in mid-1960 80 percent of all Cubans supported him completely; and that he remains personally popular to this day.[105] How had Batista fallen so far? After all, Batista had been enormously popular among soldiers and Afro-Cubans in his earlier period of rule, and under his aegis a good deal of protective "welfare" legislation was passed, increasing the well-being of *colonos* (sugar tenant farmers) and the working class.[106]

Tracing Batista's Decline

When Batista announced his candidacy for the 1952 presidential elections, Cubans no longer desired his form of rule. A *Bohemia* public opinion poll showed Batista with the support of less than 20 percent of the populace, while his main opponent, Agramonte, led the field with 20 to 35 percent. (Most notably, however, Batista was still considerably more popular among lower-class Cubans than among the upper class.) We might trace this lack of interest in Batista's candidacy to the emerging Cuban political cleavage over the issue of corruption and to the most recent Cuban upsurge in hopes for democratic renewal, especially focused on the Ortodoxos and Eddy Chibás.[107] Batista's 1950s reentry into political life, therefore, began and ended in an unpopular fashion. The striking feature of his rule when this period began, as many observers have noted, was his lack of mass organized support *or* opposition.[108] Yet by the time of his downfall, in late 1958, most observers were struck by the *universal* disgust with the Batista regime: Draper referred to a "universal revulsion" which even permeated the armed forces, while a number of commentators could also observe a decisive volte-face even among members of the upper class, who formerly had at least tolerated his rule.[109] How had such massive changes come about?

In regional terms, the core of resistance to Batista always lay outside the city of Havana. That core almost surely resided in the city of Santiago de Cuba and in the Sierras of Oriente Province. This is not to deny the great importance of the Havana urban underground, their many acts of violence, and many lost lives. Yet Havana remained largely in Batista's control until the very end, while the Havana opposition flowed largely from the autonomous campus of the University of Havana. (How common this pattern has been in revolutions more generally, where the capital city has so typically been the strongest center of power for the incumbent government.) Santiago was a different story. During Batista's 1954 pseudo-elections, its citizens chanted vivas to Fidel Castro, then languishing in one of Batista's prisons for his attack at Moncada. More generally, the further one moved socially and geographically from Havana, the more pervasive was the opposition to the regime; and the closer one got to 1958 the more open was the complaining. Hence, in one early 1958 bus ride through Camagüey Province, the driver cursed Batista for the lousy roads, generating a vehement political discussion, notable for lacking a single defender of the regime. Everybody talks that way, the reporter argued. The Oriente city of Bayamo turned decisively against the regime in 1957 following a severe bout of government repression, while open anti-Batista demonstrations in Santiago—during the August 1957 visit of new U.S. ambassador Earl Smith to that city—led Batista to impose severe censorship. The Cienfuegos naval revolt the following month also took place far from the center of Batista's power. The best evidence of the opposition's greater regional strength in eastern Cuba is the direction of the guerrillas' offensive of mid-1958: they swept the country from east to west, not the reverse.[110]

We may indicate three separate classes who initially supported Batista during his 1933–1944 incumbency. The upper class welcomed his reimposition of order on Cuban society, so close to revolution in 1933. The organized working class, including the Communist-influenced labor unions, welcomed the populist labor reforms that Batista pushed through during his earlier "populist period," which had the nice bonus of securing for Batista substantial labor peace throughout his administrations. Finally, Batista had a strong popular following among the cane-cutting and other Afro-Cuban lower classes, since he was a mulatto himself and his father had been a cane cutter. "Lower-class boy makes good" often provides a good formula that generates strong lower-class support for populist politicians, as Huey Long demonstrated in Louisiana.

Batista lost the bulk of upper-class and Afro-Cuban support by 1958, and a substantial part of his working-class backing as well. Let us consider each in turn. Sheer reliance on military force and fiscal corruption as the two pillars of his rule "eventually alienated most of those upper-class Cubans who had originally accepted and even welcomed his rule." A decisive turning point in upper- and upper middle-class hostility came when Batista rejected the overtures of the Society of the Friends of the Republic (SAR) to get him and the opposition to sit down and talk in 1955. His intransigence hardened the opposition of the middle class and began to turn the upper class against him. The children of the elite consistently ridiculed Batista for his mulatto background, and their upper-class parents eventually moved from a tolerant position to one of opposition. They eventually abandoned the position of one Havanan, who in April 1958 reluctantly accepted this "thief of millions" and instigator of police brutality, largely because at least he and his peers could work with the dictator, and a change could be worse. Instead, by December 1958, they more often reasoned like the wealthy Havana businessman who said, "I've been pro-Batista all along, but now I realize he has to go. We can't support him now, the Cuban people are overwhelmingly against him."[111]

One can certainly overstate working-class support for Batista through 1958. Bonachea and San Martín, in particular, have done much to resurrect workers' roles in the urban fighting, in providing a substantial portion of the urban underground in Oriente Province (especially Santiago), and in sheltering the Havana urban guerrillas from Batista's terror.[112] Nonetheless, as a class, the urban workers largely remained outside the struggle until the very end; the failure of the April 1958 general strike may be one rough index of this. The bulk of regime violence was absorbed by the peasants of the Sierra and by the student and other underground revolutionaries in the capital, who were largely from middle-class backgrounds. The bulk of the opposition money came from those who had it: exiles and the middle and upper classes. If Batista retained *some* degree of support in any classes, those would be the upper class and the urban working class.

Such was less true among the Afro-Cuban lower classes. As late as 1957, Afro-Cubans, peasants, and cane cutters spontaneously demonstrated on Batista's behalf following his April brush with death in the DR's palace assassination attempt. We even have a ready index of their favor and disfavor: the use of figurines and necklaces associated with the practice of *Santería*, the Afro-Christian religious system that roughly parallels Haitian *vodoun* or the variants of Brazilian *macumba*. During the heyday of Batista's popularity with the *santeros*, well into 1957, they made wax figurines of him to celebrate his ascendancy. By early 1959, a mere week after Batista's flight from Cuba, they still made figurines, but now in the image of Fidel Castro, and sent red, white, and blue beaded collars to bedeck and protect the guerrillas, in celebration of Castro's victory (thus providing a particularly colorful and graphic illustration of "shifting loyalties").[113]

Looking at the organizational axis, Batista's firmest supporters were probably the United States government, the Cuban armed forces, and the Cuban Communists (PSP)—strange bedfellows indeed. The United States began to pull away from Batista in the summer of 1957 and may have supported the Cienfuegos naval revolt in September. By early 1958 the U.S. imposed an arms embargo on Cuba, since Batista was using those arms for internal repression rather than, in accord with U.S. law, for foreign defense. That arms embargo—and the symbolic more than the material impact it conveyed—created a notable drop in the morale of the armed forces, further deflating what little fighting spirit they had displayed in the past. Batista had made the army his personal tool in the 1930s. Now, Batista's increasing use of terror caused "revulsion" even in the armed forces, which in the end just "evaporated" under Castro's guerrilla assaults. Finally, the Communist-Batista "pact" of 1938 had helped both parties: the PSP got open access to, and influence in, the labor union movement, while Batista got labor peace. The PSP stayed, more or less, with Batista as late as mid-1958, when they began to pull away. For example, although they declared themselves neutral when Castro called for a nationwide general strike against Batista in April 1958, evidence suggests that the PSP worked actively to undermine its success. Thereafter they sought and eventually achieved a slow rapprochement with the Castro's M-26 until his victory at year's end, and substantially increased their organization's power in the decades since the revolution.[114]

Other organizations never gave Batista such strong support, and therefore had to go shorter distances to move into opposition. From 1933 until 1957, the University of Havana provided the most unchanging core of opposition to the various Batista governments: in 1933, at the time he seized power; throughout the later years of that decade; and even at the time of his 1952 coup, when most other opposition voices were muted. University students generated the main urban opposition to Batista in Havana, the Directorio Revolucionario, who lost more dead to Batista's terror than did Castro's own followers. Their attempt to assassinate Batista in April 1957—a move that Castro opposed—failed in its goal only by mischance. Nonetheless, that attack shattered Batista's aura of invincibility among Cubans and was probably the decisive inflection point in his descent from grace and, ultimately, power.[115]

By early 1958, other formal organizations with broad support among Cubans, especially "respectable" Cubans, also began to turn decisively against the regime. In February, the Bishops of Cuba asked Batista to resign to end the shedding of Cuban blood, while in March the Committee on Civic Institutions did likewise. In early March, the bishops and the cardinal reiterated their plea, calling for a government of national unity, and within a week thirteen Cuban judges protested the regime of force.[116]

Tracing Castro's Ascent

By those months in early 1958, a number of commentators could trace a shift of loyalties in Castro's direction; one reporter in March argued that a majority of the population now seemed to sympathize with Fidel. The overall shift of attitudes in the Cuban populace that appeared in a number of contexts—from bishops' conclaves to bus-ride arguments—suggests a watershed in the loyalties of the Cuban populace as of the first three months of 1958. That watershed properly led Claude Julien to the characterization that began this chapter: "Castro's success . . . was in the first place a moral victory among the people," against an opponent, moreover, who was increasingly viewed as immoral and amoral.[117]

Castro's increasing authority among the Cuban populace was not simply something brought from the mountains down to the cities, as Guevara and Debray suggested in their postrevolutionary writings on guerrillas and the *foco* theory of revolution. In its beginnings, Castro depended in fundamental ways upon support from the urban wing of the M-26, and most particularly upon the work of Frank País, whose death in 1957 removed from the movement a most important rival to Castro for leadership of the opposition. New members, supplies, and funding regularly came from País's Santiago support group up to the Sierra Maestra during 1957, enabling Castro's guerrillas to survive during a year that saw them at times in near-desperate straits.[118] Moreover, massive opposition tended to flow out of middle-class segments of urban Cuba, as seen most clearly in the middle-class composition of the leadership of the opposition: Castro's M-26 commanders, as I documented in chapter 2, and those of the DR came overwhelmingly from middle-class backgrounds. Middle-class opposition was seen in a more routine form in the revolutionary role of the Civic Resistance Movement, which served as the urban auxiliary to the M-26, and whose members were largely from the middle and upper classes: businessmen, professors, teachers, and civil servants.[119]

The strongest supporters of the revolutionary cause were the peasants of the sierras of Oriente Province, for reasons I explored in chapters 6 and 7 above. Evidence strongly suggests that, as early as 1957, the squatters and some other peasants of those regions had come to recognize Castro's guerrillas as their new government, but a government that was far more just than any they had ever known. During the revolution, dual power was created first and strongest among the peasants of the Sierra, who early on came to obey the guerrillas' directives rather than those of the Batista government.[120]

As other classes and organizations began to desert Batista, they increasingly provided active recruits, not just passive sympathy, for Castro's revolutionary movement. By the summer of 1958, the urban underground movement itself had some ten thousand members who provided a variety of shelter, support, and sabotage services, and some thirty thousand persons contributing cash on a regular basis.[121] A full year before that perhaps sixty thousand citizens of Santiago attended the funeral of Frank País, murdered by Batista's police, and a spontaneous general strike called as a response to his death brought Santiago to a standstill on 1 August 1957.[122] While the April 1958 national general strike was, by contrast, a clear failure—in part due to Batista's careful preparation, in part due to the Communists' betrayal and Castro's lukewarm support—active support for the guerrillas in the mountains still grew sharply just before the summer offensive (our best chroniclers describe the underground's efforts as "frantic").[123] One last general strike, called in the days just following Batista's departure in early 1959, shut down Havana and consolidated Castro's claim to power against the threat by certain sectors of the armed forces to seize power in a preemptive move.[124]

Most striking in shifts of support were the desertions of large portions of the armed forces to the insurgents. Diana Russell attempted to quantify the degree of such disloyalty and found it appreciable. Moreover, many Cuban *puro* military officers, who had suffered under Batista's patrimonial control of the armed forces, were in opposition by the mid-1950s. Notable here is Colonel Ramón Barquín López, who was jailed after Batista discovered a plot against his rule; later Barquín was to throw in his lot with Castro in late 1958–early 1959, when some military men and the U.S. government sought him as a less radical alternative to the Castro regime then clearly coming to power. Finally, the rank-and-file soldiers regularly deserted to Castro's cause as well. In the last year of the struggle, Batista was forced to employ soldiers from western Cuba in the campaigns in the east, for eastern Cubans had become too unreliable as fighters in their home territory. In mid-1958, a visitor to Raúl Castro's camp reported, "I saw government soldiers, still wearing their uniform blouses, waiting to join Raúl's army."[125]

Less surprising, but more solid, was the university's opposition to Batista, as we have seen. From 1952 to 1956, university students carried the brunt of the (often terroristic) opposition to Batista, using bombs and bullets to attack the regime and disrupt routines. Students were protected from the most severe reprisals by the University of Havana's tradition of autonomy, which Batista occasionally violated, but which only Castro would utterly remove. In Mexico, on 30 August 1956, Castro and José Echeverría, the leader of the DR student resistance, signed a revolutionary pact to pursue simultaneous uprisings against Batista when Castro landed. Throughout the next two years these two prongs of opposition to Batista continued to operate, mostly independently. The DR might well have provided a third alternative to the "Batista or

Castro" choice that Cubans confronted in 1958, yet they never really contended for national power. The inevitable confrontation came from late 1958 until early 1959, as Ché Guevara faced down the rural DR guerrillas in Las Villas Province and Castro forced them to disarm shortly after securing power in early 1959.[126] In those maneuvers, Castro made certain that the Cubans would face a situation of dual power, and not of triad power, where the choice for Castro would be less compelling.

FAILURES OF DUAL POWER

In virtually all Latin American nations guerrilla movements emerged during this decade, but very few came to a point where they seriously challenged or worried incumbent governments. As we saw above (chapter 4), guerrilla movements secured strong peasant support in selected rural areas of Guatemala, Colombia, and Venezuela. Where they did secure such peasant support, regional guerrillas in fact became effective rural "governments" in the areas they dominated for shorter (Guatemala) or longer (Colombia) periods of time.[127] In that modest sense, then, those guerrillas *did* achieve dual power in selected areas. More striking, however, and distinguishing them from the Cuban experience, was their failure to expand such dual power to other rural regions or to create a parallel process among urban populations. Of the three cases in question, surely the Guatemalan guerrillas came closest to that *nationwide* "revolutionary situation" of which Tilly wrote, the Venezuelan guerrillas less close, and the Colombian guerrillas still further from the commanding heights of power. We will closely analyze the first two cases and then discuss the Colombian, Peruvian, and Bolivian failures in briefer compass.

Guatemala: The Failed Flirtation with Dual Power

> [The guerrillas] . . . are fighting for the land . . . in the end they're going to win, because everybody is for them.
> —Guatemalan soldier hunting guerrillas, 1965

> . . . the guerrillas were rapidly becoming effective government.
> —Report to Judy Hicks, 1966

> Even under conceivably favorable conditions for revolution, such as prevailed in Guatemala, the politically active segments of the population weren't interested in a solution of the guerrilla type.
> —Robert Lamberg, 1971[128]

Of all 1960s guerrilla movements, those in Guatemala came closest to the revolutionary seizure of power. In retrospect, it has become very common on both the left and the right to belittle their chances during that decade.[129] Yet at the time many observers saw critical points of inflection in which Guatemalan military regimes of the 1960s were sorely threatened by popular rebellion. The most notable urban instance came in early 1962, when widespread street riots, supported but not controlled by the PGT and the nascent guerrillas, were finally put down.[130] Nationwide, a number of observers in 1965—admittedly most of them on the left—detected a swing in popular opinion away from the regime and toward the guerrilla movements. The Red Cross and other organizations nearly gave them recognition as a "legitimate force," while the press began to turn against the government and to publish FAR communiqués.[131]

More than anything else, the 1966 presidential elections reversed that move toward greater guerrilla support among the populace. As one guerrillaphile source put it: "Méndez campaigned as a reformer, the inheritor of the 1944 Revolution. He made repeated half-hearted promises of negotiating with the guerrillas. All these factors combined to give him considerable popular support. These factors also fed into existing confusion about elections among the Left, especially within the PGT, which saw the prospect of another national democratic government."[132] In those elections, the FAR guerrillas and their largely urban Communist allies, the PGT, split over support for Méndez versus abstention from sham electioneering, and the FAR rural guerrillas were largely destroyed by the ensuing counterinsurgency campaign of late 1966 and early 1967.

Overall popular support for the guerrillas was never more than sketchy throughout the entire decade. When the PGT finally abandoned the armed struggle in 1968, they argued that the revolutionary process was now in a "critical phase" and added that "[a]fter more than four years of armed struggle we have succeeded in winning neither active participation nor meaningful support of the masses."[133] One important class component of that failure was the guerrillas' lack of success in striking resonant chords among the Guatemalan working class, shown by the weakness of their urban support network and by the social makeup of those who eventually joined the guerrilla movement: former military officers; university- and party-related intellectuals and activists; and *Ladino* peasants.[134] While the FAR sought their support, the middle classes never decisively deserted the incumbents in favor of the guerrillas and were a crucial component in the election of Méndez in 1966. Moreover, when the struggle became ever more terroristic on both sides in the late 1960s, part of that electorate moved to the *right*, perhaps ensuring the 1970 electoral victory of rightist candidate Arana Osorio.[135] Finally, all signs indicate that the upper class provided the most consistently violent opponents of the guerrillas, a pattern continuing to this day (the contrast with Cuba here is striking). Moreover, several have chronicled close upper-class involvement with the military death squads that appeared during the 1966–1967 counterinsurgency campaign. In a remarkably candid reply to a question about death-squad violence, one right-wing Guatemalan congressman noted, "The regime should not find it remarkable when the bourgeoisie organizes itself in order to take the law into its own hands."[136]

The Guatemalan guerrillas had done rather better at striking down roots among regional peasantries until the mid-1960s, yet failed completely in at least two attempts to recruit support in the indigenous highlands of northwestern Guatemala. Moreover, the ideological conservatism of those regions became apparent in the 1966 elections, when the Indian village highlands were the most consistently conservative voting areas of the entire nation. One Marxist analyst conceded that "Indian peasants . . . are, by and large, not politically active." Such conservative voting patterns probably reflected a combination of cultural traditionalism, landlord coercion, and patron-client relationships in the highlands, a conservative pattern certainly subject to later disruption and decay.[137] Yet in the late 1960s, the guerrillas also lost support even in their earlier strongholds. In the 1966–1967 situation and its aftermath, an FAR guerrilla leader in one breath notes that their (then) rivals in Izabal, the MR-13 guerrillas, had "lost their audience among the popular sectors that supported them," yet in another breath, he chronicles the FAR's own loss of peasant support in the Sierra de las Minas: "Presently we find ourselves in a phase where the social forces from which we could count on support have adopted a counterrevolutionary position."[138] In regional terms, all chroniclers of the movement acknowledge the guerrillas' restricted loci of operations: the northeastern departments, in particular Izabal, Zacapa, and Alta Verapaz. Their weakness in the capital city was evident throughout the struggle, as was their aforementioned failure in the western highlands. Elsewhere in the nation, their "presence" was virtually nonexistent. Indeed, if one takes the time to decipher the language of orthodox Communists, the PGT (guerrilla allies) themselves conceded their regional weaknesses publicly in 1965, only claiming the northeast as a focus of armed struggle with the regime.[139]

Along the organizational axis, the guerrillas suffered on several major counts. First, as I showed in chapter 5, the U.S. government stepped up military aid and training to Guatemala in the mid-1960s, and largely organized the counterinsurgency campaign that wiped the guerrillas out as major political actors for more than a decade. (How different from U.S. actions in Cuba.) Second, the military consolidated itself as a radically anti-guerrilla organization just before and during that campaign and has remained so ever since. The military participated in civic-action programs, begun in 1960 before confronted with a guerrilla opposition, in order "to elevate the living standards of the people, as a way of effectively combating communist propaganda that tries to exploit the ignorance and poverty of underdeveloped areas." Moreover, the military used focused civic-action programs, and not just terror, in its 1966–1967 counterinsurgency campaigns.[140] Finally, the stability of the Guatemalan military in the face of insurgency almost surely has particular historical roots, traceable to recurrent attempts in the past to arm the populace to serve as a counterforce to politically suspect soldiers, including the 1954 shipment of arms from Eastern Europe. The army intercepted that shipment at dockside and, later that year, stood aside when General Castillo Armas invaded Guatemala from Honduras with U.S. support.[141] The presence of some Communists in the Arbenz government, combined with 1950s cold-war ideology and the arms-shipment incident, have combined to make the Guatemalan military among the most profoundly anticommunist in the world.

Finally, the Guatemalan bishops were and continue to be among the most profoundly conservative prelates in all Latin America: both before and after the Medellín Conference of 1968. As late as the early 1980s, the Guatemalan archbishop continually refused to make any public condemnations of regime violence. That silence was only less obvious in the 1960s, before the spread of Liberation Theology and radical forms of Catholic action.

In conclusion, the Guatemalan pattern is a pivotal one, for in that nation revolutionaries seemed to be reaching a tipping point of dual power in the mid-1960s. Within a short period of time, however, the prospects for success dimmed almost completely. Prospective working- and middle-class supporters apparently deserted them to vote for a reformist politician in 1966, and their peasant supporters were either killed or turned against them in 1967. The U.S. government, the military, and the church consistently and strongly opposed any guerrilla successes. Those events should only serve to confirm what analysts should have noted all along: Even when dual power is on the historical agenda, the decisive vote doesn't always go to the revolutionaries.

Venezuela: A Breath of Dual Power

> Looked at from a purely class point of view it could be said that, during the years 1960–63, the working class and peasantry were defending a moderate but active government against assault from political groups composed, for the most part, of intellectuals, students, career-politicians and people who had come down in the world.
>
> —Luis Mercier Vega[142]

Despite the markedly different character of Venezuelan political life, that nation also saw the birth of a guerrilla movement that struck deep roots in selected rural areas, and also hinted at dual power in other areas of the country. Massive unrest during 1960 and 1961 in Caracas lent plausibility to left-wing claims that repression by the Betancourt regime was producing a revolutionary countermovement in the capital.[143] On the other hand, observers such as Mercier dismissed the riots of 1960 as an "explosion of violence that no one could call a popular insurrection."[144] Where is the truth here? Did the (undeniable) urban unrest in Caracas really augur, for a time, a revolutionary upheaval among the urban masses comparable to, say, Petrograd in 1917? The evidence suggests not.

Our starting point should focus on the differences between Guatemalan military rule during the 1960s and Venezuelan electoral democracy. Whereas the Guatemalan coup of 1954 ushered out that nation's sole historical experiment with reformist, electoral democracy, the Venezuelan civil-military coup of early 1958 ushered in a period of reformist, electoral rule, such as Venezuela had only ever experienced in the brief period from 1945 to 1948.

Betancourt's AD party could hardly be called "conservative" at this time. The party was born as a quasi-socialist party and retained socialist rhetoric and some policies when in power from 1945 to 1948. For example, the AD government had pioneered the fifty–fifty profits split with the foreign oil companies, the first major concession ever wrung from that foreign elite.[145] Indeed, when Betancourt returned to take the presidential sash in 1959, $1 billion in capital fled the country, fearing a new wave of "socialism." Throughout his five-year term, Betancourt pursued a policy of social and economic reforms—especially in education and land distribution—while resolutely repressing violence and quasi-insurrectionary activity in the capital. His successor, fellow *adeco* Raúl Leoni, was then elected to the presidency in 1963, with a much narrower plurality, coming to office largely on the basis of votes in rural areas.

Throughout this first unbroken decade of electoral democracy, opposition to the AD governments was highly vehement and vocal, but the bulk of government and opposition activity was *within* the legal system and the electoral process.[146] Obviously, the very "openness" of the Venezuelan electoral system—one that Guatemalans could only glimpse briefly in 1966—provided a political space for the moderate opponents of the regime, weakening any attractions that the radical left might have held for them. (Most radical critics of the Betancourt regime fumed about this political feature, rather than analyzing it.)[147] Venezuelan political actors mostly attempted to secure governmental power through legal and electoral channels, and not by setting up a parallel government or counter-state as a path to dual power. The major exception to this "loyal opposition" was the guerrilla movement and its parent organizations, the PCV and the MIR, who envisaged themselves as a counter-state.

Where could we encounter hints of dual power favoring the insurgent opposition to Betancourt's version of electoral democracy? First of all, the capital had voted overwhelmingly against his candidacy in 1958, giving him but 12 percent of the vote. While this does not indicate a revolutionary form of opposition, the Betancourt regime was especially weak in the various poor *barrios* of Caracas, where the nonunionized working class and other poor groups largely resided. Second, the guerrillas succeeded in building up small rural areas of guerrilla "government" in several areas of the countryside, most notably in the hills of Lara and Falcón states.[148] Finally, there is a mass of evidence indicating that the Central University in Caracas not only over- whelmingly lined up against the Betancourt regime, but also specifically pro- vided key resources for the revolutionary struggle.[149] Those areas of support, however, never coalesced into a national movement toward dual power, as each faltered in turn, in part because each branch of revolutionary activity was eventually cut off from the others.

In regional terms, the headlines were always grabbed by the actions of the Caracas-based Unidades Tácticas de Combate (UTCs—Tactical Combat Units), the urban "terror" wing of the FALN, whereas the rural *tomas* (brief village seizures) and engagements with the military eventually came to have only faint resonance in the newspapers published in the capital. UTC activ- ity was never successfully coordinated with rural actions by the FALN guer- rillas in the countryside. Nothing resembling simultaneous urban and rural uprisings—as in Nicaragua—ever occurred in Venezuela. The urban riots occurred mainly in the years 1960–1962, the rural guerrilla movement from 1963 to 1967. Moreover, the UTCs decayed noticeably as political actors after they lost support in the barrios, and again after the Leoni government occupied the Central University in 1966. The rural fronts, for their part, began to lose steam when their ties to urban areas began to decay; the with- drawal of PCV support and the occupation of the Central University, in the years 1965–1966, were especially damaging blows to the insurgency. Rural insurgency seemed to have grown because the state historically possessed only a weak administrative apparatus in rural areas, rather than because of the guerrillas' own effectiveness at mobilization.[150]

The peasantry and (to a lesser degree) the working class were the AD gov- ernments' strongest sources of support from 1958 to 1968.[151] In addition, the shift of Betancourt's administration rightward from its earlier leftism appar- ently assuaged the fears of the Venezuelan upper class and of foreign capital. In any event, that upper class was a far less important political actor than its counterparts elsewhere, and its position was certainly to Betancourt's right, not left.[152] Hence they were certainly not potential allies for the guerrilla movement (contrast the Cuban case). In the middle classes, despite an appre- ciable flow of out-group politicians, university students and professors, and a few others into the ranks of the guerrillas, the highly educated professionals and intellectuals remained predominantly with the political system; indeed, they tended to be AD political supporters.[153]

In the urban lower classes, a bifurcated pattern emerged in the early 1960s. The organized working class, represented in unions and labor confederations, was the second largest single source of support for AD governments, and the insurgent left gained no substantial support among the Venezuelan working class, paralleling the Guatemalan experience. After 1958, the Communists declined from a position of influence over 15 to 20 percent of labor union members (from 1958 to 1961) to no more than 5 percent by 1966.[154] In contrast, the support for the UTCs in the Caracas *barrios* for some time seems to be beyond dispute. University students, who later would provide most UTC members, had built up a network of barrio support and social prestige during the earlier struggles against the Pérez Jiménez regime.[155] The two groups' shared hostility to the Betancourt government—which replaced the massive 1958 welfare-spending program in Caracas (the *Plan de Emergencia*) with an austerity program—led to a continued antigovernment alliance early in the Betancourt administration.

This support bears some structural resemblance to support in the Nicaraguan towns for "*los muchachos*" during the Sandinistas' insurgency against Somoza, and hence we should briefly analyze the Venezuelan failure to expand in a similar way, and the final loss of barrio support for urban insurgency. First, even left-wing observers like John Gerassi and ex-guerrilla Petkoff saw the political dangers to a movement whose major insurgent technique was killing policemen; such killings of policemen, often relatively poor men from the urban barrios, could be expected to alienate a good part of the barrio population from the insurgency.[156] Talton Ray indicates results damaging to leftist hopes for support:

> Almost all the murdered policemen were barrio residents. In many instances, they were shot to death while walking home from work or sitting in their ranchos at night; families, friends and neighbors were witnesses. Some of those killed were elderly men who had been working for the force for years before AD came into power and were considered about as politically harmful as traffic cops. When the FALN ambushed a train just outside Caracas in September 1963, and machine-gunned to death four national guardsmen—all the sons of poor families—the disgust was especially strong because, for a barrio youth, it was a sign of social advancement to launch a career with the national guard.[157]

Hence we can better understand Petkoff's later, rueful references to "absurd deformities in our actions [which] awakened hatred in the population toward us."[158]

As Ray makes abundantly clear in his closely argued analysis of barrio life and politics—he worked there from 1961 to 1964—the barrio residents were acutely resentful of the AD government and voted strongly for Wolfgang Larrazábal (architect of the *Plan de Emergencia*) in 1958, and against the AD in 1963. Yet their voting was heavily aimed at eliciting government welfare-spending directed in the barrios, and not toward revolution. The far left lost further support when, having been squeezed out of government posts by the Betancourt regime, the posts that the left could use to reward barrio supporters with spending and patronage, they proceeded to sabotage some projects linked to the regime, earning them the enmity of some barrio residents. Evidence of the barrios' political orientation, along with that of other Venezuelans, came in December 1963 when over 90 percent of the Venezuelan electorate voted, despite FALN demands for abstention and their violent preelection wave that killed dozens and wounded a hundred. Most Venezuelans (68 percent) voted against AD's presidential candidate, Leoni, but he became president with a plurality of the presidential vote.[159] Both major guerrilla leaders, Petkoff and Bravo, conceded that the turnout in the 1963 elections and the retention of the presidency by AD were political defeats, if not disasters, for "the popular movement."[160]

The loss of peasant support added the *coup de grace* to a guerrilla movement rapidly becoming moribund. The accidental death of key Lara leader Argimiro Gabaldón, followed by the PCV's withdrawal from the armed struggle, led to a sharp drop in the strength of the guerrilla front in that state, exacerbated by the internal struggles for power that followed. Once again, that decay in an entire front was confirmed by a former participant, José "El Gavilán" Díaz, when he came down from the mountains to surrender in August 1965: "The guerrillas in Lara, upon the loss of their leaders, especially Argimiro Gabaldón, are on the way to their total disappearance."[161] In Falcón, home of the second strongest guerrilla front, strong peasant support and patterns of informal guerrilla "government" slowly gave way to the disintegration of the guerrilla movement into a largely inactive core group who consistently sought aid from Cuba, rather than combat with the military.[162]

Clearly the largest single obstacle to the spread of dual power in rural Venezuela was the decades-old presence there of Acción Democrática itself. Peasants were the single largest, and most dependable, of AD's groups of supporters, and were no threat to desert en masse to the guerrillas.[163] No other guerrilla movement in the region faced such a thoroughly unfavorable rural milieu as did the Venezuelan insurgents. As a result, the Betancourt government could mobilize its rural backers *for* the regime, when faced with riots or military revolts organized *against* the regime with the support of the left. Twice the Betancourt government bussed in large groups of peasants from the countryside to Caracas, perhaps one hundred thousand strong, to demonstrate their solidarity with his regime, and some peasants reportedly rose up to back the AD government during the two military revolts of 1962.[164]

Those military revolts, at Carupano and Puerto Cabello, were the last gasp of the left within the armed forces. In fact, they elicited popular indifference more than supportive uprisings. Many officers who led the revolts fled to the interior to join the guerrilla forces.[165] From that point on, the military stayed firmly on the side of the regime, with the main hints of discord coming from rightists, not leftists. With the killing of the four guardsmen in September 1963, the army was finally allowed freer rein in the anti-guerrilla struggle, which became quite violent, and often terror laden, despite Venezuela's nascent democratic institutions. The elite troops within the army (the *cazadores*) and the political police (DIGEPOL, or General Directorate of Police) were particularly virulent in their anticommunism and, scattered evidence suggests, in their violence as well.[166]

In addition to the military, other critical organizations also stayed with the regime. Given the alternatives of military coup or communism, the church decided to side with the government from 1958 to 1963.[167] Although the AD and its left-wing opponents fought for control of a variety of organizations, including labor unions, professional associations, and journalistic organizations, the AD generally won those battles, and in the labor unions in particular the PCV had to form its own counter-organizations to retain any influence at all.[168]

Finally, the Central University was a hotbed of anti-regime ideology and activity throughout the Betancourt years and into the Leoni presidency, until Leoni ordered it occupied in late 1966, proclaiming that university autonomy would no longer be interpreted to give it "extraterritoriality" (that is, as a safe haven for guerrillas or terrorists). University student linkages to the barrios during the fight against Pérez Jiménez had led to their high prestige in those neighborhoods, so high that, when the police forces of the capital collapsed following the 1958 fall of that regime, student-organized "brigades of order" became the de facto police force of much of the capital, surely looking like a counter-state in embryo.[169] For reasons we have already explored, the links of support among students, UTC urban guerrillas, and barrio residents had largely fallen apart by 1963. In fact, the brief political strength of the studentry reflected the temporary power vacuum created by the dictator's 1958 fall more than it did their own resources. As political parties resumed shape and electoral competition, university politics were elbowed aside firmly to a peripheral role in the national scene, and students themselves gained strong influence only in those parties that lacked other core sources of support: the PCV and the MIR.[170]

In summary, Venezuela showed only hints, more modest than in Guatemala, of leaning toward dual power, especially in the urban barrios from 1958 to 1962. Yet those residents, in the end, were interested more in welfare-state spending by political parties than in revolutionary insurrection, and the left lost support there by 1963, the very year in which they were increasing their presence in rural areas. Yet in rural areas the guerrillas largely faced "occupied ground," since AD's support among the peasantry was widespread and firm. Overall, the persistence of reformist, electoral democracy continued to generate alternatives for the populace—including potential support groups for the far left such as the barrio residents, the working class, and the peasantry—making the growth of a counter-state not just unlikely, but perhaps almost unthinkable to Venezuelans not on the far left of the political spectrum.

"Oases of the Armed Struggle" : Colombia, Peru, and Bolivia

> All these Cubans, these Peruvians, these Argentines, who tried to mount a model guerrilla front in Bolivia—a country that had barely gotten over a revolution—were supported only by a few students in La Paz and a few miners in Oruro.
>
> —Jean Lartéguy[171]

While Bolivia is an extreme variant, Robert Lamberg's description of the guerrilla experience in many nations as mere "oases" is an extremely apt one, for few signs of dual power ever emerged in our remaining three cases, and virtually no evidence that groups other than scattered ones among the peasantry ever regarded the guerrillas with more than curiosity and some occasional good will.

The Colombian guerrillas remained throughout the 1960s and 1970s the most purely rural guerrilla movement of any we have seen. Their historical origins go back to *La Violencia* and other forms of peasant mobilization in and before the 1950s. Like La Violencia itself, the guerrilla movement remained a purely rural phenomenon, with no resonance among urban dwellers, save for select groups of university students scattered through Colombia. We must trace this striking failure to the continued existence of Colombia's two traditional political parties, the Liberals and the Conservatives, even if their political conflict was almost completely muted under National Front governments from 1958 to 1974. However, the failure of the National Front regime to consolidate the same degree of support as did the old political parties led to a sharp weakening of central government legitimacy in the 1960s. Yet the nation saw no parallel improvement in the guerrillas' political position, in part because there were three competing groups who sought to subordinate and damage each other at various times, in part because military civic action actually weakened peasant support for the insurgents in some rural areas.[172] Unlike Bolivia and Peru, guerrillas in Colombia had relied on deep and fairly widespread peasant support for decades as the 1980s arrived, but never secured anything more than that rural presence.

In Peru, the struggle for the establishment of electoral democracy had apparently been won with the 1963 election of Fernando Belaúnde Terry to the presidency. The parties of the left, including the Commmunists (PCP), had participated in that election. Indeed, in the course of "centering" itself in search of greater electoral success, the APRA party had alienated its left-wing caucus, APRA Rebelde, which later was to organize the MIR guerrilla movement. The Communists, for their part, voted only in a minority for "the armed struggle" in the early 1960s, despite the power of Cuban imagery elsewhere in Latin America, and disgruntled revolutionaries under the leadership of

Héctor Béjar left the party to form the Army of National Liberation (ELN), with its subsequent guerrilla *foco* in Ayacucho.

As in Colombia, there were some minor resonances far from the Andean *focos* in favor of the guerrilla movement, especially in the universities, but those were only whispers of revolution in a society struggling with a shot at reform-oriented democratic rule.[173] The major social groups and classes did not support the guerrilla movement. Despite the proposed reforms threatening some of their long-standing privileges, the Peruvian upper classes stood by the regime when it was confronted with a revolutionary insurgency. The surest index of this was their rapid purchases of a government bond issue floated specifically for the purposes of funding the counterinsurgency. Sales of these "anti-red" bonds reached 84 millon *soles* by late August, 121 million by late September (the exchange rate was about 26 *soles* to the dollar).[174] While Héctor Béjar would argue that revolutionary elements of the petty bourgeoisie were the main proponents of revolution, one is instead struck by their paucity of numbers, excepting again the case of university students.[175] As in Venezuela and Guatemala, the working class once again was virtually absent from the ranks of the 1965 revolutionaries, reflecting the latter's striking weaknesses in and neglect of urban areas. Despite Luis de la Puente's prediction that the lumpenproletariat of the urban *barriadas* would explode like a bomb given a revolutionary clarion call, those areas were silent in 1965.[176]

Only the Campa Indians (for a time) and the peasantry in Béjar's locale provided any peasant support to the insurgents; such support, moreover, was feebler and more fleeting than elsewhere in the region, although not as completely absent as in Bolivia.[177] In La Convención (Cuzco) and the nearby regions, despite de la Puente's year-long organizing efforts, no such support was forthcoming for the MIR's Pachacútec front. As the letter of a disillusioned guerrilla revealed, the front attracted few peasants, and most of them cooperated after being given large sums of money. Several later deserted and helped the military to destroy the *mirista* guerrillas on the nearby Mesa Pelada.[178]

Both regionally and organizationally, the Peruvian guerrillas exhibited a striking narrowness of support. All observers agree on the virtual absence of any kind of urban support network, let alone an urban insurrection. At most, as Lamberg observed, a few bombs were exploded in urban areas, for the urban network was almost strictly "an intellectual activity." Perhaps a few demonstrations were also held at universities; nothing more.[179] Organizationally, the MIR received some token support from Fidel Castro abroad, and little more.[180] Peru's almost-infinite variety of left-wing parties and splinter groups produced position papers on the guerrillas, but little other tangible support or activity; the Communists' (PCP) "critical support" meant nothing except agreeing that revolution was a good thing, but insisting that the guerrillas were using the wrong strategy at the wrong time.[181] Béjar analyzed the situation most acutely: The "profound divisions" of the left—which themselves were reflected in the noncooperation of two rival guerrilla groups—continued to cripple overall revolutionary strategy, reducing it to nothing save fragmentation and wordiness.[182] The large-scale press in Peru, especially *La Prensa*, was rabidly anti-guerrilla; the contrast with Cuba's *Bohemia*, a scant seven years earlier, is striking. The military may not have stood unwaveringly by Belaúnde, as their coup of 1968 would reveal, yet they never broke ranks vis-à-vis the guerrillas and systematically and (at times) ruthlessly pursued their counterinsurgency. Finally, the Peruvian archbishops stood firmly against "communist subversion" and condemned the insurgents and communism on 29 August 1965 before a crowd of 25,000 Indians in Huancayo—near the operations area of the MIR in Junín.[183]

Instead, the main political actors throughout 1963–1968 were the Belaúnde government, the APRA-dominated congressional opposition, and a politicized military. Given such powerful contenders, the guerrilla insurgencies were insignificant indeed; they were used by APRA to score political points against Belaúnde and, further still, to drive a wedge between the Belaúnde government and the military. By doing so, leading *aprista* Haya de la Torre sought to make APRA look more acceptable to the military that had so adamantly opposed its ascent to power over the previous third of a century.[184] Despite that tripartite division within the government and the state, the very reformism of Belaúnde's electoral democratic experiment indicated that the guerrillas had timed the insurgency very badly. Several observers have traced the Peruvians' lack of a revolutionary response precisely to their orientation toward the expected reforms of the new democratic government.[185]

In Bolivia, the tin miners had persisted as an organization outside the effective control of the central government ever since the revolution of 1952 and the subsequent nationalization of the mines. Armed and capable of self-defense during and after the revolution (as were groups of peasants),[186] they did indeed constitute something resembling "dual power" in Bolivian society, especially given the striking weaknesses of the Bolivian state, both before and after the revolution. The economic drains that the mines made upon state finances probably augured an eventual confrontation. It came. The military, rebuilt with U.S. aid since the 1950s, confronted the miners over "sovereignty" in the mines in 1964, with the first of several massacres of miners that would eventually reestablish violent state control, if not legitimacy, over the mining portions of Bolivian society.[187] The Bolivian army, or more precisely René Barrientos, finally seized power from the revolutionary MNR in a 1964 coup, and Barrientos was confirmed in office in a 1966 election, with deep support among the peasantry, especially in the Cochabamba Valley.[188] Another bloody confrontation in the mines came in the midst of Guevara's insurgency, in mid-1967. Throughout that year, however, Barrientos consistently threw his political opponents off balance, alternating carrots and sticks, and thereby consolidating his position. Notably, the Communist parties were legal, and the Soviet-line one (PCB) took part in the 1966 elections in a combination front party.[189] The weakness of the guerrillas, along with the strength afforded the government by the support of the armed forces and the peasantry, helped Barrientos to weather a temporary storm, and then to rule without serious political challenge until his accidental death in a helicopter crash in 1969.

Ché Guevara had in fact hatched his "South American strategy"—revolution in Bolivia as a catalyst for a continent-wide revolution—in 1963 and, like so many guerrillas elsewhere, failed to alter that strategy to changed political conditions.[190] Several commentators had pointed to Bolivia as a nation "ripe" for (another) revolution, including Régis Debray. Yet in 1968, after Guevara's death, Debray spoke from a Bolivian jail cell (after his conviction for aiding the insurgency during a visit to the *foco*), remarking wistfully that "[t]his thing of nationalism is very important" while noting the "peculiarities" of the "heterogeneous" and "revolutionary officers" in the Bolivian army.[191]

Socially, regionally, and organizationally the guerrillas failed to secure support from Bolivians. The peasantry as a class voted heavily for Barrientos in 1966 and had good relations with the military, one-fifth of whose manhours had been spent in rural civic action in 1963.[192] The peasant confederation, moreover, pledged their support to Barrientos in mid-1967 in the midst of the regime's unease over the insurgency.[193] Both sympathizers and critics of Ché's *foco* point to the peasant support enjoyed by Barrientos, and the utter lack of support for the guerrillas.[194] They were indifferent, if not hostile, to Ché's guerrillas, and many informed on him throughout the campaign. The tin miners had been strong supporters of the revolutionary MNR since 1952, although that support had weakened when their union leader, Juan Lechín, was passed over for the MNR's presidential nomination in 1964 and then expelled from the party after protesting the slight. Still, their opposition to Barrientos and the military over mine policy should not be confused with support for the guerrillas; of the latter there is very little evidence.[195] Furthermore, the urban middle classes also had exhibited a unified opposition to the guerrillas and could be expected to do so in the future.[196]

Regionally, the guerrillas had no support in *any* area of Bolivia, most certainly not the countryside. Only the faintest echoes of sympathy appeared during the insurgency, for example in the Technical University in Oruro (a tin-mining region), and the guerrillas' urban network simply failed to function or was wrecked by raids and arrests.[197]

Related to the guerrillas' striking urban weaknesses was their complete lack of organizational supporters,[198] epitomized in Ché's estrangement from the local Communist party (PCB) over Cuban domination of the Bolivian insurrection. The PCB did not support the insurrection or earlier Cuban revolutionary "suggestions" (thereby earning the epithet *mierda* from Fidel Castro). While some individual members of the PCB helped the insurgency, others were later expelled from the party for such activity.[199] The opposition MNR party, despite its hostility to the ruler who had ousted them from power, actually opposed the guerrilla movement and warned its members against any contacts with the insurgents. At most the various leftist groups expressed verbal "solidarity" with Ché's revolution, and gave no other tangible support.[200] (The resemblance to the Peruvian left's response is probably structural rather than accidental: each leftist group was struggling for *open* power and influence, under relatively nonrepressive conditions, against a reformist, elected government with substantial popular support. Under such conditions, endorsement and open support for insurrection would lead to immediate repression and the closing down of such open opportunities for mobilizing support.)

The military also clearly presented a unified front against the guerrilla insurgency and showed no signs of splitting apart within the officer corps, despite the sorry performance of the troops early in the campaign. Moreover, the high command initially resisted, rather than welcomed, U.S. aid for the counterinsurgency campaign and bristled nationalistically at the "reactionary press and media organs" who suggested that the United States really commanded "the glorious Bolivian army."[201] Nonetheless, as I showed in chapter 5, the United States gave clear, if measured, support to the Bolivian counterinsurgency from the start.

Striking in each of the three preceding cases is a pair of features: (1) a rural-based guerrilla movement with few or no ties to urban support groups, hence vitiating any chances for the expansion of a wing of dual power in urban centers; and (2) a regime with reasonably deep political support among the lower classes in society. Belaúnde had won his election with peasant support in the southern Sierra; the Colombian parties each continued to draw on their deep cross-class bases of support, despite increased abstention through the 1960s; and Barrientos, a native Quechua speaker and former author of civic-action programs in rural areas, was wildly popular among the peasants, especially in the Cochabamba Valley. Taking these three cases together with the Venezuelan case, we must agree with Loveman and Davies that Guevara's original thesis—that it is futile to start an insurgency against an elected regime because other political avenues have not been exhausted—stands supported by the evidence of the 1960s.[202]

However, the further evidence of Cuba and Guatemala strongly suggests that the existence of electoral democracy is not a necessary condition for the failure of revolutionaries to seize power. Both were "military dictatorships" in the conventionally accepted sense of the term, thereby suggesting that only *peculiar types of dictatorships* are especially vulnerable to insurgent revolutionary assaults: *patrimonial praetorian* regimes, or *mafiacracies*. For the moment we will suspend such analyses, until we can reflect upon the Nicaraguan revolution against the Somoza regime (chapter 11) and finally put regime strengths and weaknesses in an overall comparative context in chapter 12.

PART III

Guerrillas and Revolution since 1970 —Testing Theories on the Second Wave

There is nothing new under the sun.
—Ecclesiastes (1:9)

CHAPTER 9

The Origins of the Second Wave

> It has been proven that the Sierra Maestra can never be recreated
> outside of Cuba, that the Cuban revolution was an exceptional
> phenomenon which will never reappear in the same form.
> —Jean Lartéguy (1970)[1]

BEGINNING as early as 1966, and growing louder yet after Ché Guevara met
his death in a schoolhouse in La Higuera, Bolivia, observers began to announce "the end" of Latin American rural guerrillas as viable political movements. Many such analysts, revolutionary friends and foes alike, proclaimed
a strategic shift to urban "guerrilla" activity, seen as a more defensible and
potentially successful form of revolutionary strategy, given the increasingly
urban character of Latin America's population structure. With the subsequent
crushing of urban guerrilla activity throughout the "Southern Cone"—the
Tupamaros in Uruguay, the MIR in Chile following Allende's fall, Marighella's urban guerrillas in Brazil, and the Montoneros in Argentina—theorists found themselves increasingly without revolutionary options. For more
than a decade since that period, however, both analysts and revolutionaries
have "rediscovered" rural guerrilla warfare. Any suggestions in 1980 that
"the guerrilla" had died with Ché in that Bolivian backwater would have
seemed absurd.

The bulk of guerrilla insurrectional activity since 1970 has once again been
located in the countryside. While revolutionary victors in the region have
always enjoyed urban support as well—impressively so in Nicaragua—it will
not do to suggest that the Nicaraguan revolution was an urban revolution, as
more than one scholar has suggested in comparing it to the Iranian revolution
against the shah.[2] Such theories only achieve plausibility if we completely
ignore the rural historiography of the Nicaraguan revolution from 1960 to
1977, for the Sandinistas themselves have termed the *montaña* the "crucible
of the revolution"; as Omar Cabezas put it in his widely read book, fire came
from the mountain. Jeffrey Gould's recent and careful historical work on
rural Chinandega demonstrates just how much scholars miss by seeing the
Nicaraguan revolution as an "urban" one. More sociologically, and more
damaging to these urban interpretations, Jeffery Paige has shown that the
urban, lower-class insurrections so crucial to the Nicaraguan revolution
were fundamentally rooted among recently displaced peasants who often

continued to work as migrant laborers in the countryside; thus even the urban aspects of the revolution were strongly colored by rural events and processes and conform to Paige's predictions concerning migratory labor and revolution.[3]

Finally, in sheer military terms one must note that the discrete urban uprisings of 1978 *were* crushed. Only in 1979, when Somoza *also* had to disperse and thus weaken his armed forces in battles against at least five different rural-based guerrilla fronts, did the revolutionaries seize power.[4] Just as we have already seen in Cuba, urban events and loyalty shifts *did* affect revolutionary outcomes in our next five cases. Yet only in partnership with peasant-supported and rurally based guerrilla armies did revolutionaries seize power in Nicaragua.

In this and the chapters that follow, I will discuss in some detail the major revolutionary movements of the 1970s and 1980s. My procedure will differ in some details from the one that I pursued earlier in this work. For the most part I will eschew systematic comparison of failed with successful guerrilla movements, insofar as peasant support is concerned. I will, however, pursue a comparison of the complete victory of the revolutionaries in Nicaragua with the failures of their contemporaries in El Salvador, Guatemala, Peru and, in lesser compass, Colombia. I will also attempt to draw out fundamental parallels in the Cuban and Nicaraguan revolutions, as well as contrasts with failures elsewhere, in order to bolster my causal explanation of revolutionary success in those two instances.[5] Since there is far greater continuity between the earlier and later periods in the Colombian case, I will have considerably less to say about Colombian guerrilla movements in the sections to follow. The most noteworthy patterns there since 1970 have been the following: (1) considerable regional diversification of the various guerrilla organizations beyond the locations of their 1960s origins; (2) the emergence of M-19 as a new guerrilla group; (3) the massive increase in guerrilla numbers up to the early 1980s, and some declines since then; (4) the continued failure of such a strongly entrenched guerrilla movement to provide any real political threat to incumbent governments.[6]

A Brief Historical Review

In Nicaragua, opposition to the thirty-year-old Somoza family dynasty foundered in the 1960s despite sporadic guerrilla efforts. In the early 1970s, however, the Sandinista National Liberation Front (FSLN) revitalized itself with growing peasant support in the mountainous north central region. The centrist faction would eventually cement over a three-way split within the FSLN, appealing to their common opposition to Somoza. Middle-class and even capitalist opposition to Somoza grew as well, especially after the regime looted international relief funds sent following the 1972 Managua earthquake, and also because of Somoza's continued refusal to share real power with other social groups or parties. By 1978, civil and guerrilla opposition to Somoza finally coalesced into a semblance of unity, joining in demanding his ouster. Insurrection in various forms, both urban and rural, continued to grow until the regime fell in July 1979.

In El Salvador, an extended period of military rule since 1931 began to decay in the early 1970s. A number of guerrilla groups engaged in irregular warfare against the military, apparently unhampered by a series of internal splits. The three largest groups have been the Popular Forces of Liberation— Farabundo Martí (FPL), born of a 1970 split within the Communist party; the Revolutionary Army of the People (ERP), formed of Christians and Communists in 1971; and the Armed Forces of National Resistance (FARN), which split from the ERP in 1975. At the same time, general opposition to military rule grew with the electoral frauds of 1972 and 1977 and the brutality of the Romero government (1977–1979). The guerrilla groups gradually reached a certain modus vivendi and even cooperation (1979–1981), and with one other group merged to form the Farabundo Martí National Liberation Front (FMLN). An alliance deepened between the FMLN and their civil allies, the Democratic Revolutionary Front (FDR), whom the guerrillas partially dominated. Resistance grew even further after a new "reformist" civilian-military junta seized power in late 1979. A guerrilla "final offensive" of early 1981 failed to oust the government from power, and the active revolutionaries withdrew mainly to the countryside. Upon accession to the U.S. presidency in early 1981, Ronald Reagan promptly renewed economic and military aid to the incumbent government and increased it to massive proportions. Elections for a Constituent Assembly in 1982 lent some new legitimacy to the government, as did the later legislative and presidential elections of 1984 and 1985. Important opposition groups such as the FDR were (self-)excluded from those elections, under conditions of widespread death-squad violence, and the guerrillas demanded electoral boycotts. While the insurgents' numbers grew to perhaps ten thousand combatants in the early 1980s, their political fortunes declined after 1982, stabilizing since then at a lower level of activity and support, keeping a dynamic stalemate with the government, with neither side able to make inroads upon the core of its opponent's strength. Peace talks, joined intermittently after late 1984, did not bear fruit, while civil opposition to President José Napoleón Duarte's government increased somewhat after 1985. By 1988 civil resistance was still growing in El Salvador. The right-wing ARENA's gains in elections in that year and 1989 came as the governing Christian Democrats (PDC) lost support, while the old FDR group partially broke ranks with the guerrillas of the FMLN to participate in civil and electoral activity as the Convergencia Democrática. A major military campaign by the guerrillas to "invade" and control key urban centers in November 1989 failed to produce a corresponding civilian uprising and produced fierce urban fighting, hundreds of guerrilla deaths, and substantial army terror. It resulted only in a renewal in 1990 of peace talks between the ARENA-controlled government and the FMLN guerrillas.

In Guatemala, after periods of dormancy and urban terrorism in the late 1960s, various offshoots of the FAR reemerged in the 1970s, primarily in the Indian-populated western highlands, as more or less thinly veiled authoritarian governments came and went. Among the later guerrilla groups were the Guerrilla Army of the Poor (EGP), the FAR (again), and the Organization of the People in Arms (ORPA). After sustained growth to 1982, reaching over six thousand combatants in some estimates, a violent counterinsurgency campaign under General Efraín Ríos Montt again reversed guerrilla fortunes, although they may have retrenched slightly up until the 1985 election of civilian president Vinicio Cerezo. Cerezo's administration, despite his inability to push through substantial social reforms, was characterized by the continued decline or relative insignificance of guerrilla activity, with some hints of resurgence in early 1990.

In Colombia, the fortunes of the various guerrilla groups—the FARC, formerly linked to the Soviet-line Communists; the ELN, formerly Castroist and recipient of Cuban aid; and the Chinese-line EPL—waned toward 1970, but waxed anew in the new decade. The M-19 (19th of April Movement) guerrillas emerged following the allegedly fraudulent elections of 19 April 1970, which cost the new ANAPO party at least a share of the power monopolized by the Liberals and Conservatives. The M-19 was a radical splinter group from ANAPO, initially solely urban, but later spreading somewhat to rural areas; it, too, grew in the early 1980s, despite strong military counterefforts. By the early 1980s, some estimates put the total number of Colombian guerrillas at seven thousand. However, a downward inflection in the guerrillas' political fortunes began with the mid-1982 election of President Belisario Betancur and subsequent amnesty offers. Since then, other guerrillas have been lured from the struggle with cease-fire armistices and the option of participating in the electoral process, which the FARC in part accepted for a time. Throughout this period both the newly civilized ex-guerrilla left, represented in the Unidad Patriótica party, and the guerrilla regions themselves suffered recurrent death-squad terror. Several guerrilla groups finally unified in 1988, but the M-19 abandoned the armed struggle in early 1990 to participate in civilian politics. Still, in early 1991, the FARC and ELN, perhaps totaling eleven thousand members, were able to launch a major military strike, aimed at derailing the meetings of a newly elected (with M-19 delegates) constituent assembly.

During the 1970s in Peru, university people organized a Maoist guerrilla group, *Sendero Luminoso* (Shining Path) with substantial peasant support in the southern Sierra. Beginning in Ayacucho, *Sendero* spread and grew by the mid-1980s to as many as two thousand to seven thousand members and many more supporters, despite its extreme violence and ideological rigidity. By 1985–1986, however, various indicators suggested that *Sendero* was beginning to lose some of its rural support, even as it increased its presence in poor *barrios* of various towns and stepped up its military activities nationwide.

WHO WERE THE SECOND-WAVE GUERRILLAS?

Class and Education

> The majority [of the Sandinista leaders] come from the most comfortable families of Nicaragua and are from universities . . . and a high proportion of them have been educated by the Jesuits.
>
> —José Fajardo (1979)[7]

In appendix B I have gathered biographical data on the leaders of the post-1970 guerrilla movements in Nicaragua, El Salvador, Guatemala, Colombia, and Peru. While we will later observe important differences from the earlier period, for the most part we must agree here with Ecclesiastes. Once again we find confirmation of Alvin Gouldner's generalization about revolutionaries: They are drawn disproportionately from the intelligentsia, not only highly educated, but also largely involved in the production of theories.[8] While not all were socially located within that stronghold of intellectual activity, the university, many were immersed in two other realms where the commitments to ideas and beliefs are a central component of day-to-day life: politics and the church. And once again, as we shall see, the rank and file of the movements were overwhelmingly composed of peasants under the leadership of such intellectuals. While some have suggested that these later movements have provided more opportunities for peasants to rise to leadership positions, especially in the Guatemalan EGP, Peru's *Sendero*, and various Salvadoran groups, one should instead be impressed by the degree to which the university educated retain control over the highest "levers of power" within guerrilla organizations.

This is especially true of Nicaragua, which some in their revolutionary élan have declared to be "a new kind" of revolution.[9] Whatever the case for its outcome, in its origins the Nicaraguan revolution conforms *most* strongly to Gouldner's position—that revolutionary leaders are drawn overwhelmingly from the intellectuals, the "new class"—and to my own position, that guerrillas are drawn disproportionately from upper- and upper middle-class backgrounds, and from similar occupations on their own account. As in Cuba, there are exceptions to the generalization about social origins—Omar Cabezas and Carlos Nuñez in Nicaragua, and Facundo Guardado in El Salvador stand out in this regard—but otherwise the correlation between privileged class origins and university education, on the one hand, and domination of revolutionary leadership, on the other, is striking.

Claims made in a guerrilla zone of El Salvador that "leadership arises directly out of the local peasant population" may apply to local, mid-level leadership (cadres) in selected regions of that nation; indeed, it probably applies as well to the EGP and ORPA in Guatemala and to *Sendero* in Peru. Yet the evidence above shows that it definitely does not apply to the national, higher-level leadership of the Salvadoran FMLN, or to its component parts, or (probably) to the upper leadership in Guatemala and Peru.[10]

If the leadership of the second wave was drawn from privileged groups in society, just as in the first wave, the rank and file also resembled their historical predecessors in class origins. Virtually every report from the countryside, including a wealth of on-the-scene reports by journalists, confirms the largely, often overwhelmingly peasant composition of the guerrilla armies, which came to number in the thousands in the 1970s and 1980s, perhaps reaching ten thousand in El Salvador in the early 1980s. In El Salvador, Peru, Colombia, and Guatemala, the reports were all the same: the guerrilla combatants were largely peasants. In Nicaragua, moreover, a sample of Sandinista members—probably skewed toward urban fighters—confirms substantial participation by the urban lower classes, especially in the urban informal sector of the economy. In Peru, Guatemala, and especially El Salvador, friendly visitors made the plausible claim that, in guerrilla strongholds, the categorical distinction between guerrillas and peasants had largely dissolved, with part-time peasant militias and various peasant support activities integrating peasant and guerrilla into a unified force against army and regime forces.[11] The Salvadoran guerrillas put it most succinctly: "Our mountains are the people."[12] Oddly enough, the evidence on this count is rather *less* persuasive for the case of Nicaragua, despite a number of revolutionary memoirs, even though there, too, peasants provided the core of rural supporters and participants.[13]

We should attend to some minor variations worthy of note. In Colombia, the ELN, the EPL, and the FARC continued into the 1970s and 1980s to be numerically dominated by peasant combatants, and the FARC's peasant leadership also largely survived into the 1980s. Nonetheless, the FARC's Marulanda noted that there had been an appreciable broadening of the guerrillas' ranks, now including a larger number of urbanites: workers, intellectuals, students, professionals, doctors, lawyers, professors, and priests. The Colombian M-19 also claimed that its core rank and file came from simple people, largely workers. This claim was made elsewhere with little supportive evidence, yet was here more plausible due to M-19's historical emergence from ANAPO, which had strong electoral support among the Colombian urban lower classes in the early 1970s.[14] In Nicaragua, several of the urban insurrections against the Somoza regime began as spontaneous Indian uprisings in the Indian suburbs of Monimbó (in Masaya) and Subtiava (in León) and later culminated in more massive, organized insurrections in those cities, and others such as Matagalpa, toward the end of the Somoza regime. While many of these people were technically located, in class terms, in the "urban informal" sector and among Marx's lumpenproletariat—as were the bulk of ANAPO supporters in Colombia—we should recall that Paige has traced the social origins of many to peasants displaced by the expansion of cotton production.[15] In Peru, most *senderistas* are from provincial peasant backgrounds (parents or grandparents), although they themselves have above-average education, including their well-known attendance and recruitment at the regional University of Huamanga, where *Sendero* was born.[16]

Gender and Ethnicity

If the class and educational composition of the post-1970 guerrilla movements resoundingly echoes Latin America of the 1960s, as well as other times and places, such is not the case for gender and ethnicity. In fact, both women and Indians, as disprivileged status groups within their societies, made substantial inroads into guerrilla movements in the two decades following the death of Ché Guevara.

Over the last decade, Norma Stoltz Chinchilla, Jane Jaquette, and Linda Lobao [Reif], among many others, have especially expanded our understanding of "women's place" in Latin American revolutionary movements. Lobao's work probably now defines the state of our knowledge. She and others have documented the striking expansion of women's revolutionary roles since 1967. In no other fashion does the second wave of guerrillas differ so thoroughly from the first wave. In the first wave, as I have documented in chapter 2 above, women's roles were limited in sheer numbers, in percentages, and in the scope of their participation. Since 1970 the changes seem clear. There are now far more women revolutionaries, in absolute numbers as well as percentages, and they are far more likely to participate in combat and leadership roles. One might in part trace this shift to a common guerrilla strategic shift from a *foco* theory of revolution, which implies a quick road to victory, to something more like "Prolonged Popular War" (the Nicaraguan term), which implies a greater emphasis on sheer, long-term accumulation of human support, sometimes all done in subterranean fashion (in Nicaragua, "accumulation of forces in silence").[17]

The percentages of women combatants reported for the 1970s and 1980s are truly striking: 30 percent of the Sandinista Army toward the end of the insurrection; one-third of the forces of the FMLN (combined) guerrillas in El Salvador; and *one-half* of all *senderista* combatants in Peru.[18] Percentages tell only part of this story. The late Edith Lagos has been termed—probably mistakenly—"the intellectual mentor" of *Sendero* in Peru. The late Mélida Anaya Montes ("Ana María") served as second in command of the FPL, El Salvador's largest guerrilla organization, and on the joint FMLN command, prior to her murder by her FPL rivals in 1983. By the 1980s, a journalist interviewing the FARC guerrillas in rural Colombia was told that women now fought side by side with men and got no special privileges, something observed by no Colombian analyst during the 1960s. When the Colombian M-19 elected its new leaders in 1985, one of the eight was a woman (Vera Grave), and the organization said that it had no "woman problem." Eight ELN women carried out a 1979 *toma* (armed seizure) of a movie theatre in downtown Bogotá, followed by armed propaganda before their captive audience. Among the female Nicaraguan *comandantes* were Dora Téllez, Mónica Baltadano, and Leticia Herrera, and four of the seven Sandinistas who commanded during the battle of León were reportedly women.[19]

On the other hand, there is some contrary information. One of the recurring points of Cabezas's account of his experience in the hills of Nicaragua is the absence of women, and when Nora Astorga was sent to a Sandinista training camp near the Costa Rican border in 1978, only 4 of the 80 trainees were women. For Guatemala, while we certainly have evidence of some female participation in the EGP and ORPA guerrillas, we apparently lack evidence of a scope comparable to the percentages proposed above for other nations. In the Peruvian jails holding people accused of terrorist activities, mostly from *Sendero* or similar groups, only 80 were held in the women's prison, out of a nationwide total of 855 such prisoners.[20] Each of these instances suggests a sharply lower participation rate for women than the strikingly high percentages produced by the revolutionaries, typically for western intellectual consumption, especially for feminist academics in the United States and elsewhere. Such contrasts should alert our critical faculties. Was this part of a revolutionary public-relations campaign? Was this an instance in which male guerrilla leaders or selected female representatives told foreign academics precisely what they wished to hear? In short, this instance might parallel that famous sequence from the Russian Revolution, in which the Bolshevik delegation came to negotiate for peace with the Germans, with a worker, a sailor, and a peasant on the revolutionaries' panel. Crane Brinton reports the denouement: "When, however, the negotiations really got going after a recess, the Russians dropped their ornamental sailor, worker, and peasant, and were represented by men of course not the social equals of the high-born Germans opposite them, but, one suspects, their cultural superiors. . . ."[21] The question is therefore clearly raised: Were women in these Latin American cases merely ornamental or were they thoroughly integrated into the movement?

While widespread evidence from Cuba, Nicaragua, and Communist countries surely demonstrates that women do *not* share equal power with men under socialism, despite formal regime commitments to gender equality, does this therefore imply a rejection of the Latin American evidence on increased female participation?[22] It does not. I am still persuaded that a quantum leap occurred in women's participation in Latin American revolutionary movements, roughly between 1965 and 1975, and that there were even hints of feminist resistance to male domination as early as 1964.[23] Feminism, in a sense, *had* to emerge sooner or later on the radical left, due to the patent cultural contradiction between an ideology of equality and brotherhood (I use the latter term advisedly) and the obvious subordination of women. The "opening up" of the left to women was a worldwide process,[24] in which Latin Americans clearly partook, and that *abertura* was accelerated by the needs of revolutionaries for support during prolonged periods of revolutionary activity. Even so, equal female participation in power politics may well suffer, as it has in many past instances, whenever military considerations become paramount.[25] They often do become paramount, both in the course of revolutionary insurgency and in the revolutionary defense of power once acquired. Military pressure and militaristic activity do not seem to be good for gender equality. This may well explain the underrepresentation of women in revolutionary leadership during and following the seizure of power. Still, the continued *non*participation of Cuban women at the commanding heights of the Cuban polity should give both scholars and advocates pause in any rush to proclaim the woman-empowering character of Latin American revolutionary movements.[26]

If women entered the ranks of the revolutionaries in droves during the second wave, so, too, did another hitherto excluded and exploited status group, the Indians. Nowhere has this been clearer than in Guatemala and Peru. In the case of Guatemala, we should recall that the 1960s guerrillas were overwhelmingly concentrated in *Ladino* areas of northeastern Guatemala and succeeded only in forming a single guerrilla column from the indigenous people, led by Pascual Ixtapá, former *alcalde* (mayor) of Rabinal, in a largely Kekchí area of Alta Verapaz. The EGP and the ORPA guerrillas—who notably *both* were offshoots and remnants of the 1960s guerrillas—reforged their insurgent movements with long periods of underground work during the early-to-mid 1970s. They then both emerged as strong guerrilla movements late in that decade, and continue, despite setbacks from 1982 to 1984, to provide a substantial insurgent challenge to Guatemalan politicans, whether military or civilian.

EGP and ORPA are, by consensus, the strongest of the second-wave guerrilla movements in Guatemala, with the FAR and the Communists (PGT) fielding numerically inferior forces. Both EGP and ORPA developed strong bases of peasant support and recruitment in the Indian highlands of western Guatemala. EGP laboriously built up its indigenous support in the "transverse strip" of northwestern Guatemala, particularly in the "Ixil Triangle" and El Quiché Department.[27] In striking parallel, ORPA built its support in the central-west highlands, also largely among the indigenous populations, in San Marcos, Totonicapán, Quezaltenango, and Sololá, especially near Lake

Atitlán. Both groups also altered their pure Marxist theory to fit their actions, insisting that under Guatemalan conditions, they were pursuing not just a class-based socialist revolution, but also simultaneously a "national" revolution of Indians against their historical Hispanic oppressors.[28] Several aspects of the Guatemalan struggle have become clear since the birth of these new movements. First, the guerrillas have met and recruited the Indians through the medium of Indian languages, like Kekchí, Mam, and Cakchiquel. Second, the guerrilla combat units came to be, it is widely agreed, composed largely, sometimes overwhelmingly of peasant Indian forces, in some cases as high as 99 percent. Third, the mid-level leadership is largely recruited from the Indian peoples as well, although there is little evidence for their nationwide leadership in the various movements.[29]

In Peru, despite the secrecy surrounding its membership and operations, the historical origins of *Sendero Luminoso* have now become substantially clear. Its organizational leadership and origins lay in the University of San Cristóbal de Huamanga, usually known as the University of Huamanga. Huamanga from its origins was intended to be a community-oriented provincial university, serving the needs of the people in surrounding areas of Ayacucho Department. As such, a high proportion of the students were not from white, upper- and middle-class Peruvian families—the Peruvian norm—but rather were the children and grandchildren of Indian peasants, whose lingua franca was typically Quechua, rather than Spanish. Huamanga's ties to indigenous communities were further strengthened by its educational extension and other outreach programs branching into the surrounding countryside. Many Huamanga students from indigenous backgrounds were recruited into *Sendero*, which politically controlled student and faculty organizations there by the early 1970s. When *Sendero* lost control of Huamanga in 1974, it went underground. Meanwhile, its closet-members returned to the Sierran Indian communities, often as teachers, and became community members, often intermarrying into the local population. In this manner, the indigenous population of Ayacucho moved, in some places overwhelmingly, into support for *Sendero* when it went public around 1980. As in Guatemala, there is widespread agreement that the membership is largely, perhaps overwhelmingly Indian in origins and Quechua speaking or bilingual, even though the highest leaders originated outside the region and the department. Moreover, much of the mid-level leadership, again paralleling Guatemala, apparently comes from the Indian population as well. In short, whereas the 1960s Peruvian guerrillas only had sporadic luck in recruiting from the Indian peasant population, *Sendero* has struck deep roots into the indigenous peasantry of Ayaucho and other departments, completely reversing the guerrilla failures of the 1960s in Sierran Peru.[30] In both Guatemalan cases, and in Peru as well (the latter by drawing on Andean mythic traditions[31]) the guerrillas have reshaped their ideology to target the Indian population and its specific hopes and needs.

Our remaining nations had relatively smaller Indian populations, and therefore the question of indigenous participation was less relevant and less pronounced.[32] Nonetheless, these latter cases raise interesting questions and challenges. In Nicaragua, we can see a clearly bifurcated pattern. The Sandinistas put down fairly deep roots into the Subtiavan Indian *barrio* in León through their careful organizing efforts of the early 1970s. Indian *barrios* in, first, Monimbó (outside Masaya), and then Subtiava rose against Somoza in early 1978, and were bloodily suppressed. The first was spontaneous, the second in part led by the Sandinistas, but both bespoke mass pressures more than Sandinista leadership, and both areas joined in the Sandinista-led insurrections during the following year.[33] Overall, one is impressed by the Sandinistas' ability both to organize insurrection and to join up with and nurture existing insurrectional activity. The other side of Sandinista-Indian relations, however, concerns their failures with the Miskito Indian populations of eastern Nicaragua. Not only did the Sandinista guerrillas fail in one early *foco* attempt in a Miskito region in the east, but they also succeeded in sharply alienating large numbers of Miskitos following the revolution, pushing Miskito resistance fighters into an alliance with the *contra* resistance. Later the Sandinistas began to mend fences with the Miskitos, with some partial successes along those lines.[34]

In El Salvador, the largest indigenous populations have historically been in the western highlands, with smaller numbers in an interior band stretching into eastern El Salvador. The western Indian peasantry rose up in revolt in 1932 but were violently suppressed in the subsequent military repression, known as the *matanza*, which took fifteen to thirty thousand lives. In the succeeding fifty years, that area was politically quiescent; indeed, the very speaking of the Pipil variant of Nahuatl tended to disappear when white people were within earshot, and some variants of Indian dress tended to vanish as well. These western highlands have been the areas of El Salvador in which the latter-day revolutionaries have garnered the *least* success, and most observers trace that "peace" to memories of the earlier terror.[35]

ORGANIZATIONAL ORIGINS

Once Again: The University and Revolution

During their early revolutionary years the Sandinistas had argued that university life itself produces revolutionary consciousness, almost paralleling my argument in chapter 3.[36] Therefore we should attempt again to give such a perspective our systematic attention and analyze information on university enrollments as we did before. We should again keep in mind that the Latin American tradition of university autonomy protected certain student anti-regime organizing efforts, especially in Nicaragua, where Somoza generally

TABLE 9-1

Guerrilla-Student Linkages and University Enrollments in Latin
America during the Second Wave, 1965–1975
(in rank order, by size of increase)

Country	Enrollments		% Increase
	1965	1975	
Ecuador	13,728	170,173	1,140%
El Salvador	**3,831**	**26,909**	**602**
Brazil	155,781	1,089,808	600
Costa Rica	5,824	32,483	458
Nicaragua	**3,042**	**15,579**	**412**
Honduras	2,148	10,635	395
Venezuela	43,477	185,518	327
Cuba	20,573	82,688	302
Mexico	133,374	520,194	290
Colombia	44,403	167,503	277
Panama	7,091	26,289	271
Chile	43,608	149,647	243
Paraguay	5,833	17,153	194
Peru	**64,541**	**186,511**	**189**
Guatemala	8,459	22,881	170
Bolivia	13,996	34,350	145
Argentina	222,194	536,959	142
Uruguay	16,975	32,627	92
Dominican Republic	6,606	11,773	78
Haiti	1,607	2,467	54

Source: United Nations, Statistical Yearbook, 1977 (pp. 336–44) and 1984
(pp. 261–68).

Boldface indicates nations meeting two conditions: (1) a strong guerrilla
movement after 1975; (2) strong linkages between those movements and university students, faculty, and/or organizations.

respected university autonomy. The University of San Carlos in Guatemala
and the National University of El Salvador, however, proved themselves to
be far more vulnerable to regime and death-squad violence. Indeed, in those
two cases, there is serious question whether the universities could *continue* to
provide any kind of haven for guerrilla-related activity during the later period
of guerrilla war, especially after the closing of the National University in El
Salvador in mid-1980, and the "open-season" for killing students at San Carlos in 1977–1978 and in 1980.[37]

In my earlier analysis, I found that those nations with the strongest 1960s
ties between guerrillas and university students—Venezuela, Peru, Guate-

mala, and Colombia—were also the very nations that had seen the greatest explosions in university enrollments during the preceding decade. Did that pattern repeat itself for the second wave? For El Salvador, we know that (ex-)students from the National University (in San Salvador) were overrepresented among the leadership, while in Nicaragua there was comparable disproportion from the National Autonomous University in León. In both nations, enrollment in those two universities—given their "weight" in national university life—is likely to be reflected in nationwide enrollment growth. Information from Guatemala, Colombia, and Peru is notably thinner, and we expect that the student-guerrilla connection has been substantially weaker in the first two cases, because the guerrilla movements have had such weak ties to urban groups and areas since the mid-1970s (the exception is the Colombian M-19, which moved from its urban beginnings to a rural presence). That is, the Guatemalan and Colombian guerrillas have been *overwhelmingly* rural in their orientation and recruitment since 1975. For the case of Peru, however, all observers agree that *Sendero* is dominated by former students and professors from the University of Huamanga in Ayacucho Department, *Sendero's* birthplace.

The correlation between strong student-guerrilla linkages and an earlier explosion of university enrollments is apparent for the second-wave movements. From 1965 to 1975, El Salvador and Nicaragua ranked high (2 and 5), as we would expect. Colombia, Peru, and Guatemala did not (10, 14, and 15). For Peru, the question should *not* be overall enrollments, but those at Sendero's birthplace, the University of Huamanga. Enrollments there rose very rapidly from 700 students in 1963 to 15,000 in 1972—five times the capacity of the university facilities—especially following the radicals' 1968 victory in university elections and their subsequent adoption of open-enrollment policies. Such growth (over 2,000 percent) would easily place Huamanga at the top of our list. Therefore, the three nations with the *closest* student-guerrilla ties in the latter period had indeed exhibited earlier university enrollment explosions. The hypothesis from chapter 3 is supported here as well.[38]

Once Again: Guerrillas as Left-Wing Splinter Groups

In the 1950s and 1960s, guerrilla organizations routinely (1) emerged from already mobilized political organizations of the left and center, including the various communist parties; (2) had alternating histories, varying by both time and place, in which the communist parties committed themselves to or distanced themselves from "the armed struggle," depending upon the political opportunities available to them for other forms of legal political activity, including union organizing and electoral campaigning. The patterns of the

1970s and 1980s throughout Latin America have resoundingly supported that empirical generalization, even in nations that I have not closely analyzed for this study.[39]

In Nicaragua, the organizational origins of the Sandinistas clearly lie in the Partido Socialista Nicaragüense, the Communist party of Nicaragua. The two major founders of the FSLN[40]—Carlos Fonseca and Tomás Borge—emerged from a critical wing of the PSN youth group, Juventud Revolucionaria Nicaragüense (Revolutionary Nicaraguan Youth, or JRN). The Juventud Patriótica Nicaragüense (Patriotic Nicaraguan Youth, or JPN), a left-wing student group at the National Autonomous University of León, also contributed not only the other FSLN cofounder, Silvio Mayorga, but leading FSLN cadres such as José Benito Escobar, Julio Buitrago, Doris Tijerino, Rigoberto Cruz, and Casimiro Sotelo as well.[41]

The JRN and the JPN formed the core of the FSLN at the time of its founding in 1961. Indeed, those very origins help in part to resolve the hotly-debated question of whether the Sandinistas were "Marxist-Leninists." Of course part of the leadership was, but the Sandinistas grew as a movement because of their symbolic addition of other Christian and strictly national issues to their Marxism. Notable here are their opposition to the U.S. presence and their self-identification as the heirs of Sandino himself, both of which could be concretely, rather than abstractly, embodied in their opposition to the consecutive rule of Luis and Anastasio Somoza Debayle (1956–1979). (There is a family resemblance here to Castro's M-26 revolutionaries, who could draw on the proximate legacy of Eddy Chibás, and the distant one of José Martí, as "symbolic partners" in their struggle against Batista.)

A third organizational source of the early FSLN came from young members of the Conservative party, which had engaged in sporadic armed resistance to the Somoza family's (nominally Liberal) rule since the 1930s. Another such Conservative generation came of age in the 1950s and provided some important cadres to the FSLN in its early days: Edén Pastora (later known as Comandante Cero), and Ernesto and Fernando Cardenal.[42]

After their initial formation, the FSLN received additional organizational "recharges" from various other structured groups in Nicaragua, while in turn influencing the political direction those groups would take. These were especially important during its organizational doldrums of the late 1960s and early 1970s. First, they received influxes from the cohorts of left-wing students who together attended Moscow's Patrice Lumumba University, where they formed two cells to analyze and plan for a Nicaraguan revolution. Among those attending were later party stalwarts such as Henry Ruiz. Others studied and trained together in Cuba as well.[43] Second, the FSLN and key student organizations developed an even closer symbiotic relationship during the late 1960s, strengthening the student ties apparent at the movement's inception. At the university level, the FSLN created the Federación Estudiantil Revolucionario (Revolutionary Student Federation or FER), which later won the university elections at León and, with an electoral victory in 1970, came to dominate the university students' federation, the Consejo Universidadio [sic] de la Universidad de Nicaragua (University Council of the University of Nicaragua, CUUN). The CUUN victory gave the FSLN easy access to typewriters and mimeo machines, whereas in the past they had had to steal them. More importantly, it gave them a ready recruitment channel at León to funnel funds, supplies, cadres, and messages between the university and the guerrillas. Later the FER and other Sandinista front-organizations like the Comités Cívicos Populares (People's Civic Committees) would provide the organizational access for the FSLN into urban Indian *barrios* such as Subtiava in León.[44] Moreover, FSLN influence among students soon extended beyond the universities into the *colegios* among high school students, especially in León.[45] Finally, exemplifying the special links between the Sandinistas and left-wing Christians to which many chroniclers have pointed, we should note that the Movimiento Cristiano Revolucionario (Christian Revolutionary Movement) came to be, in the words of Sandinista sympathizers, "a legal arm of the FSLN." A second Christian source of FSLN cadres and support lay in the monastery at Solentiname, run by Ernesto Cardenal, which became a mobilizer of revolutionaries prior to its occupation and destruction by Somoza's forces.[46]

The organizational origins of the Guatemalan guerrillas are rather easier to summarize, for each major group can be traced back to the guerrilla movements and front organizations of the 1960s. Those predecessors survived in stunted form into the new decade, and then regained strength as the 1970s progressed, finally resulting in a far stronger insurgency than had ever existed in the 1960s. The ORPA guerrilla movement shows the clearest precedents: its founders were the remaining members of the 1960s FAR's "Regional de Occidente" (Western Regional Organization), which split from the parent group in 1971 over revolutionary strategy. It continued its work in the Indian regions of the west—San Marcos, Totonicapán, Quezaltenango, and Sololá—and finally went public in 1979, with strong Indian support and membership.[47]

The other large-scale guerrilla organization, the EGP, also derived from the original FAR: "In March 1967 former members of the FAR living in Cuba, Mexico and Europe began to draw up discussion documents and critically assess the guerrilla experience of the 1960s. By the end of the decade the EGP's founding nucleus had been formed and on 19 January 1972 the first contingent of the new organisation entered Guatemala to start a people's war in the northeast."[48] From that point on, Mario Payeras's *Days of the Jungle* provides a vivid account of the early, difficult years of organizing a guerrilla insurgency in the transverse strip of northwestern Guatemala, especially around the "Ixil Triangle" in El Quiché Department.

These two patient organizers of guerrilla warfare were soon joined by another "veteran" of the 1960s guerrilla struggles, the Communists themselves (the PGT). The virulent 1960s debates over the appropriateness of the armed struggle to "Guatemalan conditions" were repeated when in 1978 the "PGT Leadership Nucleus" broke away from the main body of the party and, under the leadership of Mario Sánchez, embraced the armed struggle. The remaining part of the PGT came slowly to the armed struggle through 1981 and 1982.[49]

The original FAR did not completely disintegrate during its period of urban "terrorism" in the late 1960s. In 1972 it restructured itself to pursue "mass activity," rather than short-term revolutionary goals, and gained some influence in labor unions. After a period of supporting mass mobilization in cities during the mid-1970s, it returned to develop a more rural strategy of mobilizing the peasantry, with its main weight in El Petén, the sparsely populated northern panhandle of Guatemala.[50]

Finally, there is evidence, albeit only fragmentary and suggestive, that certain other organizations have served to channel members toward the guerrilla movements since the latters' origins. The Comité de Unidad Campesina (Committee for Peasant Unity, or CUC) developed during the 1970s as a form of Indian resistance to political and military oppression and had its greatest strength among the migratory workers of the highlands: the very workers who Paige and others suggest are the core of support and recruits for the guerrillas. This indicates at least an ecological overlap between the two groups; it suggests possible organizational influences as well.[51] After the violence at San Carlos in 1977–1978, a student group broke away from its PGT connections—at a time when the PGT opposed the armed struggle—to form the Frente Estudiantil Revolucionario Robin García (Robín García Revolutionary Student Front, or FERG), which may or may not have had close ties to the guerrillas.[52]

The Salvadoran guerrillas also have clear origins in preexisting political groups, including the Communist party of El Salvador (PCS).[53] The first of the guerrilla groups arose initially in a split from the Communist party in 1969, taking shape as the FPL, led by Salvador Cayetano Carpio, in the years 1970–1972. This is the largest overall group in size, but second to the ERP in number of guerrilla combatants. The FPL remained bitterly opposed to the PCS well into the late 1970s, and perhaps a residue yet remains, despite their formal cooperation in the FMLN since 1980. The FPL also "quickly recruited radicalized members of the Christian base communities and persecuted union activists" at the start and later would organizationally dominate its corresponding mass or front organization, the Bloque Popular Revolucionario (Popular Revolutionary Bloc, or BPR).[54]

The largest guerrilla group and second largest organization is the ERP, formed in 1971 and led by Joaquín Villalobos (René Cruz) since the late

1970s. The ERP blended together three clear organizational antecedents: (1) a splintering from the Communist youth group, perhaps even from the FPL guerrillas themselves; (2) young dissidents from the Christian Democratic Party (PDC) (whose centrist leader José Napoleón Duarte would be elected president in 1985); and (3) members of a left-wing student organization known as El Grupo (The Group), whose membership may have overlapped with either or both of the first two groups.[55]

Other, smaller revolutionary groups have emerged since that time. The first was the FARN guerrillas, who split with the ERP over ideological disagreements and the ERP's execution of Roque Dalton and another ERP militant. The FARN thereafter took over the ERP's front organization, the FAPU (for United Popular Action Front), and the ERP only three years later would form a new group, the LP-28 (Popular Leagues of 28 February). (The FAPU was the first of the popular fronts, from which several others, including the BPR, emerged.) Thus, by 1978, each of the three main guerrilla groups had its own corresponding popular organization.[56] The fourth main guerrilla group, the Partido Revolucionario de Trabajadores Centroamericanos (Revolutionary Party of the Central American Workers, or PRTC), formed in 1976 under a Trotskyist ideology and may have been another splinter group of the ERP guerrillas and of the Communists.[57] Finally, the Salvadoran Communists belatedly joined the armed struggle, establishing their guerrilla organization in the years 1977 to 1979.[58]

All the above-named guerrilla groups would eventually join a new umbrella organization, the FMLN, by the years 1980 to 1981, yet the actual unity of this organization remains a matter of serious dispute, for the ERP and the PRTC in particular have at times pursued tactics that their colleagues reject, such as the former's kidnapping of local government officials and the latter's café bombing in the capital. Moreover, there was through the 1980s only fragmentary evidence of strategic coordination of true military actions among the various components of the FMLN; perhaps the November 1989 insurrection finally showed such true unity. Finally, further groups have at times emerged since the early 1980s, usually splintering off from existing revolutionary organizations. The most prominent case was a militant splinter group that broke off from the FPL when its moderate wing came to dominate the group in the wake of the in-group murder of Comandante Ana María (Mélida Anaya Montes) and the subsequent guilty suicide of FPL chief Cayetano Carpio.[59]

Earlier I traced the origins of the three main Colombian guerrilla movements: the FARC (to the "peasant republics" and the Communist party); the EPL (to the Peking-line Communist party); and the ELN (to the short-lived Castroist movement, the MOEC). While each of these groups operated into the 1980s, one major new guerrilla group appeared in the interim, the Movimiento 19 de Abril (April 19th Movement, usually known simply as

M-19). Although later denying such origins, the M-19 clearly emerges from the populist party led by ex-dictator (1953–1957) Gustavo Rojas Pinilla, the Alianza Nacional Popular (ANAPO). The M-19 began as "the armed wing of ANAPO" and, indeed, was self-described at the time as "a dissident and revolutionary splinter of ANAPO."[60] ANAPO splintered after its loss—fraudulently, its members claimed—in the 1970 Colombian presidential election to the National Front candidate, with the dissidents first forming ANAPO Socialista, and later the M-19, which itself apparently splintered later on as well.[61] Oddly enough, the M-19 may have had much less publicized ties to and origins in an already existing guerrilla organization, the FARC, which claimed that the M-19 really grew out of the urban wing of the FARC guerrillas. Indeed, longtime FARC leader Jacobo Arenas argued sharply that "We provided the men, we provided the money, and we provided the ideas" for M-19, although they could not resolve "internal contradictions" with M-19 leader Jaime Bateman. Perhaps, after all, the M-19 always had been a kind of FARC fifth column within ANAPO, with the M-19 later splintering from the FARC, only to show hints of reuniting in the early 1980s.[62]

Sendero Luminoso, Peru's Maoist guerrillas, can be organizationally traced all the way back to the movements of the 1960s. Formed in a split with the Communists, Héctor Béjar's ELN began a guerrilla *foco* in 1965 in Ayacucho Department. One (inactive?) branch of the ELN was the "ELN—Huamanga Command," to which some have traced *Sendero's* origins, probably erroneously.[63] The ELN itself split over the *foquista* strategy in 1965. In 1966, future *Sendero* leader Abimael Guzmán Reynoso and his clique formed the first Peruvian Maoist group out of part of the PCP—the record is somewhat unclear—and called itself the Partido Comunista del Peru—Bandera Roja (Communist Party of Peru—Red Flag). This group in turn expelled Guzmán and his "bumpkins" (ca. 1968–1970), or they withdrew and adopted a new name, "The Communist Party of Peru in the Shining Path [*Sendero Luminoso*] of Mariátegui," named after the famous Peruvian Marxist of the early 1900s. Thereafter the group would pursue a relatively straight, if highly patient, line to the guerrilla explosion of 1980, drawing on the human and material resources afforded them by their control of the University of Huamanga and the university's influence in highland Indian villages.[64]

In table 9-2, I have summarized the previous lengthy discussion by demonstrating parallels for the individual cases from the 1970s and 1980s. Just two types of organizational predecessors, Communist parties and other guerrilla organizations, capture the large majority of the organizational forerunners of the regional guerrilla movements; the remaining groups formed as splinter groups from noncommunist parties, or from other, mostly student-dominated, political groups. In all these respects the guerrilla movements of the 1970s and 1980s provide resounding confirmation for the theses I advanced in chapter 3 for the 1950s and 1960s. The guerrilla movements do not

TABLE 9-2
Organizational Precursors of the Second-Wave Guerrilla Movements

Nation/ Movement	Communist Party	Other Guerrilla Movement	Other Party	Student Organization
Nicaragua				
FSLN	Yes		Partly (Conservatives)	Yes (JPN; FER)
Guatemala				
EGP	Partly	FAR		
ORPA	Partly	FAR		
FAR	Partly	Revival of FAR		
El Salvador				
FPL	Yes			
ERP	Yes (Youth)	FPL?	Christian Democrats	
FARN		ERP		
PRTC	Yes?	ERP?		
Colombia				
M-19		FARC	ANAPO	
Peru				
Sendero	PCP (Soviet) PCP (Maoist) Bandera Roja	ELN?		

Sources: See text and notes.

originate, therefore, merely in explosions of discontent among the unorganized masses but are found rather more clearly among (1) those individuals already imbedded in political organizations and, more specifically (2) among "marginal political elites," as Theda Skocpol termed them in her study of revolutions.[65]

THE ORIGINS OF THE SECOND-WAVE MOVEMENTS

As in the first revolutionary wave, the second wave of guerrilla activity continued to be influenced by the model of the Cuban revolution, now including the transformations of Cuban society effected during the 1960s. Sandinistas Carlos Fonseca and Manlio Tirado both confirmed the influence of "The Cuban people's rebellion . . . even before its victorious outcome" (that is, during the late 1950s), while accounts of both the prerevolutionary and postrevolutionary Sandinista movement point to Ché Guevara as the single most important icon for revolutionary Nicaraguans.[66] Similar events occurred on the left in both Guatemala and El Salvador, where the Communists suffered splits because of their initial unwillingness to follow "the Cuban Road." In the latter case, Salvador Cayetano Carpio, who formed the first Salvadoran guerrilla group after a bitter split with the Communists, put his position succinctly in an interview: "Did you renounce the Communist Party?" ["Yes."] "Why?" "For the Cuban Revolution."[67]

In both the 1960s and the 1970s, strong guerrilla movements appeared where the state appeared unresponsive to the revolutionaries; yet in the first period the eruption was due largely to state clampdown, while in the latter period it occurred more because civil society had shifted its views of the state. Thus, if strong guerrilla movements in the 1960s appeared as a reaction to the *reimposition* of nonrevolutionary or counterrevolutionary governments, then their 1970s counterparts—in Colombia, Nicaragua, Guatemala, and El Salvador—appear to be responses to the *persistence* of the old regime.[68] I have diagrammed the differences between the two periods, and the similarities within periods, in figure 9-1.

I stress "old" regime, because the governments in those four nations looked increasingly archaic in a regional context, and I stress old "regime" because they were also (though less) distinctive in denying real political participation to new contenders pounding at the gates of power. In the language of political science, these regimes faced "crises" of participation with which their "old" institutions were incapable of dealing, and guerrilla warfare was freshly available in the cultural repertoire as a revolutionary option. Only in Paraguay and Haiti did similar regimes persist without engendering strong guerrilla movements (although both regimes have since fallen to nonrevolutionary successors). Yet both Paraguay and Haiti have peculiar sociopolitical histories, distinguished by strong, personalistic, authoritarian control over both politics *and* society, which has worked against mass countermobilization.

In Nicaragua, Guatemala, and El Salvador, personal or military dictatorships of long duration—reaching back to the 1930s in Nicaragua and El Salvador—persisted in denying any institutional share of power even to "respectable" middle-class opposition parties, let alone the lower classes. In Colombia, political outsiders were excluded from power through 1974 by the National Front coalition, which may have retained power in 1970 through electoral fraud. Not until the 1982 elections was a "nonofficial" candidate finally chosen president. In response to a "closed" political system in all four countries, guerrilla movements were initiated in the 1970s, if not before, by disaffected intellectuals and marginal political elites.[69]

Finally, Peru remains a special case among the later guerrilla movements: there an extremist ideology has proven a "functional alternative" to the patent political exclusivity found elsewhere, in contributing decisively to the creation of revolutionary sentiment. A combination of Maoist dominance of the regional University of Huamanga and a subsistence crisis in the Andes produced the powerful guerrilla movement *Sendero Luminoso*, radically differ-

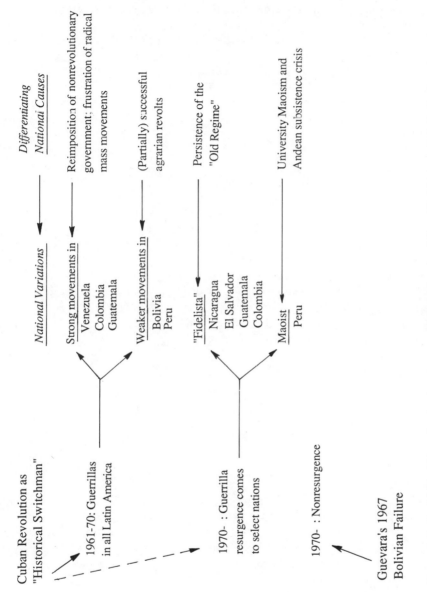

Figure 9-1. Social Conditions for the Appearance and Early Stages of Guerrilla Movements in Latin America

ent in many ways from its counterparts elsewhere. The affinity between the Maoist message of peasant war against the cities and the Sierran conditions typically conducive to peasant millenarian revolt has led to a merger of the two eschatologies in a powerful revolutionary movement with apocalyptic overtones.[70]

CHAPTER 10

The Structures of Peasant Support
in the Second Wave

> The peasant is an agent of forces larger than himself, forces
> produced by a disordered past as much as by a disordered
> present.
>
> —Eric Wolf

IF PEASANT support was not random in the first wave of guerrilla movements, it was not in the second wave either. As we saw in chapters 6 and 7,
peasant support for guerrilla movements tended to be higher in regions that
exhibited certain types of characteristics: (1) they had land-tenure structures
featuring relatively high rates of sharecropping or squatting; (2) they had
recent or long-term histories of assaults on the landed security of peasant
cultivators; (3) they had long-term histories of resistance to central authorities; and (4) they displayed social and cultural structures that provided revolutionaries with ready access to a sympathetic peasant population.

Those features were, surprisingly, replicated in the second wave of guerrilla movements with few exceptions. The main difference in the analyses
that follow is the absence of countries with weakly supported guerrilla movements from the comparison; we have no Bolivia, no Peru in the second wave.
Therefore, our second-wave comparisons rely solely on intra-national differences in peasant support, rather than on the international comparisons that
supplemented my earlier analyses. A second difference lies in the general
exclusion of Colombia from the analyses to follow. The 1980s Colombian
guerrillas are essentially continuities of the 1960s movements, even though
certain movement organizations now control areas that others dominated in
the earlier period. The sheer persistence of these movements over a quarter
century through regions of the Colombian interior strongly suggests that my
Colombian analyses of the earlier chapters still pertain to those movements.
The main difference lies in the spread of insurgency to several new areas of
the interior, which is to be expected of any long-term movement. Yet for our
theoretical purposes, we are more interested in the earlier "crucibles" of revolution and less interested in those areas that board a revolutionary bandwagon
at later stages. Similar strictures apply to the Salvadoran case, where the
regions of guerrilla influence shifted somewhat from 1982 to 1988.

AGRARIAN STRUCTURES AND REVOLUTION

According to Jeffery Paige's analysis, which I earlier supported in a modified form, we would expect that sharecropping regions would provide a haven for revolutionaries superior to that of most other regions. Along with share-croppers, moreover, I suggested and provided evidence that squatter-dominated regions would provide similar levels of support. At this point, we should note that Paige predicted a second type of revolutionary cultivator, structurally similar to the sharecropper in confronting a wage-paying, economically weak landlord: the migratory estate laborer. Unlike his sharecropper counterpart, however, the migratory estate laborer is associated with nationalist (i.e., anticolonial) revolutions rather than with socialist revolutions.[1] Thus we have three types of cultivators, all of whom we expect to be revolutionary. While that list may seem over-copious, it excludes certain cultivators in whom other theorists have sought the rural counterpart of Marx's revolutionary subject; in particular it excludes the "middle peasant," who has secure access to a plot of land (Paige's "smallholder"), as well as the true rural proletariat, those who face *capitalist* (i.e., owners of capital, not just land) landlords.[2] As we shall see, the migratory estate laborer now moves to the center of our analysis, for regions supplying such laborers have moved to the forefront of revolutionary activity in Latin America since 1975, the year Paige's book was published.

There were two fundamental loci of revolution in the anti-Somoza resistance. One such area, the "crucible of the revolution" in the words of one Sandinista, was the *montaña* of north-central Nicaragua, whose guerrilla areas John Booth has independently identified (which is of use for our analysis to follow).[3] In those rural areas the Sandinistas began securing widespread peasant support—following a decade of failures in other areas—in the late 1960s, strengthening such support into the mid-1970s. The second locus of revolution in Nicaragua was the cities of the north and west, where major anti-Somoza uprisings—a number of them independent of Sandinista control or influence—began in 1978 and continued off and on until the regime fell on 19 July 1979. Among the important urban insurrectionary centers were Matagalpa, León, Masaya, Chinandega, and Estelí.

The data in table 10-1 support the proposition that squatter areas provided special support for the FSLN guerrillas in the *montaña* during the 1970s in Nicaragua. In those departments that served as major rural guerrilla havens from 1971 to 1977—Matagalpa, Jinotega, Nueva Segovia, and Zelaya—36 percent of the cultivators were squatters, versus but 8 percent nationwide. Moreover, as the second set of data shows, within each of these locales, the percentage of squatters was at least eleven points higher in the guerrilla zones than elsewhere. The only nonguerrilla zone in these departments with a high

TABLE 10-1

Nicaragua: Proportion of Squatters in Guerrilla Zones and Other Areas

	Number of Units		% Squatter-Held
	Total	Squatter	
	1. Across Departments		
Nicaragua	88,223	16,049	18.2%
Guerrilla departments	*33,309*	*11,929*	*35.8%*
Matagalpa	14,620	4,927	
Jinotega	6,772	2,116	
Nueva Segovia	4,003	1,296	
Zelaya	7,914	3,590	
Other departments	*54,914*	*4,120*	*7.5%*
	2. Within Departments, by Municipio		
1. Matagalpa	14,620	4,927	33.7%
Guerrilla zones	*10,422*	*4,652*	*44.6%*
Matagalpa	4,516	1,721	
Esquipulas	416	37	
Matiguás	2,754	1,811	
Muy Muy	417	8	
San Dionisio	345	165	
San Ramón	1,974	910	
Other areas	*4,198*	*275*	*6.6%*
2. Jinotega	6,772	2,116	31.2%
Guerrilla zones	*5,759*	*2,058*	*35.7%*
Jinotega	5,267	2,030	
San Rafael del Norte	492	28	
Other areas	*1,013*	*58*	*5.7%*
3. Nueva Segovia	4,003	1,296	32.4%
Guerrilla zones	*2,040*	*1,066*	*52.3%*
Jalapa	795	236	
Murra	599	503	
Quilalí	646	327	
Other areas	*1,963*	*230*	*11.7%*
4. Zelaya	7,914	3,590	45.4%
Guerrilla zones	*3,373*	*1,733*	*51.4%*
La Cruz de Río Grande	994	852	
Prinzapolka	1,274	602	
Waspán	1,105	279	
Other areas	*4,541*	*1,857*	*40.9%*
Rama	1,948	1,414	72.6%
Except Rama	2,593	443	17.1%
5. Madriz[a]	4,870	458	9.4%
Guerrilla zone	*1,308*	*229*	*17.5%*
Telpaneca	1,308	229	
Other areas	*3,652*	*229*	*6.3%*

TABLE 10-1 (*cont.*)

	Number of Units		% Squatter-Held
	Total	Squatter	
3. Guerrilla Municipios versus Rest of Nation			
Guerrilla Zones *(Municipios)*	22,902	9,738	42.5%
Rest of Nicaragua	65,321	6,311	9.7%

Sources: For maps of FSLN rural zones, see Booth, *The End and the Beginning*, pp. 117 (1971–1977 period), 149 (1977–1979 period, "Eastern Front" in Rama); for corresponding departments and *municipios*, see either Nuhn et al., *Zentralamerika* (maps and lists in back pocket of volume), or Nicaragua, Dirección General de Estadística y Censos, *Censos nacionales, 1963: Volume 3 (?)—Agropecuario* (Managua, 1966), pp. i–ix for maps; in same volume, see table 3, pp. 9–19, for the land tenure data used above.

ª Madriz is excluded from the "Guerrilla Departments" in section 1 because only one of its nine *municipios* was involved.

percentage of squatters was the municipio of Rama, in Zelaya, which contained more than three-fourths of all the squatters *not* found in Zelaya's 1971–1977 guerrilla zones. As it happens, the Sandinistas later established their Eastern Front there in the 1977–1979 period. Overall, if we compare the *montaña* guerrilla *municipios* to the rest of the nation, the pattern is a marked one: squatters comprised 43 percent of the cultivators in all guerrilla municipios, but only 10 percent elsewhere in Nicaragua. This ecological analysis strongly suggests a striking parallel to the Cuban revolution: the crucible of the revolution in each case lay within the squatter population in a peripheral region of the country.

While sharecropping forms of tenancy are unimportant throughout Nicaragua, there is clear evidence of the growth of migratory labor there from the 1950s on. There and in our other nations, we cannot examine their "weight" in agriculture with our accustomed degree of arithmetical precision, for such laborers do not appear as such in the agricultural censuses on which I rely for data: since they do not even "possess" a plot of land in the regions where they harvest crops, they do not appear as landed residents of such areas. Indeed, they may instead appear as cultivators in *other* regions of a nation, where they work their sub-family plots to secure some subsistence, then migrating to work elsewhere to provide the balance of their familial needs.

Paige himself has done the legwork in establishing the connection between Nicaraguan migratory labor and the second, urban locus of revolution. He shows that migratory labor became more important as cotton cultivation increased in western Nicaragua from 1950 onward.[4] The majority of peasants displaced by the growth of cotton estates had to find residence elsewhere, and a substantial portion of them ended up as residents in the peripheral *barrios* of the towns and cities of northwestern Nicaragua. From there many migrated to the cotton districts to pick cotton at harvest time, while retaining an "urban" residence. He argues that the major anti-Somoza uprisings in these cities from 1977 onward apparently were closely tied with this displaced peasant population. (Some other displaced peasants, moreover, wound up in those rural areas of north-central Nicaragua which I just discussed.) Oddly enough, therefore, the "urban" nature of the Nicaraguan revolution does not, in the end, refute the theses about rural guerrillas and revolution advanced in this book. Instead, "Nicaragua, which might at first seem to be an exception to the conventional sociological wisdom that the peasantry is the decisive class in revolution, may in fact be the exception that proves the rule. The predominantly urban Nicaraguan revolution may have involved substantial participation by a new rural proletariat swollen to overwhelming size by the dynamic growth of the cotton export sector."[5] In addition to Paige's own analysis, other scholars have independently verified the role of displaced peasants in creating a cotton-picking migratory labor force in the towns of northwestern Nicaragua.[6]

We should also consider the revived 1970s–1980s Guatemalan guerrilla movements. The guerrilla renaissance there has been concentrated in the largely Indian areas of the western highlands, especially Chimaltenango, El Quiché, Huehuetenango, Quezaltenango, and San Marcos. While these areas are not foci of sharecropping, we do find the prevalence of our third type: the migratory estate laborers, who typically leave their own villages, where land is inadequate for their needs, and migrate to harvest one or more (export) cash crops, especially coffee in the piedmont regions farther south. Indeed, the highland areas of Guatemala provide the largest proportional stream of migratory labor to be found in the world. By the early 1980s, an estimated six hundred thousand migrated annually from the highlands to harvest cash crops for three months of the year.[7] Once again, Paige has applied his own theory to illuminate the rooting of the later guerrilla movements in the Guatemalan highlands, and he has carefully documented the strength of the guerrilla movements in the very departments that are the greatest "exporters" of migrant labor to the coffee piedmont.[8]

The home regions of migrant laborers clearly have provided the core of the stiffened Guatemalan guerrilla resistance since 1975, as Paige, Black, and others have shown. Nonetheless, there as in Nicaragua, there is also an appreciable squatter component to the guerrilla resistance as well. Along the northern transverse strip of Guatemala, especially in the Ixil Triangle of El Quiché, peasant colonizers had begun to immigrate in the 1960s and especially the 1970s to carve new agricultural areas out of the jungle, simultaneously seeking escape from the social repression and overpopulation of highland villages farther to the south. Some of the migrants even went as far north as El Petén.

Those peasants often squatted on unclaimed land, and thought themselves the rightful "owners" of the plots they began to cultivate. Both the peasant squatter-colonizers of the Ixil Triangle and those around Panzós became the victims of, first, land grabs and forced evacuations and, later, peasant massacres when those very zones became the targets for mineral exploitation, cattle estate development, and highway building during the 1970s. The "Zone of the Generals," as it came to be called, did indeed come to enrich generals and an elite few others, but often at the expense of the squatter population that had come to reside there. Their resistance to evacuation and massacre has apparently dovetailed with the guerrilla resistance in several places.[9]

Unlike our earlier analysis of Guatemala for the 1960s, Salvadoran census data provide no support for the thesis that the prevalence of tenancy is related to support for revolution in the Salvadoran countryside. Those departments of El Salvador with the greatest guerrilla presence and, by all on-the-spot accounts, the greatest and most widespread peasant support by late 1983 and early 1984 were *not* areas with exceptionally high rates of tenancy. Those departments included especially Chalatenango and Morazán, and also Cabañas and Usulután.[10] (Even if we add other "guerrilla departments" to the analysis, such as La Unión and San Vicente, no such relation systematically obtains.) While it is true that the census data do not allow us to separate out sharecroppers from other kinds of tenants for our analysis, the fact remains that neither squatters nor tenants are more prevalent than normal in the guerrilla zones of El Salvador.

On the other hand, there is good reason *not* to focus on squatters and tenants for the Salvadoran analysis, since their absolute and relative numbers are relatively small given the nature of, and changes in, El Salvador's agrarian structure. The last thirty-five years have witnessed a most thorough uprooting of that nation's peasantry and their increasing conversion into rural wage workers.[11] The bulk of the Salvadoran peasantry seem to have become either landless or so land-poor they must do wage work to supplement family income. Furthermore, evidence suggests that they, like their Guatemalan counterparts, have largely become migratory estate laborers. What remains vague in most analyses of El Salvador's rural milieu, unlike the Guatemalan case, is the regional distribution of those migratory laborers. Robert Williams provides the last pieces in the puzzle:

> Every country of Central America has its zones of peasant refuge. There is great diversity between zones and within zones. Some peasant communities are so prosperous that no one has to migrate to the coast for harvest. In other communities 70 to 80 percent of the work force must migrate to find work. Except for a few fertile river valleys, the northernmost section of El Salvador, constituting one-fifth of the country's surface area, is one zone of the latter type. The soil is rocky, the mountaintops have long been deforested, road networks are poor, and in the pockets of

soil between rocks, people plant corn, beans, and sorghum. During the dry season they migrate to the coast to pick export crops, only to return in time to plant their own subsistence crops when the rains begin. . . . This zone of El Salvador, which for years provided the coast with an abundant supply of harvest labor, became a stronghold of support for the FMLN in the late 1970s.[12]

Therefore in both Guatemala and El Salvador, peasant support for guerrillas after 1970 has not been found in centers of cash-cropping; instead such support has been garnered in northern regions of those nations that provide migratory labor to other zones.

Finally, we come to the Peruvian case, where we do not find supporting evidence for the agrarian structure hypothesis. The land reforms carried out by the military government during its "revolution from above" (1968–1975) destroyed most of the Peruvian landed elite, and thereby the opportunities for sharecropping or migratory labor arrangements. Such changes came to the highlands as well, including Ayacucho where Sendero Luminoso was born. Nonetheless, and perhaps most noteworthy, that particular area of the Sierra was not especially well served by the military's land reform, and large numbers of peasants remained land-poor or landless there even after execution of the nationwide land redistribution.[13]

AGRARIAN TRANSFORMATIONS AND THE RUPTURE OF THE MORAL ECONOMY

Before considering evidence on the rupture of the moral economy, we should consider Paige's strongly argued critique of Scott's thesis, found in the former's analysis of revolution in Guatemala.[14] Paige summarizes Scott's theory thusly: "Peasant revolution occurs when the subsistence minimum is endangered and village security systems and patron-client ties destroyed by (a) ecological pressures (b) the demands of the state or (c) the growth of markets."[15] In the analysis that follows, Paige provides evidence and argument supporting his position that the highlands revolutionary upheaval of the 1970s and 1980s (that is, guerrilla warfare), according to Scott's theoretical logic, should have come instead in the 1930s, when a combination of growing population and commercialization, plus increased demands by landlords and the state—Paige argues the two were virtually indistinguishable in Guatemala—imposed a severe subsistence crisis upon the peasantry. Yet revolution came instead almost fifty years later when, he continues, there may even have been an easing up of the subsistence crisis.

On the face of it, Paige has produced a sharp critique of "moral economy" theory. A closer reading, especially of Scott's writings, however, suggests not only that Paige's critique is less than persuasive, but also that there may well be a kindred spirit between his own theory (especially concerning migratory estate labor) and moral economy theory that makes them complementary rather than contradictory in their theoretical implications: the very process of peasant dislocation and uprooting may be the impetus to the creation of a migratory labor force, as Paige showed for Nicaragua above.

First, Scott denies that he is formulating a causal theory of revolution, try as Paige and Popkin may to make it so.[16] Indeed, both in that theoretical statement and in more detail in later work, Scott does an important service by detailing the *non*revolutionary responses of peasants to violations of their moral economy, as well as the structural conditions under which peasants are likely to choose those avenues of action rather than revolutionary ones.[17] Instead, it is best to understand Scott's self-appointed task as creating a theory of peasant *moral outrage*.[18] Under certain, carefully delimited conditions, however, such moral outrage can take the behavioral avenue of rebellions and peasant uprisings, such as those he describes. However, there are many nonrevolutionary options as well: religious sects,[19] self- and mutual-help systems, and "scavenging" (among which Scott includes "raiding the cash economy," i.e., working for wages).[20] Second, an important element that could conceivably shelter the peasant from the full effects of subsistence pressures—which Paige includes in his rendition of Scott's theory—is the protection afforded the peasantry by community "insurance" institutions and especially by patron-client relationships with landlords. In a work published before his book, Scott and coauthor Benedict Kerkvliet placed special emphasis upon the decay of patron-client relationships in generating a peasantry "ripe" for rebellion, as age-old patterns of reciprocity increasingly break down into nakedly exploitative relationships: as the paternalism seeps out of patron-client relationships, the clients (i.e., the peasants) are likely to feel moral outrage and become prime candidates for anti-landlord uprisings.[21] Despite his apparently cogent critique of Scott, Paige never really demonstrates that village insurance systems or patron-client relationships broke down in Guatemala during the depression of the 1930s; that is, he never demonstrates that crucial middle term of his own statement of Scott's theory.

How then should we evaluate Scott's theory, and Paige's critique of Scott? First, we should look for an assault on the peasants' moral economy, rooted in subsistence pressures on the land. One extreme form that we might seek is the physical dislocation of peasants from any position on the land whatsoever. While such processes are (virtually) absent from Scott's own work—perhaps reflecting the greater landed security of peasant cultivators in Southeast Asia—such processes have become rampant in many areas of Latin America, especially since World War II. If anything constitutes a rupture of the peasants' moral economy, it is surely the loss of land itself. Moreover, there is evidence from Latin America that a "little tradition," corresponding to the moral economy Scott found in Southeast Asia, does indeed prevail among the Latin American peasantry, who view access to the land as something that should be dependent upon use for human life (e.g., "land to the tiller") and not simply dependent upon legally documented ownership.[22] Second, we should be on the lookout for disruption of the peasants' protective institutions, including especially the decay of the protections provided by patron-client relationships with landlords. Finally, we should look for some kind of outside mobilizing agent (such as guerrillas) to help support active peasant resistance, for without such a protective umbrella, peasant resistance is likely to be bloodily suppressed, or take the nonrevolutionary forms I mentioned above. In this respect, I parallel Paige's own discussion of the contexts providing support for his serf-based "agrarian revolts", which he argues are only likely to occur if some outside forces cause a weakening of the landlord class or provide new strength to the serf population, or both.[23]

Let us first consider the case of the Guatemalan guerrilla movements of the 1970s and 1980s, which Paige considered a refutation of the moral economy perspective. Considering it instead in terms of the three elements I have just outlined above, we find that all three are present in force and, moreover, that the timing is right to produce the revolutionary upsurge of the 1970s and 1980s.

First of all, let us consider assaults on landed security and subsistence. The assault on the landed security of the peasantry in the Guatemalan highlands, especially in the northern transverse strip across the highland Indian departments, became intense in the 1970s, as dozens of chroniclers have now documented. Indian settlers and sometimes older Indian villagers in the "Zone of the Generals" were uprooted from their lands in what soon resembled a large-scale assault on the peasants' very access to land. Many of the chroniclers, moreover, have further linked this process of disruption to widespread peasant support for the guerrillas in the northwest, and Paige himself has discussed the land grabs in the very region that provided a guerrilla haven.[24] Further intensifying the subsistence crisis was the level of population growth in Guatemala, which was at its highest point in history.[25] Paige himself has reproduced documentation showing that the subsistence "crisis," if measured simply by population pressure, was 50 percent greater in El Quiché Department by the mid-1970s than it had been around 1930.[26] There is more systematic documentation of a food crunch, for the acreage devoted to peasant farmland in the nation fell by 26 percent from 1970 to 1980, while the acreage devoted to export crops rose by 45 percent in that same decade.[27] The population crunch, allied with the increased absolute numbers *and* percentages of land-poor and landless among the peasantry, are almost surely responsible for the falling levels of per capita food consumption among the peasantry, which Charles Brockett and others have documented. Using the U.N. minimum of 2,236 calories daily, 45 percent of the Guatemalan people fell below that subsistence level in 1965, a proportion that increased sharply in the period under consideration: to 70 percent below the minimum in 1975, and 80 percent by 1980. Brockett has also linked such conditions "backward," to decreased peasant access to the land, and "forward," to increased levels of malnutrition among the Guatemalan peasantry.[28] All the above evidence may not be enough to document a subsistence "crisis," but it surely suggests a sharply worsening state of affairs for the Guatemalan peasantry into the 1970s and 1980s.

Compounding those subsistence problems, and perhaps causally related to them, has been the decline in patron-client ties between elites and peasants in the Indian highlands. Other analysts of the Guatemalan situation, not caught up as we are in the testing and refuting of alternative theories, found those changes worthy of note in their analyses of repression and revolution in Guatemala. Writing of peasant dislocations since the mid-1970s, one group noted:

> Fields and homes of poor campesinos began to be burned, and families were brutally thrown off lands they had cultivated for years. The traditional *patrono-colono* relationship, involving mutual obligations between landowners and workers, as well as the belief that the situation was fated and unchangeable, gradually gave way to a modern, wage relationship.
>
> These developments contributed to the deterioration in living conditions in the rural areas as pressure on the land increased. Many more people were forced to seek out seasonal work on the plantations under new conditions.[29]

Note how such changes now dovetail with Paige's own analysis of migratory estate labor, rather than leading to theoretical divergence. The authors later reiterate the point and make the timing far more precise for our theoretical purposes: "The change in the exploitation was even more intense after 1945 and again after 1965 as successive attempts at modernization and development ruptured old, paternalistic relationships between traditional landowners and Indian laborers. Today [ca. 1982] the essential relationship between wealthy landowners and Indians revolves around a wage paid for seasonal labor, with few of the trappings of mutual obligation and fatalism involved in the old forms of servitude."[30] The authors also link the increased levels of exploitation to increased and intense support of the Indian populace for the highlands insurgency. Black and his collaborators echo a very similar view, noting that "traditional rural relationships crumbled fast as the expansion of cotton and sugar lands and peasant dispossession swelled the ranks of the migrant rural semi-proletariat to 49% of the total rural labor force by the 1970s."[31] Indeed, in their outlines, these arguments show a series of striking parallels to the works of Scott and Kerkvliet noted above, and to their discussion of the conditions giving rise to peasant rebellion in Burma, Vietnam, and the Philippines.[32]

Finally, we do have evidence that there has been a major shift in the political orientation of the highlands, strongly suggesting a collapse of the old state and patronage controls over peasant political activity. Those very regions that have been the core of recent revolutionary activity were the core of electoral support for conservative parties as late as the 1960s. Adams showed that the strongest support for the conservative military-parties in the 1966 elections (when civilian reformer Méndez won the presidency) came from the highlands—the very same Indian highlands that were to harbor revolutionaries in the succeeding decade.[33] An Indian *guerrillera* named Lucia outlined the changes that took place in the interim, again suggesting the collapse of already-fragile patron-client ties:

> They used to use us in elections. They would haul us over in trucks to vote, as if we were some kind of animals. So that we would vote they would promise us things and then after voting they would forget all that we asked for. In contrast, now we are clear and convinced that this is not the road that will take us to victory. Now we realize that these elections are a lie. So now the government does not haul us around in trucks, not because they do not want to, but because we do not let them. . . .[34]

Arriving in the mid-1970s and working quietly for several years, the guerrillas finally provided the third element of our theory: organizational defense and the impetus under which open peasant rebellion could finally coalesce. Barring such an arrival, it is unlikely that a "highlands war" could have emerged with the same force and presence. Under those nurturant conditions, however, many Indian villagers, and even entire villages, flocked to the guerrillas, sometimes coming to form columns in which 99 percent of the participants were highlands Indians from a variety of language and village backgrounds.[35]

Just as Paige pairs Eric Wolf and James Scott to reject their moral economic theories, so can we follow Davis and pair them again, but in an acceptance of all Wolf's major principles, for Guatemala displays all the classic elements for a rebellious peasantry: (1) capitalist dislocation, (2) conditions worsened by population growth, with (3) the state losing control over peasant activity, and (4) the peasants linking up with revolutionary organizations.[36] Far from providing a refutation of Scott's moral economy approach, the Guatemalan experience of the last two decades suggests one of its most striking confirmations.

As in Guatemala, our best guide to the rupture of the moral economy in Nicaragua—although he doesn't frame his analysis in those terms—is Robert G. Williams's *Export Agriculture and the Crisis in Central America*. There he documents the 1960s displacement of the peasantry in Eastern Matagalpa Department—especially in the municipio of Matiguás, but also in San Ramón and Matagalpa municipios—as corn and bean growers were ousted by the Somoza government to make way for the development of cattle ranching and the beef-export industry. In that very same area, the Sandinistas finally began to establish a substantial base of support late in the decade, and several important guerrilla *focos* of the period saw action in that region: Pancasán, El Bijao, and Zinica. Williams links the peasants' support for the guerrillas, in neat conformity with my own perspective, to that process of displacement. Moreover, other participants and observers have also tied that process to the growth of peasant support in the region, as well as to the subsequent focus of counterinsurgency efforts there.[37]

If cattle provided an impetus to rupture the peasants' moral economy, clearly cotton did so as well. We have already discussed Jeffery Paige's analysis of that process, which involved both elements in that rupture. First came the conversion of the labor relationship from a patron-client pattern to a contractual one; in the words of Salmerón, quoted approvingly by Paige: "Cotton production modified the patron-worker relationship substituting the buying and selling of labor power in an impersonal market for the individual personal relationship which had existed between land owner and peon."[38] Paige, Jaime Wheelock, and others also confirm the second step in the process, the massive displacement of former peasant cultivators as labor-extensive cotton cultivation replaced more labor-intensive forms of agriculture, with the consequences we have already discussed: the mass displacement of peasants from the cotton areas to the cities of the northwest.[39]

As Wheelock and others have shown, a substantial part of the migration in this period, as well as in an earlier era when coffee cultivation produced similar displacements, was not to the cities but rather to the relatively unpopulated mountainous interior of north-central Nicaragua, the very area that was to become the rural crucible of the revolution. That historical migratory wave undoubtedly lies behind the census pattern we have already seen: the proportional predominance of squatter agriculture in such areas. In those regions of the mountainous interior lived peasants who often had themselves been displaced by such agricultural shifts, "campesinos [for whom] the land was a dream." Their families might have been displaced by the coffee expansion of the late 1800s and early 1900s, or the cotton expansion of the 1950s, or the more recent cattle expansion. No matter, for the effect was to violate sharply their moral economy. And that sense of injustice was kept alive, as Cabezas indicates in his further portrait of the mountain peasant:

> The first thing we would ask was if they owned the land they lived on, and the answer was always no, it belonged to the 'rich folk.' . . . The landowners, or the fathers or grandfathers of the landowners, had over a period of years gradually been stripping the campesinos of their land. So the generation of campesinos we knew would tell us about how their great-grandfathers had owned land. . . . The landowners had appropriated the land through a process of violent evictions, or through legal means.[40]

Thus Nicaragua, where three different regions, affected by three different crops, shows the revolutionary effects of the displacement, often violent, of peasant cultivators from their personal ties to landlords and their age-old rights to the soil.

For El Salvador, our analysis will have a degree of precision. First, let us note again that the northern, largely FMLN-controlled departments of El Salvador, notably Chalatenango and Morazán, have and had been exporters of migrant labor to other areas of El Salvador, as well as to the Guatemalan and Nicaraguan cotton zones, for some time.[41] Second, the changing land-tenure system over the last forty years has produced sharply decreased numbers of landholding and *colono* peasants—the latter being the most likely candidates for patron-client ties—while the numbers and percentages of landless and land-poor peasants have increased to perhaps the highest percentages in Latin America. Moreover, those changes now proceed most rapidly in the guerrilla departments.[42] These processes have been far more extreme than in neighboring Honduras, which may explain the greater degree of peasant radicalism and support for guerrillas in El Salvador.[43] Third, the northernmost areas of El Salvador have become "zones of peasant refuge," as Williams calls them, since their poorer, hilly soils are not suitable for lowlands cotton and sugar plantations, or even for the coffee grown at higher elevations: four guerrilla-zone departments (Morazán, Cabañas, Chalatenango, and La Unión) are the very areas of El Salvador with the lowest percentages of land devoted to farming, and they are among the minority designated unsuitable for coffee.[44]

Since so much rural proletarianization has taken place in El Salvador, the earlier moral economy associated with landholding or *colono* status has largely become a thing of the past. We would expect to find radicalism where the number of farmers is still relatively high and the relative number of agricultural workers (i.e., those not possessing any land) is low. Such areas are still, as it were, "in process," and I noted above that the rate of proletarianization was most rapid in the northernmost departments. These are also the very departments that are the last refuge of *relatively* high percentages of peasant landholders (even though the migratory labor streams indicate an inability to meet subsistence needs with those parcels).[45] These are the very peasants who have the most to lose with any further disruptions of the moral economy; they may have taken refuge there precisely because of earlier disruptions thereof; and since the early 1970s they have had the additional edge of the protection of the guerrillas.

The ratio of agricultural workers to farmers within each department provides a measure of vulnerability to disruption of the moral economy (a process that we know proceeds apace): where the ratio is high (far greater than 1.0) we expect little radicalism; where the ratio is low, with the number of farmers larger and closer to the number of wageworkers in a more bifurcated agrarian structure, we expect to find more radicalism. In conformity with this hypothesis we find a negative correlation between the worker/farmer ratio and the degree to which guerrillas control a department (I measured the latter by the percentage of each department's rural landholders living in guerrilla-controlled zones). Dropping the urban capital from the analysis, the Spearman rank correlation between the worker/farmer ratio and the degree of guer-

TABLE 10-2
Farmers, Agricultural Workers, and the Guerrilla Movement in El Salvador

Department	A % of Landholders Living in Guerrilla- Controlled Zones[a]	B Agricultural Workers (Number)	C Farmers (Number)	D Ratio: B/C
Chalatenango	89%	9,036	14,781	0.6
Morazán	59	16,210	8,730	1.9
Cabañas	32	5,318	10,649	0.5
La Unión	31	17,585	10,723	1.6
Usulután	26	28,889	10,020	2.9
San Vicente	24	11,426	7,927	1.4
Santa Ana	19	39,357	7,933	5.0
San Miguel	15	29,964	13,960	2.1
Cuscatlán	8	16,580	5,264	3.1
[San Salvador][b]	[0]	[18,356]	[5,777]	[3.2]
La Paz	0	16,547	6,893	2.4
La Libertad	0	34,528	6,118	5.6
Ahuachapán	0	26,009	3,840	6.7
Sonsonate	0	30,849	3,693	8.4

Rank Correlation of Columns:	A with D	A with B	A with C
Spearman's rho	$r = -.79$	$r = -.62$	$r = +.80$
(corrected for ties)	$r = -.81$	—	—
p-values	$(p < .01)$	$(p < .05)$	$(p < .01)$

Sources: See note 46.

[a] NON-GUERRILLA MUNICIPIOS: Chalatenango—Nueva Concepción; Morazán—Chilanga, Jocoro, Lolotiquillo, San Carlos, San Francisco Gotera, Sensembra, Sociedad, Yamabal, Yoloaiquín; GUERRILLA MUNICIPIOS: Cabañas—San Isidro, Sesuntepeque; La Unión—Anamorós, Concepción de Oriente, Lislique, Nueva Esparta, Polorós; Usulután—Jiquilisco, Jucuarán, Puerto El Triunfo, San Agustín, San Dionisio; San Vicente—Santa Clara, Tecoluca, Tepetitán; Santa Ana—Metapán; San Miguel—Carolina, Ciudad Barrios, San Antonio de Mosco; Cuscatlán—Oratorio de Concepción, San José Guayabal, Suchitoto.

[b] Largely urban capital area dropped from analysis.

rilla control is −.81. (That is, as the relative percentage of workers goes up, guerrilla control goes down; as the relative percentage of workers goes down [and thus farmers up], guerrilla control goes up.) The degree of departmental guerrilla control is also positively related to the *number* of farmers, and negatively related to the number of workers, whether we employ Spearman's *rho* or Kendall's *tau* (all Z-scores exceed 2.0 in absolute value, indicating greater than 20 to 1 odds that such a pattern could have occurred by chance).[46] This finding is cross-sectional in nature, and the data from two different census periods, yet it suggests that regions embroiled in such processes of peasant uprooting are likely to be radical "hotbeds" (See table 10-2).

In Peru we encounter our first evidence of a true subsistence crisis. Ayacucho Department had always been one of the poorer Peruvian areas, even among the Andean departments. When land reform came to Peru, including the Sierra, following the 1968 military coup, moreover, Ayacucho was not well served thereby. As David Scott Palmer has shown, land reforms touched at most 15 to 20 percent of the needy, because Ayacucho had smaller and fewer haciendas, more Indian communities, and a low priority assigned it in the reform program. He also notes that some provinces of Ayacucho later to become Sendero strongholds had no program whatsoever: Cangallo, Victor Fajardo, and parts of Huanta.[47] Peasant living standards in Ayacucho have fallen sharply due to parcelization of land and declining terms of trade with the coastal areas. Cynthia McClintock has also contributed to our understanding of the increasing depth and breadth of the subsistence crisis in Ayacucho over the last twenty years. Perhaps the single best measure is per capita income, which fell *20 percent* in the 1970s to about $60 to $70 by the early 1980s; this in a population that was already living in "fourth world" conditions. It may therefore be no accident that "[a]gricultural incomes in three Ayacucho provinces of early core support for Sendero—Huanta, Huamanga, and Cangallo—were lower than for all but 9 of Peru's 155 provinces."[48] Here is the truest subsistence crisis we are apt to find in the entire hemisphere, and here the strongest support for Sendero Luminoso.

What of the moral economy and that crucial middle term of the theory, peasant indignation? There is fragmentary evidence that any patron-client relationships with landlords here had long since disappeared. Increasingly in Sierran Peru from the 1950s onward, however, peasants and peasant communities turned their eyes to the central government for succor in their battles for subsistence. Evidence for this came in 1963, when Fernando Belaúnde Terry came to the presidency in part by carrying the peasant vote in the southern Sierra. More striking, the single greatest wave of land invasions in Peruvian history began on the very day that Belaúnde took the sash of office: clearly the Peruvian peasantry had been brought into national politics in search of solutions to their agrarian problems.[49] The Ayacucho peasantry, however, just as clearly found no redress in the agrarian reforms of the next decade.

Yet were they content with their lot, continuing to subsist within the context of Indian communities or individually carving out a living from the Sierra? Some evidence suggests not. First, by the early 1970s the level of intercommunity legal disputes over land in Ayacucho was strikingly high when compared to other Peruvian departments, reflecting perhaps the Ayacucho peasants' "image of the limited good" and their orientation to governmental authority to resolve such disputes.[50] Second, peasants in one region, later allegedly a Sendero support zone, reported highly negative responses to a 1980 survey inquiring into community progress: 92 percent reported that their community had made no achievements in recent years.[51] Third, two peasant confederations demanding more radical agrarian reforms began to sink roots in Ayacucho during the 1970s, complemented by a "skyrocketing" vote for the Marxist left there during national elections.[52] All these patterns suggest a pair of phenomena: increasing discontent with social conditions (which we must surely link to the subsistence crisis), and an increasingly national orientation in seeking solutions to those problems. Under those conditions of accelerating decay in agricultural subsistence, Sendero Luminoso would put down deep roots, especially when wedded with further conditions I will analyze in the next two sections.

TAPPING REBELLIOUS CULTURES

In chapter 7, we found that areas historically supportive of rebellion were also likely to be supporters of revolutionary guerrilla movements, even though those pasts had little to do with socialism or Marxist theorizing. As we move to the second wave, we can discern a certain degree of confirmation of that pattern, especially for Nicaragua, but that pattern is far from uniform.

The adoption of the label "Sandinista" by the mostly Marxist Nicaraguan revolutionaries offends the sense of purity of some analysts, who have noted that Sandino himself was certainly no Marxist. Most noteworthy, Sandino rejected any partnership with Salvadoran Communist Farabundo Martí. Even allowing for those observations, however, the claiming of the title "Sandinista" involves far more than revolutionary cant or postmortem attempts to convert Sandino into a crypto-Marxist: to wit, it involves a basic ecological correlation. John Booth's accounts of those two periods reveals that the very areas of the FSLN's rural bases and peasant support were rough palimpsests of Sandino's own movement a half century earlier. At the time of the 1932 elections, for example, Sandino's forces controlled the departments of Estelí, Jinotega, Matagalpa, and Nueva Segovia; the last three were all FSLN rural strongholds in the 1970s. Other chroniclers have also confirmed that correlation for various areas, one arguing that that very history was one decisive feature for choosing that region for the rural insurgency.[53] Other chroniclers have confirmed the Sandino legacy in more specific rural areas of the north, including Matagalpa, Ocotal, the La Tronca-La Luz area, and others.[54]

As in Cuba, the relationship was more than ecological, for that history was converted into personal contacts and cultural heritages. Various Sandinistas have provided further accounts showing that many residents of those regions continued to keep those memories alive, creating a culture of resistance to Somoza's National Guard.[55] As Omar Cabezas put it, "[t]hey had a Sandinista history, a history of rebellion against exploitation, against North American domination. They interpreted rebellion in a primitive, gut-level way. . . ." This statement was not merely revolutionary fluff, as several accounts show. An eighty-year old former collaborator of Sandino's resistance helped Cabezas's band in the Ocotal area in the early 1970s. Even before the FSLN was born, an old Sandino man named Ramón Raudales had attempted to foment a 1958 revolution in the far north after crossing over from Honduras, but he was betrayed and killed. One of the original trainers of Carlos Fonseca's nascent FSLN guerrillas was Colonel Santos López, who had been a member of Sandino's "Angel Corps" (a group of children and teenagers who fought with Sandino), and he and other "old Sandinistas shared with us their experiences, which fell on a soil hungry for seeds and new perspectives" in the early 1960s. López also led the early *foco* attempts at Río Coco and Bocay. Finally, Cabezas links this supportive culture in part to the peasants' historical loss of their lands: "So the generation of campesinos we knew would tell us about how their great-grandfathers had owned land. And the story of what happened was passed down from great-grandfather to grandfather to father to son. They were now a generation without land."[56]

There is more to the Nicaraguan legacy of resistance than Sandino himself. An urban component stems from a long historical rivalry between León and the two successive capitals of Nicaragua, first Granada (until 1852) and then Managua. When independence left the province of Nicaragua acephalous in 1823, then-more powerful León had tried to subordinate the provincial capital of Granada, and vice versa. By the late 1800s León and now Managua had become rivals and the loci of the Liberal and Conservative parties, respectively, further sharpening their historical conflicts.[57] León had historically been a stronghold of the Liberal dictator Zelaya and of Sandino, and it produced anti-Somoza uprisings in 1939 and 1948, long before its better-known participation in the 1977 to 1979 uprisings. As one reporter simply put it: "León is a city well known for rebellion."[58]

Finally, there may be an indigenous historical component to the anti-Somoza movement as well, for several major, partially independent riots and uprisings took place after 1976 in the two remaining Indian *barrios* of western Nicaragua, Subtiava in León, and Monimbó in Masaya. For Monimbó, we know that its history as a separately identified and administered Indian community dates back to the earliest days of the colony, when it was taken as a tributary pueblo (*encomienda* is the Spanish term) by one of the earliest governors of the province. Black further notes that Indian revolts against the colonial regime took place in those two cities in 1811–1812, and they must have been rooted among those specific Indian communities. And when the Sandinistas came to organize resistance in Subtiava, they consciously drew on local indigenous traditions, in presenting Augusto Sandino as the reincarnation of the historical Indian leader Adiac. The very persistence of Indian identity in those two *barrios* apparently provided a context for preserving a culture of resistance to the central government.[59]

For both the Peruvian and Colombian second-wave guerrillas the repetition or persistence of revolutionary movements, as well as a historical pattern of rebellious activity in selected regions, clearly raises the issue of historical cultures of rebellion. Paralleling my earlier discussion in chapter 7 above, the evidence indicates a rather clearer pattern of historical cultures of rebellion in Colombia than in Peru, yet still suggestive in the latter case.

The three 1960s Colombian guerrilla movements all apparently persisted into the 1980s as organizations—although reports on the Maoist EPL become increasingly scant—but not necessarily in the same regions of Colombia. (The M-19 began as an urban guerrilla group and then tried with some success to shift their main operations to rural areas.) By the early 1980s the FARC, still by far the largest of the guerrilla organizations, had eight fronts spread around the same western interior that had provided its earlier theater of operations. Interestingly enough, the FARC now actually dominated areas of Santander and the Antioquia-Córdoba border zones that had previously harbored the ELN and EPL guerrillas, respectively. On the other hand, a FARC spokesman indicated that the ELN had moved into areas formerly dominated by the FARC and was even using the same local residents as contact persons.[60] Maps of guerrilla zones continue to suggest an overwhelming presence in the coffee interior and an underwhelming one elsewhere, with some new areas now added to zones of long-standing guerrilla strength. Therefore, if the 1960s guerrillas already had displayed a correlation with historical patterns of rebellion, that pattern persisted into the 1980s, with some additional zones added to the insurgency.

In Peru, *Sendero*'s center of initial support lay in or near the area of Béjar's Ayacucho guerrilla *foco* of 1965 which, as I suggested in chapter 7, had at least tenuous connections to earlier Andean uprisings and a major peasant movement there in the 1920s. One can concede, following McClintock, that Ayacucho as a region has a lesser such history than Cuzco or Puno, yet still reject the next step in her logic, which asks why rebellion did not break out in those latter places rather than Ayacucho. As I argued in part 1, guerrilla movements do not "break out" spontaneously from rural social conditions but are rather produced through the interaction of revolutionary mobilizers and peasants subject to specific social forces.[61] In the next section, and drawing heavily on McClintock's and Palmer's work, I will outline the special organizational access that made revolution come to Ayacucho rather than to Puno or Cuzco, even though it subsequently spread to other Andean regions. Finally, and oddly enough, there is a fragment of evidence suggesting that *opposition* to *Sendero* in turn has at least partial historical roots in exceptionally closed and isolated Iquichanos communities of the upper Sierra: when their village chiefs (*varayocs*) gathered publicly in early 1983 to oppose the anti-market exactions and policies that *Sendero* imposed on their communities, they did so in the very locale where they had opposed the declaration of

Peru's independence from Spain and the colony's proposed republic over 150 years before.[62]

It is no accident (as they say) that in both Peru and Guatemala the socialist revolutionaries had added to their ideologies overtones of a race war of Indians versus Spanish, for both countries had large, unassimilated Indian populations that had stymied guerrilla mobilizing efforts in the 1960s. In the 1970s, the revolutionaries consciously began to employ Indian religion, myth, and symbol in order to strike more responsive chords among the Indian peasants; when wedded to the subsistence "crises" that were emerging among the highlands peasantry in both nations (as we saw above) we might expect such symbols to find a ready, even eager audience. Such symbolic congruence has been especially noteworthy in Peru, where the Communists had expelled (later *Sendero* leader) Abimael Guzmán from the party in 1970 for "occultism," among other things, because he already was making appeals to local customs and messianic traditions.[63] While McClintock and Eckstein have both entered demurrals about the importance of indigenous "culture" in effecting such Indian mobilization in Peru, other close investigators are struck by *Sendero*'s employment of pre-Columbian mythic imagery in both argument and art. Included in the argument is an appeal to an Andean tradition of millennial cycles, awaiting the hour when the head of the dead Sapa Inca will be reunited with the body, and the Quechua will rise again; included in the artwork is the recurring use on pamphlet covers of a sequence of four mountain peaks, each higher than the preceding, symbolizing the four main stages of *Sendero*'s revolution, but clearly meant to echo an identical pre-Columbian symbolic motif.[64]

The Guatemalan revolutionaries, in a manner remarkably parallel both to *Sendero* and to the Nicaraguan revolutionaries in Subtiava, also tried to draw on pre-Columbian traditions. The ORPA revolutionaries near Lake Atitlán report that one Indian oral tradition teaches that "some day men would come down from the mountains to liberate the people," a tradition repeated in variant forms among many of the post-Mayan peoples, including the Mam, Cakchiquel, and Tzutuíl.[65] The Hispanic guerrilla leaders certainly needed some cultural assistance in those highlands for, beginning in the 1600s, villages had begun to reconstitute themselves as Indian communities with little welcome given to outsiders.[66] Unlike their Bolivian and Peruvian indigenous counterparts, however, the Guatemalan Indians had not displayed a long history of major peasant uprisings that might have provided fertile ground for modern revolutionary appeals.[67] Instead, their history of cultural resistance to outsiders seems to have been the prevailing response, until their wedding— perhaps to be short-lived, in both the temporal and the mortal sense—to the guerrillas in the 1970s and early 1980s, prior to the counterinsurgency wave begun in 1982.

Finally, in El Salvador we find a case that fails to fit any notion of historical cultures of rebellion. Like the Guatemalan northeast in the 1960s, however, El Salvador did have a revolutionary movement of its own, in the peasant-cum-Communist uprising of 1932, centered in the western coffee-producing areas of Sonsonate and Ahuachapán. In both cases the uprisings were put down in a terroristic fashion by the government: the *matanza* of 1932 in El Salvador, where 10,000 to 30,000 peasants died; and the terror-filled counterinsurgency campaign in Guatemala from 1966 to 1968. While guerrilla-based revolution has failed to restore itself in that region of Guatemala since the 1960s, the results of 1932 in El Salvador have been even more sustained and striking: peasants stopped speaking Pipil within earshot of non-Indians; they stopped wearing Indian dress; and they were subjected to laws forbidding the gathering of more than three persons in a public place. The elders stopped even speaking of the events of 1932 and would grow silent when the issue was raised. The paired set of events in both countries suggests a revolutionary-sobering thesis: Perhaps extreme levels of violence against the citizenry may have the historically effective result of stifling insurrectionary activity. Those areas of western El Salvador, while still showing land hunger, have been the ones least responsive to and supportive of the FMLN guerrilla movement.[68] These paired Guatemalan and Salvadoran patterns may parallel early modern European events succinctly summarized by Charles Tilly: "In general, when a European state temporarily trained its full repressive power on its internal enemies . . . the enemies subsided."[69]

STRUCTURES OF ACCESS TO THE PEASANTRY

The resource mobilization (RM) view of social movements suggests that the kind of discontent nurtured by social conditions, such as the three just discussed, is *not* enough to generate a social movement. Discontent is always present in social systems, and the problem instead is to organize people, and to get them to commit their resources—time, money, energy, even their lives—to the goals of the movement, and not to workaday routines. Resource mobilization theorists, moreover, have noted that social movements often appear when outsiders enter a social system and begin to mobilize the resources of those who by themselves might not be able escape the constraints of everyday life. That is, there are the mobilizers and the mobilized.[70]

Such a perspective has an intrinsic appeal for the study of guerrilla movements, for two reasons. First, only rarely does peasant discontent transmute itself into guerrilla war without the intervention of revolutionary intellectuals in rural areas. Second, RM theory directs our attention to the fundamental bifurcation within guerrilla movements, between the radical middle-to-upper class mobilizers who lead such movements and the poor peasants who come to make up the rank and file. Intellectuals are free to mobilize resources for a variety of reasons: Their locations within autonomous universities protect them ideologically and physically from government repression and influence; as economically privileged individuals, they have far greater resources in the first place, hence more resources are "free" to commit to nonsubsistence activity; and their cultural repertoires were especially likely to change following the Cuban revolution, and hence they were ideologically geared to make great sacrifices in the service of revolution. Moreover, quite apart from mere hypothesis, we have already seen in chapters 3 and 9 that rapid increases in university enrollments were in fact related to the degree of student-guerrilla links.

If the mobilizers are to mobilize peasant resources in the service of revolution, however, they must have access to the peasantry. As we saw in chapter 7, such access is not a given of social structure. Instead, varied patterns of peasant-outsider social linkages and cultural influence generated different degrees of access to peasant resources during the first wave of guerrilla movements. Certain features of social and cultural structure channeled the peasants and the guerrilla leaders into alliances, while other features functioned as structural obstacles to such alliances. Such features included political party influence in a region, kinship and patron-client ties, strategic political alliances against a common enemy, the advocacy or opposition of respected religious personnel, and (non)membership in minority ethnic and religious groups. Where impediments were few and facilitation great, guerrillas were generally more successful in securing peasant support, but not very successful where the reverse was true. Indeed, some peasants were "available" for mobilization, and some already in the guerrillas' camp, yet others were hostile to the guerrillas and quite unavailable for radical mobilization.[71] Furthermore, to put it in classic colloquial form, much depended on who "got there firstest with the mostest": guerrillas secured peasant support only with difficulty where *other*, hostile political groups had arrived earlier and themselves forged peasant alliances.[72] Guerrillas thus fared better on virgin soil or friendly terrain than they did on occupied ground.

Rather than discuss the patterns by nation, and in order to highlight the theoretical issues raised by structured access to the peasantry, I will discuss the second-wave guerrilla movements in terms of the varied forms employed to give guerrillas and governments access to peasant resources. The variety of such forms is appreciable, yet there remains that pattern of underlying regularity that I outlined in chapter 7: some *preexisting* patterns of social organization generate strong personal ties of *attachment* between insurgents and peasants, while others do not, and similar structures can channel peasants and governments into anti-guerrilla alliances. Here I will again probe those regularities in the most manageable fashion, by discussing how organized social activity in the various institutional spheres of life—family, religion, politics, education, etc.—either channeled the guerrillas and peasants toward or away from one another.

Language Ties

Language itself, although not often treated by sociologists as an institution, is indeed the most basic institution of them all in that it enables communication, that most fundamental of all social processes.[73] Language variations naturally result in the emergence of a basic form of social organization, the speech community, where membership and exclusion can readily be defined by one's tongue. In Latin America, such speech communities have been most closely associated with Indian languages such as Nahuatl (in Mexico), modern variants of Maya such as Mam, Kekchí, and Cakchiquel (in Guatemala), Quechua and Aymara (in Peru and Bolivia), and Guaraní (Paraguay). In most of those cases, the most segmented indigenous communities with the fewest ties to outsiders have been precisely those whose members speak little or no Spanish and who reside in relatively isolated or undesirable areas. The access of white, Spanish-speaking nationals to many such Indian communities has been limited for centuries now (especially in parts of Guatemala, Peru, and Bolivia), and such strictures apply as well to the white, Spanish-speaking, middle- to upper-class guerrilla leaders who sought to mobilize the peasant populace to insurgency. These issues were fundamental to the 1960s failures of guerrillas in the Guatemalan and Peruvian highlands, for the Indian populations in both cases—with minor exceptions in Alta Verapaz, Guatemala, and Junín, Peru—rejected the Spanish-speaking guerrilla mobilizers as both strangers to the region and outsiders to the local speech communities.[74]

In contrast, both the Peruvian and Guatemalan insurgents of the 1970s and 1980s approached and addressed the highlands Indian populations in their own languages and their own terms. Davis and Hodson nicely summarize the Guatemalan insurgency's recruiting procedures: "During armed propaganda meetings, the guerrillas wear native dress and speak the Indian languages. Although they destroy property and kill local political bosses, landowners, liquor merchants, and military personnel, they never terrorize the general population." Both Morán and Payeras, leaders of the EGP guerrillas, confirm the systematic, sometimes arduous process of rebuilding the guerrilla movement with a base of Indian cadres rather than Hispanic ones. Indeed, one early recruitment session failed miserably when the population of an Indian town near Usapantán "barricaded themselves behind their dialect." The earliest membership in Payeras's nascent front numbered fifteen, including four Achí and Cakchiquel Indians. When attempting to reconsolidate the front following an army offensive, the main duties were given to an Ixil Indian named

Fonseca, who had the crucial linguistic advantage of having learned Spanish on the coast, thus having feet planted firmly in both Guatemalan worlds (when captured, however, he was tortured and yielded up information that set the cause back several months). The EGP later reported that they confronted the language problem directly by using local recruits to organize in their home areas—a practice sharply at variance with the outsider recruiting typical of the 1960s—speaking Indian languages in order to achieve that goal, while Spanish was used as the common tongue to communicate among the various Indian-guerrilla communities that spoke mutually unintelligible dialects.[75]

The language ties between Peru's *Sendero* and the Andean village communities were yet more intense, because the recruitment of local Quechua speakers was less "artificial," being based on channeling Quechua-speaking children and grandchildren of Indian peasants into the University of Huamanga, and often later sending them back to do teaching and educational extension in their home villages. Yet they often returned to their home villages as members of *Sendero Luminoso*, no longer as simple peasants. Indeed, there were about 5,000 teachers in Ayacucho by 1981, "as many as half of whom had studied in the *Sendero*-controlled education program in the university." Unlike virtually every other guerrilla movement, *Sendero* had little need to go to the countryside, for the countryside had come to them; virtually all leaders, save for Guzmán himself, had been born in Ayacucho.[76]

Educational Ties

Indeed, that experience suggests another form of institutional tie that was absolutely fundamental in generating peasant support in Peru, but used elsewhere only for obtaining middle- and upper-class recruits. I speak here of the organizational resources provided by the university, which has far greater autonomy and institutional independence in Latin America than in the United States and most of Europe. In part due to such autonomy, universities were *the* major 1960s recruiting ground for guerrillas in several nations, especially Venezuela. Yet even the revolutionary support rendered by the University of Caracas pales beside the overwhelming role of the University of Huamanga in generating a peasant-supported guerrilla movement in the Peruvian highlands, as every chronicler has confirmed. In response to McClintock's earlier query—why didn't revolution come to Puno or Cuzco as it did to Ayacucho?—an RM theorist could give the answer: Discontent was not enough, whether based on rebellious cultures or subsistence crises, for resources still had to be channeled in a revolutionary direction, and only *Sendero* of Huamanga provided the organizational structure to do so.[77] Indeed, we can essay a Weberian thought experiment and ask what *would* have happened had there been *no* regionally oriented and Indian-recruiting University of Huamanga, which after all was reestablished in 1959, shortly before *Sendero*'s appearance. While thought experiments can never be confirmed, an answer strongly suggests itself: no University of Huamanga, no *Sendero Luminoso* rebellion.

Religious Ties

The second wave saw new forms of religious influence favorable to the guerrilla forces as well. Before 1970, the Church hierarchy clearly supported governments in Peru, Colombia, and elsewhere (but not in Cuba, where they requested Batista's resignation in early 1958).[78] After 1970, part of the Church shifted in a manner crucial to peasant loyalty. The Medellín Bishops' Conference of 1968 paved the way for liberation theology, leading local priests, in particular, to view revolutionaries in a far more congenial light. Subsequently Comunidades Eclesiales de Base (CEBs or base communities) helped to spread liberation theology through the region, wherever Catholicism was strong. Such influence could now provide, not an impediment ("opiate") to guerrilla-peasant alliances, but rather a *nihil obstat* or even an *imprimatur* for revolution. That this might have destabilizing effects in the region was obvious to all. Whereas a few Protestant evangelicals had proselytized on the guerrillas' behalf in 1960s Colombia and Guatemala, now even members of the Catholic hierarchy came to denounce regime violence, as in the case of (later assassinated) Archbishop Romero in El Salvador and Archbishop Obando y Bravo in Nicaragua. Even moderate bishops like Romero's successor in El Salvador and the conservative Guatemalan bishops were led to criticize regime violence.

At the village level we can see the special role of CEBs, of Maryknoll missionaries, and others in providing religious backing to peasant organizing efforts in Guatemala, El Salvador, and Nicaragua.[79] Tommie Sue Montgomery, who has studied this issue as closely as any, indicates the political effects of the CEBs: ". . . there emerged a clear correlation among the development of the CEBs, the political radicalization of the people, and the presence of political organizations."[80] This process clearly took place first and foremost in Nicaragua, beginning in the late 1960s, where the hierarchy's opposition to Somoza's continued rule dovetailed with the massive and widespread role of CEBs and other grass-roots religious organizations in providing symbolic support and leadership to the opposition (especially after the Managua earthquake of 1972), as well as cadres for the insurgency. The link to the Sandinistas is by now also well known. In Montgomery's succinct summary: "The FSLN in Nicaragua organized in many areas, but people became most radical where CEBs were present."[81] Since the Nicaraguan events now generate a well-known consensus, I will say rather more about the to-date unsuccessful revolutions in Guatemala and El Salvador, where the processes have nonetheless been strikingly similar.

In El Salvador, the church had traditionally been at best a minor institutional source of social order, yet the post-Medellín years left little doubt that the CEBs were now serving to channel their members into revolutionary organizations. (As Weberians have understood better than Marxists, religion is not always and everywhere an opiate.) Montgomery herself terms such cases "innumerable," clearly suggesting such a structured connection between CEBs and the guerrilla movement. Moreover, "[d]ozens of the revolutionary leaders have been catechists or delegates" (of the word), including some later murdered by death squads. James LeMoyne also confirms the connection between CEBs and the guerrilla movement for the department of Cabañas, a major guerrilla stronghold, and indeed more general evidence suggests that there may be a nationwide, ecological correlation between the strength of CEBs and the strength of the rural insurgency. The strongest argument has been made by Douglas Kincaid, who argues that the CEBs served to recreate solidary communities from the residues remaining in El Salvador, thus providing a key lever to bring solidary peasants into revolutionary activity. Finally, several observers—rarely on the left—have suggested that formal Church organizations, including human rights organizations, have indirectly served the interests of revolutionaries through guerrilla infiltration and manipulation.[82]

In Guatemala, traditional church influence was probably stronger than in El Salvador, yet recent decades have seen changes parallel to those in its neighbor. One particular obstacle to revolutionary mobilization was the conservative Catholic hierarchy—perhaps the most conservative in Latin America—where hand-in-glove relationships between the episcopate and military dictators, and Archbishop Casariego's refusal to condemn regime violence, finally led seven exasperated bishops to resign in 1979. Still, striking religious change was coming to Guatemala. The radicalized CEBs of the 1970s and later grew especially strong in El Quiché, and it may be no accident that the Indian highlands were also the previous strongholds of Maryknoll missionaries, who had earlier been expelled by the Guatemalan government and charged with fomenting revolution under the guise of missionary work. Outside of El Quiché, however, CEB growth was far more fragmentary. While fragmentary, the alliance of Catholic clergy with the political opposition (not necessarily revolutionary in kind) grew during the 1970s, and accelerated after the Panzós massacre of 1978. The government's response to such a growing alliance was to condemn the church for inciting the peasants to rebellion; the death squads' response was to begin killing priests, at least twelve up through the end of 1982 alone.[83] While the overall rural pattern remains considerably more befogged than in El Salvador, the evidence suggests a similar phenomenon: CEBs and even missionaries may have channeled peasants into revolutionary activity. Finally, there is also evidence that both Catholic Action and the Indian-community *cofradías* (religious sodalities) also served to bring village members closer to revolutionary organizations.[84]

These political trends produced bizarre religio-political realignments, where the far right could be found assassinating an archbishop (Romero of El Salvador), and where the celebration of Catholic mass in the Guatemalan highlands came to be seen virtually as subversive activity under the rule of a Protestant evangelical general, Efraín Ríos Montt, whose Bible-thumping yet terror-filled rule finally elicited the first negative Catholic hierarchical response to a military dictator.[85] There may have been some connection between his evangelical Protestantism and counterinsurgency, for villages converting to such beliefs may have gone over to counterrevolutionary sentiment as well.

Family Ties

Rare are the kinds of family connections, or even the patron-client connections, in the second-wave insurgencies that we found in Venezuela in particular during the first wave of guerrilla movements. The reasons should be obvious, for rarely do the "mobilizers" of revolutionary activity come from peasant backgrounds or have peasant family ties. Hugo Blancos, coming from intact families with an upper-class father and a peasant mother, are exceptionally rare. Instead, family connections more commonly would work themselves out through second-order family ties, as peasant leaders would commit themselves to an elite-led armed struggle and bring with them the commitment of friends and family; the prototype for this pattern is Crescencio Pérez in Cuba.

In Nicaragua and Peru, family connections were important in securing greater peasant support for the insurgency. In the former case they followed some initial organizing efforts (and therefore were not the "preexisting" linkages that I have focused on in this section), while in the latter such ties preceded organization, thereby providing exceptional depth of support for *Sendero* in certain Andean peasant communities.

In Nicaragua, family ties between the insurgent leadership and the more moderate middle- to upper-class opposition are well known, and were exceptionally strong and important to the insurgency. Yet in the countryside family ties also worked *en cadena* (in a chain-link effect), as Henry Ruiz put it, to propagate the insurgency through areas of rural Nicaragua. This process did not come readily, for it was arduous to isolate and insulate the rural insurgents and their supporters from the *somocista* informers and the *jueces de mesta* (the rural constabulary) in the early years. Yet once the peasants' confidence was gained, reported Ruiz, "we established some organizational units, that we called *en cadena*, which were of a familial type, sometimes of blood familiarity, sometimes of political familiarity . . . creating there a chain that would continue sustaining the structure of what later became guerrilla support bases." Black adds that a single friendship established in an area could ripple to generate family sympathy and later village and hamlet commitment in each locale. Quite a similar process took place in Subtiavan communities near León where the Sandinistas had undertaken "organization in silence." Once cadres had been recruited in Subtiava, "we started penetrating other barrios in León, through the relatives of Subtiavans who had moved there."[86]

In Peru, *Sendero's* direct family ties to the peasant communities of Ayacucho were exceptionally strong, without parallel in any other guerrilla movements of the last half-century. Because the "countryside" had come to attend the University of Huamanga, and because many students of indigenous backgrounds and tongues joined *Sendero* there under the power of its message and its leader Guzmán, they returned to their communities with family ties already present. If lacking such local ties, instead they often came to the villages under educational extension programs to open up schools and teach children, and often stayed in those villages and married into them. Thus when *Sendero* decided to take the step of open insurrection in Ayacucho in 1980, they had intact a fairly dense network of cadres dispersed through a number of Andean villages in several provinces of Ayacucho, and rather clearly they used those cadres to mobilize village support for the insurgency. In light of such a rural presence, where *Sendero* both provided valuable resources to the villages (before and after the 1980 outbreak) and had deep family ties to those selfsame villages, why should anyone be surprised at the level of peasant support for the insurgency?[87]

Political Ties

In our survey of the 1960s movements, we observed that governments and guerrillas often had channels to the peasantry through pre-existing parties or other political organizations. In general, those features were scarcer for the second-wave of guerrilla movements. The reason is clear: Nicaragua, El Salvador, and Guatemala each had had for decades highly repressive regimes which hindered the mobilization of any political opposition, surely, but also failed themselves to mobilize any systematic political following among the nation's peasants. The pattern is the classic authoritarian one, and hence should not surprise us. Such a sociopolitical pattern, however, has the result of leaving vast tracts of the national political patrimony "virgin soil" (as I put it earlier) for potential political mobilizers. If radicals arrived first, therefore, they would not face the occupied political ground in rural areas that proved such an obstacle to guerrilla movements of the 1960s in Venezuela, Bolivia, and Colombia.

ORGANIZING VIRGIN SOIL

When political mobilization came to rural Nicaragua, the only real, organized political presence was the Sandinistas. The Conservative party had in good part become an empty shell, trotted out at the occasional election to make the "Liberal" Somoza dynasty look like a real democracy; while Conservative loyalists still opposed Somoza, they could do little effectively through their party organs, and hence it should not surprise us that many Conservative youth of the 1950s and 1960s became Sandinistas. Somoza certainly had his "ears" (*orejas*) and his rural constabulary, but both were only a fragmentary presence in rural Nicaragua.[88] Into this virgin soil came the Sandinistas, where they struck down deep roots—sometimes after initial setbacks—doing exceptionally well, as we saw, where Sandino's opposition "party" had ruled fifty years before.

In Peru, a wave of political organization came to the Andes beginning in the 1950s, and the new peasant voters were decisive targets of the campaigners in the elections after 1960. Ayacucho Department, however, was relatively isolated, and had few major haciendas, and thereby attracted little of the political activity of the early 1960s. When organization finally came to the area in the 1970s, it came in the form of Marxist-oriented and -affiliated grass-roots peasant organizations which the Velasco military government failed to control, and which helped to orient and shift leftward peasant politics in the region, which by 1978 and 1980 had among the highest vote for Marxist parties in Peru. In a real sense, however, *Sendero Luminoso* was the first political party (for that is what it considers itself) to mobilize the peasantry of certain areas of Ayacucho; thus when national politics came to this portion of the Sierra, those who "came firstest with the mostest" were not the representatives of a mildly left reformist party, but instead those of a Maoist-left agrarian revolutionary party of crypto-guerrillas. The consequences of that different history of political organization became sharply etched after 1980 when guerrilla warfare came to Ayacucho.[89]

In Guatemala and El Salvador, the rural absence of any real "popular parties," and the sole existence instead of periodically mobilized parties representing only different factions of the military or of the upper class, left effective political vacuums in many rural areas, which the guerrillas were later to fill.[90] Such political vacuity could only be increased, and the rural populace made more receptive to populist or revolutionary appeals, by the ongoing process of peasant despoliation in both nations which I described above as a "rupture" of the peasants' moral economy. Such processes could effectively destroy the *personal* political followings of many landlord-patrons, without introducing any modern political *party* structure to take its place.[91]

Not all political linkages were created out of whole cloth during the second wave, for both guerrillas and governments tried to secure peasant cooperation through existing organizational structures, sometimes in parallel fashion through competing organizations. In the extreme case of El Salvador, as Baloyra noted, both sides of the political conflict were fully activated in rural villages *before* the outbreak of civil war.[92]

Existing peasant organizations were one form through which such competition could take place. Virtually no such organizations helped either insurgent or regime in Nicaragua, yet in Peru, Guatemala, and especially El Salvador, they became highly relevant to the insurgency and the counterinsurgency. In Peru, while no formal party had successfully mobilized peasant activity in *Sendero's* later theater of operations, two different peasant confederations had mobilized radical discontent there in the 1970s; one of them began under government auspices but was cut off when its members elected an anti-regime leader in the late 1970s. *Sendero's* own success surely fed off the radical discontent mobilized by the confederations, even if the existence of any direct organizational linkages between them and *Sendero* remains a mystery.[93]

In Guatemala, there arose direct, violent competition for access to peasant resources in the countryside. A newly formed peasant organization, the Committee for Peasant Unity (Comité de Unidad Campesina, or CUC) began in 1978 to mobilize peasant opposition to the dictatorial regime. The CUC had its strongest roots among the partly proletarianized highland migratory workers—the very same group whom we identified as the strongest guerrilla supporters—and fragments of suggestive evidence indicate that, as repression increased, the CUC served as a channel into the guerrilla movements as well. The very solidarity of Indian villages, moreover, meant that when Indians went over to revolutionary activity, they often did so as entire villages.[94] On the opposing side, the government continued to employ the *Comisionados Militares* (Military Commissions) of the 1960s, composed of former soldiers in rural villages, as a kind of vast, and sometimes armed, spy network in the countryside, giving a series of dictatorial regimes information on the countryside vastly superior to that of many other nations with weak administrative apparatuses in rural areas. To those more traditional forms of rural presence, the Ríos Montt government would add Civilian Patrols, which peasants were pressured to join in order to patrol for and pursue rural insurgents, especially in the western highlands. We must surely trace the successes (perhaps limited) of Guatemalan counterinsurgency since 1982 to the strong presence that such political institutions provided in rural areas for a series of Guatemalan military governments.[95]

In El Salvador, too, the government began to try to establish institutions exactly mirroring the Guatemalan *Comisionados Militares*. This was hardly necessary, however, for the government up through 1980 had access to the countryside through ORDEN (Organización Democrática Nacionalista) and, after its dissolution, through its thinly disguised successor, the Broad National Front (FAN) led by Roberto D'Aubuisson. Begun semi-secretly in 1961–1965, ORDEN was composed at least in part of former members of the National Guard, who often joined the village branch of ORDEN after returning from their tours of duty. ORDEN's membership also overlapped with that of the Army Reserve. Among other things, ORDEN members were responsible for periodic patrols of their canton areas, thus again paralleling the Guatemalan pattern. ORDEN did not depend for its members' loyalty solely on patriotic experience but on the dispersal of real material favors, including occasionally land: when the interim junta began its land reform program in the early 1980s, the lands expropriated often went to ORDEN members and members of the more conservative peasant union, the UCS.[96]

THE PERSONAL BECOMES POLITICAL

Indeed, in Peru, Guatemala, and El Salvador, there is clear evidence of a repetition of a 1960s phenomenon: revolutionary conflicts overlying old personal and political conflicts at the village level. We saw evidence of such phenomena in the 1960s in Colombia, Venezuela, and Guatemala, where old personal conflicts predicted who would line up with whom when revolutionaries arrived on the scene. (These exactly parallel the "residues" of old feuds that Charles Tilly found partially underlying the pattern of conflict in the Vendée.)

In Guatemala, we have reports paralleling those of the 1960s, with members of the Civilian Patrols using their newfound weapons and power to even old personal scores or as a cover for extortion.[97] Yet in El Salvador, the process goes far deeper than that, for we see a political alignment of several features of rural village life: the radical peasant organization FECCAS (standing for the Christian Federation of Salvadoran Peasants), base communities, and ultimately the guerrilla movement seemed to have had at least partial interconnections. On the other hand, ORDEN, the death squads, the more conservative Union of Peasant Workers (UTC), and the government-military forces also seemed to have various interconnections. Moreover, some of those membership differences apparently were linked to peasants' positions in the rural class structures, with more politicized "middle" peasants in FECCAS and others in ORDEN. All such alignments tended to create new, ideologically supercharged versions of long-standing, and previously milder, village political conflicts.[98]

Finally, in Peru we can locate organized village resistance to *Sendero* in certain villages of the upper highlands that historically have had conflicts with Indian villages lower down. Not only were some of these communities royalists when other areas were up in arms against Spanish authority over 150 years ago, but their conflicts with "lowland" communities continued still. Most famous is the community of Iquichanos, which killed and expelled many members of *Sendero* (afterwards, and accidentally it appears, killing a group of reporters who came to verify that story). They would have nothing to do with the very guerrilla group so deeply supported in other Andean peasant communities. As Mario Vargas Llosa put it, "[t]he knowledge that their rivals in the valley help *Sendero Luminoso*, willingly or unwillingly, is cause enough to predispose the Iquichanos against them." The Peruvian government also took a page from the Central American textbooks, by beginning to form village patrols composed of ex-military men.[99]

CONCLUSIONS

Rather than discuss the preceding four sections in great detail again, I have summarized the findings in table 10–3.

TABLE 10-3
Peasant Support for Second-Wave Guerrilla Movements:
Do Regional Characteristics Predict a Radical Peasantry?

	Type of Social Influence in Rural Areas			
Country	Agrarian Social Structures	Agrarian Disruption	Rebellious Cultures	Preexisting Social Linkages
Nicaragua	Yes: (1) squatters (north-central); (2) migratory labor (northwest)	Yes	Yes (north-central)	Few, except CEBs
El Salvador	Yes: migratory labor	Yes	No	Yes: (1) CEBs; (2) FECCAS
Guatemala	Yes: migratory Indian labor	Yes (Crisis)	No	Yes?: (1) CUC; (2) CEBs
Peru	No	Yes (Crisis)	Yes?	Yes: (1) university; (2) villages/ town; (3) family

Sources: See text.

While no nation displays in full flower all four characteristics leading to a rebellious peasantry, *all* display *several* of the correlates leading to peasant support that we have come to expect based on the theories and evidence put forward in chapters 6 and 7.

Yet the question remains for Nicaragua as it did for Cuba in the earlier period. If these four nations—and Colombia as well—are structurally similar in the sources and degrees of peasant support, then how do we explain the revolutionary success of the Nicaraguan insurgency, and the failures to seize power elsewhere? As we shall see in the following chapter, not only can we account for such different outcomes, but the structured reasons for the Sandinistas' success bear striking resemblances to those behind Castro's success two decades before.

CHAPTER 11

Regime Weaknesses and Revolution in the Second Wave

> By 1974 these great, oligarchic, economic groups were ready to share power with Somoza, but what happened was that Somoza did not wish it. Then at the same time we could raise the banner of national liberation and unite all the people. One didn't try to say "Well, it is a class struggle." No! "It is a struggle for democracy and national liberation, against the Somocista dictatorship."
>
> —Jaime Wheelock[1]

WE HAVE already seen how Cuban society and politics created a regime that was weaker in the face of insurgency than its counterparts elsewhere. I will argue here that the Nicaraguan political system was also sharply differentiated from those in its 1970s–1980s counterparts in El Salvador, Guatemala, Peru, and Colombia. In this chapter I will first suggest a series of more or less sharply etched parallels with the Cuban revolution. Then I will contrast the Nicaraguan outcome with that in El Salvador (to date). There follows a comparison of the Salvadoran events with the more apt parallel of Guatemala. I will then briefly outline some changes in the political regimes of Peru and Colombia since the 1960s and suggest how such changes affected the political systems there, with regard to strengthening or weakening regimes that had already survived the first wave of insurgency. Finally, I will try to tie all these comments together, relating them to the writings of Skocpol on states and social revolutions.

THE NICARAGUAN REVOLUTION AND CUBAN PARALLELS

The Somoza regime of 1970s Nicaragua displayed a series of parallels—some of them quite remarkable, some of them nearly unique in the region—with the Batista regime of the 1950s in Cuba. Each political system had a long-term historical weakness in two basic institutions: political parties and institutionalized-professional militaries. Moreover, with the installation of dictatorships in the 1930s in each nation, the civilian branch of the state itself underwent a deepening or creation of widespread corruption, so that it, too, became less and less a servant of civil society, and more and more the direct spoils-source of the patrimonial dictator or president. As in Cuba, we can relate those political weaknesses to certain social weaknesses of civil society, for Nicaragua also displayed a history of weak coherence in the upper classes, and a virtual absence (until the 1960s) of anything resembling a middle-class movement for political reform.

Weak Upper and Middle Classes

> The National Guard, trained and initially paid and led by the United States, formed the core of a state that did not reflect the interests of the traditional landed oligarchy, the modernizing coffee bourgeoisie or even foreign capital. Its origins were strategic and military, not economic.
>
> —Jeffery Paige[2]

Since before independence sharp social divisions have riven the Nicaraguan upper classes, due in good part to dual regional locations in Granada and León. At independence the politically active upper classes of those two towns each attempted to subject the rival to its own political domination. Those attempts became embodied in the political-organizational rivalries between the Liberal (León) and Conservative (Granada) Parties.[3] In contrast to Cuba, therefore, Nicaraguan upper-class incoherence took on a deeper form in the open, deep conflicts between two major factions.

Marxists have reasonably linked some shifts in Nicaraguan politics to shifts in the power of different upper-class segments. The return of the Liberals to power under Liberal dictator José Santos Zelaya (1893–1909) should be linked to the growing economic power of a new coffee-based upper class, and the relative weakening of the economic fortunes centered around Granada. With the United States' interventions in 1909 and 1912, its unseating of Zelaya, and its mostly continuous occupation of Nicaragua (1912–1933), came an "artificial" restoration of the Conservatives to power, a power incongruous with their ongoing economic relegation to a second-class status as an upper-class power.[4] The series of portraits drawn of Nicaragua under Zelaya and up to the ascension of Somoza in the 1930s suggests a growing fragmentation within the Nicaraguan upper classes, for a whole series of intra-party struggles now were added on to the more traditional and organized conflicts between the Granadan Conservatives and the León Liberals (the powerful coffee interests were linked to the Liberals, but not without influence in its rival as well).[5]

The coming to power of Anastasio Somoza García, first to the head of the National Guard, and later to the presidency with his ouster of President Juan Bautista Sacasa and his own "election" (1936), was made possible, as in Cuba, by the sheer incoherence of other social and political groups. Unlike Cuba's Batista, there is a much clearer connection with the United States' intervention: the United States may have pressured Sacasa to appoint Somoza to head the Guard, and withdrew only a short time before Somoza's seizure of power.

With Somoza's seizure of power in Nicaragua, the period of upper-class contestation over state power came to an end. Instead, the upper classes were relegated to strictly economic roles within society, and increasingly took shape in three separate economic groups, each centered on a different bank: the Banco de América Group linked to the old Conservative party, the Banco Nicaragüense Group linked to the León Liberals, and the Somoza-controlled Banco Nacional. Under the last Somoza, this third group's control over portions of the economy became so massive that talk of Nicaragua as the Somozas' "family patrimony" was only an exaggeration, not an absurdity. The Somozas used their absolute dominance of state and government power to achieve economic preeminence in Nicaragua, thus reversing the usual Marxist expectation. The Nicaraguan upper class would only again play a major role in politics in its 1970s contribution to the downfall of Anastasio Somoza Debayle.[6]

Of the Nicaraguan middle classes we need say far less, for they simply were not effective political actors in Nicaragua until after 1950. Due to the sheer underdevelopment of the Nicaraguan economy, the salaried middle class as well as the independent professionals, merchants, and shopkeepers were but a small fraction of the employed until that time. When the former, salaried group finally began to grow, moreover, they did so largely under the auspices of the growing Somoza family empire, employed often in either his private businesses or in official government service.

The Somozas' autocratic, corrupt rule offended the middle classes (as Batista's rule had done in Cuba), while the political "emptiness" of Somoza's own Liberal party and its Conservative party "rival" (which struck pacts with the Somozas in 1950 and 1971 in exchange for some positions in government) left a vacuum in oppositional politics which a number of "bourgeois" groups—among them the Sandinistas—increasingly filled in the 1970s.[7] One might say that, if the Nicaraguan upper classes exited from power contention with the 1930s consolidation of the first Somoza regime, the nation's middle classes entered contention for power around 1960 in opposition to the direct heir of that regime. Yet they entered politics in circumstances in which all but revolutionary pathways had been closed off.

The Weaknesses of Nicaraguan Parties and the Military

> Somoza deliberately fostered military corruption to put enmity
> between the Guard and the public, and to create an officer corps in
> which the principal criterion for promotional success and personal
> enrichment was unconditional loyalty to "El Jefe."
> —Claribel Alegría and D. J. Flakoll[8]

As Woodward argued, during much of the first thirty years of independence "there were virtually two governments operating in the state, one in León and the other in Granada." One might reasonably speak of class "fractions" here, if only because the Granadan Conservatives' power was rooted in the merchants and the traditional landholding "aristocracy" of colonial days, while the León Liberals' resources were located in the cattle-ranching sector of the economy. The failure of the Nicaraguan Liberals to dent the strength of the governing Conservatives in the nominal capital of Granada, later Managua, broke out in open near–civil war in 1853. In 1855, the Liberals finally turned in exasperation to invite and contract the American filibuster William Walker to help them seize power. The subsequent events—including Walker's seizure of power and the Nicaraguan presidency and his introduction of slavery into the nation—led to a brief flicker of Central American unity as the five republics (at times only the Conservatives) joined forces in 1857 to oust Walker, who was later executed in Honduras when he essayed another such adventure. The Walker affair thoroughly discredited the Liberal party in Nicaragua (and in other nations whose Liberals had welcomed his intervention), leading to a long period of uninterrupted (1857–1893) rule for the Nicaraguan Conservatives and similar Liberal twilights in other nations.[9]

Perhaps as a result of such intra-class conflicts, the Nicaraguan state was always weakly developed and only began to grow to appreciable size and strength under the Somoza regime; in fact, it could well have been the weakest state apparatus in all Latin America until 1900. Thus in Nicaragua, unlike Cuba, state weaknesses derived more from upper-class conflicts than from sheer social-class incohesion. Only around 1900 do these political parties built upon warring upper-class factions begin to decay.

THE DECAY OF POLITICAL PARTIES IN NICARAGUA

The seemingly endless conflicts between the two parties, from 1824 to 1842,[10] were followed by the more serious skirmishes culminating in the Liberals' invitation to William Walker. Nonetheless, a number of commentators have noted the ideological emptiness of those conflicts, one pointing out that, even in comparison to other Central American nations, "In Nicaragua Liberalism . . . was almost purely regional."[11] That purely regional basis of difference could not sustain such parties indefinitely. The Conservative rulers (1857–1893), in fact, increasingly adopted policies right out of the Liberal canon, so that by the end of this period the parties were ideologically almost indistinguishable.[12]

Liberal José Santos Zelaya's period of iron-fisted, centralizing rule (1893–1909) began when the Conservatives divided among themselves over a presidential choice. Under Zelaya, the Nicaraguan state was clearly strengthened and centralized for the first time in that nation's history. But such strengthening came at the expense of the older, oligarchic pattern of political contention. Zelaya systematically suppressed Conservatives and regularly seized their properties under his rule, but he also quickly alienated his Liberal supporters as well.[13] As Woodward astutely noted, the rise of Liberal dictators throughout the region meant a breakup of the former political and economic dominance of the old upper classes.[14]

The 1909 revolt in Bluefields which finally brought down Zelaya's regime united strange bedfellows: Conservative groups who traditionally dominated that particular area, led by Emiliano Chamorro and Adolfo Díaz; the United States government, whose indignation was fired in part by the capture and execution of two U.S. mercenaries serving in the Conservative rebel forces; and anti-Zelaya Liberals led by the erstwhile governor of that area, Juan J. Estrada.

The United States' intervention of 1909 and the occupation of 1912–1925 led to the "dissolution" of the nascent and strengthening Nicaraguan state apparatus, reversing the gains of the Zelaya years. It reversed the long-term decline in the Conservative party, whose older and lesser wealth had been long transcended by that of the coffee planters. On the other hand, and paradoxically, the U.S. intervention accelerated the process of political party factionalization, with the parties dividing again and again into those groups willing and those unwilling to back, work with, or even talk to the foreign occupation forces. Finally, such events led to the switching of party loyalties more regularly, as the labels became increasingly meaningless. A renewed U.S. occupation of the late 1920s, with a large military force of marines, led to a brief hardening of Liberal versus Conservative divisions, when the Liberals formed and supported a "Constitutionalist Army" against the newly elected Conservative president. Nonetheless, the resulting attempts at U.S. diplomatic negotiation by Henry L. Stimson in 1926–1927 led to the "Peace of Tipitapa" where, in Neill Macaulay's expert view, "Both parties supported American intervention."[15]

THE NICARAGUAN NATIONAL GUARD

Prior to the creation of the *Guardia Nacional* by the United States in 1925, the Nicaraguan state had never possessed a true national army in a full century of independence. Instead, "party-sponsored armies continued to contest for national power through the nineteenth century."[16] This pattern is truly exceptional in Latin America. While Zelaya began to build up a centralized military power that none might have challenged had the process continued, the U.S. occupation effectively ended that process. When Dana Munro wrote of Nicaragua in the 1910s, he estimated at most two to three thousand men were still under arms there.[17] The United States later would create the guard with an eye to solving the problem of Conservative-Liberal contention with an independent national organization.

The appointment of Anastasio Somoza García ("Tacho") to head the guard would later culminate in his personal control over that armed force and over Nicaragua itself. This ending was not written in stone, and some evidence suggests that he yielded to military pressure on some occasions in the early years in order to stay abreast of the new military force.[18] By the mid-1930s Somoza had begun to consolidate his control over the guard, a control paralleled after his death (1956) by his sons Luis and Anastasio Somoza Debayle ("Tachito"). There were parallels to Batista's contemporary actions in Cuba during the 1930s and 1940s. First, Somoza the elder would remove from the National Guard any officer who gained in popularity with the men or who exhibited substantial personal ambition. Second, he also removed from the guard or otherwise derailed (e.g., through exile to remote provincial posts) those who sought the "modernization" of the officer corps, such as formal training in a military academy.[19] Third, he created a whole series of specialized privileges for the members of the National Guard. For those who were willing to toe the Somozas' line and be dutiful and unambitious order takers, many perquisites were forthcoming, including separate schools, hospitals, stores, and residential areas, later to be supplemented by truly impressive levels of graft wrung out of the civilian population. By the end of the dynasty the Guardia directly controlled the revenues of many government agencies, and its members owned perhaps 10 percent of all the cultivable land in Nicaragua.[20]

The structural weakness of such an armed force also paralleled that of Cuba. An organization so utterly dependent on a person—rather than roles, such as commander in chief, or general, or joint chiefs of staff—becomes so oriented toward that control that it lacks organization and purpose when such control disappears. Thus it happened in Cuba from 1944 to 1952, and Batista's 1950s return from "exile" could not restore his authority. In Nicaragua, Somoza suffered a heart attack in the late 1970s and went to the United States for medical care. In his absence the same kind of organizational decay that occurred in Cuba cropped up almost immediately in the guard, as members of the officer corps began jockeying for postmortem power, as did members of Somoza's Liberal party.[21]

The soldiers, unlike their Cuban counterparts, had received a great deal of counterinsurgency training, often in the United States (see chapter 5, especially table 5-9). They fought more effectively in the 1960s, however, when their opponents were largely rural and piecemeal: the 1960s Sandinista *focos*, when no mass political movement existed. Even in the last two years of insurgency (1978–1979), when they faced a large-scale insurgency and a mass political opposition, the guard clearly fought more vigorously and more bloodily than Batista's soldiers ever had. Perhaps they did so because they stood only to lose out with a shift to any other form of political regime.[22] The Cuban army's fate during the struggle seemed to be rather less tied to the outcome of the war. On the other hand, the *Guardia* was never as solidary and disciplined, as a whole, as the armies that fought guerrillas in many other nations, including most of South America.

Moreover, the National Guard had several features that structurally weakened it as the war progressed. First of all, its privileges isolated it even more from its fellow citizens than the Cuban military had been, and thus it could draw even less on popular support. Second, its looting of Managua and of relief funds during and after the 1972 earthquake is widely perceived as the decisive downward inflection point in its remnants of legitimacy.[23] Third, the culture imbued in the guard during its training—that "the people" were the guard's enemy—made it spectacularly ill suited to draw on national, popular symbols and popular support if it were to pursue a non-Somoza alternative; even less than the Cuban armed forces could the *Guardia Nacional* claim to represent the *patria*. Finally, sharp splits were appearing between the officer corps and the enlisted men (known as *rasos*); George Black describes the former's treatment of the latter simply as "appalling." Tomás Borge noted an increasing demoralization of the rank and file as the struggle progressed, and during the final insurrection "acute" officer-*raso* splits emerged in the guard. For one thing, Somoza Debayle's emphasis on, and extra-special funding of special elite units controlled closely by the family—including one commanded by his son—left a very bad taste in the mouths of members of the grunt units. The elite units became like an "army within the army," to borrow Black's apt phrase. As early as August 1978 there were widespread reports of large-scale desertions from the guard, although Somoza denied them.[24]

Parallel Patrimonial Praetorian Regimes: Mafiacracy in Cuba and Nicaragua

> Somoza converted Nicaragua into a nation ruled by the principles
> of the Sicilian mafia, assuring himself that he would be the
> undisputed "godfather" of the criminal empire he had created.
> —Claribel Alegría and D. J. Flakoll[25]

We might begin by noting an element of contrast between the Batista and Somoza versions of mafiacracy. Fulgencio Batista never came to control property to anywhere near the degree that the younger Somoza did. The reason should be clear: citizens of the United States controlled exceptionally large portions of the Cuban economy, and as such were relatively immune to corrupt patrimonial seizures. In Nicaragua, in contrast, U.S. economic interests were paltry indeed in any comparative perspective, and Somoza could enrich himself and his family to extremes without stepping on the toes of Americans. Regardless of property ownership, however, the upper class was not the "ruling class" in either of these societies.

If the ruling class did not rule in these mafiacracies, who did? As the two regimes consolidated their power, the state and government increasingly seemed to free themselves from their moorings in civil society. In a situation in which all class-based forces were markedly weak it was possible for the state to loose itself from control by "civil society" once the upper class was eased from power. Since these governments did not generate revenue primarily through direct taxation of the populace, that structural linkage and source of discontent was sharply reduced.[26] Most fundamentally, the post-1930s Cuban and Nicaraguan governments worked through a combination of personalized military control and an individualized system of patronage, corruption, and graft. Mark Falcoff has nicely termed the Nicaraguan variant a *patrimonial police state*. It is the political exclusion of the upper class, the personal character of rule, the extreme personalization of control over the military, and the high levels of corruption that define these mafiacracies, and such characteristics also fit well with Alain Rouquié's concept of *patrimonial praetorianism*.[27] Under such conditions, politics tended to "individualize" rather than to "class-ify" in both Cuba and Nicaragua.

Corruption has been widely discussed in both Cuban and Nicaraguan historiography. The Cuban system revolved around control of the national lottery and around the spoils system of political appointments, each of which supplied literally tens of millions of dollars in graft for the lucky winners. In Nicaragua, the system of corruption existed at the highest levels, with Somoza *père*'s personal enrichment at the expense of the Nicaraguan upper and middle classes, eventually securing Somoza *fils* a substantial fraction of the national patrimony. The latter's land was estimated at some 2 million acres, incorporating perhaps one-fifth of national agricultural production on his estates. As early as 1961, he owned a reported 274 properties, including 46 houses, 69 haciendas, 76 other urban lots, 13 industries, and 16 unfarmed landholdings, as well as foreign properties. This pattern was reproduced on an ever-smaller scale down through the ranks of the National Guard, until one encounters rank-and-file guardsmen obtaining graft trickling down from their superiors or protection money directly from citizens.[28] The entire Cuban pattern revolved around the spoils of enormous, sugar-derived, central-government revenues and how they would be allocated in patrimonial fashion. In Nicaragua, we see instead the privatization of the dictator's control of production, not simply of government revenues.

Beyond his preeminence in the economy and the military were Somoza's control of the party system itself, achieved by taking over the Liberal party in the 1930s and thereafter squeezing out or coopting the Conservatives. Occasionally, Somoza and the Conservatives even made formal agreements (e.g., in 1950 and again in 1971) to parcel out to the latter certain political posts and resources. Tension over such agreements did surface now and again, but Somoza Debayle's intransigence tended to grow in the latter years of his regime.[29] This attitude is best summed up by the following Somoza anecdote: The dictator was confronted with a co-opted Conservative party opponent who had lost a clearly fraudulent vote count; he called Somoza a sonofabitch and demanded that the dictator admit that the Conservative had won the election; Somoza conceded, "You won the election, but you lost the count. And the bigger sonofabitch is he who loses what he's won." Batista, by contrast, worked outside of the largely decadent Cuban party system. The difference surely reflects the stronger institutional continuity in the Nicaraguan party system, dating back to preindependence days.

This entire pattern increasingly indicated, therefore, a political system regularly, even increasingly closed to all but personal favorites of the patrimonial dictator, who moreover was increasing his ownership and seizures of large portions of the national economy. It was under such sociopolitical conditions that a revolutionary resistance emerged in the 1960s: the Sandinistas. That revolutionary resistance would largely fail on its own—as events through 1977 surely suggested—but would gather momentum and power as it forged a cross-class alliance in the late 1970s that would lead ultimately to the unseating of the dictator and to social revolution in Nicaragua. It is to that opposition that we now turn.

Structural Weakness, National Resistance

> Somoza was like a precious jewel through which all the contradictions of the people were focused.
>
> —Carlos Fonseca Amador[30]

The parallel events in Nicaragua and Cuba are quite striking. In both cases the more radical element of the opposition (Castro's guerrillas and the Sandinistas) ended up in an alliance with more moderate political actors, including middle- and upper-class–based political groups, whose joint venture focused on the ouster of the dictator and the establishment of an electoral and constitutional regime. In each case, the political program agreed upon in this "joint venture" was more moderate than that favored by radicals in the movement (Raúl Castro and Ché Guevara in Cuba; the Proletarian Tendency and the Prolonged Popular War factions of the Sandinistas). Moreover, the program was more moderate than that espoused by guerrillas in other nations whose experience most closely paralleled them: Castro's message was more moderate than that of his 1960s imitators in Venezuela, Guatemala, Colombia, Peru, and Bolivia; the Sandinistas' joint program with the "bourgeois" opposition, especially voiced through the group of The Twelve (*Los Doce*), was more moderate than those espoused by any Salvadoran guerrilla force, or by the various Colombian and Guatemalan groups, and most certainly more moderate than the wild-eyed Maoism of Peru's Sendero Luminoso. In both Cuba and Nicaragua, the combination of moderate allies and a moderated message produced improved media access for the opposition, voiced most regularly in Cuba's *Bohemia* and even more vigorously in Nicaragua's *La*

Prensa, but also echoed in the treatment of respected foreign periodicals, notably the *New York Times*.

Those three features, moderate allies, moderated messages, and mass media access, fed and fueled one another, consistently increasing the strength of the opposition and furthermore weakening the willingness of the United States' administrations (of Eisenhower and Carter, respectively) to continue supporting dictatorships under American domestic pressure to support democratic movements abroad. In 1957 and 1977, respectively, the U.S. government began to back away from the Batista and Somoza regimes, leading to a sharp decline in the morale of each regime and its defenders, in particular the armed forces. In both cases, the symbolic impact on morale was far greater than the material effect on weapons. In the very end, those same administrations would seek more or less frantically for more palatable political alternatives to the guerrillas acceding to power: the CIA sought Colonel Ramón Barquín López to take power in Havana and withhold it from Castro, and the Carter administration sought to keep the National Guard in existence and to install what critics came to call *"somocismo sin Somoza"*—the Somoza system without Somoza. Each such attempt failed, and the revolutionaries came into power. Afterwards, each radical core of revolutionaries squeezed out of power the moderates who had accompanied them to power, as the regime moved in the direction of socialism. Some of those moderate rebels would later oppose the socialist regimes in word and deed. Most notable here were Huber Matos of Cuba, formerly a military leader of Castro's insurgency, and Edén Pastora, "Comandante Cero" during the Sandinista seizure of the National Palace, yet later the leader of one of the anti-Sandinista armed groups.

Just as Batista began his rule as a populist, so Somoza García's rise to power also involved "a kind of social revolution," as Mark Falcoff has argued. It was he, and not Zelaya or Sandino, who decisively broke the back of upper-class political hegemony in Nicaragua and supplanted the former ruling class—whatever the source of their incomes: coffee, cattle, or finance capital—with his own family's dominance of state, military, and party.[31] There is thus a certain parallelism in the rise of the two figures to power, with mafiacracy replacing a more upper-class–dominated form of government.

When revolution came to Nicaragua from 1977 to 1979, there were fewer class overtones to the struggle than in the first Somoza's own consolidation of power. So close an analyst of the region as James Dunkerley has also drawn the connection between the shift in FSLN ideological strategy from a "class-oriented" approach to a "popular" approach, keyed to the value of "patriotism," and the improved fortunes of the Sandinista-led resistance after 1977.[32]

As early as 1975, a journalist pointed to a shakiness about Nicaraguan politics that had real echoes of Cuba, complete with the "disenchantment of the middle class, the bureaucracy and the United States, plus a guerrilla catalyst."[33] By late 1978, foreign journalists in their interviews with Nicaraguans turned up the same kind of pattern that had been found in Cuba less than a year prior to the seizure of power: "popular sentiment is overwhelmingly behind the Sandinistas."[34] Somoza in fact had encouraged a national resistance to form by refusing to negotiate in good faith with the opposition, just as Batista had refused.[35] Government intransigence in both cases thus could produce a situation for the *moderate* opponents of the regime in which *no hay otra salida*: there is no other way out.

THE SOURCES OF NATIONAL RESISTANCE: MODERATION AND THE MEDIA

As in Cuba, the very *personalism* of the regime provided a highly visible, very nonabstract target on which the populace could focus their grievances. This was no mere accident of history or simply a feature of personality but was tied to the patrimonial features of the regime, for patrimonial praetorian regimes in a sense *need* that single individual to dispense patrimonial rewards and punishments, to keep the whole system going. Because of the inherently personal features of the regime, the people needed to make no leap of abstraction to find an enemy. Somoza as the target meant that resistance to him implied a negation of what he stood for. If he stood for fraudulent democracy, the opposition campaigned for real democracy. If he stood for random constitution making and unmaking, the opposition could campaign on a platform of respect for constitutional principles. If he robbed from the modestly prosperous and the rich alike, then those groups could be counted on to support his ouster.

Of those groups, the Sandinistas were formed with a rather clear Marxist-Leninist orientation,[36] but two fissures arose within the Sandinistas in 1975–1976, about the time when unity figure Carlos Fonseca died in combat. The Proletarian Tendency pursued a working-class–oriented revolution along traditional Marxist lines, headed by Jaime Wheelock. The Prolonged Popular War faction instead pursued a quasi-Maoist strategy of rural- and peasant-oriented insurrection.[37] The third FSLN group, the Insurrectional Tendency, or Terceristas, as they are better known, did not simply choose a middle way but instead argued strongly for a "policy of tactical alliances" with other groups in Nicaragua; that is, they argued for the subordination of ideological differences to pursue the goal of ousting Somoza.[38]

By the year 1978, the official Sandinista ideology had lost much of its original Marxist, revolutionary flavor, as many analysts have argued and as many texts can show.[39] For example, even so partisan an insider as José Fajardo noted (prior to the victory) that the Fidelista and Marxist "tints" with which the FSLN was colored at its birth were reduced to "timid tones" by the time of its 1978 ideological manifesto.[40]

The organizational embodiments of this ideological *rapprochement* with the "bourgeois opposition" were varied, but the most important one was the group of The Twelve, known as *Los Doce*. The Twelve were viewed by the

Sandinistas and by the public as a sort of "bridge" between the more moderate and more radical strands of the anti-Somoza opposition and comprised upper- and middle-class Nicaraguans, many from business or university occupations. They did a great deal of the public-relations work for the Sandinistas abroad—the Cuban parallel was the group in the United States led by the moderate Mario Llerena[41]—and surely helped to secure for the Sandinistas some of the foreign supporters who came to back them.[42] The Twelve, however, were more than simply a symbolic bridge between the moderates and radicals, for four of the members of the group were in fact members of the FSLN, and some of the other members of the group did not know of those affiliations.[43]

Both ideologically and organizationally, then, the FSLN began to establish systematic linkages with other anti-Somoza organizations. I have no desire to recount here the numerous groups and regroupings that took part in political dialogues and insurrectionary activity from 1978 until the revolutionary seizure of power in July 1979, for that task has been well accomplished by those better suited to that task.[44] I merely wish to reiterate here what each of those studies shows in a systematic fashion: that the FSLN secured an alliance with moderate, often "bourgeois" segments of society to join in a movement to oust Somoza. That unity was more checkered than in Cuba, for certain competing groups appeared in the last several years of the Somoza regime that later became insignificant in the final contestation for power; notable in this regard was the upper-class–dominated group known as UDEL (the Democratic Liberation Union), which lost political clout and support after 1978, especially to the FSLN-oriented MPU (United People's Movement).[45]

Thus both moderate allies and a moderated ideology came to dominate opposition politics in Nicaragua after 1977. Both cause and consequence of this union was the special access to the mass media that the opposition enjoyed. No other guerrilla movements of the second wave would have such access to the "great bourgeois press" (as the Marxists termed it in several nations), but such friendly media coverage was readily forthcoming to virtually all the anti-Somoza opposition in Nicaragua. A historical accident contributing heavily to this fact was Pedro Joaquín Chamorro's position as the editor of *La Prensa*, Nicaragua's most important newspaper by far. The Chamorro family were old Conservative party rivals of the déclassé Somoza family—whose ancestor was a bandit when a Chamorro had been president— and Chamorro himself was a veteran of schoolyard brawls with Somoza Debayle in his childhood.[46] The only other guerrilla movement in this entire period with such sympathetic media coverage was Fidel Castro's 26th of July Movement in Cuba, as I documented in chapter 8. That parallelism is no accident; it derives from the increasingly national and moderate (and hence "respectable") nature of the opposition to mafiacratic rule.

The sustained fire poured on the Somoza regime by *La Prensa* served to undercut any of Somoza Debayle's claims to legitimacy. Like the Cuban press, *La Prensa* was indeed silenced by censorship periodically, yet such censorship was lifted on several occasions, so the newspaper could fuel the opposition. The last major censorship period, a state of siege, was lifted on 5 September 1977 under pressure from the Carter administration.[47] Even under censorship, however, *La Prensa* could transmit at least a symbolic statement of opposition; one typical ploy was to publish a photo of Ava Gardner in the spots where the censor had excised text.[48] During this period, the sub-director of *La Prensa* could proclaim, "I'm a Sandinista" (while denying FSLN membership). After the revolution, Sergio Ramírez conceded that the FSLN regularly fed inflated or altered figures to the media or even "falsified the news. . . . We considered any method justifiable."[49]

In addition to the press, the Sandinistas began radio broadcasts in September 1978 and viewed "Radio Sandino" as an "essential medium for creating and accelerating revolutionary conditions." By mid-1979 it had become the *principal* means for sending messages to the insurrectionary groups, as well as coded messages to the regional fronts. Nor did they have to rely on domestic radio alone in the close geography of Central America, for they could employ Costa Rica's "Radio Reloj" as well. The Sandinistas even argued that the use of radio went beyond simple communication, in helping to create a culture of resistance to the Somoza regime.[50]

THE CLASS AND INSTITUTIONAL COMPONENTS OF THE RESISTANCE

John Booth has contributed sketches of the class and institutional (e.g., church, press, university) components of the rebellion, and Carlos Vilas has described in detail the class composition of the FSLN itself. Of the latter, it is worth noting that the working class, while clearly evident, was less well represented in the FSLN—whether we look at parental or individual occupations—than were the urban "petty bourgeoisie," especially those in the urban informal sector.[51] Still, the pictures that emerge from these and other accounts is that everyone seemed to be involved in the opposition, with particularly strong loci in the university, selected towns (León and Matagalpa), and in the countryside as well.[52]

Somoza's supplanting of the old upper-class rulers of Nicaragua set up a potential source of opposition that never went away. Just as the Cuban upper class looked down on Batista as a mulatto, and the son of a lower-class cane cutter to boot, the Nicaraguan upper class viewed Somoza García's rise to power and his mafiacratic regime as the triumph of *mala educación* (bad breeding).[53] That opposition became activated with the government's response to the 1972 earthquake in Managua, as businessmen spoke of the "mafia-type" atmosphere in government during post-quake reconstruction.[54]

At that time the small independent businessmen of the capital apparently turned decisively against the regime. Indeed, Henri Weber went so far as to argue that bourgeois groups were in the forefront of the opposition until very late in the struggle. In 1978, UDEL and other bourgeois groups were the prime movers in organizing general strikes in January and August.[55]

Shifts in Somoza's policies tended to harden upper- and middle-class opposition to the regime as well. The UDEL opposition group has been described by Marxists as constituting "the" middle-class's organized opposition to the regime.[56] As usual, one of the themes hammered at in middle-class–oriented appeals was the colossal corruption of the regime; anticorruption appeals are recurrent elements in the ideologies of Latin American middle-class parties.[57] The middle class was moreover strongly hit by price increases and higher sales taxes after 1972, and Eduardo Crawley has tried to paint a composite portrait for us of the Somoza-dependent, middle-class bureaucrat coming to turn against the regime.[58]

The FSLN also managed an appreciable mobilization of urban lower-class groups against the regime, in part effected by their "accumulation of forces in silence" during the 1970s. I say "in part" here because the urban insurrections against the Somoza regime were often spontaneous lower-class or mass (especially Indian) uprisings which the Sandinistas did not lead and did not spark. They did, however, try to move to the vanguard and to fuel these uprisings once they had begun. Such largely spontaneous popular uprisings—which really have no parallel in the Cuban revolutionary process—came in January 1978 following the assassination of Pedro Joaquín Chamorro, again in the urban *barrio* of Monimbó in February of that same year, and yet again in the September insurrection in Matagalpa.[59]

Institutional actors turned regularly against the Somoza regime as well. The Catholic Church, the universities, chambers of commerce, and the press all came openly to oppose Somoza by 1978, and we have already touched on some of these groups. As early as 1972, Somoza had dissolved Congress and replaced it with "three-man rule," yet the Church refused to bless the dictator's triumvirate and no bishop attended the ceremony.[60] In March 1977 and again in January 1978 the bishops condemned the terror tactics of the regime, including its use of torture, rape, summary executions, and the persecution of priests. They even criticized the maldistribution of national wealth in the latter attack.[61] While the Church never threw its lot in clearly with the Sandinistas, identifying most closely with the Broad Opposition Front (FAO), the common ground it shared with the national minimalist program of 1978 made it at least part of the national movement to oust Somoza.[62] If the church hierarchy so clearly supported the ouster of Somoza, the argument applies *a fortiori* to the base communities and parish priests who came at times to work hand in glove with the FSLN.[63]

The university was also central to the opposition, as I showed in chapter 9 above. One important element that allowed such opposition at least some rein was the autonomy of the University of León. Somoza, like Batista two decades before, generally respected the principle of autonomy, and the schools and universities alike became key recruiting grounds and seedbeds for the Sandinistas, while the university community in León organized and led various antigovernment rallies. The FSLN, after being elected to head the student government in its university alter-ego, could then have access to type-writers, mimeo machines, and university supplies to help with its campaign of opposition.[64]

In Nicaragua, if anything, the opposition of civic and business groups to the regime was more open and more vigorous than in Cuba. Both the "civic stoppage" following the Chamorro assassination (January 1978) and the general strike later that year were clearly supported by the business community and more than that: the Chamber of Commerce actually helped to organize and launch both of those major oppositional events.[65]

At the very end even the military was no longer quite the bulwark that it had been. When Somoza capitulated to the demands made following the sei-zure of the National Palace, there ensued a coup attempt by disgruntled mem-bers of the National Guard.[66] While most observers have commented on how well the guard fought until the very end, George Black instead observed that the officer-raso splits became "acute" as the insurrection continued.[67] Others noted that, in many provincial outposts near the end, soldiers simply refused to fight, and low morale and desertion came regularly in the regime's last several months.[68]

Perhaps the final straw was the ending of U.S. military and economic aid to the regime, which had already experienced several years of tense relations with the Carter administration over human rights issues. While the United States formally ended all economic and military aid to the regime in early 1979, "[M]ilitary aid had been negligible for some time even before last Sep-tember [1978]."[69] The Carter administration had earlier voted against loans to Nicaragua from the Interamerican Development Bank, thus providing a "psy-chological shock" to the Somoza regime; that shock was to be echoed in the regime's response to the later, complete cutoff of aid, and both of those shocks precisely parallel the response of the Batista regime to the same U.S. actions twenty years before. Again in parallel to Cuba, the U.S. denial of arms shipments to Somoza did not appreciably damage either regime's mili-tary fighting capability; it merely enriched foreign arms' suppliers who, in the Cuban case, included Czechoslovakia, in the Nicaraguan case, Israel, Argen-tina, and Guatemala.[70] As a fillip to U.S. opposition, a group of mediating Latin American nations, including Venezuela and Costa Rica, also called for Somoza's resignation as early as September 1978.[71]

The Emergence of Dual Power

Relatively early in the insurrection, the Sandinistas came to control large stretches of the mountainous countryside in which they effectively operated as the government: peasants in such regions followed their directives rather than those of government, a sure sign of the presence of dual power.[72] In the insurrectionary process from January 1978 onward, the cities were the main loci of pitched battles between the Somoza regime and the popular rebels. Those struggles increasingly dovetailed with and came under the control of *los muchachos*—the Sandinistas—as the end of the Somoza regime neared in early 1979. Matagalpa and León in particular underwent intense aerial bombardments because they "went over" to the Sandinistas at a relatively early part of the insurrection; indeed, they were clearly "Sandinista" by September 1978. One of the main organizational forms the FSLN proto-government was taking at this time was the United People's Movement (MPU), a mass organization intimately tied to the lower classes and to the urban uprisings.

As early as October 1977 FSLN documents revealed a proposed "revolutionary cabinet"—The Twelve—to govern Nicaragua after the defeat of the regime. Upon Somoza's discovery of this, The Twelve fled Nicaragua, but they later returned in the summer of 1978 after Somoza made some human rights concessions in response to Carter administration pressures. On the other hand, the opposition coalition between the FAO and the FSLN fragmented later in that year as mediation talks with Somoza failed. The Sandinistas began to distance themselves somewhat from their "bourgeois" partners and align more closely with the MPU. Insurrection against the Somoza regime grew through the first six months of 1979, and the guard's resistance began to weaken. In early June, Nicaraguan revolutionaries based in neighboring Costa Rica announced that they had formed a Governing Junta of National Reconstruction, and by 9 July they had begun negotiations with the United States over the post-Somoza transition—a sure sign of dual power and authority shifts. The five-person membership included three Sandinistas—but not all three were publicly known to be FSLN members at that time, notably Sergio Ramírez Mercado—and two others: Violeta Barrios de Chamorro (widow of the slain publisher) and Alfonso Robelo. The ideological span of the junta's membership encapsulates that of the opposition itself. With the opening up of negotiations between the U.S. government and the revolutionary Junta, the United States had effectively recognized that group as the future government of Nicaragua. The Somoza era ended soon afterwards, on 19 July 1979, after Francisco Urcuyo led a brief flicker of an interim government.[73]

In table 11-1 I have summarized the parallel processes of revolution in Cuba and Nicaragua. Both societies contained weak political structures—the praetorian patrimonial regime or mafiacracy—in the years just preceding the

TABLE 11-1

Prerevolutionary Parallels in Nicaragua and Cuba

	Nicaragua	Cuba
A. Class Incohesion		
	Upper classes in open conflict since at least 1800; rooted in regional and economic differences between Granada and León; increased fragmentation after 1893.	Upper classes show no political cohesion; rooted in different national origins: Cuban versus U.S. versus Spanish immigrant.
	Middle class small, insignificant to 1950; thereafter mobilized into politics against Somozas, in civic and revolutionary opposition.	Middle class large, yet unable to mobilize behind middle-class or populist parties.

Common Pattern: Weak, incohesive, middle- and upper-class politics pave the way for patrimonial dictatorship to seize power. Contribution of U.S. political and military intervention.

	Nicaragua	Cuba
B. Political Institutions		
	Coherent upper-class parties show increasing internal conflicts under Zelaya and aftermath. U.S. occupation accelerates process, Somoza coup completes it (1936).	No continuity in party politics, as new parties repeatedly displace old ones. Ortodoxo revival derailed with death of Eddy Chibás, 1951.
	No national military ever institutionalized in 1800s, just party-armies. U.S. creates professional National Guard, but Somoza converts it into personal tool, bulwark of the family rule, 1932–1979. Guard shows signs of dissent, decay in late 1970s.	U.S. establishes national military ca. 1916. Thereafter army, generals both politicized by own actions, by presidents' manipulation. Batista coup completes politicization, personalization of his control. Army decay visible after 1952.

Common Pattern: Both had weak parties and a never-professional, never-national army. Party and military weaknesses allow dictator to seize power without effective opposition. Military is (re)constituted as personal tool of dictator, blunting all domestic opposition

TABLE 11-1 (*cont.*)

	Nicaragua	Cuba
C. Widespread Corruption	Theft from middle and upper classes. Graft, kickbacks, protection money via National Guard. Greater overall.	Looting of national lottery. Spoils system of no-show government jobs. Graft, kickbacks. Less overall.

D. Resulting Political Structure

Common Pattern: Mafiacracy, a.k.a. the patrimonial police state (Falcoff) or patrimonial praetorianism (Rouquié). Distinguishing political features:

1. Personal, rather than party-based rule
2. Upper class does not rule (perhaps attacked)
3. Personal domination of armed forces, which become almost private armies
4. Massive corruption, enrichment of ruler and personal associates
5. Violent attacks on political opposition

E. Regime's Shaping of the Political Opposition

Common Pattern: Personal nature of rule engenders easier identification of common enemy, facilitates formation of a mass opposition. Upper-class opposition engendered by property assaults, attacks on family members, déclassé character of ruler. Middle-class opposition fueled by similar features, plus regime corruption. Cross-class opposition united by democratic, constitutionalist, anti-dictatorial imagery; divisive issues downplayed. Such imagery gives them access to mass media, plus good press in the U.S.A., where national pressures arise to withdraw support for dictator, which occurs within last two years of dictatorship.

revolution. Those political weaknesses, in turn, are related as in Cuba to a history of class incoherence and U.S. politico-military intervention. Largely due to the regime's traits, the emerging opposition movements were pressured toward and eventually moved toward a cross-class and multi-institutional form of opposition to the personalized dictatorial regime, uniting on behalf of constitutional, electoral, and democratic principles. I do not deny differences between the two regimes, or between the two post-revolutionary outcomes; but the *fact* of revolution in those two societies can logically be explained only by their similarities, not their differences. I leave for others the task of explaining the differences in the emerging postrevolutionary regimes, simply noting that we have a model for such explanation in Skocpol's treatment of postrevolutionary outcomes in Russia and China.[74]

The governing theme throughout the entire first part of this chapter has been what John Stuart Mill called the "method of agreement": arguing for many similarities in two cases with similar outcomes, in this case social revolution. I have tried to show how the Cuban and Nicaraguan patrimonial praetorian regimes came to similar revolutionary ends precisely because they were such regimes, and quite apart from the many differences between the two societies. In doing so, I have also tried to show how certain aspects of Cuban and Nicaraguan social and political history, first, made it likely that such regimes would emerge and, further, that the very sociopolitical characteristics of society and polity in interaction would lead to an effective, revolutionary-cum-moderate challenge. We now move to Mill's second method, the "method of difference", to consider why the outcomes in Nicaragua, on the one hand, and El Salvador and Guatemala, on the other, have been so different.

REVOLUTION AND FAILED REVOLUTION IN CENTRAL AMERICA

> Our final offensive two weeks from now will be backed by all Salvadorans.
>
> —FMLN spokesman, January 1981[75]

> You know, in Nicaragua all the people were against Somoza. In El Salvador, what you have had building up is a real class war.
>
> —Ambassador Robert E. White[76]

> [Edén Pastora] argued that conditions in El Salvador were very different from those in Nicaragua. . . . the Sandinistas had led a largely middle-class insurrection against a family dictatorship. In El Salvador, however . . . they could not count on the support of the middle class. Mr. Pastora predicted disaster. The offensive was launched in January 1981. Mr. Pastora proved correct.
>
> —James LeMoyne[77]

> The revolutionary coalition of the FDR-FMLN, despite its incorporation of middle-class groups, is conducting a struggle that has all the hallmarks of class warfare. The representative associations of the upper class have not affiliated with the revolutionary front; instead they have exerted considerable pressure on the state to remain steadfast in its attempts to suppress the revolutionary forces.
>
> —Manus Midlarsky and Kenneth Roberts[78]

> Another factor for unity against Somoza was Somoza himself; a visible personal head, always the same, of a long-standing bloody

> dictatorship, which made the union of all opposed to it much
> easier. . . . But in El Salvador, against whom is the general
> alliance to take place?
>
> —Gabriel Zaid[79]
>
> [T]he masses are not insurrectionary.
>
> —FMLN spokesman, late 1983.[80]

Diplomats, present and former combatants, journalists, and social scientists
have all turned their attention to the different outcomes to date of revolutionary exertions in Nicaragua and neighboring El Salvador. Here we must pursue
what John Stuart Mill called the method of difference: What conditions of
those two societies have led to such disparate outcomes? By far the most
favored analytical path when confronted with this theoretical issue has been
what I shall call in chapter 12 the "imperial prop" thesis: The United States
withdrew support from Somoza, and he fell to a popular insurgency; the
United States threw all its economic and military weight behind Salvadoran
governments from 1981 to the present—$618 million in 1987 alone[81]—and
they have withstood the popular insurgency, although they have not destroyed
it. As I write these words, the right-wing ARENA government and the FMLN
guerrillas are negotiating for peace at talks in Mexico, a far cry from the
FMLN's revolutionary triumphalism of early 1981. Why did the Salvadoran
revolutionaries fail?

I will argue here and in chapter 12 that a third Central American case,
Guatemala, casts very strong doubt on U.S. support as the *single, decisive*
cause of failure in El Salvador.[82] Guatemalan social and political structures
were very akin to those of El Salvador, and each regime faced a large-scale
insurgency. Both regimes have, to date, weathered those insurgencies, even
though the United States had withheld—and the Guatemalan military government refused—military aid during the strongest years of the Guatemalan insurgency, unlike the massive U.S. aid to El Salvador. Thus these societies
with very similar "outcomes" differ greatly in the very condition that some
scholars argue as decisive to the defeat of insurgency.

Nicaragua and El Salvador Contrasted

To that illogical conclusion I wish to contrast a very different interpretation.
El Salvador's class structure and political system were both very unlike those
of Nicaragua. The Salvadoran polity can best be termed a *collective military
regime* from the early 1950s until 1979–1982, and the military governors
ruled in de facto alliance with a solidary Salvadoran upper class. That regime
"cracked open" during the 1979–1982 "reformist" period when a series of
civil-military juntas ruled El Salvador, but emerging from that period was a
constituent assembly (elected in 1982) that produced competitive elections

for national offices in 1984, 1985, 1988, and 1989, pitting the centrist Christian Democrats against a number of right-wing groups, the largest of which was ARENA. Paralleling these new alignments were a series of sociopolitical divisions within the Salvadoran class structure that were the antithesis of the cross-class alliances that had ousted Batista and later Somoza. Hence the Salvadoran polity during the 1980s moved increasingly, albeit only partially—the left was excluded in the early elections, and only partly present in 1988 and 1989—in the direction of *electoral democracy*. The results, paralleling my arguments of chapter 8 above, were a series of Salvadoran political systems that were relatively strong in the face of revolutionary challenges, unlike the patrimonial praetorian regimes of Cuba and Nicaragua.

SOCIAL CLASSES AND POLITICAL ACTORS

Nicaragua had a long period of rule by essentially a single family dynasty, whereas Salvadoran politics had been controlled for decades in what was essentially an alliance between the officer corps of the military, on the one hand, and the "oligarchy," "fourteen families," or simply the upper class of that nation, on the other. The unity of the Salvadoran upper class derived primarily from its control of coffee cultivation, which in the past century has led to spin-offs into coffee processing, and then into exports, manufacturing, and finance. Careful scholarship has confirmed the repetition of the same family names controlling the various key subsectors of the economy, strongly suggesting that there is a social reality to talk about a Salvadoran "oligarchy," even if the number of families involved is much larger than that famous fourteen. Moreover, the unity of that Salvadoran elite survived even the unrest of the 1970s and the partial economic reforms and civil war of the 1980s.[83]

While the Salvadoran upper class ruled the economy, the military ruled the polity. The officer corps of the army technically held the positions of political power, but throughout those earlier decades they allowed or the upper class enforced an economic veto over any undesirable policies; a notable case here is the latter group's "shouting down" of an agrarian reform proposal in 1975–1976.[84] Whereas the Nicaraguan military was dominated by the Somoza family, the Salvadoran military had various currents of thought, but was ruled mostly by men coming from a single *tanda*, or academy graduating-class cohort, at any given point in time.[85] With the 1979 coup and various ensuing proposals for and enactments of reform, upper-class opposition in league with *parts* of the officer corps succeeded in derailing or limiting the reform process, largely through massive violence fueled by extreme anticommunism.[86] Increased military dissatisfaction with upper-class politics—reflected in the former's rebuff to ARENA's "fraud" charges after the 1985 elections—has only reduced, not eliminated, upper-class power in the state.

In the history of other nations in Latin America, such upper-class domination of national politics, in league with the military, tended to produce a populist opposition movement, led and supported by the middle classes, but also enlisting substantial backing from workers and the peasantry; so, too, in El Salvador. From the 1960s to 1980, the single most important popular opposition to Salvadoran military rule was the Christian Democratic party (PDC), whose major personality by 1980 was the former mayor of San Salvador, José Napoleón Duarte. Nicaragua lacked the kind of Christian Democratic party that Duarte led in El Salvador, which gained power from the masses *against* oligarchic rule. Duarte was apparently cheated out of the presidency in the 1972 election and was beaten and exiled after popular protests followed his "defeat." As none other than Communist party (PCS) leader Shafik Jorge Handal noted, "The Christian-Democratic Party, until recently an important force at elections, did not become a party of the bourgeoisie: it found it had to pursue a populist policy, proclaim the slogan of a 'revolution of the poor,' look for support among the working masses, and form an alliance with the CPS [Communist party]."[87] At least some portion of its populist heritage—surely providing a declining level of support between 1984 and 1988—generated some mass support for the Christian Democrats and José Napoleón Duarte during the entire 1980s period of civil war.

POLITICAL CHANGES SINCE 1979

With the disruption of the collective military regime during the years 1979–1982, shifts in the major political actors of El Salvador have been paralleled by shifts in the political loyalties of various social classes. The result has been to create a political spectrum of left, center, and right, with corresponding strengths among the various social classes. The populist heritage of the Christian Democrats, and the history of political patronage by the right, have split various social classes on the issue of revolution. On the left, deep support among the marginalized northern peasantry (see chapter 10 above) plus substantial urban support have lent to it exceptional strengths as well. Hence no single "party" can make persuasive claims to speak for "the" Salvadoran people.

To refer to the Christian Democrats as a just another "rightist power bloc"[88] in Salvadoran politics is to choose anathema over analysis, for that party throughout the 1980s could count on *some* substantial political support, including votes, from the middle and working classes and from the peasantry.[89] As for right-wing parties, the (former) members of the peasant paramilitary organization known as ORDEN (Nationalist Democratic Organization)—at one time 100,000 strong—tended to support, not the Christian Democrats or the FMLN guerrillas, but the far-right military party the PCN (Party of National Conciliation) or ARENA, and often joined the death squads as well.[90] The middle classes were and are also divided in tripartite ways between the revolutionaries, the Christian Democrats, and ARENA, and may have supported the last-named group because it controlled the disbursement of political patronage jobs in the capital, while many of them voted against the Christian Democrats in 1989, complaining of corruption during the Duarte years.[91]

The Salvadoran left by 1981 was composed politically of the various guerrilla groups in the FMLN and their "mass" (or front) civilian organizations concentrated in the capital and certain rural areas, gathered together in the Democratic Revolutionary Front (FDR). Socially, we have already seen that the guerrilla leadership was drawn from the highly educated middle and upper classes, and the bulk of the rank and file from the peasantry, with substantial numbers from the working class as well. Yet each of those social classes also lent considerable support to the FMLN's political opponents. By the elections of 1988 and 1989 the left began to show signs of fragmentation, not unlike those that were tearing apart the Christian Democrats at the same time. For one thing, the absolute numbers of guerrillas were down from their peaks of 1983–1984. Second, recurrent elections have put pressure on the alliance between the civic revolutionaries of the FDR and the guerrillas of the FMLN. That alliance was always a suspect one, in good part because the guerrillas controlled the real levers of power within the joint command, as well as the guns.[92] The 1988 elections actually brought some members of the old FDR, notably Guillermo Ungo and Rubén Zamora, back into domestic political life and also brought into higher relief the tensions that had always existed between at least parts of the FDR and the Marxist-Leninist guerrilla leadership. The 1988 and 1989 elections did not produce an open split in the left, despite Ungo and Zamora's public criticisms of certain FMLN acts of violence, but did outline the increasing independence of the newly formed left-wing party, Convergencia Democrática (Democratic Convergence), from the soldiery of the FMLN.[93]

Strong geographical evidence further outlining the weaknesses of the left is their widely acknowledged and sharp decline in urban areas, especially the capital, after the January 1981 offensive. That weakness is damaging to those theories suggesting that the guerrillas could have won the war in 1983 or thereabouts if the United States had not propped up the tottering Salvadoran military, for at that time the revolutionaries were as weak in the cities as at any time in the 1980s.[94] How could they win a revolution with virtually no urban component to the insurrection? In contrast, their *greatest* strength in the cities had been in 1980 and January 1981, when their "final" insurrection was put down by the military, yet *before* the United States restored any substantial military aid to the Salvadoran regime. Even then, the revolutionaries exhibited substantial weaknesses in the cities: in their own documents at that time they said that the "popular sectors are becoming progressively confused . . . affected by the defeatist attitude" and further called "vast sectors of the population . . . unaware" of guerrilla advances in the countryside.[95]

After 1985 they very gradually began to regroup in the capital, where they remained weak until 1989.[96] In November 1989, however, the FMLN launched a major uprising in the capital that, in the eyes of some observers, showed their substantial urban strengths and almost brought them victory. Closer examination suggests otherwise: (1) most of these "urban" fighters apparently came from outside the capital, especially from rural areas to the north near Guazapa volcano; (2) they were joined by some underground urban cadres who promptly lost their covers, and often their lives, in the insurrection (which cost the guerrillas many hundred dead); (3) no one seriously claims that the urban *barrio* residents widely joined in the insurrection, and some observers argued—this was disputed—that the guerrillas used civilians as "cover" and at times prevented them from fleeing the firefight areas (the contrast with Nicaragua's urban uprisings of 1978–1979, which the people did join with, is instructive here);[97] (4) the armed forces vigorously, sometimes indiscriminately, fought and eventually suppressed the uprising; among the terror tactics were bombing of *barrios* and the murders of six Jesuit priests.[98] Following the failure of the uprising, the "orders" from the five Central American presidents to end the fighting (December 1989), and the Sandinistas' loss in the Nicaraguan national elections (March 1990), the FMLN's prospects looked ever bleaker.[99] The guerrillas again sat at the bargaining table with their most despised enemies, ARENA, and that outcome certainly does not suggest that they were on the verge of victory scarcely six months before; rather that sequence suggests that the November uprising was the last gasp of the guerrillas' hopes for a military victory, and may even have been intended, not to secure victory, but simply to force the new government of Alfredo Cristiani into political negotiations, for the FMLN is making fewer nonnegotiable demands now rather than more.

THE RESULTS: CLASS WAR, NOT REVOLUTION

Let us now unite those contrasts to make a coherent interpretation of the Salvadoran guerrillas' failure to date. The Salvadoran insurgency began against a collective military regime that governed hand in glove with the upper class, not against a patrimonial praetorian regime like Batista's Cuba or Somoza's Nicaragua. Only patrimonial regimes tend to elicit cross-class, populist uprisings that isolate the government from all organized support; an uprising against an upper-class–backed military regime will instead tend to take the form of a class war. That is precisely what happened in El Salvador. That turn to class warfare hardened any wavering upper-class reformists against the insurgency. There is no greater difference from Nicaragua: there the upper class turned against the regime from "the left" beginning in 1972; in El Salvador, the upper class instead had been united to support the old military regime, and then turned against any "reformist" governments, attacking them from the right. In doing so, the the Salvadoran upper classes took with them into the far-right opposition a substantial part of the bureaucratic middle classes of El Salvador as well, and part of the ORDEN-oriented peasantry to boot; there is no other way to account for the substantial electoral support that the ARENA party and the PCN consistently have gathered since 1982.

The hardening of class warfare in El Salvador has stiffened the political intransigence of the officer corps and of the upper class against any form of compromise with the "communists." To understand the virulence of such feeling, we must refer to a decisive date of Salvadoran history: 1932, the year of the peasant and Communist uprising and the subsequent massacre of rebels and innocents, known as the *matanza* (killing). That historical event has created the strongest anticommunist sentiment in Latin America and has provided some of the social "glue" that kept the military and the upper class in alliance for a half a century. Nicaragua had no such decisive confrontation with communism. Instead, it had Sandino's populist guerrilla war against the American occupation forces. Sandino's symbols were nationalist ones, not class-divisive ones, and came to be employed by the self-proclaimed heirs of Sandino (the *Sandinistas*), in opposition to the Somoza family dynasty at whose doorstep patriots could lay Sandino's assassination. All the symbols of nationalism, patriotism, self-government, and democracy lay with the opposition in Nicaragua, where the last Somoza, bereft in the end of all but some military supporters, finally fell to a cross-class opposition that united the vast majority of the Nicaraguan population.

EL SALVADOR: A CONTINUING STRUCTURAL WEAKNESS

Despite an apparent transition from a military regime toward ever more competitive electoral democracy, El Salvador has not succeeded yet in establishing a solid democratic regime. Venezuela made precisely such a transition during the 1960s and was able to do so because foreign ownership of heavily taxed oil resources simultaneously weakened the domestic upper class and strengthened the state apparatus. The upper class was thus unable to block the transition to reformist democratic rule and the virtual disappearance of true conservative parties. In contrast, the persistence of the military and the upper class as key political actors in El Salvador, despite recurrent elections, suggests that Salvador remains primarily a "mixed case" of different regimes, halfway between collective military rule and electoral democracy. The coffee-based, largely domestic capitalist class of El Salvador is simply too firmly rooted in the Salvadoran economy and society to be "voted out" of its pre-eminent role in society and politics.[100]

In fact, the regime both benefits and suffers from its curious mixture. The heritage of collective military rule (from 1932 to 1979), in strong alliance with highly conservative upper-class elements (whom Baloyra terms the "disloyal right"), has led to a virulent opposition by both partners to the guerrilla insurgency. They are most unlikely to sunder ranks with each other, as occurred in Cuba and Nicaragua, and the state is thereby strengthened. On the other hand, the successive 1980s elections served to legitimate the government of President José Napoleón Duarte, and the guerrillas became *politically* weaker through the decade, as Ché Guevara would have predicted, since electoral alternatives existed, widening to include part of the left in 1988 and 1989.

However, this blend has a central weakness, which Baloyra has clearly outlined: The disloyal right has the will and the structural capability—given its presence in the state and especially the armed forces—to oppose, block, limit, derail, or sabotage reforms, particularly agrarian reforms.[101] In this respect, they structurally resemble the upper classes of France and China, who staved off state reforms, but only at the final expense of triggering social revolution. Also like the elites of France and China, the Salvadoran elite have been able to block reforms because they are firmly lodged in the state itself, most evident in their ties to the military—and the ties of both to the death squads—but also visible in upper-class control of the judiciary and now of the governing ARENA party as well.[102]

The final result of the Salvadoran insurgency remains unwritten at this time, but one possible (yet still unlikely) outcome would provide a very precise parallel to Skocpol's analysis of France. There is yet the chance that the Salvadoran upper class will so sabotage all attempts to reform the economy and polity of that nation that they will critically weaken the state, precipitating El Salvador into the very revolution that that selfsame upper class has fought so violently to avoid. Such *unanticipated consequences* of purposive social action (in this case, of the upper classes) are precisely what Merton and Skocpol have taught sociologists to look for, and they may yet augur revolution for El Salvador.[103] Revolutions are not necessarily "made" by the revolutionaries themselves; they sometimes come unlooked for and unwanted.

Guatemala and El Salvador Compared

We can understand the Salvadoran failure better by its many similarities to Guatemala than by its many differences with the successful Nicaraguan revolution.[104] Those similarities strengthen our conclusions that collective military regimes, in alliance with the upper class, provided exceptional resistance to guerrilla insurgencies, even those with thousands of combatants.

The closest structural and historical parallel to Salvadoran politics in this century lies thus in Guatemala, not in Nicaragua. Both Guatemala and El Salvador have experienced the following. (1) There were long periods of collective military rule, in El Salvador from about 1950 to 1982, in Guatemala from 1954 to 1985. (2) Periodic fraudulent or highly restricted elections took place that allowed the military to govern with a democratic façade that fooled no one; these were held every four years in Guatemala, every five in

El Salvador, and were occasionally punctuated by military coups when things failed to run according to plan. (3) Military governments existed that, while not being staffed by members of the upper class, served to reclaim, protect, and extend upper-class claims to property and upper-class legal controls over the labor of the lower classes. (4) There were exceptionally strong levels of anticommunism within the military and the upper classes in both nations. A long period of military rule in Guatemala began by overthrowing the Arbenz government at the height of the cold war (1954), a government with Communists (PGT members) in an administration that moreover had just tried to import arms from Eastern Europe. Guatemalan governors have been second only to those of El Salvador in the virulence of their anticommunism since that time. (5) There have been occasional political *aberturas* (or openings) to parties of the middle-class or populist opposition, although rarely were they allowed to take office or to govern in unimpeded fashion (notably in Guatemala, 1966, and Salvadoran electoral frauds of 1972 and 1977).

Opposition politics have also strikingly resembled each other in the two nations. (1) Guerrilla movements emerged out of older and failed left-wing movements and parties in the early 1970s and included the most important guerrilla groups as of 1988: the FPL, ERP, and FARN of El Salvador, and the FAR, EGP, and ORPA of Guatemala. (2) Guerrillas formed umbrella organizations around 1980 which did not really unify them militarily, or eliminate ideological differences; the Guatemalan URNG formed in imitation of the Salvadoran FMLN, and their ideological-unity statements are virtually identical.[105] (3) Every group named above is a Marxist-Leninist group, although several reject the tutelage of the USSR (notably the ERP and ORPA). (4) Each group has or had areas of exceptionally deep and appreciably widespread peasant support in the countryside, which fueled and continues to fuel the insurgency; by the early 1980s the Salvadoran guerrillas could field perhaps ten thousand combatants, the Guatemalan guerrillas perhaps six thousand, and those numbers far exceeded the size of either the Nicaraguan or the Cuban guerrilla forces one year prior to their victories. (5) Most importantly, each guerrilla movement failed to seize power in the early 1980s despite its strengths, and both have declined in numbers and strength from those peaks.[106]

The Guatemalan guerrillas in the 1980s have clearly been both stronger and closer to unity than their counterparts in the 1960s, and we already saw in chapter 10 the deep roots they put down in the western Indian highlands. Those advantages have been offset, however, by increasing government strengths—peppered with occasional weaknesses—achieved during that very same time. One of the central achievements in extending its control was the military's expansion and deepening of their presence in rural areas in 1982 and 1983, through their twin programs of civic action, including bread and beans (and occasionally land) for cooperative villagers, and the formation of Civil Defense Patrols, which by 1984 encompassed perhaps five hundred thousand villagers.[107]

Changes in the nature of the Guatemalan regime in the late 1970s at first seemed to augur well for the revolutionaries, but then each successive regime shift created ever greater political obstacles to revolution. In terms of the regime types I discussed above, the government of General Romeo Lucas García (1978–1982) increasingly departed from the form of "collective military rule," elsewhere so effective in suppressing guerrilla movements, toward an increasingly personalized form of rule, indeed toward patrimonial praetorianism. As we saw above and in chapter 8, such personalized military regimes are vulnerable to cross-class revolutionary challenges and to internal decay. The Lucas regime showed some—but only some—evidence of all the features that eventually brought down the Batista and Somoza regimes. First, grumbling and discontent grew in the armed forces itself, and the regime's solidary front against the opposition splintered perceptibly. Second, the upper class began to grumble against the "bureaucratic bourgeoisie," those army officers who enriched themselves not only through their privileged access to political and administrative offices, but increasingly to land and other economic resources as well. Third, the opposition itself began to show greater unity under the Lucas regime, with separate mass organizations composed of peasants, students, or workers multiplying and/or showing increasing signs of cooperation; i.e., elements of a cross-class opposition movement began to form.[108] The net result of all these processes was an increasing loss of all civilian support for the regime from the 1970 election of Arana Osorio until 1982.[109]

In 1982, however, political events began to turn decisively against the chances for revolution. General Efraín Ríos Montt came to power in a coup in March 1982, joined by junior officers who opposed Lucas's attempt to handpick his political successor. Ríos Montt's reputation was at the time quite clean; indeed, even the left could argue that he had been cheated out of his "victory" in the 1974 election, which the military high command gave instead to General Kjell Laugeraud.[110] Yet Ríos Montt was responsible more than anyone else for destroying the chances of the revolutionaries. While continually proclaiming in public his commitment to the Bible and to evangelical Christianity, his government pushed through all the elements of the counterinsurgency campaign in the countryside: bread and beans for cooperative peasants; terror against the peasantry in guerrilla core areas (taking thousands of lives in the highlands and creating hundreds of thousands of refugees in less than two years); and the formation of the obligatory Civil Defense Patrols.[111] The guerrillas' numbers fell perhaps by half, and by 1985 their leaders were discussing the errors they had committed, with rueful references to their false "triumphalism." They added that "[n]ow we don't think triumph is on the doorstep," and that they had underestimated the "force of the military regime, its army, its repressive apparatus, the paramilitary bands."[112]

Yet Ríos Montt constituted an obstacle to any kind of new regime consolidation, due both to his bizarre personality and strange public statements, and to his evangelical leanings. He was ousted from power in August 1983 by Defense Minister Oscar Mejía Victores. The government that ensued can best be understood as a transition team: with the guerrillas now firmly pushed to the margins of politics, yet military government still in disrepute, the new administration "rectified the excesses stemming from Ríos Montt's government and engaged in a graduated retreat from public administration," which would culminate in the election of civilian president Vinicio Cerezo, a Christian Democrat, in December 1985.[113]

In terms of regime types, the Guatemalan polity was shifting back into a collective military form, in order to make the transition to democratic rule, with the first real participation by centrist parties (although not the left) since 1966. While Cerezo promised reforms, enactment was at best quite modest; this suggests a Salvadoran-style political stalemate between Cerezo and his electoral supporters, on the one hand, and the military and upper class on the other. Nonetheless, there is no questioning the ability of the new electoral process to raise hopes. As one peasant woman put it, "I pray to God we get a good government, one with a conscience, not like the thieves and murderers" [we had before]. Both the elements of hope and of political stalemate clearly echo El Salvador since 1984. The shift to electoral democracy, whatever the "outputs" of that process, has served only further to weaken the guerrillas, who demonstrated a near-desperation for negotiations with the Cerezo government, because as a political force in the nation they were nearly spent.[114]

I have summarized the preceding complex series of political comparisons in table 11-2. Those various comparisons—with Nicaragua, Guatemala, Venezuela, and finally France—have had a clear theoretical purpose: to explain simultaneously (1) the national structural causes for the failure of the Salvadoran revolutionaries, as well as (2) other structural causes that have lent them continued exceptional strengths vis-à-vis the various incumbent regimes they have faced since 1980. In conclusion, the Salvadoran guerrillas failed to seize power for reasons like those of the parallel failure of their Guatemalan counterparts, for both faced regimes at least partially characterized by collective military rule and were not strong enough to overcome the strengths of such regimes. Nonetheless, the Salvadoran guerrillas continue to mount the strongest insurgent threat to the polity in all of Latin America precisely because of structural weaknesses in the Salvadoran polity: the structured ability of the upper class to stave off fiscal and political reforms that might have weakened the radical elements of the opposition in favor of the reformists. Because of such upper-class obstructionism, the Salvadoran polity has not

TABLE 11-2
Strengths and Weaknesses of Salvadoran Political Regimes: Changes, Comparisons, and Contrasts

	A. STRENGTHS		
	Strong Political Regimes		Weak Regime
	El Salvador 1950–1979(–1990)	Guatemala 1954–1985	Nicaragua 1936–1979
Regime type	Collective military	Collective military	Patrimonial praetorian
Upper-class stance toward regime	Alliance	Alliance	Exclusion, then opposition
Class structure of opposition	Some intellectuals; many peasants; some workers	Some intellectuals; many Indian peasants; fewer workers	Cross-class
Consequences	Class war; no revolution	Class/race war; no revolution	Mass uprising and social revolution
	B. WEAKNESSES		
	Weak Political Regimes		Strong Regime
	El Salvador ([1975–]1979–1990)	France (1787–1789)	Venezuela (1958–1988)
Regime type	Collective military mixed with democratic	Agrarian proto-bureaucracy	Democratic government; bureaucratic rentier-state
Upper-class strengths in the state	Crucial economic power; crucial political power in state (military, judiciary), government (ARENA, PCN parties); coffee industry decisive	Revived political rights to peasant incomes; controlled officer corps of military, and *parlements* ("judiciary"); weak peasant tax-base, upper-class tax exemptions decisive.	Weak vis-à-vis foreign capital, domestic state, political parties; massive oil revenues decisive.
Fate of reform attempts	Mostly blocked by upper class	Blocked by upper class	Many carried out by mass-based political parties
Consequences	Massive revolutionary movement	Social revolution	Reforms from above

been able to consolidate democracy in the manner of Venezuelan governments since 1958, but instead, weakened by upper-class obstructionism within the state itself, has shown hints, if only hints, of facing the kind of revolutionary downfall experienced by the French monarchy and aristocracy precisely 200 years ago.

DÉJÀ VU IN COLOMBIA AND PERU: INSURGENTS AND ELECTIONS

Both Colombia and Peru saw a striking guerrilla revival by 1980, and insurgents achieved numerical strengths heretofore unachieved. Indeed, those numbers were only exceeded by the Salvadorans, of all the other guerrilla movements in this thirty-year period, even if we include the successful insurgents of Nicaragua and Cuba. By the early 1980s, the various Colombian guerrilla groups had perhaps seven thousand under arms, and Peru's secretive and hermetic *Sendero Luminoso* had at least several thousand fighters.[115]

Despite those increased strengths, certain other guerrilla weaknesses and regime strengths make social revolution an unlikely outcome for both Colombia and Peru. While I will discuss each case in some detail below, we should first observe some similarities in both nations. First, in each case the guerrillas have displayed a high level of sectarianism which makes it difficult to form stable alliances even within the left, let alone with other more moderate groups in society; that ideological sectarianism then blocks the formation of cross-class alliances with moderates such as we saw in Cuba and Nicaragua. Second, the armed forces in each nation have remained highly solidary backers of regimes, at least insofar as counterinsurgency is the issue. Third, each nation has regular experience with electoral democracy, which strengthens the claims made by governments that they truly represent, rather than simply repress, the populace. Finally, and in response to U.S. policymakers who view guerrilla threats as nothing but Soviet adventures in Latin America, there is good evidence that guerrillas in both nations have relied overwhelmingly on internal resources for their insurgent activities. Certain groups, moreover, such as Peru's *Sendero*, have even rejected aid from the Soviet bloc and other Marxist outsiders.

Colombia: Waiting for Revolution

> We know that we're not yet a threat.
> —Manuel Marulanda, FARC leader, ca. 1984

Despite the most impressive numbers of guerrilla fighters outside of El Salvador, Colombia's guerrillas have been the weakest *political* challengers to incumbent regimes of all the second-wave movements. This certainly requires some explanation. First of all, and echoing the 1960s, the guerrillas have remained profoundly divided among themselves, despite recurrent intimations that unity, like the lord, "cometh soon." By the late 1960s there were already unity talks among the guerrillas, and even announcements of imminent or actual unification in 1973, 1978, and 1981. Yet by 1983 or 1984, longtime FARC leader Jacobo Arenas would once more announce that there was no unity yet, but add, "We're talking."[116] As if to reinforce the image of sectarianism, the individual groups themselves split up on a number of occasions: the ELN was virtually torn apart in the 1960s by murderous internal intolerance; the EPL split into at least three groups in 1975; the M-19 urban-guerrilla group—the "new" guerrillas of the second wave—apparently began as the urban wing of the FARC (with links to the ANAPO party), before they, too, split off from their parent organization, only later to hold unification talks with them(!); and finally the M-19 itself split apart early in the 1980s.[117] The guerrillas have throughout the last quarter century spent more time in competition with one another than in cooperation—epitomized perhaps in organizations "taking over" territory formerly controlled by their rivals[118]— and this has weakened any chance they might have of defeating the incumbent regime. It is tempting to relate the sectarianism of the left to the violent sectarianism of the nation's past, to interpret it as a leftist version of the "hereditary hatreds" between Liberals and Conservatives that have historically dominated Colombian political life. In 1988 the guerrillas finally formed an umbrella group to negotiate with the government over true democratization, yet the ELN and EPL continued to hedge their commitments to the new organization.[119] Moreover, in early 1990 the M-19 guerrillas, who had often been intransigent in previous negotiations with Colombian governments, turned over their weapons to representatives of the Socialist International and gave up the armed struggle, while planning participation in the next national elections.[120] The M-19 then proceeded to outpoll its well-established Liberal and Conservative rivals in those elections, which were held to create a constituent assembly. When that assembly was about to meet in early 1991, some eleven thousand guerrillas of the FARC and ELN launched a major series of military actions to protest their exclusion from the political process. Clearly, unity was still a distant dream for Colombia's revolutionaries after a quarter century.

The Reagan administration consistently tried to trace Colombian guerrilla strengths back to their supposed links to drug traffickers and massive revenues derived therefrom. On this score there is some occasional evidence for guerrillas "taxing" drug activity or even growing coca plants to generate revenues. Still, the overall pattern is one of *conflict*, not cooperation between the political guerrillas and the drug lords. That conflict was best summarized when drug kingpins formed their own death squad named *Muerto a Secuestradores* (MAS—Death to Kidnappers) in order to tame one of the guerrillas' favorite revenue-raising techniques: kidnap of the rich to elicit huge ransom payments (commonly used by the FARN in El Salvador and several other groups as well).[121] Such conflicts with organized crime as well as the military can only weaken the guerrillas, not strengthen them.

If the guerrillas have been weakened by splits despite their impressive numbers, Colombian governments have only been strengthened by the continuity of electoral democracy there. The National Front coalition between

Liberals and Conservatives, installed in 1957–1958 to defuse La Violencia, formally ended with the 1974 elections, although a less explicit continuation of it has partially prevailed into the 1980s. Nonetheless, a more competitive brand of politics returned to the national scene in 1980, when Belisario Betancur, a "maverick" Conservative (as one analyst termed him), was elected to the presidency. Betancur ran a populist campaign which secured him substantial votes among the urban poor, and then espoused nationalist, nonaligned principles once in office. For one thing, he was a major driving force behind the region-wide Contadora intitiatives to limit military spending, restore electoral democracy, and restrict the U.S. presence in Latin America.

Betancur's attempts to end the guerrilla war with a series of signed truces and governmental amnesties largely failed, yet nonetheless they substantially defused portions of the insurgency. So persuaded was the FARC by this policy that it proceeded to form its own political party, the Unidad Patriótica (UP) or Patriotic Unity, in order to compete in national elections. However, the linking of amnesties and truces to cease-fire campaigns has not persuaded the armed forces, which retain a good deal of independence from civilian governments in the pursuit of counterinsurgency. Military violations of the truces were justified because the army high command resisted the implication that truce-signing guerrillas should be allowed to maintain armed groups independent of the control of the national military, and rumors of a coup attempt were especially heavy in late 1984. Since the mid-1980s many members of the UP have been assassinated, including several presidential candidates. Betancur was succeeded in office by Virgilio Barco in 1984, who also received a "strong electoral mandate." Yet there was an upsurge during his administration in truce violations, unordered army violence, and assassinations of leftist politicans, all quite apart from the virulent violence associated with the drug trade and attempts to stamp it out.[122] Despite the upsurge in intransigence, the Colombian government did not show the slightest danger of caving in to the political insurgents—not even in early 1991—being more clearly threatened by narco-violence than by revolutionary war.

The guerrillas themselves candidly admitted that they had very little hope of political success in the near-term, unless "a revolutionary situation" were to arise. That admission was all the more impressive coming from both Manuel Marulanda and Jacobo Arenas, decades-old leaders of the FARC, which could field some five thousand guerrillas in the mid-1980s and boast some twelve thousand members overall.[123] In class terms, the guerrillas surely retain their stongest support and membership among the marginalized peasantry of Colombia, but they still do not have or claim any zones of guerrilla control.[124] The Colombian army even dislodged them from their main rural refuge in late 1990. Despite peasant membership, however, most FARC guerrillas are in fact in the *jungle* and "don't have direct contact with the population," noted Arenas. Moreover, despite the massive levels of peasant political mobilization in Colombia in the 1970s and 1980s, taking the form of peasant unions pressing for new economic and political gains, the FARC remained completely separate from those activities by 1980.[125] While the FARC talked of the increasing diversity of its membership in the 1980s, it remained an overwhelmingly peasant group, with virtually no resonance among other social classes. As if to confirm regionally the guerrillas' over-whelmingly rural and peasant support bases, they never—except for M-19, which moved a good part of its operations to the countryside in the 1980s— have had any urban presence to speak of; Marulanda rather conceded in the 1980s that there was no urban FARC at all.[126]

Not only did the guerrillas compete with and occasionally fight with other guerrilla organizations, but they found little organizational assistance from outsiders to boot. I have already noted the essential bifurcation of the peasant-dominated rural guerrillas from the peasant political organizations of the 1970s. The Colombian Catholic Church, in a deeply Catholic nation, has remained on the side of the regime throughout a quarter century of guerrilla activity, despite the now-regular defection of priests into the guerrilla ranks, following the 1965 example of Camilo Torres.[127] As I discussed at the end of chapter 8, the Colombian press was historically and virulently anti-guerrilla, in a media world dominated by the two major parties, and that hostility con-tinued into the 1970s and 1980s, when there was finally a slight loosening of press restrictions on guerrilla reporting, resulting in highly revealing inter-views such as those collected by Manuel Arango.[128] The military high com-mand and the soldiery, for their part, continue the patterns established in the 1950s: a highly solidary military, clearly united against the guerrillas (if oc-casionally at odds with civilian presidents) and willing to engage and pursue the guerrillas in long-term counterinsurgency campaigns.[129]

In accord with the discussions of chapter 8 and the second-wave cases discussed in this chapter, we must trace the strength of the Colombian regime to the persistence there of electoral democracy for more than three decades since La Violencia ravaged the nation in the 1950s. Despite high rates of abstentionism at the polls, especially in the 1960s, Colombian citizens in urban areas have indicated no resonance with the call to the armed struggle, preferring (until M-19's recent success) to cast their votes for the traditional parties, and occasionally for modest mavericks from those parties such as Betancur. Colombia remains a profoundly violence-ridden nation, with the courts and other areas of government threatening to collapse at times. Even so, violence is not revolution, only a portion of the revolutionary process, and "the revolutionary situation" remains a distant, vague image on the hori-zon. Arenas and the FARC simply await revolution, virtually helpless to create it.[130]

Peru: Sendero Luminoso, *Sectarianism, and Democracy*

> Sendero's ideological fanaticism is well-known. Senderistas consider themeselves Gang-of-Four Maoists. They are so fanatically Maoist that they paint slogans on Andean village walls proclaiming "Death to the Traitor Deng Xiaoping," despite the fact that most Ayacucho peasants have never heard of the Chinese leader.
>
> —Cynthia McClintock[131]

In *Sendero Luminoso* (Shining Path), Marxism that is truly Albanian in its virulence has come to the Latin American revolutionary process. Because of that fact, *Sendero* has engendered a large number of ever-deeper and stronger social-scientific analyses to which I can only add footnotes here. I shall draw heavily on that groundwork and reorganize for my own purposes the information provided therein.[132] Because of the high quality of other works by Cynthia McClintock and David Scott Palmer, I can be mercifully brief about *Sendero*.

Sendero Luminoso is a far, far stronger guerrilla group than existed in Peru in the 1960s. It can boast thousands of members, whose dedication to the organization has a quality nigh-religious in fervor; there are no Latin American parallels to such commitment. Still, its strengths are sharply limited in regional terms. It began in the hinterlands of Ayacucho Department, and was generated by a Communist splinter group rooted in the University of Huamanga, as I argued in chapters 9 and 10. Its exceptionally deep support in certain provinces of Ayacucho spread somewhat to contiguous areas of the highlands, but that spread soon came mostly to a halt. It further succeeded in establishing a presence in coca and drug-trafficking areas around Tingo María in the upper Huallaga Valley. Nonetheless, attempts to spread to areas such as Cajamarca, Puno, and perhaps Apurímac seem to have failed: some local peasants accepted any benefits the closet-*Senderistas* could offer but rejected their attempts to politicize the peasantry when they came out into the open.[133] Despite recurring fears of its opponents and heady claims by its proponents, *Sendero* remains more weakly supported in urban areas—exploding bombs and assassinating people requires little in the way of support—where its greatest presence has been felt in the prisons, not the streets. Some peripheral *barrios* of Lima are, however, *Sendero* strongholds now.[134] Moreover, *Sendero*'s level of support in its Ayacucho birthplace clearly declined in the mid-1980s: measured by the commentary of interviewed peasants (where "a plague on both your houses" came to be a growing sentiment); seen in the declining levels of abstentionism and spoiled ballots at the polls in that department; and shown by the decreased vote for parties of the Marxist left, if we compare 1985 to 1980 or 1978.[135] There is no question, however, that since the mid-1980s *Sendero*'s strictly military activity has continued to increase.[136]

The utter sectarianism and sheer "orneriness" of *Sendero* is the root cause of its limitations. It has systematically lambasted and even assassinated, not just government officials and peasant villagers in the highlands, but even members of Marxist and social-democratic political parties. They had shown virtually no concern about the attitudes of other Peruvians concerning the future of the nation, until they emitted hints (only) of willingness to address the issue of their lack of "appeal" with a public statement issued in 1988.[137] That unusual public appeal, however, only further reinforced their sectarianism, in its call for class warfare and its attacks on traitorous revolutionaries like Fidel Castro and the Chinese leadership.

Had such a movement confronted a patrimonial praetorian regime, or a collective military regime, it still would have failed due to its utter lack of political allies.[138] Instead, *Sendero* began its public operations in 1980, the very year in which Peruvians got their first newly elected government since 1963. Just as in 1963, they elected Fernando Belaúnde Terry to the presidency, with widespread popular support among many Peruvian classes and groups. By the end of his term in 1985, Belaúnde's administration had been so disastrous—with a failing economy and no hint of a solution to *Sendero* as yet—that he took his party down in ruins with him. Nonetheless, his sucessor as president was Alan García Pérez of the APRA party, whose populist credentials and lower-class voting support were more pronounced than Belaúnde's had been. In both elections, the most distinctive feature of Peruvian politics was the widespread and somewhat successful participation of *Marxist* parties (a dozen or so in 1980) in the process.[139]

What does all this mean? *Sendero Luminoso*, the most profoundly sectarian mass revolutionary movement Latin America had yet experienced, was trying to overthrow a state and a series of elected governments in the wrong nation at the wrong time. Peru probably had—along with Venezuela and Costa Rica—the most wide-ranging legalized political spectrum in all Latin America, one in which, moreover, the left could and did make certain inroads, including a score of seats in the legislature in 1980.[140] Furthermore, surveys of the citizens in Lima in 1982, 1984, and 1986, showed only a small and decreasing minority of citizens in favor of socialist revolution (13 percent to 6 percent), with a vast and increasing majority favoring a democratically elected political regime (69 percent up to 88 percent).[141] Those Lima findings parallel decreasing support for *Sendero*'s brand of revolution in Ayacucho itself. The main gainers, initially, in the face of the economic and political setbacks of both 1980s presidents, were political *parties* further to the left of the incumbent ruler. García ran against Belaúnde's record by proclaiming himself for *social* democracy rather than simply representative democracy. As García's own problems increased and his popularity waned from its enthusiastic levels of 1985, the main political beneficiary became, not the hope-fully expectant *Izquierda Unida* (United Left),[142] but a vaguely moderate Alberto Fujimori, who defeated conservative Mario Vargas Llosa in the 1990 presidential race.

More than any other case we will encounter in these three decades of insur-gency, *Sendero Luminoso* best illustrates the principle that there are *political*, not just social and economic obstacles to revolution, and further confirms Ché Guevara's early thesis that a revolutionary who wishes to succeed should not begin that revolution against a popularly elected democratic government.

CONCLUSIONS: REGIME WEAKNESSES AND REVOLUTIONARY SUCCESS

If we combine the observations of this chapter with those made earlier in chapter 8, a clear correlation emerges: Patrimonial praetorian regimes, or mafiacracies, have shown themselves to be strikingly vulnerable to revolu-tionary overthrows because of their peculiar lack of supports in civil society, and because of their corresponding tendency to elicit cross-class opposition to the patrimonial ruler. Collective military regimes allied to the upper class, in contrast, have shown themselves consistently able to suppress revolution-aries, even those with deep and widespread peasant support and substantial military firepower. Finally, elected democratic regimes appear to be the strongest of all in the face of insurgency, and they achieve this strength largely because the populace becomes *indifferent*, if not actively hostile, to the insurgents' cause, preferring to vote into power new governments if the present incumbents demonstrate ineptitude or rascality; the ability to throw out the current crop of scoundrels remains the strongest impediment to the spread of insurgency in nations with electoral institutions.

What does all this mean, in terms of developing a theory of Latin American revolutions? First, we have identified a "new" type of regime that has proven itself vulnerable to revolution, one clearly different from the agrarian proto-bureaucratic systems that fell to revolution in France, Russia, and China.[143] Furthermore, the vulnerability of that peculiar type of regime was recognized in part by Ché Guevara and later in a more systematic form by Goldstone, and by Loveman and Davies, when the latter authors referred to the vulnerability of "Caribbean-style dictatorships" (à la Batista in Cuba or Trujillo in the Dominican Republic).[144] Second, we have further shown that other types of political regimes in the region are markedly less vulnerable to revolution: even when confronted with insurgencies of equal or greater strength than dictators faced in Cuba or Nicaragua, both collective military regimes and democratic regimes have demonstrated a consistent ability to suppress the insurgency or simply to tap out its strength over longer periods of time.

My emphasis on the vulnerabilities of certain types of regimes to revolu-

TABLE 11-3
Comparing Revolutions in Skocpol's Structural Terms

Cases	France, Russia, China	Iran	Cuba, Nicaragua
Regime type	Agrarian proto-bureaucracy headed by hereditary monarch	Rentier-state-cum-patrimonial absolutist rule	Mafiacracy, i.e., patrimonial praetorian dictatorship
State-dominant class relations	Landed elite lodged within the state (France,China)	Monarchy excludes, even attacks, upper class	Dictatorship excludes, even attacks, upper class
Taxation of masses?	Yes	No	Little
External Pressures?	Yes (massive in Russia)	Modest U.S. pressure (at end) for regime shift	Loss of external support
Weakened Armed Forces: Source?	Recurrent or intense war	Patrimonial meddling weakens esprit de corps	Patrimonial meddling weakens esprit de corps
Key structural weakness	Upper class blocks state, fiscal reforms	Monarch-state is focus of cross-class demands, unrest	Personal dictator is focus of cross-class unrest
Sources of lower-class insurrection (internal versus external)			
(a) Lower-class solidarity? (internal)	In peasant villages (France,Russia)	In urban bazaars	Unimportant (some role in Cuba)
(b) Mobilization by outsiders? (external)	Rural China, by Red Army	Unimportant	Dispersed rural squatters and/or urban *barrios*, by guerrillas

tion is meant to echo and build on Theda Skocpol's analyses of revolutions in France, Russia, China, and Iran. In table 11-3, therefore, I have presented in rough outline the regime weaknesses that contributed to the three "Great Revolutions," to the religiously oriented revolution against the shah of Iran, and to the revolutions that ousted patrimonial dictators in Cuba and Nicaragua. As we can see in this comparison, there are a number of clear parallels between the structural weaknesses of the shah's rentier-state regime and the patrimonial praetorian regimes of Batista and Somoza, and in the necessity in all three cases for consciously mobilized revolutionary oppositions to bring such regimes to the ground. In Iran, the solidarity of the shah's military and civil service were weakened by his constant shifting of personnel to prevent anti-monarch alliances from forming; the echoes of Batista and Somoza are clear here. In Iran solidary anti-regime opposition arose from the dense social networks of the bazaars, where the shah's "reforms" helped to forge a unified opposition among damaged merchant groups, outraged religious leaders, and ordinary urban citizens, whose courageous and solidary protests in the face of regime violence finally brought the regime down. The Cuban and Nicaraguan counterparts to the fundamentalist clerics were the guerrilla leaders who mobilized peripheral peasants and certain urban groups; they, too, had certain counterparts in a secular, left-wing, guerrilla opposition to the shah (whose importance in the whole revolutionary process is a subject of much debate). Overall, the parallels in the weaknesses of the Cuban and Nicaraguan regimes to the shah's rentier state are fairly dense, and Jeff Goodwin and Theda Skocpol have already created a master concept to integrate such parallels.[145]

This development of a theory of Latin American revolutions has not yet come to an end. The relationships between peasant support, military strength, regime type, and foreign intervention in contributing to those final outcomes—social revolution or not?—still remain unclear. Which if any of those variables are necessary to revolution, and which are not? Furthermore, which of the four correlates of peasant support are theoretically necesary, and which, if any, are superfluous? In the next and final chapter I wish to deal with the cases, variables, and models developed in chapters 4 through 11; to pull all the strands of argument together; to introduce, for comparative purposes, other Latin American "control" cases not systematically analyzed in this work; and finally to come up with a clear theory that remains true to the cases we have analyzed, but that nonetheless results in a theory that can help us to sort out the winners, losers, and also-rans of Latin American revolutionary movements.

CHAPTER 12

Winners, Losers, and Also-Rans:
Toward an Integration of Revolutionary Theories

> There's a lot going on out there.
> —Ian Craib

Transcending the Quantitative versus Qualitative Debate: Boolean Algebra and Macro-causal Analysis

For some time now, sociologists and other analysts of society have engaged in deep debate over whether and to what degree the analysis of society should be done in a quantitative or a qualitative fashion. The debate sometimes takes on shrill overtones, with qualitative scholars railing against the subhuman "positivism" of the work of "number crunchers," while the quantitative scholars view qualitative work as prescientific in nature, generating research, as one economist said of political science, in which the "plural of anecdote is data." Clearly, those scholars whose work is purely qualitative, yet who still try to make inferences about social causes and effects, are quite vulnerable to selecting only those social or historical facts that confirm their theses, while (perhaps unconsciously) missing contrary or anomalous findings.[1] The recurring problem for qualitative scholars is how to draw causal inferences *carefully*, rather than impressionistically. On the other side, however, several sociologists who are masters of statistical analysis have written ringing critiques of mindless number crunching, and have even shown that the application of routine statistical controls can produce the very *opposite* of the correct results when applied to nonexperimental data.[2] Statistical analysis of multiple cases and multiple variables, therefore, provides no sure escape from problems of causal inference. What, then, can be done?

Such methodological problems generated by comparative analysis have not gone unaddressed in the sociological community. Oddly enough, two rather different works, whose authors come from sharply variant styles of sociological research, have found a common ground in the writings of John Stuart Mill. By going backward they appear to have succeeded in thinking forward. Mill suggested two basic techniques for comparative analysis, the *method of agreement and the method of difference*. In the method of agreement one collects all known cases in which a similar outcome is present (let us call it X, which could stand for "peasant revolt"). Now these cases (read: societies) may otherwise greatly differ from one another. They may differ with respect to the presence of other conditions A, B, C, and D, yet be alike with respect to condition E. If so, then we may infer that E is therefore the cause of their similar outcomes. Mill himself thought that the method of agreement should be used with caution and suggested that one make use of the more powerful logical tool, the method of difference. In the method of difference, one does not necessarily have to take cases with all possible outcomes, nor is it dependent on a random sample of existing outcomes. Instead, one takes societies that are otherwise quite similar but differ with respect to that final outcome: one ends up with outcome Y, the other with outcome not-Y ("social revolution" could be the variable). These societies may both share conditions A, B, C, and D, but differ *only* with respect to E; in that case, it is the presence or absence of E (or perhaps the "nature" of E) that has determined those different outcomes.

Theda Skocpol and Margaret Somers in 1980, and Charles Ragin in 1987, have arrived at similar positions in espousing a return to Millian logics of analysis in comparative studies, and each carefully outlines the Millian methods I just discussed.[3] The first authors term their preferred tool "macro-causal analysis," while Ragin has employed Boolean algebra to systematize his Millian logics. Moreover, Ragin has made an especially spirited defense of this method—not simply that "it's the best we can do when we only have a few cases"—but defending it as a technique superior to statistical analyses on several interpretative grounds. For one thing, Ragin's suggested alternative allows conditions to remain contextualized—that is, it allows variables to remain inherently dependent on the presence or absence of others for their effects—whereas statistical procedures can only achieve the same type of understanding through the introduction of interaction terms into the equations. (For the uninitiated, an interaction term creates a new independent variable out of quantitative variables A and B, typically through the product of A and B, called AB; or ABC out of three variables, etc.) In statistical procedures, just 7 independent variables and all possible interaction terms thereof would produce a model with over 100 independent variables. Massive interpretative problems would then ensue due to the loss of degrees of freedom and an increase in multicollinearity (i.e., intercorrelations between various independent variables and between them and the dependent variable). To put it simply, Ragin's alternative naturally allows the researcher to deal with conjunctural and contextual situations, whereas such conditions only further constrain the general linear model and its variants.[4]

Ragin has taken the ideas resurrected by Skocpol and Somers—and, in truth, used semiconsciously by many comparative researchers in the Weberian tradition—and systematized them through the use of Boolean algebra.

(The quantophobic reader is asked to stay a while; this won't hurt much.) That daunting label hides a deceptively simple approach to analysis. First, it begins by taking each case, which in this work is one of two things: a *region* of a country in a particular period in time; or a *nation* in a particular period. Next, it establishes the *presence or absence* of the outcome that one wishes to study; for our purposes here I will treat two outcomes: peasant support for guerrilla movements and the sucessful revolutionary seizure of power. Having done that for outcomes, we follow a similar procedure for the supposed *conditions that are thought to produce* the outcome. In contrast to statistical procedures, the absolute number of such conditions does not affect the validity of this form of comparative analysis; more variables only make the later logical transformations more complex. The hypothetical causes then become the columns of a table (labeled *A*, *B*, *C*, etc.) with the supposed outcome usually as the last column, while the various cases under study, let us say nations, become the rows of a table, known as a *truth table*. Each case is then assigned a 1 (one) if the condition is present, and a 0 (zero) if the condition is absent. Table 12-1 (below) provides such an example.[5]

From this point on, the table is analyzed systematically through a series of "reductions." Those reductions are nothing but a series of attempts to establish which conditions are *necessary and sufficient to produce either outcome* (e.g., failure or success). "Necessary" means that a condition must be present, or the outcome will not occur; it may, however, have that effect only in the context of other, supporting conditions. "Sufficient" means that the occurrence of this condition alone will produce the outcome in question; this does not preclude the existence of other conditions, or sets of conditions, that might also be sufficient. Since social phenomena are complex, rare is the cause both sufficient and necessary for the effect. What we might hope for instead is to isolate a few conditions—Occam's Razor so enjoins us—that together are sufficient for revolution, and each individually necessary.

The entire procedure of Boolean reduction, when finished, produces a series of "scenarios" specifying which set *or sets* of conditions produce, for example, social revolutions (that is, outcome = 1); the exact same procedure can specify the set or sets of conditions that lead to revolutionary failures (outcome = 0).[6] For example, from a list of twenty-eight cases that I produce in table 12-3, the process of reduction leads to many fewer final scenarios in table 12-4: one only leading to a successful outcome, and three different ones with unsuccessful outcomes.

A BOOLEAN ANALYSIS OF THE SOURCES OF PEASANT SUPPORT

As I noted in my opening comments to chapter 6, many are the interpretations seeking to answer Theda Skocpol's nicely posed question, "What Makes Peasants Revolutionary?" From the perspective I have adopted, as well as that of Boolean algebra, the unique answer implied by the word *what* and by the treatments of Skocpol, Paige, Popkin, and Jenkins is not necessarily an end to be pursued. As the evidence in table 12-1 can attest through casual inspection, guerrilla movements secured strong and sustained peasant support under a variety of circumstances in Latin America. *There is no single social condition that predicts peasant support in every circumstance.* That is, no single such condition, be it Paige's "agrarian structure" or the moral-economic "agrarian disruption," serves as an infallible guide in all instances.

While Paige's theory, even given my substantial modifications, certainly and surprisingly predicted a "revolutionary" peasantry in a large number of cases, it failed to turn up any structural correlates of peasant support in Las Villas Province in Cuba, where the *Directorio Revolucionario* secured substantial peasant support in 1958; or in Huila, Colombia, home of a historically rebellious peasantry; or most certainly in Ayacucho, birthplace of *Sendero Luminoso*—where sharecropping, tenancy, and perhaps even squatting were all largely gone by the 1980s (although land hunger certainly remained).

On the other hand, agrarian disruption has not always been present where we encountered such peasants. There is simply no evidence either way for Las Villas, Cuba, and probably not for Huila, Colombia. More striking yet is the experience of guerrilla havens Lara and Falcón in Venezuela where, if anything, the government was distributing lands to a not-particularly-land-hungry peasantry throughout the 1960s while substantial numbers of them nurtured guerrilla movements in the hills.

Advocates of the other two conditions, rebellious cultures (column C) and peasant linkages (column D), are few indeed in the field of sociology or of peasant studies, even though each such cause would seem to have a prima facie case on the basis of existing sociological research.[7] Those causes, too, are not present in every situation where guerrillas received substantial peasant support. The Nicaraguan guerrillas had few preexisting linkages to the mountain peasants, and we may doubt whether the Guatemalan guerrillas of the ORPA movement (1970s) had substantially better organizational access to peasant resources. Indeed, of all second-wave movements, only Peru's *Sendero Luminoso* clearly had exceptional linkages to the peasantry prior to the insurgency. We could also apply similar restrictions to the "rebellious culture" argument, but I have no wish to be tedious. A simple inspection of table 12-1 or table 12-2 will confirm all the above.

Before "reducing" this particular table we can note that sustained peasant support (excluding Junín and Ayacucho in 1960s Peru) was not forthcoming to *any* guerrilla movement unless that region was characterized by at least two, and usually three or even more such social conditions (Las Villas may be an exception here, yet we have too little information to judge conditions concerning agrarian disruption and rebellious cultures.)

TABLE 12-1
Predicting Regional Peasant Support for Guerrilla Movements: A Boolean Truth Table
(0 = trait is absent; 1 = trait is present)

Case	Favorable Conditions				Outcomes
	(A) Agrarian Structure	(B) Agrarian Disruption	(C) Rebellious Cultures	(D) Peasant Linkage	High Levels of Peasant Support
First Wave					
Cuba					
1. Oriente	1	1	1	1	1
2. Las Villas	0	0?	0?	1?	1
Venezuela					
3. Lara	1	0	1	1	1
4. Falcón	1	0	1	1	1
Guatemala					
5. Zacapa	1	0	1	0?	1
6. Izabal	1	1	0	1	1
Colombia					
7. Tolima, Caldas, and Valle	1	1	1	1	1
8. Huila	0	0	1?	1?	1
9. Santander	1	1	1?	1	1
Peru					
10. La Convención	0	0	0?	0	0
11. Ayacucho	1?	1?	1	0	0?
12. Junín	1?	0?	1	1	0?
Bolivia					
13. East	0	0	0	0	0
Second Wave					
Nicaragua					
14. N. Central (rural)	1	1	1	0?	1
15. Northwest (towns)	1	1	1?	0?	1
El Salvador					
16. North	1	1	0	1?	1
17. West	0	0?	0?	0	0
Guatemala					
18. Northwest (EGP, FAR)	1	1	0	1?	1
19. West (ORPA)	1?	1?	0	1	1
Peru					
20. Ayacucho	0	1	1	1	1

Sources: Text, chapters 6, 7, 10.

TABLE 12-2

Multiple Conditions Underlying Peasant Support for Guerrilla Movements, 1956–1990
(1 = trait present, 0 = trait absent)

Cases (Lines, Table 12-1)	A Agrarian Structure	B Agrarian Disruption	C Rebellious Cultures	D Peasant Linkage	Frequency
Outcome 1: High Levels of Peasant Support (= 1 in Tables 12-3, 12-4)					
Variant 1: #1, 7, 9 (all 4 conditions)	1	1	1	1	(3)
Variant 2: #14, 15	1	1	1	0	(2)
Variant 3: #6, 16, 18, 19	1	1	0	1	(4)
Variant 4: #3, 4	1	0	1	1	(2)
Variant 5: #20 (3 conditions only)	0	1	1	1	(1)
Variant 6: #5	1	0	1	0?	(1)
Variant 7: #8 (2 conditions at most)	0	0	1?	1?	(1)
Variant 8: #2 (1–2 conditions at most)	0	0	0	1?	(1)
Outcome 2: Moderate Levels of Peasant Support (= 0 in Tables 12-3, 12-4)					
Line #11	1?	1?	1	0	(1)
Line #12	1?	0?	1	1	(1)
(At most 2 clearly present)					
Outcome 3: Low Levels of Peasant Support (= 0 in Tables 12-3, 12-4)					
Lines #10, 13, 17	0	0	0	0	(3)

Source: Table 12-1.

Minimization: Shaving Variables with Occam's Razor

We can begin to find out whether any particular *combination* or a few combinations of conditions emerge that can simplify our understanding of the thirteen different successful outcomes of table 12-1. First, in table 12-2, I have pooled similar cases from table 12-1, to indicate eight different patterns of "success" (i.e., strong peasant support) that emerged in that first table. The reader will note that variants 7 and 8 are problematic. We can now begin to "minimize" these data. Minimization is simple and straightforward: if two scenarios have identical outcomes, yet differ *only* on the presence/absence of a *single* condition, then that condition cannot be decisive in producing the shared outcome; therefore it can logically be dropped, and the two scenarios combined to make one, with one less contributing condition. Put simply, this is Occam's Razor in action, with a very clear, standardized procedure. This process should be performed on all possible variant-pairs, until the number of conditions is reduced by one for all possible combinations. The procedure should be repeated to reduce the number of conditions even further if possible. Minimization should continue until no further scenario pairing-and-elimination procedures are possible. If a condition is present, we code it as capital A,B,C, or D; if absent, as lower-case a,b,c, or d. If we focus on the cases for which we have the clearest information, variants 1 through 6 in table 12-2, the minimization proceeds as follows (final scenarios appear in **boldface**):

1. Variants 1 & 2: *ABCD* combines with *ABCd* to produce *ABC*
2. Variants 1 & 3: *ABCD* combines with *ABcD* to produce ***ABD***
3. Variants 1 & 4: *ABCD* combines with *AbCD* to produce *ACD*
4. Variants 1 & 5: *ABCD* combines with *aBCD* to produce *BCD*
5. Variants 2 & 6: *ABCd* combines with *AbCd* to produce *ACd*
6. Variants 4 & 6: *AbCD* combines with *AbCd* to produce *AbC*

If we now consider the more ambiguous cases, variants 7 and 8, we can reduce the complexity slightly as well (no. 9 below is especially ambiguous):

7. Variants 4 & 7: *AbCD* combines with *abCD* to produce *bCD*
8. Variants 5 & 7: *aBCD* combines with *abCD* to produce *aCD*
9. Variants 7 & 8: *abCD* combines with *abcD* to produce ***abD (?)***

In the second round—reducing conditions from three to two—several further reducations are possible:

> *ABC* (1st combination) with *AbC* (6th combination) produces ***AC***
> *ACD* (3rd combination) with *ACd* (5th combination) produces ***AC*** as well
> *ACD* (3rd combination) with *aCD* (8th combination) produces ***CD***
> *BCD* (4th combination) with *bCD* (7th combination) produces ***CD*** as well

We have therefore come to a first conclusion concerning the conditions under which peasants have supported guerrilla movements. Those conditions are clearly multiple rather than singular. In Boolean terms, we can express it "algebraically," with the plus sign ($+$) below meaning "or," and the equal sign ($=$) meaning "occurs under conditions":

AFTER MINIMIZATION

Peasant Support = ABD + AC + CD + abD(?)

That is, peasant support came under a variety of conditions to guerrilla movements, including the presence of the two (probably) sets of three determinants, and two sets of two determinants each. Let us put this in prose. Peasant support came when conducive agrarian structures were combined with agrarian disruption in an area with substantial preexisting linkages joining guerrillas to the peasantry (**ABD**); peasant support could also be obtained where conducive agrarian structures were joined to a historically rebellious peasantry (**AC**) or where such a rebellious peasantry was previously linked to the proto-guerrillas before the insurgency (**CD**). In one more dubious finding, the preexisting organizational linkage might itself be a determinant, but only in the absence of of both conducive agrarian structures and agrarian disruption (**abD**).

What Does It All Mean?

First of all, none of the four variables underlying peasant support has dropped out of analysis after applying basic Boolean algebraic procedures. The greatest import of this finding is that all sociological theories that seek to identify "the" source of peasant radicalism are fruitless pursuits after an unrealistic theoretical monism. Robert Merton's warnings to those seeking "functional indispensability" are still good advice.[8] Skocpol's suggestion that Paige's theory ("agrarian structure," condition A) only works by bringing in a whole series of contextual variables—the kind that she systematically explicates in her own analysis of social revolutions—is not necessarily supported here, for Paige's theoretical predictions "work," so to speak. Neither she nor anyone else has ever successfully challenged the correlations between different agrarian structures and different types of collective resistance that are the heart of his findings. Similar strictures apply to Jenkins's rejection of Paige's work in favor of moral economy theory ("agrarian disruption," condition B).[9] On the other hand, Paige's and Popkin's rejections of moral economy theory are also shown to be premature attempts at theoretical closure against competing explanations.[10] Similar comments could be made about Marxists whose love of "class analysis" leads them to ignore other important social conditions that cannot be reduced to the narrow economic confines of Marxist theory: rebellious cultures and peasant linkages (conditions C and D).

If we reread our Weber, we can find clues as to the human motivations lying behind these four different sources of peasant support for guerrilla movements. One of Weber's least appreciated typologies is that of the different ideal types of social action. In considering the range of social action, Weber identified four different ideal types that he thought most useful for such analyses: (1) *calculating rationality* (or *zweckrationalität*), where an individual weighs the various means to a given end, and chooses the most "efficient"—in doing so, one also takes into account various competing ends; (2) *value-based rationality* (or *wertrationalität*), in which one chooses action based on a commitment to some central value, whatever the consequences that may ensue; (3) *affectual orientations*, in which acts derive from some emotional commitment of the actor, such as love or hate; and (4) *traditional orientations* based on the (cultural) traditions of a social group. Extreme forms of this type border on action that instead is pure, asocial habit, not a traditional orientation. Weber not only rejected the idea that pure rational action was the *only* analytically relevant model for behavior, he even argued that pure calculating rationality was one of the less common forms of behavior, the "tip of the iceberg." The most common forms of behavior are rather those lower down on the list, rather than those higher up.[11]

A surprising outcome of this research is that the four different conditions underlying peasant support for guerrillas tend to align with the four different Weberian ideal-types of social action. This alignment, although not absolute, suggests that those four conditions are *not* simply a laundry list accidentally falling into place for this particular work (which is how I initially viewed them). Such alignment of conditions and motivations in these four types suggests that a "deep [motivational] structure" pervades each of the four conditions underlying revolutionary peasantries, as follows:

Peasant support for guerrillas based on:	*Is largely related to Weber's:*
(A) Specific agrarian structures	Calculating rationality
(B) Disruption of the moral economy	Value-based rationality
(C) Preexisting linkages to the peasantry	Affectual orientations[12]
(D) The presence of rebellious cultures	Traditional orientations

Following Weber's advice, I am not arguing that each of these cases is completely intelligible in terms of a single motivational structure, but that they are mostly so. For example, assaults on the security of peasant cultivators clearly indicate strongly the sheer defense of self-interest and land (calculating rationality) as well as moral indignation at the assault on perceived rights to subsistence (value-based rationality). And the latter cannot be reduced to the former, for the peasant rage so commonly found in the countryside cannot logically be explained by the cool calculation of the rational actor model.

If this argument is sound, we can now relate it back to the Boolean findings concerning peasant support. Since peasant support came only when multiple conditions were present, peasants tended to support guerrilla movements only when multiple levels of motivation were involved, and not solely when "rational self-interest" was in play. Another way of saying this is that, for peasants to take the step of supporting revolutionaries, that behavioral shift must be "overdetermined" rather than simply responding to a single kind of motivational pressure.

This logic is consistent with a variety of social perspectives that have emphasized the sheer inertia of everyday social life, and the difficulty in mobilizing people for collective action; Sartre once nicely termed such everyday patterns of behavior the "practico-inert." As Tilly argued, reactive or defensive forms of collective action (typically carried out by the lower classes in society) are generally threat-responsive rather than opportunity-responsive. The findings here suggest that mobilization to collective action must come at many levels of motivation as well.[13] Finally, this finding dovetails with a comment by Robin Williams, where he noted that the stability of a social system is typically enormously overdetermined, not yielding readily to light pressures for change.[14]

FAILURE AND SUCCESS IN LATIN AMERICAN REVOLUTIONARY MOVEMENTS

Having established the conditions underlying peasant support for guerrilla movements, we can now address the main issue: Why did some revolutionary guerrilla movements succeed in coming to power, in Cuba and later in Nicaragua, while their contemporaries and imitators failed to do so? As we have seen throughout this work, peasant support was not enough to bring the revolutionaries to power, important though it might have been as a contributor to the outcome. In chapter 5, moreover, I tried to show that the sheer military strength of guerrillas and governments, respectively, and military aid from the United States were also at best contributory factors in the outcomes. Finally, in chapters 8 and 11, I probed the distinctive features of the Cuban and Nicaraguan regimes that fell to the revolutionaries, arguing that precisely such features made them vulnerable to cross-class revolutionary alliances led militarily by rural-based guerrilla organizations. This is clearly the place to pull together those multiple strands of argument and, once again through Boolean algebra, to establish the conditions for revolutionary success and failure in the region.

Alternative Theories of Latin American Revolutions

Before we do so, however, we should pause and consider alternative views of revolutionary failure and success and discard them for their various insufficiencies. In most alternative views, sheer partiality is the main limitation, although each tends to have its own kinds of political blinders.

We should first examine the cases studied closely in this work, as well as other Latin American nations, so that we might more closely approximate the "universe" of cases for Latin American since 1956.

In table 12-3, lines 1 to 9 and 16 to 18 pose no problems, for those cases are all closely discussed in this work. Argentina has had at least three failed guerrilla movements: an unsupported *foco* in 1963 in the interior, under the elected regime of Arturo Illia; the *Montoneros* of the 1970s, who apparently had substantial support among the urban working class of Córdoba; and the ERP (Revolutionary Army of the People), who put down at least modest roots among the Tucumán peasantry (lines 10, 12, and 15). Both of the 1970s groups succumbed to severe repression unleashed by the Argentine military after the death of President Juan Perón and under the rule of his wife Isabel

TABLE 12-3
Revolution or Not in Latin America: A Boolean Truth Table
(0 = trait absent; 1 = trait present)

Cases	Favorable Conditions					Outcomes
	(A) Guerrilla Attempt	(B) Peasant/ (Worker) Support	(C) Guerrilla Military Strength	(D) Patrimonial Praetorian Regime	(E) Government Loses U.S. Support (1 = yes)	Social Revolution?
I. Winners: Successful Revolutions						
1. Cuba, 1956–59	1	1	1	1	1	1
2. Nicaragua, 1971–79	1	1(P,W)	1	1	1	1
II. Also-Rans: Other Guerrillas with Peasant Support						
3. Venezuela, 1960s	1	1	1	0	0	0
4. Colombia, 1960s	1	1	1	0	0	0
5. Guatemala, 1960s	1	1	1	0	0	0
6. Colombia, 1970–90	1	1	1	0	0	0
7. Peru, 1980s	1	1	1	0	0	0
8. Guatemala, 1975–90	1	1	1	0	1	0
9. El Salvador, 1975–90	1	1(P,W)	1	0	0	0
10. Argentina, 1974–78	1	1	0	0	1	0
11. Brazil, 1970s	1	1	0	0	0	0
12. Argentina, *Montoneros*	1	1(W)	1	0	1	0
13. Mexico, 1970s	1	1	0	0	0	0
14. Uruguay, *Tupamaros*	1	1	1?	0	0	0
III. Losers: Failed Guerrilla Movements						
15. Argentina, 1958–63	1	0	0	0	0	0
16. Peru, 1965	1	0	0	0	0?	0
17. Bolivia, 1967	1	0	0	0	0	0
18. Nicaragua, 1958–63	1	0	0	1?	0	0
19. Dom.Republic, 1963	1	0	0	0	0	0
20. Ecuador, 1962	1	0	0	0	0	0
21. Haiti, 1960s	1	0	0	1	1	0
22. Paraguay, 1958–59	1	0	0	1	0	0
23. Honduras, 1965	1	0	0	0	0	0
24. Brazil, 1960s (urban)	1	0	0	0	0	0
IV. Absent Rural Guerrilla Movements						
25. Costa Rica	0	0	0	0	0	0
26. Panama, 1959–85	0	0	0	0	0	0
27. Panama, 1985–89	0	0	0	1	1 (1988)	0
28. Paraguay, 1960–89	0	0	0	1	0	0

Sources: See chapters 4–11 for lines 1 to 9 and 16–17; for others, see this chapter's text and notes.

who succeeded him, eventually seizing power for themselves. In Brazil, a group of rural guerrillas began to secure some peasant support in the Amazon interior in Araguaia, Pará State, during the 1970s, but succumbed rapidly to the first counterinsurgency campaign against them (line 11). Similarly, the urban-guerrilla Tupamaros of Uruguay could trace their lineage back to the organization of sugar workers in the interior province of Artigas. Later they would have some spectacular media successes in the early 1970s against the then-decaying democratic government. But when the military was unleashed against them, their organization fell apart with startling rapidity (line 14). In Mexico, rural guerrillas in the state of Guerrero rather clearly had peasant support in that old haven of banditry, yet they posed no political challenge to the political hegemony of the PRI (Institutional Revolutionary Party) (line 13). Various small-scale *foco* attempts of the late 1950s and 1960s failed in their imitative attempts to repeat Fidel Castro's successes and were quickly wiped out (lines 18–23). Carlos Marighella's attempt to create a post-*foco* form of revolution in the region, by unleashing his urban guerrillas against the Brazilian military government, also fell rapidly to government repression (line 24). Finally, minimal or no guerrilla movements characterized the politics of Costa Rica throughout this period, and Panama apparently as well, while Alfredo Stroessner's ever-tightening control (1954–1989) over Paraguayan society and politics also seemed to stave off even the appearance of guerrilla threats after 1960 (lines 25–28).[15]

Can alternative theories of revolution in Latin America explain both the failures and the successes of revolutionaries in the region? That crucial failure/success issue is precisely the one most readily avoided in careless or ideological attempts at explanation. The coding of the additional cases just discussed, in terms of the five variables I have emphasized here, can lay the groundwork for the systematic evaluation of competing explanations.

HYPOTHESIS 1: THE *FOCO* THEORY

The *foco* theory of revolution was suggested in Ché Guevara's famous theses on revolution, where he argued that popular forces can defeat the army, that they can create rather than await the conditions for revolution, and that the countryside was the proper revolutionary venue for Latin American conditions.[16] This theory of revolution was advocated by both Guevara and Régis Debray[17] and became widely known and criticized as the Guevara-Debray theory of revolution. Throughout the 1970s and 1980s, the second-wave guerrillas trumpeted their rejection of the *foco* theory, in proposing an alternative approach to revolution called "prolonged popular war."

Despite the presumed, extreme ideological disjunction between these two "schools" of revolutionaries, they actually resemble each other greatly in terms of the conditions outlined in table 12-3. Both assume that the main determinant of success lies in the simple attempt at guerrilla warfare. Both

approaches largely or completely ignore the specific conditions of the peasantry and variations in types of political regime. Indeed, Ché Guevara at least
amended his theory in other writings, in suggesting that democracies were a
"strong" political regime in the face of revolution, while military regimes or
civilian dictatorships were not. My own analysis supports a different division: Mafiacracies are weak, and other regimes tend to be stronger.

Table 12-3 in no way supports the contention that the mere attempt at insurgency (column A) guarantees success in that attempt. It strongly suggests that
the actions of peasants (B), the type of political regime (D), and the strength
of the United States' backing for regimes (E) all influence such outcomes.
Moreover, since the military strength of guerrillas (C) is also highly correlated with levels of peasant support, that influence too is largely ignored.
Both the impatient advocates of the *foco* theory and the patient revolutionaries speaking of prolonged wars simply do not address these issues, and their
positions cannot predict revolutionary failure and success.

HYPOTHESIS 2: "EL PUEBLO UNIDO JAMÁS SERÁ VENCIDO"

That revolutionary chant translates as: "The united people will never be
defeated." Here the proponents espouse a stronger position and focus more on
the actions of nonguerrillas, and less on the revolutionaries proper. This thesis emphasizes the crucial role of popular support, of the "hearts and minds"
of the masses. Yet it, too, shares a crucial failing in ignoring the actions of
nonrevolutionaries and the peculiar strengths of certain types of military regimes to suppress revolution through sheer force. Events in rural Guatemala
during the 1980s are bloody evidence indeed that this thesis can be tragically
mistaken. As I argued carefully in chapters 8 and 11, it was *not* the differences in levels of peasant support that helped the Cuban and Nicaraguan insurgents to win, but rather the nature of the regimes they faced. It was the
nature of the Cuban and Nicaraguan regimes themselves that made it highly
likely that the "pueblo" would indeed become "unido" against the Batista and
Somoza dictatorships; it was not simply a creation of popular action alone,
but in part derived from the peculiar sociopolitical context of an entire nation.
Furthermore, if the slogan means that a revolution can be carried to victory by
the support of the common people alone, despite the potential opposition of
the middle and upper classes, then it is almost surely wrong. The Mexican
and Bolivian revolutions were both populist revolutions, supported by the
peasantry or workers, yet led by men of the middle and sometimes upper
classes.[18] As I argued clearly in chapters 8 and 11, one distinctive feature of
both Cuba and Nicaragua was the desertion of (at least substantial parts of)
the middle and upper classes from the regime, and their alliance, however
uneasy, with the revolutionary opposition. That simply has not happened in
contemporary El Salvador, Guatemala, nor most certainly in Peru, or is it

likely to happen. The "Also-rans" of panel II in table 12-3—all revolutionary failures despite popular support—provide telling refutation of both this and the previous theory.

HYPOTHESIS 3: OUTSIDE AID TO GUERRILLAS IS DECISIVE

The Reagan adminstration and various conservative groups were very strong advocates of this position in the 1980s, arguing that the mere interdiction of supplies to the revolutionaries would suffice to destroy them. In more extreme variants, they further suggest that the revolution is "nothing but" an outcropping of Communist-fomented revolution in the third world. In academic writings that support this type of perspective, the intended effect is largely achieved through extensive discussion of the *external* connections of Latin American revolutionaries, wedded to a curious obliviousness to two *internal* features: (1) the internal history of these revolutionary organizations; and (2) the domestic social and political events, processes, histories, and structures of those societies, such as I have examined throughout this work.[19] All such theories can do is count soldiers and military budgets and propose giving more resources to such regimes to compensate for the external resources the guerrillas bring to bear. They assume that guerrilla warfare is simply a battle of purses. Such thinking in part produced the colossal U.S. failure in Vietnam.

The internal political and military history of Latin American guerrilla movements—including their highly variable relationships with Soviet-line Communist parties—makes risible the suggestion that guerrilla movements are "nothing but" Soviet adventures in Latin America. The nigh-unbroken record of internal schisms, rivalries, mutual excommunications, and even internal killings that guerrillas have exhibited in so many nations—Peru, Colombia, Venezuela, Guatemala (1960s), and El Salvador—makes such one-sided notions more than risible: they are pathetic.

Yet even the less extreme position, that revolutionary movements depend upon external support to survive and flourish, seems untenable. The events of the second wave provide excellent evidence for rejecting the contention. The second-wave guerrilla movements have been on the whole much stronger than those of the 1960s, yet external aid has been utterly irrelevant in several cases. The Guatemalan guerrillas, especially ORPA, have been virtually cut off from all external aid, including that notoriously available from Cuba. The various Colombian guerrillas have survived largely without external aid for two decades. Peru's *Sendero Luminoso* has operated even more independently of outside assistance, caustically attacking the credentials, and occasionally the persons, of other Marxist groups.[20] While some Cuban and perhaps indirect Soviet aid clearly reached guerrillas in Nicaragua and El Salvador,[21] the obsession of U.S. policymakers and conservatives with that aid far,

far outweighs the importance of such aid in the process of revolution in those two nations. Peasant support has been a far more important and consistent correlate of guerrilla military capability than has the extent and level of outside military aid (note the parallelism of columns B and C in table 12-3).

In sum, hypothesis 3 tends to emphasize setting limitations upon the military capabilities of guerrilla organizations (condition C), either by intercepting the shipment of foreign aid to such organizations, or by decreasing the relative importance of such aid through sometimes massive compensatory aid to the military forces that the guerrillas oppose. This viewpoint simply ignores the structures of peasant support (condition B) and differences in political regimes (condition D), although it does implicitly suggest strong and continued U.S. support for existing regimes (condition E).

HYPOTHESIS 4: THE UNITED STATES AS COUNTERREVOLUTIONARY PROP

Perhaps no theory is more widely held by the left in Latin America and in the United States itself than that U.S. military aid (in particular) to Latin American regimes has been the main cause of revolutionary *failures* in Latin America since 1960. The growth of counterinsurgency emphases and training under the Kennedy administration, in particular, was thought to be a decisive policy shift allowing Latin American governments to wield newly enhanced powers against their internal enemies.[22] James Petras put it succinctly in the 1960s, focusing on a narrower target, by arguing that U.S. military missions "are responsible for the suppression of popular movements."[23] Few have appreciated, however, that precisely this same thesis has been adopted by the political right, inverted, and then used to explain the *success* of revolutionaries in the region as well. It began with the "Cuba betrayed" and "we lost Cuba" commentary in the 1960s. An almost identical flow of argument appeared again when the Sandinistas came to power in Nicaragua in July 1979. None other than Jeane Kirkpatrick has put this view forcefully: "What did the Carter administration do in Nicaragua? *It brought down the Somoza regime*" (emphasis in the original).[24] Revolutionary theory-making can certainly make strange ideological bedfellows: we now have the Petras-Kirkpatrick theory of revolution.[25]

Nor is this thesis totally lacking evidence. The U.S. government withdrew support from Batista, and Castro won; it continued and sometimes increased support in various nations during the 1960s, and guerrillas lost. It withdrew support from Somoza, and the FSLN came to power, but later threw enormous military aid behind the Salvadoran regimes after 1980, and the revolutionaries have been kept in check. Have we indeed found the master variable? Before we accept this thesis we might do well to consider two countries that each received massive U.S. military aid dwarfing anything that any Latin American nation had ever received: Iran and South Vietnam.[26] Military aid hardly made them proof against revolution. How, then, could much lesser aid provide such a defense in Latin America? Now that we have paused, we can consider the evidence more systematically.

The evidence from table 12-3 gives us pause in this rush to simplify. First of all, this theory ignores the whole issue of the presence or absence of a substantial internal challenge to the regime. In the absence of such a challenge, U.S. support seems to be utterly irrelevant to the regime's continuity. Haiti consistently received insignificant levels of military aid throughout the Duvaliers' years, yet no one suggests that the "withdrawal of U.S. support" caused a revolution there (line 21). Nor was Stroessner's Paraguay an especially gifted recipient of such military aid, yet Stroessner ruled that nation until deposed by his longtime number two in early 1989, when the dictator tried to fire him (lines 22,28).

Revolutionaries have even failed where they made the guerrilla attempt, succeeded in securing some popular support, and faced a regime from which the United States government had withdrawn military support. U.S. military aid to Argentina fell to insignificant levels in the 1970s at least until the decade's end; yet those were the very years in which the military unleashed an extraordinarily violent campaign against the guerrillas (and the Argentine citizenry) that utterly crushed the revolutionaries.[27]

One of the strongest counterexamples lies in the same region as Nicaragua and El Salvador, which supposedly confirm the "imperial prop" thesis: Guatemala. In the Carter years, the administration's emphasis on human rights issues led it to cut off military aid to that government; in fact, U.S. pressure on such issues led the military rulers indignantly to accuse the U.S. of meddling in Guatemala's internal affairs, and to refuse such aid. In fact, in 1986 a Guatemalan general encouraged Sandinista leader Daniel Ortega to "keep screwing over the *gringos*."[28] Not until the mid-to-late-1980s was substantial U.S. aid restored to Guatemala.[29] Yet during that very "dry" period the Guatemalan military fought a violent counterinsurgency against the guerrillas that was also highly effective in reducing guerrilla numbers and effectiveness. If U.S. aid is decisive, why didn't the Guatemalan military regimes fall to an insurgency fielding thousands of combatants with deep support among the peasantry of the Indian highlands?[30]

Finally, the case of Manuel Noriega in Panama also raises crucial issues about the importance of U.S. support. There the Reagan administration did not simply withdraw support in 1987–1988, it actually invoked massive financial sanctions against the regime, which had begun to acquire all the traits of mafiacracy or patrimonial praetorianism: echoes of Somoza, Trujillo, and Duvalier hung all about Noriega. Despite the "weak form" of regime in Panama, a general strike, open-armed invitations from some opposition Panamanians for yet greater U.S. intervention, and open and massive U.S. government opposition, the Noriega regime weathered the storm, only succumbing when the Bush administration launched an all-out invasion of Panama in December 1989. The missing element here was any kind of organized guerrilla movement and its accompanying cross-class alliance. The urban middle classes who took to the streets of Panama City in anti-Noriega demonstrations lacked the military resources or deep lower-class support to carry through Noriega's ouster.[31]

To sum up, the "Petras-Kirkpatrick theses" seem initially persuasive, but a closer look at the regional universe of cases in the end dissuades us from accepting them. Once again, such a theory ignores the different strengths of varied regimes in the face of revolution, confirmed by Argentina in the 1970s and by Guatemala in the 1980s, despite the withdrawal of U.S. military aid in both cases. Those regimes were strong *qua* special types of regimes, not *qua* recipients of imperial largesse. Furthermore, a striking feature that emerges in table 12-3 is that even a patrimonial praetorian regime (condition *D*) that experiences a withdrawal of U.S. military support (condition *E*) does not necessarily thereby become a casualty of revolution: witness Haiti under the Duvaliers and Panama under Noriega.

HYPOTHESIS 5: REGIME WEAKNESSES CAUSE REVOLUTIONS

Theda Skocpol has been the premier advocate of this thesis, and has raised for us all the right issues. She has argued forcefully that the French, Russian, and Chinese revolutions occurred because their agrarian proto-bureaucratic regimes collapsed due to internal pressures from the upper classes and/or external pressures from rival nation-states. Only afterwards did revolutionary organizations take over the process of revolution.[32] Skocpol is on far weaker ground, however, when she extends that claim to say that "historically no successful social revolution has ever been 'made' by a mass-mobilizing, avowedly revolutionary movement."[33] The Bolivian revolution of 1952 seems to be a good counterexample, and Castro's insurgency in Cuba can only be excluded by a very heavy and restrictive emphasis on the qualification "avowedly revolutionary."[34] In the very year her book was published, moreover, mass-mobilizing revolutionaries came to power in Nicaragua and Iran. It is to Skocpol's credit that she conceded the differences for the case of Iran and proceeded to demonstrate how political mobilization—based on a historical culture of resistance and defiance and wedded to structured popular religious networks—confronted a peculiar type of political regime (the shah's "rentier state") and produced the religious revolution against the shah.[35]

From the point of view of table 12-3, Skocpol's formal argument combined an emphasis on regime weaknesses (column *D*) and on independent peasant uprisings (roughly columns *A* + *B*). Whereas my "peasant insurrections" stem from guerrillas mobilizing peasant followers successfully, her peasant insurrections came independently of outside mobilization. That is, conditions A, B, and D must all be present for revolutionaries to seize power. For Skocpol, regime collapses *allowed* peasant insurrection to occur in an unimpeded way in France and Russia; mobilization was not crucial. In terms of table 12-3, condition D allowed conditions $A + B$ to occur, and that sequence provided the two main causes of revolution.

There is, however, a clear structural resemblance here to one of Skocpol's cases: China. In China, as her own analysis makes clear, the Chinese peasantry rose up only after being mobilized by Mao's Red Army. The delay came because social structures in the Chinese countryside reduced the autonomy and the solidarity of peasant villagers.[36] Her Chinese case rather more clearly parallels Latin American events in this respect: a guerrilla attempt at peasant mobilization (condition A) successfully secured massive peasant support (condition B) following the collapse of a weakened political regime in the preceding years (condition D). In Latin America, likewise, the mobilization of peasant support against the regime was not enough to secure victory. Yet against particular types of (weak) regimes, the revolutionaries could weld together a cross-class alliance that brought down the regime. In Latin America, therefore, peasant mobilization preceded and was instrumental in destroying the old regime; in Skocpol's French and Russian cases, by contrast, the old regime fell by itself first, and then peasant uprisings ensured it would not rise again.

Finally, both Skocpol's explanation and my own focus on the international context of revolutions (condition E). Whereas she emphasizes the pattern of international conflicts and wars in weakening old-regime states, the Latin American pattern has involved the weakening or collapse of international alliances, when the U.S. withdrew support from the Batista and Somoza regimes. In *States and Social Revolutions*, therefore, Theda Skocpol asked almost all the right questions and may well have given correct answers for the Eurasian cases she considered. For Latin America, we can take her lead, reorder and slightly reconceptualize the problem of revolutionary failure and success, and begin to come finally to a full understanding of Latin American revolutions.

A Theory of Latin American Revolutions, 1956–1990

EXPLAINING SUCCESSES: CUBA AND NICARAGUA

We can now evaluate the twenty-eight cases of table 12-3. First, I shall reduce them to manageable numbers by combining identical patterns. Second, I will apply Boolean minimization to eliminate unnecessary variables from the list of causes. Third, I will finally search for prime implicants to eliminate redundant forms of explanation.

The pattern of success for Latin American revolutions is revealed simply through casual inspection. While in other cases we could find as many as four of the conditions present (Argentina) and three conditions present in many cases (most of panel II), only in Cuba and Nicaragua were all five conditions present, and only in those nations did the revolutionaries seize power in the thirty-five-year period we are now reviewing. In Boolean terms:

Successful Social Revolution = ABCDE.

That is the crux of this entire work, finally boiled down to an extreme Boolean shorthand. Put into prose rather than letters: revolutionaries came to power in Latin America from 1956 to 1990 only when a rural-based guerrilla movement secured strong peasant support in the countryside and achieved substantial levels of military strength; if that movement also faced a patrimonial praetorian regime (a.k.a. *mafiacracy*), then it was structurally pressured to seek, and succeeded in securing a cross-class alliance against the patrimonial dictator who, lacking the social bases of support to resist such an alliance, in the end fell to a national resistance; under such conditions the United States tended to withdraw support from the dictatorship because of the symbolic and social pressures exerted by the constitutionalist and electoral symbols under which the revolutionaries and their more moderate allies united.

A careful examination of table 12-3, however, suggests a yet deeper parallel to and support for Skocpol's theory. While several other cases did indeed have even four conditions present, yet not all five, only in Cuba and Nicaragua did a specific *pair* of conditions converge: a peasant-supported guerrilla movement (*B*) confronting a patrimonial praetorian regime (*D*). Those conditions are close analogues of Skocpol's key conditions: regime collapse followed by peasant insurrections. This does not mean, however, that we can easily collapse the theory down to just two variables, for two reasons. First, lacking control cases, we cannot say that the other three conditions in Cuba and Nicaragua were superfluous; they *may* still have been necessary, and Ragin himself argues that Boolean algebra should be applied thoughtfully rather than mechanically.[37] Second, given the close contextual interrelations among the five conditions—see below—it would be difficult to remove any one variable as if it were an isolated influence.

EXPLAINING FAILURES

Any theory of revolution remains incomplete unless it also explores Mill's method of difference in greater depth. We can also treat revolutionary failure as an outcome requiring explanation and study. We wish also to understand the varied conditions under which revolutions did not occur in Latin America. Since these patterns are multiple rather than singular, we shall have to employ Boolean techniques to reduce the complexity. First, let us consider the main patterns from table 12-3 (remembering that lower-case letters indicate the absence of a condition, capitals its presence).

Pattern	Cases from Table 12-3
1. *abcde*	Lines 25,26
2. *abcDe*	Line 28
3. *Abcde*	Lines 15–17,19,20,23,24
4. *ABcde*	Lines 11,13
5. *AbcDe*	Lines 18,22
6. *ABCde*	Lines 3–7,9,14
7. *AbcDE*	Line 21
8. *ABCdE*	Lines 8,12
9. *abcDE*	Line 27
10. *ABcdE*	Line 10

To proceed with Boolean minimization, we must now combine all possible pairs that differ on the value of but one variable, but that share similar outcomes. All the above are failures, so the outcome is held constant. We can carry out the following minimizations:

Patterns 1 & 2: *abcde* combines with *abcDe* to produce **abce**.
Patterns 1 & 3: *abcde* combines with *Abcde* to produce **bcde**.
Patterns 2 & 5: *abcDe* combines with *AbcDe* to produce **bcDe**.
Patterns 2 & 9: *abcDe* combines with *abcDE* to produce **abcD**.
Patterns 3 & 4: *Abcde* combines with *ABcde* to produce **Acde**.
Patterns 3 & 5: *Abcde* combines with *AbcDe* to produce **Abce**.
Patterns 4 & 6: *ABcde* combines with *ABCde* to produce **ABde**.
Patterns 4 & 10: *ABcde* combines with *ABcdE* to produce **ABcd**.
Patterns 5 & 7: *AbcDe* combines with *AbcDE* to produce **AbcD**.
Patterns 6 & 8: *ABCde* combines with *ABCdE* to produce **ABCd**.
Patterns 7 & 9: *AbcDE* combines with *abcDE* to produce **bcDE**.
Patterns 8 & 10: *ABCdE* combines with *ABcdE* to produce **ABdE**.

A second round of minimization is also possible, as follows:

Patterns 1 + 2 & 3 + 5: *abce* combines with *Abce* to produce **bce**.
Patterns 1 + 3 & 2 + 5: *bcde* combines with *bcDe* to produce **bce** as well.
Patterns 2 + 5 & 7 + 9: *bcDe* combines with *bcDE* to produce **bcD**.
Patterns 2 + 9 & 5 + 7: *abcD* combines with *AbcD* to produce **bcD** as well.
Patterns 4 + 6 & 8 + 10: *ABde* combines with *ABdE* to produce **ABd**.
Patterns 6 + 8 & 4 + 10: *ABCd* combines with *ABcd* to produce **ABd** as well.
Pattern 3 + 4 is irreducible in this second round, and remains **Acde**.

After the second minimization, then, we are left with but four patterns of failure: **Acde**, **bce**, **bcD**, and **ABd**.

PRIME IMPLICANTS: THE SECOND BLADE OF OCCAM'S RAZOR

We can now ask ourselves if there exists any explanatory redundancy in the four patterns of failure above. I do not wish to burden the reader with a forty-cell table showing the true "prime implicants," from among the four scenarios just produced, paired up with the original set of ten scenarios (also called "primitive expressions").[38] Suffice it to say that there is some redundancy in the four prime implicants I have generated: expression **Acde** can be dropped from the analysis, because the same variables are "captured" by the other expressions. An inspection of table 12-3 can confirm that the twenty-six failed cases are all "covered" by the three remaining expressions.

Therefore we can now specify the multiple scenarios in which revolution did not occur (" + " indicates logical or):

Absence of Revolution = ABd + bce + bcD

(i.e., nonrevolution has three different variant patterns)

Table 12-4 summarizes the conditions for both revolutionary success and revolutionary failure in Latin America, after completion of both minimization procedures. When guerrillas actually attempted to foment revolution in Latin America in that thirty-year period, two patterns of revolutionary failure tended to emerge. In variant A (**ABd**), the guerrillas did indeed secure substantial peasant support in the countryside, but popular support alone was not enough to carry them through to victory. They faced an unweakened form of political regime—either an electoral democracy or a collective military dictatorship—and failed in their attempt. Military strength is irrelevant, and U.S. support for the regime simply falls out of the analysis and becomes irrelevant to the outcome. Why? Because some of those regimes retained U.S. support, while some lost it, yet all of them defeated or at least have stood off the insurgents. The cases here were every "also-ran" in panel II of table 12-3.

In variant B (**bce**), the guerrillas usually essayed attempts against stronger regimes supported by U.S. backing and failed. Peasant support was absent in every one of these cases, either because the peasantry was unwilling to do so, or because no revolutionary movement seeking such support made an appearance. Guerrillas here also lacked substantial military might, in any event. The cases for this variant where guerrilla movements were present included Argentina, Peru, Bolivia, and various lesser *focos* of the 1960s, and Brazil and Mexico in the 1970s. In the remaining instances, guerrillas simply made no substantial appearance in Costa Rica and Panama after about 1960, and that fact itself perhaps merits an explanation (which I shall leave for others).

Variant C (**bcD**) is a most interesting case, for it contains every case of a patrimonial praetorian regime that did not fall to revolution: Nicaragua (1958–1963), Haiti, Paraguay (twice), and Panama under Manuel Noriega.

TABLE 12-4

Conditions for the Success and Failure of Revolutionary Guerrilla Movements in Latin America, 1956–1990
(1 = trait present, 0 = trait absent, — = irrelevant)[a]
(All #s refer to lines in table 12-3)

Different Scenarios	(A) Guerrilla Attempt	(B) Peasant/ (Worker) Support	(C) Guerrilla Military Strength	(D) Patrimonial Praetorian Regime	(E) Government Loses U.S. Support (1 = yes)
Social Revolution					
(#1, 2: Cuba, Nicaragua)	1	1	1	1	1
Guerrilla Failure: Three Variants					
(A) Strong regime versus strong guerrillas; U.S. support irrelevant (#s 3–14)	1	1	—	0	—
(B) Weak or no guerrilla attempt; U.S.-backed regime (#s 15–17, 19, 20, 23–26)	—	0	0	—	0
(C) Weak regime-type, but strong guerrillas absent (#s 18, 21, 22, 27, 28)	—	0	0	1	—

Source: Table 12-3, plus textual discussion and notes.

[a] "Irrelevant" means that the variable dropped out in the process of Boolean minimization. Why? Because there were two original subtypes within the scenario that had identical outcomes but that differed on the condition described as (—): present in one group, absent in the other; therefore that condition logically could *not* have produced the the outcome *within the context of that scenario*. In other contextual circumstances it could well be relevant.

In the absence of a strong guerrilla movement (either absent or weakly supported guerrillas), those regimes did not succumb to revolution, and U.S. support for the regime once again becomes irrelevant to the outcome.

Conclusions: The Contextual Conditions for Social Revolutions in Latin America

We have arrived at the end of our theoretical narrative, with a macro-causal analysis, supported by the systematic tools of Boolean algebra, demonstrating the conditions under which revolutions have occurred or failed to occur in Latin America since 1956. Like Skocpol, I would like to enter a demurral here about uncritical attempts to extend this logic beyond Latin America, to "test it" in other areas—not that I have been without thoughts about such extensions, especially to the Philippines, where the Marcos regime looked suspiciously like the biggest mafiacracy of them all and fell to an urban, cross-class insurrection that the rural Communist insurgency failed to link up with.

The virtue of the macro-causal and Boolean approaches is their case-oriented nature. Each case remains contextualized, and the impact of each "condition" or "variable" is not ripped out of context, but instead depends for its impact upon the presence or absence of other conditions. To put it in simpler terms, each scenario that emerges describes a structure of interrelated conditions, rather than a list of variables. I would like to end this work by exploring briefly the contextual interrelations for successful revolutions in Latin America.

It should be obvious that peasant support for revolutionaries (condition B) depends upon having revolutionaries available to support (condition A). While peasant revolts over the issues of land and tribute have been common-place in the region, only rarely in Latin American history has the peasantry on its own risen up to confront a political regime over the nature of the political system. The main exception here remains that of Emiliano Zapata's (and per-haps Pancho Villa's) followers during the Mexican revolution.[39] Conditions A and B therefore remain heavily interrelated, with B dependent upon A. We should note again the contrast with Skocpol's study: there peasant insur-rection with revolutionary consequences was not elite-dependent in either France or Russia but arose out of the constitution of rural communities in those nations.

Peasant support is also intimately correlated with the military strength of guerrilla movements (conditions B and C). That very correlation, which I believe to be largely independent of the degree of outside military aid to the guerrillas, strongly suggests the aphorism of the Salvadoran guerrilla move-ment: "Our mountains are the people." Why should this be the case? As I noted in chapter 5, guerrilla warfare is the most labor-intensive form of war-fare, and more peasant support translates into a greater number of eager and ready peasant combatants. Moreover, massive peasant support means not only bodies for combat, but also personnel for all the ancillary activities of warfare: lookouts, guides, civil-defense specialists, food growers and provid-ers, and even munitions manufacturers.[40] The labor-intensive nature of guer-rilla warfare—as shown in Vietnam—strongly suggests that we might expect a "deep" contextual relationship between levels of peasant support and the military strength of the insurgency.

On the other hand, high levels of peasant support for an insurgency are highly context-*independent* of the support of other social groups and classes for revolution. The cross-class nature of opposition that tends to emerge in the face of patrimonial praetorian regimes is largely dependent upon precisely that *national* political context. Peasant support, as we have seen, derives instead from the *regional* contexts that different peasants inhabit. Those two types of support for revolution, in the language of statistics, are largely "orthogonal" to one another, and neither one readily converts into the other. This suggests a more or less yawning chasm between the nature of peasant responses to insurgency, and the conditions activating upper-, middle-, and even working-class opposition to incumbent regimes.

Finally, most writers have simply ignored the contextual link between the presence of a patrimonial praetorian regime and the withdrawal of U.S. support from such regimes (conditions *D* and *E*). Because of the conflicting tugs of U.S. democratic values and the desire for stable non-Communist governments in the region, various American administrations have experienced love-hate relationships with dictators, especially patrimonial ones. Mark Falcoff sketched that approach-avoidance history for the Somoza dynasty, while the reader should remember that Dominican dictator Rafael Trujillo ("our son of a bitch") was eventually (evidently) assassinated under CIA auspices.[41] Similar comments pertain rather clearly to the regimes of Batista, Duvalier, and Noriega as well. When a radical-cum-moderate alliance appeared in both Cuba and Nicaragua, and espoused democratic, electoral, and constitutional principles, the United States government was pressured both by American citizens and by its own professed values to endorse the constitutional opposition, or at the very least to stop supporting a dictator whose entire history was a slap in the face of such values. Several successful revolutionaries candidly conceded that, when Batista and Somoza both fell, U.S. "imperialism" was temporarily "disoriented," or words to the same effect.[42] The change of political position by the U.S. government was not simply a historical accident but derived in good part from the shifting political scenes in Cuba and Nicaragua themselves. Hence I believe it to be a fundamental misunderstanding to think of this variable in isolation from the other conditions of revolution in Latin America; and that is precisely the error committed by proponents of the "imperial prop" theory of revolution (hypothesis 4 above).

In this work I have tried to advance the study of Latin American revolutions on several grounds. I have shunned the "area studies" approach which ignores general theory in its rush to establish the supposed uniqueness of each case, each event. As my references throughout I hope have demonstrated, we have much to learn from general theory. I have also tried to avoid the Balkanized silliness of school making that has proven such a burden to clear sociological thought. As Henry Fielding said in *Tom Jones*, "[W]e do not disdain to borrow wit or wisdom from any man who is capable of lending us either. . . ." Instead, I embrace the position of Walter Wallace, who has shown that sociologists in their actual research adopt a limited variety of explanatory devices.[43] Finally, I have sought to integrate a variety of existing theories, without simply creating a "laundry-list" theory of revolution (we have enough of those already). Especially in this final chapter I hope I have simultaneously succeeded in establishing the theoretical utility of a variety of sociological theories and in integrating them into a unified theory of Latin American revolutions. I hope I have suceeded in getting a handle on the whole elephant.

Profiles of Guerrilla Leadership

Name	Birth Year	Father's Occupation	Own Education/ Occupation	Political Party (former)
Cuba, 1956–1959				
Fidel Castro Ruz	1926	Plantation owner	Lawyer	Ortodoxo
Ernesto "Ché" Guevara	1928	Architect/Engineer (Mother: member of old aristocracy)	Doctor	
Camilo Cienfuegos			Tailor and salesman	
Raúl Castro Ruz	1931	Plantation owner	Social science student	Communist
Frank País (urban)	1934	Baptist minister	Teacher	Acción Nacional Revolucionaria
Huber Matos			Rice farmer/schoolmaster	
Guillermo García			Peasant	
Ramiro Valdés		"Poor family"	Student/white-collar worker	
Crescencio Pérez		Mountain peasant	Cattle dealer/squatter leader	Auténtico
Celia Sánchez		Dentist	Accountant	
Vilma Espín	1930	Physician	Chem. engineer?/architect?	
Juan Almeida			Bricklayer	
Efigenio Amejeiras			Cab driver	
Dermi[n/t]io Escalona		Provincial bourgeoisie		
Delio Gómez Ochoa		Landowner	Law student	Ortodoxo
Victor Mora			Mountain peasant	
José Ponce			Printer/designer	
Ciro Redondo			Student	
Augusto Martinez Sánchez			Lawyer	
René Ramos Latour			Accountant	
Ramón Paz Barroto			Miner	

Name	Birth Year	Father's Occupation	Own Education/ Occupation	Political Party (former)
Universo Sánchez		Peasant	Peasant?/small businessman?	
Marcelo Fernández			Medical student	
Humberto Sori Marín			Lawyer	
Armando Hart Dávalos		Supreme court	Lawyer	
Faustino Pérez		Middle peasant	Medical student	
Enrique Oltuski	1931	Middle class	Engineer	
Pedro Miret	1928		Engineering student	
Julio Martínez Páez			Surgeon	
Rene Vallejo			Doctor	
Jorge Ribas			Engineer	
Faure Chomón (DR)			Student	

Venezuela, 1961–1970

Name	Birth Year	Father's Occupation	Own Education/ Occupation	Political Party (former)
Douglas Bravo (Falcón)	1933	"Modest merchant"	Cement worker/law student	PCV/Central Committee (out in 1966)
Elías Manuit(t) Camero (Falcón)			Police instructor/army captain	
Fabricio Ojeda (Trujillo-Portuguesa)	1927	"Modest family"	Journalist/deputy in parliament	URD
Argimiro Gabaldón Márquez (Lara)		General/Hacendado	PCV militant	PCV
Teodoro Petkoff (Lara/Falcón)	1931	Chemical engineer (Mother: doctor)	Economics student/ parliament deputy	PCV
Luben Petkoff (Yaracuy)	1933	Chemical Engineer (Mother: doctor)	Printer	PCV
Hipólito Acosta Blanco (Falcón)	1929	Hacendado	Lawyer	PCV (?)
Domingo Urbina (Falcón)		Hacendado	PCV Activist	PCV
Juan Vicente Cabezas (Portuguesa-Trujillo)	1933		Engineer	PCV
Gregorio Lunar Márquez (Lara)			Geological engineer	PCV
José "El Gavilán" Díaz (Lara)	1910		AD union leader	(AD), MIR

Name	Birth Year	Father's Occupation	Own Education/ Occupation	Political Party (former)
Lino Díaz (Lara)				
Américo Martín (Miranda)	1938	Architect	Student/Student Federation president	(AD), MIR
Moisés Moleiro (Miranda)			Student	(AD), MIR
Freddy Cárquez (Lara)			Medical student/ doctor	PCV
Francisco Prada (Llanos)	1933		Sociologist/social worker	(AD)
Carlos Betancourt (Miranda)			Student	MIR
Argelia Laya (Lara)	1926	Rural poor; urban poor	Teacher	(AD)/PCV
Hernán Cortés Mujica (Lara)			Doctor	(AD), (URD) PCV
Juan Bautista Arena (Falcón)			Evangelical minister	
Máximo Canales (Miranda)				
Héctor Pérez Mara- cano (Miranda)			Student/Student Federation president	(MIR)
"Negro Antonio" (Miranda)				
Antonio Zamora (pseud?) (Llanos)		Owner of two ranches	Former officer in National Guard	PCV
Julio Escalona (Oriente)			Student/Student Federation president	MIR
José "Chema" Saher (Falcón)	1943	State governor (Falcón)	Student	PCV
Pedro Vegas Castejón (Falcón)			Major, National Guard	PCV
Angela Zago			Psychology student	PCV
Iván Daza (Lara)	1947	Journalist	High school student	
Félix Farías Salcedo			University student	PCV
Manuel Aguajo Ortega			Army major	
Héctor Fleming Men- doza (Oriente)			Lieutenant, naval infantry	
Albornoz Gutiérrez			Air force officer	
Juan Moncada Vidal			Lieutenant colonel	
Alfredo Maneiro (Oriente)			Student leader	PCV

Name	Birth Year	Father's Occupation	Own Education/ Occupation	Political Party (former)
Argenis Bravo (Falcón)		Hacendado (?)		
Pedro [or Ramón] París Aldana (Lara)		"Well-known family," Lara		
Eloy Pérez Silva			University educated (Chile)	
Edgar Gabaldón Márquez (Lara)		General/Hacendado		
Nery [or Nelly] Carrillo (UTC—Caracas?)				
Baltazar Ojeda Negrete (Falcón)	1944			
Juan Mariño (Falcón)				
José Carmelo Mendoza (Lara)				PCV
Juanita Villavicencio (Lara)				
José Rodríguez Flores (Portuguesa)				
Germán Lairet (Cuban contact)			Lawyer	PCV
Tulio Martínez Delgado	1939		Army lieutenant	
Pedro Medina Silva (Puerto Cabello revolt)			Naval captain	
Jesus Teodoro Molina (Carupano revolt)			Naval captain	
Tirso Pinto (Lara)			High school student	PCV
Trina Urbina (Falcón)	1928		Textile worker	PCV(?)
Octavio Acosta Bello (Falcón)			Army officer	
Guatemala, 1962–1970				
Luis Augusto Turcios Lima (FAR)	( )[a]	Watchmaker (Mother: office worker)	Army—second lieutenant	
Marco Antonio Yon Sosa (MR-13)	( )[a]	"Upper middle class"—transport	Army—lieutenant	

Name	Birth Year	Father's Occupation	Own Education/ Occupation	Political Party (former)
Julio César Macias Mayora (César Montes)—(FAR)	1942		Law student/PGT Central Committee	(JPT)
Camilo Sánchez (FAR)	c. 1940–1945	Peasant	High school (minimum)	JPT
Luis Trejo Esquivel				PGT
Carlos Paz Tejada			Army—lieutentant colonel	
Emilio Román López (Pascual Ixtapá)— (FAR)			Town mayor, Alta Verapaz	
Oliverio Castancda			Guerrilla leader; Right-wing deputy in parliament	
Augusto V. Loarca			Army—lieutenant colonel; Arbenz's general staff	
Alejandro de León Aragon			Army officer	
Otto René Castillo			Poet	
Bernal Hernández				

Colombia, 1964–1970+

Name	Birth Year	Father's Occupation	Own Education/ Occupation	Political Party (former)
Fabio Vásquez Castaño (ELN)	1929	Peasant	4th Grade +/Cuba scholarship	(MOEC)
Manuel Marulanda Velez, aka Pedro Antonio Marín, aka "Tirofijo" (FARC)	1928	Peasant	Ex-army officer/ peasant/bandit/guer-rilla (Marquetalia)	PCC Central Committee
Camilo Torres Restrepo[b] (ELN)	1929	Doctor (one of nation's "24 Families")	Priest/sociology professor	(PCC Youth; MOEC)
Victor Medina Morón (ELN)			Engineer	(MOEC)
Jacobo Arenas (Luis Morantes)— (FARC)	1924	Peasant?	2 years school; Presi-dential Guard	PCC
Juan de la Cruz Varela (FARC)			Peasant/bandit/ guerrilla (Icon_onzo)	(Liberal; Gaitanista)
Pedro León Arboleda (EPL)			Journalist	(PCC)/ PCC-M-L

Name	Birth Year	Father's Occupation	Own Education/ Occupation	Political Party (former)
Pedro Vasquez Rendón (EPL)		"Middle class"	Student	PCC-M-L
Ricardo Lara Parada (ELN)		Worker		
Heliodoro Ochoa (ELN)			Student	(PCC-Youth)
Julio César Cortes (ELN)			Medical student	
Heriberto Espitia (ELN)		Peasant		(PCC-Youth)
Ciro Trujillo Castaño (FARC)		Peasant(?)	Guerrilla (Paez)	PCC Central Committee
Isauro Yosa	c. 1910	Peasant(?)	Peasant guerrilla (Marquetalia)	PCC Central Committee
Oscar Reyes, aka Januario Valerio (FARC)		Peasant(?)		PCC Central Committee
Julio Portocarrero (ELN)			Student	
Domingo Lain (ELN)			Priest	
Jaime Velásquez García (FARC)	1931		Surgeon/National University	
(Maj.) Hernando González (FARC)			Student/guerrilla (Riochiquito)	PCC-Youth
Luis Rovira (ELN)				
Mario Hernández				
José Merchan (ELN)				
Mariela Amaya y Paulina González (ELN)			University graduate	

Peru, 1965–1966

Name	Birth Year	Father's Occupation	Own Education/ Occupation	Political Party (former)
Luis de la Puente Uceda (MIR-Cuzco)	1926– 1965	Hacendado	Lawyer; political activist	(APRA)
Héctor Béjar Rivera (ELN)	1934		Student-fine arts; poet; journalist	(PCP)
Guillermo Lobatón Mille (MIR-Junín)	1927– 1966	Working class	Sociology at Sorbonne; journalist	(APRA?)
Gonzalo Fernández Gasco (MIR-Piura)	1920		Lawyer; professor	(APRA)
Máximo Velando Gálvez (MIR-Junín)	1942– 1965		Economics student in Argentina; peasant organizer	(APRA?)

Name	Birth Year	Father's Occupation	Own Education/ Occupation	Political Party (former)
Ruben Tupayachi (MIR-Cuzco)				(APRA?)
Froilan Herrera (MIR-Junín)	1937		Student	
Máximo Lazo Orrego (MIR-Junín)	1947		High school student	
Elio Portocarrero Ríos (MIR-Piura)	1941		Law student (Trujillo)	
Albino Guzmán (MIR-Cuzco)	1935		Student-Cuzco; peasant	
Juan Zapata Bordero (ELN)				(FIR)
Ricardo León (ELN)				

Quasi-Guerrilla Leaders in Peru, Pre-1965

Name	Birth Year	Father's Occupation	Own Education/ Occupation	Political Party (former)
Hugo Blanco Galdos (Cuzco, 1956-63)	1933	Lawyer (Mother: peasant)	Agricultural engineer; tenant farmer; peasant organizer	(POR, FIR) Trotskyist
Javier Héraud Pérez (Madre de Dios, 1963)	1942–1963	"Great Bourgeois" family	Poet	

Bolivia, 1966–1967 (nom de guerre)

Name	Birth Year	Father's Occupation	Own Education/ Occupation	Political Party (former)
Ernesto "Ché" Guevara (Ramón)	1928	Architect/Engineer (Mother: old upper class)	Doctor; government minister	
Juan Vitalio Acuña Nuñez (Joaquín)	1920	Peasant	Cuban CP-Central Committee	CP-Cuba
Guido Peredo Leigue (Inti)	1938		High school/PCB officer	PCB
Eliseo Reyes Rodríguez (Rolando)	1940			
Antonio Sánchez Díaz	1927		Doctor; Cuban CP Central Committee	CP-Cuba
Rolando Quindela Blez (Braulio)	1936			
Roberto Peredo Leigue (Coco)	1939		High school; cab driver; PCB officer	PCB

Sources: Sources are widely scattered. For concentrations of information, see as follows: CUBA—Carlos Franqui, *The Twelve* (New York: Lyle Stuart, 1968), pp. 17–19; Ramón L. Bonachea and Marta San Martín, *The Cuban Insurrection, 1952–1959* (New Brunswick, N.J.: Transaction, 1974), pp. 103–4, 252; Günter Maschke, *Kritik des Guerillero* (Frankfurt: S. Fischer, 1973), p. 73; Enrique Meneses, *Fidel Castro* (New York: Taplinger, 1966), pp. 54–55; Hugh Thomas, *Cuba: The Pursuit of Freedom* (New York: Harper and Row, 1971), pp. 1043–44 (contrast to profiles of Moncada attackers, listed on pp. 1546–47); Theodore Draper, *Castro's Revolution: Myths and Realities* (New York: Frederick Praeger, 1962), pp. 42–43; and Neill Macaulay, "The Cuban Rebel Army: A Numerical Survey," *Hispanic American Historical Review* 58, no. 2 (May 1978): 289–91. VENEZUELA—Above all, consult Luigi Valsalice, *Guerriglia e Politica: L'esempio del Venezuela, 1962–1969* (Florence, Italy: Valmartina Editore, 1973), pp. 235–58; see also Judith Ewell, *Venezuela: A Century of Change* (Stanford, Calif.: Stanford University Press, 1984), pp. 146–51; Antonio Zamora, *Memoria(s) de la guerrilla venezolana* (Caracas: Síntesis Dosmil, 1974), pp. 139–49; François Maspero/Douglas Bravo, *Avec Douglas Bravo dans les maquis vénézuéliens* (Paris: François Maspero, 1968), p. 23; and Daniel Levine, *Conflict and Political Change in Venezuela* (Princeton, N.J.: Princeton University Press, 1973), pp. 149–80. GUATEMALA—The best source is Gabriel Aguilera Peralta, *La violencia en Guatemala como fenómeno político* (Cuernavaca, Mexico: CIDOC, 1971), pp. 2/19, 2/26–27; see also João Batista Berardo, *Guerrilhas e guerrilheiros no drama da América Latina* (São Paulo: Edições Populares, 1981), p. 356; also the chapters on Guatemala in Richard Gott, *Rural Guerrillas in Latin America* (Harmondsworth, England: Penguin, 1973); Robert F. Lamberg, *Die castristiche Guerilla in Lateinamerika* (Hannover, Germany: Verlag für Literatur und Zeitgeschehen, 1971); and Fritz René Allemann, *Macht und Ohnmacht der Guerilla* (Munich: R. Piper, 1974). COLOMBIA—Again, there are few good central sources. Perhaps the best is Manuel Arango Z., *FARC: Veinte años—De Marquetalia a la Uribe* (Bogotá: Ediciones Aurora, 1984), pp. 51–54, 61, 70–71, 86–88. See also the chapters on Colombia in the three works just cited for Guatemala. On the leadership of the peasant republics, from which the FARC guerrillas in large part emerged, see Lamberg, *Die castristiche Guerilla*, pp. 91, 98. PERU—Lamberg, *Die castristiche Guerilla*, pp. 109–15; Berardo, *Guerrilhas e guerrilheiros*, pp. 162–68; Gonzalo Añi Castillo, *El secreto de las guerrillas* (Lima: Ediciones 'Mas Allá', 1967), p. 186; Manuel Castillo, "Las guerrillas en el Peru," *Estudios* (Buenos Aires) 581 (April 1967): 162–64; Peru, Ministerio de Guerra, *Las guerrillas en el Peru y su represión* (Lima?: Ministerio de Guerra, 1966), pp. 45–46. BOLIVIA—Ernesto 'Che' Guevara, *The Complete Bolivian Diaries of Che Guevara and Other Captured Documents*, edited and with an introduction by Daniel James (New York: Stein and Day, 1968), pp. 324–25; and Luis J. González and Gustavo A. Sánchez Salazar, *The Great Rebel: Che Guevara in Bolivia* (New York: Grove Press, 1969), pp. 234–43. The former work lists all Cuban participants and the latter all (known) Bolivians as well. The fates of all, and backgrounds of some, are discussed in Berardo, *Guerrilhas e guerrilheiros*, pp. 183–86.

Note: Where not otherwise specified in the column headings, words in parentheses generally indicate geographical locations.

[a] Varying birth dates given or implied in the literature for Turcios Lima and Yon Sosa. Aguilera places their birth dates in 1942 and 1929, respectively; ICOPS in 1924 and 1934; and Gott in 1941 and 1938(?). Given the usual emphasis on their youth and occasional reference to Yon Sosa being somewhat older than Turcios, I am inclined toward 1941 or 1942 for Turcios and 1938 for Yon Sosa as the most probable birth years, which would make them eighteen to nineteen and twenty-two, respectively, at the time of the revolt on 13 November 1960.

[b] Never a guerrilla *comandante* but included here for symbolic importance to ELN.

Social Origins of Guerrilla Leadership: Post-1970 Period

Name/Group/ "nom de guerre"	Year of Birth(– Death)	Occupation/Education of:		Party of Origin
		Father	Self	
Nicaragua, 1960–1979: The Sandinista Leaders				
Carlos Fonseca Amador	1936– 1976	Property admin- istrator (Mother:cook)	Student leader; party leader	PSN Youth (Communists)
Tomás Borge Martínez/GPP	1930	Pharmicist (Mother: shop- keeper)	Student leader (law student)	PSN Youth
Silvio Mayorga	1936– 1967	?	Student leader	PSN Youth
Humberto Ortega Saavedra/TI	1946/7	Accountant, export-import business (Mother: cashier)	Jesuit University	
Daniel Ortega Saavedra/TI	1944/5	(same)	Jesuit University— law	
Henry Ruiz Hernández/GPP	?	"Modest fam- ily"	University education (incl. USSR)	
Bayardo Arce/GPP	1949	Journalist	Student leader; jour- nalist	
Luís Carrión Cruz/TP		Millionaire	University education (in U.S.)	
Jaime Wheelock Roman/TP	1946	Wealthy land- owners	Student; essayist, his- torian	
Carlos Nuñez Téllez/ TP	1951	Carpenter (Mother: sales- woman)		
Eduardo Contreras Escobar	1945– 1976		German university— economics, engineer- ing	
Ricardo Morales	?–1973		Sociology professor	

Name/Group/ "nom de guerre"	Year of Birth(– Death)	Occupation/Education of: Father	Occupation/Education of: Self	Party of Origin
Edén Pastora Gómez/ TI "Comandante Cero"	1937	Middle class	University—medicine	Sandino Revolutionary Front
Sergio Ramírez Mercado	1942	Musician; small coffee planter (Mother: teacher)	Professor; writer (U.S. educated)	
Ernesto Cardenal Martínez	1925/6	Old upper class	Jesuit priest; poet	
Fernando Cardenal Martínez	1935	Old upper class	Trappist priest; philosophy professor	
Miguel d'Escoto Brockman	1934/5	Actor; Somoza diplomat	Maryknoll priest	
Moisés Hassán Morales	1942	"Petty Bourgeois"	Physics Ph.D; university dean	
Plutarco Hernández Sancho	1944– 1978	Congressman (Costa Rica)	University student (incl. USSR)	
Nora Astorga	1949	Rich landowner (Grandfather: Somoza's cabinet)	University student (incl. U.S., Italy); lawyer	
Joaquín Cuadra Lacayo	c. 1952	Corporate lawyer	University student	
Dora María Téllez Agüero	1955	Government bureaucrat (Mother: professional of upper-class origin)		
Omar Cabezas	1950	Homemade soap maker (Mother: "simple" family)	University student	
Leticia Herrera		Worker, founder of Syndicalists (Mother: worker)	Soviet University	
Alvaro Baltadano		Wealthy coffee planter, businessman		
Mónica Baltadano	1954?	(same?)	University student	

Name/Group/ "nom de guerre"	Year of Birth(– Death)	Occupation/Education of:		Party of Origin
		Father	Self	
El Salvador, 1970– : *The FMLN and Its* *Components*				
Salvador Cayetano Carpio/FPL & FMLN Command/ "Marcial"	1920– 1983		Seminarian; Communist party school-Moscow; Bakers' union leader; PCS secretary general	PCS (Communists)
Joaquín Villalobos/ ERP & FMLN Command/ "René Cruz"	1951		University—economics	
Rafael Arce Zablah/ ERP	c. 1950– 1975	Army colonel	Student leader	
Eduardo Sancho Castaneda/FARN & FMLN command/ "Fermán Cienfuegos"	1947		University—medicine, sociology; "dapper businessman"	PCS
Ernesto Jovel Funes/ FARN	1956– 1980		Lawyer; labor organizer	
Mélida Anaya Montes/ FPL & FMLN command/"Ana María"	1925– 1983	"Simple working family"	Ph.D.; professor; schoolteacher; union leader	PCS
Jorge Shafi(c)k Handal [varies]/PCS	1930	Wealthy Palestinian immigrants	University—law; PCS general secretary	PCS
Facundo Guardado/ FPL?	1954	Peasant?	Peasant fieldworker	
Fabio Castillo Figueroa/PRTC			University student leader; Ph.D.; government junta member (1961–66)	PCS
Salvador Guerra Firma				
Roque Dalton García/ ERP/"Julio Delfos Marín"	1935– 1975	Upper middle class	University—law; poet, historian; PCS Central Committee	PCS
Rogelio Bazziglia/ FPL?				PCS
Roberto Roca/PRTC			Student leader	
Salvador Samayoa	c. 1950	Professionals (both parents)	Catholic University; professor; government minister	

Name/Group/ "nom de guerre"	Year of Birth(– Death)	Occupation/Education of: Father	Occupation/Education of: Self	Party of Origin
Román Mayorga Quiróz			University rector; government junta member (1979–80)	PDC
Guillermo Ungo		Educated middle class	Lawyer; government junta member (1979–80)	PDC
Ana Guadalupe Martínez/ERP			Writer(?)	
Leonel González			Schoolteacher	
Colombia, 1970– : The M-19[a]				
Jaime Bateman Cayón/ "Pablo"	1941–1983	"Old money"	Architecture student	PCC (Communists)/ANAPO
Carlos Toledo de la Plata	1932	"Certain wealth"	Surgeon; journalist; congressman	ANAPO
Iván Marino Ospina Morón		"24 Families"? (mother)		
Luis Francisco Otero Cifuentes				
Rosemberg Pabón	c. 1948	Peasants	Professor	ANAPO?
Carmenza Cardono Londono	c. 1955		Doctor	
Rafael Artega		"Some resources"		
Carlos Duplat Sanjuan			Television actor	
Guatemala, 1970– : The URNG and Its Components				
Pablo Monsanto/FAR	1946			FAR-1960s
Rolando Morán/EGP				PGT (Communists)/FAR-1960s
Rodrigo Asturias/ ORPA/"Gaspar Ilom"	1940	Writer and Nobel Laureate	University	FAR-1960s
Sebastian Aguilar/ ORPA				

Name/Group/ "nom de guerre"	Year of Birth(– Death)	Occupation/Education of: Father	Occupation/Education of: Self	Party of Origin
Peru, 1979– : Sendero Luminoso				
Abimael Guzmán Reynoso	1934	Middle class	University; Ph.D; professor	PCC (Communists); *Bandera Roja* (BR)
Julio César Mezzich Eyzaguirre			University—medicine; Peasant organizer	(same?)
Laura Zambrano Padilla/"Meche"	1944		Schoolteacher	
Maximiliano Durán Araujo			Professor	PCC?/BR? leader
Luis Kawata Makabe			Professor	PCC?/BR?
Edith Lagos	1962– 1982		University Student	
Luis Medina	1954			
Osmán Morote				
Julio Casanova				

Sources: Sources are widely scattered and information especially fragmentary on Guatemala and Peru. For concentrations of information, see as follows for each nation. NICARAGUA: Pilar Arias, *Nicaragua: Revolución*, pp. 215–21; Shirley Christian, *Nicaragua: Revolution in the Family*, passim; Diederich, *Somoza and the Legacy of U.S. Involvement in Central America*, passim. EL SALVADOR: *Latin America Weekly Report* (26 October 1984), p. 6; James LeMoyne, "The Guerrilla Network," *New York Times Magazine*, 6 April 1986, 14–20 + ; Armstrong and Shenk, *El Salvador*, pp. 131–32; *Punto Crítico* (Mexico City) 132 (May 1983): 31; Shirley Christian, "Rebel Factions," in Falcoff and Royal, *Crisis and Opportunity*, pp. 233–45; Michael Radu, "The Structure of the Salvadoran Left," *Orbis* 28 (Winter 1985): 673–84; Zaid, "Enemy Colleagues," 13–40; Mario Menéndez Rodríguez, *Voices from El Salvador* (San Francisco, Calif.: Solidarity, 1983). COLOMBIA: Berardo, *Guerrilhas e Guerrilheiros*, p. 148; "El M-19 elige a sus dirigentes," *Proceso* (Mexico City) 436 (11 March 1985): 40–44; *Latin America Weekly Report*, (3 October 1980), p. 11 and (12 August 1983), pp. 9–11; *Latin America Political Report* (26 January 1979), p. 27. GUATEMALA: *Latin America Weekly Report* (16 March 1984), pp. 2–3; Richard Gillespie, "Anatomy of the Guatemalan Guerrilla," *Communist Affairs: Documents and Analysis* 2–4 (October 1983): 490–96. PERU: *[Latin America] Weekly Report* (10 August 1984), p. 6; Thomas G. Sanders, "Peru between Democracy and the Sendero Luminoso," *Universities Field Staff International Reports* (1984, no. 21); Palmer, "Rebellion in Rural Peru," 127–46.

Note: GPP = Prolonged Popular War; TI = *Terceristas*; TP = Proletarian Tendency

[a] See appendix A for leaders of other movements.

Notes

Chapter 1
Introduction

1. Walter Laqueur, *Guerrilla: A Historical and Critical Study* (Boston: Little, Brown, and Co., 1976), pp. 4–30.

2. Bibliographies of major works appear in Laqueur, *Guerrilla* and, for more militarily oriented works, in Colonel Virgil Ney, "Guerrilla Warfare: Annotated Bibliography," *Military Review* 41 (November 1961): 97–112, and "Guerrilla Warfare," *Military Review* 42 (May 1962): 73–82.

3. Robert Sansom, *The Economics of Insurgency in the Mekong Delta of Vietnam* (Cambridge, Mass.: M.I.T. Press, 1970); Eric R. Wolf, *Peasant Wars of the Twentieth Century* (New York: Harper and Row, 1969), chap. 4; Jeffery M. Paige, *Agrarian Revolution: Social Movements and Export Agriculture in the Underdeveloped World* (New York: The Free Press, 1975), chap. 5; James C. Scott, *The Moral Economy of the Peasant: Rebellion and Subsistence in Southeast Asia* (New Haven, Conn.: Yale University Press, 1976); and Samuel L. Popkin, *The Rational Peasant: The Political Economy of Rural Society in Vietnam* (Berkeley: University of California Press, 1979), esp. chap. 6.

4. While there are many, many country studies, and many general works giving narrative accounts of the events in several different nations, works devoted to explanation and analysis are still few and far between. Two good ones: Che Guevara, *Guerrilla Warfare*, edited with an introduction by Brian Loveman and Thomas M. Davies, Jr. (Lincoln: University of Nebraska Press, 1985), where the editors "test" Guevara's implicit theories against a number of case studies; and Robert G. Williams, *Export Agriculture and the Crisis in Central America* (Chapel Hill: University of North Carolina Press, 1986). While the latter work is not about guerrilla movements per se, it contains a systematically repeated theoretical analysis explaining peasant support for guerrilla movements in Guatemala, Nicaragua, and El Salvador. There exist a number of narrative articles on guerrillas and/or revolution in individual countries, along with a few paired comparisons; a good rule of thumb is that the Marxist analyses generally address the more interesting sociological issues, while not necessarily giving the correct answers.

5. Among the most solid and important works collecting a series of case studies, inevitably divided into country chapters rather than theoretical divisions, are the following: Fritz René Allemann, *Macht und Ohnmacht der Guerilla* (Munich: R. Piper, 1974); João Batista Berardo, *Guerrilhas e guerrilheiros no drama da América Latina* (São Paulo: Edições Populares, 1981); Richard Gott, *Rural Guerrillas in Latin America* (Harmondsworth, Eng.: Penguin, 1973), which is simply a reissue of his work, *Guerrilla Movements in Latin America* (London: Nelson and Sons, 1970); Robert F. Lamberg, *Die castristiche Guerilla in Lateinamerika: Theorie und Praxis eines revolutionären Modells* (Hannover, Germany: Verlag für Literatur und Zeitge-

schehen, 1971); Jean Lartéguy, *The Guerrillas* (New York: The World Press, 1970); Luis Mercier Vega, *Guerrillas in Latin America: The Technique of the Counter-State* (New York: Praeger, 1969); and the edition of Guevara, *Guerrilla Warfare*, edited and with case studies by Loveman and Davies. Other shorter or less important "comparative" surveys are cited below and listed in the final bibliography.

6. Seymour Martin Lipset, *Revolution and Counterrevolution: Change and Persistence in Social Structures*, rev. and updated ed. (Garden City, N.Y.: Anchor/Doubleday, 1970), chap. 2; Susan Eckstein, "The Impact of Revolution on Social Welfare in Latin America," *Theory and Society* 11 (1982): 43–94; Theda Skocpol, "Old Regime Legacies and Communist Revolutions in Russia and China," *Social Forces* 55, no. 2 (December 1976): 284–315. Both the Eckstein and Skocpol pieces, the first in abridged form, perhaps the second as well, appear in Jack Goldstone, ed., *Revolutions: Theoretical, Comparative, and Historical Studies* (San Diego, Calif.: Harcourt Brace Jovanovich, 1986), pp. 280–307 and 218–38, respectively.

7. Wolf, *Peasant Wars*; Paige, *Agrarian Revolution*; Tilly, *From Mobilization to Revolution* (Reading, Mass.: Addison-Wesley, 1978).

8. Theda Skocpol, *States and Social Revolutions: A Comparative Analysis of France, Russia, and China* (Cambridge: Cambridge University Press, 1979).

9. Skocpol, *States and Social Revolutions*, pp. 292–93.

10. Walter L. Goldfrank, "World System, State Structure, and the Onset of the Mexican Revolution," *Politics and Society* 5 (1975): 417–39; for more attention to rural variations, see his "Inequality and Revolution in Mexico," *Social and Economic Studies* 25, no. 4 (December 1976): 397–410; his clearest statement is perhaps "Theories of Revolution and Revolution without Theory: The Case of Mexico," *Theory and Society* 7 (1979): 135–65; an abridged version appears as "The Mexican Revolution," in Goldstone, *Revolutions*, pp. 104–17.

11. Theda Skocpol, "What Makes Peasants Revolutionary?" *Comparative Politics* 14 (April 1982): 361–67; see also Jeff Goodwin and Theda Skocpol, "Explaining Revolutions in the Contemporary Third World," *Politics and Society* 17, no. 4 (December 1989): 489–509.

12. This is the major thesis of Robert H. Dix, "Why Revolutions Succeed and Fail," *Polity* 16, no. 3 (Spring 1984): 423–26, where he argues that the nature of the Cuban and Nicaraguan regimes virtually generated the negative coalitions that overthrew them.

13. Dix, "Why Revolutions Succeed and Fail," esp. 438.

14. Alain Rouquié, *The Military and the State in Latin America*, trans. Paul E. Sigmund (Berkeley: University of California Press, 1987), chap. 6; my main previous references to mafiacracy appear in unpublished conference papers, now revised as chapter 7 of Timothy P. Wickham-Crowley, *Exploring Revolution* (Armonk, N.Y.: M. E. Sharpe, 1991); see Guevara, *Guerrilla Warfare*, for commentary and case studies by Loveman and Davies.

15. Skocpol, *States and Social Revolutions*.

16. Arthur Stinchcombe has noted this for Skocpol's analysis of the geographic distribution of peasant revolts in France during the revolution; cf. Arthur L. Stinchcombe, *Economic Sociology* (New York: Academic Press, 1983), pp. 12–14. Skocpol is rather more attentive to such regionalisms in her analysis of revolts in the Russian case, with her focus on the "Black Earth" regions where insurrection was concen-

trated. For evidence that regional differences were central to peasant support for the Chinese Red Army, and furthermore that support declined in some regions while growing in others at different stages of the revolutionary war, see Roy Hofheinz, Jr., "The Ecology of Chinese Communist Success: Rural Influence Patterns, 1923–1945," in *Chinese Communist Politics in Action*, ed. A. Doak Barnett (Seattle: University of Washington Press, 1969), pp. 3–77, esp. p. 33.

17. See especially Goldfrank, "World-System" and "The Mexican Revolution."

18. Theda Skocpol and Margaret Somers, "The Uses of Comparative History in Macrosocial Inquiry," *Comparative Studies in Society and History* 22, no. 2 (April 1980): 174–97.

19. Skocpol and Somers, "The Uses of Comparative History," 191–96.

20. (New York: The Free Press, 1969).

21. (New York: Vintage, 1981 [1957]).

22. Williams, *Export Agriculture*, pp. 63–66, 129–52.

23. Here the reader must be referred to a wonderful gem of a work: David Hackett Fischer, *Historians' Fallacies: Toward a Logic of Historical Thought* (New York: Harper and Row, 1970). My "historians' fallacy" is not the same that Fischer discusses on pp. 209–13.

24. James Dunkerley, *Power in the Isthmus: A Political History of Modern Central America* (London: Verso, 1988), p. 338.

25. Something like this thesis appears, hidden mostly behind the narrative form, but sometimes out in the open, in Gott, *Rural Guerrillas in Latin America* and more clearly in James Petras, "Revolution and Guerrilla Movements in Latin America: Venezuela, Colombia, Guatemala, and Peru," in *Latin America: Reform or Revolution?*, ed. James Petras and Maurice Zeitlin (Greenwich, Conn.: Fawcett, 1968): 329–69. This theme is clearer still in Michael T. Klare and Nancy Stein, *Armas y poder in América Latina* (México, D.F.: Serie Popular Era, 1978).

26. The clearest list of failings is Robert F. Lamberg, "Consideraciones concluyentes en torno a las guerrillas castristas en Latinoamérica," *Aportes* 25 (July 1972): 107–18; various comments about failings also pepper Lartéguy, *The Guerrillas*.

27. Lamberg, *Die castristiche Guerilla*; Allemann, *Macht und Ohnmacht*, pp. 421–39; and both Lartéguy, *The Guerrillas*, and Mercier, *Guerrillas in Latin America*, both passim.

28. Skocpol and Somers, "Uses of Comparative History," 184–85.

29. *Past and Present* 70 (February 1976): 30–75.

30. Those "methods" come from the writings of John Stuart Mill; cf. Skocpol and Somers, "The Uses of Comparative History," 183–85.

31. Skocpol and Somers, "The Uses of Comparative History," 181–87.

32. The authors place Charles Tilly's *The Rebellious Century* between the parallel and the macro-causal poles and Perry Anderson's *Lineages of the Absolutist State* between the parallel and contrast-oriented poles.

CHAPTER 2
WHO ARE THE GUERRILLAS?

1. Robert K. Merton, "Three Fragments from a Sociologist's Notebooks" *Annual Review of Sociology* 13 (1987): 2–6.

2. *Daily Journal* (Caracas), 15 November 1962; Angela Zago, *Aquí no ha pasado nada* (Caracas: El Sobre, 1972), p. 56; Lartéguy, *The Guerrillas*, p. 61; Donn Munson, *Zacapa* (Canoga, Calif.: Challenge, 1967), p. 154; *La Prensa* (Lima), 15 October 1965, 8; Alphonse Max, *Guerrillas in Latin America* (The Hague: Interdoc, 1971), p. 39.

3. Sara Beatriz Guardia, *Proceso a campesinos de la Guerrilla "Túpac Amaru"* (Lima: Impresiones y Publicidad, 1972): 47–63. For an estimate of a Guatemalan peasant majority, see Munson, *Zacapa*, p. 154; for the 90 percent estimate for one unit, see Adolfo Gilly, "The Guerrilla Movement in Guatemala II," *Monthly Review* 17 (June 1965): 37. For Cuba, see Ché Guevara, "Guerra y población campesina," *Bohemia* 45 (10 November 1967): 4. For Venezuela, see Luigi Valsalice, *Guerriglia e Politica: L'esempio del Venezuela, 1962–1969* (Florence, Italy: Valmartina Editore, 1973), p. 218.

4. Joel S. Midgal, *Peasants, Politics, and Revolution* (Princeton, N.J.: Princeton University Press, 1974), pp. 242–43; E. J. Hobsbawm, *Bandits* (London: Trinity, 1969), pp. 24–29, and idem, *Primitive Rebels* (New York: W. W. Norton, 1965), p. 18; Charles A. Russell and Capt. Bowman H. Miller, "Profile of a Terrorist," *Military Review* 57 (August 1977): 23–24.

5. See the articles by various authors in SCAAN (Stanford Central America Action Network), eds., *Revolution in Central America* (Boulder, Colo.: Westview, 1983), pp. 379–434, esp. pp. 382, 407, 416–17.

6. Carlos Saíz Cidoncha, *Guerrillas en Cuba y otros países de Iberoamérica* (Madrid: Editora Nacional, 1974), p. 126; Hugh Thomas, *Cuba: The Pursuit of Freedom* (New York: Harper and Row, 1971), p. 1042; Valsalice, *Guerriglia e Politica*, pp. 237–58; *El Nacional* (Caracas), 9 November 1964; Régis Debray, *Strategy for Revolution*, ed. Robin Blackburn (London: Jonathan Cape, 1970), p. 90; *Daily Journal* (Caracas), 9 October 1963; Munson, *Zacapa*, p. 141.

7. *El Nacional* (Caracas), 15 November 1962; Jaime Arenas, *La guerrilla por dentro* (Bogotá: Tercer Mundo, 1970), p. 45; see pp. 166–67 for the case of "Mariela."

8. Jo Freeman, *The Politics of Women's Liberation* (New York: David McKay, 1975), pp. 56–62. In one case in Guatemala, the reporter notes that the only female present made breakfast; see Munson, *Zacapa*, pp. 144–45.

9. Nancy Reeves, "Women of the New Cuba," *Monthly Review* 12 (November 1960): 387 (quote), 392.

10. Valsalice, *Guerriglia e Politica*, p. 214 n. 19; Angela Zago, *Aquí no ha pasado nada* (Caracas: El Sobre, 1972), pp. 46–48, 53; Robert Rogers and Ted Yates, "The Undeclared War in Guatemala," *Saturday Evening Post* 239 (18 June 1966): 33.

11. Of this there is little doubt. An enormous body of research on sex differences in aggression is summarized by Eleanor E. Maccoby and Carol N. Jacklin, *The Psychology of Sex Differences* (Stanford, Calif.: Stanford University Press, 1974), chap. 7.

12. Alvin W. Gouldner, *The Future of Intellectuals and the Rise of the New Class* (New York: Continuum, 1979), pp. 53–57.

13. See, for example, Teodoro Petkoff, "Pre-Election Climate in Venezuela (An Interview with Comrade Teodoro Petkov [sic])," *World Marxist Review* (England) 11 (April 1968): 29.

14. See Skocpol, *States and Social Revolutions*, chap. 3, for a discussion of the conditions that allowed such peasant uprisings during the French and Russian revolutions; see also my discussion of such issues in *Exploring Revolution*, chap. 5 and 6.

15. See chapter 3. In Chile and Uruguay in the year 1964, both relatively advanced countries, perhaps only 0.8 percent (workers and peasants) and 4 percent, respectively, of the students were from the working class; cf. Roque Dalton, "Student Youth and the Latin American Revolution" *World Marxist Review* (England) 9 (March 1966): 30, 33. Very low working-class (not to mention peasant) enrollments, if not necessarily Dalton's (undocumented) minuscule numbers, are confirmed in various contributions to Aldo Solari, ed., *Estudiantes y política en América Latina* (Caracas: Monte Avila, 1968), pp. 33–40, 121–31, 164, and 246, providing data or estimates from various universities in the region.

16. Dalton, "Student Youth," 33.

17. Luis J. González and Gustavo A. Sánchez Salazar, *The Great Rebel: Che Guevara in Bolivia* (New York: Grove Press, 1969): 234–43, plus additional information from Daniel James's edition of Ché Guevara's Bolivian Diaries, *The Complete Bolivian Diaries of Che Guevara and Other Captured Documents* (New York: Stein and Day, 1968).

18. For example, Héctor Béjar locates the guerrilla leadership in the "impoverished and powerless sectors of the petty-bourgeoisie." See his *Peru 1965* (New York: Monthly Review, 1968): 51–52.

19. François Maspero, ed., *Avec Douglas Bravo dans les maquis vénézuéliens* (Paris: François Maspero, 1968), p. 44; James Petras, "Revolution and Guerrilla Movements in Latin America: Venezuela, Colombia, Guatemala, and Peru," in Petras and Maurice Zeitlin, eds., *Latin America: Reform or Revolution?* (Greenwich, Conn.: Fawcett, 1968), p. 354.

20. Béjar, *Peru 1965*, pp. 51–52; General Armando Artola Azcarate, *¡Subversión!* (Lima: Editorial Jurídica, 1976), p. 93.

21. Thomas, *Cuba*, pp. 24–25, 1546–47; Theodore Draper, *Castro's Revolution: Myths and Realities* (New York: Praeger, 1962), p. 11.

22. For example, Petras, "Revolution and Guerrilla Movements," p. 345, writes of 1965 Peru that "as the mass peasant movement could not defend itself and was an easy target, guerrilla forms of struggle emerged." In writing that passage, Petras conflates Blanco's mass peasant movement with the MIR guerrillas a year or two later; the MIR and ELN focos most certainly did not "emerge" from the peasantry, or from the peasants' experience, with the possible exception of Junín.

23. In Russian, *narod* means people. In fact, the *narodniki* endorsed an even more radical project than their erstwhile comrades, who had also sought to mobilize the Russian peasantry, for they sought to live in the villages and learn *from* the peasants, rather than convert them to revolutionary ways. For the differences, see Richard Pipes, *Russia under the Old Regime* (New York: Charles Scribner's Sons, 1974), pp. 273–74.

24. Concerning the mechanisms involved in such recruitment see Timothy P. Wickham-Crowley, "The Rise (and Sometimes Fall) of Guerrilla Governments in Latin America," *Sociological Forum* 2, no. 3 (Summer 1987): 473–99; reprinted as chapter 2 of my *Exploring Revolution*.

25. The various percentage estimates are from Günter Maschke, *Kritik des Guerillero* (Frankfurt: S. Fischer, 1973), pp. 79–80 (low); Thomas, *Cuba*, p. 1043 (medium); and Robin Blackburn, "Prologue to the Cuban Revolution," *New Left Review* 2 (October 1963): 77 (high). The most careful estimates of troop strengths at various points in time are in Neill Macaulay, "The Cuban Rebel Army: A Numerical Survey," *Hispanic American Historical Review* 58, no. 2 (May 1978): esp. 288–89. Castro once claimed—hyperbolically but perhaps still roughly indicative of the political climate in Oriente Province—that all the youth of Santiago would flock to join him if he could supply them with weapons; see Daniel M. Friedenberg, "Notes on the Cuban Revolution," *New Republic* 138 (17 February 1958): 15.

26. *Daily Journal*, 13 February 1963; Valsalice, *Guerriglia e Politica*, p. 216, Maspero, *Avec Douglas Bravo*, p. 54; Norman Gall, "Teodoro Petkoff: The Crisis of the Professional Revolutionary—Part 1: Years of Insurrection," *American Universities Field Staff Reports—East Coast South America Series* 16, no. 1 (January 1972): 12; Jean-Claude Guénier, "Luttes au Vénézuela," *Partisans* (Paris) 37 (April–June 1967): 84.

27. Walter Schump, *Las guerrillas en América Latina: El principio y el fin* (Buenos Aires: Punto Crítico, 1971), p. 51; Adolfo Gilly, "Guerrilla Movement in Guatemala II," 37; Munson, *Zacapa*, p. 154; Lartéguy, *The Guerrillas*, p. 107. For demurrals on such high estimates, see Lamberg, *Die castristiche Guerilla*, pp. 55–56, and Saíz, *Guerrillas*, p. 185.

28. Boris Goldenberg, "Kommunismus in Lateinamerika: Die Kommunistiche Partei Kolumbiens," *Der Ostblock und die Entwicklungsländer* (Vierteljahresberichte—Forschungsinstitut der Friedrich-Ebert-Stiftung) 21 (September 1965): 246–47. Henceforth VJB-FFES. Lartéguy, *The Guerrillas*, p. 135; Allemann, *Macht und Ohnmacht der Guerilla*, pp. 57–58.

29. For the first fifteen named individuals, see Mario Ménendez Rodríguez, "Colombia: ¡Al ataque!" *Sucesos* (Mexico City) 1777 (24 June 1967): 12–68; for the last nine, see Arenas, *La guerrilla por dentro*. See also Lartéguy, *The Guerrillas*, pp. 94, 136; Lamberg, *Die castristiche Guerilla*, p. 94; Allemann, *Macht und Ohnmacht*, pp. 258, 261.

30. See *La Prensa* (Lima), 11 July 1965, for the minister's comment.

31. On the ELN, see Arenas, *La guerrilla por dentro*. On Cuba, see Ramón L. Bonachea and Marta San Martín, *The Cuban Insurrection, 1952–1959* (New Brunswick, N.J.: Transaction Books, 1974), p. 103. On Camilo Sánchez, see Camilo Castaño, "Avec les guérillas du Guatemala," *Partisans* (Paris) 38 (July–September 1967): 150.

32. Laqueur, *Guerrilla*, p. 54; Lartéguy, *The Guerrillas*, p. 226; Lamberg, *Die castristriche Guerilla*, p. 138; Norman Gall, "Revolution without Revolutionaries," *The Nation* 203 (22 August 1966): 145; Gott, *Rural Guerrillas in Latin America*, pp. 293–96; Allemann, *Macht und Ohnmacht*, pp. 241–42; Jaime López, *10 años de guerrillas en México, 1964–1974* (Mexico City: Editorial Posada, 1974).

33. González and Sánchez, *The Great Rebel*, pp. 234–43; Artola, *¡Subversión!*, p. 77. For "Negro Antonio," see appendix A for Venezuela.

34. For 1960s Guatemala, see Allemann, *Macht und Ohnmacht*, p. 476 n.47 and Gall, "Revolution without Revolutionaries," 145.

CHAPTER 3
THE SOCIAL AND POLITICAL ORIGINS OF THE GUERRILLA MOVEMENTS

1. For typical examples of this mode of thought, see Rogger Mercado, *Las guerrillas del Peru* (Lima: Fondo de Cultura Popular, 1967), p. 171; Petras, "Revolution and Guerrilla Movements," p. 345; and Teodoro Petkoff, "Pre-Election Climate," 29.

2. For the suggestion that all studies of social movements should pay attention to the questions of "when," "where," and among which social groups or locations movements occur, see Robin M. Williams, Jr., "Relative Deprivation versus Power Struggle? 'Tension' and 'Structural' Explanations of Collective Conflict," *Cornell Journal of Social Relations* 11 (Spring 1976): 31–38.

3. Debray, *Strategy for Revolution*, p. 93; Béjar, *Peru 1965*, pp. 60–61; Maspero, *Avec Douglas Bravo*; *El Nacional*, 25 May 1964; Alfredo Guerra Borges, "The Experience of Guatemala: Some Problems of the Revolutionary Struggle Today," *World Marxist Review* (England) 7 (June 1964): 11; *La Prensa*, 19 June 1965, p. 1.

4. Arenas, *La guerrilla por dentro*, p. 14; Gott, *Rural Guerrillas*, pp. 393–94.

5. Allemann, *Macht und Ohnmacht*, p. 133, discusses the kidnapping. For a sampling of guerrilla manifestoes and ideologies, the best sources are Gott, *Rural Guerrillas*, passim, and Mercier, *Guerrillas in Latin America*, chap. 1.

6. One Chilean noted trenchantly: "We were for Fidel until we heard the balalaika." On the shift from pure admiration of the Cuban revolution after 1960–61, see Boris Goldenberg, *The Cuban Revolution and Latin America* (New York: Frederick A. Praeger, 1965): 319–20.

7. The following discussion draws heavily upon Charles Tilly, *From Mobilization to Revolution* (Reading, Mass.: Addison-Wesley, 1978), pp. 151–58, 224–25; Moore, *Injustice*, pp. 100–1, 125, 458–62; and Ralph Turner and Lewis M. Killian, *Collective Behavior* (Englewood Cliffs, NJ: Prentice-Hall, 1957), pp. 123–24, 523.

8. Sartre grasps this sense of inevitability by terming any status quo the "practico-inert."

9. Lamberg, *Die castristiche Guerilla*, pp. 15–16; for the original essay see 'Ché' Guevara, "Guerra de Guerrillas: Un Método" *Cuba Socialista* (September 1963).

10. The reasons for this are discussed below.

11. In order, these terms are from Turner and Killian, *Collective Behavior*, p. 120; Neil J. Smelser, *Theory of Collective Behavior* (New York: Free Press, 1962), pp. 79–130; and George S. Pettee, *The Process of Revolution* (New York: Harper, 1938), p. 78.

12. Pettee, *Process of Revolution*, p. 78; Robert K. Merton, *Social Theory and Social Structure*, 3d ed. (New York: Free Press, 1968), pp. 284–85. Contrast Ché Guevara, for whom the decision to embrace Marxism was not a conversion, but rather like "the abstraction of a proof." See John Womack, Jr. " 'El Che' Guevara," *New York Review of Books* 16 (28 January 1971): 8.

13. Valsalice, *Guerriglia e Politica*, p. 3; Gall, "Teodoro Petkoff I," 16; Norman Gall, "Teodoro Petkoff: The Crisis of the Professional Revolutionary—Part II: A New Party," *American Universities Field Staff Reports—East Coast South America Series* 17, no. 9 (August 1973): 5.

14. Alfredo Peña, *Conversaciones con Américo Martín* (Caracas: Editorial At-

eneo, 1978), p. 82. On p. 5, Martín refers to his guerrilla years as a crazy thing to have done.

15. Karl Mannheim, *Ideology and Utopia* (New York: Harcourt, Brace and Co., 1936), pp. 136–39, and also his "The Problem of Generations," in *Essays in the Sociology of Knowledge*, ed. Paul Kecskemeti (London: Routledge and Kegan Paul, 1952), pp. 315, 318.

16. See the review essay by Lewis Feuer, "University Marxism," *Problems of Communism* 27, no. 4 (July–August 1978): 65–72.

17. Again see Solari, *Estudiantes y política*, pp. 33–40, 124; Arthur Liebman, Kenneth N. Walker, and Myron Glazer, *Latin American University Students: A Six Nation Study* (Cambridge, Mass.: Harvard, 1972), p. 41; Dalton, "Student Youth," 30. Working-class enrollment figures for European universities around 1960 are: France, 7 percent; Italy, 11 percent; and Spain, 5 percent. Carlos Rangel Guevara, *The Latin Americans* (New York and London: Harcourt Brace Jovanovich, 1977), p. 213. In a vein similar to Rangel, Lartéguy noted that there were no peasants where Camilo Torres served as professor of sociology; see his *The Guerrillas*, p. 129.

18. Mannheim, *Ideology and Utopia*, pp. 138–39; Dalton, "Student Youth," 30.

19. Gláucio Ary Dillon Soares and Loreto Hoecker, "El mundo de la ideología: La función de las ideas y la legitimidad de la política estudiantil," in Solari, *Estudiantes y política*, pp. 338–41. Goffman's concept and discussion appear in his essay "On the Characteristics of Total Institutions," in *Asylums* (Garden City, N.Y.: Anchor, 1961), pp. 1–124.

20. Barrington Moore, Jr., *Injustice: The Social Bases of Obedience and Revolt* (White Plains, N.Y.: M.E. Sharpe, 1978), p. 482.

21. Mario Góngora, "Origin and Philosophy of the Spanish American University," in *The Latin American University*, ed. Joseph Maier and Richard W. Weatherhead (Albuquerque: University of New Mexico Press, 1979), pp. 17–64.

22. Valsalice, *Guerriglia e Politica*, p. 213; Solari, *Estudiantes y política*, pp. 82, 264–67; *La Prensa*, 11 July 1965, 1; *New York Times*, 24 October 1962.

23. For example, during the ouster of dictators, as in 1933 Cuba and in 1957–58 Venezuela; cf. Daniel Levine, *Conflict and Political Change in Venezuela* (Princeton, N.J.: Princeton University Press, 1973), p. 151.

24. Solari, *Estudiantes y política*, pp. 98–99; Liebman et al., *Latin American University Students*, p. 51.

25. Levine, *Conflict and Political Change*, pp. 171–74; Manuel Castillo, "Las guerrillas en el Peru," *Estudios* (Buenos Aires) 581 (April 1967): 167.

26. Orlando Albornoz, *Ideología y política en la universidad Latino-Americana* (Caracas: Instituto Societas, 1972), p. 136; Liebman et al., *Latin American University Students*, p. 125.

27. Solari, *Estudiantes y política*, p. 62; Liebman et al., *Latin American University Students*, pp. 106–09, 125; Valsalice, *Guerriglia e Politica*, p. 212. Concerning the image as savior of society, one scholar described de la Puente's leanings as "messiah-like"; cf. Lamberg, *Die castristiche Guerilla*, p. 113; Mannheim, "The Problem of Generations," p. 318.

28. Allemann, *Macht und Ohnmacht*, p. 416; Turner and Killian, *Collective Behavior*, p. 212. See as well the section on "Youth" below.

29. Pettee, *Process of Revolution*, pp. 68–75; Levine, *Conflict and Political Change*, pp. 161–62, 207.

30. Bonachea and San Martín, *The Cuban Insurrection*, pp. 175–79; Castillo, "Las guerrillas en el Peru," 165–66; for other Peruvian examples see Peru, Ministerio de Guerra, *Las guerrillas en el Peru y su represión* (Lima: Ministerio de Guerra, 1966), pp. 39–40, 44. On Colombia, see Arenas, *La guerrilla por dentro*, pp. 23–39.

31. *Daily Journal*, 12 April 1962; Mercier, *Guerrillas in Latin America*, p. 68 (quote); Venezuela, Oficina Central de Información, *Six Years of Aggression* (Caracas: Imprenta Nacional, 1967[?]), pp. 66–68.

32. Lamberg, *Die castristiche Guerilla*. See the organizational charts following each country study.

33. Bonachea and San Martín, *The Cuban Insurrection*, pp. 60, 39–40; Thomas, *Cuba*, pp. 801–3, 824–25, 867–68; Maschke, *Kritik des Guerillero*, p. 73.

34. Petras, "Revolution and Guerrilla Movements," p. 356 (quote); Robert F. Lamberg, "Kommunismus und Castrismus am Scheideweg: Stationen des Differenzierungprozesses bei den Linksradikalen Lateinamerikas (1966–1967)," *VJB-FFES* 20 (June 1965): 380. Such half-truths and biased fact selection unfortunately mar Petras's otherwise interesting article. Despite a number of intriguing sociological analyses, it is not a very reliable source of information on the guerrillas, especially due to his failure to document his narrative. The limitations may derive, however, from the paucity of sources available when he wrote the piece. On the MIR majority, see Lamberg, *Die castristiche Guerilla*, p. 74, and compare Peña, *Américo Martín*, p. 42. On the remaining points, see Robert A. Alexander, *The Communist Party of Venezuela* (Stanford, Calif.: Hoover Institution Press, 1969), pp. 138, 70–74; *Newsweek*, 12 August 1963, 40; *Daily Journal*, 7 June 1962 and 3 November 1965; Jesus Faría, "After the Government Crisis in Venezuela," *World Marxist Review* (England) 9 (June 1966): 28; Gall, "Teodoro Petkoff II," 5.

35. On the 1960 revolt, see [Marco Antonio Yon Sosa], "Breves apuntes históricos del Movimiento Revolucionario 13 de Noviembre (I)," in *Movimientos revolucionarios de América Latina (I): Documentación propia*, 2nd ed., edited by Información Documental de América Latina (henceforth INDAL) (Caracas: INDAL, 1972), pp. 104–7; although not identified here, Yon Sosa earlier had published this article in Cuba. For other information, see Lamberg, *Die castristiche Guerilla*, pp. 52–63, 67, and/or Gott, *Rural Guerrillas*, pp. 138–41. When the FAR was breaking with the PGT in 1968, César Montes noted acerbically that the PGT had supplied the ideas and the FAR the dead.

36. For the Arenas quote, see Manuel Arango Z., *FARC: Veinte años—De Marquetalia a la Uribe* (Bogotá: Aurora, 1984), p. 30; for the guerrilla diary, see "Colombia en las montañas," *Bohemia* (Havana), 4 February 1967, 4–11 +, quote on p. 10.

37. On the rivalries, see Allemann, *Macht und Ohnmacht*, p. 272; *New York Times*, 27 May 1984, 11.

38. Gott, *Rural Guerrillas*, pp. 293–96, 308; Allemann, *Macht und Ohnmacht*, pp. 258–59; Arenas, *La guerrilla por dentro*, pp. 17–20.

39. Lamberg, *Die castristiche Guerilla*, pp. 93, 102; Arenas, *La guerrilla por dentro*, p. 161.

40. APRA stands for Alianza Popular Revolucionaria Americana—American Pop-

ular Revolutionary Alliance; Peña, *Américo Martín*, p. 34, demonstrates that influence was reciprocal between the two movements.

41. Allemann, *Macht und Ohnmacht*, p. 201; Béjar, *Peru 1965*, pp. 48, 69–73; Artola, *¡Subversión!*, p. 20; Lamberg, *Die castristiche Guerilla*, p. 108. Leon G. Campbell, "The Historiography of the Peruvian Guerrilla Movement," *Latin American Research Review* 8 (Spring 1973): 56–57. A number of these authors noted that the bitter rivalry between APRA and the Communists was partially carried over to their political offspring as well, creating a barrier to MIR-ELN cooperation that was never effectively breached.

42. Edgar Millares Reyes, *Las guerrillas: Teoría y práctica* (Sucre, Bolivia: Imprenta Universitaria, 1968), p. 70; González and Sánchez, *The Great Rebel*, p. 59. Similarly, the Argentine guerrilla groups were largely drawn from left-wing *peronistas*; cf. Lamberg, *Die castristiche Guerilla*, p. 139, and Allemann, *Macht und Ohnmacht*, p. 408.

43. Alan Riding, "Guatemala: State of Siege" *New York Times Magazine* (24 August 1980): 29; *New York Times*, 27 May 1984, p. 11; Allemann, *Macht und Ohnmacht*, p. 157 (quote).

44. Theda Skocpol, "France, Russia, and China: A Structural Analysis of Social Revolutions," *Comparative Studies in Society and History* 18 (April 1976): 175–210. The idea of an "intrinsic elite" is from Pettee, *Process of Revolution*, pp. 10–13. See also Lamberg, *Die castristiche Guerilla*, p. 36.

45. Jean Piaget, "The Moral Development of the Child," in *Six Psychological Studies* (New York: Random House, 1967), pp. 68–69.

46. Parallel to this argument, E. J. Hobsbawm found that rural bandits are also drawn from the young, unmarried, and uncommitted among the peasantry; cf. his *Bandits*, pp. 24–29.

47. Mannheim, "The Problem of Generations," pp. 292–300.

48. Piaget, "Moral Development," p. 68.

49. Solari, *Estudiantes y política*, p. 153.

50. Petras, "Revolution and Guerrilla Movements," p. 348.

51. See Anthony Oberschall, *Social Conflict and Social Movements* (Englewood Cliffs, N.J.: Prentice-Hall, 1973), p. 129, where he argues that mobilization is easier the more a collectivity is segmented (read: isolated) from the rest of society, and the more extensive are the intra-collectivity ties.

52. Joseph A. Kahl suggested the Cuban parallel to me in a private communication.

53. For the scope of the agrarian reform, and its effects in increasing agricultural production in the early to mid-1960s, see Venezuela, Oficina Central de Información, *La Reforma Agraria en Venezuela* (Caracas?, 1967?), esp. pp. 21–29. Political critiques of the accuracy of these data appeared in the early 1960s, followed later by similar conclusions drawn by scholars; a common theme is that many "reforms" only involved giving titles to squatters already in full possession of government-owned land (also a common pattern, one might add, in the history of the United States' frontier areas). Even giving a heavy discount to official data, however, the efforts were appreciable, especially considering that 70 percent of all Venezuelans lived in cities at the time. For school enrollments, see Levine, *Conflict and Political Change*, pp. 114–15 and Jorge I. Domínguez, *Cuba: Order and Revolution* (Cambridge,

Mass.: Belknap Press of Harvard, 1978), pp. 166–68. In the late fifties and early sixties, Cuba increased literacy from about 70 percent to about 96 percent of the adult populace by sending thousands of teachers to the countryside. Betancourt also sent teachers to the countryside, teaching one million persons to read in three years; cf. *El Nacional* (Caracas), 5 March 1962; *Daily Journal* (Caracas), 22 June 1965 and 23 May 1963. He did not send them on so massive a scale, but neither did he close down other schools in carrying out the literacy campaign, which reduced illiteracy from 56 percent to 26 percent by 1962; see *Time*, 28 December 1962, p. 19. By 1971, Venezuela's official illiteracy rate was 16 percent; see Inter-American Development Bank, *Socio-Economic Progress in Latin America—Annual Report 1971* (Washington, D.C.: IDB, 1971), p. 326.

54. The best analytical account of this period is Levine's *Conflict and Political Change in Venezuela*, on which I have relied heavily for this discussion and analysis.

55. E. J. Hobsbawm, "The Revolutionary Situation in Colombia," *World Today* 19 (June 1963): 248–58; Major General Gerardo Ayerbe Chaux, "La rebelión en Colombia," *Revista de las Fuerzas Armadas* (Colombia) 10 (November–December 1964): 253; for one reference to 70 percent abstention in the 1968 national elections, see *Latin America* (London), 22 March 1968.

56. See James C. Davies, "Toward a Theory of Revolution," *American Sociological Review* 27, no. 1 (February 1962): 5–19, for the original version of the theory.

57. Again see Oberschall, *Social Conflict and Social Movements*, p. 129.

58. For a good summary, see Robert F. Lamberg, "Kubas Einfluss auf Lateinamerika," *Der Ostblock und die Entwicklungsländer (VJB-FFES)* 20 (June 1965): 136–51.

CHAPTER 4
VARIABLES AND MODELS

1. Wolf, *Peasant Wars of the Twentieth Century*, and Paige, *Agrarian Revolution*, are among the most notable studies.

2. The most important example of the latter is the collectivization of agriculture, usually both bitterly and violently opposed by peasants wherever it is undertaken. This procedure is usually defended by the government with the transparent lie that the peasants themselves requested collectivization.

3. Tilly, *From Mobilization to Revolution*, pp. 70–72, 79–80, 95–97. Hofheinz, "Chinese Communist Success," suggests the following measures of guerrilla influence: security, social mobilization, and participation mobilization. He measures security by the length of time without defeat in a region; social mobilization by circulation of the guerrillas' newspaper and attendance at their school; and participation mobilization by the numbers joining the Communist party or Mao's army. He also suggests two measures of movement strength: estimated numbers and spatial dispersion of the movement; cf. pp. 21–22, 38–52. Gil Carl Alroy, *The Involvement of Peasants in Internal Wars* (Princeton, N.J.: Princeton University, Center for International Affairs, Woodrow Wilson School, 1966), pp. 23–25, also suggests criteria for distinguishing various degrees of peasant commitment to the struggle.

4. Nathan Leites and Charles Wolf, Jr., *Rebellion and Authority: An Analytic Essay on Insurgent Conflicts* (Chicago: Markham, 1970), pp. 41–42, 86–89.

5. For overall Latin American estimates, see Barry Lando, "Latin-American Guerrillas," *Atlantic Monthly* (December 1967): 26, and Lamberg, "Kommunismus und Castrismus," 387. For Bolivia, the best single summary is Mercier, *Guerrillas*, p. 35. For Colombia, see Lamberg, *Die castristiche Guerilla*, pp. 94–96, 99, 102; Allemann, *Macht und Ohnmacht*, pp. 256–57, 273–74; Mario Menéndez Rodríguez, "Colombia: ¡Ni un paso atrás! ¡Liberación o muerte! (Fabio Vásquez Castaño)," *Sucesos* (Mexico City) 1778 (1 July 1967): 50. For Cuba, by far the best source is again Macaulay, "The Cuban Rebel Army"; all other sources are markedly inferior. For Guatemala, see Allemann, *Macht und Ohnmacht*, pp. 171, 190; Gilly, "Guerrilla Movement II," 12–13; and Lamberg, *Die castristiche Guerilla*, pp. 55–56, 60, 64. Also see Lamberg's book, pp. 116–17, on Peru, and pp. 76, 79, 81 for Venezuela. Also for Venezuela, see *Time* (24 July 1964): 36; Antonio Zamora, *Memoria(s) de la guerrilla venezolana* (Caracas: Síntesis Dosmil, 1974), p. 132; Valsalice, *Guerriglia e Politica*, pp. 139–40, 193; Klaus Lindenberg, "Zur Krise der revolutionären Linken in Lateinamerika: Das Beispeil Venezuela," *Vierteljahresberichte—FFES* 33 (September 1968): 289; Benedict Cross (pseud.), "Marxism in Venezuela," *Problems of Communism* 22 (November–December 1973): 59, 68; and Gall, "Teodoro Petkoff I," 12.

6. Macaulay, "The Cuban Rebel Army," 289.

7. Private communication from Michael Smith; he has been studying Peru's Sendero Luminoso closely for some time now and notes that their level of supporter backing is even higher than this ten-to-one ratio.

8. The best source for these assertions is Guevara, *Complete Bolivian Diaries*, including the introduction by Daniel James.

9. On the Cuzco *foco*, see *La Prensa* (Lima), 1 October 1965, p. 6; Allemann, *Macht und Ohnmacht*, pp. 207–8, 429; Mercado, *Las guerrillas*, pp. 168–69; and Héctor Béjar, *Peru 1965*, pp. 86–87. For Ayacucho, also see Béjar, pp. 100–1, 105, 109–11, plus his "Bilan d'une guerilla au Pérou," *Partisans* (Paris) 37 (April–June, 1967): 97, and "Ne pas surestimer ses forces," *Partisans* 38 (July–September, 1967): 113. For Junín, see Gott, *Rural Guerrillas*, pp. 422–23 (Lobatón's quote), and Allemann, *Macht und Ohnmacht*, pp. 207–8, 429.

10. Allemann, *Macht und Ohnmacht*, p. 178; Gilly, "Guerrilla Movement II," 12–13.

11. *Look* (4 February 1958): 30; Lt. Colonel Harold R. Aaron, "Why Batista Lost," *Army* 15 (September 1965): 68.

12. Menéndez, "Colombia: ¡Ni un paso atrás!," 50.

13. Such reports appear almost exclusively in newspapers, and certainly not in the guerrillaphile sources of the period. See *New York Times*, 5 May 1962; Institute for the Comparative Study of Political Systems (ICOPS), *The Venezuelan Elections of December 1, 1963—Part I: An Analysis*, by John Martz (Washington, D.C.: ICOPS, 1964), p. 13; *Daily Journal* (Caracas), 10 March 1962, 6 May 1962, 11 May 1962, 29 August 1962, 27 January 1963, 13 February 1963; and *El Nacional* (Caracas), 14 October 1962 and 16 October 1962.

14. Allemann, *Macht und Ohnmacht*, p. 71.

15. James D. Cockcroft and Eduardo Vicente, "Venezuela and the FALN Since Leoni," *Monthly Review* 17 (November 1965): 36–37; Angel Raúl Guevara, *Los cachorros del Pentagono* (Caracas: Salvador de la Plaza, 1973), p. 94; Jacobo Arenas, *Diario de la resistencia de Marquetalia* (Bogotá?: Abejón Mono, 1972), p.

67; Artola, *¡Subversión!*, p. 66; Bonachea and San Martín, *The Cuban Insurrection*, p. 105; Valsalice, *Guerriglia e Politica*, pp. 126–27; *Daily Journal* (Caracas), 13 November 1964 and 20 December 1964; *El Nacional* (Caracas), 12 November 1964; Rogers and Yates, "Undeclared War," 32; Allemann, *Macht und Ohnmacht*, pp. 256–57.

16. The documentation of the terror itself and of peasant response thereto is substantial, and I cannot treat it adequately here, but see my "Terror and Guerrilla Warfare in Latin America, 1956–1970," *Comparative Studies in Society and History* 32, no. 2 (April 1990): 201–37; a slightly altered and expanded version appears in my *Exploring Revolution*, chap. 3. Other sources on terror: on Peru, see Béjar's discussion in *Peru 1965*; for Guatemala, see Castaño, "Avec les guérillas du Guatemala," 144. On the role of government terror in creating new guerrillas, see Friedenberg, "Notes on the Cuban Revolution," 15, and (Colonel) Ramón Barquín López, *Las luchas guerrilleras en Cuba*, 2 volumes (Madrid: Plaza Mayor, 1975), 1:319, both for Cuba; for Venezuela, see Zago, *Aquí no ha pasado nada*, pp. 173–74, and Debray, *Strategy for Revolution*, p. 103; for Colombia, see Arenas, *La guerrilla por dentro*, pp. 22–23, and Jaime Velásquez García, *Contrainsurgencia y guerra revolucionaria* (Bogotá: Tinta Roja, 1975), p. 118.

17. Leo Heiman, "Guerrilla Warfare: An Analysis," *Military Review* 43 (July 1963): 27.

18. Tilly, *From Mobilization to Revolution*, p. 114.

19. Thought experiments involve conditions contrary to fact, and as such cannot be resolved by empirical means. Yet they do suggest theoretically stimulating scenarios. One of Max Weber's most famous ventures along such lines was to consider the probable long-term effects on Western civilization had the Greeks lost to the Persians at the Battle of Marathon, and had the Persians subsequently followed said conquest with the usual cultural transformations they imposed upon their colonies. Weber argued that the whole path of Western civilization would have been sharply altered.

20. For examples of near-disasters for Castro's rebels, see Bonachea and San Martín, *The Cuban Insurrection*, pp. 251–60, 266–78.

21. Occam's razor places a value on simplicity, especially when choosing between competing scientific explanations: "Entities should not be multiplied unnecessarily." This principle, for example, was one basis for preferring the Copernican view of the solar system to the Ptolemaic view, in an era before accurate astronomical measurement could confirm the superiority of the former.

22. Merton, *Social Theory and Social Structure*, pp. 86–91.

CHAPTER 5
THE ROLE OF MILITARY POWER

1. Representative of this "school" are Gott, *Rural Guerrillas*, and Petras, "Revolution and Guerrilla Movements."

2. Richard Kiessler, *Guerilla und Revolution: Parteikommunismus und Partisanenstrategie in Lateinamerika* (Bonn-Bad Godesberg: Verlag Neue Gesellschaft GmbH., 1975), pp. 1, 353.

3. For a general discussion of the relative importance in sociological analysis of "intrusive elements" and the social systems they affect, see Ralph H. Turner, "The

Quest for Universals in Sociological Research" in *Research Methods: Issues and Insights*, ed. Billy J. Franklin and Harold W. Osborne (Belmont, Calif.: Wadsworth, 1971), p. 35.

4. Joseph Loftus, *Latin American Defense Expenditures, 1938–1965*, Rand Research Memorandum, No. RM-5310-PR/ISA (Santa Monica, Calif.: Rand Corporation, 1968). I have extended his figures, corrected a few of them, and adjusted them for inflation in my thesis; cf. "A Sociological Analysis of Latin American Guerrilla Movements, 1956–1970" Ph.D. diss., Cornell University, 1981, chap. 5. My own data are presented here.

5. In addition to Loftus's and my own estimates, see (for data after 1965) United Nations, *Statistical Yearbook*, various editions, always using the latest available data for each given year. Exchange rates per U.S. 1960 $ are as follows: Cuba, 1.02 pesos; Venezuela, 3.35 bolivares; Guatemala, 1.00 quetzales; Peru, 26.76 soles; and Bolivia, 11.885 pesos. For the Cuban data, all years are fiscal years, not calendar years.

6. Loftus, *Defense Expenditures*, pp. vii–viii, comes to similar conclusions after comparing military spending to the levels of internal and external violence; only Venezuela, in his view, seems to provide an exception.

7. See the data in *Statistical Abstract of Latin America* 18 (Los Angeles: UCLA Latin American Center, 1977), pp. 160–61, table 1-1; for Latin American national population figures, see United Nations, *Statistical Yearbook* 18 (1966): 80–81.

8. United Nations, *Statistical Yearbook* 18 (1966): 80–81. All data are in 1960 U.S. dollars. Loftus, *Defense Expenditures*, p. 59, reports somewhat different figures, but the broad patterns are substantially the same, except for the inversion of the Peruvian and Guatemalan data in the rankings.

9. See Loftus, *Defense Expenditures*, p. 87, for armed-forces personnel, and the same U.N. source for population. In this paragraph, all national data are for 1965, save for Cuba, where 1958 or 1960 data are employed.

10. Segunda Sección Académica de la ESG, "El destacamiento aerotrasportado en un asalto para destruir un base de apoyo de guerrilleros" *Revista de la Escuela Superior de Guerra* (Peru) 13 (April–June 1966): 63–79.

11. D.E.H. Russell, *Rebellion, Revolution, and Armed Force* (New York: Academic, 1974), develops the thesis that the (dis)loyalty of the armed forces lies at the crux of revolutionary success or failure. On German soldiers' morale in World War II, see Morris Janowitz, *Military Conflict* (Beverly Hills, Calif.: Sage, 1975), pp. 177–220.

12. Moore, *Injustice*, pp. 82–83.

13. Russell, *Rebellion, Revolution, and Armed Force*, passim; also see the capsule summary in Tilly, *From Mobilization to Revolution*, pp. 214–16.

14. Writing as a former Cuban officer, Ramón Barquín, *Luchas guerrilleras*, expresses particular personal bitterness over Batista's unwillingness to professionalize the armed forces.

15. For more on the Cuban and Nicaraguan military regimes, see chapters 8 and 11.

16. Erving Goffman notes this in his original essay on total institutions; cf. *Asylums*, pp. 119–21.

17. The image of the army as the final bulwark against a descent into barbarism is

clear in Evelio Buitrago Salazar, *Zarpazo the Bandit: Memoirs of an Undercover Agent of the Colombian Army* (Tuscaloosa: University of Alabama Press, 1977).

18. Richard L. Maullin, *Soldiers, Guerrillas, and Politics in Colombia* (Toronto: Lexington, 1973), pp. 113–16; Allemann, *Macht und Ohnmacht*, p. 274.

19. There is an interesting postscript to Bolivia, 1967: a radical critic asserted that the officers supporting Hugo Banzer's conservative military coup of the early 1970s were drawn largely from the those trained by U.S. advisors during the 1967 insurgency.

20. Norman Gall, "The Legacy of Che Guevara," *Commentary* 44 (December 1967): 32.

21. González and Sánchez, *The Great Rebel*, pp. 103–4.

22. In the period since 1967, however, the military has been plagued by left- and right-wing conflicts, factionalism, and drug-based corruption.

23. On the *cazadores'* response to encountering some captured guerrilla suspects see Guevara, *Los cachorros del Pentagono*, pp. 53–54.

24. Munson, *Zacapa*, p. 21.

25. Malcolm Deas, "Guerrillas in Latin America: A Perspective," *World Today* 24 (February 1968): 78.

26. Richard N. Adams, *Crucifixion by Power* (Austin: University of Texas Press, 1970), p. 249.

27. Lartéguy, *The Guerrillas*, pp. 88–89, and Adams, *Crucifixion*, pp. 266–67, 468–69. Two suggestive experiments demonstrated that situations of authority, command structures, and even simple role assignments may be effective in eliciting compliance in the performance of supposedly unthinkable actions: the Milgram shock experiments and the Zimbardo prison experiment, in which a "guard" self-described as a pacifist prior to the experiment tormented and even force-fed inmate(s); cf. Stanley Milgram, *Obedience to Authority* (New York: Harper and Row, 1974) and Moore's comments on this study in *Injustice*, pp. 94–100; Philip G. Zimbardo, "The Mind is a Pirandellian Prison," *New York Times Magazine*, 8 April 1973, 38–40+.

28. Edwin Lieuwen, "Militarism in Latin America: A Threat to the Alliance for Progress," *World Today* 19 (May 1963): 198; *El Nacional* (Caracas), 4 May 1962.

29. United States Department of Defense, Security Assistance Agency, *Foreign Military Sales and Military Assistance Facts* (April 1974): 12, 16–19.

30. In 1970, the U.S. had some $75.5 billion in direct investments in foreign countries, of which $11.1 billion, or about 15 percent, was in Latin America. U.S. trade with Latin America in 1965 amounted to about 15 percent of all U.S. foreign trade. Net economic assistance to Latin America from 1948 to 1978 totalled $7.2 billion, or about 10 percent of the global assistance total of $70.2 billion. See U.S. Department of Commerce, *Statistical Abstract of the United States 1979* (Washington, D.C.: U.S. Govt. Printing Office), tables 1497, 1511, 1504, respectively.

31. Maullin, *Soldiers, Guerrillas, and Politics*, p. 103; U.S. Senate, Committee on Foreign Relations, *United States Military Policies and Programs in Latin America* (Washington, D.C.: U.S. Govt. Printing Office, 1969), pp. 44–45.

32. Maullin, *Soldiers, Guerrillas, and Politics*, p. 94; U.S. Senate, *U.S. Military Policies*, p. 64.

33. U.S. Senate, *U.S. Military Policies*, pp. 73–74.

34. See U.S. Department of Defense, *Foreign Military Sales and Military Assistance Facts* (December 1977): 19–20, 23–24, 28–30 for data sources. Separate data for the 1950–1967 period and for fiscal years 1968–1977 appear for the following categories: (1) MAP deliveries/expenditures, excluding training; (2) the acquisition cost of excess defense articles delivered; and (3) deliveries/expenditures on international military education and training. Therefore the training share of the MAP program is equal to (3) divided by the total for all three categories. This percentage, for appropriate years, can then be applied, country by country, to the MAP data in the source for table 5-3. The resulting overall training share for Latin American MAP aid (12 percent) is somewhat higher than the 10 percent reported by the Stockholm International Peace Research Institute (henceforth SIPRI), *Arms Trade with the Third World* (New York: Humanities Press, 1971), pp. 165–66. For more details on the calculations and the exclusion of certain expenditures, see Wickham-Crowley, "A Sociological Analysis," chap. 5.

35. Domínguez, *Cuba: Order and Revolution*, p. 151.

36. This is precisely the argument of domestic arms merchants in the United States: if you refuse to sell to certain buyers on moral grounds, then others will, especially nations like France, Britain, or other major vendors.

37. See U.S. Department of Defense, *Foreign Military Sales* (April 1974): 16–17. All data are for fiscal years and in current dollars.

38. U.S. Arms Control and Disarmament Agency, *World Military Expenditures and Arms Transfers, 1963–73* (Washington, D.C., 1975[?]): 70.

39. Klare and Stein, *Armas y poder*, pp. 120, 159–60.

40. Lt. Colonel Milton Delfín Cataldi, "Las guerrillas," *Revista Militar del Peru* 17 (March–April 1962): 74; Lamberg, *Die castristiche Guerilla*, p. 44, and idem, "Consideraciones concluyentes," 116–17.

41. "Armies Can Be Builders," *Army Information Digest* 20 (February 1965): 16–19.

42. Eduardo Galeano, "With the Guerrillas in Guatemala," in Petras and Zeitlin, eds., *Latin America*, p. 373; Klare and Stein, *Armas y poder*, pp. 94–95.

43. This followed the confirmation of guerrilla activity there; see Gott, *Rural Guerrillas*, pp. 526–27 for details.

44. Guevara, *Los cachorros del Pentagono*, p. 46; Galeano, "With the Guerrillas," 371; Mercado, *Las guerrillas*, pp. 221–22.

45. Gott, *Rural Guerrillas*, p. 526; Georgie Anne Geyer, "The Blood of Guatemala," *Nation* 207 (8 July 1968): 10.

46. Petras, "Revolution and Guerrilla Movements," pp. 352–53.

47. On the sizes of the military missions, see U.S. Senate, Committee on Foreign Relations, *Survey of the Alliance for Progress—The Latin American Military*, prepared by Edwin Lieuwen (Washington, D.C.: U.S. Govt. Printing Office, 1967), p. 36; for changes in the sizes of the missions, see U.S. Senate, *United States Military Policies*, pp. 57–58, 77.

48. Thomas, *Cuba*, p. 1028.

49. *Daily Journal* (Caracas), 18 March 1967; Maspero, *Avec Douglas Bravo*, p. 53; Manuel Cabieses Donoso, ¡*Venezuela, okey!* (Santiago, Chile: Ediciones del Litoral, 1963), pp. 235–58; Lindenberg, "Zur Krise," 289–90.

50. *Daily Journal*, 22 April 1967.

51. On this last point, see José Cardona Hoyos, "Civil War in Colombia?" *World Marxist Review* (England) 7 (July 1964): 93.

52. Bolivia might even be described as a proxy fight between Cubans and Americans over the shape of the Bolivian polity.

53. David L. Graham, "Guatemala's Shrine of Blood," *Nation* 194 (2 June 1962): 497 +; Ron Chernow, "The Strange Death of Bill Woods," *Mother Jones* (May 1979): 39; Munson, *Zacapa*, pp. 95–96.

54. Colonel George S. Blanchard, "Special Warfare—NOW!" *Army Information Digest* 19 (January 1964): 20–26. On the 1965 MTT missions, see Gott, *Rural Guerrillas*, pp. 568–70.

55. For typical Peruvian allegations, see Guardia, *Proceso a campesinos*, p. 15; Mercado, *Las guerrillas*, p. 179; Américo Pumaruna, "Peru: Revolución, insurrección, guerrillas," *Pensamiento Crítico* (February 1967): 95; and *La Prensa*, 12 September 1965. For the Colombian exception, see Munson, *Zacapa*, pp. 62–63.

56. The source for Venezuela is Douglas Bravo, who even lied to his Cuban allies; cf. Maspero, *Avec Douglas Bravo*, p. 36; while assertions by Bravo and other guerrillas may be treated with less skepticism on other matters, on these issues one approaches all claims with special caution. The source for Bolivia is Albert-Paul Lentin, "Des Experts de Punta del Este aux 'Bérets Verts' de Santa Cruz," *Partisans* (Paris) 37 (April–June 1967): 126, where he claims that "entire units" of Green Berets engaged Ché's guerrillas in Bolivia. Guevara's diaries support no such allegations. A much more selective role for U.S. combat personnel is implied by Allemann, *Macht und Ohnmacht*, p. 404, where he says that occasionally U.S. officers were "present in the ranks" at the close of the Bolivian campaign. The charge that Guevara was "executed by the CIA" is not even supported by the article bearing that title; cf. Michèle Ray, "The Execution of Che by the CIA," *Ramparts* 6 (March 1968): 21–37. Compare Gott, *Rural Guerrillas*, pp. 553–54, for a different view of events by another left-wing critic of U.S. policy. See the information supplied by Colonel John D. Waghelstein, "Che's Bolivian Adventure," *Military Review* 59 (August 1979): 44, who argues that Barrientos gave the order to execute Ché against advice from the United States.

57. See *Nation* 206 (4 March 1968): 291; Munson, *Zacapa*, pp. 52, 58–59, 201–2; and Allemann, *Macht und Ohnmacht*, p. 187 for a few examples.

58. Castaño, "Avec les guérillas du Guatemala," 151, 154; Lartéguy, *The Guerrillas*, p. 111; Orlando Fernández, "Situación y perspectivo del movimiento revolucionario guatemalteco," *Pensamiento Crítico* 15 (1968): 9.

59. This analysis bears some resemblance to some systems analyses, e.g., Leites and Wolf's *Rebellion and Authority*. Since I find that the systems' language of "inputs" and "outputs" adds little to our understanding of phenomena, I will forgo such argot here.

60. Leites and Wolfe, *Rebellion and Authority*, pp. 21–25; Laqueur, *Guerrilla*, pp. 263, 313.

61. In the following discussion I will avoid such value-laden terms as "intervention," which are generally used when the writer believes that the donor or the recipient is illegitimate in claiming the right to deal in such aid. When approval is present, we usually encounter terms such as "fraternal assistance" or "socialist internationalism," to use phrases preferred on the left. The right has its own jargon.

62. Octavio Arizmendi Posada, "Latinoamérica: Guerra de guerrillas," *Istmo* 27 (July–August 1963): 56; Lt. Colonel Harold R. Aaron, "The Export of Revolution to Latin America," *Army* 15 (June 1965): 96–97; Lando, "Latin-American Guerrillas," 26; William Ratliff, *Castroism and Communism in Latin America, 1959–1976* (Washington, D.C. and Stanford, Calif.: American Enterprise Institute for Public Policy Research and Hoover Institution on War, Revolution, and Peace, 1976), p. 42.

63. Lando, "Latin-American Guerrillas," 26; Gall, "Revolution without Revolutionaries," 149; *New York Times*, 8 September 1965; *Time*, 22 January 1965, 30; Daniel James, "Latin America: How Many Vietnams?" *National Review* 19 (5 September 1967): 950.

64. Norman Gall, "The Continental Revolution," *The New Leader*, 12 April 1965: 4; Lamberg, "Kubas Einfluss auf Lateinamerika," 147.

65. Barquín, *Luchas guerrilleras* 1:220; Thomas, *Cuba*, p. 986.

66. *Hispanic American Report* 11 (September 1958): 496; *Newsweek*, 24 February 1958, 54; Barquín, *Luchas guerrilleras* 1: 231; James E. Bond, *The Rules of Riot: Internal Conflict and the Laws of War* (Princeton, N.J.: Princeton University Press, 1974), p. 85.

67. *Daily Journal* (Caracas), 3 July 1967; *El Nacional* (Caracas), 22 April 1965; *New York Times*, 14 December 1964; 19 May 1967, 11; Allemann, *Macht und Ohnmacht*, pp. 145–46.

68. To put these figures in perspective, our numbers on military aid to Venezuela from the U.S. were $6.1 million in 1965 and about $800,000 in 1967. See table 5-3.

69. On the sums of money involved, see *Daily Journal*, 11 April 1965; *New York Times*, 17 October 1965; Allemann, *Macht und Ohnmacht*, p. 156; on Bravo's reliance on Cuban aid in general, see Gall, "Teodoro Petkoff II," 20; Valsalice, *Guerriglia e Politica*, p. 117; for the quote, see *New York Times*, 6 November 1964.

70. *Daily Journal*, 4 November 1963; Kenneth O. Gilmore, "Cuba's Brazen Blueprint for Subversion," *Readers' Digest* 87 (August 1965): 67–75; Allemann, *Macht und Ohnmacht*, pp. 142–43.

71. *Daily Journal*, 18 and 19 November 1964; 13 and 19 May 1967; Allemann, *Macht und Ohnmacht*, pp. 154–55; Zago, *Aquí no ha pasado nada*, p. 17; Gall, "Teodoro Petkoff II," 3; Valsalice, *Guerriglia a Politica*, p. 189. For some of the contents of the Cuban volunteer's diary, see Allemann, pp. 155–56.

72. Gott, *Rural Guerrillas*, pp. 53–54.

73. Alan Howard, "With the Guerrillas in Guatemala," *New York Times Magazine* (26 June 1966): 16, 18, 20; Allemann, *Macht und Ohnmacht*, pp. 172–73.

74. Lartéguy, *The Guerrillas*, p. 160; Maullin, *Soldiers, Guerrillas, and Politics*, pp. 23–24; Allemann, *Macht und Ohnmacht*, p. 261; Lamberg, *Die castristiche Guerilla*, p. 103; Arenas, *La guerrilla por dentro*, pp. 155, 195.

75. See the numerical estimates discussed at the beginning of this section.

76. Peru, Ministerio de Guerra, *Las guerrillas en el Peru*, p. 30; Artola, *¡Subversión!*, pp. 28–31, 85. Artola outlines the "typical" program.

77. See Martin D. Gensler, "Cuba's Second Vietnam: Bolivia," *Yale Review* 60 (Spring 1971): 345–46. Radio Havana reported 3,800 Green Berets in Bolivia (up from its earlier report of 100) and denied Cuban ties to the Bolivian guerrillas, describing the movement as a "purely Bolivian explosion."

CHAPTER 6
THE SOURCES OF PEASANT SUPPORT I

1. See Jeffery M. Paige, *Agrarian Revolution* (New York: Free Press, 1975); James C. Scott, *The Moral Economy of the Peasant* (New Haven: Yale University Press, 1976); Eric Wolf, *Peasant Wars of the Twentieth Century* (New York: Harper, 1969); Barrington Moore, Jr., *Social Origins of Dictatorship and Democracy* (Boston: Beacon, 1966); E. J. Hobsbawm, *Bandits* (London: Trinity Press, 1969), and *Primitive Rebels* (New York: W. W. Norton, 1965); Samuel Popkin, *The Rational Peasant* (Berkeley, Calif.: University of California Press, 1979), Theda Skocpol, *States and Social Revolutions* (Cambridge, England: Cambridge University Press, 1979), and her "What Makes Peasants Revolutionary?" *Comparative Politics* 14, no. 2 (April 1982): 351–75.

2. J. Craig Jenkins, "Why Do Peasants Rebel?: Structural and Historical Theories of Modern Peasant Rebellions," *American Journal of Sociology* 88, no. 3 (November 1982): 467–514; Skocpol, "What Makes Peasants Revolutionary?"; Jeffery M. Paige, "Social Theory and Peasant Revolution in Vietnam and Guatemala," *Theory and Society* 12, no. 2 (November 1983): 699–737.

3. Robert K. Merton, "Manifest and Latent Functions," in his *Social Theory and Social Structure* esp. pp. 86–91; Paige, *Agrarian Revolution*, pp. 40–45, esp. p. 42; Skocpol, *States and Social Revolutions*, esp. pp. 155–57.

4. The entire preceding discussion is based on Paige, *Agrarian Revolution*, chap. 1, with the exception of my coda on squatters.

5. Wolf, *Peasant Wars*, chap. 7, or idem, "On Peasant Rebellions," *International Social Science Journal* 21, no. 2 (1969): 286–93.

6. Paige, *Agrarian Revolution*, p. 42.

7. Jenkins, "Why Do Peasants Rebel?" 489 n.3.

8. Hofheinz, "The Ecology of Chinese Communist Success," pp. 60–62.

9. Goldenberg, *Cuban Revolution*, pp. 124–25; Domínguez, *Cuba*, pp. 429–33.

10. A late-1958 *foco* was set up on the opposite end of the island, in Pinar del Río, which happened to be the sharecropping center of Cuba (see table 6-1). That foco may have been an example of the "bandwagon" effect late in that year, rather than a key area of independent development. Unfortunately, the *municipio* geography for Pinar del Río makes it virtually impossible to sort out rebel-held areas from "other" zones, although there does seem to be little or no correlation with sharecropping regions in this case. For the events there, see the memoir by Neill Macaulay, *A Rebel in Cuba: An American's Memoir* (Chicago: Quadrangle, 1970); for one "guerrilla map" that includes that provincial front, see Lt. Colonel Harold R. Aaron, "Why Batista Lost," *Army* (September 1965): 67. For maps of the layout of *municipios* within each province, the only ready source I have encountered is Vicente Baez, ed., *Enciclopedia de Cuba* 14 volumes (Madrid: Playor, 1975), vols. 9–11 for each Cuban *municipio* and its departmental location (prior to the reorganization effected by Castro in the 1970s).

11. Lowry Nelson, *Rural Cuba* (Minneapolis: University of Minnesota Press, 1950), pp. 20, 112, 154, 171; Barquín, *Luchas guerrilleras*, 1:327–29; Thomas, *Cuba*, p. 906; Goldenberg, *Cuban Revolution*, p. 155; Domínguez, *Cuba*, pp. 429–37.

12. Ché Guevara, *Reminiscences of the Cuban Revolutionary War* (New York: Monthly Review, 1968), pp. 246–47; Bonachea and San Martín, *Cuban Insurrection*, p. 271; Allemann, *Macht und Ohnmacht*, pp. 84, 461; Domínguez, *Cuba*, pp. 345–46, 441–45.

13. Venezuela, *Censo agropecuario 1961: Parte A*, table 2.05, pp. 50–56. The high guerrilla-support districts listed in table 6-4 collectively report 57 percent of their census respondents involved in coffee production, versus just 26 percent for the nation overall.

14. Valsalice, *Guerriglia e Politica*, chap. IV.

15. Jenkins, "Why Do Peasants Rebel?" 489 n.3.

16. See especially Adams, *Crucifixion*, map between pp. 138 and 139; Allemann, *Macht und Ohnmacht*, p. 159; and Lamberg, *Die castristiche Guerilla*, p. 71. Neither Allemann nor Lamberg correctly places the Sierra de las Minas, which in reality runs almost directly along the Zacapa border with Alta Verapaz and then with Izabal. In addition, Adams's map assigns no. 4 to two different Zacapa *municipios*. The northeastern one is correctly labeled Gualán, and the smaller southwestern one is Huite, and should be numbered 10. The Mico Mountains in Izabal—the major haven for the MR-13—run parallel to the long southeastern shore of Lake Izabal, roughly on the municipal borders separating Puerto Barrios and Morales *municipios* from Livingston and Los Amates, and then on toward the southwest.

17. See Gall, "Revolution without Revolutionaries," 145; Allemann, *Macht und Ohnmacht*, p. 170; and Lamberg, *Die castristiche Guerilla*, p. 54 for accounts of the events there.

18. See Guatemala, *Censo agropecuario 1964*, 1:71, 121–22, 173, 274, 283 for data on San Mateo and Huehuetenango.

19. Colombia, Departamento Administrativo Nacional de Estadística (DANE), *Directorio nacional de explotaciones agropecuarios (Censo agropecuario) 1960: Resumen nacional* part I (Bogotá, 1962) and part II (Bogotá, 1964).

20. Colombia, DANE, *Explotaciones agropecuarias* part II, pp. 22–23.

21. Many scholars have linked the events of *La Violencia* to the later guerrilla movements, but few have successfully linked either to regional agrarian structures. To probe for such a relationship, I correlated the number of violent events (1958–63) in each department with the 1960 percentage of lands held by sharecroppers (the events data come from Germán Guzmán Campos, Orlando Fals Borda, and Eduardo Umaña Luna, *La Violencia en Colombia*, 2 vols. (Bogotá: Tercer Mundo, 1962 and 1964), 2:301–26). The Spearman rank correlations were + .68 for sharecropped land and + .65 for all rental forms. Regressing events on sharecropping, I found a Pearson correlation of + .39, with Norte de Santander as a major negative outlier. If that department is dropped, the correlation rises to + .68. Some of the violence, though, may be due to a contagion effect, wherein a dialectic of vengeance and counter-vengeance itself produces violence, rather than social structure alone. We can eliminate this "contagion" or "vendetta" effect by using the natural log of the number of events rather than the absolute number (assigning 0 or 1 event a score of 0), as suggested by Paige, *Agrarian Revolution*, pp. 100–103. In that case the two Pearson correlations just discussed get even stronger, rising to + .48 and + .71, the latter without Norte de Santander in the analysis. This strongly suggests a structural relationship between sharecropping and La Violencia and, by extension, between sharecropping and the later guerrilla movements.

22. For the inaccurate maps, see Lamberg, *Die castristiche Guerilla*, p. 106, and Allemann, *Macht und Ohnmacht*, p. 243. Allemann's map also shows shading into Norte de Santander, where in fact there was little or no ELN activity prior to 1970. For the location of ELN "events," see Arenas, *La guerrilla por dentro*, pp. 199–204; for political maps of Colombia showing *municipio* locations, see Colombia, DANE, *División político-administrativa de Colombia 1967* (Bogotá, 1967).

23. Gott, *Rural Guerrillas*, p. 282; Colombia, Ministerio de Defensa Nacional, *Memoria al Congreso* 1966 (pp. 3, 82–83); 1967 (pp. 5–6, 107–8); 1968 (pp. 3, 70); 1969; 1971 (pp. i–ii, 31–33, 38–39); see also Maullin, *Soldiers, Guerrillas and Politics*, p. 36.

24. On the EPL, see the Ministerio de Defensa's *Memorias* cited in note 23, as well as Comité de Solidaridad con los Presos Políticos, *Libro negro de la represión: Frente Nacional 1958–1974* (Bogotá: Gráficas Mundo Nuevo, 1974), the reports for 1968–1970, esp. p. 81. The *Libro negro* is an excellent supplementary source on guerrilla "events" and their locations, not only for the EPL, but for other guerrilla bands as well.

25. If one compares these estimates with accurate information for the two departments whose census data we do possess—Caldas and Cundinamarca—the comparison suggests that the estimates are not, in fact, very reliable at all.

26. Merton, *Social Theory and Social Structure*, pp. 86–91.

27. Guzmán et al., *La Violencia* 1:62; Maullin, *Soldiers, Guerrillas, and Politics*, p. 15, 48–49.

28. Guzmán et al., *La Violencia*, 1:120–21; Buitrago, *Zarpazo*, p. 19; Maullin, *Soldiers, Guerrillas and Politics*, p. 13.

29. Wickham-Crowley, "A Sociological Analysis of Latin American Guerrilla Movements," pp. 309–14.

30. Béjar, *Peru 1965*, pp. 88–95, 99–100.

31. Gott, *Rural Guerrillas*, pp. 415–31, Artola, *¡Subversión!*, p. 48. On the conflicts between Indian *comunidades* and the peasants resident on hacienda lands, see F. LaMond Tullis, *Lord and Peasant in Peru* (Cambridge, Mass.: Harvard, 1970), p. 82.

32. Béjar, "Ne pas surestimer," pp. 111, 113; Artola, *¡Subversión!*, p. 77.

33. Béjar, *Peru 1965*, pp. 79–81, 84, 86–87. Other information supporting the position that the Cuzco *foco* received support inferior to that of the other two sites can be found in Mercado, *Las guerrillas*, pp. 168–69; Norman Gall, "Peru's Misfired Guerrilla Campaign," *The Reporter*, 26 January 1967: 38; Lamberg, *Die castristiche Guerilla*, p. 116; and Allemann, *Macht und Ohnmacht*, pp. 208–9, 429.

34. Artola, *¡Subversión!*, p. 100.

35. Dwight B. Heath, Charles Erasmus, and Hans C. Buechler, *Land Reform and Social Revolution in Bolivia* (New York: Praeger, 1969), pp. 325, 327, 328. On an 1878 land reform in the Santa Cruz region, see Lamberg, "Ché in Bolivia," p. 30.

36. Mercier, *Guerrillas*, p. 134; Guevara, *Complete Bolivian Diaries*, p. 59. See also Esser, "Guevaras Guerilla," 325–26; Lamberg, "Che in Bolivia," 30. For quite a different interpretation, see Gott, *Rural Guerrillas*, pp. 556–58. His discussion of the matter of landlordism and revolution in Bolivia is disingenuous at best.

37. Scott, *Moral Economy*, and James C. Scott and Benedict J. Kerkvliet, "How Traditional Rural Patrons Lose Legitimacy (in Southeast Asia)," *Cultures et Developpement* [*sic*] 5, no. 3 (1977): 501–40.

362 · Notes to Chapter 6

38. Reference group theory originated in the massive study of the U.S. military during World War II by Samuel Stouffer et al., *The American Soldier* (Princeton, N.J.: Princeton University Press; 1949). An extended refinement and discussion of the concept appears in Merton, *Social Theory and Social Structure*, pp. 335–440.

39. Paige, *Agrarian Revolution*, pp. 1–40, 45–48.

40. Domínguez, *Cuba*, pp. 429–33, 441–45.

41. Nelson, *Rural Cuba*, pp. 20, 112; Domínguez, *Cuba*, pp. 429–33. For a map indicating the distribution of squatters (*precaristas*) in Cuba, see Cuba, *Memoria del censo agrícola, 1946*, p. 99.

42. Domínguez, *Cuba*, pp. 436–37; Barquín, *Luchas guerrilleras*, 1:317.

43. An account of Venezuela's agrarian history during that time period appears in John Duncan Powell, *Political Mobilization of the Venezuelan Peasant* (Cambridge, Mass.: MIT Press, 1971), pp. 71–72, 90–94, 104, and also pp. 166–70, for the responsiveness of the government to peasant demands; see as well Gerrit Huizer, *The Revolutionary Potential of Peasants in Latin America* (Toronto: Lexington, 1972), pp. 108–14, who also provides the data on the land invasions.

44. Huizer, *Revolutionary Potential*, pp. 108–14. The best discussion of the Miranda *foco* is in Valsalice, *Guerriglia e Politica*, pp. 141–43.

45. Wickham-Crowley, "Sociological Analysis of Latin American Guerrilla Movements," 392–96.

46. See Adams, *Crucifixion*, p. 396; Allemann, *Macht und Ohnmacht*, p. 166; and Comité Interamericano para Desarrollo Agrícola (CIDA), *Guatemala: Tenencia de la tierra y desarrollo socio-económico del sector agrícola* (Washington, D.C.: Pan American Union, 1965), pp. 36–52.

47. Adolfo Gilly, "The Guerrilla Movement in Guatemala I," *Monthly Review* 17 (May 1965): 10.

48. CIDA, *Guatemala*, p. 53.

49. See Salomon Kalmonovitz, "Evolución de la estructura agraria," p. 170 (on *jornaleros*), and Hector Tamayo, "El problema agrario," p. 221 (on INCORA's "adjudications"), both in Mario Arrubla, ed., *La agricultura colombiana en el siglo XX* (Bogotá?: Andes, 1976); Feder, *Rape of the Peasantry*, chaps. 22, 24.

50. Instituto Colombiano de Reforma Agraria (INCORA), *Seis años de reforma social agraria en Colombia, 1962–1967* (Bogotá: INCORA, 1968), p. 18.

51. Pierre Gilhodès, "La Violence en Colombie, banditisme et guerre sociale" *Caravelle* 26 (1976): 78.

52. On the Michigan student's research, I am indebted to a private conversation with Charles Tilly, ca. 1980; Kalmonovitz, "Evolución," p. 181, presents Lorenz curves suggesting a less equal distribution of coffee lands in 1970 than in 1932, with 1954 more like the latter year.

53. For the listing of violent events, see Guzmán et al., *La Violencia* 2:301–26. For coffee production figures, see William P. McGreevey, "Exportaciones y precios de tabaco y café," in *Compendio de estadísticas históricas de Colombia*, ed. Miguel Urrutia and Mario Arrubla (Bogotá: Dirección de Divulgación Cultural, 1970), p. 210.

54. Guzmán et al., *La Violencia*, 1:124.

55. Huizer, *Revolutionary Potential*, pp. 114–24; Paige, *Agrarian Revolution*, pp. 175–82; Campbell, "The Historiography of the Peruvian Guerrilla Movement," 45;

La Prensa, 1 October 1965; and the summary analysis by Mercier, *Guerrillas in Latin America*, p. 148.

56. I will not be considering the impact of land reform efforts up to 1965. I could locate no source indicating land distribution in 1963 and 1964 by department, and several writers suggest that very few titles were passed out prior to 1965, and not many more in the following three years.

57. Béjar, *Peru 1965*, p. 58; David Chaplin, ed., *Peruvian Nationalism* (New Brunswick, N.J.: Transaction, 1976), p. 297; Huizer, *Revolutionary Potential*, pp. 119–24; *La Prensa*, 13 October 1965; and Tullis, *Lord and Peasant*, p. 82.

58. Béjar, *Peru 1965*, passim.

59. Tullis, *Lord and Peasant*, pp. 70–72; Cynthia McClintock, "Sendero Luminoso: Peru's Maoist Guerrillas," *Problems of Communism* 32, no. 5 (September–October 1983): 19–34.

60. James W. Wilkie, *Measuring Land Reform*, Supplement to the Statistical Abstract of Latin America (Los Angeles: UCLA Latin American Center, 1974), pp. 41, 55.

CHAPTER 7
THE SOURCES OF PEASANT SUPPORT II

1. George Homans, "The Frisians in East Anglia," in his *Sentiments and Activities* (New York: Free Press of Glencoe, 1962), pp. 158–81; Etienne van de Walle and John Knodel, "Europe's Fertility Transition," *Population Bulletin* 34, no. 6 (February 1980): esp. 29–36.

2. Walter L. Wallace, *Principles of Scientific Sociology* (Hawthorne, N.Y.: Aldine, 1983); Jeffrey C. Alexander, *Theoretical Logic in Sociology*, 4 volumes (Berkeley: University of California Press, 1982–1984).

3. Charles Tilly, *The Vendée* (Cambridge, Mass.: Harvard, 1964), p. 191.

4. Saíz, *Guerrillas en Cuba*, pp. 103–4.

5. For a general statement, see Laqueur, *Guerrilla*, pp. 393–97; for cultures of resistance and Mao's guerrillas in China, see Hofheinz, "Chinese Communist Success," 62–64, 73–74; for early Norman England (!), see John Beeler, "XIIth Century Guerrilla Campaign," *Military Review* 42 (August 1962): 41–42; on rural resistance in the Piedmont to federal authority in American history, see Tom Wolfe, "The Last American Hero," in *The Kandy-Kolored Tangerine-Flake Streamline Baby* (New York: Farrar, Strauss, and Giroux, 1963), pp. 161–63.

6. Blackburn, "Prologue to the Cuban Revolution," 88–89; V.A., "Cuba: A Peasant Revolution," 188; "La guerra clandestina," *Boletín del Ejército* 7 (November–December 1956): 62–67; Laqueur, *Guerrilla*, p. 56–57; Thomas, *Cuba*, pp. 245–46, 254, 319; Allemann, *Macht und Ohnmacht*, p. 62.

7. Thomas, *Cuba*, p. 523; Robert J. Alexander, *Communism in Latin America* (New Brunswick, N.J.: Rutgers, 1957), p. 274.

8. Domínguez, *Cuba*, pp. 435–36, 613; Cuba, Academia de Ciencias de Cuba y Academia de Ciencias de la URSS, *Atlas Nacional de Cuba* (Havana, 1970), p. 129.

9. Barquín, *Luchas guerrilleras* 1:327, 317; Allemann, *Macht und Ohnmacht*, pp. 71, 394; Thomas, *Cuba*, p. 808 and his "The Origins of the Cuban Revolution," *World Today* 19 (October 1963): 449; Enrique Meneses, *Fidel Castro* (New York:

Taplinger, 1966), p. 22; Domínguez, *Cuba*, pp. 429–37; Nelson, *Rural Cuba*, p. 20. Nelson in particular provides ample evidence of Oriente's poverty relative to the rest of Cuba.

10. Norman Gall suggests the hillbilly comparison. For sources on Falcón, see Valsalice, *Guerriglia e Politica*, pp. 120–24; Allemann, *Macht und Ohnmacht*, p. 139; Norman Gall, "A Cheerleader's Report," *New York Times Book Review*, 28 March 1971: 6; *El Nacional*, 28 July 1963; Robert L. Gilmore, *Caudillism and Militarism in Venezuela, 1810–1910* (Athens: Ohio University Press, 1964), pp. 52–53; Frank Bonilla and José A. Silva Michelena, *A Strategy for Research on Social Policy* (Cambridge, Mass.: MIT Press, 1967), pp. 63–64.

11. V.L., "Venezuelan National Hero," *World Marxist Review* (England) 8 (May 1965): 58; Gall, "Teodoro Petkoff II," 6; Valsalice, *Guerriglia e Politica*, pp. 131–32.

12. Zamora, *Memoria*, p. 127 and passim, recounts the experiences of a *llanero* guerrilla, whose details certainly support Valsalice's comments on the lack of organization there; cf. Valsalice, *Guerriglia e Politca*, pp. 120, 147.

13. Schump, *Las guerrillas*, p. 42, disagrees with Valsalice on the historical and contemporary strength of insurgency in the east (Oriente). See also Valsalice, *Guerriglia e Politica*, pp. 141–44, 207–8; Bonilla and Silva, *A Strategy for Research*, pp. 63–64; and Gilmore, *Caudillism and Militarism*, p. 119.

14. If there was any regional propensity to revolt, it probably lay in the eastern highlands (*la montaña*) during the nineteenth century. See Ralph Lee Woodward, Jr., *Central America: A Nation Divided* (New York: Oxford, 1976), pp. 98–102.

15. Guerra, "The Experience of Guatemala," 11; Allemann, *Macht und Ohnmacht*, p. 71.

16. Guzmán et al., *La Violencia*, 2:408, note that the Colombian homicide rate circa 1964 was *seven times* that of the United States, itself highly violent by international standards. The suggestion of the sui generis character of Colombian violence is Lamberg's in *Die castristiche Guerilla*, p. 88. Allemann even argues that Colombia's guerrilla experience is wholly (*"ganz und gar"*) derivative from its earlier experience of violence, in *Macht und Ohnmacht*, p. 244.

17. Charles W. Bergquist, *Coffee and Conflict in Colombia, 1886–1910* (Durham, N.C.: Duke University Press, 1978), pp. 158–60; Pierre Gilhodès, "Agrarian Struggles in Colombia," in *Agrarian Problems and Peasant Movements in Latin America*, ed. Rodolfo Stavenhagen (Garden City, N.Y.: Doubleday, 1970) pp. 409–10.

18. Dario Mesa, "El problema agrario en Colombia, 1920–1960," in *La agricultura colombiana en el siglo XX*, p. 114; see Gilhodès, "Agrarian Struggles," pp. 411–13 for details.

19. Guzmán et al., *La Violencia*, esp. 1:97–98, 101, 103, and 2:285.

20. Guzmán et al., *La Violencia*, 2:301–26, gives the event count by department and municipio. In old Caldas, most violence took place in the east and south, areas later to become the new departments of Risaralda and Quindio, respectively. In Valle, most violence occurred in the east, near the Tolima border. In Santander the violence was in the ELN's later area of operations, concentrated along the Magdalena River, on the western border of the department. The remainder of the department's violence is concentrated in eastern Santander, while the later ELN operated almost exclusively in the west; see Guzmán et al., ibid. 1:125, for the distribution of events during *La Violencia*.

21. Maullin, *Soldiers, Guerrillas, and Politics*, p. 14; Pierre Gilhodès, *La Question agraire en Colombie* (Paris: Armand Colin, 1974), p. 394.

22. Hugo Escobar Sierra, *Las invasiones en Colombia* (Bogotá: Tercer Mundo, 1972), pp. 103–25.

23. Wilfredo Kapsoli, *Los movimientos campesinos en el Peru, 1879–1965* (Lima: Delva, 1977), pp. 31, 74–76, and passim; Béjar, *Peru 1965*, pp. 88–89.

24. See the discussions in Béjar, *Peru 1965*, pp. 105–7, and Artola, *Subversión!*, pp. 44–80.

25. Paige, *Agrarian Revolution*, pp. 176–82.

26. Huizer, *Revolutionary Potential*, pp. 3, 88–105; Heath et al., *Bolivia*, pp. 36–49, 47 (quotation), 74, 120–22, 256–59; *Hispanic American Report* 11 (June 1959): 337.

27. A clear example in which historical rebelliousness was a conscious criterion for the choice of a *foco* site occurred with the Colombian ELN's choice of Santander; see Arenas, *La guerrilla por dentro*, pp. 16, 42, and Allemann, *Macht und Ohnmacht*, pp. 259–60.

28. See the instructive discussions and bibliographical guides in Rodney Stark, *Sociology* (Belmont, Calif.: Wadsworth, 1985), pp. 62–70, 154–57, 507–15. For a more formal view of the critical role of social networks, see Kenneth L. Wilson and Anthony M. Orum, "Mobilizing People for Collective Political Action," in *Political Sociology*, ed. George A. Kourvetaris and Betty A. Dobratz (New Brunswick, N.J.: Transaction, 1980), pp. 275–90.

29. Commandante [*sic*] Ernesto 'Che' Guevara, "Notes on the Cuban Revolution," *Studies on the Left* 1, no. 3 (1960): 77.

30. See the concise discussion of balance theory in Robert A. Baron and Donn Byrne, *Social Psychology: Understanding Human Interaction* (Boston: Allyn and Bacon, 1977), pp. 200–203, as well as Stark, *Sociology*, pp. 4–8, for examples of balanced and unbalanced triadic relationships. Among the original researchers in this field were Fritz Heider and Theodore Newcomb.

31. Barquín, *Luchas guerrilleras* 1:272-F, 309, 313, 327–30; Carlos Franqui, *The Twelve* (New York: Lyle Stuart, 1968), p. 67; Meneses, *Fidel Castro*, pp. 46 (quotes) passim; Maschke, *Kritik*, p. 76; Guevara, *Reminiscences*, pp. 50–53; Thomas, *Cuba*, pp. 902, 906, 920.

32. Bonachea and San Martín, *The Cuban Insurrection*, pp. 187–90.

33. See Benedict J. Kerkvliet, *The Huk Rebellion* (Berkeley: University of California, 1977), pp. 262–66 for the Philippines; Scott, *Moral Economy*, pp. 222–25 for Indonesia; and Alex Weingrod, "Patrons, Patronage, and Political Parties," *Comparative Studies in Society and History* 10 (July 1968): 377–400, on Sardinia and others.

34. Alexander, *The Communist Party of Venezuela*, pp. 184–85.

35. Valsalice, *Guerriglia e Politica*, p. 131; Zago, *Aquí no ha pasado nada*, entire, esp. pp. 13–15 (quote), 73, 85; Gall, "Teodoro Petkoff I and II," passim.

36. Valsalice, *Guerriglia e Politica*, p. 195–98.

37. Gilmore, *Caudillism and Militarism*, p. 47.

38. Turner and Killian, *Collective Behavior*, p. 308.

39. Allemann, *Macht und Ohnmacht*, pp. 139–40, 395.

40. Allemann, *Macht und Ohnmacht*, pp. 139–40, 395; Debray, *Strategy for Revolution*, p. 92; Gall, "A Cheerleader's Report," 6; Valsalice, *Guerriglia e Politica*, p.

123; *El Nacional*, 7 April 1963; Gall, "Teodoro Petkoff I," 13 (quote); Cross, "Marxism in Venezuela," 68; Gall, "The Continental Revolution," 7.

41. V.L. "Venezuelan National Hero," 58–59; Gall, "Teodoro Petkoff II," 6.

42. Zago, *Aquí no ha pasado nada*, p. 46; *El Nacional*, 26 and 27 August 1965; Valsalice, *Guerriglia e Politica*, p. 133.

43. Zamora, *Memoria*, pp. 48–49, 19–21 (quote).

44. Z. Martin Kowalewski and Miguel Sobrado, *Antropología de la guerrilla* (Caracas: Nueva Izquierda, 1971), p. 32; Zamora, *Memoria*, pp. 61, 146; Colonel Edward F. Callanan, "Terror in Venezuela," *Military Review* 49 (February 1969): 51; *El Nacional*, 6 April 1962.

45. See Peter L. Berger, *Pyramids of Sacrifice* (New York: Basic Books, 1974), pp. 111–32 for a stimulating discussion of the problematic nature of such upper-class persons' attempts to mobilize and "raise the consciousness" of lower-class individuals; for a related critique of such attempts, see my *Exploring Revolution*, chap. 4.

46. Arenas, *Diario de la resistencia de Marquetalia*, p. 91.

47. Russell W. Ramsey, "Critical Bibliography on *La Violencia* in Colombia," *Latin American Research Review* 8 (Spring 1973): 12, 33; Lamberg, *Die castristiche Guerilla*, pp. 89–91; Lartéguy, *The Guerrillas*, pp. 151, 158–59; Richard L. Maullin, *The Rise and Fall of Dumar Aljure* (Santa Monica, Calif.: Rand Corporation, 1968), pp. v–vi, and his *Soldiers, Guerrillas, and Politics*, pp. 30–33; Goldenberg, "Kommunismus in Lateinamerika," 246–48, 256–57; Arango, *FARC: Veinte años*, p. 112.

48. *Look*, 8 May 1962, pp. 85–90 + ; Maullin, *Soldiers, Guerrillas, and Politics*, pp. 125–26; Hobsbawm, "Revolutionary Situation," 251; *Hispanic American Report* 13 (June 1960): 395.

49. MOEC stands for "Worker-Student-Peasant Movement."

50. Allemann, *Macht und Ohnmacht*, p. 260; Arenas, *La guerrilla por dentro*, pp. 14, 35–37; Guardia, *Proceso a campesinos*, pp. 63–65; *New York Times*, 1 August 1965; Mercier, *Guerrillas*, p. 184; Artola, *Subversión!*, p. 39; Norman Gall, "Peru: Las semillas de la revolución," *Política* (Caracas) 37 (January 1965): 106–7; McClintock, "Sendero Luminoso: Peru's Maoist Guerrillas," 19–34.

51. Arenas, *Marquetalia*, pp. 67, 107–8 (quote); Arango, *FARC*, pp. 217–18 on the Páez Indians' role, and 219–30 on the campaign itself.

52. For a critique of the use of such procedures in the work of an eminent Marxist historian, see J. H. Hexter, "The Historical Method of Christopher Hill," *On Historians* (Cambridge, Mass.: Harvard, 1979), pp. 227–51, esp. 241–44.

53. Saíz, *Guerrillas en Cuba*, p. 184; Lamberg, *Die castristiche Guerilla*, p. 55; Marco Antonio Yon Sosa, "Breves apuntes históricos," *Pensamiento Crítico* 15 (1968): 137; interview with Pablo Monsanto in Marta Harnecker, *Pueblos en armas* (México, D.F.: Era, 1984), p. 241.

54. Allemann, *Macht und Ohnmacht*, pp. 172–74; Adams, *Crucifixion*, pp. 258, 268–70; Deas, "Guerrillas," 78.

55. Some secondary sources indicate that the Indians were Cakchiquel, not Kekchí. Lamberg, *Die castristiche Guerilla*, p. 58, for example, identifies Ixtapá as Cakchiquel, as does Schump, *Las guerrillas*, pp. 50–51, and Saíz, *Guerrillas en Cuba*, p. 184. This is highly unlikely, due to the FAR's location (in Alta Verapaz) and because of Ixtapá's previous office as *alcalde* of Rabinal in another Kekchí depart-

ment, Baja Verapaz. See the map of Guatemalan Indian groups in concerned Guatemala Scholars, *Guatemala: Dare to Struggle, Dare to Win*, rev. ed. (San Francisco: Solidarity, 1982), p. 9, as well as Allemann, *Macht und Ohnmacht*, pp. 178–79, and 476 n. 7; Adams, *Crucifixion*, p. 180; and Munson, *Zacapa*, pp. 160–63, all on the FAR's Kekchí influence. For information on López, see Julio del Valle, "Guatemala bajo el signo de la guerra," *Pensamiento Crítico* 15 (1968): 63; Aura Marina Arriola, "Secuencia de la cultura indígena guatemalteca," *Pensamiento Crítico* 15 (1968): 99; and Saíz, *Guerrillas en Cuba*, p. 184.

56. Gilly, "Guerrilla Movement I," 28–29 (quotation); Geyer, "The Blood of Guatemala," 8; Thomas Melville (letter to the editor) *Commonweal* 88 (20 September 1968): 613, 639; Ralph Clark Chandler, "Guerrilla Priests: A Few Kind Words," *Commonweal* 88 (9 August 1968): 525–28; *New York Times*, 28 January 1980.

57. Galeano, "With the Guerrillas," 370; Kowalewski and Sobrado, *Antropología de la guerrilla*, pp. 41–42; Allemann, *Macht und Ohnmacht*, p. 187; Lartéguy, *The Guerrillas*, p. 95.

58. The parallels to Hugo Blanco's experience organizing peasants in Cuzco are quite remarkable and may even be mimetic in their origins. On Blanco, see Wesley W. Craig, "From Hacienda to Community," Ph.D. diss., Cornell University, 1967.

59. Allemann, *Macht und Ohnmacht*, pp. 205, 196–97; *La Prensa*, 23 June 1965; Artola, *Subversión!*, pp. 44–45; Peru, Ministerio de Guerra, *Las guerrillas*, p. 16.

60. Béjar, *Peru 1965*, pp. 79–80; Gott, *Rural Guerrillas*, pp. 459–60; *La Prensa*, 12 September 1965, p. 1 (quotes) and 1 October 1965, p. 6.

61. Gall, "The Legacy of Che Guevara," 39; Artola, *Subversión!*, pp. 70–79; Lamberg, *Die castristiche Guerilla*, p. 119; Campbell, "Historiography," 46; Guardia, *Proceso a campesinos*, pp. 11–22; Peru, Ministerio de Guerra, *Las guerrillas*, pp. 53, 60, 65; *La Prensa*, 23 June 1965; Gott, *Rural Guerrillas*, pp. 390, 396; Béjar, *Peru 1965*, pp. 88–96.

62. González and Sánchez, *The Great Rebel*, p. 180; Georgie Anne Geyer, "Why Guevara Failed: An Interview with Regis Debray," *Saturday Review*, 24 August 1968: 15–16; Guevara, *Complete Bolivian Diaries*, pp. 48–49, 59, and entries of 9, 10, and 15 February, 24 March, 4 April, and 22 September 1967; from the same book, see Rolando's diary, entry of 17 April 1967; Robert F. Lamberg, "Che in Bolivia: The 'Revolution' That Failed," *Problems of Communism* 19 (July–August 1970): 30; Klaus Esser, "Guevaras Guerilla in Bolivien," *Vierteljahresberichte—FFES* 37 (September 1969): 327.

63. Guevara, *Complete Bolivian Diaries*, entry for 30 June 1967; Millares, *Las guerrillas*, p. 40; Ojarikuj Runa (pseud.), "Bolivia: Análisis de una situación," *Pensamiento Crítico* 26 July 1967: 213; Esser, "Guevaras Guerilla," 327.

64. Wolf, *Peasant Wars*, pp. 289–302, with the clearest statement on p. 290.

CHAPTER 8
REGIME WEAKNESSES AND THE EMERGENCE OF DUAL POWER

1. The following draws on Tilly, *From Mobilization to Revolution*, pp. 189–216, esp. pp. 191–93.

2. Pettee, *The Process of Revolution*, pp. 6 (first quote), 100–103; second quote on p. 100.

3. Skocpol, *States and Social Revolutions*.

4. See my concluding comments to chapter 11 here, and also my *Exploring Revolution*, chap. 7.

5. Theda Skocpol, "Rentier State and Shi'a Islam in the Iranian Revolution" *Theory and Society* 11, no. 2 (May 1982): 265–83.

6. For a recent comparative treatment suggesting that different regimes tend to elicit different types of "revolutionary" oppositions, and that only certain opponents are likely to be successful, see Goodwin and Skocpol, "Explaining Revolutions in the Contemporary Third World," 489–509.

7. Thomas, "The Origins of the Cuban Revolution," 448–60, esp. p. 460. Ché Guevara also argued for the importance of Cuba's sugar economy, yet he thought similar crops and similar social structures might be found elsewhere; cf. his "Cuba: Exceptional Case? [or Vanguard in the Struggle Against Colonialism]," *Monthly Review* 13 (July–August 1961): 56–71.

8. A useful index of this can be found in the revolutionary correspondence collected by Carlos Franqui, *Diary of the Cuban Revolution* (New York: Viking Press, 1976).

9. For a firm rejection of the use of "caste" to explain all distinctiveness of Indian history, see Barrington Moore, Jr., *Social Origins of Dictatorship and Democracy* (Boston: Beacon, 1966), pp. 334–35.

10. Domínguez, *Cuba*, pp. 129–31, documents this very concisely.

11. Fidel Castro, "Why We Fight," *Coronet* 43 (February 1958): 84–85.

12. Domínguez, *Cuba*, esp. pp. 95–109; Blackburn, "Prologue to the Cuban Revolution," 66–70; Samuel Farber, *Revolution and Reaction in Cuba, 1933–1960* (Middletown, Conn.: Wesleyan University Press, 1976), pp. 89–90, 106–114, 129–30, 152.

13. Bonachea and San Martín, *The Cuban Insurrection*, p. 8; Maschke, *Kritik*, p. 65; Allemann, *Macht und Ohnmacht*, p. 65; Thomas, "Origins," 455–56 and *Cuba*, pp. 680–85; Farber, *Revolution and Reaction*, pp. 20–22, 73–74, 168; Blackburn, "Prologue," 70–74. Samuel Doe led a later sergeants' revolt in Liberia several decades later.

14. The first concept is elaborated in Rouquié, *The Military and the State in Latin America*, chap. 6; for the second, see my *Exploring Revolution*, chap. 7.

15. One influential exposition of this theme is John J. Johnson's *Political Change in Latin America: The Emergence of the Middle Sectors* (Stanford, Calif.: Stanford University Press, 1958), where he discusses the cases of Argentina, Chile, Uruguay, Brazil, and Mexico. Barrington Moore's thesis is argued far more carefully in his *Social Origins of Dictatorship and Democracy* than I can do justice to here. The quotation is from p. 418.

16. See Michael L. Conniff, ed., *Latin American Populism in Comparative Perspective* (Albuquerque, N.M.: University of New Mexico, 1982) for a definition (pp. 13–23), theoretical analysis, and case studies of the phenomenon of Latin American populism, including cases from outside the region.

17. For a view quite close to this, see Cole Blasier, "Social Revolution: Origins in Mexico, Bolivia, and Cuba," in *Cuba in Revolution*, ed. Rolando E. Bonachea and Nelson P. Valdés (Garden City, N.Y.: Anchor, 1972), pp. 18–51, esp. pp. 48–49.

18. Lowry Nelson, "The Social Class Structure of Cuba," in *Materiales para el*

estudio de la clase media en América Latina, vol. 2, ed. Theo R. Crevenna (Washington, D.C.: Pan American Union, 1950), pp. 69–71 and Nelson, *Rural Cuba*, pp. 159–61; Farber, *Revolution and Reaction*, pp. 98–101; Blackburn, "Prologue," 70–76.

19. Thomas, *Cuba*, p. 684 and "Origins," pp. 457–58; Farber, *Revolution and Reaction*, pp. 32–33, 98–101, 104–5, 110–14.

20. Domínguez, *Cuba*, pp. 35–36; Farber, *Revolution and Reaction*, p. 99. In Weber's writings we can discern two sharply opposing forms of administration: complete privatization (feudalism) or the sharp distinction between private life and public office and resources (bureaucracy).

21. Maschke, *Kritik*, p. 60 (quotation); Thomas, *Cuba*, p. 770.

22. Carlos Manuel Raggi Ageo, "Contribución al estudio de las clases medias en Cuba," in Crevenna, *Materiales para el estudio*, 2:86.

23. Farber, *Revolution and Reaction*, p. 98; Juan F. Carvajal, "Observaciones sobre la clase media en Cuba," in Crevenna, *Materiales para el estudio*, 2:37–38; Domínguez, *Cuba*, chap. 3; Raggi, "Contribución," in Crevennna, pp. 85–86.

24. T. Lynn Smith, "Observations on the Middle Classes in Colombia" in Crevcnna, *Materiales para el estudio*, 4:1–14.

25. For background to Colombian politics, including class-related participation, see the series of articles collected in R. Albert Berry, Ronald G. Hellman, and Mauricio Solaún, eds., *Politics of Compromise: Coalition Government in Colombia* (New Brunswick, N.J.: Transaction, 1980). See especially, Mauricio Solaún, "Colombian Politics," esp. pp. 7, 16; Harvey F. Kline, "The National Front," esp. pp. 60–63; and Robert H. Dix, "Political Oppositions," esp. pp. 131–37, 149.

26. See Gilmore, *Caudillism and Militarism in Venezuela* on the older patterns. On the "Generation of 28" and its background, see Héctor Hurtado, "La clase media y el desarrollo de América Latina: La experiencia venezolana—Gobiernos de Acción Democrática," in *Clase media y desarrollo de América Latina*, by Orlando Cantuarias, Guillermo Bedregal, Héctor Hurtado, and Rubén V. Blanco, contribs., (San José, Costa Rica: Centro de Estudios Democráticos de América Latina, 1972), pp. 68–69.

27. On AD's party doctrine, see Leslie Manigat, "Venezuela," in Jean-Pierre Bernard et al., *Guide to the Political Parties of South America* (Harmondsworth, Eng.: Pelican, 1973), esp. pp. 534–37 and Hurtado, "La clase media," on the AD's petroleum policy. On expansion of education, see Gordon C. Ruscoe, "Education Policy in Venezuela," in Martz and Myers, eds., *Venezuela*, pp. 255–82.

28. On the guerrillas' self-professed middle-class origins, see Maspero, *Avec Douglas Bravo*, p. 54; on the AD's continued backing among workers, peasants, and the middle class, see Lamberg, *Die castristiche Guerilla*, pp. 73–74; Manigat, "Venezuela," in Bernard et al., *Guide*, pp. 527–28, 537–38; ICOPS, *The Venezuelan Elections*, p. 13; Robert J. Alexander, *The Venezuelan Democratic Revolution* (New Brunswick, N.J.: Rutgers, 1964), p. 91, and *The Communist Party of Venezuela*, p. 61; and Levine, *Conflict and Political Change*, pp. 152 (quote on youth), 161–62. On the lack of conservative parties, and on COPEI's backing and its leftward shift, see Alexander, *The Venezuelan Democratic Revolution*, pp. 84–87; Manigat, "Venezuela," pp. 540–45; and José A. Silva Michelena, "Nationalism in Venezuela," in Bonilla and Silva, *A Strategy for Research*, p. 75.

29. Hugo Neira, "Peru," in Bernard et al., *Guide*, esp. pp. 402–11 (quote on p. 403), and Carlos A. Astiz, *Pressure Groups and Power Elites in Peruvian Politics* (Ithaca, N.Y.: Cornell University Press, 1969), pp. 94–99.

30. See Neira, "Peru," pp. 408–12, 416–30, and Astiz, *Pressure Groups*, pp. 99–115.

31. Jean-Pierre Bernard, "Bolivia," in his *Guide*, p. 119.

32. Bernard, "Bolivia," pp. 118 (quote), 120, 132–46.

33. Nathan L. Whetten, *Guatemala: The Land and the People* (New Haven, Conn.: Yale University Press, 1961), pp. 332–33.

34. The military had initially backed Arbenz; cf. Adams, *Crucifixion by Power*, p. 190. For the 1944–1954 period and Marxisant views of the military, see Susanne Jonas, "Guatemala," in *Latin America: The Struggle with Dependency and Beyond*, ed. Ronald H. Chilcote and Joel C. Edelstein (New York: John Wiley, 1974), pp. 151–60, 198 (quote on "arbiter"); similar opinions appear in George Black, with Milton Jamail and Norma Stoltz Chinchilla, *Garrison Guatemala* (New York: Monthly Review, 1984). Non-Marxist scholars have had few reservations about coming to similar conclusions.

35. For a superb treatment of the Brazilian variants of such parties, whose political dominance began to break apart in the 1950s and 1960s, see Gláucio Ary Dillon Soares, *Sociedade e Política no Brasil* (São Paulo: Difusão Europeia do Livro, 1973), chaps. 5–6.

36. Thomas, *Cuba*, p. 684; Blackburn, "Prologue," 59–64; Farber, *Revolution and Reaction*, pp. 32–33, 98–101.

37. Domínguez, *Cuba*, pp. 44–46.

38. Raggi, "Contribución," pp. 85–86; Maschke, *Kritik des Guerillero*, p. 67 (quote).

39. For two such examples, see Maschke, *Kritik*, p. 77, and Bonachea and San Martín, *The Cuban Insurrection*, p. 84. See also Farber, *Revolution and Reaction*, passim.

40. Mauricio Solaún "Colombian Politics," in *Politics of Compromise*, ed. Berry et al., pp. 7–8.

41. Dennis Gilbert, "The Oligarchy and the Old Regime in Peru" (Ph.D. diss., Cornell University, Ithaca, New York, 1977); published in Spanish as *La oligarquía peruana* (Lima: Editorial Horizonte, 1982).

42. On Colombia, I am indebted to a private communication from Jeffery Paige. For Peru, this division has been documented for some time now. For one such example, see Astiz, *Pressure Groups and Power Elites*, pp. 48–61.

43. On Venezuelan *caudillaje* until early in this century, see Gilmore, *Caudillism and Militarism*; for the concept of the "rentier state," see Skocpol, "Rentier State and Shi'a Islam."

44. See Hugh Thomas, "Origins," 449, for the latter observation.

45. Thomas, *Cuba*, pp. 682–85, 770; Farber, *Revolution and Reaction*, pp. 89–90, 106–110, and esp. 111–14; Blackburn, "Prologue," 66–70. I have documented Domínguez's comments throughout.

46. Domínguez is a political scientist, very un-Marxist, from a Cuban emigré family. Blackburn is an English "plain Marxist," as C. Wright Mills would have put it.

Farber also came from a Cuban family and is, if anything, a Trotskyist. Thomas is a historian-journalist of roughly conservative hue.

47. Domínguez, *Cuba*, pp. 39–43, 95–109.

48. On Cuban politics in the 1950s, especially after Chibás's suicide, see Thomas, *Cuba*, pp. 770, 793–95, 881; Bonachea and San Martín, *The Cuban Insurrection*, pp. 73, 131; Maschke, *Kritik*, pp. 60, 66–67; Goldenberg, *The Cuban Revolution*, p. 111; Farber, *Revolution and Reaction*, pp. 120–30, 145–75. Most importantly, see the last selection in Farber's work.

49. These facts are well known to Cuban specialists but omitted from the uncritically laudatory works on Cuba appearing over the last quarter century. For an early look at such national comparisons, see Goldenberg, *The Cuban Revolution and Latin America*, pp. 120–21. For a more recent version, see Norman Luxenburg, "A Look at Castro's Statistics," *Encounter* 62 (March 1984): 58–62. On Cuba's slow economic growth from the 1920s to the 1950s, see Domínguez, *Cuba*, pp. 72–76, although he doesn't view the data in precisely those terms.

50. Farber, *Revolution and Reaction*, pp. 104–5, 110. By 1958, the civil service had swollen to 200,000; cf. Thomas, "Origins," 457–58.

51. For documentation, see Thomas, *Cuba*, chaps. 23–24 and passim.

52. On the importance of political power as an independent, "mobile" source of rewards in Latin American societies—as opposed to land ownership and foreign capital, which are largely immobile and inaccessible—and the contribution of such a system to unstable politics, see Merle Kling, "Toward a Theory of Power and Political Instability in Latin America," in *Latin America: Reform or Revolution?* ed. James Petras and Maurice Zeitlin (Greenwich, Conn.: Fawcett, 1968), pp. 76–93.

53. Batista therefore converted a weakened armed force into one strong enough, under his personal control, to intimidate most of the Cuban opposition. Only the university students could carry out systematic opposition in the early years, protected by university autonomy; cf. Thomas, *Cuba*, pp. 679–82, 793–95. See also, Allemann, *Macht und Ohnmacht*, pp. 65–66; Farber, *Revolution and Reaction*, pp. 73–74; Blackburn, "Prologue," pp. 70–74.

54. On the Guatemalan military, especially for the 1970s, see NACLA, *Guatemala* (Berkeley, Calif., and New York: NACLA, 1974), pp. 184–85; Eduardo Galeano, José González, and Antonio Campos, *Guatemala: Un pueblo en lucha* (Madrid: Editorial Revolución, 1983), pp. 61–63; and Black et al., *Garrison Guatemala*, pp. 48–53. Each of these publications has more polemical than scholarly intent, yet each is nonetheless highly informative about Guatemalan society.

55. On Colombian politics during this period, including *La Violencia*, see Maullin, *Soldiers, Guerrillas, and Politics*; Berry et al., *Politics of Compromise*, esp. chap. 1 by Solaún on the history of Colombian politics; and Paul Oquist, *Violence, Conflict, and Politics in Colombia* (New York: Academic, 1980). For Peru, see Astiz, *Pressure Groups and Power Elites*, chap. 6, and Henry E. Dobyns and Paul L. Doughty, *Peru: A Cultural History* (N.Y.: Oxford University Press, 1976), chaps. 10 and 11. On Venezuelan politics before and during the 1960s guerrilla period, see above all Levine, *Conflict and Political Change* and also Alexander, *The Venezuelan Democratic Revolution*. On events in and analyses of Bolivia, one should consult Lamberg, "Che in Bolivia," and Allemann, *Macht und Ohnmacht*. For all four South American na-

tions, see the detailed country studies in Bernard et al., *Guide to the Political Parties of South America*, which conveniently covers the period under review here. Concerning Guatemalan politics and the changes therein, see Adams, *Crucifixion by Power*; NACLA, *Guatemala*; and Black et al., *Garrison Guatemala*.

56. See contributor Bernard's comments on Barrientos and the elections, in his *Guide*, pp. 131–46.

57. José Nun, *Latin America: The Hegemonic Crisis and the Military Coup*, Politics of Modernization Series No. 7 (Berkeley Calif.: Institute of International Studies, University of California, 1969) and his "A Latin American Phenomenon: The Middle Class Military Coup," in Petras and Zeitlin, eds., *Latin America*, pp. 145–85; Samuel Huntington, *Political Order in Changing Societies* (New Haven, Conn.: Yale University Press, 1968), pp. 219–37.

58. For a detailed account of the inner workings of the Sergeants' Revolt, see Thomas, *Cuba*, pp. 634–50, 679–82.

59. Luis E. Aguilar, *Cuba 1933* (Ithaca, N.Y.: Cornell University Press, 1972), p. 161; Thomas, *Cuba*, p. 679.

60. Although their work is more complex than such simplisms, both Janowitz and Huntington suggest such approaches; cf. Janowitz, *Military Conflict*, pp. 136–45; and Huntington, *Political Order*, pp. 193–98. See similar comments in Marion J. Levy, Jr., *Modernization and the Structure of Societies* (Princeton, N.J.: Princeton University Press, 1966), pp. 571–605.

61. Nun, *The Hegemonic Crisis*, pp. 5–6, 8, 15–16.

62. For a superb treatment of the army and its role in Cuban politics, see Louis A. Pérez, Jr., *Army Politics in Cuba, 1898–1958* (Pittsburgh: University of Pittsburgh Press, 1976).

63. Thomas, *Cuba*, p. 680; see also Pérez, *Army Politics in Cuba*, chap. 3.

64. Thomas, *Cuba*, p. 583; Farber, *Revolution and Reaction*, pp. 73–74.

65. Pérez, *Army Politics*, chap. 5 is again a superb guide to the period; see also Thomas, *Cuba*, p. 681.

66. Pérez, *Army Politics*, chaps. 6–7; for information on the composition of the new officer corps, see pp. 85, 93.

67. For two such observations, from radically different political starting points, see Blackburn, "Prologue," 71 and Allemann, *Macht und Ohnmacht*, p. 65.

68. Blackburn, "Prologue," 70–74; Farber, *Revolution and Reaction*, pp. 20–22; and for much of the detail, Pérez, *Army Politics*, chap. 9.

69. See Pérez, *Army Politics*, pp. 125–26; also Maschke, *Kritik des Guerillero*, p. 65 and Thomas, "Origins," 455.

70. Thomas, *Cuba*, pp. 884, 961–73.

71. Farber, *Revolution and Reaction*, pp. 171–72, 152, 144; Draper, *Castro's Revolution*, p. 14; Allemann, *Macht und Ohnmacht*, p. 83.

72. On Lawrence's view, see Laqueur, *Guerrilla*, p. 170; for the quote on guerrillas, see Lamberg, *Die castristiche Guerilla*, p. 47.

73. Private communication from Jon McAdams.

74. The sources for the following are Goldenberg, *The Cuban Revolution*, pp. 111, 156; Bonachea and San Martín, *The Cuban Insurrection*, pp. 27, 35, 62–63, 92–94, 159; Maschke, *Kritik des Guerillero*, pp. 60, 81; Barquín, *Las luchas guerrilleras* 1:202, 209, 224, 226–28, 397–99; Thomas, *Cuba*, pp. 881, 919–20, 937; Armando

Gimenez, *Sierra Maestra* (Buenos Aires: Lautaro, 1959), pp. 51–52; Fidel Castro, *Revolutionary Struggle: Volume 1 of the Selected Works of Fidel Castro*, ed. Rolando E. Bonachea and Nelson P. Valdés (Cambridge, Mass.: MIT Press, 1972), 1:244–49, 343–48, 351–411 (the last for a long series of 1958 Castro writings and broadcasts); Leo Huberman and Paul M. Sweezy, "Cuba: Anatomy of a Revolution," *Monthly Review* 12 (July–August 1960): 61; Meneses, *Fidel Castro*, pp. 61–65; Allemann, *Macht und Ohnmacht*, p. 74; *New York Times*, 3 and 21 December 1956, 8 February 1957; *Newsweek*, 18 February 1957, p. 61; *Hispanic American Report* (1957), 10:243–44, 412–13, 467, 531–32, 593–95.

75. For such an argument, see Gimenez, *Sierra Maestra*, pp. 134–35.

76. The following does not rely on a detailed examination of all national newspapers in our six nations. Such meticulously detailed reading of years of news coverage is far beyond the scope of this study. Instead, my conclusions are based on a detailed reading of Venezuela's *El Nacional* and the English-language *Daily Journal* from 1962 to 1967; on similar coverage of Peru's *La Prensa* for the year 1965 and early 1966; on fragmentary reportage from news sources in Gott, *Rural Guerrillas*; and on the comments of the guerrillas themselves, who at times complained of their treatment by the "great bourgeois" press.

77. Maschke, *Kritik*, p. 101; Lamberg, "Consideraciones concluyentes," 108.

78. On politics and censorship in the Guatemalan press, see John Dombrowski et al., *Area Handbook for Guatemala*, prepared by Foreign Area Studies of the American University (Washington D.C.: U.S. Government Printing Office, 1970), pp. 204–7.

79. Rogers and Yates, "Undeclared War," 30–33; Judy Hicks, "FAR and MR-13 Compared" *Monthly Review* 18 (February 1967): 29–31; Howard, "With the Guerrillas."

80. In *Monthly Review*, see articles by Gilly, the Ehrenreichs (February 1967), and Hicks; see also Rogers and Yates, "Undeclared War," 30, and Howard, "With the Guerrillas." On the effects of tightened censorship, see Lartéguy, *The Guerrillas*, p. 103. On the guerrillas' ideological shift leftward, see Gabriel Aguilera Peralta, *La violencia en Guatemala como fenómeno político* (Cuernavaca, Mex.: Centro Interdisciplinario de Documentación [CIDOC], 1971), p. 3/4.

81. On the FAR-MR-13 split and the PGT's attempt to reenter politics, see Saíz, *Guerrillas en Cuba*, pp. 185–86. On the FAR's problems with Méndez and with its PGT allies during this period, see Kiessler, *Guerilla und Revolution*, pp. 404–5; Allemann, *Macht und Ohnmacht*, p. 434; and especially Gott, *Rural Guerrillas*, sec. I, chaps. 5–6. For the results of the 1966 elections, including breakdowns by department and *municipio*, see Adams, *Crucifixion*, pp. 205–17. Among the areas voting more for the liberal candidacy of Méndez were the southern coast, the east, and the northeast (the last housing the guerrilla movement).

82. Alexander, *Communism in Latin America*, p. 261; *Daily Journal*, 13 and 19 May 1967; Allemann, *Macht und Ohnmacht*, pp. 155–57. See *El Nacional*, 21 July 1964 on the police, and 4 October 1963 on the Encanto train attack. For the government's official published response to that incident, including photos, an account of the attack, and statements of support from various groups, see Venezuela, Presidencia, Secretaría General, *Gobierno y nación defienden en Venezuela el regimen democrático: Actos contra el terrorismo comunista* (Caracas?, no date). On the loss of

barrio support, see Talton Ray, *The Politics of the Barrios in Venezuela* (Berkeley: University of California Press, 1969), pp. 130–36 and the candid confirmation of those and other losses of support by ex-guerrilla Teodoro Petkoff, in Gall, "Teodoro Petkoff I," 15–16. In the second installment of his interview with Gall, Petkoff also describes the attempt to stop the 1963 elections as "perhaps our greatest error"; cf. Gall, "Teodoro Petkoff II," 4.

83. *New York Times*, 19 November 1961, 11 January, 14 April, and 10 October 1962; *El Nacional*, 9 May 1962, 1 February 1964; *Daily Journal*, 10 October 1962; 1 February, 19 and 21 November, and 23 December 1964.

84. For documents on FALN ideology, see Cabieses, *Venezuela okey!*, pp. 277–319; Gott, *Rural Guerrillas*, pp. 196–99; Mercier, *Guerrillas in Latin America*, pp. 216–20.

85. Faría, "After the Government Crisis in Venezuela," 28.

86. Simon Saez Mérida, "Interviewed," *World Marxist Review* (England) 6 (March 1963): 72.

87. Lamberg, *Die castristiche Guerilla*, p. 78; Peña, *Conversaciones con Américo Martín*, p. 90.

88. For one such argument, see Saez Mérida, "Interviewed," 73. Bravo and Cabieses evince similar positions in writings and interviews.

89. Alexander, *Communist Party of Venezuela*, p. 129; Valsalice, *Guerriglia e Politica*, p. 21.

90. Zago, *Aquí no ha pasado nada*, p. 93. On the internal impact of these "false" views of reality, see Peña, *Conversaciones con Américo Martín*, pp. 78–83.

91. Thomas E. Weil et al., *Area Handbook for Colombia*, prepared by the Foreign Area Studies program of American University (Washington D.C.: U.S. GPO, 1970), pp. 317–25.

92. Manuel Sepeda, "The Ability to Address the Masses," *World Marxist Review* (England) 27 (August 1984): 44–45.

93. Arango, *FARC: Veinte años*, pp. 108–9.

94. See the denial of a PCC link in Arango, *FARC: Veinte años*, p. 112.

95. For a representative series of *La Prensa* pieces on the guerrilla struggle, see 10 June, 21 June, 29 July, 4 August, 19 August, 28 and 29 September 1965.

96. For the quotation, see *La Prensa*, 21 June 1965, p. 8.

97. For texts of the first (all?) 16 issues, see Mercado, *Las guerrillas*, pp. 171–204.

98. Mercado, *Las guerrillas*, pp. 171, 177, 192 for *El Guerrillero*; Mercier, *Guerrillas*, pp. 17–27 for their July 1965 manifesto, which also overflows with Marxist language and concepts.

99. On mass communication in Bolivia, see Thomas E. Weil et al., *Area Handbook for Bolivia*, prepared by the Foreign Area Studies program at American University (Washington, D.C.: U.S. GPO, 1974): 210–14; on the accuracy and stance of *Presencia*, see also Gott, *Rural Guerrillas*, sec. 5; on the Bolivian tradition of pamphleteering, as well as on *Presencia*, see José Fellmann Velarde, *Historia de la cultura boliviana: Fundamentos socio-políticos* (La Paz: Los Amigos del Libro, 1976), pp. 453–55, 490.

100. See Egon Bittner, "Radicalism and the Organization of Radical Movements," *American Sociological Review* 28, no. 6 (December 1963): 928–40; for a journalistic

account along similar lines, see Sandy Rovner, "The Mind of the Terrorist," *Washington Post/Health*, 11 November 1986, 16. The "weatherman" underground in the United States displayed similar hermetic features; see Peter Collier and David Horowitz, *Destructive Generation: Second Thoughts about the Sixties* (New York: Summit Books, 1990), chap. 2.

101. See especially Herbert Marcuse, *One-Dimensional Man* (Boston: Beacon, 1964); Tilly, *From Mobilization to Revolution*, p. 135.

102. The following is from Tilly, *From Mobilization to Revolution*, pp. 191–93, 200–211. The three quotations are on pp. 192, 208, and 191, in the order presented.

103. Thomas, *Cuba*, pp. 1020–47 provides some of the detail, albeit scattered through his text.

104. The quote is from Maschke, *Kritik des Guerillero*, p. 60. Among the commentators noting the rapid collapse of organized opposition are Farber, Thomas, and Bonachea and San Martín.

105. Farber, *Revolution and Reaction*, p. 193 (quote); *Hispanic American Report* 13 (June 1960): 382. The poll was taken by still-independent *Bohemia*.

106. See Bonachea and San Martín, *The Cuban Insurrection*, p. 8, on popularity; Farber, *Revolution and Reaction*, pp. 91, 136–37, and Domínguez, *Cuba*, pp. 84–90 on welfare policies.

107. Goldenberg, *The Cuban Revolution*, p. 111 for the poll; Domínguez, *Cuba*, pp. 103–9 on corruption as a political issue.

108. Maschke, *Kritik des Guerillero*, p. 66; see also Blackburn, "Prologue to the Cuban Revolution," 70–74 (comments on isolation from "local class formations").

109. Draper, *Castro's Revolution*, p. 14; Farber, *Revolution and Reaction*, pp. 23–24.

110. Huberman and Sweezy, "Cuba," 48; Friedenberg, "Notes on the Cuban Revolution," 12; Bonachea and San Martín, *The Cuban Insurrection*, p. 95; "Lid Off— And On," *Newsweek*, 12 August 1957, 54–55; *Hispanic American Report* 10 (August 1957): 412–13.

111. Farber, *Revolution and Reaction*, pp. 148 (first quote), 166–68 on general loss of support and the SAR affair; Bonachea and San Martín, *The Cuban Insurrection*, p. 84, on elite children; and, for the two Havanans, "Fuse that Fizzled," *Newsweek*, 21 April 1958, 65 and "Counting Batista's Days," *Newsweek*, 22 December 1958, 40, 45.

112. Bonachea and San Martín, *The Cuban Insurrection*, pp. 6, 84–85. For more on the role of the working class in the insurrection—as filtered through Marxist lenses—see Huberman and Sweezy, "Cuba," p. 58.

113. Bonachea and San Martín, *The Cuban Insurrection*, pp. 131, 328–29.

114. On changing U.S. support for Batista, see chap. 5. On Batista's personal control and on the drop in morale following the embargo, see Allemann, *Macht und Ohnmacht*, pp. 65, 83 and Thomas, *Cuba*, p. 985; for more on the loss of fighting spirit, see "Counting Batista's Days," 40, 45. For more on the Cuban armed forces, see chap. 5 as well. On Batista, the PSP, and Cuban labor, see Farber, *Revolution and Reaction*, pp. 11–12, 84–87; Victor Alba, "Friends of the Communists: Some Curious Examples," *Problems of Communism* 10 (January–February 1961): 24–26; and Bonachea and San Martín, *The Cuban Insurrection*, pp. 210–14, 221, on the PSP's

betrayal of the general strike, one that Castro himself may have partially undermined. One other key labor group was controlled by Batista supporter Eusebio Mujal until late 1958, when a newly formed labor group began to challenge that control. Castro initially rejected the PSP's espousal of the guerrillas' program (in April 1958), as unsolicited and unwanted; cf. *Hispanic American Report* 11 (May 1958): 256 and (April 1958): 204.

115. Thomas, "Origins," 793–95; Bonachea and San Martín, *The Cuban Insurrection*, chaps. 3, 5.

116. Meneses, *Fidel Castro*, p. 73; Thomas, *Cuba*, pp. 982–83 and his "Origins," 454–55.

117. "Squeeze on Batista," *Newsweek*, 17 March 1958, 52; Lamberg, *Die castristiche Guerilla*, p. 14 (Julien).

118. On the misleading nature of the Guevara/Debray theses on revolution, see Maschke, *Kritik des Guerillero*, pp. 90–91, and Ratliff, *Castroism and Communism*, p. 35. On the importance of País's underground, see especially Bonachea and San Martín, *The Cuban Insurrection*, pp. 93–95, 138–44.

119. On the Civic Resistance, see Farber, *Revolution and Reaction*, p. 189.

120. I explore that process thoroughly in my article, "The Rise (and Sometimes Fall)," while Bonachea and San Martín provide a lucid discussion of this rise in dual power in *The Cuban Insurrection*, pp. 100–102.

121. Bonachea and San Martín, *The Cuban Insurrection*, p. 264.

122. Franqui, *Diary of the Cuban Revolution*, pp. 218–20, 258.

123. On all these issues, see Bonachea and San Martín, *The Cuban Insurrection*, chap. 10 and p. 232 (quote).

124. Franqui, *Diary of the Cuban Revolution*, pp. 484, 505–6; Bonachea and San Martín, *The Cuban Insurrection*, pp. 318–25.

125. Russell, *Rebellion, Revolution, and Armed Force*, pp. 115–20; Thomas, *Cuba*, pp. 884, 961–62, 1028–31, 1039–41; Lee Hall, "Inside Rebel Cuba with Raúl Castro," *Life* (21 July 1958): 30.

126. Farber, *Revolution and Reaction*, pp. 181–82; Bonachea and San Martin, *The Cuban Insurrection*, pp. 41–45, 54, 69; Thomas, *Cuba*, pp. 1012–13, 1033–34, 1069–70.

127. For conceptualization, evidence, and arguments on this issue, see my "The Rise (and Sometimes Fall) of Guerrilla Governments."

128. Gilly, "The Guerrilla Movement I," 30; Hicks, "FAR and MR-13," 31; Lamberg, *Die castristiche Guerilla*, p. 69.

129. For leftist critiques, see NACLA, *Guatemala* and Black et al., *Garrison Guatemala*. Lamberg's work is typical of those that suggest that the guerrillas never had a real chance to seize power; cf. *Die castristiche Guerilla* and "Consideraciones concluyentes."

130. Allemann, *Macht und Ohnmacht*, p. 169.

131. Rogers and Yates, "Undeclared War"; Hicks, "FAR and MR-13," 29–31; Howard, "With the Guerrillas."

132. NACLA, *Guatemala*, p. 184.

133. Kiessler, *Guerilla und Revolution*, p. 406.

134. On working-class weaknesses, see Lamberg, *Die castristiche Guerilla*, p. 42; A. P. Short, "Conversations with the Guatemalan Delegates in Cuba," *Monthly Re-*

view 18 (February 1967): 37; Hugo Barrios Klée, "The Revolutionary Situation and the Liberation Struggle of the People of Guatemala," *World Marxist Review* (England) 7 (March 1964): 17; NACLA, *Guatemala*, p. 186.

135. On the left's hope for the middle class, see John and Barbara Ehrenreich, "A Favorable View of the FAR," *Monthly Review* 18 (February 1967): 26–28; on the vote for Arana, see Lamberg, *Die castristiche Guerilla*, p. 68. Strongly suggestive evidence that the middle class, and perhaps the working class (urban and rural), voted for Méndez's Partido Revolucionario (PR), comes from ecological analysis of the 1966 vote, which Adams analyses in *Crucifixion by Power*, pp. 205–17. The capital city—home of the bulk of the middle class—and the coffee and banana plantation areas of the nation gave the PR the highest shares of the vote.

136. Allemann, *Macht und Ohnmacht*, p. 185 (quote); on upper-class support for Bay of Pigs invaders, see Adams, *Crucifixion by Power*, p. 261.

137. On the conservative vote, again see Adams, *Crucifixion*, pp. 205–17; for the Marxist, see Guerra Borges, "The Experience of Guatemala," 13; on the preexisting patterns of patron-client relations and clientelistic influences on voting patterns in Guatemala, see Concerned Guatemala Scholars, *Guatemala*, p. 22, and Jonathan L. Fried, Marvin E. Gettleman, Deborah T. Levenson, and Nancy Peckenham, eds., *Guatemala in Rebellion: Unfinished History* (New York: Grove, 1983), p. 286. On patron-client politics in general, see Steffen W. Schmidt, Laura Guasti, Carl H. Landé, and James C. Scott, eds., *Friends, Followers, and Factions: A Reader in Political Clientelism* (Berkeley: University of California Press, 1977), esp. pp. xxix–xxx, 140–44, 510–12. For the radical shifts in the politics of the Guatemalan indigenous highlands and their conversion into guerrilla havens, see my discussion in chap. 10.

138. Castaño, "Avec les guérillas du Guatemala," 156, 152.

139. For guerrilla strongholds, see my analysis in chap. 6 above; for the PGT's own analysis, see A. Tzul, "The Revolutionary Movement in Guatemala: Its Achievements and Prospects," *World Marxist Review* (England) 8 (April 1965): 27. One should, of course, allow for exaggeration as well.

140. "Acción cívica militar," *Revista Militar (Guatemala)* (October–December 1960): 87–91, quote on p. 87; Adams, *Crucifixion*, pp. 273–74; Munson, *Zacapa*, pp. 231–56; Castaño, "Avec les guérillas," 152.

141. Adams, *Crucifixion*, pp. 266–67, 142, 192–93.

142. Mercier, *Guerrillas in Latin America*, p. 106.

143. Most left-wing accounts of this period run along these interpretative lines; e.g., Cabieses, *Venezuela, okey!*, and Petras, "Revolution and Guerrilla Movements."

144. Mercier, *Guerrillas in Latin America*, p. 105.

145. See Alexander, *The Communist Party of Venezuela*, pp. 17, 23, on the profits split and the election results during this period.

146. See Levine, *Conflict and Political Change*, chaps. 3 and 6, for a critical yet balanced view of the political conflicts of the early Betancourt years; for electoral results from 1947 to 1968, see p. 54.

147. Representative of the literature that attacks the Betancourt regime, rather than analyzing it, are Cabieses, *Venezuela, okey!* (which was published in one edition by "FALN Publications"); Petras, "Guerrilla Movements and Revolution," pp. 337–43;

and John Gerassi, *The Great Fear in Latin America* (London: Collier, 1965), chap. 11. On the other side, Alexander, *The Venezuelan Democratic Revolution*, largely defends the administration. Levine, *Conflict and Political Change*, remained for some time the only treatment of the period that transcended such simplisms.

148. Zago, *Aquí no ha pasado nada*, provides an insider's account of one Larense area, while Maspero, *Avec Douglas Bravo*, gives an account of a visit to the Falcón front. For a discussion of conditions giving rise to guerrilla governments, see my "The Rise (and Sometimes Fall)" or *Exploring Revolution*, chap. 2.

149. Levine, *Conflict and Political Change*, chap. 6, and my detailed discussion in chap. 3 above.

150. Ex-guerrilla Petkoff is clear on the importance of urban support for the development of the rural guerrilla struggle; see his "Pre-Election Climate in Venezuela," 31; on the weak government rural presence and the opportunities it supplied to guerrillas, see Valsalice, *Guerriglia e Politica*, p. 185.

151. For further confirmation of Mercier's position on the social bases of AD support, see Bernard et al., *Guide to the Political Parties*, pp. 527–28 (membership), 537–38 (electoral support).

152. Their political support in 1963 for right-of-center candidate Arturo Uslar Pietri gathered little other support in the face of the AD and COPEI party organizations. Indeed, no Venezuelan party even calls itself a conservative party, so far has the nation moved from upper-class influence in politics. See, respectively, Alexander, *The Venezuelan Democratic Revolution*, p. 133, and Bonilla and Silva, *A Strategy for Research*, p. 75.

153. See Bernard et al., *Guide to the Political Parties*, pp. 537–38.

154. Cross, "Marxism in Venezuela," 58–59; Alexander, *The Communist Party*, pp. 61, 182–83; Levine, *Conflict and Political Change*, pp. 207–8.

155. On the university and the UTCs, see Lamberg, *Die castristiche Guerilla*, p. 77. On student-*barrio* links, see Levine, *Conflict and Political Change*, pp. 149–51; Teodoro Petkoff also confirms "considerable support" for the PCV in the *barrios*; cf. Gall, "Teodoro Petkoff I," 15.

156. See Gall, "Teodoro Petkoff I," 15–16; Gerassi is quoted in Gott, *Guerrilla Movements* (1970), p. 177; Valsalice, *Guerriglia e Politica*, p. 170 notes the lower-class position of the average policeman.

157. Ray, *Politics of the Barrios*, p. 133. The left later renounced and condemned the attack, but not immediately for public consumption; cf. Alfredo Peña, *Conversaciones con Douglas Bravo* (Caracas: Ateneo, 1978), p. 60.

158. Gall, "Teodoro Petkoff I," 16.

159. See Ray, *Politics of the Barrios*, pp. 85–87 (government as provider of welfare), 110–27 (AD's political failures in the barrios), 130–36 (the loss of support for the radical left). On casualties caused by preelection terror, see Callanan, "Terror in Venezuela," 49–56.

160. Maspero, *Avec Douglas Bravo*, p. 43; Gall, "Teodoro Petkoff II," 4.

161. See *El Nacional* (Caracas), 25 August (quotation) and 27 August 1965.

162. This pattern was confirmed in the captured diary of a volunteer Cuban participant in the Falcón *foco*, who was frustrated by the lack of "real" guerrilla activity during his stint there; cf. Allemann, *Macht und Ohnmacht*, pp. 155–57.

163. Powell, *Political Mobilization of the Venezuelan Peasant*, gives a detailed, highly systematic, social-scientific account of the mobilization process, with AD at

the center of the story. See also the comments by Allemann, *Macht und Ohnmacht*, pp. 146–47 along lines similar to my own.

164. Powell, *Political Mobilization*, pp. 139–40; ICOPS, *The Venezuelan Elections of December 1, 1963*, p. 13.

165. Valsalice, *Guerriglia e Politica*, pp. 32, 37, 40; also see Petkoff's "insider's" view (from the PCV) of the revolts, in Gall, "Teodoro Petkoff I," 11–12.

166. One quotation from a DIGEPOL agent may render accessible their political perspective: "I am the enemy of students. I've sprayed lead at the Central University. There we hunt them like rats. We're going to end this plague"; Guevara, *Los cachorros del Pentagono*, p. 43. For more on terror in the Venezuelan guerrilla war, see Wickham-Crowley, *Exploring Revolution*, chap. 3.

167. Levine, *Conflict and Political Change*, p. 110. In matters concerning religion, I might add, Levine has been and continues to be one of the best scholars of the region.

168. Alexander, *The Venezuelan Democratic Revolution*, pp. 91–95.

169. Levine, *Conflict and Political Change*, pp. 150–51.

170. Levine, *Conflict and Political Change*, pp. 145, 186–87.

171. Lartéguy, *The Guerrillas*, p. 262.

172. For some brief comments on Colombian politics during this period, see Allemann, *Macht und Ohnmacht*, pp. 386–87 (government weakness), 272 (guerrilla rivalries); Lamberg, *Die castristiche Guerilla*, pp. 92, 98, 102 (urban weaknesses, dependence of the FARC and EPL), 99 (effects of civic action); on the last topic, see as well Lartéguy, *The Guerrillas*, p. 69, where a guerrilla concedes the negative impact of civic action on rural support for the guerrillas, and Maullin, *Soldiers, Guerrillas, and Politics*, pp. 69, 79.

173. On revolutionary echoes in a few universities and high schools, see *La Prensa* (Lima), 29 August 1965, "7 Días" section, 6–11; Ministerio de Guerra, *Las guerrillas en el Peru*, pp. 39–40; Castillo, "Las guerrillas en el Peru," 164–66; Mercier, *Guerrillas in Latin America*, p. 149.

174. *La Prensa*, 28 August, 2 September, and 1 October 1965; p. 1 in each case.

175. Béjar, *Peru 1965*, p. 11. The total number of guerrillas almost surely never even reached 200; see my comments in chapter 2, and *La Prensa*, 1 October 1965, 6.

176. On neglect of the working class (whose organized segments APRA in good part controlled), see Lamberg, *Die castristiche Guerilla*, p. 118; on de la Puente's analysis of the *barriadas*, see Mercier, *Guerrillas in Latin America*, p. 147.

177. On the ELN *foco* in Ayacucho, see Béjar, *Peru 1965*, p. 109 and passim and Allemann, *Macht und Ohnmacht*, pp. 207–8; on fleeting Campa support in Junín, see Lamberg, *Die castristiche Guerilla*, p. 116 (on support) and Artola, *¡Subversión!*, pp. 78–79, for the Campas' later collaboration with the military. On levels of peasant support, see my discussion in chapter 4.

178. For general views, see Allemann, *Macht und Ohnmacht*, pp. 207–8; Lamberg, *Die castristiche Guerilla*, p. 112; and Mercado, *Las guerrillas del Peru*, pp. 94–96. On the letter and the defections, see respectively *La Prensa*, 1 October 1965, 6, and 12 September 1965, 1. Also on the defections, see Béjar's confirmation in *Peru 1965*, pp. 79–81.

179. Lamberg, *Die castristiche Guerilla*, p. 115 (quote); Allemann, *Macht und Ohnmacht*, pp. 211–12; Béjar, *Peru 1965*, p. 82.

180. Campbell, "Historiography," 55.

181. On the positions, see Guardia, *Proceso a campesinos*, pp. 23–34, and Castillo, "Las guerrillas en el Peru," 167–68 on the PCP's "critical support."

182. Béjar, *Peru 1965*, pp. 51–52.

183. On the archbishops' rally, see *La Prensa*, 30 August 1965, 1.

184. See Lamberg, *Die castristiche Guerilla*, pp. 41, 116 on the relationship between the *focos* and Peruvian politics.

185. Allemann, *Macht und Ohnmacht*, p. 213; Mercado, *Las guerrillas del Peru*, p. 95; *La Prensa*, 12 September 1965, p. 1.

186. Allemann, *Macht und Ohnmacht*, p. 217.

187. Esser, "Guevaras Guerilla," 328.

188. For the electoral results, see Bernard et al., *Guide to the Political Parties*, pp. 137–46, including a department-by-department breakdown of the vote.

189. On Barrientos's political tactics, see Millares, *Las guerrillas*, pp. 61, 70; Esser, "Guevaras Guerilla," 328; Lamberg, *Die castristiche Guerilla*, pp. 121–22, and "Che in Bolivia," 33; Allemann, *Macht und Ohnmacht*, pp. 430–31.

190. Lamberg, "Che in Bolivia," 26–27.

191. Hinting at or arguing directly for Bolivia's ripeness for revolution are Allemann, *Macht und Ohnmacht*, pp. 217–20, where he focuses (wisely, in my opinion) on the independent armed forces among miners and peasants and on the weak state; John Womack, Jr. "The Bolivian Guerrilla," *New York Review of Books* 16 (11 February 1971): 8, whose comments in retrospect seem far off the mark, especially given the newly landed peasantry and the political strengths of the now-nonrevolutionary MNR and military; and Debray, in 1964, who argued that the subjective and objective conditions were "most favorably united" in Bolivia, due to the army's destruction in 1952 (apparently ignoring its massive rebuilding effort, largely accomplished by the year he wrote); cf. Esser, "Guevaras Guerilla," 317. For Debray's 1968 jail-cell interview, see Georgie Anne Geyer, "Why Guevara Failed: An Interview with Regis Debray," *Saturday Review* 5 (24 August 1968): 15.

192. For a sense of the peasants' vote for Barrientos, see Bernard et al., *Guide to the Political Parties*, 144–45; on the military's commitment to civic action, see "Rol de las Fuerzas Armadas en la agricultura boliviana," *Revista Militar* (Bolivia) 299 (July–September 1969): 108–13, and William H. Brill, *Military Intervention in Bolivia: The Overthrow of Paz Estenssoro and the MNR*, Political Studies Series No. 3 (Washington, D.C.: Institute for the Comparative Study of Political Systems [ICOPS], 1967), pp. 29–32.

193. Millares, *Las guerrillas*, p. 40; the confederation had also supported him electorally the year before; cf. Mercier, *Guerrillas in Latin America*, p. 96.

194. On the regime's base of support in the peasantry, see Runa, "Bolivia: Análisis de una situación," 213, writing in the Cuban revolutionary journal *Pensamiento Crítico*; see also "8 de Octubre de 1967 en la Escuela de Armas," *Revista Militar* (Bolivia) 296 (October–December 1968): 78, for a quite similar military view; for other confirmations and discussion of the social conditions underlying peasant support for the regime, see Lamberg, "Che in Bolivia," 30; and Esser, "Guevaras Guerilla," 325–26, 330–31. For Guevara's own lack of peasant support, his own diaries are the best source: see Guevara, *The Complete Bolivian Diaries*, pp. 36, 59 (commentary by the editor Daniel James) and Guevara's own 1967 Analyses of the Month, for April, May, August, and September, as well as daily entries for 4 through 6 July 1967.

195. Brill, *Military Intervention*, pp. 18–23, on Lechín; on the absence of any real miner support for guerrillas, see the skeptical comments by Millares, *Las guerrillas*, pp. 45–46. No miners joined the *foco*, but a few unemployed miners were recruited; compare James's comments in Guevara, *Complete Bolivian Diaries*, p. 62, with Lamberg, *Die castristiche Guerilla*, p. 125.

196. Esser, "Guevaras Guerilla," 333.

197. See Millares, *Las guerrillas*, pp. 42, 70 (network), 50 (Oruro).

198. Lamberg, "Che in Bolivia," 33.

199. For Guevara's own analysis of the split, see *The Complete Bolivian Diaries*, entries for 31 December 1966 and Analysis of the Month for January. For the views of outside analysts, see Esser, "Guevaras Guerilla," 318–19, including the expulsions; James, in *Complete Bolivian Diaries*, pp. 62–63; Allemann, *Macht und Ohnmacht*, p. 229; Lamberg, *Die castristiche Guerilla*, pp. 124–25.

200. Lamberg, *Die castristiche Guerilla*, p. 131.

201. González and Sánchez, *The Great Rebel*, pp. 103–4; "8 de Octubre," 77 (quote). On the U.S. training of Bolivian troops, see my discussion in chapter 5.

202. See Loveman and Davies's edition and analysis of Guevara, *Guerrilla Warfare*.

CHAPTER 9
THE ORIGINS OF THE SECOND WAVE

1. Lartéguy, *The Guerrillas*, p. 261.

2. Josef Gugler, "The Urban Character of Contemporary Revolutions," *Studies in Comparative International Development* 17, no. 2 (Summer 1982): 60–73.

3. Omar Cabezas, *Fire from the Mountain*, trans. Kathleen Weaver (New York: Crown, 1985); Jeffrey L. Gould, *To Lead as Equals: Rural Protest and Political Consciousness in Chinandega, Nicaragua, 1912–1979* (Chapel Hill: University of North Carolina Press, 1990), esp. pp. 270–305; Jeffery Paige, "Cotton and Revolution in Nicaragua," in Peter Evans, Dietrich Rueschemeyer, and Evelyne Huber Stephens, eds., *States versus Markets in the World-System*, Vol. 8 in the Political Economy of the World-System Annuals (Beverly Hills, Calif.: Sage, 1985), pp. 91–114, esp. 108–10.

4. On military events, see John A. Booth, *The End and the Beginning: The Nicaraguan Revolution* (Boulder, Colo.: Westview, 1982), pp. 149, 172–75, and George Black, *Triumph of the People: The Sandinista Revolution in Nicaragua* (London: Zed, 1981), pp. 132–37, 148–62.

5. In this regard, I again consciously emulate Theda Skocpol's model for comparative analysis, as well as her own research practice; for the first, see Skocpol and Somers, "The Uses of Comparative History" and, for the second, see Skocpol, *States and Social Revolutions*, esp. chap. 1.

6. On geography and maps for the 1960s, see Lamberg, *Die castristiche Guerilla*, p. 106 and *Latin America Regional Reports—Andean Group*, 16 May 1980, p. 7; on numbers of guerrillas, see *[Latin America] Weekly Report*, 31 August 1984, with an estimate of 7,000; on the history of the M-19, see a journalist's report in Germán Castro Caycedo, *Del ELN al M-19: Once años de lucha guerrillera* (Bogotá: Carlos Valencia, 1980). On the continued guerrilla failure to mount any serious *political*

challenge to the regime, see the candid 1980s interview given by FARC leader Jacobo Arenas, where he concedes no chance of guerrilla success unless the regime suffers a sharp political reversal; cf. Arango, *FARC*, pp. 39–40.

7. *Los Sandinistas* (Bogotá: Oveja Negra, 1979), p. 27.

8. Gouldner, *Future of Intellectuals*, esp. pp. 53–73.

9. Philip Zwerling and Connie Martin, *Nicaragua: A New Kind of Revolution* (Westport, Conn.: L. Hill, 1985).

10. For the claim, made by a visitor to a guerrilla zone, see Philippe Bourgois, "What U.S. Foreign Policy Faces in Rural El Salvador: An Eyewitness Account," *Monthly Review* 34, no. 1 (May 1982): 20.

11. In this last regard, for El Salvador, see Bourgois, "What U.S. Foreign Policy Faces," 15–16. Similar accounts can be found in the scholarly and journalistic literature on the guerrilla-controlled countryside. For further documentation on peasant support and peasant relations, see my discussion of peasant support in the following chapter. A vivid film account exists in Don North's film, *Guazapa* (Washington, D.C.: Northstar Productions, 1984). For Vilas's data, see Dunkerley, *Power in the Isthmus*, pp. 263–64.

12. Robert Armstrong and Janet Shenk, *El Salvador: The Face of Revolution* (London: Pluto, 1982), chap. 8.

13. On peasant support for the insurgency in eastern Matagalpa, see Williams, *Export Agriculture and the Crisis in Central America*, pp. 129–34; for rural Chinandega, see Gould, *To Lead as Equals*, chap. 12.

14. Arango, *FARC*, p. 33; "M-19: La lucha armada posible," *Proceso* 163 (17 December 1979): 44. On urban lower-class electoral support for Gustavo Rojas Pinilla's ANAPO party, see Robert H. Dix, "Political Oppositions under the National Front," in *Politics of Compromise*, ed. Berry et al., pp. 131–79, esp. table 2 on p. 141.

15. I would like to thank John Bailey of Georgetown University for first calling my attention to the role of the urban informal sector in the Nicaraguan revolution; on the insurrections, see Booth, *The End and the Beginning*, chap. 7, or any other account of the Nicaraguan revolution; Paige, "Cotton and Revolution."

16. McClintock, "Sendero Luminoso: Peru's Maoist Guerrillas," 20; Thomas G. Sanders, "Peru between Democracy and the Sendero Luminoso," *Universities Field Staff International Reports* (1984, no. 21): 7.

17. See Linda Lobao Reif, "Women in Revolutionary Movements: Changing Patterns of Latin American Guerrilla Struggle" (Paper presented at the annual meetings of the American Sociological Association, Chicago, Illinois, August 1987). See as well her earlier, published piece, "Women in Latin American Guerrilla Movements: A Comparative Perspective," *Comparative Politics* 18, no. 2 (January 1986): 147–70. Both works contain an extensive bibliography of citations on women in such movements.

18. For these reports see, for Nicaragua, Black, *Triumph of the People*, pp. 323–24, and Patricia Flynn, "Women Challenge the Myth," in SCAAN, eds., *Revolution in Central America*, 416–17; for El Salvador see, also in the SCAAN reader, Fatma N. Çağatay and Jo-Anne Scott, "Women and Revolution: An Introduction," p. 382; for Peru, see Cynthia McClintock, "Peru's Sendero Luminoso Rebellion: Origins and Trajectory," original ms., p. 4; a revised version, without this estimate,

appeared in *Power and Popular Protest: Latin American Social Movements*, ed. Susan Eckstein (Berkeley: University of California Press, 1989), chap. 2.

19. On Lagos, see *Latin America Weekly Report*, 17 September 1982, pp. 6–7; on Colombia's groups, see Arango, *FARC*, pp. 20, 27, 87; "El M-19 elige a sus dirigentes," *Proceso* (Mexico City) 436 (11 March 1984): 40–44; "M-19: La lucha armada posible," 44; and *Colombia Report* (University of California-Irvine) 1, no. 2 (June 1979): 6–7 on the Bogotá *toma*; Black, *Triumph of the People*, pp. 323–24; Flynn, "Women Challenge the Myth," pp. 416–17.

20. Cabezas, *Fire from the Mountain*, pp. 100–101, 141–42; Gwenda Blair, "The Many Lives of Nora Astorga," *Mother Jones* 9, no. 8 (October 1984): 50; *New York Times*, 7 September 1984, on *senderistas* in prison.

21. Crane Brinton, *The Anatomy of Revolution*, rev. and expanded ed. (New York: Vintage, 1965), p. 104.

22. For the evidence on such regimes, the best single empirical source by far is Barbara Wolfe Jancar, *Women under Communism* (Baltimore, Md.: Johns Hopkins University Press, 1978), chap. 5 and appendixes, esp. the table on p. 89.

23. See my discussion of women's participation in chapter 2.

24. On the United States, see Jo Freeman, "The Origins of the Women's Liberation Movement," *American Journal of Sociology* 78, no. 4 (January 1973): 792–811, and *The Politics of Women's Liberation* (New York: David McKay, 1975), esp. chaps. 1, 2; for worldwide evidence, see Robin Morgan, ed., *Sisterhood is Global* (Garden City, New York: Anchor, 1984).

25. Anthropologists Marvin Harris and Sally Binford have argued that a society dominated by military activity, usually monopolized by men, tends to increase the subordination of women, in extreme cases evidenced by systematic female infanticide; Marvin Harris, *Cows, Pigs, Wars and Witches* (New York: Vintage, 1974), pp. 70–93 and Sally Binford, "Are Goddesses and Matriarchies Merely Figments of Feminist Imagination?" in *The Politics of Women's Spirituality*, ed. Charlene Spretnak (Garden City, N.Y.: Anchor, 1982), p. 546.

26. Jancar, *Women under Communism*, pp. 249–53.

27. We have a superb insider's account of this process in Mario Payeras, "Days of the Jungle: Testimony of a Guatemalan Guerrillero," *Monthly Review* 35–3 (July–August 1983): entire.

28. Concerned Guatemala Scholars, *Guatemala* pp. 39–40; Galeano et al., *Guatemala*, p. 160.

29. Concerned Guatemala Scholars, *Guatemala*, pp. 41, 47–54; Fried et al., *Guatemala in Rebellion*, pp. 257–87.

30. See Sanders, "Peru," esp. p. 6; David Scott Palmer, "Rebellion in Rural Peru: The Origins and Evolution of Sendero Luminoso," *Comparative Politics* 18, no. 2 (January 1986): esp. 127–28, 137–38; McClintock, "Sendero Luminoso" and "Peru's Sendero Luminoso," both passim.

31. The use of these traditions by *Sendero* has been explored by Josette Flores, in an unpublished paper written for my Georgetown course on Revolution and Society, and confirmed in private communication and evidence from Michael L. Smith, who is writing a book on *Sendero*, "The War of the Fourth Sword," with the research support of the MacArthur Foundation.

32. For the Indian proportion of the population of various Latin American coun-

tries, see any edition of the *Statistical Abstract of Latin America*, e.g., vol. 7 (1963): 23.

33. On the underground organizing efforts there, see Cabezas, *Fire from the Mountain*, pp. 36–38, 67–68 and Pilar Arias, *Nicaragua: Revolución—Relatos de combatientes del Frente Sandinista* (México, D.F.: Siglo Veintiuno, 1980), pp. 70–71; on the uprisings at Monimbó and Subtiava, see Booth, *The End and the Beginning*, pp. 158–59, or any other general account.

34. On the failed *foco*, see David Nolan, *The Ideology of the Sandinistas and the Nicaraguan Revolution* (Coral Gables, Fla: Institute of Interamerican Studies, University of Miami, 1984), pp. 24–25; Bernard Nietschmann, "The Unreported War against the Sandinistas: 6,000 Indian Guerrillas Are Fighting for Their Lands," *Policy Review* 29 (Summer 1984): 32–39.

35. See Alastair White, *El Salvador* (New York: Praeger, 1973), pp. 97–101, for the political context and events of the 1932 uprising and *matanza*; on the effects on the Indian population, see Armstrong and Shenk, *El Salvador*, p. 30 and Lydia Chavez, "El Salvador: The Voices of Anguish in a Bitterly Divided Land," *New York Times Magazine* (11 December 1983): 77.

36. Nolan, *The Ideology of the Sandinistas*, pp. 21–22.

37. Booth, *The End and the Beginning*, p. 112. On killings of university students in Guatemala, see Black et al., *Garrison Guatemala*, pp. 91–92 and Daniel Premo, "Political Assassination in Guatemala: A Case of Institutionalized Terror," *Journal of Interamerican Studies and World Affairs* 23, no. 4 (November 1981): 446–47; on El Salvador, see *Latin America Political Report* (London), 17 November 1978, pp. 356–57 and Armstrong and Shenk, *El Salvador*, p. 164.

38. See David Scott Palmer, "Rebellion in Rural Peru" and "The Revolutionary Terrorism of Peru's Shining Path" (Paper prepared for the Ford Foundation-sponsored project, "Terrorism in Context," Martha Crenshaw, director, January 1990): 10.

39. One must especially note the Montoneros of Argentina, who emerged from the left wing of the Peronist party and created a substantial urban guerrilla threat in Argentina in the 1970s. For a superb history and analysis—perhaps the best existing account of a single Latin American revolutionary movement that failed—see Richard Gillespie, *Soldiers of Perón: Argentina's Montoneros* (Oxford: Clarendon, 1982).

40. Originally the group was called the FLN, and Fonseca later added the adjective "Sandinista" to the group's name; cf. Nolan, *The Ideology of the Sandinistas*, pp. 23–24.

41. Claribel Alegría and D. J. Flakoll, *Nicaragua: La revolución sandinista—Una crónica política, 1855–1979* (México, D.F.: Era, 1984), p. 168; Nolan, *The Ideology of the Sandinistas*, pp. 18–22.

42. Nolan, *The Ideology of the Sandinistas*, p. 15.

43. Shirley Christian, *Nicaragua: Revolution in the Family* (New York: Vintage, 1986), pp. 32–35, 104.

44. All these comments are based on Sandinista sources or their supporters; see Black, *Triumph of the People*, p. 82; Alegría and Flakoll, *Nicaragua*, pp. 211–12; Cabezas, *Fire from the Mountain*, pp. 24–27, 36–38.

45. Carlos Nuñez's comments to Pilar Arias, in her *Nicaragua: Revolución*, p. 77.

46. Alegría and Flakoll, *Nicaragua*, pp. 211–13, and passim; Bernard Diederich,

Somoza and the Legacy of U.S. Involvement in Central America (New York: E. P. Dutton, 1981), p. 148.

47. For all the following groups, see the discussion in Richard Gillespie, "Anatomy of the Guatemalan Guerrilla," *Communist Affairs: Documents and Analysis*, vol. 2, no. 4 (October 1983): 490–96. On ORPA, see either of the following: Concerned Guatemala Scholars, *Guatemala*, pp. 21, 40 or Payeras, "Days of the Jungle," 13.

48. Gillespie, "Anatomy of the Guatemalan Guerrilla," 493.

49. Gillespie, "Anatomy," 491–92.

50. Gillespie, "Anatomy," 492; on the regional focus of the various groups' rural guerrilla activity, see Gillespie, "Anatomy," 493; Paige, "Social Theory and Peasant Revolution," pp. 711–22; or *Central America Bulletin*, (Berkeley, Calif.: Central America Research Institute) vol. 3, no. 7 (May 1984): Three.

51. Paige, "Social Theory and Peasant Revolution" and Concerned Guatemala Scholars, *Guatemala*, pp. 28–29, 53–54 on the CUC and pp. 37–41 on the guerrilla organizations.

52. Black et al., *Garrison Guatemala*, pp. 91–92.

53. For focused surveys of those organizational roots, see Robert S. Leiken, "The Salvadoran Left," chap. 5 in *Central America: Anatomy of Conflict*, ed. Robert S. Leiken (New York: Pergamon Press, 1984); Michael Radu, "The Structure of the Salvadoran Left," *Orbis* 28 (Winter 1985): 673–84; or Shirley Christian, "Rebel Factions," in *Crisis and Opportunity: U.S. Policy in Central America and the Caribbean*, ed. Mark Falcoff and Robert Royal (Washington, D.C.: Ethics and Public Policy Center, 1984), chap. 16.

54. Both the left and right confirm these origins; cf. Cynthia Arnson, *El Salvador: A Revolution Confronts the United States* (Washington, D.C.: Institute for Policy Studies, 1982), p. 30; Leiken, "Salvadoran Left," p. 115 (quote); R. Bruce McColm, *El Salvador: Peaceful Revolution or Armed Struggle?* (New York: Freedom House, 1982), p. 21. On the FPL's bitter relations with the PCS, see *Latin America Political Report* (London) 29 April 1977, pp. 121–22. In general, the left has emphasized the independence of the "mass organizations" allied to the guerrilla movements, while the right and center have emphasized their subordination to guerrilla groups. For an example of the latter argument in a democratic socialist periodical, see Gabriel Zaid, "Enemy Colleagues," *Dissent* (Winter 1982): 31–34 and his "Gabriel Zaid Replies," *Dissent* (Summer 1983): 357–58. Needless to say, the right has emphasized the "Communist Front" aspects of the civil organizations. Even so, splits between the civilian and military wings of the revolutionary opposition came clearly into the open in 1988–89 when Rubén Zamora and Guillermo Ungo returned to El Salvador and political life during the national elections in those years.

55. Radu, "Structure of the Salvadoran Left," 674–76; Armstrong and Shenk, *El Salvador*, p. 67; Christian, "Rebel Factions," p. 237; McColm, *El Salvador*, p. 22. On the suggestion that the ERP split from the FPL, see Enrique Baloyra, *El Salvador in Transition* (Chapel Hill: University of North Carolina Press, 1982), p. 161.

56. On circumstances leading to the FARN's formation, see Zaid, "Enemy Colleagues," 17–27; on the corresponding guerrilla and mass groups, see Leiken, "The Salvadoran Left," 113–17, or any other work on the period.

57. Radu, "The Structure of the Salvadoran Left," 676; McColm, *El Salvador*, p. 115.

58. Leiken, "The Salvadoran Left," pp. 116–17.

59. Information on the FMLN abounds. On the Carpio-line splinter group, see James Lemoyne, "The Guerrilla Network," *New York Times Magazine* (6 April 1986): 75, 79, where he also comments briefly on improved military coordination within the FMLN following Cayetano Carpio's death.

60. For the denial of its origins, see Lawrence T. Johnson, "Escape from Colombia," *Mother Jones* 6, no. 10 (December 1981): 41–42; for the two quotations, see *Latin America Weekly Report* (London), 16 May 1980, 7, and (same periodical, earlier name) *Latin America*, 20 February 1976, 64. Its denial of its origins may be related to ANAPO's later swing to the right under the control of Rojas's daughter; cf. *Latin America Regional Reports—Andean Group*, 16 May 1980, 7.

61. *Colombia Report* (University of California at Irvine, Program in Comparative Culture) 2, no. 2 (June 1980): 5; Johnson, "Escape from Colombia," 42.

62. Arango, *FARC: Veinte años*, p. 37; Johnson, "Escape from Colombia," 43.

63. In a private communication, *Sendero* expert Michael Smith denied any such linkage.

64. Palmer, "Rebellion in Rural Peru," 127–28, 135–38.

65. Skocpol, "France, Russia, China," 178, 201–5. Here Skocpol gives slightly more emphasis to their role than in her later book, *States and Social Revolutions*. My insistence that guerrilla movements emerge from those groups in society who are already organized—rather than those who are atomized and lacking solidarity, although discontented—coincides closely with the analyses of Tilly, *From Mobilization to Revolution*; Oberschall, *Social Conflict and Social Movements*; and with the resource-mobilization perspective, briefly outlined in John D. McCarthy and Mayer Zald, "Resource Mobilization and Social Movements: A Partial Theory," *American Journal of Sociology* 82, no. 6 (May 1977): 1212–41.

66. Tomás Borge, Carlos Fonseca, Daniel Ortega, Humberto Ortega, and Jaime Wheelock, *Sandinistas Speak* (New York: Pathfinder, 1982), p. 32 (quote); Manlio Tirado, *La revolución sandinista* (México, D.F.: Nuestro Tiempo, 1983), pp. 16–17; Michael Massing, "Who Are the Sandinistas?" *New York Review of Books* 35, no. 8 (12 May 1988): 53. As Leonel Rugama said during the struggle itself, "we have to be like Ché"; cf. Cabezas, *Fire from the Mountain*, pp. 11–12.

67. For the effect of Cuba on the Guatemalans, see Galeano et al., *Guatemala*, p. 150; for the interview with Cayetano, see Julio Scherer García, "Estados Unidos es el enemigo, con distintos rostros," *Proceso* (Mexico City) 199 (25 August 1980): 9.

68. I borrow that final phrase from the title of historian Arno Mayer's book on Europe at the turn of the twentieth century, *The Persistence of the Old Regime* (New York: Pantheon, 1981).

69. There is no real debate on the descriptions of the various polities. For solid accounts of earlier politics in the Central American nations, see Dunkerley, *Power in the Isthmus*. Also see Booth, *The End and the Beginning*, chaps. 3–4, or Black, *Triumph of the People*, chaps. 3–5, both on Nicaragua. For El Salvador, see White, *El Salvador*, chaps. 3 and 7, or Baloyra, *El Salvador in Transition*, chaps. 1–2; on Guatemala, see NACLA, *Guatemala* or Adams, *Crucifixion by Power*, chaps. 3–4; on Colombia, the best source by far is the edited collection by Berry et al., *Politics of*

Compromise, all on the National Front period; for a left critique of the repressive aspects of these formally democratic Colombian governments, see Comité de Solidaridad, *Libro negro de la represión*, which includes a list of all the periods in which full civil and political liberties were not in force in Colombia.

70. The best two overall treatments to date of *Sendero* in English are McClintock, "Peru's Sendero Luminoso Rebellion: Origins and Trajectory" and Palmer, "The Revolutionary Terrorism of Peru's Shining Path." Yet more work is forthcoming, including translations of key works by Peruvian scholars.

CHAPTER 10
THE STRUCTURES OF PEASANT SUPPORT IN THE SECOND WAVE

1. Paige, *Agrarian Revolution*, pp. 66–70, 211–77.

2. Eric Wolf argued that the "middle peasant" was the social focus of revolution (*Peasant Wars of the Twentieth Century*, pp. 289–92), while many Marxists have sought revolutionary potential in the landless peasantry, without being careful to distinguish those subject to capital from those subject only to the constraints of a landed elite.

3. For the "crucible" metaphor, see Black, *Triumph of the People*, p. 83; for maps, see Booth, *The End and the Beginning*, pp. 117, 149.

4. For maps of cash-crop zones in Nicaragua, El Salvador, and Guatemala, assisting the analyses to follow, see Stanley A. Arbingast, Clark C. Gill, Robert K. Holz, and Robert H. Ryan, *Atlas of Central America*, with cartography by William L. Hezlep (Austin: Bureau of Business Research, University of Texas, 1979), pp. 11, 35, 43.

5. Paige, "Cotton and Revolution in Nicaragua," pp. 91–114 (quote, 109).

6. See especially Williams, *Export Agriculture and the Crisis in Central America*, chap. 3, esp. pp. 61–63; also Jaime Wheelock Román, *Imperialismo y dictadura* (Managua: Nueva Nicaragua, 1985), pp. 84–87.

7. Black et al., *Garrison Guatemala*, p. 34.

8. Paige, "Social Theory and Peasant Revolution in Vietnam and Guatemala," 699–737. For related insiders' information, see Payeras, "Days of the Jungle," 67, on the EGP's presence in a migratory labor-base, and similar comments by another EGP leader, see Rolando Morán, "El éxodo campesino, una acción para proteger identidad comunitaria," *Proceso* (Mexico City), no. 413 (1 October 1984): 43.

9. A series of suggestive pieces of evidence can be tied together to produce this scenario; see Black et al., *Garrison Guatemala*, pp. 75–76; Paige, "Social Theory and Peasant Revolution," 733; Charles D. Brockett, "Malnutrition, Public Policy, and Agrarian Change in Guatemala," *Journal of Interamerican Studies and World Affairs* 26, no. 4 (November 1984): 488–89; Williams, *Export Agriculture*, pp. 139–42, 176–79; Payeras, "Days of the Jungle," passim; Concerned Guatemala Scholars, *Guatemala*, pp. 32–34, and passim.

10. For the data and the sources, see Timothy P. Wickham-Crowley, "Winners, Losers, and Also-Rans: Toward a Comparative Sociology of Latin American Guerrilla Movements," in Eckstein, ed., *Power and Popular Protest*, table 4.3 and the accompanying text. While many analysts have produced maps of guerrilla-controlled zones, two created for American consumption seem both fair and substantially copi-

ous in their definitions, and I have used them to identify "guerrilla zones" as of the end of 1983: see *Newsweek*, 5 December 1983 (80) and 16 January 1984 (26). For the corresponding departments and *municipios* of El Salvador, there seems to be only one written source, H. Nuhn, P. Krieg, and W. Schlick, *Zentralamerika: Karten zur Bevölkerungs- und Wirtschaftsstruktur* (Hamburg, Germany: Institut für Geographie und Wirtschaftsgeographie der Universität Hamburg, 1975), maps in back pocket of volume. Nor did the relationship hold within departments, comparing guerrilla *municipios* to those outside guerrilla-controlled zones; for a list of such areas, see table 10–2.

11. Carmen Diana Deere and Martin Diskin, "Rural Poverty in El Salvador: Dimensions, Trends, and Causes," mimeographed (International Labour Organization, January 1983), esp. part III; Harald Jung, "Class Struggles in El Salvador," *New Left Review* 122 (July–August 1980): 5–7.

12. Williams, *Export Agriculture*, p. 63, and 29 n. 39. For other suggestive evidence, see White, *El Salvador*, p. 120, and "The Little Village in Between," *Newsweek*, 14 January 1985, 17.

13. David Scott Palmer, "The Sendero Luminoso Rebellion in Rural Peru," in Georges Fauriol, ed., *Latin American Insurgencies* (Washington, D.C.: U.S. Government Printing Office, 1984), pp. 78, 82. The proportion of land reform beneficiaries was substantially lower in Ayacucho than in other Peruvian departments. For documentation, see McClintock, "Peru's Sendero Luminoso Rebellion," table 2.3.

14. Paige, "Social Theory and Peasant Revolution," esp. 701, 702–3 (quote), 723–25.

15. Paige, "Social Theory and Peasant Revolution," 703, emphasis removed.

16. Scott, *Moral Economy of the Peasant*, p. 4.

17. Scott, *Moral Economy*, chap. 7. His *Weapons of the Weak: Everyday Forms of Peasant Resistance* (New Haven: Yale University Press, 1985) appeared after Paige's 1983 article and hence could not be consulted for absolute clarity on this point.

18. For a parallel set of ideas, see Moore, *Injustice*.

19. One should note here a precise parallel with Paige's own analysis of Vietnam, where he showed that the Hoa Hao religious sect could siphon off discontent in a decidedly nonrevolutionary direction in the Mekong Delta of Vietnam; cf. *Agrarian Revolution*, pp. 324–32.

20. Scott, *Moral Economy*, chap. 5 on the depression rebellions, and chap. 7 on alternatives to revolt.

21. Scott and Kerklviet, "How Traditional Rural Patrons Lose Legitimacy," 501–40; reprinted in Schmidt et al., *Friends, Followers, and Factions*, pp. 439–58; see also Kerkvliet's own application of this logic to the Philippine Huk Rebellion, in his *The Huk Rebellion*, esp. pp. 254–56.

22. Williams, *Export Agriculture*, pp. 118–24; Scott's discussion of the peasantry's "little tradition" is especially clear in his "Hegemony and the Peasantry" *Politics and Society* 7, no. 3 (1977), esp. pp. 273–77.

23. Paige, *Agrarian Revolution*, pp. 41–44.

24. Paige, "Social Theory and Peasant Revolution," 733. As elsewhere, Williams, *Export Agriculture*, pp. 139–51, is an excellent single guide; see as well *Latin America Regional Reports: Mexico and Central America* (London), 15 February 1980, pp.

1, 3, and 8 January 1982, p. 3; Gabriel Aguilera P., "The Massacre at Panzós and Capitalist Development in Guatemala," *Monthly Review* 31, no. 7 (December 1979): 13–23; Black et al., *Garrison Guatemala*, pp. 29–30, 34–35, 74–76, 94–97; NACLA, *Report on the Americas* 12, no. 4 (July–August 1978): 44–45; Fried et al., *Guatemala in Rebellion*, p. 192 (Amnesty International); Concerned Guatemala Scholars, *Guatemala*, pp. 22, 39–41, 44.

25. From 1930 to 1950, Guatemala's population grew at a rate of 2.6 percent, while it grew at a 2.8 percent rate from 1965 to 1985; Thomas W. Merrick, with PRB Staff, "Population Pressures in Latin America," *Population Bulletin* 41, no. 3 (Washington, D.C.: Population Reference Bureau, July 1986), p. 7.

26. Paige, "Social Theory and Peasant Revolution," 724.

27. See either Black et al., *Garrison Guatemala*, p. 34, or Julia Preston, "Guatemala: The Muffled Scream," *Mother Jones* 6, no. 9 (November 1981): 47. The source of the data is the World Bank.

28. Brockett, "Malnutrition, Public Policy, and Agrarian Change in Guatemala," 477–98, esp. 486–93; the caloric intake data are from Fried et al., *Guatemala in Rebellion*, p. 88.

29. Concerned Guatemala Scholars, *Guatemala*, p. 22.

30. Concerned Guatemala Scholars, *Guatemala*, p. 48.

31. Black et al., *Garrison Guatemala*, p. 37, citing an article in NACLA, *Report on The Americas* (January–February 1980), by Edelberto Torres-Rivas.

32. Scott, *Moral Economy*, chap. 5; Kerkvliet, *The Huk Rebellion*, passim, esp. pp. 254–56.

33. Comparing maps is a simple method here: see the Conservative party vote mapped in Adams, *Crucifixion by Power*, p. 208, and the map with recorded guerrilla actions for 1983, in *Central America Report* (Berkeley, Calif.), 15 February 1985, p. 42. Paige, "Social Theory and Peasant Revolution," 712–13, provides data out of which a similar map could be constructed.

34. Fried et al., *Guatemala in Rebellion*, p. 286.

35. Concerned Guatemala Scholars, *Guatemala*, p. 54.

36. Shelton H. Davis, "State Violence and Agrarian Crisis in Guatemala: The Roots of the Indian-Peasant Rebellion," in Fried et al., *Guatemala in Rebellion*, p. 159.

37. Williams, *Export Agriculture*, pp. 129–34; Arias, *Nicaragua: Revolución*, p. 80; Amnesty International, *The Republic of Nicaragua* (Nottingham, England: The Russell Press, 1977), pp. 29, 58–59. Both Black, *Triumph of the People*, and Doris Tijerino, *Inside the Nicaraguan Revolution* (Vancouver: New Star, 1978), provide substantial accounts of insurgent and counterinsurgent events in that region.

38. Paige, "Cotton and Revolution," p. 107.

39. Paige, "Cotton and Revolution"; Wheelock, *Imperialismo y dictadura* (México, D.F.: Siglo Veintiuno, 1975), pp. 73–74, 82; for similar observations, see Cabezas, *Fire from the Mountain*, afterword by Walter LaFeber, p. 226; SCAAN, *Revolution in Central America*, pp. 24 (Jung), 228–29 (Dorner and Quiros).

40. Wheelock, *Imperialismo y dictadura* (1975): 75, and pp. 17, 28–30 on the earlier coffee expansion and peasant displacement; Cabezas, *Fire from the Mountain*, p. 209 (both quotations).

41. White, *El Salvador*, p. 120; Williams, *Export Agriculture*, p. 65.

42. Deere and Diskin, "Rural Poverty in El Salvador," pp. 7–17; T. David Mason, "Land Reform and the Breakdown of Clientelist Politics in El Salvador," *Comparative Political Studies* 18, no. 4 (January 1986): 487–516, esp. 500–501.

43. J. Mark Ruhl, "Agrarian Structure and Political Stability in Honduras," *Journal of Interamerican Studies and World Affairs* 26, no. 1 (February 1984): 33–68, esp. pp. 56–60.

44. Santiago Ruiz, "La modernización agrícola en El Salvador," *Estudios Centroamericanos (ECA)* 31 (April 1976): 156, cuadro no. 2.

45. On that last point, Williams, *Export Agriculture*, p. 63, is quite clear.

46. For the relative numbers of farmers and workers, see El Salvador, Dirección General de Estadística y Censos, *Tercer censo nacional de población 1961* (San Salvador, 1965), tables T-23 to T-37; for the number of landholders in different departments and municipios see, from the same source, *Tercer censo nacional agropecuario 1971* (San Salvador, 1974), vol. 1:1–5; for maps of zones of guerrilla control, see *Newsweek*, 5 December 1983 (80) and 16 January 1984 (26); for corresponding departments and *municipios*, see Nuhn et al., *Zentralamerika*, maps in back pocket of volume. Regression is inappropriate here, for the data are both nonlinear and heteroscedastic. In contrast, the Spearman rank correlation, like Kendall's *tau*, only requires an ordered ranking of departments, by degree of guerrilla control, and by land-tenure type; this procedure seems more in keeping with the quality of the data. Perfect correlations have values of 1.0; + 1.0 would mean that the rank ordering of departments was exactly the same on two different measures (1 and 1, 2 and 2, etc.), while –1.0 would indicate that the departments had exactly the opposite rank order on one value of the ranking as they had on the other (1 vs. 13, 2 vs. 12, and so on to 13 vs. 1).

47. Palmer, "Rebellion in Rural Peru," 136–37; for far more detail on both living standards and land reform history there, see also his dissertation, "'Revolution from Above': Military Government and Popular Participation in Peru, 1968–1972" (Ph.D. diss., Cornell University, Ithaca, N.Y., 1973), pp. 180–213. McClintock, "Peru's Sendero Luminoso Rebellion," table 2.3, reports only 11 percent of Ayacucho's rural population served by the agrarian reform, with only Cajamarca less well served (6 percent); the proportion of beneficiaries in six other departments ranged from 14 to 54 percent.

48. For most of the data, and a more detailed discussion, see McClintock, "Peru's Sendero Luminoso Rebellion," pp. 65–70, quote on 67.

49. Paige, *Agrarian Revolution*, pp. 165–66.

50. Palmer, "'Revolution from Above,'" pp. 196–99.

51. McClintock, "Peru's Sendero Luminoso Rebellion," p. 68.

52. McClintock, "Peru's Sendero Luminoso Rebellion," pp. 74–76.

53. Booth, *The End and the Beginning*, pp. 41–46, 116–21 for areas; Alegría and Flakoll, *Nicaragua*, p. 83, on 1932; Black, *Triumph of the People*, pp. 16–18, 79. Moreover, evidence suggests that the history of revolt in that region may well predate Sandino himself; cf. Black, *Triumph*, p. 15. Gould, *To Lead as Equals*, p. 295, also confirms the presence of "Sandinista political subcultures" in the central highlands. The Colombian ELN also chose Santander, and the Cubans Oriente, because of their insurrectionary pasts.

54. Amnesty International, *The Republic of Nicaragua*, p. 29; Alegría and Flakoll, *Nicaragua*, pp. 133–35; Arias, *Nicaragua: Revolución*, p. 81.

55. For one good example, see José Valdivia's account of his experiences in the La Tronca-La Luz area, in Arias, *Nicaragua: Revolución*, pp. 79–82, esp. p. 81.

56. Cabezas, *Fire from the Mountain*, pp. 220 (first quote), 169–71, 209 (third quote); Alegría and Flakoll, *Nicaragua*, pp. 147, 168 (second quote, on López); Arias, *Nicaragua: Revolución*, p. 26.

57. "Documentos relativos al origen de las discordias entre las ciudades de León y Granada de Nicaragua, año de 1823" *Revista de los Archivos Nacionales (Costa Rica)* 1 (May–June 1937): 341–55; Nolan, *Ideology of the Sandinistas*, p. 14.

58. Cabezas, *Fire from the Mountain*, pp. 225–26; *Latin America Political Report*, 13 July 1979, p. 211.

59. On the Monimbó *encomienda*, see *Colección Somoza: Documentos para la Historia de Nicaragua*, edited by Andrés Vega Bolaños, 17 volumes (Madrid: Imprenta Viuda de Galo Sáez, 1954–57), 11:146–53 (Letter from León Cabildo, 24 June 1544); Black, *Triumph of the People*, p. 15; Cabezas, *Fire from the Mountain*, pp. 36–38. Subtiava is unusual here in several ways, for at least one account describes the *barrio* as politically *somocista* prior to the Sandinistas' organizing efforts. However, Doris Tijerino's account of Subtiava's political mobilization and radicalism leaves no such impression of *somocismo*; cf. Tijerino, *Inside the Nicaraguan Revolution*, pp. 140–43.

60. "Colombia's Guerrillas Soldier On," *Latin America Regional Reports—Andean Group*, 16 May 1980, pp. 6–7; Arango, *FARC*, p. 37; for more on the persistence of earlier rebellious traditions in the interior, see Arango, *FARC*, pp. 161–70, and the listing of uprisings in Berry et al., *Politics of Compromise*, pp. 348–49.

61. McClintock, "Peru's Sendero Luminoso Rebellion," p. 81.

62. Mario Vargas Llosa, "Inquest in the Andes," *New York Times Magazine*, 31 July 1983, 36.

63. David P. Werlich, "Peru: The Shadow of the Shining Path," *Current History* (February 1984): 80–81; for an example, see *Time*, 18 April 1983, 35.

64. For McClintock and Eckstein, see their respective contributions to Eckstein, *Power and Popular Protest*; for the appeals to Andean traditions, I am indebted to an undergraduate paper written by Josette Flores, and to a private communication and some printed evidence shown me by Michael L. Smith, currently engaged in an extensive research project on *Sendero*.

65. Fried et al., *Guatemala in Rebellion*, p. 272.

66. Murdo MacLeod, *Spanish Central America: A Socioeconomic History, 1520–1720* (Berkeley, Calif.: University of California Press, 1973), pp. 326–28; Eric Wolf, *Sons of the Shaking Earth* (Chicago: University of Chicago Press, 1959), chap. 10.

67. For some information on those three nations, see chapter 7. Herbert Klein terms "innumerable" the Bolivian Indian rebellions that occurred from the late-1500s reforms of Viceroy Toledo until the Bolivian revolution of 1952; cf. *Bolivia: The Evolution of a Multi-Ethnic Society* (New York: Oxford, 1982), p. 47. Guatemalan history simply seems to lack such large-scale and widespread phenomena, and an explanation for those differences would be intriguing.

68. Armstrong and Shenk, *El Salvador*, pp. 26–30; Chavez, "El Salvador," 77.

69. Tilly, *From Mobilization to Revolution*, p. 114.

70. McCarthy and Zald, "Resource Mobilization and Social Movements," 1212–41.

71. Levine, *Conflict and Political Change in Venezuela*, pp. 226–27.

72. For example, the strong links of Liberal and Conservative parties to rural Colombia and of reformist *Acción Democrática* to rural Venezuela definitely militated against peasant support for guerrillas in those two nations. For more detail, see chapter 7.

73. For a persuasive argument that language is an institutional realm of society, see Peter L. Berger and Brigitte Berger, *Sociology: A Biographical Approach* (New York: Basic Books, 1972), chap. 4.

74. I discuss these two cases in detail in chapter 7. For further comments on the 1960s Guatemalan experience, see Gillespie, "Anatomy of the Guatemalan Guerrilla," 494, and Galeano et al., *Guatemala*, p. 160, for the retrospective comments of Rolando Morán, who participated as a guerrilla in both periods. For the lone indigenous success story there in the 1960s, see the brief comments in Thomas J. Maloney, "El impacto social del esquema de desarrollo de la franja transversal del norte, sobre los Maya-Kekchí en Guatemala," *Estudios Sociales Centroamericanos* 29 (May–August 1981): 100.

75. Shelton H. Davis and Julie Hodson, *Witnesses to Political Violence in Guatemala: The Suppression of a Rural Development Movement* (Boston: Oxfam America, 1984), p. 32; Payeras, "Days of the Jungle," 13, 29–30, 33–34 (quote), 84–88; Fried et al., *Guatemala in Rebellion*, p. 277.

76. McClintock, "Sendero Luminoso" (1983): 20, and "Peru's Sendero Luminoso Rebellion," pp. 70–72, 77–79 (quote on 78).

77. McClintock, ibid., both works. See also Sanders, "Peru between Democracy," 6; Vargas Llosa, "Inquest in the Andes," 22; and any or all of David Scott Palmer's articles on *Sendero*.

78. See my discussion of church influence in these nations in chapter 8.

79. Booth, *The End and the Beginning*, pp. 134–37; Tommie Sue Montgomery, *Revolution in El Salvador* (Boulder, Colo.: Westview, 1982), chap. 4.

80. Tommie Sue Montgomery, "Liberation and Revolution: Christianity as Subversive Activity in Central America," in *Trouble in Our Backyard: Central America and the United States in the Eighties*, ed. Martin Diskin (New York: Pantheon, 1983), p. 93.

81. For a good account, see Booth, *The End and the Beginning*, pp. 134–37; Montgomery, "Liberation and Revolution," p. 93.

82. On weak church traditions in the villages, see White, *El Salvador*, pp. 209–11; Montgomery, "Liberation and Revolution," p. 93 (both quotations); James LeMoyne, "Salvador's 'Masas' Are Feeding the Revolution," *New York Times*, 16 September 1984; Armstrong and Shenk, *El Salvador*, pp. 81–83, list locales suggesting such a correlation; James LeMoyne, "Churches in El Salvador Accused of Aiding Rebels," *New York Times*, 3 August 1986; A. Douglas Kincaid, "Peasants into Rebels: Community and Class in Rural El Salvador," *Comparative Studies in Society and History* 29, no. 3 (July 1987): esp. 480–90.

83. *Latin America Political Report*, 15 June 1979, p. 180; Montgomery, "Liberation and Revolution," p. 92; Galeano et al., *Guatemala*, pp. 242–45.

84. On Catholic Action, see Montgomery, "Liberation and Revolution," p. 87; and Robert M. Carmack, "Estratificación y cambio social en las tierras altas occidentales

de Guatemala: El caso de Tecpanaco," *América Indigena* 36, no. 2 (April–June 1976): 291–93, 301. On the *cofradías*, see J. Antonio Bran, "Organización popular y lucha de clases en el campo," *Cuadernos de Marcha* 2, no. 10 (November–December 1980): 18 (quote); also found in Fried et al., *Guatemala in Rebellion*, reading no. 35; Concerned Guatemala Scholars, *Guatemala*, pp. 34–35; Black et al., *Garrison Guatemala*, pp. 138–39.

85. Black et al., *Garrison Guatemala*, pp. 166–67.

86. Henry Ruiz, "La montaña era como un crisol donde se forjaban los mejores cuadros," *Nicaráuac: Revista Bimestral del Ministerio de Cultura*, Año 1, no. 1 (May–June 1980): 14–15, 16 (quote); Black, *Triumph of the People*, p. 79; Cabezas, *Fire from the Mountain*, pp. 36–38 (quote).

87. Palmer, "Rebellion in Rural Peru," 137–38, is absolutely clear on all these issues; McClintock "Sendero Luminoso," 26 and "Peru's Sendero Luminoso Rebellion," pp. 77–79.

88. On those *somocista* agents, see Alegría and Flakoll, *Nicaragua*, p. 164, and *Los Sandinistas*, p. 114.

89. McClintock, "Sendero Luminoso," 28–29, and "Peru's Sendero Luminoso Rebellion," pp. 70–76 and table 2.4 (electoral results, 1980–86).

90. For Salvadoran politics up to the 1970s, the best guides are White, *El Salvador*, chaps. 3 and 7, and Baloyra, *El Salvador in Transition*, chaps. 2 and 3. For Guatemalan politics of the 1960s, see the discussion in Adams, *Crucifixion by Power*, or the less detailed treatment over a longer period in NACLA, *Guatemala*.

91. For wide-ranging discussion of this and similar issues, in many regions of the world, see the contributions to Schmidt et al., *Friends, Followers, and Factions*.

92. Baloyra, *El Salvador in Transition*, p. 137.

93. McClintock, "Peru's Sendero Luminoso Rebellion," pp. 74–76.

94. Concerned Guatemala Scholars, *Guatemala*, pp. 28–29, 40 (note comments on the FAR and its role in the "mass movement"), 53–54; Montgomery, "Liberation and Revolution," p. 92.

95. Fried et al., *Guatemala in Rebellion*, p. 144 (Amnesty International); Black et al., *Garrison Guatemala*, p. 46; *Latin America Regional Reports: Mexico and Central America*, 13 January 1984; and Richard Millett, "Guatemala: Progress and Paralysis," *Current History* (March 1985): 111.

96. White, *El Salvador*, pp. 207–8, 255; Baloyra, *El Salvador in Transition*, p. 64; Armstrong and Shenk, *El Salvador*, pp. 77–78, 126, 140; *Latin America Weekly Report*, 5 September 1980; *Latin America Regional Reports: Mexico and Central America*, 15 August 1980, p. 7.

97. *Latin America Regional Reports: Mexico and Central America*, 18 February 1983, p. 8.

98. On the personal conflicts, and on FECCAS and the CEBs, see Armstrong and Shenk, *El Salvador*, pp. 100–102, 81–83; on the class-linked memberships in FECCAS and ORDEN, see Thomas Anderson's review of Carlos Rafael Cabarrús P.'s "Génesis de una Revolución," in *Hispanic American Historical Review* 64, no. 3 (August, 1984): 50–51; on the older, milder village patterns, see the interview with José Napoleón Duarte in *Playboy* 31, no. 11 (November 1984): 72. The best single source on the organizational overlap is Kincaid, "Peasants into Rebels." Georg Simmel was the first sociologist clearly to argue that multiply aligned social conflicts tend

to intensify conflict, while cross-cutting patterns tend to mute conflicts; see Georg Simmel, *Conflict and the Web of Group Affiliations*, trans. Kurt H. Wolff and Reinhard Bendix (New York: Free Press, 1955), chaps. 1 and 3, and also the exposition of Simmel's ideas in Lewis Coser, *The Functions of Social Conflict* (New York: Free Press, 1956).

99. Vargas Llosa, "Inquest in the Andes," passim, esp. 36 (quote); *Latin America Weekly Report*, 15 April 1983, pp. 4–5.

CHAPTER 11
REGIME WEAKNESSES AND REVOLUTION IN THE SECOND WAVE

1. Arias, *Nicaragua: Revolución*, p. 108.

2. Paige, "Cotton and Revolution in Nicaragua," p. 94.

3. Wheelock, *Imperialismo y dictadura*, part 6, covers the Somozas' years within the upper classes; on the nineteenth century in particular, but also the twentieth, see the contributions to Alberto Lanuza, Juan Luis Vásquez, Amaru Barahona, and Amalia Chamorro, *Economía y sociedad en la construcción del estado en Nicaragua* (San José, Costa Rica: ICAP, 1983), especially II Parte, by Vásquez, "Luchas políticas y estado oligárquico."

4. Wheelock, *Imperialismo y dictadura* (1985), pp. 122–33.

5. Vásquez, "Luchas políticas y estado oligárquico," pp. 154–55, 164–65; Wheelock, *Imperialismo y dictadura*, pp. 127–28 (including n. 12), 130–33.

6. For the clearest descriptions of the various "Banco" groups, including Somoza's own Banco Nacional, see Harry W. Strachan, "The Role of the Business Groups in Economic Development: The Case of Nicaragua" (Doctor of Business Administration diss., Harvard University, 1972), chap. 2, esp. pp. 11, 15. For the scope of their role in the economy, see p. 81, table 3:3. Wheelock, *Imperialismo y dictadura*, part 6, also provides an excellent account of the business groups and details on the Somoza economic empire, pp. 186–201. For a briefer treatment, including the bourgeoisie's contribution to Somoza's fall, see Dennis Gilbert, "The Bourgeoisie," in Thomas W. Walker, ed., *Nicaragua: The First Five Years* (New York: Praeger, 1985), esp. pp. 163–67. Harald Jung estimates that the Somoza group came to control 60 percent of the Nicaraguan economy by the late 1970s; cf. his "Behind the Nicaraguan Revolution," in SCAAN, *Revolution in Central America*, p. 22; also in *New Left Review* 117 (September–October 1979): 69–90.

7. I provide evidence of the Sandinistas' bourgeois origins in appendix B.

8. Alegría and Flakoll, *Nicaragua*, pp. 125–26.

9. For a good account of the Walker period and the splits in the upper class, see Ralph Lee Woodward, Jr., *Central America: A Nation Divided* (New York: Oxford, 1976), pp. 136 (quote), 138–46, 271. On the economic roots of divisions within the upper class, see Nolan, *The Ideology of the Sandinistas*, p. 14, or Vásquez, "Luchas políticas y estado oligárquico." For one of the tendentious accounts emphasizing official U.S. imperialism and managing to omit the role of the Liberal party, see Alegría and Flakoll, *Nicaragua*, chap. 2.

10. Diederich, *Somoza*, p. 3.

11. Thomas L. Karnes, "The Historical Legacy and the Failure of Union," in Howard Wiarda, ed., *Rift and Revolution: The Central American Imbroglio* (Washington, D.C.: American Enterprise Institute for Public Policy Research, 1984), p. 38.

12. Booth, *The End and the Beginning*, pp. 21–22.

13. For accounts of the Zelaya years emphasizing his thorough, centralizing rule, see Dana G. Munro, *The Five Republics of Central America* (New York: Russell & Russell, 1967 [1918]), pp. 88–91; Booth, *The End and the Beginning*, pp. 22–25; Diederich, *Somoza*, pp. 7–8; Woodward, *Central America*, pp. 154–55; for Marxist accounts emphasizing the "coffee-growers' hegemony" (*hegemonia cafetalera*), see Wheelock, *Imperialismo y dictadura* (1985), pp. 121–24; Vásquez, "Luchas políticas y estado oligárquico," pp. 156–63; and Hugo Cancino Troncoso, *Las raíces históricas e ideológicas del movimiento sandinista: Antecedentes de la revolución nacional y popular nicaragüense, 1927–1929* (Gylling, Denmark: Odense University Press, 1984), pp. 33–55.

14. Woodward, *Central America*, p. 168.

15. Neill Macaulay, *The Sandino Affair* (Durham, N.C.: Duke University Press, 1985 [1967]), chap. 2, quote on p. 41.

16. Ronald H. McDonald, "Civil-Military Relations in Central America," in Wiarda, *Rift and Revolution*, p. 137.

17. Munro, *The Five Central American Republics*, p. 189.

18. For example, the guard may have opposed any treaty with Sandino, due to the long and fruitless war they had fought against him, and may have been behind his assassination; on the war see Macaulay, *The Sandino Affair*, chap. 8.

19. Richard Millett, "The Somoza Regime," in Robert S. Leiken and Barry Rubin, eds., *The Central American Crisis Reader* (New York: Summit, 1987), pp. 138–40; NACLA, "Crisis in Nicaragua," *Report on the Americas* 12, no. 6 (November–December, 1978), pp. 8–9.

20. For sources and greater detail, see Millett, "The Somoza Regime"; NACLA, "Crisis in Nicaragua"; Booth, *The End and the Beginning*, pp. 54–57, 92–93; and José Fajardo's comments in *Los Sandinistas*, p. 130.

21. The clearest account of this is in Diederich, *Somoza*, pp. 137–42; the *New York Times*, 30 October 1977, part 4, p. 3, also noticed it.

22. NACLA, "Crisis in Nicaragua," p. 8.

23. Millett, "The Somoza Regime," gives a good, brief account.

24. NACLA, "Crisis in Nicaragua," pp. 8–9; Booth, *The End and the Beginning*, pp. 54–57; Black, *Triumph of the People*, pp. 52–55; *Latin America Political Report*, 18 August 1978, p. 250.

25. Alegría and Flakoll, *Nicaragua*, p. 126.

26. In the last decade before the Cuban revolution, 40 to 50 percent of federal government receipts still came from customs duties alone. In Nicaragua in the 1970s, only one-fifth of federal government revenues came from direct taxation, the rest from indirect forms such as customs duties and some sales taxes. See, respectively, Guy Bourdé and Oscar Zanetti, "Le commerce extérieur de Cuba a l'époque de la république neo-coloniale (1897–1958)," *Cahiers des Ameriques Latines* 8 (2nd semester, 1973), p. 56; Inter-American Development Bank, *Economic and Social Progress in Latin America: 1986 Report* (Washington, D.C.: IDB, 1986), pp. 408–12.

27. Rouquié, *The Military and the State in Latin America*, chap. 6.

28. On corruption in Cuba, see Domínguez, *Cuba*, pp. 93–95; Thomas, *Cuba*, pp. 564–65, 574, 581, 583, 737–38, 763; Thomas, "Origins of the Cuban Revolution," 457–58. For Nicaragua, see Falcoff, "Somoza, Sandino, and the United States," pp. 338–41; Alegría and Flakoll, *Nicaragua*, pp. 120–26 (where they, like others, com-

pare Somoza's rule directly with the Sicilian mafia); Booth, *The End and the Beginning*, pp. 54–57; Black, *Triumph of the People*, p. 209; Jung, "Behind the Nicaraguan Revolution," pp. 22–23, 26; *Los Sandinistas*, p. 130; NACLA, "Crisis in Nicaragua," pp. 8–9; Tirado, *La revolución sandinista*, p. 21; and Ruiz, "La montaña era como un crisol," 16, on Somoza's invasion of the financial sector after the 1972 Managua earthquake.

29. Booth, *The End and the Beginning*, pp. 89, 98–101; on smaller parties, see pp. 104–6.

30. This is an attributed statement rather than a direct quote, from Henry Ruiz, "La montaña era como un crisol," 14.

31. Falcoff, "Somoza, Sandino, and the United States," pp. 333–34. Save for a brief flirtation with the Nicaraguan working class in the 1940s, the Somozas never really sponsored the kinds of populist programs that Batista carried out in Cuba.

32. Dunkerley, *Power in the Isthmus*, pp. 240–44.

33. *Latin America* (London), 19 September 1975, pp. 293–94.

34. Alan Riding, "National Mutiny in Nicaragua," *New York Times Magazine* (30 July 1978): 12–15 +; S. Kinzer, "Nicaragua: Universal Revolt," *Atlantic Monthly* 243 (February 1979): 4+; *Latin America Political Report*, 6 October 1978, p. 307 (quote).

35. Mark Falcoff, "Somoza, Sandino, and the United States," in Falcoff and Royal, *Crisis and Opportunity*, p. 341; Farber, *Revolution and Reaction in Cuba*, pp. 148, 166–68.

36. Nolan, *Ideology of the Sandinistas*, pp. 36–37; or Borge et al., *Sandinistas Speak*, pp. 13–22.

37. Tirado, *La revolución sandinista*, p. 51; *Los Sandinistas*, p. 25.

38. *Los Sandinistas*, pp. 202–3

39. See Black, *Triumph of the People*, pp. 120–122 for the minimalist program of 1978; for Gabriel García Márquez's rendering, see *Los Sandinistas*, p. 147, and p. 151 on retaining some elements of the National Guard; for an influential overview of the process of public ideological moderation, see Nolan, *Ideology of the Sandinistas*. For Castro's public statement for U.S. consumption in early 1958, compare Castro, "Why We Fight."

40. *Los Sandinistas*, p. 24.

41. See Mario Llerena, *The Unsuspected Revolution* (Ithaca, N.Y.: Cornell University Press, 1978), for details on his activities.

42. Borge et al., *Sandinistas Speak*, p. 79; Black, *Triumph of the People*, pp. 104–5, uses the "bridge" metaphor.

43. Christian, *Nicaragua*, pp. 41–42; for details on The Twelve, see Booth, *The End and the Beginning*, pp. 102, 103, 113, 131.

44. Excellent accounts, each with its own quirks and sometimes biases, appear in Booth, *The End and the Beginning*; Black, *Triumph of the People*; and Alegría and Flakoll, *Nicaragua*. Dennis Gilbert has reviewed the quality of the first wave of Nicaraguan revolutionary historiography for English-language readers; see his "Sandinistas in Power," *Latin American Research Review* 19, no. 2 (1984): 214–19.

45. Jung, "Behind the Nicaraguan Revolution," p. 33.

46. Diederich, *Somoza*, pp. 14, 153.

47. Black, *Triumph of the People*, pp. 100–101.

48. Lawrence Wright, "War of Words," *Mother Jones* 8, no. 5 (June 1983): 40.

49. *Los Sandinistas*, p. 28; Wright, "War of Words," 40.

50. See the detailed comments in Black, *Triumph of the People*, pp. 168–70; see also Humberto Ortega's confirmatory comments in *Los Sandinistas*, p. 77. Regional radio broadcasts also came from the towns of León and Matagalpa after they had been individually liberated.

51. Booth, *The End and the Beginning*, pp. 97–126, 134–37, 152–54, and passim; for a summary of Vilas's findings, see Dunkerley, *Power in the Isthmus*, pp. 240–47, 263–64.

52. The last suggestion is the most suspect, due to the statistical breakdowns developed by Carlos Vilas, and reported by Dunkerley in the previous note; but Henry Ruiz stated simply that "support in the mountains was never lacking, we were never isolated from the population" from the moments of first real communication; cf. "La montaña era como un crisol," 21. A recent historical work confirms the importance of the unheralded rural components of the resistance movement, in this instance in rural Chinandega; see Gould, *To Lead as Equals*, esp. pp. 293–305, where he criticizes Vilas's study and conclusions.

53. Falcoff, "Somoza, Sandino, and the United States," pp. 333–34.

54. NACLA, "Crisis in Nicaragua," pp. 12–17; for the upper class and middle classes turning against the regime after 1972, see also Ronald H. Ebel, "The Development and Decline of the Central American City-State," in Wiarda, ed., *Rift and Revolution*, pp. 89–90.

55. Weber's argument is concisely reported in Gilbert's review of Weber's *The Sandinist Revolution*; cf. Gilbert, "Sandinistas in Power," 215–17; see reports on the attitudes and actions of industrialists and the County Chambers of Commerce in *Latin America Political Report*, 20 January 1978, p. 17 and 1 September 1978.

56. Amalia Chamorro, "Estado y hegemonía durante el somocismo," in Lanuza et al., *Economía y sociedad*, pp. 265–67.

57. On the middle class and corruption, see my comments in chapter 8.

58. Tijerino, *Inside the Nicaraguan Revolution*, pp. 125–26; Jung, "Behind the Nicaraguan Revolution," p. 26 on sales taxes; Eduardo Crawley, *Nicaragua in Perspective* (New York: St. Martin's Press, 1984), pp. 149–50, and pp. 156–57 for the composite "middle-class bureaucrat." For the new urban middle strata's opposition to Somoza the elder as early as the 1940s, see Amaru Barahona, "Intervención extranjera y dictadura," in Lanuza et al., eds., *Economía y sociedad*, p. 227.

59. The spontaneous nature of these outbursts is confirmed by Sandinistas themselves or by authors who treat their words as gospel truth; cf. Humberto Ortega's comments in Borge et al., *Sandinistas Speak*, pp. 62–64, and Black, *Triumph of the People*, pp. 108–9, 128–29. On Black's uncritical acceptance of Sandinista positions, see Gilbert, "Sandinistas in Power," pp. 218–19. Gilbert is anything but a conservative ideologue in these matters; he is a progressive yet hard-nosed scholar sensitive to uncritical writing and thinking.

60. Tirado, *La revolución sandinista*, p. 45.

61. *New York Times*, 2 March 1977, sect. 2, p. 1; *Latin America Political Report*, 20 January 1978, p. 17.

62. Black, *Triumph of the People*, pp. 318–19.

63. See my discussion of these features in part 4 of chapter 10; see also Black, *Triumph of the People*, pp. 319–20, for a succinct summary.

64. See Walter LaFeber's afterword to Cabezas, *Fire from the Mountain*, p. 225,

as well as Cabezas's own accounts of revolutionary life within the university, esp. pp. 25–27.

65. Dunkerley, *Power in the Isthmus*, p. 251; *Latin America Political Report*, 1 September 1978.

66. *Latin America Political Report*, 1 September 1978.

67. Black, *Triumph of the People*, p. 52.

68. Diederich, *Somoza*, pp. 287, 298–99.

69. *Latin America Political Report*, 16 February 1979, pp. 52–53.

70. Christian, *Nicaragua*, pp. 107–8; Mark Falcoff, "Nicaragua: Somoza, Sandino, and the United States," this version in his *Small Countries, Large Issues: Studies in U.S.-Latin American Asymmetries* (Washington, D.C.: American Enterprise Institute for Public Research, 1984), p. 63; Booth, *The End and the Beginning*, pp. 128–30, 178–79.

71. Booth, *The End and the Beginning*, pp. 130–34, 165–68.

72. For one carefully studied rural area, see the report on Chinandega in Gould, *To Lead as Equals*, chap. 12.

73. These events and accounts are drawn from Booth, *The End and the Beginning*, pp. 152–84.

74. Theda Skocpol, "Old Regime Legacies and Communist Revolutions in Russia and China," *Social Forces* 55, part 1, no. 2 (December 1976): 284–315. I cite this study as a model despite appreciable differences with some of the conclusions she draws.

75. Luis Burstin, "A Night with the FMLN," *Commentary* 79, no. 5 (May 1985): 53.

76. Jeff Stern, "The Day of Reckoning Is Coming: An Interview with Robert E. White," in SCAAN, *Revolution in Central America*, p. 118.

77. James LeMoyne, "The Guerrilla Network," *New York Times Magazine*, 6 April 1986, p. 71.

78. Manus I. Midlarsky and Kenneth Roberts, "Class, State, and Revolution in Central America: Nicaragua and El Salvador Compared," *Journal of Conflict Resolution* 29, no. 2 (June 1985): 178.

79. Zaid, "Enemy Colleagues," 29.

80. Leiken, "The Salvadoran Left," p. 119.

81. Janet Shenk, "Can the Guerrillas Win?" *Mother Jones* 13, no. 3 (April 1988): 37; for more detail on military budgets in and military aid to the various Central American nations since World War II, with yearly data from the early 1980s, see McDonald, "Civil-Military Relations in Central America," pp. 139–47.

82. Because of the space constraints of an already overlong book, I treat this topic here in sketchbook form rather than full detail; for more detail see my "Understanding Failed Revolution in El Salvador: A Comparative Analysis of Regime Types and Social Structures," *Politics and Society* 17, no. 4 (December 1989): 511–37.

83. A good condensed guide on the "oligarchy" is Dunkerley, *Power in the Isthmus*, pp. 341–50, including lists of families involved in different sectors of the economy.

84. Dunkerley, *Power in the Isthmus*, pp. 339, 373–74; also on the response of those groups to the reform proposals, see Baloyra, *El Salvador in Transition*, pp. 31, 55–60. Shirley Christian, "El Salvador's Divided Military," *Atlantic Monthly* 251,

no. 6 (June 1983): 53 describes their alliance as a trade-off of rural peace for the upper class in exchange for willingness to pay taxes, from which military corruption could prosper; she describes such corruption as "rampant."

85. On the *tandas*, see Christian, "Salvador's Divided Military," esp. 50.

86. For some of the reforms in 1979–82 and the reaction of the right, see Baloyra, *El Salvador in Transition*, pp. 78–81, 106–16.

87. Shafik Jorge Handal, "We Have No Alternative to Armed Struggle," *World Marxist Review* (England) 23, no. 10 (October 1980): 24 n. 2.

88. *[Latin America] Weekly Report*, 19 April 1985, p. 3.

89. On Duarte's and the Christian Democrats' continued support in the middle classes, we have oblique confirmation in 1983 from the Communists themselves: Jaime Barrios, "Combat Drive and Political Initiative," *World Marxist Review* (England) 26, no. 4 (April 1983): 85, and also from the strength of the PDC in the capital (see below); on splits in the working class, see suggestive evidence along these lines in *Latin America Weekly Report*, 7 September 1984, p. 6; *New York Times*, 10 November 1985, 16; and in Wally Babcock, "El Salvador: A Labor Leader's Fact-Finding Mission," *The Grapevine* (Ithaca, New York), 10–16 November 1983, p. 9, where the FMLN/FDR admitted that "labor is basically split into two camps"; on the peasantry, electoral votes from the countryside suggest the PDC's strength among the peasantry: they received their highest vote percentages in 1982 in the guerrilla-dominated departments of Chalatenango and Morazán, followed by their vote in the capital; cf. Baloyra, *El Salvador in Transition*, pp. 178, 193.

90. Dunkerley, *Power in the Isthmus*, pp. 367–68, 376.

91. The claim that ARENA has support in the middle classes is probably the most suspect; for the opinion of an expert, see Dunkerley, *Power in the Isthmus*, pp. 405–6, where he suggests middle-class support for ARENA based on patronage jobs and a promise to "solve" the war. On the effect of PDC corruption in the 1989 elections, see *Washington Post*, 18 March 1989, A22.

92. Baloyra, *El Salvador in Transition*, pp. 161–63; McColm, *El Salvador*, p. 25.

93. On Zamora, see *Washington Post*, 24 September 1987, A41; on the public criticisms, see *Washington Post*, 21 January 1989, A21. As early as 1982, Gabriel Zaid pointed to a basic tension between those with the guns and the politicians—in both the government and the opposition; cf. Zaid, "Enemy Colleagues" and "Gabriel Zaid Replies," *Dissent* (Summer 1982): 357–59; for mid-1980s tension within the left, see Enrique Baloyra, "Negotiating War in El Salvador: The Politics of End-game," *Journal of Interamerican Studies and World Affairs* 28, no. 1 (Spring 1986): 130–36.

94. Already by 1982, foreign and not unsympathetic journalists could observe that the guerrillas had increased their military strength since the early 1981 insurrection, yet they could note also the "FMLN's lack of influence outside the areas it controls directly" and that "[p]olitically they are now perhaps weaker than ever"; cf. *Latin America Weekly Report*, 2 July 1982, pp. 10–11, and 22 October 1982, pp. 5–6.

95. Mark Falcoff, "El Salvador: The U.S. White Paper Reexamined," in his *Small Countries, Large Issues*, pp. 34–44, quotation on pp. 42–43.

96. Leiken, "The Salvadoran Left," p. 118; *Latin America Weekly Report*, 22 October 1982, pp. 5–6; Chavez, "El Salvador: The Voices of Anguish," 58; Armstrong and Shenk, *El Salvador*, pp. 185–86; *Latin America Regional Reports: Mexico and*

Central America, 30 April 1982, p. 5. On rebuilding attempts in urban areas, one of the earlier reports is in *Latin America Weekly Report*, 5 April 1985, p. 1.

97. For a review of the insurrection's pattern and results several months later, especially with regard to the civilians' experiences, see Douglas Farah, "Salvador: The Last Puzzle," *Washington Post*, 4 March 1990, C1, C4.

98. *Newsweek*, 27 November 1989, 48–55 for an overview; also several issues of the *Washington Post*, 20 November 1989, A1, A28 on the costs of the uprising to the guerrillas; 18 November 1989, A1, A18–19 on the war outside the capital, where the guerrillas also came to the towns from rural areas; and 28 November 1989, A20, where the guerrillas conceded the uprising's social and human costs, admitted that the uprising aimed to exert political pressure, and did not hope for military victory.

99. Even Daniel Ortega joined in the "censure" of the FMLN signed in early December, and the FMLN indignantly rejected the declaration; see *Washington Post*, 13 December 1989, A1, A32.

100. The clearest evidence and argument on their ineradicable primacy within Salvadoran society remain Dunkerley, *Power in the Isthmus*, chap. 8.

101. Baloyra, *El Salvador in Transition*, esp. chap. 6.

102. On blockage of the latter stages of the land reform, see Dunkerley, *Power in the Isthmus*, pp. 392–96; on the judiciary's blockage of a major tax reform, see *Newsweek*, 2 March 1987, 35; on the "meeting" of the military and the upper class in the death squads, see Craig Pyes, "The Salvadoran Right," in Leiken and Rubin, eds., *The Central American Crisis Reader*, pp. 386–90.

103. Robert K. Merton, "The Unanticipated Consequences of Purposive Social Action," *American Sociological Review* 1 (December 1936): 894–904; Skocpol, *States and Social Revolutions*, pp. 14–18.

104. After preparing this argument, I came across remarkably similar views in the ongoing work by Jeff Goodwin, "States and Revolutions in the Third World: A Comparative Analysis" (Ph.D. diss., Harvard University, 1988), written under the direction of Theda Skocpol; in published form, a capsule version can be found in Goodwin and Skocpol, "Explaining Revolutions."

105. Daniel Camacho and Rafael Menjívar, "De lo corporativo a lo político: Proyectos alternativos (Guatemala y El Salvador)" in their *Movimientos populares en Centroamérica* (San José, Costa Rica: Editorial Universitaria Centroamericana, 1985), pp. 38–41.

106. On those declines, see "El Salvador: A Rebel Defector Talks," *Newsweek*, 17 June 1985, 23; "Rebels' 'drowning screams' grow louder," *Central America Report* (Guatemala City), 15 February 1985, pp. 41–43.

107. For comments on these patrols, and on the army's rural presence more generally, see Lucía Luna, "Nueva táctica del gobierno," *Proceso* 439 (1 April 1985), 44–47; comments by Montealegre and Arnson in Fried et al., *Guatemala in Rebellion*, pp. 300–301; *Latin America Weekly Report*, 16 March 1984, pp. 2–3 (for the 500,000 estimate, and guerrillas' comments on the groups); Concerned Guatemala Scholars, *Guatemala*, p. 24, on the army's first insinuations in rural areas with relief work in such areas following the 1976 earthquake; and Black et al., *Garrison Guatemala*, pp. 135–38.

108. We have a series of excellent accounts of the increasing troubles of the Lucas regime; see Concerned Guatemala Scholars, *Guatemala*, passim; Black et al., *Garri-*

son Guatemala, passim, and pp. 48–53 on internal military divisions; Galeano et al., *Guatemala*, passim, and p. 94 on increasing conflict between the army and the upper class.

109. Black et al., *Garrison Guatemala*, p. 31.

110. Concerned Guatemala Scholars, *Guatemala*, p. 61.

111. *Latin America Regional Reports: Mexico and Central America*, 25 March 1983, p. 8; Millett, "Guatemala: Progress and Paralysis," passim; *New York Times*, 13 January 1985, sec. 4, p. E3; *Central America Report* (Guatemala City), 1 February 1985, pp. 25–26 and 22 February 1985, pp. 52–53; Black et al., *Garrison Guatemala*, pp. 136–38. For a good summary of these and many previous comments, see Dunkerley, *Power in the Isthmus*, chap. 9, esp. pp. 484–97.

112. *Proceso*, 1 April 1985, p. 47.

113. Dunkerley, *Power in the Isthmus*, p. 498.

114. For the recent political fortunes of the guerrillas there, I am indebted to a private communication from Caroll Ríos; on the topic of Guatemala since the Cerezo election, see Dunkerley, *Power in the Isthmus*, pp. 498–503; *New York Times*, 10 November 1985, E3; "Guatemala: From Bullets to Ballots," *WCNY-TV* (Syracuse, N.Y.), 20 May 1986 for the citizen's quote. On Cerezo's most recent backing of talks with the rebels, see *Washington Post*, 17 March 1990, A24. The guerrillas showed some revival and a move into urban activity in early 1990, but they certainly did not approach the levels of the early 1980s; see *Washington Post*, 17 April 1990, A18.

115. In various writings McClintock puts *Sendero*'s numbers at a few thousand strong. For Colombia's guerrillas, see *Washington Post*, 24 September 1986, A18, where FARC's numbers alone are put at 5,000.

116. *Latin America*, 9 March 1973, pp. 73–74; *Latin America Political Report*, 1 September 1978, p. 272; *Latin America Weekly Report*, 24 July 1981, p. 11 (all essentially the same London journal, with a changing title); Arango, *FARC: Veinte años*, p. 36.

117. On the rivening of the ELN, see Arenas, *La guerrilla por dentro*, passim; on the EPL split, see Peter Mossman, *Campesinos und Ausbeutungsstrukturen im internationalen Konfliktfeld* (Bamberg: Breitenbach Saarbrücken, 1979), p. 145; on the FARC and M-19, see Arango, *FARC: Veinte años*, p. 37; for the latter's origins in the former and evidence of the split, and on the reported (yet false) reports of unity in 1981, see *Latin America Weekly Report*, 24 July 1981, p. 11; on splits within M-19, see *Latin America Weekly Report*, 6 February 1981, p. 11.

118. Mossman, *Campesinos und Ausbeutungsstrukturen*, pp. 144–46 summarizes these trends concisely for the mid-1970s.

119. See the articles by Olga Behar and Rafael Vergara in *Proceso* (Mexico City) 639 (30 January 1989): 40–43, esp. 41.

120. *Washington Post*, 11 March 1990, A29.

121. "Colombia Drug Cartel Waging a Lethal War," *Washington Post*, 14 November 1987, A19, A22; Merrill Collett, "The Myth of the 'Narco-Guerrillas,'" *The Nation*, 13/20 August 1988, pp. 113, 130–34; one ransom netted the FARC guerrillas $250,000, reported to Arango, *FARC: Veinte años*, pp. 45–46; in 1983 alone, the guerrillas secured perhaps $6.6 million from extortion and robbery; cf. *[Latin America] Weekly Report*, 6 January 1984, pp. 8–9.

122. A straightforward guide to Colombian politics under Betancur is Harvey F.

Kline, "New Directions in Colombia?" *Current History* (February 1985): 65–68, 83; my account is drawn largely from his expert report. See also reports of simultaneous army campaigns and amnesty offers, in *Latin America Weekly Report*, 9 April 1982, p. 12; concerning the implications of the assassination of leftist politicians on the peace process, see *Washington Post*, 24 September 1986, A18.

123. Arenas and Marulanda made their admissions to Arango, in *FARC: Veinte años*, pp. 39–40, 122; Kline, "New Directions," 66 gives the 12,000 figure; *Washington Post*, 24 September 1986, A18, provides the 5,000 estimate.

124. Arango, *FARC: Veinte años*, pp. 128–29.

125. Arango, *FARC: Veinte años*, p. 42; *Colombia Report* (University of California, Irvine) 2, no. 3 (September 1980): 2–3. Also on the peasant unions, with mention of their separateness from the guerrilla struggle, see León Zamosc, "Peasant Struggles of the 1970s in Colombia," in Eckstein, ed., *Power and Popular Protest*.

126. Arango, *FARC: Veinte años*, p. 99.

127. Arango, *FARC: Veinte años*, pp. 132–33.

128. For press hostility to the guerrillas in the mid-1970s, Mossman, *Campesinos und Ausbeutungsstrukturen*, pp. 160–62, provides some detail; see also Arango, *FARC: Veinte años*, esp. pp. 108–9 on the loosening of official restrictions on guerrilla reporting.

129. One report illustrating all these features of the military is in *Latin America Weekly Report*, 18 November 1983, p. 9. For two works that give a very strong sense of the relations between the military and civilian political elites—relations that have led to an almost complete absence of military coups in Colombia—see Maullin, *Soldiers, Guerrillas, and Politics* and J. Mark Ruhl's more recent treatment, *Colombia: Armed Forces and Society*, Foreign and Comparative Studies, Latin American Series I (Syracuse, New York: Maxwell School of Citizenship and Public Affairs, Syracuse University, 1980).

130. See the comments by Arenas and Marulanda, both suggesting a certain apathy about revolutionary prospects, in Arango, *FARC: Veinte Años*, pp. 39–40, 122, 128–29.

131. Cynthia McClintock, "Peru's Sendero Luminoso Rebellion," p. 83.

132. Throughout this section, my main source of information will be McClintock's latest statement on the group, "Peru's Sendero Luminoso Rebellion," which I will cite again below only when specific points of data are concerned.

133. The last observations were made by John Gitlitz, "Sendero Luminoso in Cajamarca, Peru" (Paper presented at the meeting of the New England Council of Latin American Studies, Harvard University, 13 October 1984). See also Palmer, "Revolutionary Terrorism," pp. 48–53 on *Sendero*'s problems in expanding into Puno and portions of Apurímac.

134. I refer here to *Sendero*'s three-prison uprising in June 1986, which was put down by the military after several days with many *senderistas* killed in the battle and 100 or more killed afterwards; cf. David P. Werlich, "Debt, Democracy and Terrorism in Peru," *Current History* 86 (January 1987): 29–33, 36–37, for this and other information on García's administration to late 1986. On *Sendero*'s urban presence, I am indebted to Michael Smith's paper "Sendero's Urban Strategy."

135. McClintock, "Peru's Sendero Luminoso Rebellion," pp. 85–88.

136. On this last point, see Palmer, "Revolutionary Terrorism."

137. "Peruvian Rebel Offers Grim Prophecy," *Washington Post*, 19 August 1988, A10.

138. Two minor exceptions are worth noting: It formed a "tactical alliance" in late 1985 with the Lima-based, bomb-planting revolutionaries of the Túpac Amaru Revolutionary Movement; and it had ties to the Peruvian Peasants' confederation of Apurímac (which, as Gitlitz noted, did not serve to convert the confederation to a pro-*Sendero* position); see, respectively, Werlich, "Debt, Democracy and Terrorism," 36, and Palmer, "Rebellion in Rural Peru," 140.

139. Werlich, "Peru: The Shadow of the Shining Path," 78–82, 90.

140. Werlich, "Peru," 78.

141. McClintock, "Peru's Sendero Luminoso Rebellion," pp. 87–88.

142. For their hopes in the 1990 national elections—later shattered by a runoff between moderate Alberto Fujimori and conservative Mario Vargas Llosa—see the article by Lucía Luna in *Proceso* (Mexico City) 647 (27 March 1989): 45–47.

143. See Skocpol, *States and Social Revolutions*, esp. chap. 2.

144. See Loveman and Davies's edition of Guevara, *Guerrilla Warfare*, where in many ways they reach conclusions similar to my own regarding the contributions of the political system to the failure and success of revolutionary movements. For earlier, similar conclusions about such regimes, see Jack Goldstone's analysis in his edited work, *Revolutions*, pp. 7–10.

145. For the analysis of Iran, see Skocpol, "Rentier State and Shi'a Islam." For pointing my nose even more toward the Iran–Latin American parallels, I am indebted to a private communication from Theda Skocpol; see also Goodwin and Skocpol, "Explaining Revolutions," 498–501.

CHAPTER 12
WINNERS, LOSERS, AND ALSO-RANS

1. See the general comments in David Hackett Fischer, *Historians' Fallacies: Toward a Logic of Historical Thought* (New York: Harper and Row, 1970), chap. 3, esp. pp. 90–97, and 289–90; for historian Christopher Hill's fall into this trap, see Hexter, *On Historians*, pp. 241–43 and passim.

2. See Arthur L. Stinchcombe, *Theoretical Methods in Social History* (New York: Academic, 1978), where he argues that comparative statistics should only be used when the processes being compared reflect "deep historical analogies"; also Stanley Lieberson, *Making it Count: The Improvement of Social Research and Theory* (Berkeley: University of California Press, 1985), esp. chaps. 3, 4.

3. Skocpol and Somers, "The Uses of Comparative History," 174–97, esp. 183–85; Charles Ragin, *The Comparative Method: Moving Beyond Qualitative and Quantitative Strategies* (Berkeley, Calif.: University of California Press, 1987), esp. pp. 12–13, 36–42.

4. Ragin, *The Comparative Method*, chaps. 1–4, esp. chap. 4; for his comments on the problem of interaction, see pp. 13–16.

5. This is an inherent difficulty of the method, which insists we obey the law of the excluded middle. As one wag once noted, "Ours is not the sort of world in which middles can be excluded unambiguously."

6. Ragin, *The Comparative Method*, chap. 6 esp. but also chaps. 7–8.

7. See my arguments supporting "peasant linkages" as a cause in chapter 7. Anthropologists, for their part, are quite willing to bristle at the notion—implied by the rejection of the "rebellious culture" argument—that culture has no influence upon behavior patterns. Any suggestion that "culture" does not influence behavior patterns suggests a curiously archaic form of thought. For reasons why the "rational actor" can provide no theoretical refuge for those who reject "cultural" arguments, see my discussion below, and my comments in chapter 4.

8. I refer here to Merton's famous essay "Manifest and Latent Functions" in his also-famous *Social Theory and Social Structure*, esp. pp. 86–91.

9. Skocpol, "What Makes Peasants Revolutionary?" 355–358, and *States and Social Revolutions*, p. 319 n. 11; Jenkins, "Why Do Peasants Rebel?"

10. Paige, "Social Theory and Peasant Revolution in Vietnam and Guatemala"; Popkin, *The Rational Peasant*.

11. Max Weber, *The Theory of Social and Economic Organization*, ed. and with an introduction by Talcott Parsons (New York: The Free Press, 1947), pp. 112–18.

12. See my argument preceding this topic in chapter 7, where I related this pattern to interpersonal balance theory in psychology. Balance theory has everything to do with affect, and nothing to do with "rational choice." Imbalance has to do with discomfort in affect, not unrealized self-interest.

13. Tilly, *From Mobilization to Revolution*, pp. 74–76.

14. Robin Williams's graduate course, Social Organization and Change, Cornell University.

15. Good guides to the lesser movements of these thirty years appear, for the earlier period, in Lamberg, *Die castristiche Guerilla*, pp. 136–61, and for the entire period, in a series of compact summaries in Berardo, *Guerrilhas e guerrilheiros no drama da América Latina*.

16. Guevara, *Guerrilla Warfare*, p. 47.

17. Régis Debray, *Revolution in the Revolution?* (New York: Monthly Review, 1967); for a number of critiques, see Leo Huberman and Paul M. Sweezy, *Régis Debray and the Latin American Revolution* (New York: Monthly Review, 1968).

18. Blasier, "Social Revolution," esp. pp. 48–49.

19. Examples of such writings are several contributions to Fauriol, *Latin American Insurgencies*, released by the Center for Strategic and International Studies, formerly affiliated with Georgetown University, and well known for its conservative ideological agenda, which led to its loss of affiliation with the university. The contributions by David Scott Palmer and by Cesar Sereseres to the volume are clear exceptions to this general statement and bespeak and focus on the authors' detailed knowledge of internal events in Peru and Guatemala, respectively. An earlier work exhibiting similar blinders was Ratliff, *Castroism and Communism in Latin America, 1959–1976*.

20. For Guatemala, scattered comments abound, but one good source is Fried et al., *Guatemala in Rebellion*; for Colombia's FARC, see Arango's interviews in *FARC: Veinte años*; for Peru, see McClintock, "Peru's Sendero Luminoso Rebellion."

21. For Nicaragua, see Christian, *Nicaragua*, pp. 103–7; Leiken and Rubin, eds., *The Central American Crisis Reader*, pp. 450–53 for evidence on each.

22. See the rather different evaluations of this shift in Willard Barber and C. Neale Ronning, *Internal Security and Military Power* (Columbus: Ohio State University Press, 1966), and Klare and Stein, *Armas y poder en América Latina*.

23. Petras, "Revolution and Guerrilla Movements," p. 353.

24. Jeane Kirkpatrick, "U.S. Security and Latin America," in Wiarda, ed., *Rift and Revolution*, pp. 344–45.

25. In fairness to Petras, he has proposed a complex, full-blown theory of revolution; cf. "Toward a Theory of 20th-Century Socialist Revolutions," *Journal of Contemporary Asia* 8, no. 2 (1978): 167–95.

26. From 1950 to 1977, U.S. Military Assistance Program (MAP) aid to Iran totaled $766 million, which was more than that to all of Latin America combined ($657 million). Needless to say, the amounts to Vietnam dwarfed even those numbers: $14.8 billion; cf. U.S. Department of Defense, Security Assistance Agency, *Foreign Military Sales and Military Assistance Facts* (December 1977), pp. 19–20.

27. U.S. Dept. of Defense, *Foreign Military Sales*, p. 20 for evidence on Haiti, Paraguay, and Argentina. For more on Argentine events during the insurgency, see Gillespie, *Soldiers of Perón*.

28. Jean-Marie Simon, *Guatemala: Eternal Spring, Eternal Tyranny* (New York: W.W. Norton, 1987), p. 177.

29. See U.S. Dept. of Defense, *Foreign Military Sales*, p. 20, and McDonald, "Civil-Military Relations in Central America," p. 146.

30. The thesis might be saved by a deep contextual comparison between Nicaragua, El Salvador, and Guatemala. In the course of such comparisons, however, what would surely emerge would be a typology of different types of political regimes, some stronger, some weaker in the face of revolution. That is, it would begin to reproduce a variant of my column D (a weak form of political regime); it would therefore confirm, not deny, my argument that regime type is a central contextual variable for predicting the success of revolutions. Moreover, any attempt, in particular, to drive a typological wedge between the Guatemalan and Salvadoran military regimes of the 1970s and early 1980s would find it difficult indeed to differentiate them: they were more similar to each other than either was to Nicaragua.

31. The attentive watchers of the evening news might have noted that the pro-Noriega demonstrators were often, sometimes largely, dark-skinned Panamanians, while the anti-Noriega groups were primarily light skinned. In Panama, as elsewhere in the Americas, such color differences tend to correlate well with class differences.

32. Skocpol, *States and Social Revolutions*, pp. 14–18 and chap. 2.

33. Skocpol, *States and Social Revolutions*, p. 17.

34. For the avowedly revolutionary aims of the Bolivian MNR, see my discussion of Bolivian society and politics in chapter 8. While Castro rather clearly muted the more radical tones of his 26th of July Movement, there was indeed much talk of "revolution" among many regime opponents, and the constitution of 1940 that Castro proposed to restore itself had some revolutionary elements.

35. Skocpol, "Rentier State and Shi'a Islam."

36. Skocpol, *States and Social Revolutions*, pp. 147–54; Himmelstein and Kimmel were among the first to point out this difference from her other two cases and its implications for theoretical consistency. See Jerome L. Himmelstein and Michael S. Kimmel, "Review Essay: States and Social Revolutions," *American Journal of Sociology* 86, no. 5 (March 1981): 1145–55.

37. Ragin, *The Comparative Method*, p. 98.

38. Ragin, *The Comparative Method*, pp. 93–98, on both minimization and the determination of prime implicants.

39. On this issue, John Womack, Jr., *Zapata and the Mexican Revolution* (New York: Vintage, 1968), provides an abundance of confirmatory evidence about the essentially elite-independent nature of Zapata's peasant movement.

40. On the last item, evidence has come to light in the last few years that the Salvadoran guerrillas have established a highly effective munitions manufacture to support their war effort.

41. Falcoff, "Somoza, Sandino, and the United States." In Trujillo's death, while a Dominican soldier pulled the trigger, the CIA apparently organized the event; see Gerassi, *The Great Fear in Latin America*, p. 197.

42. Ché Guevara, "Cuba: Exceptional Case?" provides one such case; see *Venceremos: The Speeches and Writings of Che Guevara*, edited by John Gerassi (New York: Simon and Schuster, 1968), p. 133.

43. See Walter L. Wallace, *Sociological Theory* (Chicago: Aldine, 1969) and his later *Principles of Scientific Sociology* (Hawthorne, N.Y.: Aldine, 1983). I have made my own contribution to Wallace's perspective, for the case of Marxian theorizing, in an as yet unpublished paper, "Marxian Theory via Wallace: A Bourgeois Dissection." There I show that Wallace's clearly categorized varieties of theory, found in the works of sociologists, have almost mirror images in the works of Marxian writers.

Select Bibliography

SPACE constraints prohibit a complete listing of sources here. For other bibliographies on the topic, see Vera de Lamberg's entry under "Latin America—Comparative," and Virgil Ney's under "Military." For good general guides in the "Latin America—Comparative" section, Gott, *Rural Guerrillas*, provides many references to hard-to-find journalistic sources, while Lamberg, *Die castristiche Guerilla*; Allemann, *Macht und Ohnmacht*; and the Loveman and Davies edition of Guevara's *Guerrilla Warfare* all are well documented. However, most sources have a very low "signal-to-noise ratio" and, while cited in the text, are not included here, where I list only particularly useful, informative, or theoretically stimulating sources.

The entries are grouped in subcategories according to the following headings:

LATIN AMERICA—COMPARATIVE

Allemann, Fritz René. *Macht und Ohnmacht der Guerilla*. Munich: R. Piper, 1974.

Berardo, João Batista. *Guerrilhas e guerrilheiros no drama da América Latina*. São Paulo: Edições Populares, 1981.

Bernard, Jean-Pierre, Silas Cerqueira, Nugo Neira, Hélène Graillot, Leslie F. Manigat, and Pierre Gilhodès. *Guide to the Political Parties of South America*. Harmondsworth, Eng.: Pelican, 1973.

Blasier, Cole. "Social Revolution: Origins in Mexico, Bolivia, and Cuba." In *Cuba in Revolution*, edited by Rolando E. Bonachea and Nelson P. Valdés, pp. 18–51. Garden City, N.Y.: Anchor, 1972.

Debray, Régis. *Strategy for Revolution*. Edited by Robin Blackburn. London: Jonathan Cape, 1970.

Dix, Robert H. "Why Revolutions Succeed & Fail." *Polity* 16, no. 3 (Spring 1984): 423–46.

Dunkerley, James. *Power in the Isthmus: A Political History of Modern Central America*. London: Verso, 1988.

Gall, Norman. "The Legacy of Che Guevara." *Commentary* 44 (December 1967): 31–44.

Gott, Richard. *Rural Guerrillas in Latin America*. Harmondsworth, Eng.: Penguin, 1973. Reissue of *Guerrilla Movements in Latin America* (London: Nelson and Sons, 1970).

Guevara, Ernesto 'Che.' *Guerrilla Warfare*. Introduction and case studies by Brian Loveman and Thomas M. Davies, Jr. Lincoln: University of Nebraska Press, 1985.

Harnecker, Marta. *Pueblos en Armas*. México, D.F.: Serie Popular Era, 1984.

INDAL (Información Documental de América Latina). *Movimientos revolucionarios de América Latina (I): Documentación propia*. 2d ed. Caracas: INDAL, November 1972.

Lamberg, Robert F. *Die castristiche Guerilla in Lateinamerika: Theorie und Praxis eines revolutionären Modells*. Hannover, Germany: Verlag für Literatur und Zeitgeschehen, 1971.

Lamberg, Vera B. de. "La guerrilla castrista en América Latina: Bibliografía selecta, 1960–1970." *Foro Internacional* 12 (July–September 1971): 95–111.

Lartéguy, Jean. *The Guerrillas*. New York: World Press, 1970.

Leiken, Robert S., and Barry Rubin, eds. *The Central American Crisis Reader*. New York: Summit, 1987.

Mercier Vega, Luis. *Guerrillas in Latin America: The Technique of the Counter-State*. New York: Praeger Publishers, 1969.

Nuhn, H., P. Krieg, and W. Schlick. *Zentralamerika: Karten zur Bevölkerungs- und Wirtschaftsstruktur*. Hamburg, Germany: Institut für Geographie und Wirtschaftsgeographie der Universität Hamburg, 1975.

Rouquié Alain. *The Military and the State in Latin America*. Translated by Paul E. Sigmund. Berkeley: University of California Press, 1987.

SCAAN (Stanford Central America Action Network), eds. *Revolution in Central America*. Boulder, Colo.: Westview, 1983.

Williams, Robert G. *Export Agriculture and the Crisis in Central America*. Chapel Hill: University of North Carolina Press, 1986.

BOLIVIA

Esser, Klaus. "Guevaras Guerilla in Bolivien." *Vierteljahresberichte—Forschungsinstitut der Friedrich-Ebert-Stiftung* 37 (September 1969): 315–36.

González, Luis J., and Gustavo A. Sánchez Salazar. *The Great Rebel: Che Guevara in Bolivia*. New York: Grove Press, 1969.

Guevara, Ernesto 'Ché'. *The Complete Bolivian Diaries of Che Guevara and Other Captured Documents*. Edited and with introduction by Daniel James. New York: Stein and Day, 1968.

Lamberg, Robert F. "Che in Bolivia: The 'Revolution' That Failed." *Problems of Communism* 19 (July–August 1970): 25–37.

Millares Reyes, Edgar. *Las guerrillas: Teoría y práctica*. Sucre, Bolivia: Imprenta Universitaria, 1968.

COLOMBIA

Arango Z., Manuel. *FARC: Veinte años—De Marquetalia a la Uribe*. Bogotá: Ediciones Aurora, 1984.

Arenas, Jaime. *La guerrilla por dentro*. Bogotá: Tercer Mundo, 1970.

Berry, R. Albert, Ronald G. Hellman, and Mauricio Solaún, eds. *Politics of Compromise: Coalition Government in Colombia*. New Brunswick, N.J.: Transaction, 1980.

Calvo O., Fabiola. *EPL: Diez hombres, un ejército, una historia*. Bogotá: Ecoe Ediciones, 1985.

Castro Caycedo, Germán. *Del ELN al M-19: Once años de lucha guerrillera*. Bogotá: Carlos Valencia, 1980.

Colombia, República de. Departamento Administrativo Nacional de Estadísticas (DANE). *Directorio nacional de explotaciones agropecuarias (censo agropecuario) 1960: Resumen nacional*. 2 parts. Bogotá, 1962 and 1964.

Maullin, Richard L. *Soldiers, Guerrillas, and Politics in Colombia*. Toronto: Lexington, 1973.

CUBA

Blackburn, Robin. "Prologue to the Cuban Revolution." *New Left Review* 21 (October 1963): 52–91.

Bonachea, Ramón L., and Marta San Martín. *The Cuban Insurrection, 1952–1959*. New Brunswick, N.J.: Transaction, 1974.

Cuba, República de. Ministerio de Agricultura. *Memoria del censo agrícola nacional 1946*. Havana, 1951.

Domínguez, Jorge I. *Cuba: Order and Revolution*. Cambridge, Mass. and London: Belknap Press of Harvard University Press, 1978.

Farber, Samuel. *Revolution and Reaction in Cuba, 1933–1960*. Middletown, Conn.: Wesleyan University Press, 1976.

Carlos Franqui. *Diary of the Cuban Revolution*. Translated by Georgette Felix, Elaine Kerrigan, Phyllis Freeman, and Hardie St. Martin. New York: Viking, 1980.

Goldenberg, Boris. *The Cuban Revolution and Latin America*. New York: Praeger, 1965.

Guevara, Ernesto "Ché". *Reminiscences of the Cuban Revolutionary War*. New York: Monthly Review, 1968.

Pérez, Louis A., Jr. *Army Politics in Cuba, 1898–1958*. Pittsburgh: University of Pittsburgh Press, 1976.

Ruiz, Ramon Eduardo. *Cuba: The Making of a Revolution*. New York: W.W. Norton, 1968.

Thomas, Hugh. *Cuba: The Pursuit of Freedom*. New York: Harper and Row, 1971.

EL SALVADOR

Armstrong, Robert, and Janet Shenk. *El Salvador: The Face of Revolution*. London: Pluto, 1982.

Baloyra, Enrique. *El Salvador in Transition*. Chapel Hill: University of North Carolina, 1982.

Jung, Harald. "Class Struggles in El Salvador." *New Left Review* 122 (July–August 1980): 3–25.

Kincaid, A. Douglas. "Peasants into Rebels: Community and Class in Rural El Salvador." *Comparative Studies in Society and History* 29, no. 3 (July 1987): 466–94.

Leiken, Robert S. "The Salvadoran Left." In his *Central America: Anatomy of Conflict*. New York: Pergamon, 1984.

Lopes, Gilberto. *Reportaje en El Salvador*. San José, Costa Rica: Editorial Universitaria Centroamericana, 1984.

Montgomery, Tommie Sue. *Revolution in El Salvador*. Boulder, Colo.: Westview, 1982.

White, Alastair. *El Salvador*. New York: Praeger, 1973.
Zaid, Gabriel. "Enemy Colleagues: A Reading of the Salvadoran Tragedy." *Dissent* (Winter 1982): 13–40.

GUATEMALA

Adams, Richard N. *Crucifixion by Power: Essays on Guatemalan National Social Structure, 1944–1966*. Austin, Texas: University of Texas Press, 1970.
Black, George, with Milton Jamail and Norma Stoltz Chinchilla. *Garrison Guatemala*. New York: Monthly Review, 1984.
Castaño, Camilo. "Avec les guérillas du Guatemala." *Partisans* (Paris) 38 (July–September 1967): 143–57.
Concerned Guatemala Scholars. *Guatemala: Dare to Struggle, Dare to Win*. Revised Edition. San Francisco, Calif.: Solidarity, 1982.
Fried, Jonathan L., Marvin E. Gettleman, Deborah T. Levenson, and Nancy Peckenham, eds. *Guatemala in Rebellion: Unfinished History*. New York: Grove, 1983.
Galeano, Eduardo, José González, and Antonio Campos. *Guatemala: Un pueblo en lucha*. Madrid: Editorial Revolución, 1983.
Gillespie, Richard. "Anatomy of the Guatemalan Guerrilla." *Communist Affairs: Documents and Analysis* 2, no. 4 (October 1983): 490–96.
Gilly, Adolfo. The Guerrilla Movement in Guatemala I. *Monthly Review* 17 (May 1965): 9–40.
———. The Guerrilla Movement in Guatemala II. *Monthly Review* 17 (June 1965): 7–41.
Guatemala, República de. Dirección General de Estadística. *II censo agropecuario 1964*. 2 vols. Guatemala City, 1968.
Munson, Donn. *Zacapa*. Canoga, Calif.: Challenge, 1967.
NACLA (North American Congress on Latin America). *Guatemala*. Berkeley, Calif. and N.Y.: NACLA, 1974.
Paige, Jeffery M. "Social Theory and Peasant Revolution in Vietnam and Guatemala." *Theory and Society* 12, no. 6 (November 1983): 699–737.
Payeras, Mario. "Days of the Jungle: The Testimony of a Guatemalan *Guerrillero*, 1972–1976." *Monthly Review* 35, no. 3 (July–August 1983). Also published as a book.

NICARAGUA

Alegría, Claribel, and D. J. Flakoll. *Nicaragua: La revolución sandinista—Una crónica política*. México, D.F.: Era, 1984.
Arias, Pilar. *Nicaragua: Revolución—Relatos de combatientes del Frente Sandinista*. México, D.F.: Siglo Veintiuno, 1980.
Black, George. *Triumph of the People: The Sandinista Revolution in Nicaragua*. London: Zed, 1981.
Booth, John A. *The End and the Beginning: The Nicaraguan Revolution*. Boulder, Co.: Westview, 1982.
Borge, Tomás, Carlos Fonseca, Daniel Ortega, Humberto Ortega, and Jaime Wheelock. *Sandinistas Speak*. New York: Pathfinder, 1982.

Diederich, Bernard. *Somoza and the Legacy of U.S. Involvement in Central America*. New York: E. P. Dutton, 1981.

Jung, Harald. "Behind the Nicaraguan Revolution." *New Left Review* 117 (September–October 1979): 69–90

Macaulay, Neill. *The Sandino Affair*. Durham, North Carolina: Duke University Press, 1985 [1967].

Nicaragua, República de. Dirección General de Estadística y Censos. *Censos nacionales 1963*. Vol. 3, *Agropecuario*. Managua, 1966.

Nolan, David. *The Ideology of the Sandinistas and the Nicaraguan Revolution*. Coral Gables, Florida: Institute of Interamerican Studies, University of Miami, 1984.

Paige, Jeffery. "Cotton and Revolution in Nicaragua." In *States versus Markets in the World System*, edited by Peter Evans, Dietrich Rueschemeyer, and Evelyne Huber Stephens. Vol. 8 in the Political Economy of the World-System Annuals. Beverly Hills, Calif.: Sage, 1985.

Ruiz, Henry. "La montaña era como un crisol donde se forjaban los mejores cuadros." *Nicaráuac: Revista Bimestral del Ministerio de Cultura*. Año 1, no. 1 (May–June 1980): 8–24.

Los Sandinistas. Bogotá: Oveja Negra, 1979.

Wheelock Román, Jaime. *Imperialismo y dictadura*. México, D.F.: Siglo Veintiuno, 1975. Also Managua: Editorial Nueva Nicaragua, 1985.

PERU

Artola Azcarate, General Armando. *¡Subversión!* Lima: Editorial Jurídica, 1976.

Béjar, Héctor. *Peru 1965: Notes on a Guerrilla Experience*. New York: Monthly Review, 1970. Also in Spanish.

Campbell, Leon G. "The Historiography of the Peruvian Guerrilla Movement." *Latin American Research Review* 8 (Spring 1973): 45–70.

Gall, Norman. "Peru's Misfired Guerrilla Campaign." *The Reporter* 36 (26 January 1967): 36–38.

McClintock, Cynthia. "Peru's Sendero Luminoso Rebellion: Origins and Trajectory." Ch. 2 in *Power and Popular Protest: Latin American Social Movements*, edited by Susan Eckstein. Berkeley, Calif.: University of California Press, 1989.

Mercado, Rogger. *Las guerrillas del Peru: De la prédica ideológica a la acción armada*. Lima: Fondo de Cultura Popular, 1967.

Palmer, David Scott. "Rebellion in Rural Peru: The Origins and Evolution of Sendero Luminoso." *Comparative Politics* 18, no. 2 (January 1986): 127–46.

———. "The Revolutionary Terrorism of Peru's Shining Path." Paper prepared for the Ford Foundation–sponsored project, "Terrorism in Context." Martha Crenshaw, director. January 1990.

Peru. Ministerio de Guerra. *Las guerrillas en el Peru y su represión*. Lima(?): Ministerio de Guerra, 1966.

VENEZUELA

Gall, Norman (interviewer). "Teodoro Petkoff: The Crisis of the Professional Revolutionary—Part I: Years of Insurrection." *American Universities Field Staff Reports—East Coast South America Series* 16, no. 1 (January 1972): 1–19.

412 · Select Bibliography

Levine, Daniel H. *Conflict and Political Change in Venezuela*. Princeton, N.J.:
Princeton University Press, 1973.
Maspero, François, ed. *Avec Douglas Bravo dans les maquis vénézuéliens*. Paris:
François Maspero, 1968.
Peña, Alfredo. *Conversaciones con Américo Martín*. Caracas: Ateneo, 1978.
———. *Conversaciones con Douglas Bravo*. Caracas: Ateneo, 1978.
Petkoff, Teodoro. "Pre-Election Climate in Venezuela (An Interview with Comrade
Teodoro Petkov [*sic*])." *World Marxist Review* (England) 11 (April 1968): 29–32.
Powell, John Duncan. *Political Mobilization of the Venezuelan Peasant*. Cambridge,
Mass.: Harvard University Press, 1971.
Valsalice, Luigi. *Guerriglia e Politica: L'esempio del Venezuela*. Florence, Italy:
Valmartina Editore, 1973. Also in two Spanish editions.
Venezuela, República de. Ministerio de Fomento. *III censo agropecuario 1961: Re-
sumen general de la república*. Parts A and B. Caracas, 1967.
Zago, Angela. *Aquí no ha pasado nada*. Caracas: El Sobre, 1972.
Zamora, Antonio. *Memoria(s) de la guerrilla venezolana*. Caracas: Síntesis Dosmil,
1974.

THEORY AND GENERAL

Goldfrank, Walter L. "Theories of Revolution and Revolution without Theory: The
Case of Mexico." *Theory and Society* 7 (1979): 135–65. Abridged as: "The Mexi-
can Revolution." In *Revolutions: Theoretical, Comparative, and Historical Stud-
ies*. Edited by Jack Goldstone. San Diego: Harcourt Brace Jovanovich, 1986.
Goodwin, Jeff and Theda Skocpol. "Explaining Revolutions in the Contemporary
Third World." *Politics and Society* 17, no. 4 (December 1989): 489–509.
Hofheinz, Roy, Jr. "The Ecology of Chinese Communist Success: Rural Influence
Patterns, 1923–1945." Pp. 3–77 in *Chinese Communist Politics in Action*. Edited
by A. Doak Barnett. Seattle: University of Washington Press, 1969.
Laqueur, Walter Ze'ev. *Guerrilla: A Historical and Critical Study*. Boston: Little,
Brown, and Co., 1976.
Paige, Jeffery M. *Agrarian Revolution: Social Movements and Export Agriculture in
the Underdeveloped World*. New York: The Free Press, 1975.
Ragin, Charles C. *The Comparative Method: Moving Beyond Qualitative and Quanti-
tative Strategies*. Berkeley: University of California Press, 1987.
Russell, D.E.H. *Rebellion, Revolution, and Armed Force*. New York: Academic
Press, 1974.
Scott, James C. *The Moral Economy of the Peasant*. New Haven, Conn.: Yale, 1976.
Skocpol, Theda. *States and Social Revolutions*. Cambridge: Cambridge University
Press, 1979.
———. "What Makes Peasants Revolutionary?" In *Power and Protest in the Coun-
tryside*, edited by Scott Guggenheim and Robert Weller, pp. 157–79. Durham,
N.C.: Duke University Press, 1982. Also in *Comparative Politics* 14 (April 1982):
351–75.
———. "Rentier State and Shi'a Islam in the Iranian Revolution." *Theory and Society*
11, no. 2 (May 1982): 265–83.
———, and Margaret Somers. "The Uses of Comparative History in Macrosocial

Inquiry." *Comparative Studies in Society and History* 22, no. 2 (April 1980): 174–97.
Wolf, Eric R. *Peasant Wars of the Twentieth Century*. New York: Harper and Row, 1969.

MILITARY

Callanan, Colonel Edward F. "Terror in Venezuela." *Military Review* 49 (February 1969): 49–56.
Ney, Colonel Virgil. "Guerrilla Warfare: Annotated Bibliography." *Military Review* 41 (November 1961): 97–112.
Russell, Charles A., and Captain Bowman H. Miller. "Profile of a Terrorist." *Military Review* 57 (August 1977): 21–34.
Waghelstein, Colonel John D. "'Che's' Bolivian Adventure." *Military Review* 59 (August 1979): 39–48.

NEWS SOURCES CONSULTED

Central America Report (Guatemala City)
Colombia Report (University of California, Irvine)
Current History
Daily Journal (Caracas)
El Nacional (Caracas)
El Salvador Bulletin (Berkeley)
Hispanic American Report
La Prensa (Lima)
Latin America Regional Reports: Mexico & Central America; Andean Group (London)
Latin America; *Latin America Report*; *Latin America Weekly Report*; *Weekly Report* (London; title varies)
Latin America Political Report (London)
Mother Jones
New York Times
Newsweek
Nicaráuac (Nicaragua, Ministerio de Cultura)
Partisans (Paris)
Proceso (Mexico City)
Punto Crítico (Mexico City)
Sucesos (Mexico City)
Time
Washington Post

Index

OMITTED from the index are the names of certain individual guerrilla leaders—those not otherwise mentioned in the text—whose background profiles do, however, appear in appendixes A and B.